THE CAMBRIDGE COMPANION TO
RABINDRANATH TAGORE

Rabindranath Tagore (1861–1941) is an iconic presence in Indian literature. International interest in his work soared after he received the Nobel Prize in 1913, declined thereafter, but has increased again in recent years. He practised all the major literary genres – poetry, drama, fiction, and a range of non-fictional writings. In addition, he was a song-writer, composer, painter, philosopher, educationist, social thinker, and public intellectual.

There is no one-volume guide to the range of achievements of this multi-faceted genius in English, or indeed in his own language, Bengali. *The Cambridge Companion to Rabindranath Tagore* takes on that challenging task. It contains a series of critical surveys of the chief sectors of his artistic output and its reception, followed by a number of more specialized studies on particular topics and fields of activity. The authors are among the leading Tagore experts from India and abroad. They have drawn upon the entire body of relevant material in Bengali and English, besides other languages as appropriate. They have also woven into their accounts the historical and cultural background of Tagore's time, a period of exceptional ferment and creativity for Bengal and India.

This is the first major volume on Tagore in English to take full stock of the untranslated Bengali works that comprise the greater part of his oeuvre. It includes an index of the primary works used in this collection, with full details of their complex history of transmission, as well as a substantial reading list for Tagore studies in English. It will be an indispensable guide for all scholars, students, and general readers of Tagore and his times, even those who can access his works and related scholarship in Bengali.

Sukanta Chaudhuri is Professor Emeritus, Department of English, Jadavpur University, where he founded the School of Cultural Texts and Records. Besides his work on Shakespeare and other Renaissance literature, he was chief co-ordinator of the Tagore online variorum *Bichitra*, and general editor of the Oxford Tagore Translations.

THE CAMBRIDGE COMPANION TO

RABINDRANATH TAGORE

Edited by

Sukanta Chaudhuri

Jadavpur University

CAMBRIDGE
UNIVERSITY PRESS

CAMBRIDGE
UNIVERSITY PRESS

University Printing House, Cambridge CB2 8BS, United Kingdom

One Liberty Plaza, 20th Floor, New York, NY 10006, USA

477 Williamstown Road, Port Melbourne, vic 3207, Australia

314 to 321, 3rd Floor, Plot No.3, Splendor Forum, Jasola District Centre, New Delhi 110025, India

79 Anson Road, #06–04/06, Singapore 079906

Cambridge University Press is part of the University of Cambridge.

It furthers the University's mission by disseminating knowledge in the pursuit of education, learning and research at the highest international levels of excellence.

www.cambridge.org
Information on this title: www.cambridge.org/9781108489942

© Cambridge University Press 2020

First published 2020

Printed in India by Rajkamal Electric Press

A catalogue record for this publication is available from the British Library

ISBN 978-1-108-48994-2 Hardback

ISBN 978-1-108-74773-8 Paperback

Contents

Illustrations

Notes on Contributors

Fakrul Alam is UGC Professor, Department of English, Dhaka University. He has authored *Rabindranath Tagore and National Identity Formation in Bangladesh* (2012), edited *South Asian Writers in English* (2006), and co-edited *The Essential Tagore* (2011). In 2013, he received the Translation Award of the Bangla Academy, Dhaka.

Anisuzzaman is a National Professor of Bangladesh, after retiring from Dhaka University as Professor of Bengali. His publications on Tagore include *Rabindranāth: ekāler chokhe* (2011), *Tnār srishtir path* (2016), and the edited volumes *Rabindranāth* (1968) and *Sārdhashatabarshe rabindranāth: bānglādesher shraddhānjali* (2012).

Sibaji Bandyopadhyay was Professor of Cultural Studies at the Centre for Studies in Social Sciences, Calcutta. Besides essays, he writes poems, stories, plays, novels and film scripts. His two recent English publications are *Tagores Before Tagore: A Screenplay* (2018) and *Three Essays on the Mahābhārata* (2015).

Himani Bannerji is Emeritus Professor of Sociology, York University, Canada. Her publications include *Inventing Subjects: Studies in Hegemony, Patriarchy and Colonialism* (2001), *Demography and Democracy* (2011), and 'Beyond the Binaries: Notes on Karl Marx and Rabindranath Tagore's Ideas on Human Capacities and Alienation' in *Marxism: With and Beyond Marx* (2014).

France Bhattacharya is Emeritus Professor of Bengali language, literature, and social and religious history at the Institut national des langues et civilisations orientales, Paris. She has translated several works by Rabindranath, Bibhutibhushan Bandyopādhyāy and Tārāshankar Bandyopādhyāy, as well as Bipradās's *Manasāmangal*, into French and Bhāratchandra Rāy's *Annadāmangal* into English.

Sabyasachi Bhattacharya (1938–2019) was Professor of Indian History, Jawaharlal Nehru University, Delhi; Vice-Chancellor, Visva-Bharati; and Chairman, Indian Council of Historical Research. His last books were *Rabindranath Tagore: An Interpretation* (2017) and *Archiving the British Raj, 1858–1947* (2018). He received the Rabindra Puraskar of the West Bengal Government and the Tagore Birth Centenary Award of the Asiatic Society, Kolkata.

Sourin Bhattacharya retired as Professor of Economics, Jadavpur University, Kolkata. Among his many writings on Rabindranath, the book *Keno āmrā rabindranāthke chāi ebang kibhābe* (2007) received the Sahitya Akademi Award. Five volumes of his collected works have appeared so far.

Subha Chakraborty Dasgupta was Professor of Comparative Literature, Jadavpur University, Kolkata. She has published many essays on Tagore, co-edited a collection of Tagore material from the journal *Sāhitya*, and contributed to the online Tagore variorum *Bichitra*. Most recently, she has co-edited the volume *Figures of Transcontinental Multilingualism* (2017).

Nirmalya Narayan Chakraborty is Professor of Philosophy and Dean of Arts, Rabindra Bharati University, Kolkata. His recent writings include 'Tagore and the Problem of Evil' in *The Idea of Surplus* (2016) and 'Methodology in Indian Philosophy' in *The Routledge History of Indian Philosophy* (2018).

Swapan Chakravorty held the Kabiguru Rabindranath Tagore Distinguished Chair in the Humanities, Presidency University, Kolkata. He has edited *Rabindranāth: shilparup, pāthrup, grantharup* (2011) and *Nameless Recognition: Rabindranath Tagore and Other Indian Literatures* (2011), and translated Tagore's essays on literature for the Oxford Tagore Translations (2010).

Jayanti Chattopadhyay was Professor of Modern Indian Languages at the University of Delhi. She has authored a number of articles on Rabindranath in English and Bengali. She has also worked on linguistics and women's studies.

Sukanta Chaudhuri is Professor Emeritus, Department of English, Jadavpur University, Kolkata, where he founded the School of Cultural Texts and Records. Besides his work on Shakespeare and other Renaissance literature, he was chief co-ordinator of the Tagore online variorum *Bichitra*, and general editor of the Oxford Tagore Translations.

Supriya Chaudhuri is Professor Emerita, Department of English, Jadavpur University, Kolkata. She has translated Tagore's poetry and fiction, including the novel *Jogājog*, for the Oxford Tagore Translations, and published critical essays on Tagore. Her chapter on 'The Bengali Novel' appears in *The Cambridge Companion to Modern Indian Culture* (2012).

Sobhanlal Datta Gupta retired as Surendra Nath Banerjee Professor of Political Science, University of Calcutta. He has previously been attached to Presidency College, Kolkata, the University of Burdwan, and the Centre for Studies in Social Sciences, Calcutta. His works include *Marxism in Dark Times* (2012).

Partha Ghose retired as Professor, S.N. Bose National Centre for Basic Sciences, Kolkata. His many publications, scientific and other, include the edited volumes

Einstein, Tagore and the Nature of Reality (2017) and *Tagore, Einstein and the Nature of Reality: Literary and Philosophical Reflections* (2019).

Sankha Ghosh is a major poet and essayist in Bengali, and an eminent Tagore scholar. He retired as Professor of Bengali, Jadavpur University, Kolkata. Some of his noted Tagore titles are *Kāler mātrā o rabindranātak* (1978), *E āmir ābaran* (1980), and *Nirmān ār srishti* (1982). His many honours include the Sahitya Akademi Award, Rabindra Puraskar, and Jnanpith Award.

Ashish Lahiri is Adjunct Professor, Indian Institute of Science Education and Research, Kolkata, and a writer, translator, lexicographer and historian of science. On Tagore, he has published *Rabindranāth: mānusher dharma, mānusher bijnān* (2013) and *Rabindrasangit theke rabindranāth: byaktigata ek abhijātrā* (2014).

Ananda Lal retired as Professor of English, Jadavpur University, Kolkata. He has translated six Tagore plays and about fifty Tagore poems. His other Tagoreana include *The Voice of Rabindranath Tagore* (CD, 1997) and a teleplay of *Shesher Kabitā* (2007). He has directed *Arup ratan* and *Tapati* on stage.

Shefali Moitra retired as Professor of Philosophy, Jadavpur University, Kolkata. Besides her work in philosophy and women's studies, she has published widely on Rabindranath in English and Bengali, most recently *Rabindra-nrityanātya: ekti nāribādi pāth* (2019), a feminist reading of the dance dramas.

Kathleen M. O'Connell retired as Lecturer, University of Toronto. She has published *Rabindranath Tagore: The Poet as Educator* (2012), and co-edited *Rabindranath Tagore: Claiming a Cultural Icon* (2009) and the Tagore issue of the *University of Toronto Quarterly* (2008).

Biswajit Ray is Associate Professor of Bengali, Visva-Bharati. His publications on Rabindranath include *Rabindranāth o bibekānanda: swadeshe samakāle* (2017) and *Sachalatār gān* (2019). A well-known columnist, he writes regularly for the *Ananda Bazar Patrika* about various socio-cultural aspects of Bengali life.

Aseem Shrivastava has taught economics and philosophy at various institutions in India, Norway, and the United States. He currently teaches ecosophy at Ashoka University, Delhi, and is working on the philosophical dimensions of Rabindranath's ecological vision. He is co-author of *Churning the Earth: The Making of Global India* (2012).

R. Siva Kumar is Professor of Art History at Visva Bharati, an author, and curator. His books include *Rabindra Chitravali* (2011), a four-volume compilation of Rabindranath's paintings. His curated exhibitions include *The Last Harvest: Paintings of Rabindranath Tagore*, which travelled to nine museums across the world and four in India.

Saranindranath Tagore is Associate Professor of Philosophy, National University of Singapore, and an Editor-in-Chief of *Sophia: International Journal of Philosophy and Tradition*. His publications on Rabindranath include collaborative translations in *Rabindranath Tagore: Final Poems* (2001), and 'Rabindranath Tagore's Conception of Cosmopolitanism', *University of Toronto Quarterly* 77 (2008).

Harish Trivedi retired as Professor of English, University of Delhi. He has authored *Colonial Transactions* (1995), an Introduction (1991) to Edward Thompson's *Rabindranath Tagore: Poet and Dramatist*, and essays on Tagore and the West, Tagore and Premchand, and Tagore's view of contemporaneity.

Preface

Rabindranāth Thākur (Tagore) has been a recognized figure in world literature for a hundred years and more, but the language that unlocked his genius has also hampered his global reception. Bengali is the world's seventh most widely spoken language but not a 'world language' in its cultural reach. The extent of Rabindranath's output has also told against him. The standard edition of his Bengali works runs to thirty-three large volumes and is still incomplete; his English works to four yet larger volumes but is also incomplete. Only a fraction of the Bengali writings has been translated into English, often (starting with his own versions) with more than the inevitable loss in translating great literature. Renderings in other languages, including most Indian ones, have been made from these English versions more often than not.

Thus when Bengalis claim for Tagore a place beside Dante, Shakespeare, and Goethe, their claim is predictably ascribed to cultural chauvinism, especially as shades of such chauvinism are sometimes quite apparent. His early international reputation subsided in a matter of decades. Even in India, his effective impact outside Bengal came to decline, despite the iconic status ensured by the Nobel Prize and continuing to this day. He has received some fresh attention since the late twentieth century, often for his writings and activities in other fields rather than his core literary output. However, the sweep and depth of his total achievement has scarcely been addressed – even across the entire body of scholarly work, let alone in a single exercise.

His non-literary enterprises, active and contemplative, would each have made the reputation of a lesser man: music, dance, and painting; social, historical, and political thought, with an impressive record of activism; radical thinking on education and rural development, embodied in an institution that started as a makeshift school with five students and is today a major university. Through his travels no less than his writings, he acquired standing as a global intellectual, if thereby often reducing himself to the figure of a spiritualist and 'oriental sage'. More lastingly and materially, his historic association has transformed a remote Bengal village into a thriving academic centre, tourist destination, and, yet more improbably, an economic and administrative hub. Even Shakespeare's impact on Stratford-upon-Avon has not been transformative in so many ways.

It is a fit time to present the full scope of Rabindranath's improbably manifold genius in a single integrated effort. There have been few if any such ventures even in Bengali, short of the multi-volume biographies by Prabhatkumar

Mukhopadhyay and Prashantakumar Pal. (The latter did not live to complete his work.) This book attempts the task in a single accessible volume.

It is a formidable task, given the range of issues and sheer volume of material. Each major sector of Tagore's achievement had to be covered in a single article of limited size. Even so, it was agreed that the effort should not be diluted by limiting the material to what is available in English. Every contributor to this book has drawn on the full body of relevant Bengali material, for the benefit of readers who may not themselves have such access. An attempt has been made to link Tagore's work to his times and, more crucially, each aspect of that work to all others as appropriate. Readers will find how contributors on diverse subjects stress the total nature of the man's genius as reflected in their particular sphere of interest. He could work major innovations in music and painting, drama and dance, educational and ecological practice, and indeed literary genres like the short story and the novel, precisely because he was not a specialized practitioner in any one of these fields: they are diverse expressions of an endlessly versatile sensibility whose core expression, if anywhere, is in the poetry. It is to be hoped that the brevity of each study will be compensated by the chance to consider all of them side by side.

The book begins with two synoptic pieces by the doyens of Tagore studies in both realms of Bengal, Sankha Ghosh and Anisuzzaman. This is followed by a group of relatively long pieces, each offering a critical overview of a major area of Tagore's work or reception, and then by briefer, more focused studies of particular themes and concerns. With such a huge and intricate body of material, the sheer challenge of documentation was immense. We have tried to meet it productively in a cumulative bibliography-cum-index that, we hope, will benefit all Tagore scholars, not least as a template for a comprehensive exercise in the future.

I could not have carried out this daunting editorial task without the unstinted support and patience of a distinguished body of contributors: my sincerest thanks to them all. One of them did not live to see the volume in print, though he heroically met the deadline, like all his other commitments, during his last taxing illness. In grateful admiration, I offer this volume as a tribute to the memory of Sabyasachi Bhattacharya.

Sankha Ghosh was an unfailing source of information, guidance, and moral support. This would have been a different and poorer book without his sustained silent inputs, over and above his own essay. Thanks to Supriya Chaudhuri and Ananda Lal (again, for more than their signed contributions); to Amrit Sen and Ayanendranath Basu; to Rabindra-Bhavana, Santiniketan, for supplying the illustrations; and to the libraries of Visva-Bharati, Jadavpur University, and the Tagore Research Centre, Kolkata.

Sukanta Chaudhuri
Kolkata
April 2019

Note on Conventions and Practices

SOURCES AND CITATIONS

Tagore's Bengali texts are usually cited from the Visva-Bharati *Rabindra-rachanābali*, and English texts from the Sahitya Akademi *English Writings* (details below). The few works not included in these collections are cited from other sources.

The footnotes carry references to works quoted (in original or translation) or referred to closely, but not to works only cited by title. The latter are included in the List of Tagore's Works Cited.

ABBREVIATIONS AND SHORT TITLES

RRVB   *Rabindra-rachanābali* [Bengali Collected Works] (Kolkata: Visva-Bharati, 1939–); 33 + 2 vols, in progress. The two volumes of *Achalita sangraha* (early works 'withdrawn from circulation') are cited as A1 and A2.

RRGWB   *Rabindra-rachanābali* (Kolkata: Govt. of West Bengal, 1981–2004); 16 + 2 vols. Vol. 16 contains a detailed bibliography and publication history of the Bengali works.

EW   *The English Writings of Rabindranath Tagore*, vols 1–3 ed. Sisir Kumar Das, vol. 4 ed. Nityapriya Ghosh (Delhi: Sahitya Akademi, 1994–2007).

GB   *Gitabitān*, 3rd 1-vol. ed. (Kolkata: Visva-Bharati, 1973): chiefly cited for songs not found in *RRVB*.

CP   *Chithipatra* (Kolkata: Visva-Bharati, 1942–); 19 vols, in progress.

CPBLI   *Chhinnapatrābali*, 2nd ed. (Kolkata: Visva-Bharati, 1993).

Centenary *Rabindranath Tagore 1861–1961: A Centenary Volume* (New Delhi: Sahitya Akademi, 1961).

RJPM   Prabhātkumār Mukhopādhyāy, *Rabindra-jibani* (Kolkata: Visva-Bharati): vol. 1, 4th ed., 1970 rpt. 1994; vol. 2, 4th ed., 1976 rpt. 1999; vol. 3, 3rd ed., 1990 rpt. 1999; vol. 4, 3rd ed., 1994 rpt. 2004.

RJPP   Prashāntakumār Pāl, *Rabi-jibani*, 9 vols (Kolkata: vol. 1, Bhurjapatra, vols 2–9, Ānanda Publishers, 1982–2001).

SL   Krishna Dutta and Andrew Robinson, eds, *Selected Letters of Rabindranath Tagore* (Cambridge: Cambridge University Press, 1997).

VBP   *Visva-bhārati patrikā*.

VBQ   *Visva-Bharati Quarterly.*

100 Years   Martin Kämpchen and Imre Bangha, eds, *Rabindranath Tagore: One Hundred Years of Global Reception* (Hyderabad: Orient Blackswan, 2014).

TRANSLATIONS OF TITLES

Tagore's Bengali titles are translated at their first occurrence in each chapter. Where a single short piece is being cited, the title of the collection where it appears is generally not translated there but only in the List of Tagore's Works Cited.

Titles from other writers are not translated except for special need.

Translated titles that have appeared formally in published form are printed, like original titles, in italics for volume-length works and in roman type within inverted commas for short works. Translated titles devised for this volume appear in roman type without inverted commas.

Titles that are proper names have, of course, been left untranslated; so have a few others involving a nuance or a play on words that seemed untranslatable.

DATES

Except for special reason, dates of composition and publication (usually the latter) are cited within the chapters by year only. Fuller dates – exact, approximate, or conjectural – can be found in the List of Tagore's Works Cited.

Dates usually follow the Common Era (CE); Bengali Era (BE) dates are cited only for special reason. However, in the List of Tagore's Works Cited, journals are cited by Bengali date, which is often the only way to identify a particular issue.

The Bengali year runs from CE mid-April to mid-April: for example, BE 1268, the year of Tagore's birth, covers CE mid-April 1861 to mid-April 1862. Where the precise CE year is not known, the earlier year is cited with an asterisk: for example, *1861 covers the span of BE 1268, mid-April 1861 to mid-April 1862.

Bengali months run from the middle of one CE month to the next: for example, Vaishākh is mid-April to mid-May. Again, if the precise CE equivalent is not known, the earlier month is cited with an asterisk: for example, *April 1861 for Vaishākh 1268, the month of Tagore's birth.

TRANSLITERATION

No conversion of Bengali characters to Roman can be entirely consistent without using the phonetic alphabet or diacritical marks. This book uses only one such mark, the macron over *a* (*ā*) to indicate Bengali আ. Titles of works;

words, phrases, and excerpts from Bengali texts; and certain cultural terms (for example, *ānanda*) are rendered with macrons each time they occur. Proper names include the macron only at the point of first occurrence in each chapter. Bengali has no capital letters, and none has been used in transliterating Bengali titles, phrases, and excerpts, except for the initial letter of a title.

The following equivalents have been followed:

- অ = a, আ = ā, ঐ = ai, ও = o, ঔ = au
- শ,ষ = sh, স = s
- ক্ষ = ksh
- জ্ঞ = jn
- ড় = rh
- ঢ় = rhh
- য = j, but য-ফলা = y; hence র্য = rj, র্য্য = rjy. আচার্য/আচার্য্য, ভট্টাচার্য/ভট্টাচার্য্য are always spelt with 'ry'.
- ব-ফলা = w
- nasal (chandrabindu): *n* following the consonant (thus কঁ = kna, সঁ = sna).

Words close to the original Sanskrit form and/or associations are rendered accordingly, for example, with *v* instead of *b* (Veda, Vidyāsāgar, Vivekānanda). So are words of pan-Indian currency like the names of months or of Hindu gods and mythological characters. *Va-phalā* in Sanskrit words is rendered by *v*.

Certain place-names, notably 'Kolkata', 'Jorasanko', 'Santiniketan', and 'Sriniketan', and the institutional names 'Visva-Bharati', 'Brahmo Samaj', 'Sahitya Akademi', and 'University of Calcutta' are so spelt, following the standard official forms. But book titles like *Shāntiniketan* and *Bishwabhārati* are transliterated in the usual way.

Certain place-names, notably 'Kolkata' (also 'Mumbai', 'Chennai', and so on), have been cited in their current versions irrespective of the date of reference or exact form in the source, except in direct quotation.

The system is not without anomalies, which could not be removed without creating other, arguably greater ones. We would request the indulgence of readers.

TRANSLATED PASSAGES

Authors were asked either to use Tagore's own translations of his work or to make their own. Except in very rare cases, translations by other hands have not been used. Translations carrying references only to the Bengali source (usually *RRVB*) have been made for this volume by the author of the chapter concerned. Tagore's own translations (and the few others cited) are documented in the notes.

BENGALI NAMES

Unavoidably, the familiar form 'Tagore' has been retained in place of 'Thākur'. Other personal names have been consistently transliterated following the above conventions, irrespective of individual practice (which is often hard to ascertain and can itself be variable). In a few illustrious cases, where the person concerned used another spelling, the latter follows in parentheses: thus, Michael Madhusudan Datta (Dutt), Jagadishchandra Basu (Bose), Buddhadeb Basu (Buddhadeva Bose).

When directly citing an English work, the title and author's name follow the title page even if it differs from the normal practice of this volume: thus, Bengali *Gitānjali* but English *Gitanjali*; 'Debabrata Mukhopādhyāy' in the text but 'Devabrata Mukerjea' in the reference citing the title page. This divergence also applies to the use of macrons.

As a rule, authentic Bengali forms of names have been preferred to their anglicized versions: thus 'Chattopādhyāy' and 'Mukhopādhyāy' rather than 'Chatterjee' or 'Mukherjee'. The latter forms are sometimes placed in parentheses at the point of first reference.

In accord with common practice, famous Bengalis are usually referred to by their first names: 'Bankim(chandra)', 'Sharatchandra', 'Sudhindranath'. The outstanding and unavoidable exception is the free use of both 'Rabindranath' and 'Tagore'. The latter form, familiar to most readers of this volume and current in many Indian languages, could not be dismissed.

1 Rabindranath Tagore

From Art to Life

SANKHA GHOSH

I

There is an account in Rāni Chanda's book on Abanindranāth Tagore, Rabindranāth's artist nephew, on Abanindranath's response to music. Listening to song after song, he would suddenly burst out: 'Here are you all trying to construct Rabikā's[1] biography, but his real biography is in his songs.... His whole life is contained in them. You will find his living image there among the words and the music.'[2] Much later, Niradchandra Chaudhuri seems to be saying something similar: if Tagore's songs are arranged by date, 'one can construct his mental biography from them'.[3]

The two observations sound much the same, but did the two speakers have the same thing in mind by the poet's 'biography'? Abanindranath would listen to Tagore songs like 'I can bear yet more blows' or 'Strike me more, still more, O lord', or lines like 'My sorrows are like a red lotus girding your feet',[4] and exclaim, 'No, no, not that one, sing some other song. Rabika could say things like that, he had the courage; I don't. I can only say: I have borne enough, now raise me on high, make me a lamp in your temple.'[5] The idea of a 'biography' conveyed by such a remark ('He had the courage') seems very different from that of Niradchandra. The latter mines specific songs by Tagore for direct reflections of the poet's personal life.

He discovers, for instance, how 'just as Chateaubriand could pass from France to Bengal, Rabindranath passed from Bengal to England'.[6] Which is the song conveying this piece of biography? According to Niradchandra, it is 'I know you, I know you, woman from a foreign land'.[7] Niradchandra is well aware of the very different mystical insight behind its composition, as vouched by the poet himself in his reminiscences,[8] but he does not place much reliance upon that account, as in his view, songs can only spring from sensory experience. The foreign woman, therefore, must be some blue-eyed blonde-haired beauty, not a cosmic or universal presence: if anyone thinks otherwise, 'he cannot have seen a female form in his life, or felt the touch of a woman's body against his own'.[9] Niradchandra even knows exactly what

Tagore was recalling. On 19 September 1890, he writes in *Yuropjātrir dāyāri* (Diary of a Traveller to Europe) that Englishwomen are the most beautiful on earth.[10] That perception of 1890 cannot but be the precise motive power behind this song written in 1895, with lines such as 'I have laid my ear to the sky to hear your song'.

The occasion of a single song is of little moment. What should concern us is the very idea of a particular song springing in simple causation from a particular episode of the poet's life. For Niradchandra, the language of song can never be sensorily neutral (though he admits at another point that the themes of song might be transcendent).[11] In what, then, does the history of a song inhere, its language or its theme? If we are to place any value at all on the theme, how can we ignore what the poet himself tells us about the inspiration behind the song?

Niradchandra himself writes in another context that he does not believe 'everything an author writes is linked to some event or experience of his life'.[12] If that is so, his other thesis must be discounted. Any person's life, let alone a poet's, comprises not just events but feelings and perceptions, expressed and unexpressed. Many moments of artistic creation originate in complex currents of experience, mundane and transcendent, spanning many layers of consciousness. It then becomes difficult to work back to some specific external event at the time of composition.

2

Not that there can never be a link between a poet's work and the external events of his life. When we hear songs like 'Your dead river is now in flood', or the pledge to the motherland 'Whoever might desert you, I will never do so, O mother', or the challenge to the British 'Are you so strong that you can break the bonds of fate?',[13] we have no problem in relating that surge of patriotic sentiment to the political movement against the partition of Bengal in 1905, the year of their composition. We do not have to deduce this from the words of the songs: we have external witness of the circumstances in which they were composed. Elsewhere, we can work out a connexion for ourselves. The early manuscript *Pushpānjali* (Flower Offering) contains songs such as 'Why did you come, why did you love though not loved in return?', 'The flower that withers drops from the branch', and 'Why did you make her weep?'[14] We can easily relate them to the young Rabindranath's grief at the self-inflicted death of his beloved sister-in-law Kādambari Debi. Moments of strong emotion, impelled by patriotism or bereavement, can indeed leave visible traces in a poet's work.

But we cannot conclude that all such compelling moments will find direct expression in poetry. We would then be at a loss to explain how, in the very month that his young son Shamindranāth died, the poet could address the divine in lines like these:

> Your unsullied nectar is pouring down in love, in life, in song and
> scent and light and joy, flooding the skies and the earth. Joy is waking
> in visible form on all sides, breaking all bonds: my life is brimming
> over with rich nectar.[15]

If we did not know the date, we might conclude that this song marks an especially happy moment in the poet's life. But the poet himself expresses in another song how suffering can evoke its own joy, how despair can transform into ardour: 'Let the song of joy sound on the flute of my pain. Let my boat to the other shore sail on the tide of tears.'[16]

Alongside this poem from *Balākā*, we might consider another from the same volume: 'Do you hear the roar of death from afar?'[17] What was the poet's situation in real life on the day he wrote this celebrated poem? He had returned from Kashmir only a few days earlier. He had not enjoyed his trip at all. He writes to his daughter Mirā on 19 Kārtik 1322 (5 November 1915): 'Wherever I go, I am plagued by disturbance – there isn't a moment's respite from being bothered by people. I was on a houseboat in Srinagar, but found neither peace nor joy, so I quickly escaped.'[18] Two days later, he writes in the same vein to Pramatha Chaudhuri,[19] and in another two days to Santoshchandra Majumdār that he had come, exhausted, to recoup by the river Padmā.[20] Yet, some two weeks earlier, he had written while still in Kashmir: 'I am one song after another, one life after another. I am the shining light that bursts from the shattered heart of darkness' (*Balākā* #35).

This is the varied background to *Balākā* #37. It was composed on 23 Kārtik 1322 (9 November 1915), the very day of the letter to Santoshchandra. The poem is a call to action: 'Set out, voyagers, set out: the command has come. Your stay in the harbour is at end.' They must embark 'with the world's lamentation in your ears, the demented times beating upon your head', yet raise the flag of victory through storm and thunder.[21] The mind that issues such a call must be tracked through a very different path than a direct situational link.

Again, the very day that Rabindranath is burdened with an urgent payment relating to some land, he can write: 'I lose you time and again only so that I can find you anew.... You are not a hidden presence but my very own, through all time.'[22] On the day he exhorts Mahim Thākur of the royal house of Tripurā to commit himself to his homeland's cause – tells him he cannot be indifferent to the call even if he wishes – he writes the poem 'Nirudyam' ('Indolence' or 'Disheartenment', *Kheyā*). Another time, he writes: 'I have a home in every place.' He hears the call of the earth, senses the exhilaration of each blade of grass: 'There is love in every speck of dust, there is joy in all creation.'[23] We would not have guessed that this was written at a time of deep financial stress. The very next day, he writes to Priyanāth Sen: 'I need about 12,000 rupees, but I am told the moneylender will give no more than 6,000. Of course, that's only hearsay. Try to get 12,000 or 10,000 if you can, otherwise I'll have to make do with 6,000.'[24]

The disjuncture is not always between external events and inward states. The mind itself can assume various, apparently contradictory, positions at the same time. Hence Tagore can write

> Now comes the destroyer.... Life joins in the revels of death....
> Abandon all, come as a bride in blood-red garb.[25]

on the same day as

> You jest by dressing him [the soul] in beggar's guise.... He had thought
> himself the eternal pauper, in life and death.... But at close of day,
> you drew him to your side and shared your throne with him.[26]

The very next day, 'We press forward, who can bind us?'[27] appears alongside 'Evening falls: mother, draw me to your bosom'.[28] It seems incredible that these two pieces should bear the same date, one with the lines

> My mind has spread across the skies, I am drugged with light; but
> those other people skulk behind closed doors: their eyes will be
> dazzled when they look out.

and the other

> Bring back, mother, bring back all that has been lost in this scattered
> life: let it all gather together in your darkness.

The true history of the poet's mental life lies in this tension between the opposite visions of light and darkness.

3

It is because we neglect this history that we often form wrong ideas about the poet's sensibility. The year 1905 marked the first high point of the Swadeshi movement, where Rabindranath's role has become a matter of legend. However, in the two volumes of poems that followed, *Kheyā* (1906) and *Gitānjali* (1910), he seems to be in total retreat from a life of action, conflict, and turmoil. 'Bid me farewell, forgive me [for my withdrawal],' he writes on 14 Chaitra 1312 (28 March 1906), 'I am no longer a farer on the road of work.'[29] On 29 Shrāvan 1317 (14 August 1910), in the last poem in *Gitānjali*, he speaks as 'one whose store is exhausted in the middle of his journey, whose brows are lined with loss'.[30] Such passages bear out the overt theme of renunciation: both collections strike a deeply introspective note of vigil and renunciation. This moreover was the time when each morning he would deliver a spiritual sermon to his colleagues in Santiniketan, to be collected in instalments under the title *Shāntiniketan*, and when he brought out another volume on spiritual themes actually entitled *Dharma*. The play *Rājā*, full of mystical implications, appeared in the same year as *Gitānjali*. Putting these facts together, we might well conclude that we have found the key to his mental history at this date, in a consistent narrative of retreat from the world.

For the moment, I am not raising the question of whether what we call Rabindranath's spirituality is necessarily escapist. However, to look at all his writings from this period as unidimensionally 'spiritual' is itself a restrictive approach, which has prevented us to this day from assessing Rabindranath's achievement at its true and full worth. If we look beyond those confines, we will find a body of essays on social and political issues balancing the spiritual: 'Swadeshi samāj' (Indigenous Society) alongside 'Prāchin bhārater ekah' ('The One' of Ancient India), and 'Rājbhakti' (Loyalty to the King) alongside 'Utsab' (Celebration). *Dharma* was published in 1909, but nine of its essays were written between 1902 and 1906. Over that same span of time, Rabindranath expressed these two contrary positions:

> Is our music carrying us to that more secret interior of creation,
> where all the tunes of the universe forgo all discord and disorder to
> unfold themselves, at every moment, as a single perfected raga?[31]

and

No human and no demon has the power to eradicate by sheer force of governance the famished truth in the innermost hearts of 300 million subjects.[32]

I have cited the poem in *Kheyā*, 'Bid me farewell, forgive me'. But only ten days later, he writes from Āgartalā, 'I am killing myself with traipsing round.'[33] Now he is in Agartala over the affairs of the state of Tripura, then again in Barishāl for the provincial gathering of the Indian National Congress. What appears from his poems to be a phase of spiritual renunciation is the very time that he turns again and again to matters like the relations between Hindus and Muslims, as in the essays 'Byādhi o pratikār' (Malady and Cure), 'Samasyā' (The Problem), and 'Sadupāy' (A Good Recourse), or the relations between British rulers and Indian subjects, as in 'Deshnāyak' (Leader of the Country), 'Jajnabhanga' (Spoiling the Sacrificial Ceremony), 'Path o pātheya' (The Way and the Means), and 'Deshahit' (The Good of the Country). In 1908, as chair of the provincial convention of Pābnā District, he held up before his audience the wretched condition of rural Bengal, and proposed means for its amelioration: how several villages might combine to form a circle, whose headmen could resolve local disputes in their own assemblies. At more or less the same time, he was writing devotional songs like 'I hear your footsteps, lord' and 'Play your veena in my heart', and a cosmic vision of joy like 'This great wave',[34] as also the essay 'Duhkha' (Sorrow) in *Dharma*, which reiterates the Upanishadic idea that 'the concept of sorrow and the concept of creation are inextricably linked'.[35]

4

It thus appears that during the very period marked by a deep vein of renunciation in Tagore's poems and songs, and even to some extent in his plays and essays, he also proves to be bound to social and family life by many hard, mundane commitments. There is ample evidence of this aspect of his being in his essays of the time, and in his conception of the motherland in *Gorā*. In fact, India may be called the principal character in this epic novel, composed in instalments between 1907 and 1910. The terrain it unfolds is not a land of dreams and sentiment but 'this vast, withdrawn rural India – how isolated, how constricted, how enfeebled', a land where 'the burden of inert ignorance and suffering, vast and terrifying, weighs upon the shoulders of all of us, learned and unlearned, rich and poor'.[36] This vision is brought out through the eyes of a vigorous servant of India: the protagonist Gorā, but no less his creator, the novelist himself. Gora gives living shape to the ethos that Rabindranath articulates in essays like 'Swadeshi samāj', 'Chhātrader prati sambhāshan' (Address to the Students) and 'Byādhi o pratikār' – and this in the middle of the same 'spiritual phase'. It acquires force because Rabindranath is not merely uttering his thoughts about his country; he is defining the total perception of a mature and experienced citizen.

Rabindranath understood patriotism as an engagement with the country's identity, the basis of its selfhood. Over a substantial period before and after the anti-partition movement of 1905, he evolved some methods to carry out this function. He called his countrymen to the cause; but not content with motivating others, he also tried to implement his ideas in his own principles and practice. The two fields he adjudged most critical were agriculture and education. From late in the previous century, he had been conceiving of an ideal education system for India; he now set about its implementation in his own *brahmacharyāshram* at Santiniketan. When a wider programme of national education was proposed during the anti-partition movement, he was one of its principal movers. At the same time, he involved himself directly in agricultural improvements and rural uplift on his family estates.

'Bid me farewell, forgive me,' he had written in 1906 in the 'renunciatory' volume *Kheyā*. But starting the same year, he sent some young people close to him to study agricultural science abroad: his son Rathindranāth, his friend's son Santoshchandra Majumdar, and (a little later) his son-in-law Nagendranāth Gangopādhyāy. While they were abroad, he started work at home by enlisting local youths. 'I wish to set up true *swarāj* [home rule] in every village,' he writes to Ajitkumār Chakrabarti on 29 Paush 1314 (14 January 1908), 'as a small model of what should happen across the country. It's a very difficult task, but it must be done.'[37] He engaged people like Bhupeshchandra Rāy and Jatindranāth Mukhopādhyāy in the task: 'Some lads from East Bengal have fallen captive to my lures,' he writes elatedly to Abalā Basu in April 1908. He has set them to work 'paving roads, digging ponds and drains, clearing forest land'.[38] He hopes that by the time Abala and Jagadishchandra Basu (Bose) return home, the villages on his Shilāidaha estates will be markedly improved. On 12 Kārtik 1314 (29 October 1907), twenty-three years before he witnessed the transformation of Soviet Russia, he writes to Nagendranath:

You have gone abroad to study agriculture with the resources that might have fed our famine-stricken tenants at home. If you can make up for it by ensuring a few more mouthfuls for them on your return, my mind will be assuaged. Remember that the landlord's wealth is actually the peasants': they are bearing the cost of your education by starving or half-starving themselves. It is your responsibility to repay this debt in full. That is your first task, even before the welfare of your own family.[39]

The moment he returned, writes Rathindranath, he 'whisked me off to Shilaidaha and set me to work'. Sitting on boat-deck while proceeding from Shilaidaha to Patisar, he would tell Rathindranath of 'the social, ethical and economic plight he had seen in village after village of Bengal – the various problems of their daily lives, how he had tried to resolve them, and what he planned to do in future'.[40] Rathindranath and his associates set to work: Rabindranath sent instructions without fail, even when he was far away. He might write:

> There is a rice-husking mill in Bolpur. It would be useful to acquire one like that for use here [on his estate at Patisar]. I was thinking what *industry* one might teach to the local farmers.... I need to know whether *Pottery* can count as a *Cottage Industry*. Try to find out about this – whether we could set up a small furnace and engage all the people in a village to work it collectively.... Another possibility is to teach them to make umbrellas.[41]

Again, he writes to Nagendranath on 30 Phālgun 1316 (14 March 1910): 'Kushtiā is a promising place to set up a *Co-operative Dairy* with our tenants.... I am awaiting your arrival to start such projects.'[42] And to Bhupeshchandra Ray on 17 Shravan 1315 (1 August 1908): 'Encourage the tenants to plant pineapple, banana, date palms and other fruit trees around their houses and on the embankments between their fields. You can make very strong thread from pineapple leaves.'[43]

Rabindranath writes these missives even while composing the songs in *Gitānjali*, the sermons in *Shāntiniketan* and the play *Shāradotsab* (Autumn Festival), with *Rājā* (The King) and *Dākghar* (*The Post Office*) soon to follow. His sermon on 11 Māgh 1316 (24 January 1910) at the Brahmo festival of Māghotsav addresses God in these words: 'Whatever is beautiful, beneficent and lasting in me is where you manifest yourself within me. Everything else is precious only insofar as they contribute to this manifestation.'[44] Only nine days later, he instructs Nagendranath: 'There's no end to the things to do: to get the farmers to start co-operative farming, to set up banks, to build hygienic dwelling-houses for them, to free them from debt, to arrange for their children's education, to ensure their security in old age, to build roads and dams, to solve their water supply problems, to unite them in mutual help.'[45]

5

Is there really any contradiction between these aspects of Rabindranath's sensibility? Is there no deeper link between the spiritual life and the social? If we observe carefully, we may find that his spiritual thought has a social basis, and his social thought is empowered by spiritual motivation. The two are linked and balanced, the apparent contradictions resolved at a nodal point where all the strands of his life come together.

Whenever Rabindranath talks of India's development, he evokes the image of a vast country in decline, underscoring the disjuncture between its pervasive plight and the agenda of its political institutions. What can the country mean to the common people when there is no guiding force in their unfed, untaught lives? Living in the midst of an unrelenting 'nothing', they have been drained of all self-confidence. Ten years' close observation of the Bengal countryside underlies Rabindranath's philosophy of rural life in *Gorā* (1910), charged with a sense of its impoverishment and self-abjection. He adjudged it a principal task of Indian politics to free the common people from this demeaning state and infuse them with a belief in themselves. His social philosophy thus leads him to conceive of an inner force, a force within oneself (*ātmashakti*). To acquire this *ātmashakti* becomes the chief aim of his political thought in the first decade of the twentieth century. In the play *Prāyashchitta* (1909), Dhananjay rouses the subjects to rebel against the king, but is frustrated to find them relying on him alone, not on their own power.

Once we grasp this aspect of his thought, we realize that what might seem like Rabindranath's withdrawal from society is actually a distinctive expression of his social being. The 'effective means' (*sadupāy*), 'remedy' (*pratikār*) and 'resource' (*pātheya*) of which he talks in his political writings are attainable only through this internal resource of *ātmashakti*.

Ātmashakti is fulfilled in social endeavour, but it springs from the heart of one's private sensibility. Rabindranath says in the Maghotsav sermon 'Chiranabinatā' cited earlier:

We must renew our youth every moment, we must be reborn in Him again and again, minute to minute – as a poem attains its movement by adding one metrical foot to another, revalidating the underlying metre every time, achieving beauty by co-ordinating every part to the whole. That is what we must do as well.[46]

The notion of 'co-ordinating every part to the whole' contains his basic philosophy of life, a life that finds emancipation in moving outward from the centre to the totality.

This perception enables us to understand how he can write on the same day of darkness and light, destruction and nurture, outward and inward movement. The being in beggar's garb can be endowed with internal wealth. But where is the seat of that internal life? Who is the maharaja at whose gate the beggar will stand? The being beyond the confines of the 'I', inhering in an all-pervasive 'not-I', is the being decked in royal robes that can welcome and relieve the beggar. When one responds to that welcome, one can look outward, imbued with the inner force of *ātmashakti*, and say eagerly, 'Now comes the destroyer.' The protecting maharaja becomes one with the destroyer; life plunges into a festival of death.

The strands of our 'scattered life' are to be upgathered into a fulfilling darkness – like the darkness in the play *Rājā*, the soul's secret chamber where one nurtures one's being. That retreat into darkness is not in conflict with the call to march forward: there is unbroken traffic between the external collective being and the interiorized, individual self. We cannot chart this exchange by a straight graph. Our social existence and its representation in art are linked but also separated by the unending flow of our everyday experience – sometimes minute and trivial, sometimes momentous; now sensory, now beyond the senses. A single poem might synthesize all these diverse elements: in that case, it cannot simply reflect the poet's external life as suggested by Niradchandra Chaudhuri. Rather, we must look for the poet's life in his work in the way proposed by Abanindranath, where we view all the elements together and admire the 'courage' of the poet who could engage with them all. The poet's life is borne on the pulse-beat of that courageous heart.

Translated by Sukanta Chaudhuri from 'Shilpa theke jiban' in Dāminir gān *(Kolkata: Papyrus, 2002).*

NOTES

1. Short for 'Rabikākā', 'Uncle Rabi'.
2. Rani Chanda, *Shilpiguru abanindranāth* (Kolkata: Visva-Bharati, 1972), 137.
3. Niradchandra Chaudhuri, *Ātmaghāti rabindranāth* (Kolkata: Mitra o ghosh, 1996), 23.
4. Respectively: *GB*, 'Pujā' #224, *GB* 'Pujā' #228, *Gitāli* #28.
5. Chanda, *Shilpiguru abanindranāth*, 137. The last words echo a line from yet another Tagore song, 'The touchstone of fire' (*GB*, 'Pujā' #212).
6. Chaudhuri, *Ātmaghāti rabindranāth*, 23.
7. *GB*, 'Prem' #86.
8. *Jibansmriti*, RRVB 17:389–90.

9. Chaudhuri, *Ātmaghāti rabindranāth*, 21.

10. This superlative praise in the original text was toned down in the version in *RRVB* 1:604.

11. Chaudhuri, *Ātmaghāti rabindranāth*, 24, 57.

12. Ibid., 57.

13. Respectively: *GB*, 'Swadesh' #5, #25, #44.

14. Respectively: song from the musical drama *Māyār khelā* (The Sport of Illusion), *RRVB* 1:256; *GB*, 'Prem' #387; *GB*, *Rabichchhāyā* #26, p. 882.

15. *Gitānjali* #6, *RRVB* 11:9.

16. *Balākā* #20, *RRVB* 12:41.

17. *Balākā* #37, *RRVB* 12:60.

18. *CP* 4:62.

19. Ibid., 5:204.

20. *Desh*, Pujā issue (*sharadiyā*), 1362 (1955), 28.

21. *Balākā* #37, *RRVB* 12:61–2.

22. *GB*, 'Pujā' #45.

23. *Utsarga* #14, *RRVB* 10:16.

24. *CP* 8:151.

25. *Balākā* #2, *RRVB* 12:3–4.

26. *Gitimālya* #106, *RRVB* 11:209.

27. *Balākā* #3, *RRVB* 12:5.

28. *Gitimālya* #107, *RRVB* 11:209.

29. 'Bidāy' (Farewell), *Kheyā*, *RRVB* 10:150.

30. *RRVB* 11:123.

31. 'Utsab', *RRVB* 13:339.

32. 'Rājbhakti', *RRVB* 10:440.

33. *CP* 13:51.

34. Respectively: *GB*, 'Puja' #399, #409, #322.

35. *RRVB* 13:400.

36. *Gorā*, ch. 26, *RRVB* 6:276–7.

37. Rudraprasād Chakrabarti, ed., *Bhakta o kabi* (Kolkata: Paschimbanga bānglā ākādemi, 2007), 10.

38. *CP* 6:90–1.

39. *Desh*, Pujā issue (*shāradiyā*), 1362 (1955), 9.

40. Rathindranath Tagore, *Pitrismriti* (Kolkata: Jijnāsā, 1960), 239–40.

41. Ibid., 246–7. In this and later excerpts, words in italics are in English in the original Bengali text.

42. *Desh*, 3 Agrahāyan 1362 (November 1955), 164.

43. *Purbāshā*, Tagore issue, 1348 (1941), 114.

44. 'Chiranabinatā' (Eternal Youth), *RRVB* 14:505.

45. *Desh*, 24 Kārtik 1362 (November 1955), 9.

46. *RRVB* 14:499.

2 A Garland of Many Tagores

ANISUZZAMAN

I

Rabindranāth's collection of poems *Shesh saptak* appeared on the poet's seventy-fourth birthday, 25 Vaishākh 1342 (8 May 1935). Anticipating the pre-planned date of publication, he writes in poem #43:

> The twenty-fifth of Vaishākh flows on, carrying the tide of birthdays towards the day of death. Sitting on that moving seat, a craftsman weaves, along the borders of many small births and deaths, a garland of many Rabindranaths.[1]

Rabindranath lived another six years after writing this poem. There was no slackening of his creative powers during this period. More flowers were added to the garland even after his death. The flowers are not all of the same colour, size, or scent. They do not even always match each other when viewed side by side.

2

Rabindranath's close associate W.W. Pearson tells an anecdote about Tagore and Gāndhi. He asked both of them the same two questions: what did they consider their greatest virtue and greatest vice? Gandhi returned an evasive answer. Tagore's was both pungent and profound: to both questions, he replied, 'Inconsistency.'[2]

This could not have been said in jest. It is neither possible nor desirable for a man who lived to be eighty, whose life testified to unmatched creativity, vast experience, and unending stimuli, to be entirely consistent. His views changed over time, as did his sense of values: that was only natural. But more than that, his actions and utterances sometimes seem truly inconsistent or even self-contradictory.

Rabindranath first went to England in 1878 in order to qualify for the Indian Civil Service like his elder brother Satyendranāth or else to be a barrister. After a year and a half, he returned without any training or qualification. Among the things that most impressed him in England was the freedom enjoyed by its women. In the serialized account of his travels published in the journal *Bhārati*, he extolled the independence enjoyed by Englishwomen and the free mingling of men and women in English society, in contrast to the situation back home, which 'reduced half the humans in society to the level of beasts'.[3] Dwijendranāth Tagore, the editor of *Bhārati*, added some acerbic comments in disagreement. Rabindranath, too, did not hesitate to attack his elder brother in kind.

Yet, some years later, writing in the journal *Bhārati o bālak* (Āshārhh 1296, *June 1889) after hearing the woman scholar and reformer Panditā Ramābāi's lecture in Pune, Rabindranath declared the difference between men and women to be ordained by nature: men were superior in physical strength and intelligence, women in looks and emotive power. He confidently opines that there have been no great women poets or musicians because women can never be the intellectual equals of men; hence, 'The current outcry against patriarchy seems to me not only unjustified but harmful.' Going further, 'If a man treats his devoted wife brutally, it does not humiliate the woman but glorifies her.'[4]

Two years later, Rabindranath wrote the verse play *Chitrāngadā* (published 1892) where the princess Chitrāngadā, brought up as a male, discovers her womanly identity on encountering Arjuna, the hero of the *Mahābhārata*. At the end, she tells Arjuna that she does not have the flower-like tenderness demanded of women, but she does have 'the undying, unchanging heart of a woman'. She then declares proudly:

> I am not a goddess, nor am I a weak insignificant woman. I am not one you can worship and raise high, nor one you can neglect and have follow you. You will come to know what I am only if you let me travel with you down perilous roads, share your challenging thoughts and partake of your sternest vows, if you make me your companion in joy and sorrow.[5]

Arjuna was overcome with admiration on hearing this, as we may be towards both Chitrangada and her creator. Chitrangada's words anticipate the speaker of the much later poem 'Sabalā' (The Empowered Woman, 1928): 'God, why should you not let woman rule over her own fate?'[6] Still later (1936), in the essay 'Nāri' (Woman) in *Kālāntar*, he comments on the way women's lives were extending to areas formerly closed to them: 'At the start of a new era, women have come forward to take up the task of moulding a new civilization', correcting the age-old imbalance in gender roles.[7] All this might make us conclude that Tagore has set aside all his earlier prejudices and reservations about women. But when between these last two works, in the short novel *Dui bon* (Two Sisters, 1932), he cites unnamed authorities for dividing all women into two categories, mothers and lovers, we cannot but be nonplussed at the contradiction. We would not have expected such simplism from the creator of so many diverse and individualized women characters from Binodini in *Chokher bāli* (Grit in the Eye) to Lābanya in *Shesher kabitā* (The Last Poem), indeed two such different women as Harimohini and Ānandamayi in the same novel, *Gorā*.

We may also consider a related matter. Towards the end of the nineteenth century, Rabindranath engaged in polemics with Akshaychandra Sarkār and Chandranāth Basu on the subject of Hindu marriage. He took a humane and rational stand, which led him to firmly oppose child marriage. In the essay 'Hindubibāha' (Hindu Marriage) (1887), he cites Dr William Carpenter in a manner that indicates he held girls should not be married until they had attained puberty, somewhere between the ages of thirteen and sixteen.[8] Yet in the very first year of the new century, he married off two of his daughters in quick succession: Mādhurilatā, then little more than fourteen, and Renukā, eleven and a half. The former's husband had been practising law for six or seven years, and the other had qualified as a doctor. The difference in age between husband and wife was not in accord with Tagore's professed views. He was also opposed to dowry, yet he agreed to such a payment to his eldest son-in-law, that too in cash. A complication was caused when the poet's father, Debendranāth, who was expected to provide the money, refused to do so, though he contributed 5,000 rupees after the marriage. The second son-in-law demanded that Tagore fund his homeopathic studies in America. Tagore's biographer Prabhātkumār Mukhopādhyāy suspects that the man had married chiefly with this end in view.[9] Tagore obliged and sent him on his way when the wedding was scarcely over. The youngest daughter, Mirā, was also married at fourteen, in 1907. Her husband too went to America at Tagore's expense, though the poet was then in straitened circumstances. In a letter to his son Rathindranāth,[10] Tagore remarked on this son-in-law's shallowness of intelligence and personality.

3

In his reminiscences *Jibansmriti* (1912), Rabindranath writes: 'I never had any truck with the religion practised in our household – I did not accept it.'[11] Yet in 1880, before he was twenty, he composed seven devotional songs in one go for the Brahmo Samaj, followed it up with many more, and acted many times as the *āchārya* or spiritual preceptor at the Brahmo festival of Māghotsav. In 1884, Debendranath appointed him secretary of the Ādi ['Original'] Brahmo Samaj to which this branch of the Tagores belonged. The biographer Prabhatkumar recounts that 'the young Rabindranath set about his duties as secretary with great enthusiasm and diligence; his excess of ardour led to a battle of words with Bankimchandra'.[12] It is around this time (1894) that, in an essay on Rāmmohan Rāy, Tagore calls Brahmoism 'a religion for the world'.[13] His eldest son-in-law, Sharatkumār Chakrabarti, had to embrace Brahmoism at the time of marriage, and Rabindranath personally initiated his youngest son-in-law, Nagendranāth Gangopādhyāy, from another branch of the Brahmo Samaj to that to which the Tagore family belonged. During the censuses of 1901 and 1911, he strongly proclaimed his belief that Brahmos were Hindus.

Yet he says that he found himself asking whether he had sincerely adopted the Brahmo ideal or only assumed it as a 'mask' fashioned from an 'artificial average' of thought and belief, obscuring 'the living face of truth'. The moment this doubt assailed him, he declares, he cut off all connection with his 'church'.[14] It is indeed true that Tagore never clung to any institutional religion, but he held positions of authority in the Brahmo Samaj and in due course appointed his son-in-law Nagendranath as its secretary. He drew inspiration from the Upanishads all his life, was deeply influenced by medieval saints and mystics like Kabir, and, though he never adopted the Bāul way of life and worship, he imbibed a great deal from the mystic pietism of Baul songs. He followed no particular faith, no guru, no religious text, no mantra, committing himself rather to what he called the religion of man. In 1926, perturbed by religious riots and divisions, he wrote: 'Honest atheism is much better than this terrifying deluded religion.... I cannot see any solution except to burn all India's misguided religious faith in the flames of atheism and make an absolutely fresh start.'[15] Around the same time, he wrote in the poem 'Dharmamoha' (The Illusion of Religion, *Parishesh*): 'Smite with thunder the walls of the prison of religion, / Bring the light of wisdom to this unfortunate land.'[16]

Yet during one phase of his life, when he first moved from Shilāidaha to Santiniketan, Rabindranath was deeply immersed in Hindu orthodoxy. His nephew Balendranāth had conceived of a residential school for *brahmachāri*s (celibate learners and devotees) at Santiniketan, but was not able to implement the idea. Rabindranath now took up the project. It was the period of his devotional poems in *Naibedya* and essays on social principles in the journal *Bangadarshan*. Inspired by the ancient Indian ideal of the *tapovana*, or forest retreat, and a concomitant celibacy, he set up his *brahmacharyāshram* at the end of 1901. The programme was strongly affected by the views of Brahmabāndhab Upadhyāy. Brahmabandhab's exchanges with Rabindranath began when, under a pseudonym, he wrote an effusive review of *Naibedya* in the journal *The Twentieth Century*. Born into a brahmin family, Brahmabandhab joined Keshabchandra Sen's Nababidhān ('New Order') Brahmo Samaj. On his travels in Sind to propagate Brahmoism, he converted first to Protestant and then to Catholic Christianity, reverted to Hinduism in 1898 and became a monk, subsequently took up arms against British rule, and died while on trial for sedition.

In the system set up by Brahmabandhab, the boys of the *brahmacharyāshram* had to wear saffron clothes, chant the *gāyatri mantra*, meditate morning and evening, eat no meat or fish, wear no shoes, and use no umbrellas. They sat down to eat in groups separated by caste. It was Brahmabandhab who set up the practice of calling Rabindranath 'Gurudeb'. While living at Shilaidaha to manage the family estates, the poet had engaged three tutors for his children: Jagadānanda Rāy, Shibdhan Vidyārnav, and a Mr Lawrence. The first two joined the *brahmacharyāshram*; the third expectedly could not, though he later taught briefly at Santiniketan. Brahmabandhab, a man of restless mind, soon left the place. Some time after, a problem arose when Kunjalāl Ghosh joined as a teacher. The boys had to touch the teachers' feet at the start of class: how could brahmin boys touch the feet of a *kāyastha* teacher? The headmaster Manoranjan Bandyopādhyay asked Rabindranath to resolve the problem. The poet decreed that students should touch the feet of brahmin teachers and only offer a *namaskār* to the others. In fact, he thought it best if Kunjalal did not teach classes on a regular basis but looked after matters like the students' meals: he would then not count as a *guru*.

It took time for Rabindranath to cast aside such discriminatory orthodoxy. How and when he achieved this appears in a letter of 1911 about admitting a Muslim student. The movement against the partition of Bengal, when Hindus and Muslims marched together in protest, had happened in the interim, with Rabindranath playing a prominent part. He had also composed the novel *Gorā* in the intervening years. He now writes to Nepālchandra Rāy, a teacher at Santiniketan:

> You eat bread prepared by Muslim bakers; what crime has the Muslim student committed? ... In the *tapovana* of ancient times, tigers and cattle drank together at the river. If Hindus and Muslims cannot drink the same water, side by side, in our modern *tapovana*, all our spiritual meditations (*tapasyā*) will be proved a sham.... Accept this boy happily and confidently, praising the one God of all humankind.[17]

The boy did not come after all, but a change in outlook gradually grew evident. In 1909, Rabindranath wrote to Ajitkumār Chakrabarti about the observance of *rākhi-bandhan* – wearing coloured wrist-bands as a token of love and friendship, widely practised during the 1905 anti-partition movement – wishing that the Buddha, Christ, and Muhammad might be unitedly present in his ashram on the occasion.[18] From 1910, Christmas began to be celebrated at Santiniketan. Christians like Charles Freer Andrews, a lifelong friend of Tagore as of Gandhi, and William W. Pearson took up residence in 1914. When Maulānā Shaukat Ali came to Santiniketan in 1920 during the Khilāfat Movement (primarily to meet Gandhi, who was there at the time), the brahmin scholar Bidhushekhar Shāstri took him in to meals with everyone else. The transformation of the *brahmacharyāshram* into Visva-Bharati was initiated in 1918 and came into effect in 1921. Defining its ideals, Rabindranath declared the goal of cultivating Vedic, later Hindu (Purānic), Buddhist, Jain, Muslim, and Zoroastrian learning side by side, with Western learning as an accompaniment.[19] His plan was epitomized in the Sanskrit verse that became the motto of the university: *yatra vishvam bhavatyekanidam*, 'where the whole world meets in one nest'.

4

In late 1925, Carlo Formichi, professor of Sanskrit at the University of Rome, came to Santiniketan as a visiting scholar. Earlier that year, Formichi had acted as Rabindranath's interpreter and companion when the poet visited Italy on his way home from South America. Formichi was close to Mussolini, who used the opportunity to gift a large collection of books to Visva-Bharati, as also to send the orientalist scholar Giuseppe Tucci there at the Italian government's expense. Rabindranath was overjoyed by these gestures, as also when the Italian government offered to host his own visit to Italy. He took up the offer, met Mussolini on two occasions, and professed himself deeply impressed by the development he saw in Italy. His praise was published in the Italian papers, perhaps somewhat overtinged. He later heard from Romain Rolland about the real nature of the fascist state and met some of its victims. He condemned fascism in a letter to Andrews that was published in the *Manchester Guardian*. Formichi wrote a rejoinder to which Tagore replied in turn. He was then reviled in the state-controlled Italian press.

'I have to pass through a purification ceremony for the defilement to which I submitted myself in Italy,' wrote Tagore to Romain Rolland on

13 July 1926.[20] Yet Tagore seems to have never quite lost his regard for Mussolini. After meeting Formichi again a long time later, in New York in 1930, he wrote to his son Rathindranath:

> He [Formichi] still feels deeply towards me. He shed tears as soon as we met. I asked him whether it would be possible for me to return home via Italy. He said the misunderstanding could be cleared by my writing a single letter to Mussolini. I told him I would do so.[21]

It was long uncertain whether the letter was actually sent, but the late Bikāsh Chakrabarti of Visva-Bharati traced it to the state archives in Rome and published a facsimile.[22] Rabindranath writes there: 'I earnestly hope that the misunderstanding which has unfortunately caused a barrier between me and the great people you represent, the people for whom I have genuine love, will not remain permanent, and that this expression of my gratitude to you and your nation will be accepted. The politics of a country is its own, its culture belongs to all humanity.'[23] The sentiments are admirable, but in this context, they may sound too much like an expression of regret for his earlier criticism of the fascist ruler. We cannot tell what led Rabindranath to write such a letter. His motives remain inscrutable.

5

This inscrutability shows also in the more basic matter of the poet's attitude to his own English translations of his work. The circumstances of publication of the English *Gitanjali: Song Offerings* (1912) are well known. The title page clearly says these are 'prose translations made by the author from the original Bengali manuscript'. There are similar declarations in the next two volumes, *The Gardener* and *The Crescent Moon* (both 1913), but in no publication that followed. *The Collected Poems and Plays of Rabindranath Tagore* (1936) nowhere mentions that these works are translations or that they represent a small fraction of Tagore's full 'collection' of poems and plays. Buddhadeb Basu (Buddhadeva Bose) calls this omission 'not only unliterary (*asāhityik*) but dishonest'.[24] More crucially still, it is not stated that among the contents, *The Post Office* is actually translated by Debabrata Mukhopādhyāy and *The Cycle of Spring* by C.F. Andrews and Nishikānta Sen. Later, Kshitishchandra Sen, the translator of *Rājā* as *The King of the Dark Chamber*, goes similarly unacknowledged. These translations were, and often still are, credited to Rabindranath by default. Were these omissions entirely owing to the publisher, Macmillan, or must the poet share the blame by his tacit consent? Some early reviewers raised questions about the original language, without finding a response in subsequent editions.

The Nobel award citation described Tagore's self-translations into English as 'in a real and full sense ... belong[ing] to English literature'.[25] Did the appreciation he received in the West arouse an ambition in him to be numbered among English writers? An incident of 1915 confirms the possibility. Robert Bridges wanted to modify the language of a poem from the English *Gitanjali* for inclusion in Bridges's 'anthology in English and French', *The Spirit of Man*. Tagore initially demurred at any modification, declaring to William Rothenstein that having won fame as a writer in English, 'I feel extreme reluctance in accepting alterations in my English poems by any of your writers'.[26] However, he relented in the end.

Yet on 6 May 1913, he had written to his niece Indirā that he was mystified by his acclaim in the West: 'It's so obvious that I can't write English that I don't even have the vanity to feel ashamed about it.'[27] Even in 1921, he deplored the inadequacy of his translations in a letter to Edward Thompson[28] and wrote to the same Rothenstein in 1932 that he felt ashamed at seeking resort to another language.[29] To Sturge Moore in 1935, he confessed that he had come to see the futility of stepping outside his natural sphere in quest of fame,[30] and to Amiya Chakrabarti on 6 January 1935 that it is not only futile but also foolish, as though he were deceiving himself.[31] Yet at this very time, he was preparing the *Collected Poems and Plays*, and effusively thanked the publisher on its appearance in 1936.

6

We think of Rabindranath as the poet of life. 'I do not wish to die in this beautiful world,' he wrote in early life; in his middle years, 'What I have seen, what I have received, are beyond compare'; and late in life, echoing a Vedic hymn, 'This sky is full of sweetness, full of sweetness the dust of this earth'.[32] Yet at least once in his life, he underwent a phase of deep depression and rejection of life. In 1914, crowned with international fame, he wrote to his son:

I am driven night and day by thoughts of death and the wish to die. I feel I have done nothing and never will, that I have lived entirely in vain. I also feel despair and distrust towards everyone else.... I was on the point of *deliberately* committing *suicide* [italicized words in English] – I had no jot of pleasure in life. I seemed to be flinging away whatever I touched.... It's like the dense coils of a bad dream.[33]

However, he continued, 'Never fear, I'll break out of it: the remedy is there in my own heart.... I have no doubt I shall emerge from the cave of death into which I was sinking, and come out into the light once more.' He shortly left for Shilaidaha and, as always, found the 'light' of solace there.

7

At a reception on his seventieth birthday, the poet described himself as the 'harbinger of variety' (*bichitrer dut*).[34] He had long viewed himself in this light. On 13 July 1893, he wrote to his niece Indira from Shāhjādpur:

> I can never really tell what should be my proper work. Sometimes I feel I can write lots of short stories, not too badly either, and with pleasure to myself. Sometimes ... I think a lot of thoughts that cannot be expressed in poetry. They would be best expressed in something like a diary.... Sometimes it's necessary to pick quarrels with our countrymen on social issues; when I see no-one else taking up the unwelcome task, I am led to do it myself. And then I feel, hang it all, let the world look after itself: making up little poems in metre and rhyme comes happily to me, so let me abandon everything else and do just that in my own private corner. My state is like that of a conceited young woman with a lot of lovers, none of whom she can bear to give up.[35]

He continues in this vein, even alluding to the visual arts, to which he would not turn for another thirty-five years. He concludes by professing greatest attachment to his 'childhood love', poetry. But as we know well, he never confined himself to poetry at any point of his life. He repeats the idea of his 1893 letter in one of 7 March 1931, again to Indira: 'I am like a man with many wives, I can't deal with all of them at the same time.'[36] The only difference is that the lovers are now spouses.

There is no one else in Bengali cultural history, and few in the world, who has worked with such assured success in so many fields of art and culture; moreover, his transactions in each have continually taken new forms. His poetry has undergone many revolutions: in *Sonār tari*, *Kshanikā*, *Balākā*, *Punascha*, and *Janmadine*. The reader is led inexorably from each phase to the next. The mature novels – *Gorā*, *Ghare-bāire* (At Home and in the World), *Chaturanga* (Quartet), *Jogājog* (Relationships), and *Shesher kabitā* (The Last Poem) – are separated by miles from each other; *Gorā* and *Chaturanga* have found no successor in the intervening century.

Rabindranath began writing plays on the five-act Shakespearean model. Over a lifetime of experimentation, he proceeded to dispense with all division of acts and scenes, all stage furniture. The action takes place against a blank white backdrop: there are no soliloquies, no excess of deaths and languishment. These plays might owe something to the symbolic drama of the West, but the yield on that investment is astonishing. Again, Tagore is effectively the progenitor of the Bengali short story, but here too, a vast distance separates the first stories from the last. Who else could have made a literary genre of the private letter? The range of his nonfictional prose defies description. The body of his songs, and sometimes individual songs, interweave dramatically contrasting items: north Indian and south Indian classical music, Western music, devotional *kirtan*s, Baul songs, and other folk songs. The dance dramas he innovated in late life similarly combine many elements in a totally new synthesis: a range of Indian dance forms, with others drawn from Sri Lanka, Java, and Bali.

The world of his paintings, again, is utterly different from all these. He started painting when close to seventy. To look at it another way, he composed nearly 2,200 songs over some sixty-five years but over 2,000 paintings in just twelve. These relative figures indicate why his nephew, the artist Abanindranāth, compared his uncle's career as painter to a volcanic eruption.[37] There is little of the graceful or picturesque in the landscapes and human figures in Rabindranath's paintings: the humans are almost uncouth, the animals disturbing. This has led some critics to premise that his paintings are absolutely unrelated to his literary works;[38] others have linked them in oppositional terms, as products, respectively, of the unconscious and the conscious.[39] One scholar has applied the Sanskrit terminology of the classical aesthetics of *rasa*, finding in the songs and poems the *shringār* (erotic), *hāsya* (comic), *karunā* (arousing pity), and *shānta* (peaceful, serene) *rasa*s, and in the paintings the *bhayānak* (fearsome), *bibhatsa* (odious), and *adbhuta* (marvellous) *rasa*s.[40] Some discern a dark element in the poems, songs, and plays and assimilate this to the use of dark colours in the paintings; others find in the paintings not only the dark, sinister, and inauspicious but also the beautiful and life-enhancing. The painter Jāmini Rāy observed that, as a painter, Rabindranath was totally European.[41] The latter himself said that his paintings were not for his own country.[42] Sending the paintings to Paris in 1930 to be exhibited for the first time, he expressed the hope that people might at last realize he was no less occidental than oriental.[43] The excitement generated by the paintings in France and Germany in the 1930s makes one speculate that outside the

Bengali-reading world, Tagore might come to be better known one day as a painter than as a poet.

Yet we may rightly hesitate to say that Tagore's paintings point in one direction, and all his other works in all forms and modes in another. Traffic flows down endless, unimagined paths between the many worlds of his creativity. To say even this is to leave out of account the wide-ranging field of his practical activities: rural development, agricultural innovation, a school that became a university, and worldwide travel that embraced not only artistic and cultural exchanges but also explicit, sometimes acrimonious political pronouncements.

Towards the end of the poem from *Shesh saptak* with which I began, the poet writes:

> Within my expression of myself there lies much that is incomplete, much that is tattered and torn, much that is neglected. The image of myself made within and without, of good and bad, clear and hazy, famous and unknown, fulfilled and futile, in complex combination, reflected in your respect, your love, your forgiveness – I accept it on this birthday as my final identity. As I depart, this mental image remains in your hearts: I will not pride myself that it lies in the hands of time.

The poet is being too modest here. It is time, the mediator of fame, that has steered the boat laden with his life's work into a harbour beyond the reach of time. We must take stock of every item of that cargo. We must look at the garland of many Tagores not as a string of disjunct elements but as an organic, integral whole.

Tagore 150th Anniversary Lecture, Chittagong University. Translated by Sukanta Chaudhuri.

NOTES

1. *RRVB* 18:89–90.
2. See Manindrakumār Ghosh, 'Parihāspriya rabindranāth', in *Sāmayiki* (1977; rpt. Kolkata: Dey's, 1991), 103.
3. *Yurop-prabāsir patra* (Letters of a Sojourner in Europe) (Kolkata, 1881), 128–9. These controversial passages were omitted in the later, recast version of the work entitled *Pāschātya-bhraman* (Visva-Bharati, 1936), and from both current editions of Tagore's *Rachanābali* (Collected Works), though appended in *RRWBG* 16:1123–4.

4. 'Ramābāier baktritā-upalakshe', *Samāj*, *RRVB* 12:450–3.
5. *RRVB* 3:200.
6. *RRVB* 15:41.
7. *RRVB* 24:382.
8. *RRVB* 12:431.
9. *RJPM* 2:34.
10. Letter of 26 August 1907, *CP* 2:13.
11. *RRVB* 17:377.
12. *RJPM* 1:205.
13. *RRVB* 4:520.
14. *The Religion of Man*, ch. 7, 'The Man of My Heart', *EW* 3:129.
15. 'Dharma o jarhatā' (Religion and Inertia), *RRVB* 33:195–6.
16. *RRVB* 15:285.
17. *RJPP* 6:247.
18. *RJPM* 2:277.
19. *RJPM* 3:27.
20. *SL* 329.
21. Letter of 21 November 1930, *CP* 2:204–5.
22. Bikash Chakrabarti, *Ingrejite rabindranāth o anyānya prabandha* (Kolkata: Punascha, 2010), 207, 221–2.
23. Letter of 21 November 1930, *SL* 394.
24. Buddhadeb Basu, 'Ingrejite rabindranath', in *Kabi rabindranāth* (1966; rpt. Kolkata: Dey's Publishing, 1980), 88.
25. Nobel Prize website, https://www.nobelprize.org/prizes/literature/1913/ceremony-speech/, accessed 21 March 2019.
26. Letter of 4 April 1915, *SL* 161.
27. *CP* 5:19.
28. Letter of 2 February 1921: Uma Das Gupta, ed., *A Difficult Friendship* (Delhi: Oxford University Press, 2003), 128.
29. See Chakrabarti, *Ingrejite rabindranāth*, 44–5.
30. See ibid., 47: letter in Rabindra Bhavana archives, Santiniketan.
31. *CP* 11:131.
32. Respectively: 'Prān' (Life), *Karhi o komal*, *RRVB* 2:31; *Gitānjali* #142, *RRVB* 11:111; *Ārogya* #1, *RRVB* 25:41.
33. Letter of 25 September 1914, *CP* 2:32, 34.
34. *RJPM* 3:438.
35. *CPBLI* #107.
36. *CP* 5:80.
37. See Rāni Chanda, *Shilpiguru abanindranāth* (Kolkata: Visva-Bharati, 1972), 79.
38. See Somendranāth Bandyopādhyāy, *Rabindra-chitrakalā* (Kolkata: Dey's, 2009), 59.

39. See Shankha Ghosh, *Nirmān ār srishti* (Santiniketan: Rabindra Bhavana, 1982), 95–9.
40. Shobhan Som, *Tin shilpi* (Kolkata: Bānishilpa, 1985), 122–3.
41. Quoted in Bandyopadhyay, *Rabindra-chitrakalā*, 230.
42. See Maitreyi Debi, *Mangpute rabindranāth* (1943; rpt. Kolkata: Rupa, 1967), 103.
43. Letter to Nirmalkumāri Mahalānabish, 18 August 1930: Rabindranath Tagore, *Nijer kathā*, ed. Amitrasudan Bhattāchārya (Kolkata: Mitra o ghosh, 2011; rpt. 2015), 270.

Part I
Overviews

BISWAJIT RAY

Rabindranāth Tagore, the first non-European Nobel laureate in literature, had a long life (1861–1941) that may be divided into two almost equal phases in two very different eras. The first phase relates to the emergence of colonial and political modernity in Bengal; the second to an age of wars, revolutions, and what he termed a 'crisis in civilization'. Tagore was influenced by Western modernity from his formative years, yet he came to condemn the engulfing evils of Western colonialism and militant nationalism. The attack, however, was in a constructive spirit, admitting the benefits of engagement with the West: 'As our encounter with the British has warmed our heart up, the dying forces of our lives are getting conscious again.'[1]

THE INHERITANCE

The impact of Western rationalism led educated Indians, with support from some Europeans, to think of reconstructing society. Major social reforms like the regulation banning *sati* or widow-burning (1829) and the Hindu Widows Remarriage Act (1856) had taken place before Rabindranath's birth, and institutions for female education set up. But benevolence was hardly the goal of the colonial agenda. The East India Company drained India's wealth for individual and collective profit. Its economic policy forced Indians to supply raw materials cheaply to England and buy back finished products at a higher price. Indigenous craftsmen were robbed of their livelihood to provide cheap labour in the new colonial city of Calcutta (now Kolkata). Lord Cornwallis's Permanent Settlement Act (1793), which permanently impoverished India's peasantry, had its earliest and most pernicious impact in Bengal. Rabindranath observed that the colonial rulers looked upon India as an 'eternal pet-cow in their royal barn'.[2]

Historians often talk about the 'Bengal Renaissance' of the nineteenth century, but like many terms drawn from Western intellectual idiom, its application is problematic. Some early Marxist scholars have stigmatized the period as an age of compradors, Rabindranath and his forefathers among them. By this view, a particular class of Indians, mostly upper-class English-educated Bengali Hindus, improved their lot socially and economically in this period: it was a Renaissance for them and them only.

Rabindranath was the scion of a land-owning family, but the privileged, protected ambience of his family mansion at Jorasanko, in the northern part of the burgeoning city of Kolkata, was not cut off from community life. The boy Rabi bonded more intensively than might be expected with family retainers like Shyām, an elderly helping hand, and Abdul Mājhi, a fisherman: in his autobiographical writings, they are portrayed in the same emotive register as the Bengali elite and educated middle-class *bhadralok*. The poet's grandfather actively pursued wealth, and his father assiduously protected his landed legacy. But that legacy also involved a social commitment recognized and creatively activated by Rabindranath, while supervising his family estates in eastern Bengal and later in his initiatives at Santiniketan. Nikhilesh, the caring landlord in *Ghare-bāire* (At Home and in the World), embodies this ideal.

Although belonging to the priestly brahmin caste, the Tagores were considered 'degraded' in caste terms because of alleged Muslim connections in a previous century. But wealth, even more than caste, was becoming the new mark of status in the changing times. Kolkata was the new seat of Lakshmi, the goddess of wealth; English was ousting Persian, the language of the Mughal court, as the language of power. The stigma of 'degraded' caste was more than compensated by the new wealth acquired by the poet's grandfather, Dwarakānath (1794–1846), through dealings and sometimes direct collaboration with the British. He bought landed property, founded a bank, and engaged in opium trading, coal mining, shipping, and indigo planting. A friend of the scholar and reformer Rāmmohan Rāy, the 'father of modern India', Dwarakanath also learnt English, was active in social reform, became a member of the international elite, and hosted lavish parties. His wealth and status earned him the sobriquet of 'Prince', though he held no such formal rank.

Rabindranath seems to have been embarrassed by his 'princely' grandfather: he even asked his biographer Prabhātkumār Mukhopādhyāy to relegate Dwarakanath to an appendix. He was uneasy with ostentatious wealth, and wrote against the opium trade in which his grandfather participated. Not that he was opposed to private property as such: in this respect, neither Rabindranath nor Gāndhi was a socialist. The radical humanist Manabendranāth Rāy criticized the poet on this score. In his essay 'City and Village', Rabindranath uses two contrasting mythological figures to critique the capitalist economy: he rejects Kubera, the Mammon-like demigod of selfish acquisition, in favour of Lakshmi or S[h]ri, the benevolent goddess of prosperity for the entire people.[3] He named his institute of rural reconstruction 'Sriniketan' (*niketan*, abode).

Though uneasy about his grandfather, Rabindranath paid due tribute to his *bābāmashāi* (respected father) Debendranāth (1817–1905). Debendranath too set out in the family business, but the influence of Rammohan Ray soon engaged him in social and religious reform. Nineteenth-century Bengal was a melting pot of Eastern and Western ideas. Restoring the Indian past in the new light of Western modernity became a mode of collective self-assertion for many educated Bengalis of the time. Besides campaigning against widow-burning, Rammohan founded the Ātmiya Sabhā (Society of Companions) to revive the worship of Brahma, the formless non-dualistic God of the Upanishads. The association offered prayers to Brahma in intimate gatherings. On Rammohan's death in England in 1833, Debendranath took the lead in promoting 'Brāhmadharma', institutionalizing its practices in the Tattwabodhini Sabhā (Society for the Propagation of Truth) in 1839. Though he preached against idolatry, he once made an alliance with the orthodox Hindu leader Rādhākānta Deb against the foreign Christian missionaries. This indicates how cultural nationalism was latent in his religious programme. Rabindranath was grateful to his father for inspiring an ardent interest in the Upanishads and reverence for the *swadesh* or motherland.

Dwarakanath's untimely death was a blow for Debendranath. He dissociated himself from the family businesses, deciding to support his household solely on the revenues from his landed property. He thereby ensured financial security without the distracting compulsions of commerce, allowing him to diversify his social and religious activities. He preached a sophisticated form of indigenous religion all over India, published the philosophical journal *Tattwabodhini patrikā*, and set up Bengali *pāthshālā*s (elementary schools). These activities won him the title of 'Maharshi' (great sage) from his countrymen.

Rabindranath, eighth son and fourteenth child (of fifteen) of Debendranath and Sārada Debi, was born on 7 May 1861 (25 Vaishākh 1268 by the Bengali calendar). Among his brothers were Dwijendranāth the philosopher, Satyendranāth the first Indian member of the Indian Civil Service, and Jyotirindranāth the dramatist, a man of many parts and Rabi's special mentor; among his sisters, the talented writer Swarnakumāri.

In 1857, four years before Rabindranath's birth, India saw an uprising variously labelled a soldiers' mutiny and India's first war of independence. The dream of independence, if it existed at that date, was brutally crushed, and India was placed directly under the British crown. The Hindu *bhadralok* of Kolkata, the new colonially educated salariat and professional class, had dissociated themselves from the prospect of rebellion and anarchy; the British found new ways to reward them and consolidate their support. New avenues of education and employment were opened up, and three universities (including that of Calcutta, as it is still called) set up in the three 'Presidencies' of the new Indian empire. Long before that, an institution had been founded to hegemonize the Indians: Hindu (later Presidency) College, established in 1817 not by the British but by the Hindu Bengali elite. Its alumni played a notable part in the birth of a new Bengali culture in the earlier nineteenth century.

Dwarakanath had a role in setting up the college; Debendranath was its student for some time. In their respective ways, they were both deeply affected by its social impact and spirit of reform. While largely conforming to the colonial *status quo* in their external lives, the Hindu *bhadralok* asserted a new sense of nationhood in their inner domain of family, society, and culture. (Muslims effectively joined their ranks only from the 1880s.) They initiated major social reforms and public debates about the Hindu way of life. This new imaginary of nationhood could not but challenge the rulers' agenda in many ways, at least implicitly. It marked a profound and, in the long term, truly momentous engagement with Western modernity.

Many major Bengali writers of the time worked for the colonial government and judiciary. The novelist Bankimchandra Chattopādhyāy (Chatterjee) was a deputy magistrate; the poets Michael Madhusudan Datta (Dutt), Rangalāl Bandyopādhyāy, Nabinchandra Sen, and Hemchandra Bandyopādhyāy were lawyers; and the dramatist Dinabandhu Mitra was postmaster-general. Yet all these servants of the Crown expressed nationalist sentiments in their writings and a commitment to their own society. Debendranath's second son, Satyendranath, joined the Indian Civil Service in 1864. An admirer of Mary Wollstonecraft, he was eager to effect a 'vindication of the rights of woman' in Indian households. The traditions of the Tagore family were overturned by Satyendranath and his wife, Jnānadānandini, who accompanied her husband to his workplace at Mumbai against Debendranath's strictures. Debendranath travelled all over India as a preacher but seems to have spared little thought for his housebound wife. His children, too, rarely enjoyed his company. On his visits home, he was treated with patriarchal deference. Armed with the cachet of his professional success, Satyendranath challenged this ethos, setting an example for his brothers.

Rabindranath was less self-assured. He and his wife Mrinālini had to compromise with their elders for the sake of harmony. He generally fell in with his father's regressive decisions, partly no doubt because of his economic dependence on Debendranath. The Brahmo Samaj was opposed to child marriage, but Rabindranath married off his daughters at an early age to ensure their annuities from family funds. The Maharshi also sent Rabindranath to dissuade Sāhānā Debi, widow of Rabindranath's nephew Balendranāth, from marrying again.

Yet in his own way, Debendranath did his duty and more by his youngest surviving son. After Rabi's sacred thread ceremony, he took the eleven-year-old with him on his travels through northern India, giving father and son an opportunity to bond. After Rabi's marriage, he supported the couple and their children by engaging Rabi to manage their estates in eastern Bengal from 1890. He also gifted his son some land at Birbhum that he had bought from a local landowner to build a spiritual retreat called 'S[h]āntiniketan' (home of peace). This was where Rabindranath would set up his unique centre of alternative education.

GROWING UP: LITERATURE AND THE NATION

Young Rabi was admitted to several Kolkata schools in turn. They uniformly failed to engage the sensitive, introvert boy, not least because their language was English. He was finally educated at home by a battery of teachers in different subjects. Yet his elders did not abandon hope of his formal education: he was dispatched to England in 1878 to be trained in law. He attended some classes at University College, London, watched plays and operas, and savoured English society and culture before returning to India without a qualification. But his experiences abroad helped him to mature as a writer: his letters home to his beloved sister-in-law Kādambari, Jyotirindranath's wife, were serialized in *Bhārati*, a Tagore family periodical edited by Dwijendranath. In that age, Bengali books were generally written in a chaste (*sādhu*) form of the language, but both the diction and the grammatical register of this early travelogue are colloquial (*chalit*).

Rabindranath and his illustrious elder brothers briefly followed in their father's religious footsteps. They attended regular prayer sessions of the Brahmo Samaj, which already featured Rabi's devotional songs. He was elected secretary of the Ādi (Original) Brahmo Samaj in 1884, and later briefly edited its periodical, the *Tattwabodhini patrikā*. Gradually, however, he freed himself from the constraints of the Samaj. He recalls this transformation in his Oxford Hibbert lectures, *The Religion of Man* (1930). Initially, he was delighted to be elected secretary despite his youth, but this joy soon turned to a burdensome sense of duty. To his disappointment, the hymns he wrote for the Samaj took on 'the many-thumbed impression of orthodox minds'.

> At last I came to discover that in my conduct I was not strictly loyal to my religion, but only to the religious institution. This latter represented an artificial average.... After a long struggle with the feeling that I was using a mask to hide the living face of truth, I gave up my connection with our church.[4]

The keyword in this confession is 'artificial average'. In every sphere of life, Rabindranath preferred the individual signature to the institutional 'thumbed impression' erasing one's personal choices. In 1924, a year before Sergei Eisenstein's film *Battleship Potemkin*, Rabindranath published his play *Raktakarabi* (Red Oleanders), ending in a revolution of mine workers forced into nameless machinelike toil in a gold-mining city. In 1930, the poet visited post-revolutionary Russia. He was elated by the welfare of the proletariat but did not forget to warn the Soviets about the political mould in which they were trying to set 'humanity':

> Man has two sides: on the one hand, he has his independent self, on the other he is related to everybody else. If one leaves out either of these sides, what remains is unreal.[5]

This synthesis of the 'independent' and the 'related' self grew out of the religious, political, and literary debates of nineteenth-century Bengal – its tussle between tradition and individual aspiration, the latter subsumed in a modernity that gradually became many modernities. The tension between the individual and the collective stamped itself on the young poet's mind.

After the Maharshi's death in 1905, Rabindranath gradually freed himself from conservative family restraints. He encouraged his son Rathindranāth to marry the widow Pratimā Debi. But this liberation in private life was anticipated in his writings: his poetry focused from its earliest phase on romantic love, and his early short stories brought out the waste and pathos of constricted lives, especially among women. In the later nineteenth century, *sāhitya* (literature: literally 'with-ness' or social consciousness) became a new means for young moderns to meet their social obligations: this may have provided Rabindranath with additional reason for a literary career. An introvert young adult without conventional academic education, he could acquire confidence and social standing by propagating new themes and concerns, with the language to convey them.

In the nineteenth century, the Bengali language won prominence over other modern Indian languages for historical reasons. An article by the Englishman John Beams, translated in Bankimchandra's journal *Bangadarshan*, offered the equivocal praise that 'Bengali literature in comparison to the literature of other provinces of India excels and elevates its standard almost to the rank of European literature'.[6] Beams also proposed a Bengali literary academy. His idea came true in 1893 in a 'Bengal Academy of Literature', fittingly renamed in 1894 by the Bengali equivalent, Bangiya Sāhitya Parishat. Rabindranath became an active member and, in 1894, its vice-president; Satyendranath was elected president in 1900.

Beams's assertion of the pre-eminence of Bengali was based on reality. Bengal was the seat of the British government and, since the days of the East India Company, its most important trading zone and a major field for the missionaries' evangelical zeal. Fort William College was set up in Kolkata for 'civilians' to learn the language; grammars, textbooks, and other works were published for the purpose. Most crucially, missionary and civilian activity, most importantly at the Baptist Mission in Shrirāmpur (Serampore), led to the virtual start of Bengali printing with movable type.[7] Before that, literature had mostly circulated orally in traditional poetic forms like the *pnāchāli*, *mangal-kābya*, *padābali*, and *gitikā*, performed at gatherings (āsars) under the patronage of local lords. Manuscripts were the preserve of a literate minority for special purposes. Both production and consumption of literature were transformed with the coming of print. Not the least outcome was that literature could now support private reading.

The young Rabindranath commented on the print medium in the allegorical fantasy 'Lekhā kumāri o chhāpā sundari' (Miss Script and Madame Print), mourning how the personalized manuscript has succumbed to the uniformity of print. The subject continued to engage him: he brings out its deeper implications in the 1932 poem 'Patra' (The Letter).[8] He deplores the shackling of 'poetry to be heard' by the chains of sight; moreover, the 'ogre of the printing press' smears the poetic sky with ink, crowding out the intervals separating poems either as composed or as recited in more spacious times. But print might have its compensations. In the 1895 poem '1400 sāl' (The Year 1400), he imagines someone reading his verses a hundred years later, and through that reader, he sends his greetings to the new poets of that age.

Before Rabindranath, the cultural transformations worked by print were most intensively discussed by Bankimchandra Chattopadhyay, the leading writer of his age. Bankim's discourse turns on practical issues like the cultivation of good taste through 'good books' and the forging of patriotic bonds among readers by the circulation of printed texts. He founded the journal *Bangadarshan* in 1872 as part of this literary agenda, designed to sweep the courtyard of Bengali culture clean of 'bad *bat-talā* literature' (that is, pulp literature).

Rabindranath admired Bankim, and modelled his early novels *Rājarshi* and *Bauthākurānir hāt* on Bankim's historical fiction. However, his attitude to his literary idol Bankimchandra was many-layered. Bankimchandra was drawn to the Hindu revivalist movement that arose in Bengal in reaction to the new, intellectually sophisticated monotheism most influentially spread by the Brahmo Samaj. His 'revivalist nationalism' imagined the motherland as a mother goddess, as in his celebrated hymn 'Vande mātaram'. Rabindranath respected Bankim's literary genius but persistently questioned this revivalist discourse. Fierce arguments between their camps broke out in periodicals like *Sanjibani* and *Bangabāsi*. The two writers might be said to follow opposite trajectories. Bankim, a romantic novelist, gradually became a strong proponent of Hindu religion and nationhood. Rabindranath, on the contrary, started out within a formulated religion and celebrated his motherland's golden past but came to seek a truth beyond chauvinism and religious institutionalism.

His three elder brothers Dwijendranath, Satyendranath, and Jyotirindranath were keen participants in cultural activities of nationalist bent. Nabagopāl Mitra, a champion of Hindu nationalism, started a 'Hindu *melā*' (fair) to showcase national culture through traditional sports, crafts, and performances. The Tagores knew Nabagopal well: Debendranath had funded his English weekly, the *National Paper*. Dwijendranath was associated with the Hindu *melā* from the start; Jyotirindranath wrote for it the song 'Mile sabe bhāratsantān' (All India's children, gathered together); Rabindranath read there his poem 'Hindumelāy upahār' (A Gift for the Hindu Mela) extolling the Hindu past. It was modelled on poets like Hemchandra Bandyopadhyay, Rangalal Bandyopadhyay and Nabinchandra Sen, who extolled India's past glory and mourned her present decline in a style and diction influenced by Western poetry. The young Rabindranath so far fell in with them as to write a hostile review of *Meghnādbadh kābya*, the epic masterpiece (modelled on Milton) of the greatest of the new poets, Michael Madhusudan Datta (Dutt), whom Bankim's *Bangadarshan* had adjudged the 'national poet of Bengal'. It is worth note that barring some juvenilia, Rabindranath composed no epic or other long poem, and few of even moderate length.

Kadambari Debi, Jyotirindranath's wife and young Rabi's close companion, introduced him to the work of Bihārilāl Chakrabarti, who initiated a new lyricism in Bengali poetry. Rabi was deeply drawn to this model. In an obituary for Biharilal, he wrote:

> If [Bankim's journal] *Bangadarshan* is the morning sun of modern Bengali literature, little *Abodhbandhu* [the journal for which Bihārilāl wrote] may be called the morning star. People were yet to awake at that dawn, [but] a morning bird had started to sing [in] a melody of its own. I do not know what history might say, but I heard there for the first time the voice of an individual in Bengali poetry.[9]

History might not have paid Biharilal such attention if he had not been a decisive influence on Rabindranath.

Modernity had two aspects for Rabindranath: it was both contemporary and beyond time. He saw Biharilal as reacting to the cultural nationalism of his time by asserting a private, individual voice. Rabindranath found his own inner voice in a quasi-mystical experience of 1882, described in his reminiscences, leading him to compose the poem 'Nirjharer swapnabhanga' (The Awakening of the Waterfall).[10] It was a moment both temporal and eternal: temporal as located on the axis of time, eternal as expressing a voice within. This was the true starting point of his poetic journey.

His poems evoked a mixed response among readers. Shortly before 'Nirjharer swapnabhanga', Bankimchandra had garlanded Rabindranath in a distinguished gathering for the latter's early collection *Sandhyāsangit* (Evening Songs, 1882). Not all readers were so appreciative. Conservative Sanskrit pundits laughed at his allegedly impure and even incorrect Bengali, as they had earlier laughed at Bankim. This was part of the continuing controversy between those who viewed Bengali as a dependent offspring of Sanskrit and those who asserted its independent entity. Among the latter, though in different veins, were the three greatest prose writers of the century, Rammohan Ray, Ishwarchandra Vidyāsāgar, and Bankimchandra. Bankim pronounced that simple and lofty, indigenous and Sanskritic, high and low language should all be used as the subject demanded, with the basic aim of lucidity and comprehensibility. Words can be drawn from various sources such as English, Persian, Arabic, and Sanskrit, or even rustic and primitive diction, if it aided clarity.[11]

This was the spirit in which Rabindranath wrote the poems in *Karhi o komal* (Sharps and Flats, 1886), which the conservatives lampooned. He employed images and descriptions of unprecedented intimacy. This paved the way for the full-fledged Romantic utterance of *Mānasi* (Woman of the Mind, 1890), the firstfruits of his maturity. From 1890 to 1913, he experimented continually with both poetic diction and range of themes. Besides intimate lyrics, he wrote narrative poems, chiefly based on tales from the past. His growing reputation reached heroic proportions when he won the Nobel Prize for literature in 1913 for the English volume *Gitanjali: Song Offerings.*

THE CHANGING WORLD, A CHANGING LIFE

This creative growth was held in tension against many factors in Rabindranath's private and public life during these twenty-four years. His wife, Mrinalini, died in 1902, leaving behind five young children of whom the middle daughter, Renukā, died in 1903, and the younger son Shamindranāth in 1907. Debendranath too passed away in 1905. Shamindranath's death, in particular, affected Rabindranath deeply; yet six weeks later, he had controlled his grief sufficiently to write: 'There is so much sorrow, want and abjection all around us that I feel ashamed to be overwhelmed by my personal grief or consider myself to be specially unfortunate. When I think of our country's present state and its future, it draws me out of my own sorrow.'[12] He did not disown his private bereavement but did not allow himself to be paralysed by it, rather turning his thoughts outward to the general human condition.

In fact, the year 1905 saw a great political crisis in Bengal, which plunged the poet into the most actively political phase of his life. The British planned to split Bengal in two parts, with the aim of dividing the Hindus from the Muslims. People across the province rose in protest, their chief rallying force being Rabindranath's first great cycle of patriotic songs. The poet's nephew, the artist Abanindranāth Tagore, has described the magical impact of these songs on the crowds.[13] Composed in simple Bengali and set to folk tunes, they proved to affect public sentiment more powerfully than political speeches. They demonstrated the force and utility of the mother tongue, to whose advance Rabindranath had already made a major contribution. In later life, he adopted the same strategy with the colloquial *chalit* register of prose as a binding force across classes and communities.

The Indian National Congress was founded in 1885, largely through the efforts of the Englishman Allan Octavian Hume. In its early days, it was the resort of an English-educated Indian elite eager to prove its nationalist credentials. (Satyendranath Tagore was a member.) Rabindranath was all too aware of the disjuncture of this privileged conclave from the common folk, particularly after he witnessed the miserable condition of the latter during his years managing the family estates in eastern Bengal. This encounter with village life is reflected in his early short stories, which he cited in his defence when accused of indulging in poetic romanticism. He also initiated some practical measures for the villagers' welfare; later, he invested the greater part of his Nobel prize money in a rural co-operative bank.

The experience of rural life also taught him the importance of the mother tongue for the welfare of the common people: how else could they make their voice heard? This, in turn, called for a greater role of the mother tongue in education, as he argued at the Rājshāhi Association in 1892. He was strongly supported by, among others, Bankimchandra and Gurudās Bandyopādhyāy (Banerjee), the first Indian vice-chancellor of Calcutta University, although the latter's efforts were defeated in the university senate. Rabindranath was a member of a panel that reported on the issue after circulating a public questionnaire under the aegis of the Bangiya Sahitya Parishat. Yet his commitment to the cause led him into a great misjudgement: in his 1898 essay 'Bhāshābichchhed' (Linguistic Separation), he urged the people of Assam and Odisha to merge their linguistic identities with the Bengali, causing great protest and resentment. He corrected this hegemonic outlook towards neighbouring languages in course of time, and came to support Gandhi's proposal to make Hindi India's *lingua franca*, but his basic advocacy of the mother tongue for education and culture never faltered. It was central to his programme at Santiniketan, though not at the cost of the many other languages taught there.

As English became the language of power and knowledge, some Bengali authors tried to use it creatively. Madhusudan and Bankimchandra both started their literary careers in English but soon turned to their mother tongue. Rabindranath took a different path. His literary life was firmly rooted in Bengali from beginning to end; but when the time was ripe, he adopted English to carry his harvest to the West. On a seminal visit to England in 1912, he took with him a volume of his own English renderings of his poems. These won the admiration of a circle of friends, including W.B. Yeats and the painter William Rothenstein. Unsurprisingly, the vein that found the readiest reception was that which, commencing with *Naibedya* (Prayer Offerings, 1901), reaches its height in *Gitānjali* (1910). Here human love transforms itself in diverse ways into love of the divine, both as lord and as beloved. Rothenstein circulated the drafts among influential connoisseurs of poetry. The published volume, brought out in 1912, bore the title *Gitanjali: Song Offerings* but contained poems from ten Bengali collections (including the then unpublished *Gitimālya*). In his introduction, Yeats writes how he carried the manuscript everywhere for days, reading it in trains, buses, and restaurants. Perhaps what attracted him and his Western contemporaries was the complete contrast to the frenetic and competitive milieu of the West, as reflected in Rabindranath's own response to London:

> At what tremendous speed are all the streets of London moving! How gigantic is the mind whose external image is this speed! They are tugging at time and space with great force, this way and that.[14]

This uncompromising difference of theme and purpose may have been the crucial factor behind the Nobel award for the English *Gitanjali* in 1913. The prize not only won him international celebrity but also ensured his impregnable prestige at home.

Yet just as he seemed to be reaching the pinnacle of acclaim, a new generation of Bengali poets turned against him for new reasons. They were close observers of world politics and ardent readers of continental literature. They were also disillusioned by the economic depression following the First World War. For them, Rabindranath was the exponent of an outdated *rabiyānā* ('Rabindrism'), a vintage concoction of literary spiritualism and unreal sublimity. Achintyakumār Sengupta, author of *Kallol jug* (The Kallol Age), blames Tagore in his poem 'Ābishkār' (Discovery) for obstructing the path of the new generation. These young writers published their work, often celebrating carnal love or attacking economic disparities, in a new generation of periodicals like *Kallol* (Waves), *Kālikalam* (Pen and Ink), and *Pragati* (Progress). In Rabindranath's view, this was crude realism masquerading as modernism. A controversy sprang up on these issues: the *Kallol* and *Kālikalam* brigade crossed swords with the *Shanibārer chithi* (Saturday Letter) group led by Sajanikānta Dās, not only a monumental reader but an expert lampoonist who turned his talent to cutting use. A literary convention was called at the Tagore mansion in Kolkata, in Rabindranath's presence, to debate the issues of realism, modernism, and the writer's social responsibilities. Later, the leftist Indian Progressive Writers' Association, with chapters in London and Kolkata, also kept its distance from Tagore's overwhelming presence where, they might have felt, they did not have the freedom to be themselves.

Yet the modernists could not but acknowledge his formidable genius: in fact, many formed close bonds with him. Amiya Chakrabarti was his secretary for ten years and a valued associate. Sudhindranāth Datta also interacted closely with him and was entrusted with drafting the introduction to an *Oxford Book of Bengali Verse* that Rabindranath was asked to edit but that sadly did not materialize. Buddhadeb Basu (Buddhadeva Bose), who had declared in 1938 that the age that produced Tagore was long over,[15] was invited to Santiniketan in the poet's last days. He recounted the visit movingly in a book entitled *Sab peyechhir deshe* (In the Land of All I Want – that is, Utopia). Sadly, Rabindranath did not live to see it, but he had already replied to his young contemporaries in the poem 'Samayhārā' (Beyond Time, 1939). He pictures himself there as a superannuated dollmaker, but a voice 'from beyond the lion-gate of Orion' tells him that his toys are bespoke by a new age, and a fairytale princess is coming to buy the lot.[16]

Yet Rabindranath, always sensitive to new stimuli and ready to change course like a mighty river, found modernism a rejuvenating force with which he played hide and seek. In his novel *Shesher kabitā* (The Last Poem, 1929), the protagonist Amit Rāy disparages him as an outdated survival and pits against his poems those of the fictitious Nibāran Chakrabarti, actually Amit's *nom de guerre*. But Amit, of course, is Rabindranath's own fiction, and in the collection *Mahuyā* published the same year, the poems reappear in their true identity as the poet's own work! Three late stories, collected as *Tin sangi* (Three Companions, 1941), and the still later 'Badnām' (Ill Repute) and 'Pragatisanghār', written shortly before his death, are examples of modernist writing that testify no less to his innovative power to the end.

By this time, Rabindranath had changed decisively to *chalit bhāshā*, the popular or colloquial register of Bengali, in his fiction and much other writing. He had tried out the mode in some early series of published letters but (excluding dramatic dialogue) made a formal literary start only with the short story 'Strir patra' (The Wife's Letter, 1914) and the novel *Ghare-bāire* (At Home and in the World, serialized 1915–16). Both were published in *Sabuj patra* (The Green Leaf, but also The Fresh Page), a journal started in 1914 under the editorship of Pramatha Chaudhuri, husband of Rabindranath's favourite niece, Indirā Debi, to whom, during his years in east Bengal, he had addressed a series of letters (*Chhinnapatra*, meaning both 'Torn Leaves' and 'Torn Letters', later expanded as *Chhinnapatrābali*). Pramatha had started a movement to make *chalit bhāshā* the medium of literature and other formal writing. Rabindranath was converted to the cause and wrote many such pieces, most importantly fiction, for *Sabuj patra*.

'Strir patra' and *Ghare-bāire* are both first-person narratives – the latter in three voices, one a woman's. Long before this, Bankimchandra had employed first-person narrative in his novel *Rajani* but not in conjunction with *chalit bhāshā*. By combining the two, Tagore not only accommodated the female speaking voice in literature but used it to express a vocal protest against patriarchy. In 'Strir patra', Mrināl leaves her husband's home on realizing that her views counted as nothing there. It was not easy to write such a socially subversive story in Bengal at that time. For Tagore, *chalit bhāshā* was the language of the mind, not simply of the tongue: he used it to bring into the open the suppressed anger and protest at the heart of Bengali womanhood.

It was alleged that Tagore had insulted Bengali women by dragging them out of the home and involving them in extramarital relations. Nothing could have been farther from his intentions, but in both the stories, he raised questions about the patriarchal institution of marriage. The *Sabuj patra* phase initiated the modernity of thought and expression that reaches its high point in the stories of the late collection *Tin sangi*.

Even this radical change is as nothing to the extraordinary new venture he took up when well in his sixties. In 1928, after four years of intensive doodling begun in the manuscript of *Purabi*, he began to experiment with the brush despite having no formal training in art. This 'volcanic eruption'[17] of creativity in a new medium resulted in a corpus of over 2,000 paintings, first publicly exhibited in Paris in 1930 – while he was running a major programme of education and social reconstruction, travelling extensively in India and abroad, and engaging with matters of great public moment, not to mention the pursuit of literature.

The exhibition of paintings was made possible by the support of the French artist André Karpeles and the Argentinian writer and cultural personality Victoria Ocampo. He addressed Ocampo as 'Vijayā', an Indian equivalent of her first name, and dedicated to her the poetical collection *Purabi*. Ocampo writes:

> When Tagore lived in San Isidro I was impressed by the copy-book where he was writing his *Puravi* poems in Bengali.... That copy-book, I think, was the beginning of Tagore the painter, of his urge to translate his dreams with a pencil or a brush. I took such delight in his doodles that it encouraged him to go on.[18]

THE SAMĀJ, THE NATION, AND THE WORLD

The words 'public' and 'nation', taken from Western political parlance, became current among the English-educated political class of India from the early twentieth century. Rabindranath took a different approach, partly owing to his intimate encounters with folk forms as a creative writer, composer, and performer. In the essays 'Rangamancha' (The Stage) and 'Swadeshi samāj' (Indigenous Society), he explains his idea of *lok* (folk) and *samāj* (society). The folk imagination does not rely on realistic stagecraft and props to create a dramatic illusion. Rabindranath charges European practice with robbing Indian spectators of this imaginative genius. In the second essay, as in other writings before and after, he stresses the need to build an Indian *samāj* (society) instead of a 'nation'. However, he soon realized that it was impossible to advance these ideas in the muddied waters of Bengal politics. The communal harmony evinced during the anti-partition movement was soon threatened by tensions. The youth were turning to violent means in their fight for independence, while their elders were affected all too often by narrow-mindedness and the search for short-term gains. Hence, after the anti-partition movement, Rabindranath turned more and more to his own distinctive means of political engagement, chiefly through writings and speeches, with only occasional public participation. Most importantly, he projected his vision of a total development of society and personality, subsuming the conventional spheres of the political, economic, and cultural, by founding Visva-Bharati.

The Nobel award extended Rabindranath's role beyond the purely Bengali or Indian. He was now an international figure whose opinions and actions carried force for both India and the world. He utilized this position to raise his voice against social and political injustice in a two-part agenda: on the one hand, to sustainedly oppose the Western model of avaricious nationalism, 'militarism' (*militaritwa*) and destructive imperialism; on the other, to advance ideas and institutions to counter these conjoint evils.

For Rabindranath, imperialism based on nationalism was the root curse of the twentieth century. The idea of the nation was, for him, a crucible of militant capitalism that alienated people not only from nature but also from their fellow humans, promoting only the material interests of a particular group within a defined territory. Poem #64 of *Naibedya* was given the title 'Jugāntar' (Change of Era) in the anthology *Chayanikā*. The poem, composed on 31 December 1900, begins: 'The century's sun has set today amid blood-red clouds.' In the essay 'Birodhmulak ādarsha' (An Ideal Based on Conflict) written about the same time, Tagore elaborates on the same image of blood:

> Europe's cheeks are florid with the blood of mounting militarism. Can it be a sign of health? Do we not see daily how the malady of nationalism, like swelling obesity, is invading its heart, its core being, its religious principles?[19]

This conflict of nations had to be excluded from India at all cost. At the same time, to conceive of an exclusively Hindu India would destroy the social integrity of the subjugated *samāj*. Instead, Rabindranath held out a message of universalism. In the novel *Gorā* (1910), Bengali readers encountered for the first time a message of universal humanity, even if set in an Indian frame. Gorā, earlier a Hindu nationalist and revivalist, ends with a vision of pan-Indianism leading on to universalism on discovering his mixed Indian and European parentage: 'a mantra of worship to the god who belongs alike to Hindu, Muslim, Christian, and Buddhist, whose temple doors are not closed to any race, any person' – a 'god of India' (*bhāratbarsher debatā*).[20] This expanded view of India provides the foundation on which Rabindranath constructs his internationalist ideal.

Rabindranath preached his humane gospel against nationalism, violence, and greed to audiences in East and West alike, and even to extremist movements in India. A focal point was his consistent condemnation of the misdeeds of colonial rule in India. After the massacre of unarmed Indians at Jaliānwālā Bāgh in Punjab in 1919, he gave up his knighthood (conferred in 1915) in protest.

Two vital issues occupied him ceaselessly: harmony between Hindus and Muslims, and the extremism of one current of the Independence Movement. Particularly in the 1930s, Hindu–Muslim tensions escalated in colonial India, with the British fomenting the Indians' own abuse of institutional religion for nationalist politics, and leading finally to a demand for two separate nation states. By contrast, the teachings of medieval Indian saints provided an alternative model of religious practice based on love and exchange. Rabindranath wrote an introduction to Kshitimohan Sen's 1929 lectures at Calcutta University on 'The Religious Traditions of Medieval India'. Medieval precedent altered Rabindranath's view of the nineteenth-century pietist Rāmkrishna. During Ramkrishna's birth centenary in 1936, Rabindranath chaired a session of a religious parliament and delivered a lecture on India's traditional religious harmony, alluding specially to the premodern saints. He also composed a four-line poem on Ramkrishna as successor to that saintly tradition.

There was an economic and class dimension to the religious conflicts. Muslim peasants were often cheated by their Hindu landlords in collusion with government officials and sometimes even opportunistic *swadeshi* leaders. This cynical exploitation is described in the novels *Gorā* and *Ghare-bāire*. Again, though Rabindranath continued to revere the extremist freedom fighters for their courage and sacrifice, he could not support their pursuit of violence, which often destroyed the lives of common people.

Ghare-bāire has another distinction: for the first time, Rabindranath employs three narrative voices, following the example of Bankimchandra's *Rajani* (1877), itself professedly modelled on Wilkie Collins's *The Woman in White* (1859). The presence of multiple narrators enables Rabindranath to set Nikhilesh, the benevolent landowner, opposite Sandip, the duplicitous *swadeshi* leader who even abuses Bankim's hymn 'Vande mātaram', a rallying cry of the Independence Movement. Literary and political issues are deeply enmeshed here, as in the novels *Gorā, Chaturanga* (*Quartet*, 1916), and *Chār adhyāy* (*Four Chapters*, 1934). Rabindranath's literary constructs are not only a vehicle for his politics; their humane ethos infuses that politics with a synthesis all his own.

On a different plane, Rabindranath's relations with Mahatmā Gandhi were complex in many ways. He argued vehemently with 'Bāpu' on many basic issues but never lost his esteem for the man who transformed the Congress Party from a club of moderates to a national party of the entire Indian people. He offered hospitality to Gandhi's followers in 1914–15 on their first arrival in India from South Africa, when few were willing to shelter them. In 1940, during Gandhi's last visit to Santiniketan, the poet handed him a letter requesting him to protect Santiniketan after his death. Yet the ethos of Santiniketan diverged from the Gandhian model of national schools, which, Rabindranath told Gandhi, had too limited an objective.[21] Instead, the poet invited scholars from the world over to help him build his new university, and at the same time to learn something from the creative aspects of Indian culture. He also opposed Gandhi's advocacy of the spinning wheel as a focus for indigenous economic enterprise. Rabindranath argued that this might serve a symbolic function but would not seriously challenge the Lancashire cotton mills.

Two younger nationalist leaders, Jawāharlāl Nehru and Subhāshchandra Basu (Subhas Chandra Bose), were also dear to Rabindranath. Subhash, in particular, he knew from the latter's college days: when Subhash was rusticated from college for political protest, Tagore wrote to the authorities in his defence. Subhash's later politics did not always win his support, but there is ample evidence of the affection and respect between them. In January 1939, Subhash was given a reception at Santiniketan after being elected President of the Indian National Congress. He returned there again after falling out with other leaders of the Congress. Nehru, too, was in Santiniketan at the time, and both leaders held discussions with Tagore. This could not resolve the conflict: Subhash was expelled from the Congress. When the convention centre Mahājāti Sadan (Hall of the Great Nation) was set up by Subhash after his expulsion, Tagore laid the foundation stone.

The conservative patriot-politician Chittaranjan Dās was perplexed by Rabindranath's anti-nationalist stance. He also crossed swords with him on gender issues. He was so incensed by Rabindranath's story 'Strir patra', where a spirited woman leaves her husband and marital home for an unknown world, that he published a counter-tale by another conservative nationalist, Bipinchandra Pāl, in his magazine *Nārāyan*. Clearly, Chittaranjan and Bipinchandra were unable to see the connexion between their brand of nationalism and patriarchy.

Rabindranath's own stand on women's issues was not unequivocal by any means, but especially in his fiction, he treats women with sensitivity and an empathy beyond the reach of legal reforms and social practices. His novels *Jogājog* (*Relationships*) and *Shesher kabitā* (*The Last Poem*) appeared in 1929, the same year as Virginia Woolf's *A Room of One's Own*. There is no evidence that Tagore knew of the last (though Woolf knew of Tagore and had reviewed the English *Gitanjali*); but it may be significant that Kumudini in *Jogājog* is a victim of marital rape, while Lābanya in *Shesher kabitā*, in a rare act for a woman in that age, rejects her ardent wooer, the highly eligible, supremely egotistical Amit Ray, for the humble Shobhanlāl. Rabindranath also created a new model of sensitive masculinity. The British held Indian males in contempt for their alleged effeminacy. In reaction, Indian writers not only told heroic stories of old kings and warriors but also created figures of aggressive manhood. In Rabindranath, however, figures like Bihāri (*Chokher bāli*), Nikhilesh (*Ghare-bāire*), Shribilās (*Chaturanga*), and, to some extent, Bipradās (*Jogājog*) are men of strong character who can defy norms but who never act violently, aggressively, or domineeringly.

VISION AND CREATION

Rabindranath devoted himself to a creative alternative agenda by giving shape to his ideal *samāj* at Santiniketan. This institution developed through many phases. Founded on a somewhat simplistic model of the ancient *tapovana* or forest hermitage, it burgeoned into a multifaceted centre working constructively in the cause of universal humanity. On 11 October 1916, he wrote from Chicago to his son Rathindranath:

> The school at Santiniketan has to be made the meeting-place between India and the world. The days of narrow chauvinistic nativism are coming to an end. Preparations for the great *yagna* [sacrificial worship] to mark the union of all the world's nations must be made on the plains of Bolpur.[22]

Santiniketan became the territory of many innovative disciplines and pursuits beyond the conventional curriculum. Tagore writes in 1919:

This school will practise agriculture, cattle farming and weaving to high standards. By adopting the co-operative model for economic sustenance, it will bond closely with the students, teachers and surrounding inhabitants through the ties of livelihood.[23]

In another direction, art and music came to be equally important parts of the activities.

One by one, Santiniketan came to attract persons as capable, and in due course as eminent, as Kshitimohan Sen, scholar of early Indian religion; Bidhushekhar Shāstri, Sanskritist and Indologist; Haricharan Bandyopādhyāy the lexicographer; Prabhatkumar Mukhopadhyay, Tagore's biographer and historian of Visva-Bharati; and the artist Nandalāl Basu (Bose). Dissolving provincial and national boundaries, persons from across India and many other countries joined the community. Mahāsthabir from Sri Lanka taught Buddhist philosophy; Kapileshwar Mishra from Mithilā, Pānini's Sanskrit grammar; and Hājāri Prasād Dwivedi, Hindi. Alex Aronson, a German Jew, found refuge in Santiniketan from the Holocaust. The French orientalist Sylvain Levi came too, besides many from Britain: Charles Andrews, William Pearson, Leonard Elmhirst, and Arthur Geddes. Links increased with China and Japan as well. The Chinese youth Tan Yun-Shan came to stay in 1928; Visva-Bharati's Cheena Bhavana was set up with his assistance in 1937. In every way, the hermitage was blossoming into a universal society. Nehru sent his daughter Indirā to Visva-Bharati; Abdul Gaffar Khān, the 'Frontier Gandhi', sent his son to study art at Kala Bhavana. Vijaykrishna from Mālābar joined as a student, as did Narbhup and Chāru from Dārjeeling.

The poet's personal and family life was set against this backdrop. After his wife's death, Santiniketan became his usual abode. He divided his stay between a number of adjacent houses of contrasting plan and appearance but bound by a common architectural vision: all of them single storeyed but with different floor levels, hence never too hot in the summer nor cold in the winter. The furniture was built at trifling cost, often from discarded materials like an upturned packing box made into a table, but with an elegance that became the hallmark of the place. The whole community, the poet himself in particular, was designedly housed in a style contrasting with colonial Kolkata. He even wished to be buried in the soil of Santiniketan – a wish not to be fulfilled.

Rabindranath's vision was ahead of his time in other respects as well. He wrote his play *Muktadhārā* (The Freed Stream, 1923) long before the modern environmentalist movement. The crisis in *Muktadhārā* begins when a big dam is built over a stream, cutting off a community from their supply of water. The story might remind us of the water politics of our own time. Nature provides resources for all, but humans rob one another as they do in other spheres. Rabindranath, the ambassador of world peace, raised his voice in protest and appeal, but the crisis intensified in his own land and across the world.

During his last twenty years, Rabindranath travelled worldwide, preaching against nationalistic hegemony and aggression, be it in the East or the West. He realized that the version of nationhood spawned by Western capitalism was turning into an escalating crisis for humankind. His experiment in alternative living at Santiniketan did not attain completeness for many reasons, not least because it was hard to convince people that it would succeed in larger communities. He also studied other alternative models for humane living and social organization. He shared his anxieties with personalities like Romain Rolland and Albert Einstein, though his meetings with the latter were philosophical rather than political. Both of them alerted him to the dangers of fascism, but when invited to Italy by Mussolini, he accepted, being imperfectly aware of the nature of the regime. Pictures of the poet with Mussolini made a good propaganda point for the fascist government, even if Rolland's expostulations later made Rabindranath issue a recantation. In a general way, Tagore was sceptical about modern political and religious institutions but retained faith in cooperative enterprise. He was impressed by the progress of post-revolutionary Russia (which he visited in Stalin's day, again to the alarm of liberal Europeans). The positive changes in Persia also attracted his attention.

Back home in Santiniketan, however, he was apprehensive about the future of the institution he had founded, owing to the death of dedicated workers, lack of funds, political turmoil, and his own ill health. He felt, moreover, that the ideal of universalism had not been adequately embodied in the place. On Gandhi's last visit to Santiniketan in February 1940, Rabindranath pressed a letter into the Mahatma's hand at parting, beseeching him to take care of his 'life's best treasure' when he, Rabindranath, was no more. The prospect of death had troubled him ever since he suddenly fell unconscious on the evening of 10 September 1937: on recovery, he felt he had returned from 'extinction's cave'.[24] In a poem in *The Modern Review* responding to *Prāntik*, Dilipkumār Rāy, son of the poet and dramatist Dwijendralāl, described Tagore as a 'Bird of Fire' who 'in the dark of sleep … cannot nest', whose 'flame-wings burn the dusk'.[25]

Death came on 7 August 1941 (22 Shrāvan 1348 of the Bengali era). In the preceding years, the poet had felt mounting concern at the violence, intolerance, and competitive greed engulfing the world. It was nearly two years into the Second World War. He was also deeply perturbed over the Spanish Civil War. He published an appeal on 3 March 1937 in the Kolkata paper *The Statesman* appealing to 'the conscience of humanity' to support the Spanish People's Front. Japan's imperial aggression in China was a third major cause of anguish, leading to some acrimonious exchanges in 1938 with the Japanese poet Yone Noguchi. 'Sabhyatār sangkat' ('Crisis in Civilization', 14 April 1941), Rabindranath's last Santiniketan oration, is a cry of despair. In a poem written twelve days before his death, the sun asks the same question, who knows to whom, on the first and the last day of the world: 'Who are you?' On neither day is there an answer.[26]

In the only two poems Rabindranath wrote thereafter, he moderates that total incertitude; but this poet of positive values ends his days still facing challenges and seeking answers. We may recall a passage in the 1933 lectures *Mānusher dharma* (The Religion of Man).[27] There, to define the human condition in contrast to an animal's, Rabindranath borrows a term from Buddhist philosophy: humanity is *anāgārik*, 'without a home'. The animal has a den to bide in; humanity's lot is the road.[28] The human quest never ends in time.

NOTES

1. 'Ingrāj o bhāratbāsi' (The English and the Indians), *RRVB* 10:394.
2. Ibid., *RRVB* 10:390.
3. *EW* 3:513.
4. *The Religion of Man*, ch. 7, 'The Man of My Heart', *EW* 3:129.
5. 'The Soviet system' (1931), *EW* 4:426; tr. of *Rāshiār chithi*, 'Upasanghār' (Letters from Russia, Conclusion).
6. Beams's original English article cannot be traced. The Bengali appeared as 'Bangiya sāhitya samāj, anusthān patra' in *Bangadarshan*, Āshārhh 1279 (*June 1872).
7. There was a brief disjunct episode of earlier Bengali printing by the Portuguese.
8. *RRVB* 16:18.
9. 'Bihārilal' (1894), *RRVB* 9:412.
10. *Jibansmriti* (Reminiscences), *RRVB* 17:396.
11. Bankimchandra Chattopadhyay, 'Bānglā bhāshā' (The Bengali Language), in *Bibidha prabandha: rachanābali*, ed. Alok Rāy et al. (Kolkata: Paschimbanga bānglā ākādemi, 2015), 4:205.
12. Letter to Jagadishchandra Basu, 8 January 1908, *CP* 6:55.
13. Abanindranath, *Gharoā*, in *Abanindra rachanābali* (Kolkata: Prakāsh bhaban, 1973), 1:71.

14. 'Landane' (In London), *RRVB* 26:515. This essay of 1912 was recast in 1939 for inclusion in the collection *Pather sanchay.*

15. As Tagore himself complains in a letter to Amiya Chakrabarti, 30 December 1938, *CP* 11:222.

16. *RRVB* 23:106.

17. As phrased by Abanindranath Tagore: see Rāni Chanda, *Shilpiguru abanindranāth* (Kolkata: Visva-Bharati, 1972), 79.

18. Victoria Ocampo, 'Tagore on the Banks of River Plate', in *Centenary*, 40.

19. *RRVB* 10:595.

20. *RRVB* 6:571.

21. See Leonard K. Elmhirst, *Poet and Plowman* (Kolkata: Visva-Bharati, 1975; rpt. 2008), 6.

22. *CP* 2:70.

23. *Bishwabhārati* #1, *RRVB* 27:346.

24. *Prāntik* #17, *RRVB* 22:18.

25. Dilipkumar Ray, 'To Rabindranath: On Reading "Prantika"', *Modern Review*, March 1938, 313.

26. *Shesh lekhā* #13, *RRVB* 26:49–50.

27. This is different from the 1930 English lectures with a synonymous title.

28. *RRVB* 20:394.

4 Tagore's Poetry

An Overview

SUKANTA CHAUDHURI

Rabindranāth Thākur (Tagore) practised nearly every literary form, but his primary mode is lyric poetry. He defines his artistic persona in its terms: all his other work takes its bearings from it. He wrote no epics, virtually no long poems of any kind. Of some 4,500 poetical items, nearly 2,200 are songs, and many more song-like though not set to music.

The poems cover an extraordinary formal range. Traditional Bengali verse-forms like the *payār* couplet appear along with blank verse and the sonnet, derived from the West though assimilated in Bengali by Rabindranath's day. There is a huge range of lyric stanza-forms. His later poetry employs a distinctive type of irregular couplets as well as *vers libre*. This variety contrasts markedly with the uniform style and structure of Rabindranath's own English versions, couched in a formalized, somewhat archaic poetic prose. They hold no clue to the formal energy and versatility of the originals.

The English selection also creates the misleading image of a largely religious or spiritual poet. Undoubtedly, a sustained vein of philosophic spirituality runs through his poetry. He wrote many hymns for the Brahmo Samaj, the reformed Hindu community to which his family belonged. His poetry shows profound assimilation of the Vedas and Upanishads. But it mostly upholds no doctrinal religion and is often incompatible with any. He consistently finds a spirit immanent in nature and human life. The interaction of the natural with the supra-natural is presented in many veins, from the theistic to a kind of refined animism.

A great many poems address human matters pure and simple, human love above all. His own art is a regular theme. There is some political poetry, from local satire to fierce attacks on the global order. Many poems concern the inner life and external situation of women, complementing his fiction and essays on the subject. There is an unsuspected amount of humour, whimsy, and nonsense.

Rabindranath's poetry comprises a whole universe of themes and concerns. This chapter is a very brief overview of a vast, hugely varied, mostly untranslated, and intellectually complex body of poetry. That poetry does not evolve in a straight graph. It is full of repetitions, expansions, conjunctions, and even reversals. Its intellective element is as crucial as its vast store of imagery, rich veins of description (above all of the Bengal landscape), and unfailing engagement with human lives and minds. Tagore is a prime example of the major poet as defined by T.S. Eliot, one whose work is greater in sum than the total of its parts.[1]

Rabindranath has some early poems of remarkable power, like 'Tarakār ātmahatyā' (The Suicide of a Star), on the self-destruction of a star that cannot bear its unbroken radiant happiness, or 'Rāhur prem' (Rāhu's Love), a harrowing study of possessive sexuality. But by the poet's own account, a turning point came in 1882, somewhere between these two poems. Standing on a balcony in Kolkata at sunrise, he 'felt a veil pass from before his eyes', showing the world in a new light.[2] Using the trope of a spring bursting from its source, he celebrated this vision that filled him with new creative energy, an urge to break all confines. 'Nirjharer swapnabhanga' (The Spring Wakes from Its Dream) grew from 201 to 267 lines but was then pruned in stages to 43. Understandably, the mature Rabindranath felt a growing distance from it, while granting it due historical space. He similarly abridged 'Srishti, sthiti, pralay' (Creation, Stasis, Destruction), which anticipates however remotely the cosmic vision of his later work. In the early poetry as a whole, his biggest innovation is in devising lyric stanza-forms and the prosody to make them possible. In this task, his most celebrated predecessor was Michael Madhusudan Datta (Dutt), the first major poet of modern Bengal; and perhaps the most influential, the relatively obscure Bihārilāl Chakrabarti.

The early work offers other verse-models as well. *Karhi o komal* (Sharps and Flats, 1886) has sonnets alongside the customary lyrics; some of the latter double as songs. Even earlier, there are accomplished poems – again, often with a parallel life in song – in *Bhānusingha thākurer padābali* (Bhānusingha Thākur's Verses, 1884), where the young poet imitates medieval Vaishnav poetry in the Brajabuli language of the poet Vidyāpati. This anticipates his later work: most memorably in poem #19 addressing death as a lover, as Krishna was Rādhā's lover. But the real breakthrough comes in *Mānasi* (1890).

EARLY MATURITY: LOVE, NATURE, HUMANITY

A major advance in *Mānasi* is prosodic. Rabindranath adopts a new principle of syllabification enabling a lively, supple flow and intricate nuances of tone. There is also a crucial intellectual advance. *Mānasi* has poems on many subjects, but for the first time, it binds a core body of poems by certain common concerns. The new prosody enables the lyric to treat serious themes without collapsing under their weight. For more sustained thought or narration, the traditional *payār* couplet is endowed with a new mobility, allowing sensitive changes of verbal register.

'Mānasi' means 'woman of the mind'. The poems are in high-Romantic vein, with marked philosophic idealism. (The influence of Shelley has been noted, though Keats was Rabindranath's favourite English poet.) As the poet explains in an introductory piece, he constructs an image within his mind through hope, language, and love.[3] The phrase he uses, the feminine *mānasi-pratimā*, primarily means the mental image of a woman. At its most elevated, the love he celebrates has an almost cosmic origin: 'We two have floated down love's tide from its source in the heart of primal time.'[4] The poet is alive to the unreality of such love in worldly terms. Many pieces, from the tender to the comic, project the frustrations of immature romanticism, like the dialogue between the sexes in 'Nārir ukti' (The Woman's Words) and 'Purusher ukti' (The Man's Words). The same dialogue is implicit in 'Nishphal kāmanā' (Fruitless Desire), expressing the male lover's distress. Again, his romantic love is exalted to a cosmic plane:

As the infinite mystery of heavenly light trembles in the lonely star, so the flame of the soul's mystery trembles in the darkness of those eyes.

However, those depths are beyond the lover's reach: all he can hope for is a little laughter, a few words and glances, a hint of affection. He cannot offer the infinite love that would make him deserve more. He tells himself,

A human being is not food for your hunger.... The lotus blooms for God and the universe.... Will you sever it from its stem with the sharp knife of your desire?[5]

But the reality check cannot negate the ideal love in these poems. It merges with the life-principle of nature and the universe.

Other major themes are broached in *Mānasi* and developed in the volumes that follow, from *Sonār tari* (The Golden Boat, 1894) through *Chitrā* (The Many-Pictured One, 1896)[6] and *Kalpanā* (Imaginings, 1900) to *Kheyā* (The Ferry, 1906). We first find here the vivid yet thought-laden descriptions of nature that is one of Rabindranath's most celebrated veins. *Mānasi* (like *Bhānusingha thākurer padābali*) often celebrates the rains, inspired by the monsoon settings of Kalidāsa's poem of parted love, the *Meghadutam*, and Vaishnav poetry on the love of Krishna and Radha. Vaishnav poetry contributes specially to the philosophic, even mystic nuances that play about the depictions of love, even at its most erotic or passionate – or, as in 'Barshā jāpan' (Passing a Rainy Night, *Sonār tari*), in a half-ironic contemporary middle-class setting:

> 'A dark rainy night: the deep thunder roars.'[7] ... The picture rises to my mind of Vrindāvan of old, and Radha's solitary dream.... The rain grows stronger, the clouds rage, the sound of crickets fills the earth. I cannot tell how the heart feels on this dense dark night, mingling dream and waking.[8]

Mānasi has a still more striking image of feminity in the womb of nature: the mythical Ahalyā, turned to stone and buried underground, now restored to life as an erotic yet primally innocent figure recalling (as has been noted)[9] Botticelli's Venus rising from the sea:

> Exquisite, unclad, mysterious form, the fullness of youth bathed in the freshness of childhood.... You rise from the blue waters ... like the first sunrise.[10]

Nature itself can be of primordial power: 'O ocean, our first mother, the earth is your child, the only daughter of your bosom.'[11] Rabindranath already shows a sense, unprecedented in Bengali poetry, of nature as a total entity:

> Cruel Nature, we search for your heart. So many flowers, so much light, so much scent and music, but where is your love? ... You do not know your own extent, your own mystery.[12]

Equally, he views each minute creature as a separate sentient being:

> How the blossoms on their beautiful stems are rapturous with blind joy! With what deep, spontaneous elation do the trees, creepers, grass

and lichens rejoice in the fresh sunlight, like contented infants tired with suckling, smiling in happy sleep.[13]

Or he can paint what, extracted from its conceptual frame, appears a total but uncomplicated landscape:

> The mango grove is full of copper fruit, its thick undergrowth covered with clustered flowers. The scent of the *champak* wafts from the woods to my window. The shadeless *deodār* sighs dreamily.... The empty plain stretches in the sun, a hot dry path winding through it; but the woods alongside are full of light breezes, the scent of flowers, and soft green shade.[14]

Love is plotted against myth and classical poetry, nature, and the cosmos. Shiva's destruction of the love-god Madana, far from curbing the power of love, has scattered it through creation ('Madanbhasmer par', After the Burning of Madana, *Kalpanā*). But love also appears in purely human contexts, most sustainedly in the sonnet-like poems in *Smaran* (Remembrance, 1903) recalling the poet's dead wife, but also in living relationships in all keys: rejection and frustration:

> I thought he had called me, remembered me through the ages.... Alas, that night is departed: how can I bring it back?[15]

but no less intimacy:

> to drink in the eye's nectar with the eye, to feel the heart with the heart: all else is lost in the dark.[16]

or a full-throated eroticism:

> Today my vineyard is laden with clustered fruit.... Tear and pluck them with your oyster-red nails.... Burst the ripe fruit with your lips, with your teeth.[17]

Love and nature are conjoint. Their worlds intermingle – sometimes lightly and suggestively, often in open and complex association. Perhaps the most striking instance is a titanic figure of female sexuality, the celestial dancer Urvashi:

Your body's grace is washed with the world's tears; your feet are tinged with the heart's blood of the three worlds. Your hair unbound, you have lightly placed your lotus-feet upon the unfolded lotus of universal desire.[18]

THE SPRINGS OF POETRY; CREATIVE SELVES

Another crucial link between the human world and created nature, both earthly and cosmic, is through the poet's own art. The 'woman of the mind' can be his muse, his 'treasure sought since birth – poetry, fair vine of the imagination'.[19] But these romantic flights embellish a challenging intellectual construct.

A good starting point is 'Bhāshā o chhanda' (Words and Rhythm), a narrative poem in the collection *Kāhini* (1900). Sanskrit tradition ascribes the birth of poetry to the verses uttered by the hermit Vālmiki on seeing a hunter kill a mating crane. This leads Brahmā, the god of creation, to send the sage Nārada to enjoin Valmiki to compose the *Rāmāyana*. Valmiki explains to Narada the basis of his art. All nature is bound in harmony, hymning the divine in a language exceeding human speech; but transformed through metre into poetry, human language can

> ascend like fire, floating beyond earthly limits, uplifting the ponderous earth itself, raising speech to the heaven of thought, the human to the shrine of the gods.[20]

The idea extends through all of Rabindranath's work. Much later in *Purabi* (1925), rising higher in the cosmic scale, he sees the sun as the original poet (*ādi kabi*, a title given to Valmiki):

> My mind is the flute you play beside the sea of dark emptiness, destroying that gloom. Its stops break into music with the colours of the clouds, the flowers of the groves, the murmur of the spring. Its beat inspires the rhythm of life in my every limb.[21]

It is only one stage back to the primordial Word, a concept as rooted in the Upanishads as in the Bible. But a concomitant idea is that poetic utterance strives towards silence, a fulfilment beyond speech: 'Now make your loquacious poet mute.'[22] Even the loftier 'language' of nature culminates in the silence of the Himalayas:

Your aspiration, having reached its last limit, loses its voice, forgets all its music. Your wordless hymn ... pours down in a stream.[23]

There is a countering factor, however. 'You have gifted song to the bird; it sings only that song but gives nothing more. You have gifted me my voice, so I gift you something more: I sing my own songs.'[24] The poet's art reflects the creative power of a divine universal artist. But the latter's creation would be futile if human perception did not activate its latent being: 'It is the colours of my consciousness that make the emerald green and the ruby red.... I looked at the rose and said "Beautiful", and beautiful it was.'[25]

That last excerpt, from 'Āmi' (I, *Shyāmali*), is of much later date. I cite it here to introduce another seminal idea in Rabindranath: a notion of many selves, many 'I's, reaching outward from the individual 'I' to answering presences in other people; thence to all created objects; to the cosmic powers creating and ordering those objects; and sometimes to a theistically conceived God. The poet's private being is extended and transcended as he seeks to identify himself through these stages with a 'universal I' (*bishwa-āmi*). He will thereby lose his own being but achieve a universal selfhood.

In *Sadhana*, Rabindranath links the Upanishads to Christ's words, 'Before Abraham was, I am':[26]

This is the eternal *I am* that speaks through the *I am* that is in me. The individual *I am* attains its perfect end when it realizes its freedom of harmony in the infinite *I am*.[27]

This recalls Coleridge's theory of the imagination. For Coleridge, the core reality is the 'infinite I AM': the divine is everywhere, implicit in all creation. Humans perceive the world by participating in this common being through the faculty of 'primary imagination': we know all other things by assimilating them to our own being, our 'I'. 'Secondary imagination', special to the poet, works a more intensive synthesis where the identities of separate objects are dissolved and recreated, or at very least idealized and unified.[28]

Rabindranath never cites Coleridge's theory, but lines like these serve to illustrate it:

Present in the young light of the new dawn, I open my rapt eyes to the sky; hidden in the sad rays of the silent evening, I inhabit the heights of the human heart.[29]

There is an 'I' in every creature and object across the scale of being, reflecting the one all-embracing Self: the *ātman*, the true and total self beyond the *aham*, the ego or lesser self. The poet creates by validating this order in his own consciousness. Rabindranath even comes to read his early 'Nirjharer swapnabhanga' as celebrating the release of the lesser self into the universal.[30] In a 1918 song, the poet's 'I' gazes at the 'I' who 'floats beneath the sky on the waves of time' and flows also through soil and water, fruit and flower. 'I am free, replete, serene, radiant'[31] – which 'I' is this? The poet projects his private self into the universal self. Equally, he receives the universe within his being:

> The same life-force whose waves flow night and day through my veins rushes to conquer the world. It dances in exquisite rhythm through the universe. In silent joy, it infuses a million blades of grass in the pores of the soil, breaks out in leaf and flower.[32]

These poems reflect the single greatest influence on Rabindranath, the Upanishads. Their profound impact on him is best gauged from his own account in *Sadhana* (1913). 'This deity who is manifesting himself in activities of the universe always dwells in the heart of man as the supreme soul.'[33] The end of the human soul is to blend with nature and humanity, hence with this deity.

Such ideas reach their height in Rabindranath's later poetry. But already in his early middle period, they acquire a uniquely personalized form in a crucial development, extending literally to the last poem he composed.

JIBAN-DEBATĀ, THE GOD OF LIFE

'Niruddesh jātrā' (Voyage without Destination, *Sonār tari*) presents a mysterious *bideshini*, a woman from a foreign land. She has lured the speaker onto a golden boat sailing endlessly without a destination. Yet he knows that one day she will abandon him.

This combination of the 'woman of the mind' with the *femme fatale* of European Romanticism may or may not be the figure who steers a golden boat (*sonār tari*) in the volume's title poem. She offers no feminine allure: in fact, Bengali pronouns being gender-neutral, only the English version indicates it is a woman.[34] The boat moors where the speaker is waiting with the harvest of his field. It takes that harvest on board and departs, leaving him abandoned.

The stranger-woman is a recurrent figure in Rabindranath, traceable to a snatch of song heard in his childhood.[35] That memory inspired an 1895 song to a *bideshini*: 'I have seen you on autumn mornings and spring nights, and within my heart.... I have travelled the world to this new land: I am a guest at your door.'[36] That last line is echoed by a voyager to the palace of a foreign princess in the 1927 verse-tale 'Sāgarikā' (Woman by the Sea, *Mahuyā*). In the earlier bizarre verse-tale 'Sindhu-pāre' (Beside the Sea, *Chitrā*), a veiled woman makes the spellbound narrator ride with her to a sumptuous palace where she finally unveils herself. The astonished narrator bursts out: 'Are you here too, god of my life (*jiban-debatā*)?'[37]

Starting from *Chitrā*, Rabindranath's poetry abounds in bewilderingly various *jiban-debatā* figures. They can be female or male, lover or beloved or both, worshipped or worshipper or both, deeply interiorized but also latent in earthly or universal nature. But it is always a personalized god: that is the point of the concept. In a special version of the play of 'I's, the *jiban-debatā* is intimately linked with the poet, a second self yet separate and autonomous. It guides and fulfils the poet's being but thereby also fulfils its own. In a late preface to *Chitrā*, Rabindranath calls it his 'joint self, like a binary star': 'its purpose is fulfilled through me, in my joy and sorrow, my good and evil.'[38]

The poet links the song from his childhood memory with another by the Bāul poet Lālan Fakir: 'The unknown bird goes in and out of the cage.' The Bauls are a cultic community of Bengal. The unknown bird is a trope for their *maner mānush* ('man of the mind'), the viscerally mystical power or presence that Rabindranath renders as 'the divine which is in Man'.[39] His god (*debatā*) is so closely interfused with the human entity (*mānush*) as to humanize and personalize the god more than to spiritualize the human in any conventional sense; rather, it charges the latter's core identity with existential meaning and energy.

In the poem called 'Jiban-debatā' (*Chitrā*), the immaterial god fulfils his own longing by entering the poet's soul. The soul, in turn, fashions their marriage bed with the colours, sounds, and scents of all creation, sings songs of the seasons for the god on his once-remote throne. The poem ends in the languor of a satisfied union. Rabindranath translates the entire poem in *The Religion of Man* and comments: 'I felt that I had found my religion at last, the religion of Man, in which the infinite became defined in humanity and came close to me so as to need my love and co-operation.'[40]

Two Upanishadic premises are transformed here. First, the divine needs the human no less than the human the divine. This godly need is born not of lack but of plenitude, to actualize the divine power to create and contain all things. 'That inherent want is he himself, and so he is in so many ways, in so many forms, giving himself.'[41] Hence the 'king of kings' woos the human soul: 'Your love would be futile were it not for me.'[42]

This implies an extraordinary parity between creator and created. In *Mānusher dharma* 3, Rabindranath cites *Brihadāranyaka upanishad* 1:4:10: 'He who thinks "The god I worship is one, and I am another" ... is ignorant like a beast.'[43] The divine triumphs in its human manifestation. Rabindranath extends the idea to humble mundane life: the god does not dwell in 'hymns and worship and devotion' but in the lives of toiling men.[44]

The second point follows. The divine is linked to the natural and human by bonds of love: 'our individual soul has been separated from the supreme soul ... not from alienation but from the fullness of love.'[45] The *jiban-debatā* and the human host bond through love, even erotic love. In a letter to the philosopher Brajendranāth Shil (Seal), Rabindranath says that his mental climate was generated by the confluence of the Upanishads with Vaishnav poetry.[46] The union of divine and human in the love of Radha and Krishna melds with the Upanishadic union of the divine with the human soul in a construct entirely the poet's own, the *jiban-debatā*. His father, Debendranāth, read the Upanishads alongside the Persian poet Hafez, inspiring him to view his God 'with a love full of the ardour of intense passion, steeped in rich sweetness'.[47]

As often as not, the *jiban-debatā* is female: sometimes a serene ideal figure, anadyomene not like Venus but like the goddess Lakshmi who also rose from the sea, seated on a lotus;[48] sometimes a beguiling, even seductive figure blending with the foreign woman and *femme fatale* already mentioned. Her various beauties are the changing splendours of the universe; but within the poet's soul, she is serene and solitary.[49]

The *jiban-debatā* is a presence both internal and external, across the universe and within the poet. The poet bonds with nature and the elements through this divinity, and also interiorizes it in subjective terms. To say this is to convey nothing of the imaginative power of the construct; also its intellectual complexity, drawing opposites into synthesis, justifying all contradictions as integral to that synthesis even while they endow the poetry with immense figurative richness. The *jiban-debatā* must rank among the great philosophical tropes of world literature.

VIGIL, TRYST, WORSHIP

A motif linked to the *jiban-debatā* is the arrival of a visitor – god, ruler, or lover. The arrival might be unexpected, the very possibility dismissed, as with the royal guest in 'Āgaman' (The Coming, *Kheyā*). Or it can be eagerly awaited – sometimes in hope of union, sometimes for almost certain disappointment. In two companion pieces in *Kheyā*, 'Shubhakshan' (The Auspicious Hour) and 'Tyāg' (Sacrifice), a girl adorns herself for the prince passing by her window. She throws down her jewels: they are crushed by his chariot wheels while he rides heedlessly by.

In its most frequent and suggestive version, the wait becomes a woman's vigil for her lover. The most celebrated examples are three songs set on stormy nights, from the triad *Gitānjali* (1912), *Gitimālya*, and *Gitāli* (both 1914). In *Gitānjali* #20, the soul awaits her tryst with the 'friend of her heart', who crosses forests and rivers to reach her. In *Gitimālya* #67, he arrives as the storm wrecks the beloved's doors; she sees him next morning in the desolation of her shattered room. *Gitāli* #33 is often associated with these two songs, though not clearly about any tryst. Here the speaker travels through a stormy night towards an unknown city he or she may reach at daybreak.

Arrival implies journeying. Many poems feature a traveller who spurns the comforts of home for the spell of the road, an uncertain journey to an unknown but irresistible goal. The call of the unknown stirs not only immoveable subjects such as trees but also the earth-bound human spirit:

I am restless with thirst for the afar.... O you the afar, the great afar,
I hear your plaintive flute. I forget I have no wings but am bound to
one spot.[50]

The guest in the soul's shattered home can be a sublime and radiant figure, a god to worship rather than a lover to embrace: 'O radiant one, you have stormed my door and come. Victory to you!'[51] More prominently than before, *Gitānjali*, *Gitimālya*, and *Gitāli* feature a removed, elevated divinity alongside the intimate lover-god. The former figure, projected in quasi-biblical phrasing, dominates the English *Gitanjali*, encouraging the view of Rabindranath as a poet of simple piety or 'oriental mysticism'. This formally devotional phase occupies only a short period from *Naibedya* to *Gitāli*.

Naibedya (*Worship-offering*, 1901) is Rabindranath's first volume of poems devoted largely (though not exclusively) to spiritual themes. They are tight sonnet-like structures, as though supporting a new meditative rigour. However, the following volumes, from *Kheyā* to *Gitāli*, return to lighter free-flowing lyric forms. *Gitānjali*, *Gitimālya*, and *Gitāli* contain a high proportion of song-poems, as their titles indicate though with different thrusts: *Gitānjali*, 'song-offering', as to a god; *Gitimālya*, 'song-garland', as offered to a lover; and *Gitāli*, simply 'a collection of songs', as though in and for themselves.

Gitānjali contains a variety of material including the famous poem #106, elsewhere titled 'Bhārat-tirtha' (Pilgrimage to India), on the unity evolving through India's diverse history. But the volume's principal vein is spiritual ardour and devotion, conveyed with unusual simplicity, not to say purity, of prosody and verbal register. This cannot but affect the nature of the spirituality, whether at the pietistic or the mystical end of the spectrum. The latter, especially, generates some deeply evocative poems, sometimes linked to the soul's wait for a divine lover. In Rabindranath's own rendering:

> Clouds heap upon clouds and it darkens. Ah, love, why dost thou let me wait outside at the door all alone?[52]

Gitānjali is more compatible with conventional theism than Rabindranath's more original syntheses. This may account for its popularity, translatability, and consequent impact on the worldwide image of Rabindranath as primarily a sage or devotional poet. Its distinctive power cannot be denied, but it may not have gained such pre-eminence had the overlapping English volume not won Rabindranath the Nobel Prize.

Gitimālya and *Gitāli* show some changes in orientation. *Gitānjali* did not lack poems where the deity was not an object of worship but a friend or lover, but *Gitimālya* has more. There are more vigils and trysts, more assertions that the divine seeks the human no less than the human the divine, hence more poems assimilable to the *jiban-debatā*:

> Who is this, most deeply within me? My understanding, my emotions, are roused by his hidden touch. He brushes my eyes with his spells, and plays upon my heart-strings.[53]

Gitāli, on the contrary, was written during deep, virtually clinical depression. This accounts for a new concern with suffering and death. There are still many vigils and trysts with mystic lovers, perhaps in radiant heroic guise, but also poems of spiritual inertness and cowardice. Most often, however, suffering strengthens and purifies the soul:

> I will not turn away the guest who has come to my door in the guise of pain.... O fierce god, you tell me through sorrow that I am not little within my little self.[54]

The soul's loneliness also makes it more independent: more often than before, it sets out on a journey rather than await the coming of the god: 'If you have unbolted your door at break of day, why should I bashfully languish at home?'[55]

In the last analysis, these features modify rather than override the design perfected in *Gitānjali*. *Gitānjali*, *Gitimālya*, and *Gitāli* form a distinctive, integral phase of Rabindranath's opus. But they build on elements variously unfolding since *Mānasi*. They also reveal subtle but incremental reworkings that prepare us for the radical changes to follow.

REDEFINITIONS

The modernist poet Buddhadeb Basu (Buddhadeva Bose) found a single poetic trajectory from *Mānasi* to *Balākā* (1916).[56] But *Balākā* (A Flight of Geese) marks a watershed in many ways. The underlying change, as always, is formal. Some poems in *Balākā* retain stanzaic patterns, sometimes with novel intricacies after the restraint of *Gitānjali*, *Gitimālya*, and *Gitāli*. But most pieces embody a striking innovation, the *muktabandha* ('freely bound') form – lines of greatly varying length rhyming in couplets. There can be pauses in mid-line, more usually at line-end underpinned by the rhyme, with run-on lines subtly played off against them. The result is an immensely supple, versatile medium to accommodate virtually any subject. Its movement has an inbuilt, almost colloquial informality that moderates elevated themes and dignifies simple ones. *Balākā* demonstrates most possibilities of the form; the next volume, *Palātakā* (The Escaped, 1918), completes the range with some designedly simple narratives, almost artless in tone, with the lightest symbolic subtext where any at all. *Palātakā* also introduces a more flexible syllabification, closer to the flow of natural speech.

Henceforth a good proportion of Rabindranath's poetry is always in *muktabandha*, and its presence underlies much of the rest. That poetry carries an increasingly philosophic and even abstract thrust; *muktabandha* authenticates it in language at once familiar and poetic, melding with the common experience of nature and human life. Old themes and motifs continue till the end, often in strikingly new guise alongside entirely new elements. This may not have been possible without a revolution in prosodic practice.

But the explicit concern is with innovation of other kinds. *Balākā* opens with an invocation to youth. The second poem celebrates destruction. The third is a virtual call to revolution, deriding those who lag behind:

With bloodied feet, we will break our bonds and rush forth in sun
and shadow, while they only tangle themselves in their own nets.
They will weep, they will weep.[57]

Human and material concerns are integrated with the play of cosmic forces.
In *Balākā* #16, cities built by 'the clenched fist of wood and stone' embody
man's myriad thoughts and desires, competing with cosmic dust from 'the
huge material mass of the universe'.[58] On what plane of (im)materiality does
this notion operate? Again, the mighty Ganga is marked not by the mass of
its waters but the flow. If it were to halt for a moment, the entire universe
would be in turmoil: a 'crippled, dumb, deaf, decapitated darkness' would
overwhelm mountains of inert matter, minute atoms impaled to them in
the absence of motion.[59] On what metaphysical plane does this vision work?

The linking of earthly nature and humanity with the cosmic and even
abstract is hardly new in Rabindranath, but its metaphysical basis is now
more consistently stressed. Most of the poems in *Balākā* were written during
the First World War. The human condition is rendered with a harder realism
than before, though expressed symbolically rather than directly. It does not
lose power thereby, as *Balākā* #37 (elsewhere 'Jharher kheyā', The Storm-
Crossing) illustrates. Here voyagers battle the stormy seas of 'all sorrow
on earth, all sin and evil, all tears, all poison and violence' to uphold their
faith in humanity, peace, and beneficence, the divine truth of the One.[60]

This is not the poet's first engagement with suffering and evil. A notable
early expression was in 'Ebār phirāo more' (Now Turn Me Back, *Chitrā*),
where he turns from a withdrawn poetic life to face the pain and injustice
of the world:

Swollen audacity sucks blood from feeble breasts through a million
mouths. Arrogant self-serving injustice mocks at suffering. See the
dumb hordes with bowed heads, their dimmed faces inscribed with
the pain of a hundred centuries.[61]

Chitrā also contains 'Swarga hate bidāy' (Farewell to Heaven), the cry of a
soul in heaven that wants to exchange its cloying happiness for an imperfect
earthly life. This recalls the earlier 'Tarakār ātmahatyā'.

Yet 'Ebār phirāo more' evokes 'the victress of the world', a goddess of
virtuous beneficence (*mahimālakshmi*). This again is the *jiban-debatā*,
like the god whose advent is awaited in 'The Storm-Crossing'. *Balākā* #5
(elsewhere 'Pārhi', The Voyage) goes further: the god himself now crosses
the stormy night sea to the soul keeping vigil. It is a striking new variant

of the divine lover's tryst with the soul. Equally, the soul itself can identify with the traveller to the unknown (*Balākā* #45).

Sometimes in *Balākā*, the *jiban-debatā* resembles the intimate companion of *Chitrā*: 'I came: your bosom trembled, your anguish began.' But now their union has an elemental dimension:

> You made me blossom in the flowers, rocked me in the cradle of many shapes. You scattered me among the stars, then drew me again to your bosom.[62]

This god is intensely private even while present in all nature: the same breeze blows through the forest of *shāl* trees and the heart's garden ('Mātir dāk', The Call of the Soil, *Purabi*). The god also keeps tryst with nature in the spring, like the 'strayed traveller' in a 1916 song who converses with trees and flowers.[63] *Purabi*, like *Mahuyā* (1929), records many trysts between wind and trees, night and dawn, rain and drought, tides and the moon – always, finally, between nature and a greater spirit. 'Has he come?' the flowering tree and the forest breeze ask the poet each spring ('Pratyāshā', Expectation, *Mahuyā*). 'Banaspati' (The Great Tree, *Purabi*) even celebrates a sexual power impregnating nature. The nymph of the horizon (*diganganā*), representing the air and elements, woos a venerable ascetic tree, kissing and stripping him in a hailstorm, but then joins in a more serene consummation, seemingly transposing male and female roles:

> Let your love take form through his whole being in ever-new leaves, flowers and fruits.... Let your touch, your ultimate message, express itself in his glory.[64]

Purabi combines cosmic breadth with a deep interiority in other ways too. The new melding of the external and internal enables sustained tropes, whole philosophic allegories enfolded in literal description:

> The great tree gazes upward, contemplating perfection. Through its clustered leaves, it responds continually to the silent call of the immense, chants mantras in the murmur of its branches.[65]

Even as Rabindranath's poetry grows more abstracted and conceptual, it incorporates more and more elaborate descriptions – above all of natural scenes, but also of human events.

Related themes even touch poems for and about children in *Shishu bholānāth* (The Child Shiva, 1922). In 'Dui āmi' (The Two I's), the child imagines another 'I', a döppelganger among the clouds, riding the sunbeams or chasing the moon. This was the theme of the 1918 song cited earlier. But only in *Parishesh* (Conclusion, 1932) does the interplay of 'I's reappear significantly. There, in a poem called 'Āmi' (I – with a sequel 'Tumi', You), the poet's greater 'I' is clearly a version of the *jiban-debatā*. He had considered it part of himself but finds it is not 'imprisoned' within his being: it spans all time and space. The mystic knows of this 'I', as does the poet.[66]

Yet as a distinct entity, a 'you', this deity awaits fulfilment in the poet's life. And that life now embraces all suffering humanity:

> Your drumbeat calls me where humanity is oppressed and insulted, where light dims in the stricken heart, where the captive weeps in prison.[67]

This aligns with a nascent radicalism I will shortly discuss. The *jiban-debatā* now looks beyond the individual soul: the poet must share his god with all humanity, as already with the rest of created nature.

Shishu bholānāth offers a child's version of the *jiban-debatā*, a spirit linking the child to nature:

> Eternal child yourself, you are there with the child, carrying your bag of stuff. You launch colourful fire-balloons, and paint the sky with colourful brushes.[68]

The title poem reflects a major philosophic motif in the later poetry. Bholānāth, the 'heedless' or 'oblivious' god, is Shiva. The unruly child (*shishu*), 'liberating' his toys 'out of destruction into destruction', is like the destroyer-god, but such disorder underlies all creative harmony: 'My songs will attain rhythm if I link them with your wild dance.'[69] Shiva – especially in his aspect as Natarāj, the cosmic dancer – becomes a creative, harmonizing force, the ordering principle of the universe. The celebrated song 'Nrityer tāle tāle' (To the beat of the dance, 1927),[70] perhaps Rabindranath's most elaborate musical creation, interprets the dance of Nataraj in this light. The previous year saw *Natarāj-riturangashālā* (Nataraj's Theatre of the Seasons),[71] a linked series of songs about the seasonal cycle.

'Tapobhanga' (Broken Meditation, *Purabi*) reinvents Shiva in a remarkable new light. Madana, the love-god, was burnt in the fire of Shiva's fury when he disturbed the latter's meditation. But this is only the stern god's deceptive play: he actually surrenders to beauty. By his creational dance, he fills the springtide with colours, scents, and sensory delights.

His destructive, ascetic mode preludes a new era, a fresh cycle of youth and life. The design was latent in 'Barshashesh' (The End of the Year, *Kalpanā*), where the storm-god destroys to create:

> As the fruit emerges, shattering the petals of the withered flower, so have you emerged in exquisite, fulfilled form, breaking and scattering the old leaf-cups.[72]

In *Utsarga* #45 (elsewhere 'Maran-milan', Death-Tryst), the poet seeks death as a woman seeks her lover, in particular as Umā, Shiva's consort, sought the god.

Shiva-as-Nataraj appears all through the late poetry: vibrant but increasingly philosophized, himself a contemplative figure. He provides a foil to the incremental presence of Vedic and Upanishadic elements in Rabindranath's work.

THE LIFE OF PLANTS

In 1931 appeared *Banabāni* (The Voice of the Forest), a volume devoted to nature, especially trees. It offers a good vantage point for all Rabindranath's poetry on the subject.

Nature is a major presence virtually everywhere in Rabindranath, with the Bengal countryside as the default setting. Nature is prominent in the fiction as well, but chiefly as a backdrop to human affairs. This is sometimes the case in the poetry too, from *Chaitāli* (Poems of Late Spring, 1896) to *Punascha* (Postscript, 1932) and beyond. Still later – perhaps in *Prāntik* (On the Border, 1938) above all – nature settings are imbued with philosophic and mystical themes, but the basic engagement is with nature in and for itself.

Nature appears in purely sensory and pictorial terms, but pathetic fallacy is a regular mode, from 'Jete nāhi diba' (I Won't Let You Go, 1892):

> Earth and sky are sunk in deep sorrow.... Mother Earth clasps the smallest blade of grass to her bosom and cries, 'I won't let you go.'[73]

to 'Meghmālā' (The Cloudbank, 1935):

> The veiled morning sun lays its offering at the mountain's feet. The ascetic's meditation is broken: he forgets to be stern, and draws to his bosom the young moisture-laden cloudbank.[74]

Equally, as we have seen, the earthly landscape is linked to the primal and cosmic, as memorably in this 1896 song: 'In the vast universe, under the vast sky, in the midst of vast time, I, man, roam in solitary wonder.'[75] The cosmic landscape is gradually seen in a more sensory light, as though from a celestial viewing gallery; but the same forces pervade all created bodies:

> I have received in body and mind the vital juice cascading down the skies from creation's spring. It has coloured my life, as also the ricefields, the forest leaves, and autumn's scarf of world-weary clouds.[76]

The primal life force can also emanate from within the earth and manifest itself in earthly nature. Commencing in early poems like 'To Ahalyā', the idea grows over time. In 'Mātā' (Mother) in *Bithikā* (The Avenue), the mother's womb is compared to the hidden life-chamber of the soil. The human mother is thereby linked to all time and space, to travellers 'journeying towards the infinite across the skies'.[77]

These two elemental orders, the cosmic and the telluric, unite in the life of plants. That does not obviate a down-to-earth, companionate relation with them. It starts with the tree outside the poet's childhood nursery:

> You stand there night and day with tangled hair. Ancient banyan, do you remember that little boy?[78]

He bonds with the trees in his garden and the Santiniketan landscape, and finally with those outside his window in his old age. But these friends are also philosophers communing with the infinite. The opening poem of *Banabāni* covers the whole thematic terrain. The tree's descent from heaven brought the first life to earth, the first creative utterance breaking upon a blank, silent world. In the poet's familiar paradigm, it embodies the divine quest for earthly fulfilment. The immaterial permeates the material: transforming scientific fact into a creational trope, the tree drinks in the sun's fire, converting it to greenery. That quasi-Promethean flame impregnates human life: fired by its radiance, soothed by its shade, empowering it to challenge the gods.[79]

These ideas recur through *Banabāni* and *Bithikā*. Now captive to humans, the banyan is 'fearsome' in its primal identity: 'In my blood, I still bear the memory of the primal terror of the forest.'[80] Can this be the same tree that befriended the poet as a boy? But he still recalls the trees of his youth with gentle nostalgia, even as he sees small plants in a cosmic light: 'Its history is written by the universal scribe in minute letters in the corner of a tiny leaf. But a vast history is unfolding alongside.'[81]

Small plants and flowers are usually feminized, while large trees – banyan, *deodār*, *shāl* – are masculine, often pictured as sages or ascetics. One poem remarkably twins flower and woman as coeval: born in the primal dawn, wafted to earth on the same vital breeze. But after aeons, the flower sees in the woman the perfection of what in the plant is still only potential: 'I remain close to my origin, while you have received the message of fulfilment.'[82]

The poem is 'Pushpa' (The Flower) from *Bichitritā* (1933). This volume provides a vantage point for another crucial area of engagement.

WOMEN'S LIVES, WOMAN'S BEING

Bichitritā (The Pictured) is discussed, if at all, for its most apparent feature: each poem relates to an accompanying picture, seven of them the poet's own work, the rest by his relations and his circle. Another important feature is commonly overlooked: all the poems are about women. Even where the picture is of a flower or plant, the poet makes it symbolize some aspect of women's existence.

Women are a major presence in Rabindranath's poetry, as in his fiction and drama. But the poetry confines them much longer than the fiction to their roles as object of male attention, provider of male needs, and symbol of male ideas. A poem as late as *Balākā* #23 projects only two ideal figures, both risen from the sea: Urvashi, 'queen of the universal realm of desire', and Lakshmi, 'universal mother' and goddess of beneficence.[83]

In veins ranging from the poignant to the satiric, the early *Mānasi* had projected the constricted lives of women in that society, even while they were idealized by the male. A poem in *Chaitāli*, also entitled 'Mānasi' (Woman of the Mind), implies the tyranny of this double exaction:

> Woman, you are not God's creation alone. Man has formed you with beauty drawn from his mind.... Bestowing the garbs of modesty and adornment, the poet has made you secret and rare. Glowing desire has descended upon you. You are half human, half imagination.[84]

Smaran, commemorating the poet's deceased wife, Mrinālini, idealizes her in relation to his own life, at most regretting that he had neglected or underprized her. There is self-indulgence in his grief, even self-pity:

You can sleep today; I will wake by the door and keep the lamp lit.
You have loved me; today I, in solitude, must love you.[85]

We learn nothing about the dead woman as an independent being. Years
later, in a humbler social setting, similar neglect is recalled by a dying wife
in 'Mukti' (Liberation, *Palātakā*): 'You came home from work, then left again
to play dice with friends.' But at the point of death, she declares, 'I am a
woman, I am ennobled', and truly hears a wedding-flute, like the flute on
which Krishna called to Radha.[86] It is her own *jiban-debatā*, come to free
her from a lifetime of bleak married chastity.

Palātakā has many such women, their personalities dulled, their lives
unfulfilled. The women in *Mahuyā*, too, mostly have serving or sacrificial
roles, but a handful are of different mettle: 'Lord, why will you not grant
woman the right to conquer her own fate?'[87] The title of this poem, 'Sabalā',
can translate as 'The Empowered Woman'. In another hard-hitting piece,
the woman rejects the sordid advances of an odious lover:

> His deformed imagination squirms among his loose thoughts like
> maggots feeding on rotten flesh. – May my mind lash out at him
> with all its might![88]

The title, 'Spardhā', can mean both audacity and virtuous boldness. It is
explicitly used in the first sense of the man. Does the second sense apply
implicitly to the woman?

But there is no simple advance. In 'Sādhāran meye' (An Ordinary
Woman, *Punascha*), such a woman begs the romantic novelist Sharatchandra
Chattopādhyāy for a story about a heroine who enjoys what this woman
never will: romance, protest, and self-assertion. Other narrative poems, in
Punascha as earlier in *Palātakā*, recall characters in the short stories: women,
sometimes little girls, who dream or even struggle, then die or lose their
battle or – all too rarely – win them.

Bichitritā presents a range of women, from philosophic symbols and
cruder male constructs to independent spirits. The illustrations serve an
organic purpose. They do not simply provide pretexts for the poems, but
a commentary in another key – ironic, uplifting, piquant, or bizarre. The
most arresting contrast is in 'Kālo ghorhā' (The Black Horse). This horse is
the male libido, bearing away the object of its 'blind desire'. But the picture,
by the poet's nephew Gaganendranāth, shows an ambiguous figure, black-
veiled, black-robed, recalling the mysterious rider in 'Sindhu-pāre'. That
figure proved to be the *jiban-debatā*.

Elsewhere, as in 'Pushpa', woman is identified with primordial nature. Like nature, she places her serene fecundity at the service of man:

> Your creative genius reigns endlessly in your daily tasks. Your world [*sangsār* – also 'household'] is made wholly yours by the vital touch of your spirit.[89]

Some poems make the woman's fulfilment reliant on the patriarchal order. But others assert her sexuality, seemingly suppressed by convention but attending her till death as a shadowy companion:

> Do you not know that the dead disembodied springtime is with you day and night, unknown to you, as its own deathless shade?[90]

The accompanying picture, again by Gaganendranath, shows another woman in black veil and cloak, her face concealed except for two piercing eyes. 'Bhiru' (The Fearful One) exhorts a woman to reject her 'trembling love' and freely express her being: 'Do not remain ringed round by blind fear.... Who will endlessly protect the weakling trapped in a cage of lies?'[91]

In *Bichitritā*, Rabindranath covers the spectrum of women's lives, personalities, and situations. Many elements recur in *Bithikā*: failed relationships; the frustration of both partners at the woman's reluctant surrender; and at least one poem (again called 'Mukti', Liberation) where a failed union frees the woman from her bonds. Vigils, visits, and departures for and of the *jiban-debatā* revert to the plane of human relationships.

Rabindranath does not – how could he? – resolve the challenges of woman's complex state. But he presents aspects of that state with growing empathy. In *Patraput* #15, a lonely man meets a woman who tells him, 'You do not know me, nor I you.' He replies: 'The impulse to bridge these two unknowns is at the heart of the universe.' Their further relationship unfolds the familiar duality: the 'common identity of a woman ... now cherishing, now mocking, now hurting', and (yet again) a goddess from the sea, immanent in nature at springtime, seated beside the creator's throne.[92]

Perhaps the old binaries are brought closer by a new authenticity of tone. Later still, 'Bnāshioālā' (The Flute-Player, *Shyāmali*) presents another 'ordinary woman', 'left half-created by God'; but a flute player's music fills her with yearning, rebellion, and an unpractised sexuality:

> Hearing your call, a dispirited housebound woman has left her dark corner, casting aside her veil.... She will write you a letter, sitting

in the half-shadows of your music. But you will never know her address.[93]

Krishna played the flute to charm Radha. The woman in 'Mukti' (*Palātakā*) had heard the same music at her tryst with death.

POEM, PICTURE, ART

Bichitritā is innovative in placing the visual against the verbal, but its poems are in customary rhymed stanzas, as mostly in the earlier *Purabi, Mahuyā,* and *Banabāni.* But between *Banabāni* and *Bichitritā*, the poet takes a major formal decision: some poems in *Parishesh* and nearly all in *Punascha* (both 1932) are in *vers libre.* Rabindranath later transferred six 'rhymeless' poems from *Parishesh* to *Punascha*, but a few remain in *Parishesh* alongside stanzaic verse and the 'freely bound' *muktabandha.*

The search for a more lucid and flexible medium takes the poet again into new formal territory. He had approached it in the short prose pieces of *Lipikā* (Inscriptions, 1922), chiefly narratives but sometimes approaching prose poems. The free verse of *Punascha*, too, encourages narrative as the earlier freedom of *muktabandha* had done in *Palātakā.* But in *Shesh saptak* (The Last Octave, 1935), *Patraput* (The Leaf Cup), and *Shyāmali* (The Verdant, both 1936), free verse becomes a versatile medium for every kind of theme: in fact, some poems are altered from earlier metrical versions. The transparency of the medium offers a neutral setting for the diction and imagery. *Patraput*, in particular, is shot through with vivid visual effects.

Sometime before 1930, Rabindranath had started to paint. He had no training in art. Visual forms thus offered him a private mental space denied to his poetry and music, where he was a hostage to public expectations. But he explores this new formal world even in his poetry, bringing the certainty of line and form to bear on the intricacies of the verbal. In *Shesh saptak* #15, he privileges line (*rekhā*) and form (*rup*) over sound (*dhwani*) and thought (*chintā*). Even the divine Word parts the curtain of creation to say 'Look!' – sound yielding to sight. Creation becomes an artist's handiwork on the canvas of cosmic change and, within it, the expanse of human history. The familiar linking of cosmic and earthly creation, as of man and the created universe, is effected through the trope of art. In 'Āmi' (*Shyāmali*), cited earlier, the universal 'I' sits at a 'festival of creation, brush in hand, paint in pot'.[94]

In *Shesh saptak* #8, the cave painter is compared to this universal artist. They have both 'made their joy their truth, ignoring their own identity'.[95]

Effacing their artistic selves, they project their creation in the clarity of its own being. But the crucial clarity is that imparted – if only partially – by visual form to the inchoate emanations of the mind.

> Things are always breaking and joining, being cobbled together in the mind. Some part solidifies in thought, some part takes shape in pictures.[96]

Visual art gives form to mental phenomena that have none; yet that lack of stable form is the latter's distinction. Rabindranath is seeking a synthesis of the two, elusive meaning captured in realized form.

Shesh saptak #9 trains its sight on the 'unreachable planet' of the poet's being:

> There are gaps in the corners of the enveloping vapour, where alone the telescope can reach. What I might call my own is still undefined: when will its design be complete?

This mindscape, whose 'restless play of the invisible ... eludes the cupped hands of language', recalls the landscapes of Rabindranath's paintings:

> On all sides, the sky is full of the shadow-play of fulfilled and unsatisfied desire. Coloured shadows of many passions descend from it to the mind's plain.

But this mindscape is itself created by a universal artist, its shape still unfolding, suggestive but undefined: 'Those who said "We know" never came to know.'[97]

In a late, rare Freudian departure, the poet sees the mind's interior imaged in the primal components (*ādim upādān*) of dreams. They are suppressed in formal poetic creation, but the poet talks about them nonetheless:

> The waking state has its duties and responsibilities; sleep is irresponsible, so it can create random dreams.... Whenever it is set free, whimsies crowd around, and dreams build the nest of birds still in flight.[98]

Janmadine #20 reworks 'Words and Rhythm' on these lines. The sounds of nature mark the perfection of language. Humanity has betrayed and disrupted this order, but it can be accessed in dreams and captured in the rhythms of poetry.

Sometimes words enter the realm of dreams like thieves.... They trawl what they can and bind it in rhythm. From this the distracted intellect creates an art whose links are loose, ruptured, disordered, with no organic semblance to the order of creation.[99]

Like puppies at play, 'hordes of words run amok, breaking free of meaning'. The poem ends with nonsense words from a childhood rhyme. *Ākāshpradip* (Lamp in the Sky, 1939) had carried many echoes of such rhymes, whimsical imports of an outdated 'toymaker'; but one day, these rhymes will usher in a new age and assume epic dimensions, as the poet says in 'Samayhārā' (The Time-lost). In his last phase, Rabindranath relaxes the bonds of form and meaning but with new philosophic purpose.

Free verse is a tool to this end. Its simplicity allows the poet to describe the 'free flow' of nature without intruding his self:

Let my unbroken gaze float over creation's ocean – without speech, without effort, without thought.... Easily will I see all sights, hear all tunes.... I will blend with the outstretched ascesis of empty fields after harvest. I will focus my meditation on that silent *shāl* tree where a thousand years' life force is concealed in this instant.[100]

This is what I meant by saying that Rabindranath's philosophy is increasingly concretized in description even while growing more abstract in import.

Only six years separate *Shesh saptak* from *Janmadine*, but they cover much creative distance. Before traversing it, there is another line to trace from its beginning.

THE HUMAN CONDITION

Nabajātak (The Newborn, 1940) contains a startling piece, 'Prāyashchitta' (Reparation):

The fire of sin has spread in fierce strife between those who starve and those who gorge, as the spoils of plunder pile higher in the hell we call civilized.[101]

The poem ends in a virtual call to revolution. It fiercely indicts colonial capitalism, with Christianity as complicit: 'Hordes of weak-spirited worshippers attend church to assuage the Lord with flattery.' In *Janmadine* #22, Rabindranath returns to the attack:

Beneath vast wealth, the fire of hunger consumes the starved and half-
starved. Thirst-quenching water drying up and polluted; no clothes
for the winter; the gates of death thrown open....[102]

The world was plunged into the Second World War. India, moreover, faced
the violence and exploitation of a dying colonial order. On the eve of his
seventy-ninth birthday, the poet mourns:

The bloodied teeth and talons of savage conflict tear at the entrails
of hundreds of towns and villages. Horror darts from end to end of
the stupefied horizon.[103]

This is not the vein we associate with the poet of *Gitānjali*, but in fact,
it is there in *Gitānjali* itself and, as we have seen, in much earlier poems
like 'Ebār phirāo more'. *Gitānjali* #108 balances the idealized history of
'Bhārat-tirtha' with outrage at the degrading divisions of Indian society:

By spurning human touch, you have despised the god of humanity.
His anger will make you sit at famine's door and share rice and water
with all, made equal with all in humiliation.[104]

Set beside this age-old inhumanity is the suffering and waste of young
lives in India's freedom struggle. Can even God, asks the poet, forgive their
torturers? They discredit all saints and messiahs.[105] The same despair of
spiritual closure marks the later tale of a young girl raped and murdered:
'The godly faith of the scriptures scatters with the dust. The sky rings out:
There is no escape, no redress.'[106]

Decades earlier, as the sun set on 31 December 1900, the poet had
written:

The century's last sun has set today among blood-red clouds....
Barbarity garbed as civilization has risen from its bed of slime....
The band of poets howl, striking terror: the chorus of dogs on the
cremation-ground, fighting over carrion.[107]

Images of blood, charnel-ground, carrion, and scavenger return inexorably
as the world plunges from crisis to deeper crisis. The concern with evil and
exploitation passes more and more beyond the humane, the moral, and
the timelessly social to acquire an openly political dimension, reflecting
concerns long evident in the prose writings. *Balākā*'s new realism and sense

of evil has the First World War as its backdrop. From the mid-1930s, in the lead-up to the Second World War and the intensification of India's freedom struggle, the anguish turns more and more to anger: sometimes truly radical, touching on economic issues generally and, more particularly, on the colonial and imperial, supported by a militant nationalistic global order. 'Prāyashchitta' is anticipated in *Patraput* #16 (otherwise 'Āphrikā'), even to pillorying a complicit Christianity: while Africa was crushed under the colonizers' boots, 'across the sea, prayer-bells were ringing in their temples morning and evening in the name of a merciful God'.[108] The next poem is an even harsher attack on Japanese imperialism:

The hordes went to feast on raw human flesh at the death-god's banquet. But first they visited the temple of the merciful Buddha for his sacred blessings.[109]

In *Nabajātak*, the poem following 'Prāyashchitta' has Japanese soldiers praying to the Buddha for victory over China and Korea.[110]

The poet repeatedly deplores the festering world order. In 'Apaghāt' (Unnatural Death, *Sānāi*, 1940), the peace of the Bengal countryside is shattered by news of the Soviet bombing of Finland. In 'Pakshimānab' (Bird-man, *Nabajātak*), the aeroplane itself becomes a symbol of human arrogance and carnage, invading the one element, the air, till now inviolate. Fighter planes appear as vultures with 'machine-wings' in the apocalypse of *Prāntik* #17:

Flocks of monster birds fly from hell's river across the enraged sky – vultures avid for human flesh, their machine-wings roaring, polluting the sky.[111]

The poet prays to the judge on the throne of great time for a voice of thunder, to denounce such evil till it sinks into its self-ignited funeral pyre.

India, too, is viewed in a new light. 'Hindusthān' (*Nabajātak*) is like 'Bhārat-tirtha' turned inside-out to expose the pain, disorder, and discontinuities of Indian history. 'Rājputānā' (*Nabajātak*) lauds that province's heroic past (celebrated earlier in *Kathā o kāhini*) but deplores its defeat even then and its irrelevance under colonial rule. Most telling, perhaps, is 'Bhumikampa' (Earthquake, *Nabajātak*), on the Bihar earthquake of 1934. Rabindranath had ridiculed Gāndhi's view that the earthquake was a divine chastisement for human sin. The poet makes it a metaphor for the evil of colonial mercantilism, not, of course, its literal consequence. The wealth hidden in the earth, now catastrophically revealed, is contrasted with the wealth of crops springing from the soil: two ways of life, two value systems.

In his last years, Rabindranath turns increasingly to philosophic motifs of rebirth and renewal. But there are sporadic calls to what we can only term political revolution:

> She-snakes draw their poisoned breath on every side. The sweet message of peace would sound like a vain jest. So before I go, I call to those preparing in every home to wage war with the demons.[112]

Humankind can only be renewed by destroying the prevalent order. Indeed, it will destroy itself: 'The ghosts of past wrongdoing call forth the wrongdoing that heralds the future.'[113] It is a fearsome prospect either way.

The same trajectory of growing political articulation marks the more plentiful annals of common human existence. *Chaitāli* (1896) is full of vignettes of village life from the poet's years beside the Padmā. *Kātha o kāhini* (1908) contains tales of feudal tyranny like 'Dui bighā jami' (Two Measures of Land), and of iniquities of middle-class life like 'Purātan bhritya' (The Old Servant). The narratives in *Palātakā* and *Punascha* often have a social or even political bearing: tales of women, as we saw, but also of poor and ordinary people, of children and everyday encounters. Even the children's book *Chharhār chhabi* (Pictures for Rhymes, 1937) has such pieces, including 'Mādho', featuring a jute-workers' strike, and 'Sudhiā', about a milkman's son who defies a rapacious merchant. (Tagore had publicly supported an actual jute-mill strike shortly before.)

These poems reflect human life in Bengal and India. But only late in life does the poet integrate them into a total vision of common humanity as a political and even elemental force.

> They work in city and plain.... With roar and hum, ... in joy and sorrow, night and day, they sound the great mantra of life.[114]

Yet he also perceives that he is cut off from this inheritance. The 'world's poet' has absorbed the unheard songs of the mountains and stars but not responded to the sounds of humanity: 'The call of the various did not touch my music; there was a gap.'[115] He looks out from his Kolkata mansion to the tenements across the street, fascinated by the kaleidoscope of humble lives yet alienated from it: he cannot plunge into 'the turbid flow of this Ganga of the all'.[116]

This is not the habitual concern of Rabindranath's late poetry. It is chiefly marked by a new version of his spiritualized humanity, drawing more openly on the Vedas and Upanishads. Yet he never loses sight of the problem of evil. It is conclusively rejected in his total philosophy, but the horror of the prospect never ceases to haunt him.

> The dark night of sorrow has come time and again to my door. His only weapon, I saw, was the distorted pretence of suffering, the grotesque postures of fear.[117]

Rabindranath wrote this on 29 July 1941. He died nine days and one poem later.

THE MARGINS AND BEYOND

On 10 September 1937, the seventy-six-year-old poet suddenly fainted and collapsed. Recovering two days later, he felt he had travelled to the borders of death. His next book of poems, fitly entitled *Prāntik* (On the Border), is in long meditative lines – sometimes blank verse, a new medium for a new need, and sometimes couplets recalling *Naibedya*, his first book of poems focusing on spiritual themes.

Death is now a constant concern but seldom as mere cessation: 'Inexhaustible life / Floats on the tide of inexhaustible death.'[118] Long ago in *Sadhana*, he had cited the Upanishadic idea that death is coequal with immortality, each defined by the other.[119] Death can bring release into a cosmic realm of light and joy; or into the world of nature; or at very least, as in *Prāntik* 8, into an oblivion that is itself liberation, like the sky 'emancipated' at nightfall to silent self-realization by starlight.

Pain and the prospect of death returned in another spate of illness reflected in *Rogshajyāy* (On the Sick-bed, 1940). The next two titles, both from 1941, *Ārogya* (Recovery) and *Janmadine* (On My Birthday), suggest a revival, but it commonly takes the form of relinquishment. All through his career, Rabindranath exemplifies what Keats terms the egotistical sublime: the poet's personality is always implicit and commonly foregrounded in his work.[120] In these last volumes, the gap between the 'speaking' persona and the living poet virtually disappears. In poems on successive birthdays, he dismisses his public identity as increasingly irrelevant, seeking instead the seclusion of his inviolate self. In one such poem, 'Janmadin' (Birthday, *Nabajātak*), he wishes to surrender the 'disjunct shapes and shadows' of his art, so that he might himself become, exclusively, a work by the divine artist.[121] But the latter, too, seeks silence as his end – the silence at the heart of the cosmos. Nataraj's dance in the cosmic theatre culminates in self-extinction: the stars go out, actors discard their costumes, and Nataraj himself stands in the dark, silent and alone.[122]

Such absorbed annihilation accords with the general elevated tenor from *Prāntik* to *Janmadine*. *Prāntik* #1 defines a more positive trajectory: the herald of death stalks the darkening universe, but the curtain rises on Nataraj's dancing-floor, while a shaft of light signals the dawn of a new consciousness. The 'released' poet finds himself in the empyrean beyond the galaxies, 'on the shore of the most rarefied dissolution'.[123]

Later poems extend and vary this repertoire. The self unites with earthly nature and the outer elements, addressing itself as a visitant to the earth:

> The light that descends from ... the remote sky to the green brow of earth has kissed your sight, bound you for ever to the heavens in a bond of companionship.[124]

In *Ārogya* #2, humanity itself is the bonding force that unites the objects of nature and makes them sharers in the infinite:

> The touch of human affection (*priti*) suffuses everything, imparts a sense of immortality, makes the earth's dust full of sweetness.[125]

The last clause echoes the Vedic verse (*Rig-veda* 1:90:6–7) that had opened *Ārogya* #1: 'This sky is full of sweetness, full of sweetness the earth's dust.'[126] Vedic and Vedantic concepts had infused Rabindranath's poetry from the start, but they are now openly signposted. 'Rup-birup' (Formed and Unformed, *Nabajātak*) invokes Indra, god of thunder, in a 'veda-mantra'. The Vedic chant takes on a personal, interiorized note, as in this address to the sun (a Vedic deity) in 'the words of the sages':

> O sun, draw aside the veil hiding your radiance. Let me see the true identity of my soul within your innermost sacred light.[127]

The late poems are full of images of the sun and a still greater effulgence, even repeating – whether or not knowingly – Dante's image of a celestial rose of light.[128]

The same radiance lights up the human state, for humans are 'children of immortality' (as understood by Rabindranath, though the phrase might refer to the gods). Rabindranath repeatedly cites an amalgam of two Upanishadic passages: 'Listen, O children of immortality who dwell in the blessed realm: I have known the noble being hued like the sun.'[129] This supreme radiant being had appeared in *Gitāli*, a redeemer bursting upon the immured soul. His return is heralded in a song written on the poet's last Bengali new year:[130]

> See the supreme man come! Every quarter of the sky thrills, and the grass that springs from the earth's dust.[131]

But all humans are 'children of immortality': 'There is no gap between my soul and the joy that touches me from the heart of light.'[132] *Amrita*, immortality, is also the heavenly nectar conferring immortality. It is coextant with *ānanda*, the supreme joy pervading the universe.[133] All these motifs merge in 'Patrottar' (Letter in Reply, *Snejuti*), in a final union of sky and earth, cosmic and telluric:

> Where the radiance from the realm of light is enclosed in the vessel of *amrita* in the earth's bosom, the springtide touches the trees with its spell, and the form of the beyond-form is traced in the leaves.... The mind leaps with spontaneous joy at the playful dance of creation. That rhythm will be my salvation, letting me evade death even as I travel down death's path.[134]

In *Janmadine* #3, the floodgates of *ānanda* open to reveal 'the eternal human at one's core'.[135] This presence is the Upanishadic god but also the Baul's *maner mānush*, the mystic presence at the heart of the human state. In *Ārogya* #33, the poet wishes to cast off the covering that obscures his 'I': 'Let the clear light of consciousness pierce the mist and reveal the immortal shape of truth.'[136] Many late poems continue the familiar theme of many 'I's in new metaphysical perspectives. The poet sees himself in the upheavals of distant space but 'without the least recognition'.

> Is this some radiance beyond vision? ... The vapour surrounding it takes solid form in history in many guises: an 'I' congeals at its centre over countless years.[137]

In *Janmadine* #1, the poet contemplates the cosmic 'I', the distance between himself and himself. The poem opens, 'That day was my birthday.'[138] Which was the 'I' then born – the mundane 'I' into a new immensity or the cosmic 'I' in its mundane emanation? The title *Janmadine* is anticipated in *Nabajātak*, 'The Newborn'. Its title poem welcomes the newcomer:

What new chant have you brought to worship the human god? What song did you hear in the immortal realm from where you come?

This infant avatar of the Supreme Man[139] is less daunting but equally messianic: 'Time and again, a human child brings eternal promise of freedom's light in a new dawn.'[140] 'Human child' (*mānaber shishu*) recalls the poem entitled 'Mānabputra' (Son of Man, *Punascha*), on Christ's return to an unredeemed world; also Rabindranath's one major original English poem 'The Child' (1930), on Christ's nativity, with a Bengali version in *Punascha*.[141]

These manifestations can be seen as new facets of the *jiban-debatā*. In 'Karnadhār' (The Helmsman, *Sānāi*), the poet's union with the universal divine is celebrated in verse and language of simple intimacy, befitting a lover and companion more than a remote god. 'Badhu' (The Bride) in *Ākāshpradip*, a volume full of throwbacks to childhood, describes the poet's yearning for a fairy-tale bride. He senses her in the trees and the sky, and finally feels her touch. 'I herald the presence behind all that is visible,' she says. 'My name was written beside yours among the stars.'[142] She recurs in 'Jyotirbāshpa' (Nimbus of Light, *Sānāi*) as Rabindranath's last female figure risen from the sea. The poet knows her above all others: she is there within his heart, yet eternally remote.

There are still poems about the lover who visits the soul. In the most elaborate account, she too is female: she came once at the poet's birth and returns for a last tryst

in guise of this storm, the old scent of forests in your flowing hair....
I cannot tell the season whose message you bear, ringed round with
the darkness of death.[143]

Months before his death, the poet hunts for a mat gifted by a woman from abroad.[144] That real *bideshini* – whose language he did not know, who spoke only with her eyes – joins the imagined women from other lands who had beckoned to the poet since *Sonār tari*. The intimate, caring aspect of the *jiban-debatā* (even the care-givers during his illness seem to reflect the deity) does not dispel the exotic, seductive vision that has equally pervaded his life. That vision returns in his last poem, dictated on his deathbed:

You have spread a net of varied wiles along the path of your creations,
O deceitful one. With deft hands, you have laid a trap of false faith
in simple lives.

But philosophic power can counter her seduction:

> By this deceit you have marked out the noble of heart.... The path
> your star lights up for him is the path within himself.[145]

In Upanishadic terms, truth (*satyam*) overcomes illusion (*māyā*). Some ten
weeks earlier, he had pledged himself to an unsparing quest for truth. 'Truth
is hard; I loved the truth. It never deceives.'[146] Yet in his last poem, it is the
goddess of deceit that grants the truth-seeker his 'enduring right to peace'.
She is still his life's deity. With his last breath, the poet finds a new way to
engage with her – as her lover, thrall and adversary.

For two months, Rabindranath had been too ill to write. He resumed
with a poem celebrating a 'birthday' when God showers him with gifts. He
alludes to the creator by the title bestowed on himself: *bishwa-kabi*, 'world-
poet', to whose genius the human poet bears silent witness. Three final
pieces followed after another two weeks. I have cited the last two already.
Before them came a poem where on the first and last days of the emergence
of Being, the same question is put to it by the sun: 'Who are you?'[147] Both
times, the ancient god returns no answer.

~

The posthumous volume *Shesh lekhā* (Last Writings) contains fifteen poems.
All but two were written in the last months of the poet's life, through
increasing weakness and distraction. They do not add up to a consistent
philosophy, but grapple with many of his deepest concerns. In fact, at no
stage of his life does he adopt a consistent philosophical position. Early
on, he generates a number of ideas, motifs, and tropes of complex, hence
versatile, potential. He adds to this repertoire all his life, throwing old and
new elements into endless combinations. He anticipates himself, winds
back on himself, repeats and contradicts himself, working continually new
syntheses or refusing to work any. He does not make any easy compromise
with the premises of conventional philosophy or religion. He knows that
truth is many and changeable – which is why, in his words shortly before
death, it cannot deceive:[148] it is not hidden by but *hidden in* passing
appearances and changing processes. By the same token, the intellective
and spiritual are inseparable from the material in his work. He sets out to
be the poet of everything there is, and succeeds in improbable measure in
this impossible venture.

NOTES

1. T.S. Eliot, 'What Is Minor Poetry?' in *On Poetry and Poets* (London: Faber, 1957; rpt. 1971), 45–7.
2. *Jibansmriti* (Reminiscences), *RRVB* 17:396.
3. *RRVB* 2:117.
4. 'Ananta prem' (Eternal Love), *RRVB* 2:254.
5. *RRVB* 2:132, 134.
6. The English *Chitrā* is not a translation of this collection but of the play *Chitrāngadā*.
7. A verse from the medieval poet Jnānadās.
8. *RRVB* 3:29.
9. Shankha Ghosh, 'Dāyeri theke', *Chitrak kabitāpatrikā*, 3:3 (2002), 7.
10. 'Ahalyār prati' (To Ahalyā), *RRVB* 2:265.
11. 'Samudrer prati' (To the Ocean), *Sonār tari*, *RRVB* 3:55.
12. 'Prakritir prati' (To Nature), *Mānasi*, *RRVB* 2:144, 146.
13. 'Basundharā' (Earth), *Sonār tari*, *RRVB* 3:137.
14. 'Kuhudhwani' (The Koel's Call), *Mānasi*, *RRVB* 2:151.
15. 'Byārtha jauban' (Fruitless Youth), *Sonār tari*, *RRVB* 3:100.
16. 'Barshār dine' (On a Rainy Day), *Mānasi*, *RRVB* 2:249.
17. 'Utsarga' (Dedicatory poem), *Chaitāli*, *RRVB* 5:5–6.
18. 'Urbashi', *Chitrā*, *RRVB* 4:84.
19. 'Mānas-sundari' (The Fair Woman of the Mind), *Sonār tari*, *RRVB* 3:65.
20. *RRVB* 5:96.
21. 'Sābitri', *RRVB* 14:43–4.
22. *Gitānjali* #59, *RRVB* 11:49.
23. *Utsarga* #24, *RRVB* 10:41.
24. *Balākā* #28, *RRVB* 12:49.
25. *RRVB* 20:65.
26. John 8:58.
27. 'The Problem of Self', *Sadhana*, *EW* 2:313.
28. Samuel Taylor Coleridge, *Biographia Literaria*, ch.13.
29. *Utsarga* #21, *RRVB* 10:37.
30. 'Mānabsatya', appendix to *Mānusher dharma*. The Bengali *Mānusher dharma* (Kamala Lectures, Calcutta University, 1933) is different from the synonymously titled English *The Religion of Man* (Hibbert Lectures, Oxford University, 1930).
31. *GB*, 'Bichitra' #30.
32. *Naibedya* #26, *RRVB* 8:27.
33. *Shvetāshvatara upanishad* 4:17, as translated by Rabindranath ('Soul Consciousness', *Sadhana*, *EW* 2:295).
34. '[T]he boat crosses with a woman at the helm': *Fugitive* 1:17, *EW* 1:252.
35. See *Jibansmriti* (Reminiscences), *RRVB* 17:389–90.

36. *GB*, 'Prem' #86.
37. *RRVB* 4:118.
38. *RRVB* 4:19.
39. *The Religion of Man*, ch. 7, 'The Man of My Heart', *EW* 3:129.
40. Ibid., ch. 6, 'The Vision', *EW* 3:122.
41. Rabindranath's interpretation ('Realization in Action', *Sadhana*, *EW* 2:331) of *Shvetāshvatara upanishad* 4:1.
42. *Gitānjali* #121, *RRVB* 11:96. All *Gitānjali* references to the Bengali volume unless the English is specified. The English *Gitanjali* sources its poems from ten Bengali volumes including the as yet unpublished *Gitimālya* (1914), and poems published earlier but gathered in a volume only in the later *Utsarga* (1914).
43. *RRVB* 20:406.
44. *Gitānjali* #119, *RRVB* 11:94.
45. 'Realization in Love', *Sadhana*, *EW* 2:320.
46. Letter of 14 Kārtik 1328 (*October 1921), *VBP* 14 (1958), 264.
47. 'Sāmanjasya' (Harmony), *Shāntiniketan*, *RRVB* 15:499.
48. 'Jyotsnā rātre' (On a Moonlit Night), *Chitrā*, *RRVB* 4:24.
49. *Chitrā*, title poem, *RRVB* 4:21.
50. *Utsarga* #8, *RRVB* 10:17.
51. *Gitāli* #101, *RRVB* 11:287.
52. English *Gitanjali* #18, *EW* 1:48 (*Gitānjali* #16, *RRVB* 10:16).
53. *Gitimālya* #22, *RRVB* 11:152.
54. *Gitāli* #82, *RRVB* 11:274.
55. *Gitāli* #57, *RRVB* 11:257.
56. Buddhadeb Basu, ed., *Ādhunik bānglā kabitā*, 2nd ed. (Kolkata: M.C. Sarkar, 1956), ix.
57. *Balākā* #3 (elsewhere 'Āhwān', The Call), *RRVB* 12:5.
58. *RRVB* 12:35-6.
59. *Balākā* #8, *RRVB* 12:22.
60. *RRVB* 12:62.
61. *RRVB* 4:32-3.
62. *Balākā* #29, *RRVB* 12:51.
63. *GB*, 'Prakriti' #201.
64. *RRVB* 14:143-4.
65. 'Banaspati', *RRVB* 14:142.
66. *RRVB* 15:172-3.
67. 'Āhwān' (The Call), *Parishesh*, *RRVB* 15:185.
68. 'Shishur jiban' (The Child's Life), *RRVB* 13:69.
69. *RRVB* 13:66.
70. *GB*, 'Bichitra' #2.
71. Elsewhere titled *Rituranga*.
72. *RRVB* 7:186.

73. *RRVB* 3:52.
74. *RRVB* 19:57.
75. *GB*, 'Pujā' #337.
76. *Patraput* #7, *RRVB* 20:24-5.
77. *RRVB* 19:70.
78. 'Purono bat' (The Old Banyan), *RRVB* 9:91.
79. *RRVB* 15:117.
80. 'Bhishan' (The Terrifying), *Bithikā*, *RRVB* 19:83.
81. *Patraput* #8, *RRVB* 20:27-8.
82. *RRVB* 17:6.
83. *RRVB* 12:45.
84. *RRVB* 5:36.
85. *Smaran* #26, *RRVB* 8:99.
86. *RRVB* 13:10-11.
87. *RRVB* 15:41.
88. *RRVB* 15:55.
89. 'Shyamalā' (The Dark Woman), *RRVB* 17:19.
90. 'Chhāyāsangini' (The Shadowy Consort), *RRVB* 17:26.
91. *RRVB* 17:30-1.
92. *RRVB* 20:46-8.
93. *RRVB* 20:98.
94. *RRVB* 20:66.
95. *RRVB* 18:15.
96. *Shesh saptak* #15, *RRVB* 18:30.
97. *RRVB* 18:18-20.
98. *Ārogya* #26, *RRVB* 25:62.
99. *RRVB* 25:92.
100. *Shesh saptak* #4, *RRVB* 18:7.
101. *RRVB* 24:9.
102. *RRVB* 25:94.
103. *Janmadine* #21, *RRVB* 25:92.
104. *RRVB* 11:85.
105. 'Prashna' (A Question), *Parishesh*, *RRVB* 15:196-7.
106. 'Dhākirā dhāk bājāy' (The Drummers Play), *Ākāshpradip*, *RRVB* 23:117.
107. *Naibedya* #64, *RRVB* 8:51-2.
108. *RRVB* 20:50.
109. *Patraput* #17, *RRVB* 20:51.
110. 'Buddhabhakti' (Devotion to the Buddha), *RRVB* 24:11.
111. *RRVB* 22:19.
112. *Prāntik* #18, *RRVB* 22:19.
113. *Janmadine* #16, *RRVB* 25:85.
114. *Ārogya* #10, *RRVB* 25:51.
115. *Janmadine* #10, *RRVB* 25:77.

116. 'Epāre-opāre' (This Side and That), *Nabajātak, RRVB* 24:35.

117. *Shesh lekhā* #14, *RRVB* 26:50.

118. *Rogshajyāy* #2, *RRVB* 25:6.

119. 'The Relationship of the Individual to the Universe', *Sadhana, EW* 2:289.

120. John Keats, letter to Richard Woodhouse, 27 October 1818: *Letters of John Keats*, ed. Robert Gittings (London: Oxford University Press, 1970), 157–8.

121. *RRVB* 24:44.

122. *Ārogya* #9, *RRVB* 25:49.

123. *RRVB* 22:6.

124. *Prāntik* #13, *RRVB* 22:15.

125. *RRVB* 25:42.

126. *RRVB* 25:41.

127. *Janmadine* #13, *RRVB* 25:83.

128. Dante, *La divina commedia, Paradiso* cantos 32–3; *Rogshajyāy* #21.

129. *Shvetāshvatara upanishad* 2:5, 3:8; other partial sources.

130. Also the day when the poet's address 'Sabhyatār sangkat' ('Crisis in Civilization') was read out in Santiniketan.

131. *Shesh lekhā* #6, *RRVB* 26:43.

132. *Ārogya* #32, *RRVB* 25:66.

133. *Taittiriya upanishad* 3:6.

134. *RRVB* 22:30.

135. *RRVB* 25.71.

136. *RRVB* 25.66.

137. 'Prashna' (Question), *Nabajātak, RRVB* 24:45.

138. *RRVB* 25:69.

139. Rabindranath's phrase: *The Religion of Man*, ch. 10, 'Man's Nature', *EW* 3:144.

140. *RRVB* 24:5–6.

141. *Punascha* also carries a translation of T.S. Eliot's 'The Journey of the Magi': 'Tirthajātri' (Pilgrims).

142. *RRVB* 23:86.

143. 'Shesh abhisār' (The Last Tryst), *Sānāi, RRVB* 24:126–7.

144. *Shesh lekhā* #5.

145. *Shesh lekhā* #15, *RRVB* 26:51.

146. *Shesh lekhā* #11, *RRVB* 26:48.

147. *Shesh lekhā* #13, *RRVB* 26:49–50.

148. *Shesh lekhā* #11, *RRVB* 26:48.

5 'Something of a Musician'

Tagore's Songs

ASHISH LAHIRI

I claim to be something of a musician myself. I have composed many songs which have defied the canons of orthodox propriety and good people are disgusted at the impudence of a man who is audacious only because he is untrained. But I persist, and God forgives me because *I do not know what I do*. Possibly that is the best way of doing things in the sphere of art. For I find that people blame, but also sing my songs, even if not always correctly.[1]

A UNIQUE GENRE

Rabindrasangit is unique as a musical genre in three respects. First, here high poetry blends seamlessly into high music, producing a new synthesis, a third entity. It is this x-factor, going beyond a mere match of lyric and tune, that differentiates Rabindrasangit from any other musical genre. Several notable contemporaries of Tagore like Dwijendralāl Rāy, Atulprasād Sen, Rajanikānta Sen, and Kāzi Nazrul Islām have achieved an impressive combination of beautiful words and appropriate notes, each in his own way. But only in Rabindrasangit do we find this special communion of poetry and music, each influencing the other and losing its exclusive identity in the process.

Second, in purely musical terms, disparate elements mingle imperceptibly to form a new integral whole. The dramatist Dwijendralal Ray, who was well versed in Hindustāni classical music, wrote perceptively to Tagore on 25 March 1896, before an unfortunate rift in their relationship:

Must I be totally unable to grasp the tunes of your songs? You produce a pleasant, varied combination of *rāga*s and *rāgini*s, but it is difficult to learn.... I have successfully mastered the *rāgini*s of perhaps only two of your excellent songs.... What you do is to grind the *rāga*s and *rāgini*s into a paste of spices, and use it to cook your lyrics.[2]

This is why highly trained classical singers often find it difficult to render Tagore's apparently simple songs: the 'spices' cause the main melody to deviate arbitrarily from the standard structure of a *rāga*. Some even try to 'correct' the 'untrained' Tagore, thereby robbing Rabindrasangit of its essence. Needless to say, Tagore has been widely charged with impairing the rigour and purity of the structures of classical music.

However, no less a person than Shrikrishna Ratanjankar, foremost disciple of the legendary musicologist Bhātkhande, noted the singularity of Rabindrasangit in more positive terms: not as a travesty of classical music, but as a new and unique genre deriving from it. On 1 March 1967, Ratanjankar wrote to the eminent musicologist and musician Birendrakishor Rāychaudhuri:

> Are the musical settings of R[abindra] S[angit] called Ragas or have these tunes rules of notes (Thatas) [basic scales or frames], Vadi [the most important note of the *rāga*], Samvadi [the second most important note], swaras [pitches], catch phrases (Pakarhs) [set musical phrases], typical swarasangatis [harmonious note-combinations], occasions or seasons or hours at which these tunes (without reference to the word sense of the songs) are to be sung, etc? Most of these songs as I hear them are mixtures of Ragas of classical music. Rabindra Sangeet, if it is to be recognized as a subject of academic study must have its *own theory* [emphasis added] and text books and correct notations.[3]

Third, from a socio-historical angle, Sumit Sarkār finds it meaningful that Tagore 'belonged to the same generation as Bhatkhande and Paluskar', and finds some social parallels between them. Vishnunārāyan Bhatkhande (1860–1936) and Vishnu Digambar Pāluskar (1872–1931) 'sought, in somewhat different ways, to break down the isolation of the enclosed worlds of individual *gharānās* [lines or schools], and open classical music to educated middle-class men and women'. Paluskar recruited women from the middle classes for his *mahāvidyālayas* (colleges of music) and developed 'an easier and quicker method' of learning music. Tagore's agenda was analogous. Music formed an inalienable part of education at Santiniketan, and he 'flouted puritanical prejudices' by introducing co-education and encouraging women to sing and perform before an audience.[4]

TAGORE'S MUSICAL TOOLS

How great a musician was Tagore? To look for a serious answer, one must rephrase the question: How original was he in handling the musical tools at his disposal?

The musical ambience of the Tagore family was rich and varied. Hindustani classical music, especially the *dhrupad*, was a basic component in the education of its young members. Musicians from many parts of western and northern India flocked to the Tagore mansion at Jorasanko. Rabindranāth's precocious talent was noted very early by his elder brother and mentor Jyotirindranāth. As a boy of sixteen, he had composed such a beautiful patriotic song as 'Tomāri tare mā, snopinu e deha' (For you, O Mother, I yield my body).⁵ Jyotirindra, who excelled in playing the sitar, the violin, the harmonium, and the piano, encouraged his younger brother to stage the latter's musical drama *Bālmiki-pratibhā* (The Emergence of Vālmiki's Genius) (1881) at their Jorasanko house. With their teenaged niece Pratibhā in the role of Saraswati and himself as the robber-turned-poet Vālmiki, Rabindranath impressed the audience. His nieces Indirā, Pratibha, Saralā, and Abhijnā were all trained in both Indian and Western vocal and instrumental music. Whenever they learnt a new song, they would come running to their uncle, who obligingly used those offerings to create more songs of his own.

Rabindranath himself, however, learnt virtually nothing rigorously, only imbibing what naturally appealed to him. At the age of seventeen, he went to England and impressed his listeners with his high tenor voice. He also learnt quite a few popular English songs. When he came back, his singing voice sounded strangely foreign to his family circle. Later, he became quite a popular singer, being pressed to sing at any public function he attended. The senior poet Nabinchandra Sen has recorded in his autobiography how spontaneously Tagore would do so and how his voice 'might put a woman's to shame' by its melodious charm.⁶ Connoisseurs, however, did not fail to spot his lack of technical training.

A sizeable portion of the Tagore estate was situated in Nadiā district, the home of the Vaishnav devotional *kirtan*; another sizeable part, where Rabindranath spent some crucial formative years, was in eastern Bengal, a major seat of the mystic Bāul singers. As supervisor of these estates, he seized these opportunities to imbibe those musical forms.

With this history in mind, we can list the 'tools' he used as follows, in order of importance.

First, north Indian (Hindustani) classical music, particularly the *dhrupad*, especially of the Bishnupur *gharānā* of Bengal. This crucial and controversial element is treated separately later.

Second, the kirtan, a very rich and popular musical form of Bengal inspired by the Vaishnav devotion to Rādhā and Krishna. Tagore is eloquent about the *kirtan*: 'Poetry and music have united in a wonderful form in the *kirtan* of Bengal; its poetry complete, its music powerful.... The music doesn't simply serve as a vehicle for the poetry; its own wealth, expansiveness and dignity are forcefully expressed.'[7] Elsewhere, he finds in the Garānhātā style of *kirtan* the same 'self-restrained expansiveness' that he admires in the *dhrupad*.[8] That was probably the highest praise he could offer.

In his celebrated 1931 dialogue with Einstein, Tagore explains that the *kirtan* 'gives freedom to the singer to introduce parenthetical comments, phrases not in the original song ... some beautiful, spontaneous sentiment added by the singer'.[9] These are called *ākhar*s, which Rabindranath describes elsewhere as '*tāna*s [rapid melodic patterns added to the basic structure of a *rāga*] of words'.[10] Shades of the *kirtan* are found as a substratum in many Tagore songs; full-fledged *kirtan*s, complete with *ākhar*s and variations of *laya* (tempo), are few, but superb examples of their kind. Among them are 'Mājhe mājhe taba dekhā pāi' (I see you only from time to time)[11] and 'Āmi jene shune tabu bhule āchhi' (I knowingly remain forgetful).[12] The former also has a better-known version with a different setting.

Third, the Bānglā tappā. Taking his cue from Miān Gulām Nabi Shori of Āwadh, Rāmnidhi Gupta, fondly known as Nidhubābu, created the Bānglā tappā, mostly love songs, which became highly popular with urban Bengalis in the nineteenth century. Rabindranath shortened and simplified the typical *tappā* note-globules (called *dānā*) to enable them to express very subtle and varied emotions. One gets an idea of this reformed *tappā* from his own recorded renderings like 'Eso eso phire eso bnodhu he' (Come back, my beloved)[13] and 'Andhajane deho ālo' (Give light to the blind),[14] although these were recorded in his old age, when he had lost his voice. The latter adapts the *tappā* from its normal concern with love to a deeply spiritual theme, as do borrowings from Hindi *tappā* like 'E parabāse rabe ke' (Who will remain in this alien land)[15] and 'Hridayabāsanā purna hala' (My heart's desire is fulfilled).[16] But it is in compositions like 'Āmi rupe tomāy bholābo nā' (I won't charm you with my beauty)[17] – interestingly, meant for a male voice – 'Āji je rajani jāy' (This night that passes),[18] or 'Barho bismaya lāge' (I am filled with wonder)[19] that we find the authentic 'Rābindrik' *tappā*. Here the flourishes are controlled and entirely directed by the underlying passion. A combination of long *mirh*s (the uninterrupted glide of several notes) and short embellishments allows the elegance and the pathos to be nuanced properly.

Fourth, the modern Bānglā song, especially as instanced in the plays of the great actor, producer, and playwright Girishchandra Ghosh. The noted musicologist Rājyeshwar Mitra has shown how some of Ghosh's songs, put to music by others between 1883 and 1897, anticipate Tagore's compositions.[20] This precedent is important to note, as the refined elite tastes of his ingrained Brahmo culture kept Tagore outwardly aloof for the most part from the popular sensational fare of the Kolkata public stage. His disdain for Girishchandra is well known. In fact, Mitra thinks Tagore was not directly influenced by Girishchandra, but more generally by the popular music of the time.[21] The impact shows chiefly in the early songs, especially love songs, most of which are quite different from Tagore's mature creations.

Fifth, folk songs, especially the Baul songs of East Bengal. In 1927, while reviewing *Hārāmani* (The Lost Jewels), a collection of Baul songs edited by Muhammad Mansuruddin, Tagore writes:

> While I was at Shilāidaha, I would constantly meet and talk with the Baul groups. I have used Baul tunes in many of my songs, and mingled them in many others, consciously or unconsciously, with other *rāga*s and *rāgini*s. It should be clear from this that at some point, the tunes and words of Baul songs have entered freely into my mind.[22]

He also makes the important point that Baul songs are the common creation of Hindus and Muslims. The Baul community that engaged Rabindranath was from eastern Bengal. Those of western Bengal, particularly of Birbhum district where Tagore's Santiniketan is situated, did not find much place in Rabindrasangit, maybe because of the overly sexual nature of their religious practices.

Strangely, the rich traditions of folk-song from north Bengal and Assam (the *bhāoāiyā*, for example) did not attract Tagore. Their passionate, down-to-earth character may have held less appeal for him than the mystic other-worldliness of the east Bengal Bauls. This sublimity is clearly expressed in Abanindranāth Tagore's painting 'Rabi Bāul' where we find the poet whirling in a dance, the one-stringed Baul instrument called *ektārā* in his hand.

The Baul legacy bore fruit during the Swadeshi movement of 1905, when for a brief period, Tagore was in the forefront of the mass protest against Curzon's design to divide Bengal. Some of his celebrated patriotic songs were now composed and sung in street rallies. Sudhir Chakrabarti has noted how, keeping the Baul tune intact, Tagore would often add a *sanchāri* (the third section of a four-part song, set in a comparatively lower range of notes) that gave the song a completely original flavour.[23] Among these songs is 'Āmār sonār bānglā' (My golden Bengal),[24] a part of which is now the national anthem of Bangladesh.

Sixth, Western music. Tagore's encounter with Western music can best be understood in the context of his talks with Romain Rolland in 1926 and with Einstein in 1931. He recounts to Einstein how he had heard European music at home in his childhood but encountered it properly on first coming to Europe at seventeen. 'I had heard the music of Chopin and others at an early age,' he says; then adds candidly, 'Somehow the piano confounds me. The violin pleases me much more.'[25] But it is also a fact that as a young boy, he was much impressed by his elder brother Jyotirindranath's piano playing. In the same conversation, he criticizes Western classical music as being too rigidly constituted and deficient in melodic beauty.

'I love Beethoven and also Bach,' Rabindranath told Romain Rolland.[26] But he describes his experience of hearing Christina Nilsson,[27] the renowned Swedish soprano: her singing appeared to him like bird-call imitations, 'a kind of mimicry'. Indian rain-songs 'do not try to imitate the sound of falling raindrops. They rekindle the joy of rain-festivals, and convey something of the feeling associated with the rainy season.' He adds rather surprisingly, 'Somehow the songs of springtime do not have the same depth; I do not know why.'[28] He remarks to Einstein that in Indian music, iron rigidity applied only to the *tāla* (time), not the essential music. 'In European music you have a comparative liberty about time, but not about melody. But in India we have freedom of melody with no freedom of time.' About accompanying instruments, he says, in India 'instruments are used, not for harmony, but for keeping time and for adding to the volume and depth'. Hence, though he is 'deeply moved' by Western music as being 'vast in its structure and grand in its composition', Indian music 'touches [him] more deeply by its fundamental lyrical appeal'.[29]

This explains why there is so little influence of Western classical music on Rabindrasangit; whatever Western influence we find is of the popular lyrical variety. He composes 'Purāno sei diner kathā' (Those days gone by)[30] to the tune of 'Auld lang syne', 'Katabār bhebechhinu' (How often have I thought)[31] to 'Drink to me only with thine eyes', and several songs in the early musical dramas using other English and Scottish tunes.[32] Interestingly, he characterizes his rendering of 'Auld Lang Syne' as 'Scotch Bhupāli', assimilating the tune to the *rāga*-based structure familiar to him.[33]

Lastly, Carnatic music. Probably Tagore did not have much direct exposure to south Indian music. It was through his energetic niece Sarala, and later through singers like Sāvitri Krishnan, that he came across some wonderful Carnatic music and used it in a number of songs such as 'Ānandaloke mangalāloke' (In the realm of bliss and goodness),[34] 'E ki lābanye purna prān' (What grace suffuses my soul),[35] 'Nilānjana chhāyā' (The blue shadow of the cloud),[36] and 'Bāje karuna sure' (There plays to a plaintive tune).[37] But sometimes, in trying to accommodate the typical south Indian musical phrases, he may not have done justice to the delicate words, even in a well-known song like 'Bāsanti, he bhubanamohini' (O Spring, world-enchantress).[38] This is one of the few instances where his celebrated fusion has failed.

HALF IN LOVE: HINDUSTANI CLASSICAL MUSIC

From Tagore's discussions of music and other personal reminiscences, one cannot help feeling he has sometimes been rather unkind to the khyāl-based ustāds. He regards them as a species devoid of musical sensitivity, bent only on displaying their technical prowess. He seems not properly to appreciate the transformation of Hindustani classical music since the 1920s. What brought about this rather uncharacteristic harshness of judgement? And what was the nature of this musical essentialism? For an answer, we need to study Tagore's musical growth chart, reviewing his actual listening experience.

As noted earlier, Tagore grew up in a dhrupad-dominated ambience pervaded by the Bishnupur gharānā, the only classical gharānā of repute in Bengal. The renowned Jadunāth Bhattāchārya or Jadubhatta, Rādhikāprasād Goswāmi, and Gopeshwar Bandyopādhyāy – all of them reverently mentioned by Tagore – belonged to that illustrious gharānā. Rabindranath himself appointed Gopeshwar's younger brother Surendranāth as the official musician of the Adi Brahmo Samaj and, by default, his musical adviser and one of his major score-writers. Tagore appreciated the unusual and comparatively simple nature of the compositions of this gharānā vis-à-vis its northern and western Indian counterparts: 'If Hindustani classical music has adopted a particular style in Bengal, then the individuality of that style must be recognized. It cannot be said that it allows no room for excellence. Jadubhatta's genius is anchored in this very Bishnupuri style; one might say the same of Radhika Goswami. If listeners from western India do not like this style, that cannot be considered the final word.'[39] With the coming to Kolkata of Wajed Ali Shāh, the deposed Nawab of Awadh, in 1858, many Bengali singers rushed to attend his durbar. Only the Bishnupur gharānā (with a few exceptions including Jadhubhatta) held fast to its Bengali originality. That might be another reason why the Tagores, especially Rabindranath, were enamoured of Bishnupur.

For a brief period in his childhood, Rabindranath was trained in music by Bishnu Chakrabarti, the dhrupad singer who acquired great influence in the Brahmo Samaj; then even more briefly by the legendary Jadubhatta. But Tagore confesses that while he garnered a lifetime's riches from the master, he had little by way of rigorous practice. He was by nature a truant but brilliant pupil, an *ustād manqué*.

Rabindranath retained his natural ability in singing *dhrupad*. Thanks to his father, Debendranāth, he not only had to compose Bengali words for Hindi *dhrupad*s and sing them during the Brahmo festival of Māghotsav, but also had to teach some of the songs to others. This practice kept alive his close association with the form, though the attachment weakened after he settled in Santiniketan, and virtually disappeared some time after Debendranath's death in 1905 and Rabindranath's gradual withdrawal from the Brahmo establishment.

However, that he retained much of what he had imbibed in his youth is corroborated by no less an authority than Birendrakishor Raychaudhuri. Birendrakishor describes how at his insistence, in 1936 when Rabindranath had lost his voice, he rather reluctantly

> sang a *dhrupad* in the *rāga* Darbāri kanarhā, comprising four *tukā*s (sections) in *choutāla* beat, composed by Miān Tānsen.... It was an impeccable, top-grade *dhrupad* abounding in *mirh*s, typical of Tansen's 'son-line'. Except for Mohammad Ali Khān [a descendant of that line], I had never heard anyone sing a *dhrupad* in this style.... I said to him, 'If one who can sing like this is not an *ustād*, who is?'

Rabindranath thereupon smiled and said he had forgotten many such songs that he had memorized simply by listening to them, but he could still recall a hundred or more.[40]

Dhurjatiprasād Mukhopādhyāy and Dilipkumār Rāy tried, in their own ways, to open up for him the new possibilities, mostly *khyāl*-based, unfolding in north Indian classical music from the 1920s. We find Dhurjatiprasad trying to soften Tagore's mind towards *ustād*s by pointing out that the great Abdul Karim Khān was not a typical '*gharānā ustād* like Faiyāz Khān', because 'he sometimes forgets the *bandish*, or sings only a line or two ... and sings as his mood dictates. And how delightful are those moods!'[41]

The persuasion did not work, as borne out by Tagore's recorded encounters with three eminent figures of this *khyāl*-based renaissance. At Lucknow in 1935, he listened appreciatively to Shrikrishna Ratanjankar but was left with a question: Why did the *khyāl* have no defined form, no progress to a clear end? Ten shades of the *rāga* Chhāyānat should be rendered in ten separate songs, he opined. If you pack them into a single rendition, it does not do justice to the composition's 'dignity, consistency and grace'.[42] Again, on 23 April 1938, he declared himself fortunate to have heard Kesarbāi Kerkar sing, calling her performance a 'miracle of music only possible for a born genius'.[43] Yet six days later, he was making the old complaint: the songs had no defined form or ending. 'When the music is taking an organic and vibrant form, it's against aesthetics to stretch it at will, prune it, bang and twist it.... I don't blame Kesarbai for that, I blame this genre of music.'[44] On the other hand, at the Jorasanko mansion in presumably the late 1930s, Tagore heard Ustad Faiyaz Khan sing in *rāga* Rāmkeli, an elaborate *ālāp* and *dhrupad* followed by a *khyāl*. Kumārprasād Mukhopādhyāy has likened this encounter to that between Goethe and Beethoven. As the concert progressed, Tagore looked more and more engrossed and finally offered 21 gold *mohur*s to the *ustād*, saying, 'This man has taken away fifty years of my life'[45] – that is to say, he had presented the kind of music the poet would hear in his younger days. It is notable that Faiyaz Khan sang an elaborate *ālāp* and a *dhrupad*, which would have been to Tagore's taste. One presumes the *khyāl* that followed was not long enough to irk him. He had made a similar comment after listening to Birendrakishor play the *surshringār*: that, he said, was the kind of music he used to hear and appreciate in his youth but could no longer find.[46]

In none of these cases does Tagore belittle the artistic brilliance of the performer, but he assesses them against a preset standard of 'dignity, consistency and grace', the essence of which is proportion or balance. His chief complaint is against the arbitrary, no-holds-barred method of applying *tāna*s and stretching them out indefinitely. He felt it vitiated the basic norm of any artistic creation: restraint.

Another of his pet aversions was the tabla. He was brought up in the *dhrupadi* tradition, where the *pakhwāj* or *mridangam* provided the percussion. It is on record that he *recited* his monsoon song 'Ai āse ai ati bhairaba harashe' (There it comes, with fearsome joy)[47] accompanied by his friend Rājā Jagadindranāth Rāy on the *pakhwāj*. For a long time, Rabindrasangit singers were not allowed to sing to the tabla, and some of them, like the great Sāhānā Debi, simply could not. When in the 1930s, Pankajkumār Mallik requested Tagore to allow the tabla in his Rabindrasangit classes for All India Radio, it was with great reluctance that the poet agreed, on condition that the instrument be played as lightly as possible.

He also hated the harmonium, because of the instrument's inability to produce the *shruti*s, subtle sub-notes that lend character to both Hindustani music and Rabindrasangit. Instead, he preferred the *esrāj*. The pioneering

Rabindrasangit exponents Dinendranāth Tagore and Shailajāranjan Majumdār, and later Ashesh Bandyopādhyāy, were all skilled *esrāj* players.

The taste of the pudding, however, is in the eating. How deeply particular Hindustani songs set to various *rāga*s were embedded in Tagore's mind appears in his late compositions, when he had famously broken out of the 'golden cage' of classical music. Shailajaranjan has impressive anecdotes in this regard. He reminisces that as late as 1939, he would write the name of a *rāga*, or just something like 'song with *tāna*', on a scrap of paper and place it on Tagore's breakfast table; the next day, or maybe the same evening, gems like 'Eso go, jwele diye jāo pradipkhāni' (Come and light the lamp),[48] 'Āji tomāy ābār chāi shunābāre' (Today I long to tell you again),[49] 'Saghana gahana rātri' (The deep cloud-laden night),[50] or 'Shrābaner gaganer gāye' (Against the Shravana sky)[51] would come forth, with no sign of being bespoken compositions. In these songs, Tagore would typically deviate from the prescribed structures of the *rāga*s. For example, in 'Saghana gahana rātri', set to *rāga* Bāgeshri, he would use *komal dhaivat* (minor sixth), something forbidden in the books; in fact, a monsoon song in Bāgeshri is itself a deviation, as Tagore well knew.

Moreover, writes Shailajaranjan, 'The *tappā* form grew mellifluous in Rabindranath's voice.' Once Shailajaranjan found it hard to render the *tappā*-embellished opening of the song 'Ogo tumi panchadashi' (O moon in your fifteenth phase),[52] yet the poet insisted that the students be taught to sing it in chorus. Not unexpectedly, it was a disaster. Tagore then made a simpler version and was pleased with the performance. But later, at Shailajaranjan's insistence, he reconstructed the complex version of the line to be sung at a returning point of the opening of the song. Shailajaranjan writes with deserved satisfaction: 'I made Kanikā Mukhopādhyāy [later Bandyopādhyāy] sing that song at the next Barshāmangal (monsoon festival). Gurudev was very pleased this time too. It was recorded for the gramophone at his suggestion.'[53]

In particular, Tagore has been credited with special mastery of Behāg and Bhairavi, because the immense variations of these *rāga*s, particularly the latter, abound in his creations, as do the the *rāga*s Pilu and Khāmbāj. He dared to use *komal dhaivat* in the descending movement of 'Kothā je udhāo halo mor prān' (Where has my soul vanished)[54] set to *rāga* Miān-ki-malhār. Soumyendranāth Tagore proposed to name the resultant *rāga* Rabi-malhār. In 'Ādheka ghume nayana chume' (Kissing my half-asleep eyes, 1926)[55] he seems unwittingly to have reinvented the *rāga* Hem kalyān, independently developed by Ustād Ālāuddin Khān. In his mature creations, we often find use of the *thumri* style, as in superb examples like 'Tumi kichhu diye jāo'

(Leave me something before you go),[56] 'Khelār sāthi, bidāy dwār kholo' (My playmate, open the door of departure),[57] and 'Sakhi āndhāre ekelā ghare' (My beloved, alone in this dark room).[58] In songs like 'Din phurālo he sangsāri' (Your days are ending, O worldly man),[59] based on a *shehnāi* composition in the *rāga* Bhimpalashri, or 'Jāoā āsāri ei ki khelā' (What game is this, of coming and going),[60] there is quite extensive use of *tānas*, but these songs do not qualify as vintage Rabindrasangit.

A BLOSSOMING SONG-GARDEN

Tagore composed a little over two thousand songs, including those for his musical dramas and dance dramas, which were completely new genres on the Bengal stage. These songs have been collected in *Gitabitān* (literally 'Expanse of Songs'), arranged by Tagore in several sections: 'Pujā' ('Worship', 617 songs), 'Swadesh' ('My Country', 46 songs), 'Prem' ('Love', 395 songs), 'Prakriti' ('Nature', 283 songs), 'Bichitra' ('Various', 140 songs), and 'Ānushthānik' ('For Special Occasions', 21 songs).[61] Some sections are divided into subsections: 'Pujā' has as many as nineteen uneven subsections, 'Prem' two, and 'Prakriti' eight. Interestingly, the sub-cluster 'Gān' ('Song') is common to 'Pujā' and 'Prem', throwing light on his intermingled ideas of love, worship, and music. Within the cluster 'Prakriti', pride of place is held by the rains (115 songs), followed by spring (96). Most of the scores are available in the *Swarabitān*, a huge collective effort of many experts.

There is an undisturbed continuity of love songs throughout Tagore's life, though most of the masterpieces belong to the later years. Of the nature songs, however, he composed hardly twenty-five till 1908, when he was forty-seven; even of these, many belong to the musical dramas. But then the floodgates opened: nature songs flowed freely over the next thirty-three years, above all in the decade 1921–31 (152 out of 488 songs). In the final decade of his life, 1931–41, much of his musical creativity went into the dance dramas *Chitrāngādā* (1936), *Chandālikā* (1938), *Māyār khelā* (1938), and *Shyāmā* (1939).[62] Naturally there was a fall in the number of other songs. Even so, there are twenty-three nature songs[63] among the fifty-five composed in just over two years from his seventy-eighth birthday.

The 'Pujā' songs have a broadly reverse trajectory. After 1918, when he was fifty-seven, very few of them were sung at the Maghotsav, whereas earlier as many as twenty-three were sung in a single year, 1903, and seventeen in 1914. The later 'Pujā' songs had long started deviating significantly from the earlier, formally religious ones, in terms of both music and poetry. The earlier items had presented the image of the removed, reverend Brahmo 'high God', addressed as 'lord' (*prabhu* or *nāth*), as inculcated in his mind by his father, Debendranath. We now see a very different deity, of a highly intimate, personal, and non-institutional character. This is not surprising. Tagore confesses candidly in his autobiography, as in his memorable letters to Hemantabālā Debi, that his heart had never consented to the religious tenets of his family. Yet, dependent as he was on his father, he diligently went through the right motions, internalizing the resultant contradictions. Many lines scattered through his apparently simple 'Pujā' songs express this agony: 'How much farther is the home of bliss?' (1896),[64] 'I see no way forward in this darkness of confusion (1885),[65] or 'You are ever in my heart' (1888).[66]

It was only gradually, especially after his father's death, that he could develop his real faith, which he termed the 'Religion of Man'. Musically too, he stopped copying the classical songs of the *ustād*s: instead, he effortlessly mixed one *rāga* with another, or *rāga*s with folk tunes, the *kirtan*, and even Western tunes. The spiritually more orthodox *Gitānjali–Gitimālya–Gitāli* phase (1910–14) was characterized by a relatively simple and straightforward use of traditionally known *rāga*s, with little improvization. Later, when he had blossomed into his own, he cared little for classical 'propriety'. In his last ten years, he composed hardly ten 'Pujā' songs. Among them, however, was 'Samukhe shāntipārābār' (Ahead, the ocean of peace), originally composed for the deathbed of the boy Amal in the play *Dākghar* (The Post Office), but held back by its creator to be sung after his own death.[67]

Many consider the love songs and nature songs of Tagore's mature years, particularly the monsoon songs, as marking the pinnacle of his musical creativity. Two factors, among others, may have conjoined to make this possible. It must be admitted that the complaints laid by Tagore at the *ustād*s' door are sometimes equally applicable to his own verbal compositions. There too we find the same consummate skill and unhindered fluency, leading to overproduction and lack of restraint. But while composing songs, the natural structural rules of music forced a discipline of condensation, automatically curbing his poetic exuberance. Again, in his music he exhibits an innate sense of proportion. His best songs are an outcome of this dual check. What we characterized at the outset as the 'x-factor' owes a lot to this.

BEARERS OF A NOBLE BURDEN

As Tagore puts it, the song, in contrast to other art forms, is like a beloved daughter that her parents, after rearing her with great affection and care, have to hand over to the husband's family, never knowing what awaits her – in other words, how the artist's creation would be treated in performance.

Tagore was fortunate in this regard, despite his frequent lament that his songs had been mauled by insensitive singers. The allegation was not untrue in the earliest phase of his career as a composer, but the situation changed when singers from his own circle began to record his songs. Amalā Dās recorded as many as twenty-three between 1905 and 1915. Sahana Debi, the finest exponent of Rabindrasangit in Tagore's own view,[68] also recorded quite a few songs before she relinquished music and joined Sri Aurobindo's ashram in Pondicherry (now Puducherry). A little later, coinciding with the advance in recording technology in the 1930s, came Kanak Dās, who recorded as many as fifty-seven songs between 1926 and 1941. Santosh Sengupta also won acclaim in the late 1930s.[69]

Dinendranath Tagore had settled in Kolkata by 1929. Pankajkumar Mallik learnt the authentic tunes from him and played a major part in popularizing Rabindrasangit through his enormously popular Sunday music lessons on All India Radio. He also memorably sang Rabindrasangit in Pramathesh Baruā's popular film *Mukti* (1937). Thus Rabindrasangit gradually found its place in the cultural space of a wider public. In the next generation, its exponents trained in the classic Santiniketan ambience became a mainstay of the recording industry.

Needless to say, it was in Santiniketan that Rabindrasangit found its mother element. When Tagore made music an important part of his new model of education, he found four exceptional practitioners to carry out his programme. They were Indira Debi, his beloved niece; Dinendranath Tagore, his great-nephew; Shailajaranjan Majumdar, a chemist-turned-musician who proved the most fastidious teacher and score-writer of Rabindrasangit; and Shāntideb Ghosh, born into the Tagore culture. Dinendranath had a robust, open voice, and his pupils followed that style, akin to Tagore's own. This was the line cultivated by Shantideb. However, a change became apparent after Dinendranath left Santiniketan and Shailajaranjan was put at the helm of musical affairs. The emphasis was now on accurately reproducing minute subtleties. This called for careful attention, sometimes arguably at the cost of spontaneity. Suchitrā Mitra (née Mukhopādhyāy), a pupil of Shantideb, continued the former style, while Kanika Bandyopadhyay (née Mukhopadhyay), Shailajaranjan's pupil, followed the latter line. From the 1940s onwards, these two singers dominated the scene. The Shailajaranjan *gharānā* produced other memorable singers like Nilimā Sen, Ashoktaru Bandyopādhyāy, and Subinay Rāy. Sanjidā Khātun, also a student of Shailajaranjan, was largely instrumental in bringing about a resurgence of Rabindrasangit in Bangladesh after its liberation in 1971.

Rājeshwari Datta (née Vāsudev), although a product of Santiniketan, came into her own under the tutelage of Rameshchandra Bandyopādhyāy, the eldest son of Gopeshwar, in Kolkata. She created a very special niche of her own, elegantly rendering the more classically oriented songs. By contrast, Debabrata Bishwās (Biswas), the *enfant terrible* of Rabindrasangit with his roots in the leftist Indian People's Theatre Association, defied all classification. He did sing in the conventional mode in his earliest days, but from the 1950s, he broke away from the Santiniketan orthodoxy to develop a completely original and forceful style, hospitable to other musical practices, much to the chagrin of the purists whom he often surpassed in popularity.

CONCLUSION

Tagore's music cannot be seen in isolation from his poetry. Yet that the tunes can attain mass popularity on their own is shown by quite a few Hindi film songs from 'Naina diwāne ek nahin māne' (1950), 'Pawan chale zor' (1952), and 'Man merā urtā bādal ke sang' (1952) to 'Tere mere milan ki ye rainā' (1973) and 'Koi jaise mere dil kā' (1998). In Bengal, Rabindrasangit remains the steadiest and highest-selling segment of the recorded music market.

Considering the fact that the songs constitute only a part – if perhaps the most enduring part – of Tagore's varied lifelong activities, his output is awe-inspiring both in quantity and in musical achievement. He had no proper training, could not play any instrument, and did not know how to write a score; he could only sing spontaneously. But he was endowed with an ear – developed by exposure to multiple musical traditions since his earliest days – that could respond with equal ease to music as varied as the classical Indian *dhrupad* and Thomas Moore's *Irish Melodies*, as remote from each other as the *kirtan* and Carnatic music, or the Punjabi *bhajan* and the Baul songs of east Bengal. Even more impressively, he could fuse these elements into a true organicity far beyond mere eclecticism. Anything musical that came his way and attracted him was transformed into a new creation bearing his unmistakable signature. Nature and nurture happily conspired to produce in him a musician at the most fundamental level of his creative genius.

I am indebted to Soumitra Lahiri and Subrata Ghosh for their valuable suggestions.

NOTES

1. 'The Religion of an Artist' (1924–6, revised and combined 1936), *EW* 3:687. Emphasis added.
2. Cited in *RJPP* 4:99–100.

3. Ratanjankar's original English as quoted in Birendrakishor Raychaudhuri, *Hindustāni sangite tānsener sthān* (Kolkata: Thema, 2006), 122–3.
4. Sumit Sarkar, *Modern Times* (Hyderabad: Permanent Black, 2015), 405–6.
5. *GB*, p. 819.
6. Cited in *RJPP* 1:299.
7. 'Ārjya gāthā', *Ādhunik sāhitya*, *RRVB* 9:481.
8. Letter to Dhurjatiprasad Mukhopadhyay, 16 May 1935: 'Sur o sangati' (Tune and harmony), *Sangitchintā*, *RRVB* 28:854.
9. *EW* 3:915.
10. Remark to Dilipkumar Ray: 'Ālāp-ālochanā' (Discussions), *Sangitchintā*, *RRVB* 28:773.
11. *GB*, 'Pujā' #394.
12. *GB*, p. 847.
13. *GB*, 'Prem' #252.
14. *GB*, 'Pujā' #114.
15. *GB*, 'Pujā' #435.
16. *GB*, 'Pujā' #331.
17. *GB*, 'Prem' #90.
18. *GB*, 'Prem' #247.
19. *GB*, p. 893.
20. Rajyeshwar Mitra, *Prasanga bānglā gān* (Kolkata: Indirā, 1989), 135.
21. Ibid., 139.
22. 'Āshirbād: harāmani', *RRVB* 32:258.
23. 'Ashish Lahiri in conversation with Sudhir Chakrabarty on Musical Ideas', *Bitarkikā*, July 2014.
24. *GB*, 'Swadesh' #1.
25. *EW* 3:916.
26. *EW* 3:890.
27. The recorded text of the dialogue mentions a male singer named Milson. It seems likely that Tagore had Nilsson in mind: see note 13 in *Sangitchintā* (Kolkata: Visva-Bharati, 1985), 368. In *Jibansmriti* (Reminiscences), he describes in the same terms a concert by a singer who 'might have been Madame [Christina] Nilsson or Madame [Emma] Albani', the Canadian singer (*RRVB* 17:378–9).
28. *EW* 3:892–3.
29. *EW* 3:915.
30. *GB*, p. 885.
31. *GB*, p. 879.
32. For a list see *GB*, pp. 1025–6.
33. Āshis Basumallik, *Rabindranāther bhāngā gān* (Kolkata: Pratibhās, 2004), 178, 191.
34. *GB*, 'Pujā' #476.
35. *GB*, 'Pujā' #539.

36. *GB*, 'Prem' #258.
37. *GB*, 'Prem' #197.
38. *GB*, 'Prakriti' #239.
39. 'Bishwabidyālaye sangitshikshā', *Sangitchintā, RRVB* 28:751–2.
40. *CP* 9:544, which reprints a good part of Birendrakishor's article from *Taurjyatrik*, May 1966, 117–18.
41. Letter from Dhurjatiprasad to Rabindranath, 25 March 1935: *Sangitchintā, RRVB* 28:842.
42. Dhurjatiprasad's afterword to the volume *Sur o sangati* (1935): *Sangitchintā* (1985), 358.
43. *Sangitchintā, RRVB* 28:822, n. 3.
44. Letter to Sahana Debi, 29 April 1938: *Sangitchintā, RRVB* 28:822–3.
45. Kumarprasad Mukhopadhyay, *Kudrat Rangi-Birangi* (Kolkata: Ānanda, 1997), 160.
46. See *CP* 9:542–3.
47. *GB*, 'Prakriti' #27.
48. *GB*, 'Prakriti' #128.
49. *GB*, 'Prakriti' #127.
50. *GB*, 'Prakriti' #139.
51. *GB*, 'Prakriti' #130.
52. *GB*, 'Prakriti' #140.
53. Shailajaranjan Majumdar, *Jātrāpather ānandagān* (Kolkata: Ānanda, 2012), 104–5.
54. *GB*, 'Prakriti' #80.
55. *GB*, 'Bichitra' #93.
56. *GB*, 'Prakriti' #251.
57. *GB*, p. 856.
58. *GB*, 'Prem' #281.
59. *GB*, 'Pujā' #512.
60. *GB*, p. 856.
61. More songs (not arranged by Tagore) and the musical dramas were added in a separate volume.
62. The dance dramas *Chitrāngadā* and *Māyār khelā* were completely transformed from much earlier lyrical dramas, of 1892 and 1888 respectively. The dance drama *Chandālikā* was reworked from a prose play of 1933, and *Shyāmā* from the 'dramatized song' (*nātyagiti*) *Parishodh* (1936). The dance-drama version of *Māyār khelā* was neither performed in its entirely nor published in Tagore's lifetime.
63. Some of them in *GB*, pp. 909–12, outside the main 'Prakriti' section.
64. *GB*, 'Pujā' #416.
65. *GB*, 'Pujā' #420.
66. *GB*, 'Pujā' #422.
67. *Shesh lekhā* #1, *GB*, p. 866.

68. See his remark to Dilipkumar Ray, 'Ālāp-ālochanā', *Sangitchintā*, *RRVB* 28:799.
69. For these and more details see Siddhārtha Ghosh, *Recorde rabindrasangit* (Kolkata: Indira, 1982).

6 Rabindranath Tagore

Drama and Performance

ANANDA LAL

The overwhelmingly lopsided critical attention given to Tagore's poetry and fiction, and to a lesser extent his essays, paintings, philosophical discourses, and educational experiments, has submerged assessment of his equally outstanding achievements in the performing arts, specifically theatre and dance. And despite the fulfilment of his own prophecy about his songs outliving all his other creations in popularity, hardly any book-length scholarly analysis of his extraordinary output in music has appeared in English. The present chapter limits its scope to Tagore's plays, but that automatically embraces his work in dance as well, since his choreographic contributions formed an integral part of their productions.

I should also emphasize at the outset that Tagore did not just write his plays; he acted in and directed them, composed all their songs and music, and designed and choreographed many of them. To read them only as texts consciously blindsides oneself from all these activities. He reiterated the primacy of their performatory dimensions time and again. About his very first drama, *Bālmiki-pratibhā* (The Emergence of Vālmiki's Genius, 1881), he stressed that it 'is not a composition which will bear being read. Its significance is lost if it is not heard sung and seen acted.'[1] Towards the end of his career, he introduced his dance drama *Chandālikā* (The Chandāl's Daughter, 1938) with virtually identical words: 'It needs to be kept in mind that this play is to be seen and heard, but not read.'[2] By analogy, we can quote from his similar comments about songs. In his autobiography he observed, 'I am always reluctant to publish books of the words of songs, for therein the soul must needs be lacking.'[3] In a characteristically poetic simile, he wrote about Bāul songs, 'the best part of a song is missed when the tune is absent; for thereby its movement and its colour are lost, and it becomes like a butterfly whose wings have been plucked.'[4] It has become the norm in drama criticism to explicate play texts with a constant eye on their onstage visualization, leaving behind the old method of treating them exclusively as literature, like poetry and fiction. There can be no better exemplar of this than Tagore's huge dramatic corpus, of over seventy scripts and libretti.

Related to this imperative, we must note the flexible nature of Tagore's scripts, which he changed continuously not only between rehearsals but also between performances, as his son Rathindranāth recalls, 'much to the consternation of the actors'.[5] Publication did not make the text sacrosanct; Tagore typically revised it for revivals and brought out new editions. Precisely because he intended that his plays come to life in the theatre, he kept stage directions to a minimum – as in the texts of Shakespeare and Molière that have come down to us – knowing that the scripts formed merely a skeleton to which his team added the flesh and blood. However, since the printed texts constitute most of what survives, I must fall back on them to track his development, for the sake of convenience attempting first a periodization by genre as well as patterns of theme and content, then pointing out the salient aspects of his theatrical art in his own direction of them, and finally examining some key productions after his death.

THE PLAYS

A product of a large extended family that regularly organized a variety of in-house cultural programmes for invited audiences in its improvised courtyard theatre, Tagore had acted there before composing and staging *Bālmiki-pratibhā*, in which he performed the lead at the age of nineteen. It carried the seed of many of his later preoccupations: spiritual transformation (of the robber Ratnākar into Vālmiki, the poet of the *Rāmāyana*); an innocent child who causes this enlightenment; and the abjuring of violence and blood sacrifice. It was the first of three *gitinātya* (literally 'musical drama') – *Kālmrigayā* (Fateful Hunt, 1882) and *Māyār khelā* (Game of Māyā, 1888)[6] being the others – in which, mentored by his elder brother Jyotirindranāth, he boldly refashioned classical *rāga*s and even adapted some British folk tunes.

At the same time, he wrote heightened verse drama. *Prakritir pratishodh* (Nature's Revenge, 1884) featured a *sanyāsi* who finds truth not in renunciation but in affection for an ostracized orphan girl. Later, Tagore recognized that 'this has been the subject on which all my writings have dwelt – the joy of attaining the Infinite within the finite'.[7] *Rājā o rāni* (King and Queen, 1889) and *Bisarjan* (Sacrifice, 1890) were somewhat melodramatic five-act tragedies modelled after Shakespeare, a style that he subsequently rejected: '[O]ur attempts to imitate the blast of a hurricane led us easily into exaggeration.'[8] Nevertheless, *Bisarjan* still conveys a powerful message against idol worship, though even today most Indian directors do not have the courage to obey Tagore's iconoclastic stage direction at the end, where Raghupati throws the image of his revered goddess Kāli into the river.

Tagore largely abandoned the five-act structure soon after, in favour of single plots and short scenes. But *Chitrāngadā* (1892) remained in blank verse and radical in content, introducing a near-feminist heroine from the *Mahābhārata* for his thesis on the chimera of physical attractiveness and the true nature of love and human beauty. Mesmerized by Arjuna's masculinity, she asks for a divine boon of beauty to allure him, but then realizes that she deceived him, and finally reveals her real self to him. Its treatment of female sexuality scandalized some critics. In *Mālini* (1896), he perfected a new form, rhyming couplets, for his first drama reflecting his deep respect for Buddhist principles, again featuring a rebellious princess as protagonist.

It bears mentioning, because of a stereotypical association of Tagore with high seriousness, philosophy, mysticism, and poetry (Bengalis call him Gurudeb, 'revered guru', and Kabiguru, 'poet-guru'), that he excelled in prose comedy containing sparkling humour. Several of his short skits, collected under the titles *Hāsya-kautuk* (Comic Charades, 1885–7) and *Byanga-kautuk* (Satiric Charades, 1893–1901), provide children with ample entertainment even nowadays for school functions. He extended this farcical flair into social satire for adults in the exuberantly witty *Gorhāy galad* (Error at the Outset, 1892) and *Baikunther khātā* (Baikuntha's Notebook, 1897).

After founding the boys' ashram in Santiniketan, where he gradually relocated from Kolkata, Tagore completely rethought his approach to theatre and attacked foreign influences in the polemical essay 'Rangamancha' (The Stage, 1902). I quote below at length from its authorized English translation because he had obviously approved its rather strong wording, and because it must have made an impact on thinkers about Indian theatre when the nationally circulated monthly *The Modern Review* printed it in December 1913, the month after the Nobel Prize award, as public interest in him peaked, and before which not too many people outside Bengal had heard of him:

In the *Natyashastra* of Bharata[9] is a description of a stage, but no mention of scenes. It does not seem to me that this absence of concrete scenery can have been much of a loss....

To my mind it shows only faint-heartedness on the actor's part to seek [the] help [of scenery]. The relief from responsibility which he gains from the illusion created by pictorial scenes is one which is begged of the painter. Besides it pays to the spectators the very poor compliment of ascribing to them an utter poverty of imagination....

King Dushyanta [hero of Kālidāsa's classic *Shakuntalā*] hidden behind the trunk of the tree is listening to the conversation of Sakuntala and her companions. We for our part feel our creative faculty quite equal to imagining the tree trunk, even though its image be not bodily there.... [W]hat is the difficulty about imagining a few trees, a cottage, or a bit of a river? ...

That is why I like the *Jatra* plays [the popular traditional rural Bengali theatre form] of our country. There is not so much of a gulf separating the stage from the audience.

... [T]he European wants his truth concrete. He would have imaginative treats, but he must be deluded by having these imaginings to be exact imitations of actual things. He is too much afraid of being cheated, and before accepting any representation of imaginative truth with some amount of enjoyment he must have a sworn testimony of its reality accompanying it. He will not trust the flower until he sees the earth of the mountain top in which it has its roots.... The cost which is incurred for mere accessories on the stage in Europe would swamp the whole of Histrionic Art in famine-stricken India....

The theatres that we have set up in imitation of the West are too elaborate to be brought to the door of all and sundry. In them the creative richness of poet and player are overshadowed by the wealth of the capitalist. If the Hindu [this adjective at that time was often used as a synonym for 'Indian'] spectator has not been too far infected with the greed for realism and the Hindu artist still has any respect for his craft and his skill, the best thing they can do for themselves is to regain their freedom by making a clean sweep of the costly rubbish that has accumulated round about and is clogging the stage.[10]

Henceforth a sea change occurred in Tagore's theatrical vistas, starting with the first of his plays about the seasons, *Shāradotsab* (Autumn Festival, 1908), on the season of fulfilment. Prior to this, no major dramatist in the world had written scripts foregrounding nature. The cliché (which Tagore upheld)[11] goes that European drama depicts humankind usually in conflict with natural forces, striving to control their power. Tagore instead stressed the healing, immanent bond between nature and humanity and, as such, became the first theatrical exponent of the Green Movement much before it had become a movement. Deep ecology and environmental consciousness, so significant on paper in India's school system today, begins with *Shāradotsab* and the cycle that followed it: *Phālguni* (Play of Phālgun, Month of Spring, 1915), *Basanta* (Spring, 1923), *Shesh barshan* (Last Rainfall, 1925), *Sundar* (The Beautiful, 1926), *Rituranga* (Play of the Seasons, 1927),[12] *Nabin* (The New, 1931), and *Shrāban-gāthā* (Song of Shrāvan, Month of Rains, 1934). Gradually this genre was transformed into a song sequence; the 'play' became basically a compendium of Tagore songs on the season in question, linked by minimal dialogue and occasional recitative or prose commentary.

Also with *Shāradotsab*, Tagore turned to prose as his preferred dramatic idiom, but interspersed liberally with songs. A very productive period followed, important new plays coming out almost every year. *Prāyashchitta* (Penance, 1909) introduced a character prefiguring Mahātmā Gāndhi and propagating the political doctrine of *satyāgraha*, years before Gandhi arrived in India. The masterpiece *Rājā* (1910)[13] allegorized man's realization of the true nature of divinity, depicting the spiritual journey quite literally from darkness into light of a queen, symbolizing humanity, to meet her invisible king, symbolizing God. *Rājā* presents two main themes: that humanity becomes too attached to the artificial glitter of the material world, and that he cannot accept that God can permit tragedy into our lives. Ignorance makes him see superficially, leading inevitably to suffering and disillusionment; which finally contribute to his recognition of the duality of truth and reconciliation with God.

Achalāyatan (The Immovable Institution, 1911), which parodies the rigid, frequently unjust beliefs of orthodox Hinduism, in turn faced denunciation from conservative Bengalis, and even now finds few takers to stage its volatile subject. The moving *Dākghar* (The Post Office, 1912), about a dying boy awaiting a 'call from the king', is perhaps Tagore's best-known and most revived play internationally on account of its simplicity and universality. It, too, is interpreted by critics as an allegory of the human soul shackled in mortal form, longing for union with divinity. The metatheatrical *Phālguni*, cited above among the season plays, inserted such startling novelties as generic dialogue unassigned to specific characters.

Two of Tagore's finest and most difficult, politically symbolical works, *Muktadhārā* (The Free Stream, 1922) and *Raktakarabi* (Red Oleander, 1924), emerged in the next decade. They forcefully indict the oppression of subjugated people and exploitation of the earth's resources – *Muktadhārā* on damming rivers and *Raktakarabi* on digging mines – while embodying in their protagonists the spirit of self-sacrifice for a noble cause. It is chastening that, though Tagore raised these issues nearly a century ago, only in recent times has the world begun to rethink the value of massive dams and to realize the havoc caused by open mining. *Muktadhārā* features an upstream kingdom building a dam that would effectively reduce water supply to the downstream kingdom; the altruistic hero kills himself in demolishing the construction. In *Raktakarabi* the excavation of gold creates a society of colonization and totalitarianism characterized by fear, intimidation, and dehumanization. Yet the Raja, personifying power, joins hands with the heroine, nature's free spirit, to overturn his machine in a futile effort at the end. In *Natir pujā* (The Dancer's Pujā, 1926), Tagore again contrasted institutionalized Hinduism with the fundamental equality preached by Buddhism. Equally significant today, the play's first edition contained no male characters – a radical step in Indian theatre when society frowned on what it perceived as actresses' immorality – and had a dancer in the lead role.[14] The first European dramatic classic to feature an all-women cast came ten years later: Garcia Lorca's *The House of Bernarda Alba* (1936).

Never one to stagnate, Tagore displayed a typical restlessness in playwriting, frequently reworking earlier texts, compressing or improving them for new performances, labelling these as 'stageworthy' when published, but continuing to revise until he had convinced himself that he had done justice to the theme. Sometimes the alterations were substantial enough to warrant new titles, virtually assuming the guise of new plays. For example, he turned *Rājā* twice into *Arup ratan* (Formless Jewel, 1920 and 1935) in much tighter renderings. In 1929 he undertook his most ambitious project of this nature, completely recasting *Rājā o rāni* into *Tapati*, its heroine a powerful testament to feminism. Totally estranged from each other, the acquisitive king and captured queen stand at opposite poles of sensuality and asceticism respectively, but she attains liberty through suicide, the supreme act of renunciation that she hopes may restore peace and return him to benevolent rule. The following excerpt from one of their exchanges will also serve as a sample of Tagore's potent prose dialogue:

BIKRAM. You haven't been able to know me – you don't have a heart, woman! ... My love is vast, it's fierce, in it is my prowess – it isn't smaller than my royal power. If you could accept its glory everything would be easy. You've read the holy texts, you're God-fearing – your guru's teaching is to consider as noble the loading of duty's burden upon the shoulders of the servant of work. Forget them, those mantras in your ears. The flood of the primal Shakti upon which the bubbles of creation continue to foam, the huge waves of that Shakti are in my love – look at it, make *pranāms* to it, set afloat upon it all your deeds and misdeeds, doubts and disputes; this alone is called freedom, this alone is called destruction, this alone brings a new epoch to life.

SUMITRA. I don't have the courage, Maharaja, I don't have the courage! Your love has gone far beyond the object of your love – before it I'm extremely small. This boat of mine isn't enough to cross over the tempestuous waves that rise in the ocean of your heart – if I set it afloat while impassioned it would sink instantaneously. My position is at the door of your citizens' wealth and welfare – if you gave me a place even in the dust there, my shame would disappear. Your ears are deaf with the roar of your own waves, how would you know what insurmountable sorrows are on all sides of you? I've lost hope of explaining to you what heartrending echoes of crying move about the cavity of my heart agitatedly, day and night. When everyone on all sides is deprived, then however large a fortune you give me, it won't be to my taste. [15]

Contrary to the general misconception that Tagore had nothing to do with the commercial Bengali theatre of Kolkata, he appreciated the efforts of such young actor-managers as Ahindra Chaudhuri and Shishir (Sisir) Bhāduri to refine it, and at their request during the mid-1920s handed over several new scripts to them. Most of these he dramatized from his own fiction, understanding that its domestic realism better suited the requirements of the professional companies. Thus, he sourced the romantic comedy *Chirakumār sabhā* (The Bachelors' Club, 1925)[16] and *Jogājog* (Relationships, 1936) from novels, *Grihaprabesh* (The Housewarming, 1925) and *Shodhbodh* (Settling of Accounts, 1926) from short stories, and rewrote the earlier plays *Gorhāy galad* as *Shesh rakshā* (Saved in the End, 1927) and *Prāyashchitta* as *Paritrān* (Deliverance, 1927). The preoccupation with society also pervades the unstaged *Bnāshari* (published 1933), an ironic examination of the foibles of upper-crust Kolkata society, where witty conversation takes the place of genuine warmth and feeling.

In the last phase of his stage career, Tagore grew fascinated with the incorporation of dance into theatre. As with music, his implementation of dance resulted from a desire to liberate classical styles from strict conformity and sheer virtuosity to a heterogeneous lyricism that appealed to the emotions. Purists disapproved of his hybrid technique, but he could not be bothered with man-made regulations; he emphasized the expression of aesthetic values without any formal rigidity. Influenced by the dance dramas he had seen on trips to southeast Asia, he applied mixed choreography to fully musical texts, testing the ground with *Shāpmochan* (The Lifting of the Curse, 1931), based on the *Rājā* story; *Tāser desh* (The Land of Cards,

1933), which again satirized fossilized prejudices; and *Parishodh* (Requital, 1936), a play about a courtesan.

He crystallized the art in a triptych of what he termed *nritya-nātya* ('dance drama') upon the varying registers of love: *Chitrāngadā* (1936, reprising his earlier play of 1892), *Chandālikā* (1938, from his 1933 prose drama with the same title about a Dalit girl), and *Shyāmā* (1939, a revision of *Parishodh*, 1936). By foregrounding non-'feminine' or marginalized women in love as protagonists, he subverted the stereotypical images of romantic heroines. This is what Prakriti (which literally means 'nature'), the Chandāl daughter, tells her mother about their downtrodden condition:

Why did you give me birth,
A life full of disgrace –
Being a mother you brought this curse!
Tell me what sin I committed on whom,
Without offence this is grave injustice.[17]

These three plays have become Tagore's most commonly performed pieces in Bengali communities across the world.

Tagore named so many of his plays after their heroines that one may easily deduce that his main theme was the emancipation of women; yet not much exists by way of comprehensive scholarly examination of this subject. Other recurrent concerns in his drama also cry out for exhaustive critical attention: his environmental awareness, his protest against and reform of hidebound social or religious conformism, his political thought, even his spiritual quest. His poetic, symbolic, anti-realistic style, and the paucity of faithful translations may have inhibited analyses of these topics, but if Strindberg's expressionism or the Absurdists' existentialism can receive thorough investigation, surely so can Tagore. I proceed to clarify here the foundations underlying his recurrent themes.

The matter of anti-realism requires some elucidation, because on it pivots an understanding of Tagore's drama. Tagore argued that reality is necessarily relative; he set scientific reality and mental reality at opposite poles. Science, he believed, subjects God to analysis 'in the laboratory of reason outside our personal relationship, and then describes the result as unknown and unknowable'.[18] He continued that one cannot know a book by merely counting its pages, analysing its paper, or measuring and weighing its dimensions. Asking why 'we look upon Shakespeare's portrayal of extraordinary and powerful feelings as more truthful than the exact portrayal of every-day life', he supplied his own answer, that we find in Shakespeare 'the perennial man ... not merely the surface man'.[19] On his trip to Indonesia, he wrote in a letter that if anyone laughs at the apparent unrealism of Javanese dance, 'he needs must also laugh at Shakespeare, whose heroes not only fight in metre, but even die to it'.[20] He said about *Rājā* that 'the human soul has its inner drama, which is just the same as anything else that concerns Man, and Sudarshana [the queen in the play] is not more an abstraction than Lady Macbeth'.[21]

Consequently his realism is one of the mind, not so much of external physical action and conflict as of emotional or spiritual action and internal conflict. It depicts realistically fluctuations in mood and feeling, the progress of awareness and consciousness. It does not emphasize the development of a plot, but rather develops a pattern of symbols which reflect those fluctuations. Although Tagore makes his protagonists relinquish their self-centredness on the spiritual level through the process of suffering, on the social level he consistently espouses the cause of individualism. The dichotomy between the individual and the organization pervades his drama, with Tagore constantly choosing the former:

> All our spiritual teachers have proclaimed the infinite worth of the individual. It is the rampant materialism of the present age which ruthlessly sacrifices individuals to the blood-thirsty idols of organization.... Because men have been building up vast and monstrous organizations they have got into the habit of thinking that this turning-out power has something of the nature of perfection in itself.[22]

Thus we discover images of claustrophobia and depersonalization crowding his plays, as individuals longing for freedom try desperately to extricate themselves from the meshes of unfeeling organization and exploitation.

Tagore held that civilization had also begun to ignore the individual by becoming masculine in nature, thereby generating more wars and strife. In his opinion, the feminine principle commanded respect: a sensitivity, sympathy, and innate spirituality that eclipsed earthly desires. His heroines dominate the stage with their gentle yet powerful personalities. The other omnipresent force is an unseen one, that of the natural world. Tagore admits that Shakespeare's natural settings sometimes uncover 'a secret vein of complaint against the artificial life of the king's court'; in the tragedies, Shakespeare presents nature as malignant or ambivalent or absent altogether.[23] However, Tagore's nature is a perennially beneficent and healing power; by neglecting it or divesting ourselves of its influence, we close our eyes to the world around us and cut ourselves off from the unity of the universe. We cannot overlook this obviously ecofeminist view.

In the final analysis, Tagore's drama reveals a strong underlying current of optimism. The affirmative attitude to life, the broad humanism, the conviction about the inviolable relationship between humankind and its maker, and the deep faith in woman and the beauty of nature, all contribute to the pervasive sense of harmony and invincible spirit of hope.

THE PRODUCTIONS

I have elaborated elsewhere on Tagore's yet unacknowledged role as a harbinger of modern Indian theatre.[24] The space in the present essay does not allow me to contextualize the historical background in detail, without which one cannot comprehend his interventions fully. I can hope to merely summarize his pioneering accomplishments in the performing arts.

We must first realize and accept that Tagore's repertoire consciously constituted 'art theatre' and primarily catered to an elite audience as a serious alternative to the frequently escapist entertainment on the commercial Bengali stage, whether during the early period for invitees only to the private theatre of his ancestral mansion in Kolkata or after he moved to Santiniketan. Thus he belongs firmly with his generation of trendsetting modernist European playwrights who also disdained the grandiose excesses of their professional theatres and, every one of them (Ibsen, Strindberg, Shaw, Chekhov, Hauptmann, Yeats, Pirandello, and Jarry), either opened their own or associated with the new, avowedly independent little theatres meant for like-minded educated viewers. This rejection of popularity does not disqualify them as distanced from the common masses. Tagore knew of and praised the little-theatre movement in the West and the benefits of small auditoriums.[25]

Nevertheless, his theatrical activities with his family in their ancestral Jorasanko residence were rooted in their unquestioning obeisance to British nineteenth-century pictorial spectacle. As far as scenic qualities went, these performances showed no originality and followed the conventions of stage illusion by imitating realistic settings. Tagore's eminent painter nephew Abanindranāth Tagore recalled a production of *Bālmiki-pratibhā* that featured stuffed deer, birds made of cotton perched on real branches, and a painted backdrop of a forest scene with a boar hidden behind the trees. In a later performance, one actor entered leading a horse, while rain was made to fall on stage via a tin waterpipe overhead.[26] Yet we should not forget the fact noted by one reviewer in 1881 that 'a maiden from a respectable family acted before the public' for the first time.[27] From the beginning, the Tagores rejected the traditional practice of female impersonation and gave equal acting opportunities to their women. They even went to the other extreme: the distaff side of the family played all the parts, including those of men, in the original 1888 production of *Māyār khelā*.

The unexpected theoretical volte-face in his essay 'Rangamancha' resulted in the new dramaturgy that Tagore adopted in Santiniketan from 1908. Some of the season plays, however, capitalized on the natural surroundings available there. *Phālguni* premiered in 1915 on an open-air 'set' shorn of artificiality: 'The setting was an elaborate garden with real trees, flowers and rustic seats with a swing thrown in.'[28] It must have seemed only natural to enact plays about the seasons outdoors. When Tagore took it to a Kolkata auditorium, its artistic beauty stunned theatregoers; the historian Sukumār Sen termed it 'the most remarkable event in the history of Bengali stage ... in the current century'.[29] But a contemporary review records that decorative props were not exactly absent: 'The back drop was a blue curtain with hints of green. It was as if the forest and the sky had blended. A few stars.... A faint crescent moon.... A few branches of a tree.... A swing was attached to one of them. A few creepers, few tufts of grass.'[30] However, Tagore's niece Indirā Debi Chaudhurāni recollects it somewhat differently, her description suggesting a more symbolic *mise-en-scène*:

> In place of the earlier incongruous Western imitation, a blue backdrop had been used.... Against it, there was a single branch of a tree, with a single red flower at its tip, under a single ray of the pale moonshine.[31]

After this landmark event, it became fairly routine for a Tagore play to open in Santiniketan and transfer at a later date to Kolkata. But the most celebrated production, of *Dākghar*, does not fit this pattern. *Dākghar* had its world premiere in English as *The Post Office* in Dublin in 1913, as described later. The Bengali original was first staged on 3 May 1917 in Kolkata by the Brāhma Bālya Samāj at Mary Carpenter Hall, but Tagore was not associated with it. The boy chosen to act the lead, Āshāmukul Dās, joined the Santiniketan school that year, and Tagore cast him in the same role for his own production at Jorasanko. The first performance, on 10 October 1917, was followed by others into 1918. The scenography was the work of Tagore's other famous artist nephew, Gaganendranāth, assisted by Nandalāl Basu (Bose) and others. He designed an unusually detailed box set of a village hut with thatched roof and bamboo walls. As photos reveal, the trappings of naturalistic décor had not disappeared altogether, but one must hasten to add that they approximated more closely to an impressionistic style rather than a realistic one, and they proved the exception, for most Tagore productions dispensed with detailing in favour of minimalism.

To track that trajectory, we must return to the rudimentary origins of theatre in Santiniketan. Tagore's son Rathindranath tells us that the stage began as a 'ramshackle shed behind the Library, used as the dining hall', where 'a few rickety bedsteads' sufficed to create a platform.[32] Even after the construction of a regular hall, things did not change remarkably, for one viewer of *Rājā* in 1911 writes that there was just a raised platform with a drop scene, and the audience sat Indian-style on the floor.[33] While in the USA the following year, Tagore referred to the art design of Gordon Craig, in whose 'arrangement of the stage ... materials are few and simple and unaggressive'.[34] Much later, for a Kolkata revival of *Bisarjan* in 1923, Tagore used only a square altar with a lamp stand and flower tray upon it. The premiere of *Tapati* in 1929 occurred against the by-now ubiquitous indigo backdrop with just a couple of stools wrapped in embroidered cloth on stage. Tagore theorized this practice in his preface:

A poetic drama stakes claim upon the spectator's imagination; painting belittles that claim; the harm from that occurs to the spectator himself. The business of staging is swift, lively, mobile; scenery is its opposite; having entered unrightfully it remains in the midst of movement mute, still, delusory; by motionlessly enclosing the spectator's mental vision it keeps him thoroughly constrained. The rule of bidding farewell to the mind by setting a scene in the place where the mind should take its position has become prevalent in the mechanized age, it was not there previously.... For this very reason I do not indulge the childishness of raising and lowering scenery every now and then in those dramatic performances where I have any hand. Because it ridicules realistic truth as well as obstructs idealistic truth.[35]

Meanwhile in Santiniketan, till the end, Tagore often preferred to perform in an open-air ambience. A teacher there, Marjorie Sykes, describes one of the last performances of the dance drama *Chitrāngadā* in Tagore's lifetime:

The play takes place out of doors, the open verandah in front of the library of the *ashrama* being used for the stage. The audience sits on carpets, or on the grass, under the stars.... The musicians with their instruments sit on one side of the stage, together with the choir which is to sing the songs; and on the stage in the opposite corner sits the drummer who accompanies the dancing. There is no curtain to be lowered or raised; the stage is lighted and the action begins.

There is no scenery, but we are to know that the scene is a forest. A hunter enters, and dances a hunting scene to the accompaniment of male voices singing a hunting song. We picture the trees, the birds, the lovely surroundings. The hunter's work in the play is done, when he has called up the scene in our imagination.[36]

Most eyewitnesses of Tagore's productions have commented on the natural, spontaneous, beautiful, and elevated acting.[37] Tagore had watched the legendary Henry Irving in *Hamlet* and *The Bride of Lammermoor* in 1890 but disliked what he saw:

The actor very often exaggerates the emotional turmoil of a character by resorting to violent gesture and declamation.... A person who aims at imitating truth instead of expressing it is led to exaggerate, like a false witness in court.... The violence of his [Irving's] acting style stunned me. Such unrestrained excess destroys the clarity of the dramatic substance. It moves one externally, but I have never seen such an insurmountable barrier to entering into the heart of the matter.[38]

At the same time, Tagore disapproved of superficially naturalistic acting. A family anecdote proves this in a humorous way:

During a rehearsal of *Bisarjan*, Arunendranāth [Tagore] as Jaysingha, after stabbing himself in the chest, lay on the floor with both legs quivering. Rabindranath saw this and asked, 'Why are you shaking your legs?' Arunendranath replied, 'If I stab myself in the chest, wouldn't my body show slight tremors before I die?' Rabindranath countered, 'No, no, there is no need. We don't want such acutely realistic acting.'[39]

Believing that acting 'has the responsibility of drawing apart the curtain of naturalism to reveal the reality within',[40] Tagore emphasized the expression of this quality when directing. One of his best actresses, Sāhānā Debi (Basu), uncannily echoed almost these words when she said that Tagore's acting 'opened another world before my eyes – an inner world of beauty and truth'.[41] She has also testified to 'a wonderful understanding and easy relation between the director and the actors. Rarely ... have I seen such a singleminded devotion and team work.'[42] In fact, Rathindranath even compared their spirit to that of the Moscow Art Theatre and Abbey Theatre: 'In both of these enterprises, as at Santiniketan, it was not the individual artist so much as the effect produced by the spirit that moved the whole group of actors which impressed the audience and convinced them of the sincerity of the effort and gave them complete artistic satisfaction.'[43]

In this context we must remember the pedagogic aspect of Tagore's mature plays, which he initially directed with his schoolchildren as performers. William Pearson documented this aspect in the early years:

> At the end of each term arrangements are made for staging one of the poet's plays. The teachers and boys take the different parts.... The poet coaches the actors himself, first reading the play aloud, and then reading it over with those who are to take part. During the days when the play is being rehearsed there are not many classes held, for the boys of the whole school are always present at the rehearsals.... In this way the ideas of the poet are assimilated by the boys, without their having to make any conscious effort.[44]

Rathindranath corroborated this practice – one of the earliest Indian processes of educational theatre, a concept most theorized in twentieth-century USA:

> Father himself selected the actors after putting them through hard tests. In those days he preferred to hold the rehearsals in an open place and did not mind the whole Asrama looking on and listening. As a result, the rehearsals of plays and of music were of great educative value to the whole community and not to the participants only.[45]

In a farsighted interview much later, which proves how much of a trailblazer he was in the field of theatre in education, Tagore told his friend Leonard Elmhirst:

> The best actors will always be those who have been trained to use the whole body as a tool for the expression of thought, of emotion or of sentiment. Words, to convey the full perfection of their message, must be accompanied by the appropriate bodily movement. If our schools were run on the right lines, boys and girls would never lose

their natural gifts of bodily expression, making use for that purpose of all their limbs.

Unfortunately, today, in civilized communities, expression through movement is repressed and is no longer looked upon as quite proper.... We pay actors, therefore, to cultivate their natural gifts, and to give us the chance of experiencing the joys we crave, but can no longer achieve....

... I advise you to make the practice of drama and of the histrionic arts compulsory for all children.[46]

Tagore always composed his scripts to fit the casting pool available to him. Since his school began as a boys-only ashram, six of the first eight plays written there – *Prāyashchitta* and *Rājā* excepted – contained no female roles. Sizeable crowds of 'Boys' or 'Students' or 'Youths' figured prominently in them. Not until much later in the history of Santiniketan did the number of girls surpass that of boys, and when that happened Tagore responded appropriately, with the all-women first edition of *Natir pujā*. Meanwhile, by casting women alongside men and exhibiting these productions in Kolkata, Tagore persistently chipped away at the social perception that girls from decent, respectable families should not participate in theatre. The lead actress of *Natir pujā*, Gauri (Basu) Bhanja, recalls the unease in Santiniketan while planning the Kolkata performances: 'Girls singing and dancing on the stage may have provoked criticism, to prevent which, Gurudeb joined the cast.'[47] Thus, its final authorized edition added the part of a Buddhist mendicant or *bhikshu* that Tagore had enacted. Nevertheless, as late as Tagore's very last production, *Shyāmā* (1939), the noted writer Sajanikānta Dās used these words in his review: 'The language of the body is in no way less than the language of poetry. I had misgivings about the propriety of the students of Visva-Bharati enacting this tale of physical love.... I found the touch of genius could make everything possible.'[48]

During the 1920s Tagore developed a greater interest in stylized theatrical forms. One of the earliest manifestations of this trend was the 'mime' performance of *Arup ratan* in 1924, about which one spectator wrote:

The musicians and narrators sat in a half-circle near the wings, and down-stage were the actors miming in time with them. The threefold combination of narration, recitation and miming produced a novel and remarkable effect on the stage.

... Tagore could not fail to note the favourable effect produced by the small element of dance that it carried.[49]

We have already noticed how he began to insert dances in his season plays soon afterwards. Furthering this line of experimentation to the utmost, disenchanted by what he considered to be the limitations of the spoken word, he choreographed the full-scale dance dramas of the 1930s. Much impressed on a trip to Indonesia by Javanese and Balinese dance (which themselves had early Indian origins), he borrowed liberally from diverse traditions: mainly the lyrical Manipuri and the energetic Kathākali, which he put on the Santiniketan curriculum, thereby helping to validate their classical status at a time when they were popularly considered as folk forms, but Bharatanātyam and Kathak too, various folk styles, and other foreign sources such as Japanese dance and the Kandyan dance of Sri Lanka. Critics frequently take for granted that he set out to create his own dance form. In fact, he viewed these final works primarily as theatre, not dance, and used with the greatest catholicity whatever idioms he found suitable to convey the ideas and images. Encouraged by positive reactions, and to generate revenue for Visva-Bharati, he took some of these productions on tour outside Bengal – which he had never done before – where they overwhelmed audiences with their sheer artistry. But no research has been conducted on their impact and influence in various parts of India, since it requires acquaintance with the concerned regional languages in which reviews appeared in periodicals.

The special nature and function of Tagore songs in his drama demand some comment. Music literally circumscribes his theatre career, which started and ended with libretti that he set fully to music. Nearly every play he wrote contains original songs, sometimes numbering over twenty. They contribute significantly to the almost tangible atmosphere, build dramatic intensity, provide lyrical relief, offer choric commentary, and even present the climax through a concluding song in quite a few plays. *Arup ratan* provides a case in point of Tagore's songs as the quintessence of the theatrical experience, delineating through them the spiritual progress of its protagonist from ignorance to knowledge; they form the play in miniature, a paean to the awakening of the soul. It might even help a reader to conceive of Tagore's dramatic structure in terms of musical composition, like movements in symphonies or the elaboration of an Indian *rāga*.

NON-TAGOREAN PERFORMANCES

In this section I shall highlight the important productions of Tagore's plays directed by others in the one hundred years since he won international fame. Interestingly, the first of these came before the Nobel Prize award:

the world premiere of *The Post Office* at the Abbey Theatre, Dublin, in May 1913. No doubt it was facilitated by the nascent friendship between Tagore and Yeats, who was impressed enough by the translation to co-direct it with Lady Augusta Gregory. The influential Irish dramatist Padraic Colum, reviewing it for the *Manchester Guardian*,[50] was perhaps the first critic to link Tagorean drama with Maurice Maeterlinck, a connection that surfaced repeatedly later, though Tagore himself denied it and, indeed, the two playwrights had completely different worldviews.

The production moved in July to the Court Theatre in London, where newspapers did not quite know what to make of this new – and Indian – dramatist. The opening sentence of the review in the *Times* struck the note that henceforth dominated comment on Tagorean drama, calling it 'dreamy, symbolical, spiritual' and continuing, 'It is a curious play, leaving to a certain extent a sense of incompleteness, since it ends before its climax, rich in poetical thought and imagery.'[51] Others were openly hostile and patronizing, a vein of criticism that plagued Tagore afterwards. According to the *Westminster Gazette*,

> it is one of those elaborate attempts to be simple and elemental which are favored by those who by non-commercial drama mean drama that nobody would pay to see…. [N]o doubt it is a creditable attempt by an Indian gentleman to write a play. But it was all on one note and never moved one inch…. I cannot remember anything said by anybody to cause it to go on even for the short time that it lasted.[52]

On the other hand, trade magazines of the theatre and entertainment community proved much more welcoming. The *Era* reported: 'This delicate and mystic little piece was admirably acted … Lilian Jagoe giving a very impressive and pathetically beautiful portrayal of little Amal, … one that will long linger in the memory.'[53] The *Stage* followed suit, commending Jagoe's 'wistful' performance and praising the 'sweet simplicity' of Lennox Robinson's set:

> [I]t consisted merely of a screen or framework, with backing of contrasted hue. Thus, the exterior of Madhav's house was shown as white, with jet-black background, and the interior as of crimson colour, with deep green to represent the opening beyond.[54]

Robinson, who had joined the Abbey in 1910 and became one of its pillars for over forty years, referred to his sets as 'Gordon Craig Screens' – a reference to Craig's designs that echoed Tagore's own.[55]

Post Nobel, when Tagore's worldwide star was at its zenith for about a decade, we hear of many Tagore plays performed across the globe, but our unfamiliarity with the languages concerned hampers analysis of their reception. For instance, it would be interesting to know of the reactions to two translated versions of *The King of the Dark Chamber* simply because of the reputation of those who staged them: the Moscow Art Theatre, Prague Group (1918) and the Kammerspiele, Berlin (1921). Maria Germanova, possessed of a statuesque stage presence, acted as Sudarshanā in the former, while the legendary regisseur Max Reinhardt mounted the latter in the intimate theatre he had built, perfectly suited for 'chamber plays'. The same wish applies to two productions directed by the cosmopolitanist Georges Pitoëff in Paris – *Sacrifice* (1919), and *Dākghar* as *Amal et la lettre du roi* (Amal and the Letter from the King, translated by André Gide, scored by Darius Milhaud, 1937) – and to *Chitrāngadā* designed by the Futurist artist Enrico Prampolini in Rome (1920). For *The Post Office* at the renowned Volksbühne in Berlin (1921), we have two accessible accounts. *The Modern Review* translated a German review, which said that the audience of survivors from the First World War was touched by this 'drama of inner forces which we Westerners have almost lost'.[56] Tagore himself attended and liked it: '[A]ltogether the whole thing was a success. But it was a different interpretation from that of ours ... suggestive of a fairy-story, full of elusive beauty.'[57] Unfortunately, Tagore cancelled his trip that year to Spain, where García Lorca, Salvador Dali, and Luis Buñuel had rehearsed *Sacrificio* to welcome him, but aborted it in disappointment.

Another world premiere in English of a major Tagore play has come to light only recently, because the artists' amateur status obscured their achievement. *Red Oleanders*, the authorized translation under Tagore's name,[58] was staged in Mumbai probably in the last quarter of 1928 by the nationalist Mrinālini Chattopādhyāy, then Principal of the New High School for Girls. The Englishman who performed the Raja, Lester Hutchinson, was arrested in 1929 along with other leftist sympathizers during the Communist witchhunt in the notorious Meerut Conspiracy Case. He recalled the production facetiously in his memoirs:

> Because the play was completely incomprehensible, it was received very well by the audience.... The word *red* has only one meaning for the Indian police: ... they came to the conclusion that *Red Oleanders* must be communist propaganda.[59]

Returning to Kolkata in the 1920s, we should note the unusual elements in some of the productions on the Bengali commercial stage. *Grihaprabesh* by the Art Theatre (Star Theatre, 1925) created minor theatrical history on account of Gaganendranath Tagore's scenography, which depicted for the first time on the Bengali public stage two adjoining rooms, the action flowing swiftly from one half of the set to the other. *Shesh rakshā* by Nātyamandir (Cornwallis Theatre, 1927) featured the first use of audience participation in Bengal. The director, Shishir Bhāduri, broke the proscenium barrier in the final scene, inviting the spectators to join the wedding festivities in the play. The house responded with great enthusiasm, singing along to the marriage songs and intermingling with the cast on stage in celebration of the happy ending. However, Bhaduri's *Tapati* (1929), though critically praised, failed commercially, proving yet again that the average Bengali theatregoer's tastes were not compatible with the complexity of Tagore's serious works.

A polarization set in. The professionals looked upon Tagore as too highbrow, comprehensible only to the intellectual elite or the select coterie of people connected with Santiniketan; for their part, Tagore's disciples educated at Santiniketan more or less ignored the public stage or looked down upon it with condescension. The twain have rarely met since. The Second World War, Tagore's death in 1941, and India's independence in 1947 interrupted thinking on theatre. Meanwhile the myth grew that only those who had trained in Santiniketan could perform Tagorean drama: without their expertise these plays were unplayable. This mental block was finally dissipated only in the mid-1950s when the pathbreaking group Bohurupee,[60] in the vanguard of Kolkata's new, consciously socialistic, and committed 'group theatre' movement, started producing one Tagore play after another with astonishing facility.

Under the celebrated Shambhu (Sombhu) Mitra as director, Bohurupee commenced its assault upon the prevailing neglect of Tagore's plays with one of the most difficult, *Raktakarabi* (1954). Unanimously acclaimed in Kolkata, it toured other Indian cities, and its impact did not diminish for non-Bengali viewers. In a play that even most Bengali directors had avoided as too symbolical, the nationally respected Kannada author Ādya Rangāchārya discovered characters who 'live, talk and move like people we know in real life'.[61] A Delhi reviewer stated that it 'stood out like a grand symphony which overwhelms and sweeps you off your feet'.[62] Another critic described Khāled Chaudhuri's (Chowdhury) set and Tāpas Sen's lighting in some detail:

They used austere, highly suggestive sets which fell into an overall geometric pattern. The palace of the King ... suggested malignant strength.... The lighting was experimental and was given a liquid life of its own which rose and sank with the mood of the lines....

The overall effect was to enlarge the arena of action ... into an extra semi-abstract dimension of shadows.... Here poetry and drama were fused in a harmony that lightly walked the thin dividing line between fantasy and reality.[63]

Bohurupee staged other important plays at fairly regular intervals: *Dākghar* (1957), *Muktadhārā* (1959), *Bisarjan* (1961), and *Rājā* (1964). We cannot overestimate Mitra's contribution to the revival of interest in Tagore's drama. He recalled modestly, 'It has been my good fortune to be told by hundreds of people after they saw *Raktakarabi* ... that they realised then and for the first time what a great playwright Tagore was.'[64] He believed that 'Tagore's major plays grapple with the fundamentals' and the characters 'assume individual identities while retaining at the same time their universal, archetypal and symbolic qualities.... And it is because they have such individual personalities that the plays become eminently actable.' He therefore conceived of a more 'subjective' style of acting attuned to Tagore's poetic prose, 'in the way in which it was once so natural for Hamlet to move into a soliloquy'.[65]

The most publicized intercultural production of Tagore was the off-Broadway *The King of the Dark Chamber* by Krishna Shāh, who later became a Hollywood director. First staged at Iowa State University in 1960, it started a New York run at the Jan Hus House in February 1961, continued for months with several shows each week to full or near-capacity houses, and culminated in a South Africa tour in 1962 where a consolidated audience, estimated at over 50,000, saw it in Cape Town and Durban. It was a minor sensation. Evidently inspired, the leading critic Robert Brustein wrote:

This 20th Century Indian masterpiece, with its allegorical fairy-tale atmosphere and its highly charged poetic intensity, is a stunning theatrical work.... Clearly an inspired dramatic artist, Tagore manages to exploit all the various resources of the stage – music, mime, chorus, lyrical speech, song, declamation, gesture, makeup, costume – in a completely original manner. For in his hands, the conventions of Eastern theatre are liberating devices ..., freeing his imagination to an extent almost unequalled in modern Western tradition. Tagore's dramatic world is so multifarious that elements of broad farcical humor, sinister melodrama, and metaphysical soul-drama can jostle each other with no apparent friction; and his dramatic action is so multi-leveled that it becomes fairy tale, metaphor and philosophy all at once.[66]

One indeed wonders if this is the same Tagore to whom critics reacted ambivalently half a century previously. Brustein spoke of a 'charming and child-like naïveté' – a 'ceremony of innocence that Yeats (in his *Plays for Dancers*) and Brecht (in his *Caucasian Chalk Circle*) tried to restore to the Western theatre as a necessary antidote to the clichés of an exhausted realism'. Most of the reviewers complimented the deep baritone of Brock Peters as the Voice of the king and the Obie Award-winning grace of Surya Kumāri (the Telugu actor-singer-dancer) as his queen. Tom Driver pointed out the 'allegory of the soul' and considered the scenes in the dark chamber, done in silhouette, 'especially moving because of their bold use of the language of erotic love to express the soul's love of God'.[67]

However, exoticism may have been an important element in the production's success. The reviews dwelt more upon the sensuous, especially the visual, aspect rather than the thematic. According to Theophilus Lewis, 'As a series of stage pictures, the play will appeal to connoisseurs of lacquer and jade.... Still, one wonders if Tagore's ghost, wandering into the Jan Hus, would be pleased with a production that distracts attention from the mystical import.'[68] The *New Yorker* confirmed its superficial appeal:

> It is not so much Tagore's thought that entrances one, however, as the play's heady visual fragments – the wicked kings with their towering gold-and-white templelike hats and garish clown faces; a dancer, bare to the waist, moving slowly toward the back of the stage, his arms straight out and waving like seaweed, his back muscles revolving incredibly in opposite directions; and the terrible King himself, whom we never see, gliding in a tall, muscular silhouette through the dark chamber toward his tiny, quivering Queen.[69]

Perhaps Krishna Shah could not live up to his own aims spelt out in his programme notes:

> It is vital that the factor of novelty not become the keynote of the production. The exotic flavor of the Orient should not be unduly stressed to the detriment of the basic thesis of the play. Whatever 'spectacle' is natural to the play should be aesthetically conceived. The direction should attempt to recreate the lyrical and exciting theatre that Tagore intended.[70]

Some of his devices may certainly have been legitimate and inventive, such as the elaborate use of classical Indian *mudra*s or of a Jātrā-style chorus that also functioned physically as trees, lamps, doors, and flames. Undeniably, Shah deserves praise for exposing American audiences to a representation of Tagore's drama more authentic than anything before or since. There was the rare critical dissent, though, and it came unexpectedly from the respected journal *Theatre Arts*:

> I have been amazed by the reaction of my fellow critics ... turning their prayer wheels in ecstasy ever since this really terrible piece of tushery oozed (rather than burst) upon the unlikely surroundings of the Jan Hus House.... This is a very, very slow Indian drama full of Implications rather than Symbols.... All this takes a very long time, much of it in darkness, and the spoken words are in a kind of Poona prose poetry.[71]

Back in India, for the next four decades until the lapse of Tagore's copyright, Visva-Bharati's conservativism remained blind to theatrical exigencies and possibilities. The dogmatic imperative for granting permission to prospective producers fell on staying faithful to the authorized text, ignoring the legitimate question: what about the fruitful artistic middle ground of interpretation between bardolatry and iconoclasm? In 1984, Theatre Workshop's *Bisarjan* became a test case. The directors, Bibhās Chakrabarti and Ashok Mukhopādhyāy, took a brave step, creating a new prose script by splicing the original tragedy with appropriate passages from Tagore's own source novel and condensed English rendering, *Sacrifice*, translated back into Bengali. But this adventurous, praiseworthy idea met with rejection from many cultural bigwigs, who thought the group had taken unnecessary liberties with Tagore's sacrosanct work. The show flopped, leading to recriminations.[72]

Not surprisingly, the few imaginative productions during this period came from outside India. In 1989, Wolfram Mehring directed a minimalist German *The Post Office* in Chur, Switzerland. He then collaborated in Kolkata with the group Sangbarta in 1992 on a Bengali revival, co-directed by Sunil Dās, that travelled in India, Bangladesh, and the UK. Mehring used no set or props, barring a rectangular white 'ceiling' suspended above downstage right to indicate that the space below it was Amal's room. He applied the abstract tradition of German expressionism and converted the play into a spiritual allegory from the start, in pure white costumes. He doubled roles, deliberately slowed down the delivery of lines to achieve a stylized effect, and employed half-masks apparently to distinguish insincere characters, though he also applied them on the royal herald and physician.

In London in 1993, Jill Parvin took her cue from a 1942 performance of the same play in the Warsaw Ghetto by Jewish orphans under Dr Janusz Korczak, facing certain death at Nazi hands. Korczak had had an amazing dream in which Tagore asked him to stage *The Post Office*. Parvin set her production in that historical time and place as a play within a play where, appropriately and movingly, Korczak enacted the royal physician at the end. Her performance text in print retains the metatheatrical structure.[73]

In Dhaka in 2000, the Centre for Asian Theatre offered *Rājā* as an eye-opening experience. Nailā Āzād directed with a fluidity, *joie de vivre*, and sincerity that Tagore would have loved. It was remarkable for a young director to reveal such mastery of editing (the text chopped and rearranged liberally, for example, interchanging the first two scenes), physicalization (in a spiritual play), colour (a vivid spring palette), mass choreography (freed from the shackles of conventional Tagorean dance, yet precise), and music (full-throated solos and choruses sung by the actors themselves). The novel interpretation set up a Buddhist backdrop – justifiably, for Tagore sourced the play from a *Jātaka* tale – and portrayed Thākurdā, the grandfather figure who in Tagore often personifies the wisdom of age, not as an elder but as a priest.

Some eminent alumni of Santiniketan carried forward Tagore's theatre activism. The renowned dancer Mrinālini Sarābhāi took her dance production of *Tāser desh* by Darpana, Āhmedābad, to China in 1978. She remembers:

> On the first night, we danced Tasher Desh.... The very next morning, the Ambassador [of India] requested me to delete Tasher Desh from our repertoire. Of course, I understood, for the Tagore play showed ill effects of regimentation and here the country was China.[74]

In 1993, Ritā Gānguly directed her Delhi group, Kaladharmi, in an open-air Hindi performance of *Muktadhārā* in the Narmadā river valley, in solidarity with the 'Narmadā Bāchāo' (Save the Narmada) movement against the controversial river dam project.[75] In 2004, the Odia grassroots group Natya Chetana toured at least six dam sites in Odisha with *Muktadhārā*, adapted from a script translated by Krishnā Mohānty. Mohanty was the daughter of Mālati Devi and Nabakrushna Chaudhuri (a former chief minister of the state), founders of Bāji Raut Chhātrābās, an ashram in Āngul modelled on Santiniketan. The ashramites enacted the play.[76]

Two Kolkata group productions during the 1990s merit mention. Tagore's most evergreen comedy, *Chirakumār sabhā*, received definitive and historically accurate period-piece treatment from Calcutta Performers under

Tamāl Rāychaudhuri in 1996. And Kalapi's director, Anil Mukhopādhyāy, interpreted the rarely seen *Grihaprabesh* in 1998 as a lyrical human allegory similar to *Dākghar*. At the turn of the millennium, mime maestro Jogesh Datta slipped easily through Visva-Bharati's net, because his medium was non-verbal: Jogesh Mime Academy's *Kholo dwār* (Open the Door, 2000), based on *Raktakarabi*, forged a 'text' without words, proving the potential for conceptualizing Tagore's plays anew. Likewise, Tagore's dance dramas received innovative hybrid choreography in adaptations by Manjushri Chāki Sarkār (Sircar).

Only after the copyright regime expired in 2001 did Tagore's creative restlessness finally find fulfilment among Bengali directors collectively. Blind Opera's *Rājā* (2003) directed by Shubhāshis Gangopādhyāy stunned spectators. Tagore might never have imagined that his classic about deep inner vision versus glittering outer appearances could one day be staged by the visually impaired, and Blind Opera could not have chosen a more relevant play for themselves. Apart from the obvious resonances of a sightless Sudarshana (Sutapā Sāmanta) wanting to see her invisible Rājā, Blind Opera rendered the songs and Batu Pāl choreographed the dancers with unbelievable power. The same year, audiences were awestruck by the rock group Insomnia singing a cappella harmonies (without even acoustic instrumentation) for Best of Kolkata Campus's deconstructed *Raktakarabi*. That, and director Parnab Mukherjee's stroke of genius in placing it inside the bowels of Apeejay School's unfinished basement, made this production very different. The audience could physically suffer the sweaty, stifling darkness of Yakshapuri underground, led to the four sites installed by designer Sanchayan Ghosh as urban detritus out of cellophane and discarded computers, to the sound of loud industrial percussion.

Rangroop's *Shesh rakshā* (2005), edited by senior dramatist Mohit Chattopādhyāy to suit contemporary running time, was immensely enjoyable both for Tagore's timeless wit and for excellent performances directed by Simā Mukhopādhyāy. In 2006, Suman Mukhopādhyāy's direction of *Raktakarabi* for Tritiya Sutra came close to matching Tagore's revolutionary stagecraft. The curtain rose to reveal barbed wire on the proscenium line, separating us from the cast gathered on the other side, staring blankly or pleadingly at us, almost to set them free. It epitomized Suman's highly visual style, complemented by Shankar Debnāth's forbidding set looking like a concentration camp, of heavy cell-like doors and a huge grey sculpted head upstage literally topped by a megaphone that became the perfect medium for the Rājā's voice. But Suman's biggest achievement was to make his actors deliver the lines and even songs naturally, detonating the theory that only poetic speech *à la* Shambhu Mitra works for Tagore. All the characters instantly turned into flesh and blood.

Outside Bengal, Kalakshetra's *Dākghar* (2006) from Imphal completely transformed young Amal into a symbol. Instead of the child whom we expect, Heisnam Kanhailāl cast his sixty-year-old wife, H. Sābitri, the leading lady of Manipuri theatre. Immediately, Amal signified something else: not just the human spirit but Manipur herself, indoctrinated and languishing in ill health as the doctor prescribes the 'cure' of closing all windows. In London the same year, Myriad Productions' multiracial and interchangeable-casting experimental interpretation of *Red Oleander*[77] in English, directed by Kevin Rowntree, received appreciation from critics:

> The King … (with a postmodern flourish) is played by several of his own subjects. Four actors, joined in Chinese Dragon formation, crouch and veer behind a huge wire fence. Each repeats the martial, pincered gestures of the leader (the vivid and muscular Sally Okafor). They look like a giant scorpion trapped in a cage of mirrors, deadly and abject – the ideal body for Tagore's shadow demon.[78]

Rowntree remarked of the play: 'Eighty years after its writing, *Red Oleander* has special relevance in a world threatened by the forces of national self-interest and state control.'[79]

In the last decade, two moving Tagore productions emerged from prison therapy programmes conducted by the West Bengal Correctional Services for their inmates. *Bālmiki-pratibhā* (2010) proved how theatre can transform their lives. The director, Alokānandā Rāy, took art into the correctional home, instilling dignity and self-esteem into her once-demoralized cast and crew. They used forms they knew, like Chhau dance and cottage handicrafts, to create everything down to the costumes and props. Tagore himself could not have foreseen a more appropriate match of actor with character: Nigel Akkarā, serving time, subsequently released and now rehabilitated, performed the part of Ratnakar the robber chief redeemed into Valmiki, composer of the *Rāmāyana*. Similarly, for director Pradip Bhattāchārya in the 2014 *Yakshapuri* (the original title of *Raktakarabi*), to imply that penitentiary conditions resemble those in Tagore's allegorical town took gumption. He too demolished the notion that Tagore composed this play in a high-flown literary register unrelated to reality. Not once did the audience sense that the mostly unlettered actor-inmates spoke artificially; on the contrary, their lines flowed as though they actually conversed like this, whether in their villages or in jail. In hindsight, how forced the same speeches sound when delivered by sophisticated urban performers pretending to be rustic!

Approaching eighty years since the death of modern India's greatest theatrical creator, his dramatic works still do not enthuse enough directors as they should. Contrast this with Shakespeare in the UK and USA: so many annual Shakespeare festivals do brisk business because so many companies regularly mount new productions. In my considered opinion, Tagore is not a lesser playwright than Shakespeare. Thus, Indian theatre workers neglect their preeminent modern dramatist, and Bengalis fail to project his genius convincingly, chiefly through lack of new translations. Various stage interpretations establish the strength of a classic author; even if we disagree about the result, the debate serves to revitalize the classic through rediscovery. The other way is to consciously revive the plays that have rarely or never been done.

NOTES

1. Rabindranath Tagore, *My Reminiscences*, tr. Surendranath Tagore (London: Macmillan, 1917), 194; *Jibansmriti*, RRVB 17:381.
2. *RRVB* 25:425.
3. Tagore, *My Reminiscences*, 208; *Jibansmriti*, RRVB 17:390.
4. 'An Indian Folk Religion', *Creative Unity*, EW 2:523.
5. Rathindranath Tagore, *On the Edges of Time* (Bombay: Orient Longman, 1958), 103.
6. Years indicate first publication, not the usual convention of first performance, because some of the plays were staged much after their printing, and a few never staged in Tagore's lifetime.
7. Tagore, *My Reminiscences*, 238; *Jibansmriti*, RRVB 17:410.
8. Ibid., 183; *RRVB* 17:375.
9. The theoretical and practical manual of Sanskrit theatre.
10. Rabindranath Tagore, 'The Stage', tr. Surendranath Tagore, *Modern Review* 14 (December 1913), 543–5; *RRVB* 5:449–53.
11. For an extended treatment see 'The Message of the Forest', EW 3:385–400.
12. With the variant title *Nataraj-riturangashala* (Nataraj's Theatre of the Seasons).
13. The Macmillan translation by Kshitishchandra Sen, *The King of the Dark Chamber*, was unauthorized. Tagore was very unhappy with it, but most scholars remain unmindful of its publication history. See Rabindranath Tagore, *Three Plays*, tr. and ed. Ananda Lal (1987; 2nd ed., New Delhi: Oxford University Press, 2001), 98–100.
14. Tagore had written an all-female farce in 1897, *Lakshmir pariksha* (The Testing of Lakshmi), presumably for performance by young girls and

eventually published in *Kāhini* (1900), an anthology of short verse drama, but it does not seem to have been staged till later, in the Santiniketan phase of his life.

15. Tagore, *Three Plays*, tr. Lal, 224–5; *Tapati*, RRVB 21:147.
16. The years in this sentence indicate performance in the Kolkata theatres, not publication.
17. Rabindranath Tagore, *Chandalika*, tr. Ananda Lal, in *Shades of Difference: Selected Writings of Rabindranath Tagore* (New Delhi: Social Science Press, 2015), 98; *Nrityanātya chandālikā, RRVB* 25:165.
18. 'The World of Personality', *Personality* (1917), *EW* 2:366.
19. Letter to Lokendranāth Pālit, July 1892 ('Patrālāp', *Sāhitya, RRVB* 8:478), tr. Viswanath Chatterjee, in 'Tagore as a Shakespearean Critic', *Tagore Studies*, 1972–73, 20.
20. Rabindranath Tagore, *Letters from Java*, ed. Supriya Roy (Kolkata: Visva-Bharati, 2010), 86 (Letter 11, tr. Indiradevi Chaudhurani).
21. Rabindranath Tagore, *Letters to a Friend* (1928), *EW* 3:238.
22. 'Woman', *Personality, EW* 2:414, 416.
23. 'The Religion of the Forest', *Creative Unity, EW* 2:516.
24. Ananda Lal, 'A Historiography of Modern Indian Theatre', in *Modern Indian Theatre*, ed. Nandi Bhatia (New Delhi: Oxford University Press, 2009).
25. See Kironmoy Raha, 'Tagore on Theatre', *Natya*, Tagore Centenary Number (1961), 7.
26. Abanindranath Tagore, *Abanindra rachanābali* (Kolkata: Prakāsh bhaban, 1973), 1:133, 149, 151.
27. *Sādhārani*, 27 February 1881; tr. Raha, 'Tagore on Theatre', 7.
28. Rathindranath Tagore, *Edges of Time*, 102.
29. Sukumar Sen, *History of Bengali Literature* (New Delhi: Sahitya Akademi, 1979), 279.
30. *Bhārati*, Phalgun 1322 (*February 1916); tr. Raha, 'Tagore on Theatre', 8.
31. Indira Debi Chaudhurani, *Smriti samput* (Kolkata: Visva-Bharati, 2001), 3:26; tr. Abhijit Sen, 'Rabindranath's Theatre', in *Towards Tagore*, ed. Sanjukta Dasgupta et al. (Kolkata: Visva-Bharati, 2014), 504.
32. Rathindranath Tagore, *Edges of Time*, 98–9.
33. Sāhānā Debi, quoted by Ashok Sen, *Rabindra-nātya-parikramā* (Kolkata: A. Mukherjee, 1975), 59.
34. Letter to William Rothenstein, ?4 November 1912, in *Imperfect Encounter*, ed. Mary M. Lago (Cambridge: Harvard University Press, 1972), 58.
35. Tagore, *Three Plays*, tr. Lal, 194.
36. Marjorie Sykes, *Rabindranath Tagore* (Chennai: Longmans, Green, 1947), 108.
37. Ramananda Chatterjee, *The Golden Book of Tagore* (Kolkata: Golden Book Committee, 1931), v; Asit Hāldār and Sahana Debi, tr. Raha, 'Tagore on Theatre', 9.

38. 'Antar bāhir', *Pather sanchay;* *RRVB* 26:506.
39. Amitā Tagore, quoted by Rudraprasād Chakrabarti, *Rangamancha o rabindranāth* (Kolkata: Ānanda, 1995), 54.
40. 'Antar bāhir', *RRVB* 26:505.
41. Sahana Debi, *Ānandabājār patrikā*, 8 May 1961; tr. Raha, 'Tagore on Theatre', 9.
42. Ibid.
43. Rathindranath Tagore, *Edges of Time*, 100.
44. W.W. Pearson, *Shantiniketan* (New York: Macmillan, 1916), 61–2.
45. Rathindranath Tagore, *Edges of Time*, 99.
46. Rabindranath Tagore, 'The Art of Movement in Education', in *Rabindranath Tagore: Pioneer in Education*, ed. L[eonard] K[night] Elmhirst (London: John Murray, 1961), 105–6.
47. Gauri Bhanja, quoted by Chakrabarti, 207–8; tr. mine.
48. *Ānandabājār patrikā*, 8 February 1939, quoted by Chakrabarti, 301; tr. Abhijit Sen, 509.
49. G.D. Khanolkar, *The Lute and the Plough* (Mumbai: Book Centre, 1963), 269.
50. Padraic Colum, 'The Abbey Theatre', *Manchester Guardian*, 21 May 1913, 6.
51. 'The Irish Players', *The Times*, 11 July 1913, 8.
52. J.W., 'Royal Court Theatre', *Westminster Gazette*, 11 July 1913, 3.
53. 'The Post Office', *Era*, 16 July 1913, 14.
54. 'The Court', *Stage*, 17 July 1913, 20.
55. Lennox Robinson, *Ireland's Abbey Theatre* (London: Sidgwick and Jackson, 1951), 109.
56. Tr. by Arabinda Basu (Bose); see Tagore, *Three Plays*, tr. Lal, ix.
57. Tagore, *Letters to a Friend*, *EW* 3:310.
58. As with other translations ascribed to Tagore, a Bengali student may have drafted the bulk of the English version: see Tagore, *Three Plays*, tr. Lal, 103.
59. Lester Hutchinson, *Conspiracy at Meerut* (London: George Allen & Unwin, 1935), 33–5. See proceedings on 3 October 1929, *Meerut Conspiracy Case, 1929–32*, bound volume 3 (Meerut: Saraswati Machine Press, 1932), 76, 79, available at https://dspace.gipe.ac.in/xmlui/handle/10973/22829?show=full (accessed 17 June 2019), and the committal order of the Additional District Magistrate, 258, available at https://dspace.gipe.ac.in/xmlui/bitstream/handle/10973/33780/GIPE-118846.pdf?...2...n (accessed 17 June 2019).
60. Names of theatre groups spelt according to their own practice.
61. Adya Rangacharya, *The Indian Theatre* (New Delhi: National Book Trust, 1971), 146.
62. L.M. Thapalyal, 'Tagore on Delhi Stage', *Natya*, Tagore Centenary Number (1961), 80.

63. Shiv S. Kapur, 'Rakat [*sic*] Karabi – Notes on a Play', *Quest*, April–May 1956, 40.

64. Sombhu Mitra, 'Reflections on Tagore's Plays', *Illustrated Weekly of India*, 7 May 1961, 41.

65. Sombhu Mitra, 'Building from Tagore', *The Drama Review*, Spring 1971, 204.

66. Robert Brustein, 'Off Broadway's Trials and Triumph', *New Republic*, 6 March 1961, 21–2.

67. Tom F. Driver, 'Revolutionless Worlds', *Christian Century*, 26 April 1961, 535–7.

68. Theophilus Lewis, 'Theatre', *America*, 11 March 1961, 768.

69. Whitney Balliett, 'Off Broadway', *New Yorker*, 18 February 1961, 93.

70. Krishna Shah, 'The Director and the Play', in *Rabindranath Tagore Centenary*, ed. Rose Mukerji (production brochure, New York, 1961), 23.

71. Alan Pryce-Jones, 'Alan Pryce-Jones at the Theatre', *Theatre Arts* 45 (April 1961, 68).

72. I have recounted its history briefly in 'Tagore in Kolkata Theatre: 1986–2010' in *Towards Tagore*, 515–46. Other productions during this period are also discussed in more detail in that essay. I reviewed all the productions individually in *The Telegraph* (Kolkata): they are too numerous to cite separately here.

73. See Rabindranath Tagore, *The Post Office*, tr. William Radice (London: The Tagore Centre, 1996), 10. Martin Kämpchen contrasted the approaches of the two productions in 'Rabindranath Tagore on the European Stage', *India International Centre Quarterly* 24, Spring (1997): 1–12.

74. See Utpal K. Banerjee, 'Last of the Tagoreans', *The Pioneer*, 22 January 2016.

75. Verbal communication. Shyāmali Khāstagir, associated with the Narmada Bachao movement, had requested Ganguly to take the production to a dam site (I have been unable to verify where). For Khastagir's initiative, see Tapasyā Ghosh, ed., *Muktadhārā* (Kolkata: Akshar, 2007), 8.

76. Natya Chetana also staged it in many other places: see their *Annual Report*, 2004–5. Malati Devi (née Sen) had rehearsed for Tagore's aborted production of the play.

77. Title as in Ananda Lal's translation, used in this production.

78. Caroline McGinn, 'Red Oleander', *Time Out*, 10 July 2006.

79. Quoted by Amit Roy, 'Raktakarabi Clocks an English First', *The Telegraph*, Kolkata, 9 July 2006.

The Prose Fiction of Rabindranath Tagore

SUPRIYA CHAUDHURI

In 1877, when he was just sixteen years old and had begun to compose the lyrics that would form part of *Bhānusingha thākurer padābali* (The Songs of Bhānusingha Thākur), Rabindranāth Tagore contributed two pieces of prose fiction to the family journal *Bhārati*, then edited by his eldest brother, Dwijendranāth. The first was a romantic short story, 'Bhikhārini' (The Beggar Woman), set in distant Kashmir; the second was the unfinished novel *Karunā*, twenty-seven chapters of which appeared in *Bhārati* before the young writer was sent away to Āhmedābād in 1878 to prepare for his journey to England. These very early examples of the two genres in which Rabindranāth was later to make major contributions bear few marks of his genius. He was himself dismissive of the excess and artificiality of his youthful productions, and singled out *Karunā* in particular for its precocious display of bravado.[1] Seven years later, however, he asked the essayist Chandranāth Basu for his opinion of this early novel, to which Chandranath returned a long review praising the work's conception, its comic brilliance, and its social analyses, but pointing out numerous structural flaws, as well as lapses in continuity, characterization, and style of treatment.[2] Expectedly, Rabindranath did not permit either 'Bhikhārini' or *Karunā* to be reprinted in his lifetime. When he asked for Chandranath's comments, he had already completed another novel, this time a slender work of historical fiction, *Bauthākurānir hāt* (The Young Queen's Market, serialized 1881–2, published 1883). He continued this historical vein in *Rājarshi* (The Royal Sage, serialized 1885, published 1887).

None of these early narrative exercises would stand comparison with the fiction of his great nineteenth-century predecessor Bankimchandra Chattopādhyāy, whose extraordinary impact upon contemporary readers is memorably described in Tagore's *Jibansmriti* (Reminiscences). Recalling his own early reading, Rabindranāth speaks of his ecstatic surrender to the island romance of Bernardin de Saint-Pierre's *Paul et Virginie*, with its images of remote, sea-girt coconut groves, encountered in Bengali translation in the journal *Abodh-bandhu*: this was soon matched by the magic of Bankim's evocation of the shadowy forest lining the riverbank in his novel *Kapālkundalā*.[3] As Tagore put it, Bankim's journal *Bangadarshan* had arrived in the poet's own youth to 'ravish the heart of Bengal', making Bengali readers wait in breathless anticipation and desire for successive instalments of novels like *Bishabriksha* (The Poison Tree) and *Chandrashekhar*.[4] In his memorial tribute to Bankim, delivered as a lecture at the Chaitanya Library in 1894 and later printed in the journal *Sādhanā*, Rabindranath spoke of the indiscriminate, childish hunger with which he had devoured the *Rāmāyana* of Krittibās, the *Mahābhārata* of Kāshirām Dās, the bound volumes of the mid-century journal *Bibidhārtha-sangraha*, the *Arabian Nights*, Persian tales, the Bengali translation of *Robinson Crusoe*, the three-volume *Bildungsroman Sushilār upākhyān* (Sushilā's Story) by Madhusudan Mukhopādhyāy, Rāmrām Basu's life history of Rājā Pratāpāditya, and the tales of the *Betāl-panchabingshati*. This welter of narrative material – augmented by folktale, myth, *mangal-sāhitya* (devotional chronicles), and the Sanskrit *kāvya*s – was, as Rabindranath recalls, swept aside by the 'new savour, new joy, new life' ushered in by Bankim's prose fiction, replacing 'children's fables' such as the *Gul-e-bakāvali* and *Bijay-basanta*.[5] The impact of this early reading is traceable in Rabindranath's first exercises in fiction. *Bauthākurānir hāt*, composed in early maturity, combines a strongly critical view of the Pratapaditya legend with some elements of historical romance in Bankim's manner.

LANDSCAPES OF THE MIND: THE SHORT STORIES

Yet it was not as a successor of Bankim, and not in the form of the novel, that Rabindranath was to make his most significant contribution to prose fiction, inaugurating, for all purposes, both a new genre and a new idiom of representation. On 23 May 1884, Rabindranath undertook a river voyage on his brother Jyotirindranāth's launch *Sarojini*, setting down his experiences in a longish description the same evening. One feature of the riverbank, the regular succession of landing stages or *ghāt*s, appears to have left a deep impression on his mind, and he writes:

> How beautiful are these old, ruined *ghāt*s! One is led to forget that human beings built them: it seems that these too are part of the Ganga riverbank, like trees and weeds.... Breaking up the hard, white neatness of the original structure, Nature has established in its place a ruined, untidy grace. It seems as though the *ghāt* has a special

relationship with the village boys and girls who come here to bathe or fetch water: one is its grandchild, another its mother or aunt.[6]

This vision of the *ghāt* as a living, sentient being, bound in affective ties with the human agents who act out their histories on its steps, lies behind the short story 'Ghāter kathā' (The Ghāt's Story) published in *Bhārati* the same year. This is one of a pair of stories, the other being 'Rājpather kathā' (The Highway's Story, printed in *Nabajiban*, 1884), that recall the premises of the Victorian 'it-narrative', with the fundamental difference that the speaker is not an object in circulation but a stationary witness to human movement and change. In Rabindranath's vision, moreover, the *ghāt* and the highway are unmoving but not unmoved: they are transformed by the processes of time, share in the life of nature, and become repositories of human tales. The *ghāt* is the narrator of one of these unregarded histories, that of the young widow Kusum:

> As I start to tell one story, another washes up on the current: stories come and go, I cannot hold on to them. Only a few, like those boats made of aloe-leaves, circle round in the eddy and return over and over again; just such a tale today is circling round my steps with its burden, on the brink of going under at any moment.[7]

The short story, formally introduced to Bengali literature by Purnachandra Chattopādhyāy in 'Madhumati' (*Bangadarshan*, 1873), received early impetus from his more famous brother Bankimchandra's 'Jugalānguriya' (1874) and 'Rādhārāni' (1875). Rabindranath's gifted elder sister Swarnakumāri, a pioneer in many fields in which her brother was later to excel, also wrote and published short stories from an early date. Historians of the genre, however, argue that sustained experimentation with the form of the modern short story in India actually commences with 'Ghāter kathā' in 1884, followed by Rabindranath's contributions from 1891 onwards to the journal *Hitabādi*, edited by the positivist Krishnakamal Bhattāchārya. In 1889–90, Rabindranath took charge of his family's estates in riverine east Bengal, spending the next decade in intermittent residence at the estate house in Shilāidaha in rural Kushthiyā, in a houseboat on the river, or travelling through the countryside. This personal and imaginative relocation was of profound significance for the poet. During this period he produced fifty-nine stories, and even when he returned to the novel upon leaving east Bengal for the Santiniketan ashram in 1901, he never abandoned the short story genre, writing the draft of 'Musalmānir galpa' (The Story of a Muslim Woman) just two months before his death.

For the first few issues of *Hitabādi*, Tagore appears to have produced six or seven stories in as many weeks. At least one contemporary reader wrote to complain about the stories' lack of plot and their refusal to answer the question 'What happens next?'[8] Tagore, who believed that he had initiated the short story form in Bengali, later recalled that even the editor felt that this mode of 'high class literature' would pass over his readers' heads.[9] But he went on to contribute no less than thirty-six stories over the next four years to the new journal *Sādhanā*, edited by his nephew Sudhindranāth and published from the Tagore household in Jorasanko.

In his classic essay 'The Storyteller', Walter Benjamin contrasted the tale's self-perfecting through repetition with the impossibility of 'retelling' the short story, which, as he puts it, 'has removed itself from oral tradition' and therefore can be narrated only once.[10] Like the photograph, the short story is a type of modernist fragment, seeking to preserve the episodic and interrupted character of life itself, although it can never abandon narrative altogether. Rabindranath engages with these issues in his experimentation with this modernist form: close to the end of his life, in a letter to Hemantabālā Debi (24 September 1931), he stated, 'A story is not a photograph. Until what I've seen and learnt has died and become spirit, and then is reconstituted into the five elements again, it can't find place in a story.'[11] What he saw and learnt as he travelled across his family's estates, met tenants and villagers, and gazed upon land, river, and sky from his houseboat, is recorded in his letters to his niece Indirā during this period. Even these letters (selectively published in *Chhinnapatra* [Stray Leaves] in 1912, and in full as *Chhinnapatrābali*, 1960) have a literary resonance, and all the writings of this phase of his life – lyric and narrative poetry, short stories, and letters – mark the inception of a new register of feeling, especially a vastly expanded sense of physical space and the unboundedness of earth and sky. In the short story 'Subhā' (1893), his description of the young, mute girl sitting under a tree at noontide, looking out at the endless expanse of the natural world and feeling her kinship with it, evokes what Gaston Bachelard called the feeling of 'intimate immensity'.[12] Rabindranath's stories and letters from this period produce, for Bengal and perhaps for Indian modernity, a poetics of landscape that imbued a familiar vocabulary with enormous resources of affect, produced new ways of seeing, and inspired new modes of visual representation. The discovery of this landscape, vividly particularized yet described in terms of its most familiar and repeatable elements (clouds, water, sandbank, fields of crops), is neither accidental nor simple. It had profound consequences for modern Indian art, especially for the artists closest to him, such as Nandalāl Basu (Bose) and Binodbihāri Mukhopādhyāy.

The letters also bear witness to an intensive programme of reading, viewing, and reflection. On 8 May 1893, his birthday, which Tagore spent at Shilaidaha, he writes of a pleasant morning looking at Ravi Varmā's pictures.[13] The distance between those mythological landscapes and the ones that Rabindranath is himself describing could scarcely be greater, yet they form part, one might say, of a conscious programme of aesthetic renovation, a redirection of the eye. It is from this complex, part-imaginative, part-sensory experience that the stories of this period evolve. They create a *populated* landscape, the life of rural, riverine, pastoral Bengal, of humble individuals brought face to face, at critical moments, with the unboundedness of nature. Perhaps the best example of this – apart from 'Subhā' – is the visual and auditory *tour-de-force* of the last three paragraphs of 'Atithi' (The Visitor, 1895), describing the advent of the monsoon with its festive clamour (given extraordinary cinematographic treatment by the director Tapan Sinha in 1965). This vision is distinct from the rhetorical elaborations of Sanskrit poetry and the use of nature symbolism in Bhakti literature or Bāul songs: a closer influence might be the 'simple flute-music carrying the fresh air of field and forest' that the young Tagore had first encountered in the poetry of Bihārilāl Chakrabarti.[14] Tagore appears to be providing a phenomenological basis for viewing the physical world and representing it in terms of a still experimental, still evolving, modernist idiom. In a letter dated 21 June 1892, he writes:

> Today I've been drifting all day on the river's course ... sitting alone, silent – on both sides of the river the villages, the landing-*ghāts*, the fields of crops present ever-shifting scenes, and as they come, as they pass, the clouds float in the sky, taking on different colours at dusk, the boat drifts, the fishermen catch fish, the waters murmur ceaselessly as though in affection ... as I view all these changing pictures, the stream of imagination flows on, and on its two banks, like the distant scenes by the river, new desires are painted. Perhaps the scene before my eyes is unremarkable, a yellow barren sandbank stretches ahead, a deserted boat is moored on it, and the light-blue river, reflecting the colour of the sky, flows past, yet as I look at it, I can't describe the feeling in my heart ... in the human mind, imagination and reality weave such a complex web![15]

However, this world held tragedy as well as tenderness, and the short fiction of the period is ruthlessly unsentimental in its detailing of the cruelty, neglect, and oppression that Rabindranath found in the lives of ordinary men and women around him. Much in advance of his peers, he seems to be aware of the capacity of this new form to grasp what official history ignores: to produce nonlinear, affective, intimate, even subaltern accounts. In 'Postmāstār' (The Postmaster, 1891), based on an actual encounter at Shāhjādpur, the young man from the city, sent out to man a rural post office in a remote village, finds little to attract him in the beauty of the countryside, though he attempts conventional poetic exercises. Ratan, the orphan girl who does the household chores and looks after him in his illness, becomes deeply attached to him, but the postmaster is unconscious of her feelings, and longs only for the day when he can leave his rural exile behind him. The story shows us his indifference, yet when he does leave, a 'huge anguish' fills his heart, an anguish rising in him like the swelling of the river-tide, though he does not turn back, and consoles himself that life is made up of separations. Ratan has no such philosophy to console her: 'O poor, unthinking, human heart!' comments the author, 'its errors will never cease.'[16] Here, as in other stories of this period like 'Khātā' (The Exercise-Book, 1891), 'Chhuti' (Holiday, 1892), 'Subhā' (1892), or 'Anadhikār prabesh' (Trespass, 1894), Tagore catches unerringly the tenor of feelings that would otherwise go unrecorded, offering us an unofficial history of the emotions. In later life, it was precisely this 'feeling', this 'touch of the human heart' in treating the poorest and most neglected of subjects that he regarded as his highest achievement in a genre that had never received due recognition.[17]

Many of these stories – such as the account of the girl Umā in 'Khātā', married off at the age of nine, whose cherished exercise book, with its childish scrawls recording her efforts at self-expression, is confiscated by her husband; or the uncanny tale of Kādambini in 'Jibita o mrita' (The Living and the Dead, 1892); or the unsparing treatment of bourgeois greed and cruelty in 'Denāpāonā' (Owed and Owing, 1891) – focus on women's lives. Tagore had witnessed the nineteenth-century debates on child marriage, Hindu widowhood, female education (*strishikshā*), and women's roles in public life, some of it carried on by articulate women of the Tagore family.[18] His own position on these issues was ambivalent, yet his stories play their part in uncovering the lives of women 'hidden from history', especially those whose circumstances put them beyond the reach of the reformers. Most remarkable is the narrative voice, tender and drily satiric by turns, interrupted by the sudden vividness of human speech, as in 'Shāsti' (Punishment, 1893), ending in the single, untranslatable exclamation of a young peasant woman wrongfully sentenced to death for a crime of which she is innocent.

Yet Rabindranath could also use the speculative structure of the short story to transform a moment of impressionistic melancholy into a love story with a happy ending, as in 'Samāpti' (Conclusion, 1893), based on an incident he described to his niece Indira (4 July 1891) in prose suffused with sadness:

> The morning sunlight, the riverside and everything around it, gradually filled up with a deep sadness, like the most melancholy of morning ragas. I thought, how beautiful the earth is, yet how unbearably sad! This unknown young girl's story seemed familiar to me. There is something especially sad about bidding farewell as one is carried away by boat on the current. It is much like death – leaving the bank to be borne away by the stream – those who stand by the shore wipe their tears and return, the one who departs disappears from sight.[19]

These moments of lyric vision are powerfully infused into the stories of this period. But Rabindranath was a ceaseless experimenter with genre throughout his long life, altering fictional form as well as content. While many of the early stories have rural settings, the celebrated ghost story 'Kshudhita Pāshān' (Hungry Stone, 1895) is based on Tagore's own memories of the Shāhibāg palace in Ahmedabad. The uncanny, an element derived from folklore and village tales, is a recurrent presence. Estranging the everyday, it inflects ordinary lives with madness and horror, as in 'Nishithe' (In the Night, 1895), 'Jibita o mrita', and 'Manihārā' (The Lost Jewels, 1898), a ghost story composed in response to the importunities of the Mahārāni of Koch Bihār. The tale is a marvellous example of domestic Gothic, locating an undefined feminine desire (represented by its fetish object, jewellery) within the hollowed-out spaces of the bourgeois country house in nineteenth-century Bengal.[20]

Rabindranath was himself of the opinion that his later stories – published in the journals *Bhārati*, *Sabuj patra*, and *Prabāsi* from around the turn of the century – had gained in technique, in psychological complexity and in social relevance, but lost much of that early surplus of feeling.[21] The later fiction uses urban settings and more diversified subjects, from bourgeois stupidity to family squabbles, from masculine folly to feminine forbearance, from nationalist idealism to the plangent ecological lament of 'Balāi' (1928) and the complicated, unorthodox psychological warfare of 'Lyābaretari' (The Laboratory, 1940). With some exceptions (notably 'Balāi') the later stories engage more directly with social and political issues and rely on discursive exposition, rather than the intensity of the lyrical moment. Structural cohesion is often lacking, with the narrator frequently under strain to produce the semblance of a connected account. In fact the most powerful stories from this later phase are the ones that are already, in spirit or in structure, approaching the longer form of the novella: *Nashtanirh* (1901), dating from exactly the same year that saw Rabindranath take up the novel again in a new mode with *Chokher bāli* (Grit in the Eye, 1901), and 'Strir Patra' (The Wife's Letter, 1914) with its distinctive female voice, anticipating Rabindranath's structural deployment of Bimalā's 'autobiography' in *Gharebāire* (At Home and in the World, 1916).

'THE HARSH TOUCH OF DOMESTICITY': *CHOKHER BĀLI, NASHTANIRH,* AND *NAUKĀDUBI*

Looking back in 1940, the year before his death, to the composition of *Chokher bāli* (serialized in *Bangadarshan* 1901–2, published 1902), Rabindranath reflected on the intricate chain of mental and material compulsions that brought him to the writing of longer fiction at the turn of the century. He spoke of the 'harsh touch of domesticity' (*sangsārer rurhha sparsha*) that forced him to engage directly with the cruel facts of household life, but also of the new print world addressed by the revival of *Bangadarshan* (of which he was joint editor). For him, Bankimchandra Chattopadhyay's novel *Bishabriksha* (The Poison Tree, 1872) had decisively marked the literary universe of the earlier, greater phase of *Bangadarshan's* publication history: its influence extends to Rabindranath's own fiction from *Chokher bāli* (1901) to *Jogājog* (1929). In *Chokher bāli*, Binodini is shown to be reading Bankimchandra's novel, the study of a young widow who brings disaster into the household of Nagendra and Suryamukhi.[22] But if Bankim provided the impetus for a calculated destabilization of the bourgeois household, Rabindranath claims for himself the privilege of being the first to carry out a ruthless examination of the human heart and its domestic arrangements, mentioning 'Shāsti' and *Nashtanirh* as examples of a literature without pity (*nirmam sāhitya*). In producing a 'meteor shower' of short stories over the past decade, he had neglected the novel, which must now be wrought 'in the workshop of the new age'. It was the task of literature in this new phase (*nabaparjyāyer sāhitya*) not simply to describe events, but to bring to light their inner nature: a modernist mode of analysis through which Rabindranath set out to uncover the terrifying interior life of the household in *Chokher bāli*.[23]

This generic shift from short story to novel is also a spatial transformation, from the relatively open settings of rural Bengal to the interiors of the bourgeois home, a painful transition for the poet. In a letter to his wife Mrinālini in 1901, he spoke of his own need for 'emptiness' within the home, and he had written to Lokendranāth Pālit as early as 1891-2, expressing his weariness at the crowd of characters, incidents, and conversations in George Eliot, a writer he otherwise admired.[24] *Chokher bāli* is dominated by the possessive violence of Rājlakshmi's maternal love. Her jealousy (*irshā*) incites and makes dangerous space for her son Mahendra's sexual and emotional rapacity, as Rabindranath himself notes.[25] Two women become its targets: Āshā, whom Mahendra marries, taking her away from his friend Bihāri, and the hungry-hearted (*kshudita-hridayā*) Binodini, who enters their household as a dependent widow but rapidly forms intimate bonds with all its members. Binodini's hunger consumes both her and others in the novel, yet it is Rabindranath's remarkable achievement that he never represents the operation of desire as hers alone, assigning equal if not greater agency in the plot to Mahendra and the profoundly self-deceiving Rajlakshmi. Evident in Mahendra's careless appropriation of Asha from Bihari, as of Binodini herself, is Rabindranath's view of sexual desire as a function of egotism and self-absorption, a need directed as much towards the self as towards the other. Most unusually, given the male pairings we find here and in Rabindranath's other novels, the relationship of two women, Asha and Binodini, functions as a conduit through which Binodini can become a secret sharer, even a voyeur, at the scene of Asha's marriage.

Within the home, these relationships are articulated through complex negotiations of internal space: Binodini choosing when to appear before the male members of the household and when to withdraw herself, Asha gaining in confidence after she takes charge of the household during Rajlakshmi's illness, and Rajlakshmi attempting to control her son's affairs from her own bedroom. Spatially, the novel is ordered around the contrast of the lower floors of the house, which contain both the public apartments and Rajlakshmi's bedroom, and Mahendra's second-floor room with its marital bed and couch on the floor (*nicher bichhānā*), the latter becoming the locus of illicit desire. Contrasted with this oppressive but luxurious domestic interior are Binodini's impoverished village dwelling, Bihari's use of his rented house for an exercise in philanthropy, Annapurnā's simple residence in Vārānasi, and the occasional release and solace that the protagonists find on the terrace in the quiet of the evening.

In the fiction of his maturity, Rabindranath returns repeatedly to the intractable differences – of desire, of motive, of self-understanding – that lie at the heart of household life. The domestic triangles of *Chokher bāli* (1901–2) and *Ghare-bāire* (1915–16), the chance-ridden romantic history of *Naukādubi* (The Boat-Wreck, 1903–5), the moral fable of nativity in *Gorā* (1907–10), and the extraordinary quest-narrative of *Chaturanga* (Quartet, 1914–15) all subject the notion of the Hindu family to unbearable strain. In several of these novels, what appears to be a triangulated relationship is founded upon an inseparable bond between two men – Mahendra and Bihari, Nikhilesh and Sandip, Gora and Binay, Shachish and Shribilās – sometimes presented as a rational–emotional or spiritual–material dyad, sometimes as a deeply exploitative partnership in which one partner appropriates, in a sense, the other's emotional and erotic life. In each case, the woman protagonist is both a subject of desire and a desiring subject, the locus of an impossible longing that can never, given the nature of household life itself, be satisfied. Women's lives appear to be regulated by a special form of desire, a hunger directed not so much towards the world and its objects as towards the self's own image in consciousness. *Jogājog* (*Relationships*), more or less the last novel in this sequence, offers perhaps the harshest and most unsparing examination of family life, and it is also the only one in which the two partners in a marriage stand directly opposed to one another, unsupported by the partnerships Rabindranath had used in his earlier works.

The novella *Nashtanirh* (Broken Nest: serialized in *Bhārati*, Vaishākh–Agrahāyan 1308/April–December 1901), on which Satyajit Rāy based his great film *Chārulatā* (1964), permits a similar 'tracking' of affective relations through domestic space: the public rooms where the intellectual Bhupati meets his friends and runs his newspaper, and the inner apartments or *antahpur* where his young wife Chārulatā solaces her loneliness with the company of her unlettered sister-in-law, Mandākini, and Bhupati's young cousin, Amal.[26] After an abortive effort at garden designing, writing becomes the private space of communion between Charu and Amal, and they plan a handwritten periodical for themselves alone. Here, as in 'Khātā' or 'Strir Patra', the figure of the writing woman acquires extraordinary plangency. Charu writes in simple prose about the village of her birth, and when this composition is published in a literary journal, she receives unexpected recognition for the strength and originality of her written style (contrasted with Amal's own rhetorical excesses and her unsuccessful efforts to imitate him). Her entry, as a woman, into the world of print, is an event of some significance. But it distances her from Amal, who marries and leaves for England: communication between the two dwindles to a terse message received by telegraph. Bhupati's subsequent journeys into the *antahpur*, undertaken at untimely moments to commune with his wife, become an agonizing trajectory of frustration and disappointment. In a process that we might call the gendering or engendering of the mother tongue, Bhupati attempts to write in Bengali for his wife. Despite Rabindranath's own reservations regarding women writers, such as his elder sister Swarnakumari, author of several important early novels, about whom he wrote so dismissively to William Rothenstein, [27] it may not be too much to suggest that his own cultivation of Bengali prose owes much to his canny negotiations of gendered experience and its appropriate means of expression, finally coming to the colloquial (*chalit*) idiom, though *Nashtanirh* is written in the formal (*sādhu*) style.

Satyajit Ray was unequivocal in his belief that *Nashtanirh* was a *roman-à-clef* based on the triangular relationship between Rabindranath himself, his elder brother Jyotirindranath, and his brother's wife, Kādambari.[28] The parallels are not exact, and the story ends not in the tragedy of suicide as with Kadambari, but the desolation of psychic loss, terrifyingly captured in the spatial image used to represent Charu's withdrawal from domestic entanglements:

> In this way, Charu dug a tunnel under the entire structure of her domestic tasks and duties, and in that unlighted silent darkness she built a temple of secret grief, adorned with the garlands of her tears. Neither her husband nor anyone else in the world had any claim there. That place was as secret as it was deep, as it was beloved. At its entrance she would abandon all the disguises of her household and enter in her unadorned true form, and when she left it, she would put on the mask again and present herself in the theatre of the world's work, laughter, and conversation.[29]

In contrast to these deeply intimate portraits of marital unhappiness, set in the stifling interiors of the bourgeois mansion, *Naukādubi* (The Boat-Wreck, serialized in *Bangadarshan* 1903–5, published 1906) presents a rambling and widely distributed series of accidents and convergences, part of the 'errant' trajectories of its principal characters, Ramesh and Kamalā. Based on a set of outrageous coincidences following from the boat wreck of the title, the plot ends in destined pairings reminiscent of Shakespearean comedy, such as *The Comedy of Errors* or *Twelfth Night*. The novel captures to some extent the self-divisions of the educated Hindu gentry, aspiring to urban modernity while still tied to its conservative village roots, but fails to render the actual complexities of this process. Some plot motifs, however, make a surprising reappearance in Rabindranath's next – possibly his greatest – novel, *Gorā*.

HISTORY, IDENTITY, AND THE NATION: *GORĀ*

Gorā was serially published in the journal *Prabāsi* between 1907 and 1910, in an incomplete book form from Kuntalin Press during serialization on 3 April 1909, and from Indian Publishing House after completion on 1 February 1910, before the last instalment had appeared in *Prabāsi*. Rabindranath records his own self-submergence in this fictional enterprise, never missing an instalment, not even on the day his son Shamindranāth died, to honour what he saw as an obligation to Rāmānanda Chattopādhyāy, the editor of *Prabāsi*, who had paid him an advance of 300 rupees.[30] It is a hugely impressive and much misunderstood novel, its thin structure of plot (compounded of historical accident and bourgeois family life) made to bear an almost insupportable expository burden. Despite its emplotment of realist space to configure the career of its hero, *Gorā* is not a realist work, a point drily noted by Tagore himself in his essay 'Bāstab' (The Real, 1914).[31] It is a fable of nativity, playing upon the multiple senses of the term, akin to the foundling fictions that are also the founding fictions of the European novel from the eighteenth century onwards.

The novel's hero, Gora, is an orphan, the child of Irish parents, fostered like the two other orphans closest to him in the novel's world, Sucharitā and Binay, by the kindness of strangers. Brought into the household of Krishnadayāl and Ānandamayi at Etāwāh during the Revolt of 1857 ('Mutiny' is the term Tagore uses), Gora is himself unaware of his origin. This ignorance contrasts with our own knowledge, as readers, of his birth and adoption: an ironic awareness undermining Gora's sense of rootedness and agency. The irony is deepened by Gora's patriotic, anti-British fervour and his love for his country, expressed through a strict Hindu way of life, so that his friend Binay describes him as the very manifestation of the scriptural injunction to 'know thyself': 'the incarnate expression of India's self-knowledge'.[32] As readers, however, we are required to do more than simply note the absence of self-knowledge in Gora. His assertion of oneness with all of India, his unflinching resolve to stand in the dust with the most ignorant of his countrymen, his belief that the eternal spirit of the land is working through each one of them,[33] needs to be carefully measured against the accident of his birth. Symbolically, this produces the alien as a native – perhaps the only one whose nativity bears the stamp of its time – of the specific and historically contingent set of circumstances that generate, at a number of removes, the apparatus of the modern Indian state on the one hand and the idea of the Indian nation on the other. Tagore's own unremitting hostility to both was fully articulated only some years later.[34] But his treatment of the paradoxes of Gora's self-appointed mission compels us to discard the myths of the nation and the state while approving Gora's moral and affective ties with his land and people.

V.D. Sāvarkar's *The Indian War of Independence, 1857*, one of the first attempts to see the 1857 revolt as a national struggle for freedom, was published in London in 1909, just before the completion of *Gorā*. Rudyard Kipling's novel *Kim*, also featuring an Irish orphan fostered in India (who becomes a British spy), appeared in 1901. These works do not frame *Gorā* so much as mark its radical differences from them. For Rabindranath, the writing of *Gorā* coincided with a period of deep personal disquiet and political unrest. The partition of Bengal (16 October 1905) made Bengali Hindus a minority in both the newly formed states of Bengal (a Hindu-majority state comprising not only western Bengal and Darjeeling but the whole of Bihar and Orissā) and Eastern Bengal and Assam (a Muslim-majority state with its capital at Dhākā). Revoked only in 1911, this partition sparked off intense political agitation, notably the *swadeshi* movement advocating indigenous manufacture and boycott of British goods. Rabindranath, who had been at the forefront of the movement at its inception, leading a demonstration in the streets of Kolkata in 1905 where he tied *rākhi*s on the wrists of Muslims, found himself in active retreat from its narrowly chauvinistic premises within a year or so.[35] But his *swadeshi* novel is the later *Ghare-bāire*; by contrast, *Gorā* is set in the late 1870s, around the period of the Second Afghan War (1878–80). Nevertheless, it engages with issues of the nation, of religious and social reform, and of political identity. Gora's love for his country and his willed espousal of the Hindu way of life, with all its attendant prejudices and prohibitions, is less a nationalism than a kind of pre-emptive *swadeshiana*, 'homelandism', for want of a better equivalent. Tagore never identifies *swadeshi* with nationalism as such, and even in an early, relatively neutral article like 'Neshan ki?' (What Is a Nation? 1901), he pronounces himself content to use the English word 'nation' for an entity that has no cultural or political equivalent in India. By contrast, *Gorā* rejects both ultra-nationalist politics and colonial co-optation. In the fictional plot, the career of Gora's foster father, Krishnadayal, is presented as a type of the emergence of the native bourgeoisie, from the radical excesses of the Young Bengal group at the start of the nineteenth century, through the self-consolidation of a comprador elite drinking and socializing with the British, to a final stage of self-absorbed, conservative religious orthodoxy. Contrasted with Krishnadayal is his enlightened Brahmo schoolfellow, Pareshchandra Bhattāchārya, Sucharita's foster father and Gora's eventual preceptor. Gora stands apart from both these exemplars, and his exceptionalism serves as an opportunity for Tagore to interpret history through allegory.

The novel has the structure of a *Bildungsroman*, tracing Gora's progress from a blind identification with the nation as codified through custom and religion, to a truer understanding of human worth, and of the narrowness of a prescriptive or chauvinistic patriotism. Gora's efforts to reach out to the poorest of his countrymen remain admirable, but the orthodoxy through which he seeks to assimilate himself to Hindu India places an intolerable burden not just upon his moral intelligence but also, in the novel's romantic plot, upon his affective ties with his mother Anandamayi, his best friend Binay, and the heroine Sucharita. His willingness to sacrifice these ties in the country's cause is at odds with the 'conscience' represented by his dyadic partner Binay who, as so often in Tagore's novels, has to do his friend's emotional tasks for him (to the point of first falling in love with Sucharita and then leaving her to Gora). At the same time, Gora is exemplary in a unique sense. When he tells Binay that India is in his heart, not in Marshman's *History of India*, we realize this claim depends not upon the factual confidence of history-writing but upon a symbolic relation. The novel's symmetries are exact, and Gora's discovery of the secret of his own origin makes him in the end as free as he had earlier seemed bound.

At the start of the novel, Rabindranath quotes the first few lines of a Baul song ascribed to the nineteenth-century poet mystic Lālan Fakir: 'The unknown bird flies in and out of the cage. If I could catch it, I would bind its feet with my heart.'[36] For the Baul singer, the unknown bird is the unknowable divinity who visits our hearts but never sets up residence anywhere. The image is a spiritual one, but it might be suggested that this notion of the restless stranger becomes central to the novel's construction of human beings in relation to the world in which they make and unmake their homes. It is a part of morality, Adorno said, not to be at home in one's home.[37] Tagore would have agreed. By using a fable of identity to test notions of home, place, family, and above all the accidental liaisons of narrative, he effects a radical dissolution or disintegration of the categories of nation and narrative – argued for by Benedict Anderson as foundational for the novel itself – at the very site of their inscription.[38] Nativity, the native, and the nation are drawn into complex and precarious relations within which the idea of a homeland, or being at home in the world, are set against the willed dissolution of mental and political boundaries.[39]

AT HOME AND IN THE WORLD: 'STRIR PATRA', *CHATURANGA*, AND *GHARE-BĀIRE*

Rabindranath contributed seven short stories, among them 'Hāldārgoshthi' (The Haldar Family), 'Strir patra' (The Wife's Letter), and 'Aparichitā' (Woman Unknown), to the first seven issues of *Sabuj patra* in 1914. Several of these focus upon the condition of women, but 'Strir patra' offers a direct first-person female narrative, and Rabindranath later took pride in recalling that he was the first to take the woman's part. Formally, the story employs the monologic rather than the dialogic mode, and is told in the colloquial *chalit bhāshā*, which emerges not as a form of gendered, women's speech but a supple and responsive literary idiom. The narrator, Mrināl, emancipates herself through her own fierce intelligence and the tragic awakening she undergoes after the suicide of a young female dependant in her husband's home (a possible parallel is the widely reported suicide of the young Snehalatā Mukhopādhyāy on 29 January 1914). Everything in Mrinal's narrative is touched by her anger, as by her contempt for the social laws that bind her to a family she clearly despises. She scarcely ever mentions her husband individually, and certainly the story grants him no personal space. Conjugal love forms no part of the domestic relations she describes, though love between women is acknowledged; any reference to *bhakti* is ironic. Here, as in much of his other fiction, conjugal life is never romanticized, whatever the ideological imperatives controlling the institution of marriage as a whole. The reality of contemporary experience is likely in any case to have been equally bleak. At the end of her 'letter' Mrinal proclaims herself as free: no longer the *mejobau*, 'second daughter-in-law', of her marital family, she asserts: 'I too shall live. I have escaped.'[40]

The idea of freedom is also at the core of Rabindranath's experimental poetics in *Chaturanga* (literally, the four divisions of an army, or the game of chess), a novel in four chapters serialized in *Sabuj patra* (Agrahayan–Phālgun 1321/November 1914–March 1915; published 1916). Given the sequence of short stories that preceded them, the chapters – 'Jyāthāmashāy' (Uncle), 'Shachish', 'Dāmini', and 'Shribilās' – might have read as separate stories, but the lives and destinies of the four main characters are linked together in a narrative that goes beyond, and even transgresses, the ordinary limits of domestic or social life. The four-part structure is in tension with a deliberate triangulation of relationships in each section. Typically, three principal agents, closely tied to each other, contend over a single object of difference or desire: Jagamohan, Shachish, and Shribilas over Nanibālā in the first section; Shachish, Shribilas, and Lilānanda over Damini in the second, third, and fourth sections. Yet the novel is also a quest-narrative, with the fiery, brilliant Shachish, idolized by his friend Shribilas, as questing hero. Shachish's first mentor is his upright, atheist uncle Jagamohan; after Jagamohan's death, he gravitates inexplicably to the Vaishnavite guru Swāmi Lilananda; at the end, renouncing all mentors, he pursues his quest alone. But we are also presented with an unsparing examination of the human capacity for self-delusion in the very act of self-surrender to an ideal or a cause: unlike the principled and compassionate Jagamohan, Shachish appears to be driven not so much by idealism or a spirit of self-sacrifice but by some compulsion of the ego. This is especially visible in his treatment of Damini, a young widow left to the care of Swami Lilananda. Resentful of her situation, bitterly distrustful of the swami and his circle of devotees, Damini is attracted to Shachish at the same time as she questions his punitive, self-destructive obsession with an abstract, undefined spiritual goal. Unsurprisingly, it is the patient Shribilas who emerges as the most admirable of these three characters and is allowed, in the end, some modest human happiness.

Chaturanga's scathing rejection of traditional Hindu family life is accompanied by transgressive alternatives. The atheist Jagamohan gives shelter to the raped and abandoned widow Nanibala and welcomes plague-stricken Muslims into his home, while Damini, made the ward of her husband's guru Lilananda, forms unconventional alliances with Shachish and Shribilas, ultimately marrying the latter in defiance of his family. In consequence, the novel too breaks free of the demands of social realism, offering, instead, an extraordinary examination of psychic life, especially the exemplary self-reliance of Jagamohan, the passionately ego-driven personal quest of Shachish, Damini's desperate search for independence and personal fulfilment, and Shribilas's commitment to care. A central concern, here as elsewhere in Tagore's fiction, is the destructiveness of the male ego, especially in charismatic individuals who are convinced that all causes must give way to their solitary pursuit of an idea. Between the extremes of male abstraction and female self-absorption, we have the philanthropic Bihari in *Chokher bāli*, the patient Binay in *Gorā*, the modest Shribilas, and a host of less-prominent female characters who offer the alternative of an ethic – even a philosophy – of care. The experimental structure of *Chaturanga* allows these alternatives to be clearly examined and judged.

Ghare-bāire (At Home and in the World, serialized in *Sabuj patra*, Vaishākh–Phālgun 1322/April 1915–March 1916, published 1916) is a more openly political novel, often read as Rabindranath's most sustained critique of the *swadeshi* ideology disseminated throughout Bengal by

men like Bipinchandra Pāl and Ashwinikumār Datta.⁴¹ His disagreement
with Bipinchandra, who had already attacked 'Strir patra', was open and
acknowledged.⁴² In the novel, the cynical, amoral, and corrupt nationalist
leader Sandip is so savage an indictment of the self-deluded and self-seeking
revolutionary that his liberal friend Nikhilesh gains an overwhelming ethical
advantage, and the political argument is lost almost before it is proposed.
By contrast, the conflict of emotional and sexual interests between Sandip,
Nikhilesh, and the latter's wife Bimala is complex and profound. Sandip
is as necessary to Bimala's sentimental education as he is to her husband's
adult acknowledgment of the nature of sexual jealousy. Both politically
and affectively, Bimala recognizes in Sandip the temptations of power: the
intoxication of armed revolutionary struggle, with its opportunities for
coercion of the weak, for harassment of the strong; and the equal intoxication
of her own sexual magnetism. In the end, both these forms of power are
destructive and illusory, since they are based on types of self-delusion. The
conflict between these motives and histories is conveyed through three
narrative strands, each presented as an 'autobiography' (*ātmakathā*), in the
separate voices of Bimala, Nikhilesh, and Sandip: again, using the excuse
of first-person narrative to employ the *chalit* or colloquial idiom.

Bimala is the novel's centre in more ways than one, drawing to herself
both private emotions and social aspirations, inhabiting the domestic space
which is to become a site of contestation, and constituting herself as an
insoluble moral problem in her combination of innocence and egotism,
sincerity and delusion. Even in the eyes of the two men who tell her story,
both egotists with ends of their own to accomplish, she is a subject of
extraordinary interest, a project in whom they have invested more than
they can afford to lose. What binds these three characters together is love,
for each a mode of feeling that can only be understood in the context of a
process of social change. Bimala begins with an image of the virtuous and
devoted wife, yet this is the product of her desire for a lost unity that she
associates with her mother and with traditional modes of feeling. Within the
narrative, it is contrasted with the very different emotional responsibilities
that Nikhilesh's love would impose upon her. The novel as a whole focuses
not so much upon her emancipation but upon the project of her social and
psychological awakening.⁴³ Given the novel's historical time, Bimala's
emergence from the *antahpur* to the public rooms, from *ghar* (home) to
bāhir (outside), would not have been a radical proposition. But in any case,
Bimala never leaves the house, visits no tenants, attends no meetings, and
meets no British officials. The *bāhir* or public sphere, where Sandip and
Nikhilesh seek to leave their stamp, is encountered by Bimala only as a

disruptive entrant into her home. Her physical journey, captured in just over one minute of screen time in a memorable sequence of Satyajit Ray's 1984 film *Ghare bāire*, is from the inner quarters of the house to the sitting room where Sandip waits to meet her.

What then is the 'world' which Bimala enters in consequence of Nikhilesh's emancipatory project? Her narrative suggests that in her very first exchange of glances with Sandip, a crucial transaction has taken place, for the *bāhir* is constituted not only by society and politics in a general sense but also physically by the gaze of the other. At the moment that Bimala feels Sandip's gaze upon her, she is drawn not just to nation and cause but to the full reciprocity of that gaze. Sandip's seduction of her, as Tagore makes clear, is founded on the blandishments of the image: the figure of the resurgent nation is deliberately sexualized so as to coincide with Bimala's physical body, clad in the rich deep colours of blood and earth. That ideal, Bimala indicates in the critical re-examination of the episode she provides in her narrative, is not only false but also corrupt, as much a product of her own vanity and her eagerness to be deluded as of Sandip's specious rhetoric. At the same time, the project of the nation that draws her is also condemned. In the English essay 'Nationalism in the West', delivered as a lecture in Japan in 1916 and included in *Nationalism* (1917), Tagore had repeated his earlier question 'What Is a Nation?' but answered it this time in a strongly critical tone: 'A nation, in the sense of the political and economic union of a people, is that aspect which a whole population assumes when organized for a mechanical purpose. Society as such has no ulterior purpose. It is an end in itself.'[44] And in 'Nationalism in India' in the same volume, he reproved the implicit xenophobia of nationalism: 'for all our miseries and shortcomings we hold responsible the historical surprises that burst upon us from outside. This is the reason why we think that our one task is to build a political miracle of freedom upon the quicksand of social slavery.'[45]

Only Nikhilesh is able to place 'the world', as a freeing model, against the restrictive demands of *swadeshi* nationalism. His love too is committed to this model of freedom, attempting to project its desired object into the world it inhabits. As he says, 'I wished with all my heart to see Bimal, fully blossomed in understanding, strength, and love, in the midst of the world. I did not, at the time, realize that if one truly wishes to see a human being in wholeness and freedom, then one must abandon the hope of retaining a definite claim upon her.'[46] Nikhilesh invests all the resources of his heart in allowing Bimala a free, open space within marriage. For him this is a test of his love as of hers, a proof that this love is no fugitive and cloistered virtue but ready to take on all the dangers of the world. When he tells Bimala that she must come 'out' because, although she may not need the outer world, the outer world may need her, he projects an image of fulfilled human worth at odds with Sandip's conversion of Bimala to a nationalist icon, as also with Bimala's confusion of that world with Sandip. Yet Nikhilesh's romantic idealization is also a projection of his ego: the love that seeks to translate Bimala from *ghar* to *bāhir* is inattentive to Bimala's own desires and aspirations. Modern, sympathetic, liberal, painfully anxious to grant the woman her right to education, choice, and freedom, Nikhilesh's love is in the last analysis uncomfortably paternalistic and self-absorbed, making Bimala an idealistic project rather than a person. When the novel opens, Bimala's narrative perspective places these stages of her emotional history in the past; even later, when all three of the speakers seem to be focusing on the immediate present, Bimala's tone is retrospective. Her self-understanding is exemplary, not so much for the emancipation of women but for a project of emotional history. Her sentimental education leads her from a traditional model of womanhood to a state of radical incompleteness where the models she seeks have disintegrated, leaving her in the confusion and uncertainty that Rabindranath sees as characteristic of modernity. For Bimala, the political is the personal: her moral awakening produces a radical reordering of sensibility, shattering the boundary between private and public worlds.

REALISM, MODERNISM, AND FORM: *JOGĀJOG, SHESHER KABITĀ,* AND *CHĀR ADHYĀY*

In *Jogājog* (*Relationships*, serialized Āshvin 1334 to Chaitra 1335 / September 1927 to April 1929 in the newly founded literary journal *Bichitrā*, published June–July 1929), Rabindranath returned to the private lives of the new bourgeoisie. The first two instalments bore the title *Tin purush* (Three Generations), which would suggest a family history – that of two feuding families, contrasting the values of a decaying aristocracy with those of the new entrepreneurial bourgeoisie of late nineteenth-century Bengal. But this study of social change remained unfinished; in 1932, responding to a substantial financial offer from *Bichitrā* to 'complete' the novel, he observed that if he did take it up again, both language and feeling would be completely different.[47] As it stands, *Jogājog* combines a descriptive social realism typical of the ideology of representation in the high bourgeois novel with an unsettling psychological analysis of the sexual and moral frustrations of domesticity. Rabindranath's younger contemporary Sajanikānta Dās commented that in tracing the complex history, by turns 'subtle and gross' (*sukshma o sthul*), of Kumudini and Madhusudan Ghoshāl, the novel was simply a prelude to his planned work.[48] Deeply anguished by the breaking up (over 1928–9) of the marriage of his daughter Mirā (Atasilatā) with Nagendranāth Gangopādhyāy, Rabindranath felt that he had failed a task set him by the 'master' of his creative consciousness.[49]

At the heart of this novel's plot, as in every other sustained treatment of marriage in Rabindranath, is the unequal and frustrating encounter of two self-absorbed individuals unable to understand each other. In *Jogājog*, this encounter is made more complex and intense by its explicitly sexual character, and by the extent to which a specific physical revulsion on the one hand and desire on the other are made representative of class aspirations and antagonisms, of gendered subjectivities beyond the individual, and of the contrast between past and present. It is not surprising that the central treatment of relationships in the novel is scarcely able to carry this representational burden. At the same time, in its complex formation of personhood, it faces us, insistently and uncomfortably, with the question of the self as it is constituted in society. Kumudini and her brother Bipradās represent the impoverished but 'noble' zamindar family of the Chatterjees; Madhusudan and his brother Nabin represent the 'upstart' Ghoshals, once the Chatterjees' neighbours, who have regained land and wealth through Madhusudan's business acumen and energy. Madhusudan sees his marriage to Kumudini as a means of repaying the Chatterjees for past wrongs and asserting his own wealth and power; Kumudini, sheltered from birth, enters into it in a state of naïve self-deception. The incompatibility of these two partners in marriage then becomes the focus of the novel's plot, as Kumudini struggles to preserve a core of selfhood against the intolerable assaults of Madhusudan's greed, vulgarity, and materialism.

Rabindranath expends every resource of narrative and imaginative skill in representing Kumudini's world to us: a world compounded of childhood memories, her brother's teachings, her parents' tragedy, as well as dream, illusion, ignorance, solitude, and melancholy. Her self-knowledge, incomplete though it is in this incomplete work, struggles to come to terms with her instinctive physical and psychological revulsion from her husband, her sense of her duty as a wife, and the values implicit in her breeding. The person thus generated exceeds narrative possibility, imaginatively absorbing most of the novel's energies and dislocating its plot. At the same time, the relationship reflects conflicts of class and property, represented through manners, domestic interiors, objects, appearances, and tastes. Madhusudan is at an aesthetic and moral disadvantage, Kumudini at a physical one, asking: 'From today, is there nothing I can call my own?'[50] The question foregrounds a personal politics, powerfully articulated through domestic space, as

Kumudini attempts to delay her entry into the bedroom or to escape from it into the storeroom, the terrace, even the bathroom. The physical privation of the increasingly confined spaces in which Kumudini seeks refuge, paired with the grimy sky she sees from the terrace, reproduce in terms of domestic architecture the most oppressive features of the urban landscape. Like her husband, the city stares at her harshly 'like a strange man'.[51]

The text as it stands ends with the news of Kumudini's pregnancy, which forces her return to the Ghoshal household. That a marital relationship of such pain and conflict could be so quickly resolved by recourse to the most tired of domestic *motifs* drew a sarcastic comment from the novelist Sharatchandra Chattopādhyāy, certainly a more realistic assessor of family ties than his great contemporary.[52] Still, given the deep sense of disillusionment that fills the closing section of the novel, Sharatchandra's sceptical humour may seem a little harsh. The novel's end presents us with a Kumudini physically tied, in the cruellest way, to the Ghoshal family; its heir, carried in her womb, *embodies* the unhappiness and humiliation of her sexual submission to Madhusudan. This final entrapment returns us to marriage itself as the novel's problematic: marriage as a critical encounter, sexual and psychological, between two persons, and marriage as a contractual negotiation between families. Rabindranath's cruelly exact analysis of bourgeois marriage has necessarily to be conducted upon the person of Kumudini, though Madhusudan Ghoshal is a complex, even tragic figure, threatening to absorb more sympathy than Rabindranath is willing to grant him. His wife's resistance, her clinging to a realm of spiritual transcendence, a simple grace that fills him with longing, makes her always the unattainable object of his desire.

Jogājog thus remains Rabindranath's most sustained, most difficult, and most serious treatment of human relationships, and its open ending is a significant element of its structure.[53] Stylistically, his return in this novel to the representational techniques of bourgeois realism seems to lend solidity and depth to the world of objects, as exemplified in the descriptions of the Chatterjees' unused 'European' drawing room, the Ghoshals' town house, and Madhusudan's bedroom. But contrasted with these richly detailed interiors is a landscape of the mind, Kumudini's own memories of the countryside where she had grown up, as well as the retreat she attempts to construct, like Charulata, within herself. In fact, the novel's realist canvas is breached by a repeated recourse to the symbolic function of music and memory, allowing Kumudini to escape what Jean Baudrillard called 'the silent gaze of deceptive and obedient objects'.[54]

Almost midway through the composition of *Jogājog*, Rabindranath began a novel of a completely different kind, a blend of the drama of ideas, modernist experiment, and *roman à clef* to which he gave the name *Shesher kabitā* (*The Last Poem*, serialized in *Prabāsi* 1928–9, published August–September 1929).[55] He may have found it a relief from the oppressive domesticity of *Jogājog*: it was certainly an opportunity to engage with his critics, since the intellectual, modern, cosmopolitan hero of *Shesher kabitā*, Amit Rāy, rails against a celebrated senior poet called 'Rabi Thākur'. The novel presents an unconventional, open romantic relationship that does not even require the seal of marriage. It is a deeply experimental work, combining lyricism, parody, and stylistic innovation, and was in its time hailed as *ati-ādhunik*, 'ultra-[perhaps 'post'?]-modern'.[56] It also offers a modernist manifesto openly rejecting 'Rabi Thakur'; the episode was a later insertion, based on an actual meeting at Jorasanko on 3–4 March 1928 to which Tagore had invited young modernist poets. Despite the brilliance of his conversation, Amit Ray remains a puzzling figure, his quest for truth at odds with his patent artificiality, so that the novel's strengths are its questioning of romantic courtship and marriage as institutions, as well as its stylistic medley of dialogue, poetry, parody, and critique.

Experimentalism also leaves its stamp upon Rabindranath's last completed novel, *Chār adhyāy* (*Four Chapters*, 1934), a fiercely controversial work engaging with the politics of revolutionary terror. Written in Sri Lanka, the book attracted the attention of the colonial police, and was reviewed in 1935 by the Calcutta Special Branch for having 'exalted the revolutionary cult in Bengal', though the Home Department approved its rejection of terrorism.[57] The first edition carried a preface[58] in which Rabindranath described his last meeting with the 'Hindu Catholic' revolutionary Brahmabāndhab Upādhyāy: this was thought to be offensive to Upadhyay's memory and was later removed. Rabindranath later wrote a justification[59] for the novel, stating that the book was a love story, to which the stormy blasts of a revolutionary time had imparted 'intensity and suffering'. That tone of intensity and suffering, born out of a painful response to the crises of the present, imbues many writings of the poet's last decade, especially his last speech at Santiniketan, 'Sabhyatār sankat' ('Crisis in Civilization', 1941). Thus, though Tagore explicitly said that the political context was 'secondary' (*gauna*) in *Chār adhyāy*, we may feel that the work gains urgency, ambiguity, and tragic resonance from its historical setting, and that these qualities are not unrelated to its radical reworking of form and genre.

Chār adhyāy breaks open the diegetic structure of the novel by employing the dramatic form of dialogue between the revolutionary Indranāth and his disciples Elā and Atin, fanatically loyal to their leader, but locked into a passionate and doomed love affair. Sometimes, as in the first chapter, explicit scene directions 'place' the dialogue; but otherwise the narrative lacks in such notations, and is dominated by the intensity of spoken exchanges between Ela and Atin. It is as though the potentially distributed and expansive life-world of the novel has shrunk to the claustrophobic insulation of the terrorist 'cell', with no reference points other than the leader's commands. Indranath tells Ela what Krishna told Arjuna in the *Bhagavad gītā*: do not abandon pity, but when duty calls, abandon sentiment ('nirday habe nā kintu kartabyer belā nirmam hate habe').[60] That conflict between sentiment and duty places Ela and Atin's love at odds with Indranath's demand that each must be prepared to sacrifice the other for the cause. As the lovers hurtle forward, propelled by a kind of death wish, in a desperate trajectory of revolutionary violence, Atin must pay a terrible moral price for his loyalty. Ultimately, Ela seeks death at Atin's hands, a *Liebestod* that fuses love and death. This conclusion disturbed contemporary readers: women revolutionaries, like Pritilatā Oāddedār (Wadedar) in 1932, were capable of dying by their own hands, and Rabindranath's horrified rejection of the politics of terror had produced a deeply prejudiced account of the movement and its leaders. Nevertheless, it is arguable that the formal experiment Rabindranath carries out in *Chār adhyāy* had a profound influence on the greatest, and structurally most innovative, Bengali novel of revolutionary nationalism, Satināth Bhāduri's *Jāgari* (1946).

UNFINISHED STORIES AND AN EXPERIMENTAL CONCLUSION

Not only did Rabindranath write other novellas, such as *Dui bon* (Two Sisters, 1932) and *Mālancha* (The Garden, 1933), in the interstices of these greater works; he continued to publish short stories well into his last years, leaving 'Musalmānir galpa' (The Story of a Muslim Woman) in draft form in June 1941, two months before he died. The narrative impulse that drove him to fiction never exhausted itself, even if some major projects – like *Jogājog* – remained unfinished. His fiction, unlike his poetry, was never an assured exercise in an idiom that he had made his own, but an experimental mode, committed to reworking the genre in each instance of creative use. His fictional prose is distinguished from that of Bankimchandra by more than a transformation of the social and political landscape. Rabindranath's own writing bears witness to new subjectivities, fresh moral and psychological understandings.[61] When he spoke of the need to forge a new representational idiom at the start of the twentieth century to suit the 'literature of a new age' (*nabaparjyāyer sāhitya*), he was thinking not so much of the subjects or language of fiction separately but of the composite character of the fictional work, which, as he puts it in the context of *Jogājog*, must be addressed like a person.[62] What is most remarkable about Rabindranath's prose fiction is that there is no typical work that can be singled out as exemplary: in his novels, no less than his short stories, he is ceaselessly experimenting with form, structure, language, and, above all, with the question of what can be represented or expressed. That so great a poet should have made a lifelong commitment to the discipline of prose fiction had extraordinary consequences for the genre, opening it up beyond the requirements of realist representation to unprecedented lyric and dialogic possibilities, to new kinds of psychic attentiveness, and to the power of a uniquely responsive, constantly changing linguistic medium. In the end, Rabindranath's fiction will be remembered as a fiction of possibility, deliberately abdicating the novel's task of *representing* life-worlds for the more difficult responsibility of making it possible for us to imagine them.

NOTES

1. 'Many shameful testimonies of my youthful sportiveness remain inscribed in the blackness of printer's ink on the pages of *Bhārati* – not just the shame of immature composition but of arrogant immodesty, outlandish excess, and tricked-up artificiality' (*Jibansmriti, RRVB* 17:356). Again: 'The precociousness that I gained through my reading of such works would be vulgarly described as *jyāthāmi* [precocious impudence] – my Bengali composition *Karunā*, published in the first year's issues of *Bhārati*, was a sample of this' (MS draft of *Jibansmriti*, Rabindra-Bhavana MS 146 (i), 27); and 'I contributed a short story [to *Bhārati*], that I am embarrassed even to recall' (ibid., 34).

2. Letter from Chandranath Basu to Rabindranath, 17 Āshvin 1291 (2 October 1884): *VBP* 2, 1944, 420–3, cited *RRGWB* 16:913–15. Neither Chandranath nor the author describes the novel as unfinished, and the editors of *RRGWB* (16:915) cite opinions contesting the received view of the novel's incompleteness.

3. MS draft of *Jibansmriti*, Rabindra-Bhavana MS 146 (i), 26.

4. *Jibansmriti, RRVB* 17:333.

5. See 'Bankimchandra', *RRVB* 9:399, and especially 9:550 for sections in the original text omitted when the essay was collected in *Ādhunik sāhitya*.

6. 'Sarojini-prayān' (Voyage on the Sarojini), *RRVB* 5:490.

7. *RRVB* 14:245–6.

8. Letter from 'a poor brahmin', published in *Nabyabhārat*, Āshārhh 1298 (June–July 1891), cited in *RJPP* 3:180.

9. As quoted in Rāni Chanda, *Ālāpchāri rabindranāth* (Kolkata: Visva-Bharati, 1942), 125.

10. Walter Benjamin, 'The Storyteller', in *Illuminations*, ed. Hannah Arendt, tr. Harry Zohn (Glasgow: Fontana/Collins, 1977), 93.

11. *CP* 9:94.

12. Gaston Bachelard, *The Poetics of Space*, tr. Maria Jolas (Boston: Beacon Press, 1994), ch. 8, 183–210.

13. *CPBLI* #94. The Bengali date was 26 Vaishākh, the day following his birthday.

14. MS draft of *Jibansmriti*, Rabindra-Bhavana MS 146 (i), 26.

15. *CPBLI* #58.

16. *RRVB* 15:415. For the original of the postmaster, see *CPBLI* #62 (29 June 1892).

17. See Chanda, *Ālāpchāri rabindranāth*, 127.

18. See the dispute in 1889 between Rabindranath and his brilliant elder sister Swarnakumari, in the journal *Bhārati o bālak*, as cited in *RJPP* 3:118. Rabindranath's own daughters were married off before they were fourteen.

19. *CPBLI* #26.

20. See the conversation with Bipinbihāri Gupta, 7 Agrahāyan 1318 (23 November 1911), cited in *RRGWB* 16:938–9.

21. Interview in *Forward*, 23 February 1936, cited in 'Granthaparichay' (bibliograpical note) to *Galpaguchchha* (Collection of Stories; Kolkata: Visva-Bharati, 1991), 853.

22. *RRVB* 3:386. There are three references to *Bishabriksha* in the text of the novel, besides one in the introduction.

23. 'Suchanā' (Prefatory note) to *Chokher bāli*, *RRVB* 3:283–4.

24. See *CP* 1:53 (letter 29) on the need for *phnākā* (vacancy), at odds with the crowded interiors of bourgeois domesticity; 'Patrālāp: Lokendranāth Pālit-ke likhita' (Letters Exchanged with Lokendranāth Pālit), *RRVB* 8:466, on George Eliot's overcrowded novels.

25. 'Suchanā' to *Chokher bāli*, *RRVB* 3:284.

26. See Supriya Chaudhuri, 'Space, Interiority and Affect in *Charulata* and *Ghare Baire*', *Journal of the Moving Image* 6 (2007), 120–35.

27. Letter to Rothenstein, c. February 1914, cited in *RJPP* 6:355.

28. See the discussion in Andrew Robinson, *Satyajit Ray: The Inner Eye* (Delhi: Oxford University Press, 2004), 159.

29. *Nashtanirh*, ch. 15, *RRVB* 22:254.

30. See *RRGWB* 16:874–5.

31. Rabindranath comments sarcastically: 'People say there is a good account of traditional Hinduism in it. This makes me deduce that that must be the element of realism' (*RRVB* 23:364).

32. *Gorā*, ch. 13, *RRVB* 6:183.

33. Ibid., ch. 20, *RRVB* 6.243.

34. See his comments on 'the fierce idolatry of nation-worship' in 'Nationalism in the West', *Nationalism* (1917), *EW* 2:419.

35. The seeds of this discontent are present even in his earliest writings on the movement, for example, in 'Swadeshi samāj: parishishta' (The Society of Our People: an appendix), 1904, *RRVB* 3:557–8): 'India regards the welcoming of others into itself as self-fulfilment.... [H]aving been born into the world, I do not consider it right to turn my face away from it' [*or* 'reject my identity as a citizen of that world'].

36. *Gorā*, ch. 1, *RRVB* 6:116.

37. Theodor Adorno, *Minima Moralia: Reflections on a Damaged Life* [1951], tr. E.F.N. Jephcott (London: Verso, 2005), 39.

38. See Benedict Anderson, *Imagined Communities: Reflections on the Origin and Spread of Nationalism* (New York: Verso, 1983), and *The Spectre of Comparisons: Nationalism, Southeast Asia and the World* (London: Verso, 1998), 334.

39. For a full discussion of these issues, see Supriya Chaudhuri, 'The Nation and Its Fictions: History and Allegory in Tagore's *Gora*', *South Asia* 35 (2012), 97–117.

40. *RRVB* 23:261.

41. A number of articles written in 1907 and 1908 express Rabindranath's disillusionment with the politics of boycott: for example, the presidential address delivered to the provincial convention of Pābnā District in February 1908, 'Byādhi o pratikār' (Disease and Remedy), 'Sadupāy' (A Good Recourse), and 'Deshahit' (The Country's Good), included in *Samuha* (A Collection, 1908); 'Path o pātheya' (The Way and the Means) and 'Samasyā' (The Problem) included in *Rājā prajā* (Rulers and Subjects, 1908). He had earlier endorsed such politics with reservations, as, for instance, in 'Swadeshi samāj' (1904).

42. *RRGWB* 16:942.

43. See Supriya Chaudhuri, 'A Sentimental Education: Love and Marriage in *The Home and the World*', in *Rabindranath Tagore's The Home and the World: A Critical Companion*, ed. Pradip Kumar Datta (New Delhi: Permanent Black, 2003), 45–65.

44. *EW* 2:421.

45. *EW* 2:462.

46. *RRVB* 8:170.

47. Prashāntachandra Mahalānabish, 'Dinalipi' (Daily journal), entry for 7 June 1932, in *Rabindrabikshā* 28 (1995), 69.

48. Sajanikanta Das, *Rabindranāth: jiban o sāhitya* (1960; rpt. Kolkata: Subarnarekhā, 1988), 149–50.

49. 'There are some tasks that belong to the master of my inward being; to neglect them causes me unbearable harm and self-degradation [*abamānanā*].... In an evil hour, I began to write a story called *Jogājog*.... Days pass, I cannot find the time to write. When I am overwhelmed by tiredness and my mind

is distracted by a thousand niggling tasks, my pen cannot preserve its self-respect if I sit down to write of this world': letter to Dilipkumār Rāy, cited in Ray's *Anāmi* (Kolkata: Gurudās chattopādhyāy, 1933), 344.

50. *Jogājog*, ch. 26, *RRVB* 9:245.

51. Ibid., ch. 8, *RRVB* 9:198.

52. 'But who knew the problem was so simple – that the *lady doctor* would come and solve it in an instant?' Sharatchandra Chattopadhyay, 'Sāhityer mātrā' (Literary Standards), in *Sharat sāhitya samagra* (Kolkata: Ānanda Publishers, 1985), 2150.

53. See my discussion in 'Introduction: Subjects and Persons', Rabindranath Tagore, *Relationships*, tr. Supriya Chaudhuri (Delhi: Oxford University Press, 2005), 1–31.

54. Jean Baudrillard, 'Consumer Society', in *Selected Writings*, ed. Mark Poster (Stanford: Stanford University Press, 1988), 32.

55. According to Nirmalkumāri Mahalānabish, the plot of *Shesher kabitā* was outlined to her by the poet during a trip to Norway in 1926, and written while he was holidaying in the company of the Mahalanabishes in South India: see Nirmalkumari Mahalanabish, *Kabir sange yurope* (Kolkata: Mitra o ghosh, 1969), 146–7, and *Kabir sange dākshinātye* (Kolkata: DM Library, 1956), 69, 83–5, 89–92.

56. *RRGWB* 16:900, citing a review in *Shanibārer chithi*, Agrahāyan 1338 (November–December 1931.

57. See *RRGWB* 16:907–8, citing Home/Press/File no. 461/1935, Home/Press/File no. 156/36/1936, and Home/Political File no. 55/1/1935.

58. 'Ābhās', *RRVB* 13:541–2.

59. 'Kaiphiyat', 1937, *RRVB* 13:543–5.

60. *Chār Adhyāy*, ch. 1, *RRVB* 13:279.

61. See Supriya Chaudhuri, 'The Bengali Novel', in *The Cambridge Companion to Modern Indian Culture*, ed. Vasudha Dalmia and Rashmi Sadana (Cambridge: Cambridge University Press, 2012), 101–23.

62. In the note 'Nāmāntar' (Change of Name) published with the third instalment of *Jogājog*, Rabindranath justified the change of title, arguing that the literary work itself has the character of a person, who has to be addressed rather than described: *RRVB* 9:544–6.

8 The English Writings

An Overview

FAKRUL ALAM

THE PROLIFIC ENGLISH WRITER

Many readers of Rabindranāth Tagore might be surprised by the extent of this Bengali author's English writings. Outside the two Bengals, those who know of his Nobel Prize know also of the English *Gitanjali*, the book largely responsible for it. Some might also know of the misleadingly titled and unrepresentative Macmillan volume, *Collected Poems and Plays*.[1] However, many people will be astonished by the four folio-sized Sahitya Akademi volumes, *The English Writings of Rabindranath Tagore*, with over 3,200 pages of text. And even these are not comprehensive in their coverage.

The extent seems even more astonishing when one considers that Tagore started writing regularly in English only in his fifties. In fact, the English *Gitanjali* (1912) was his first real creative venture in the language. Its spectacular success led to more volumes of poetry in English to meet the demand in the West. It also resulted in a substantial correspondence in English with eminent admirers from across the globe. His growing fame made him an international celebrity by the mid-1910s. He began to deliver speeches and lectures all over the world, of course in English, which too ended up in print. He also engaged in public conversations and spoke up for many causes internationally in English.

Extent apart, the range of his English writings becomes apparent from a glance at the four volumes of *English Writings*. Volume 1 comprises poems, chiefly 'translations' diverging from the Bengali to varying degrees, but a few entirely original compositions (sometimes with later Bengali versions). Many poems are patchworks, recalling snatches of Bengali (often from more than one original) alongside passages that seem original to the English.

Volume 2 collects ten plays, four short stories, prose essays compiled in volume form, and talks from his visits to Japan and China in the 1910s and 1920s. The other two volumes are truly, as subtitled, miscellanies. They encompass essays, again sometimes in volume-length collections; lectures and addresses delivered in India and abroad; and occasional and miscellaneous texts – letters, speeches, tributes, prefaces, reviews, and musings, with more poems and plays, not to mention the Nobel Prize acceptance speech. There are conversations with famous personalities of the West, interviews in English given in different parts of the world, and (to quote a sectional title in Volume 4) 'open letters, messages and tributes'.

POETRY IN ENGLISH

Tagore's first book-length English publication is the English *Gitanjali*.[2] It created a stir on appearance and made his reputation in the West. There was more than one reason for its sensational impact. It was the eve of the First World War, when European intellectuals were registering their despair at a mechanical civilization that seemed on the verge of collapse. The *Gitanjali* poems, through their calming, meditative articulation of the individual soul seeking union with the infinite, promised to salve at least a little of the anxiety of a literary public apprehending Armageddon. More crucially, it was, in the words of the modernist poet Buddhadeb Basu (Buddhadeva Bose), Tagore's acute critic and lifelong admirer, 'a miracle of translation'. Buddhadeb implies this was because Tagore had feelingly gathered and transformed poems, mostly devotional, from several Bengali volumes,[3] and made them 'bloom anew on a foreign soil'[4] through immense thought, time, and effort.

Tagore worked on the Bengali *Gitānjali* while convalescing from illness, prior to a planned trip to Europe for medical treatment in 1911. He also utilized this leisure to mull over the form and diction that would make the poems acceptable to English readers. As he later wrote to his niece Indirā Debi, 'I felt a kind of urge to regenerate in my mind, in another language, the feast of *rasa* once aroused within me by the winds of inspiration.'[5] This creative impulse continued during the voyage to England. He used the ample time on shipboard to further polish the English renderings he had chosen to represent him in the West.

Not surprisingly, then, the English *Gitanjali* won acclaim as translations, eliciting admiration from practising poet-critics such as W.B. Yeats and Ezra Pound. Tagore cast the poems in a mould that was to appeal to readers brought up on the King James Bible: the expressive, hymn-like compositions would recall their church-going experience. Yet the medium also evoked the robust prose poetry of Walt Whitman. Taking considerable liberty with the Bengali sources – the kind of liberty only a creative writer could exercise with his own work – Tagore made the English versions almost original compositions or, at the very least, considerably reworked versions of the intricate, emotionally intense, and musically rich Bengali poems. Using parallelism, internal rhyme, alliteration, assonance, and consonance, weaving sounds together through devices such as anaphora and the refrain, Tagore reached a formula whereby the musical and lyrical elements of the originals would be substantially retained in their English versions.[6]

The India Society in London brought out a limited edition of the English *Gitanjali* in November 1912; its success led to Macmillan republishing it a year later. A perceptive review in the *Times Literary Supplement* (*TLS*) suggests why the poems might have captivated the poetry-reading intelligentsia of the West:

> In reading them one feels, not that they are the curiosities of an alien mind, but that they are prophetic of the poetry that might be written in England if our poets could attain the same harmony of emotion and idea.... As a poet should be, he is so simple that anyone can understand him; yet this does not mean that there is little to understand.[7]

Spurred by the Nobel award, several English poetical volumes appeared over the next few years. *The Gardener* (1913), *The Crescent Moon* (1913), and *One Hundred Poems of Kabir* (1914) followed *Gitanjali* in quick succession. However, Tagore's reputation as an English-language poet began to decline steadily and even sharply among the very poets and critics who had once praised and promoted him. By the end of the decade, Yeats, Pound, and other established literary figures, who had once chorused their approval, now seemed to compete in disparaging every new volume directly or indirectly, or damning them with silence.

The diminishing of the poet's popularity is evidenced by the ever dwindling number of volumes. Macmillan published *Fruit-Gathering* in 1916, *Lover's Gifts and Crossing* in 1918, *The Fugitive* in 1921,[8] and the first Tagore anthology in English, *Poems from Tagore*, in 1921. The next volumes of translated poems would not be by the poet but by associates and admirers like Kshitishchandra Sen, Nagendranāth Gupta, and Bhabāni Bhattāchārya.[9] However, in 1931, Tagore would publish his only substantial original poem in English, *The Child* (translated into Bengali as 'Shishutirtha'). A volume simply titled *Poems* came out posthumously in 1942, with a few translations by the poet-critic Amiya Chakrabarti and the rest by Tagore himself.

Why did the English *Gitanjali* succeed so spectacularly and the later volumes fail by comparison? The reasons must be sought in their contents, and the largely unchanging mould in which the poet continued to cast them, as also in the changing taste of the Western anglophone readership, overwhelmed around this time by the masterpieces of Modernism appearing one after another. *Gitanjali* has its share of awkward and unidiomatic language, but Tagore's chosen model of the prose poem, with deft use of repeated sounds, creates a solemn music in keeping with the intense, spontaneous, and almost rhapsodic devotion of the Bengali originals: that is to say, form complements content in these translations. The unhurried and meticulous manner of composition, with Yeats's editorial emendations, helped to ease out the infelicities (though manuscript evidence shows that Yeats's interventions were minimal).[10] Finally, the volume is endowed with a substantial unity of structure. It seems designed as a narrative: the narrator progresses from a desire to unite with God to the union itself, overcoming all barriers including the fear of being separated by death.[11] The last set of poems (#86 to #103) show the poet about to cross over to the other world and embrace eternity.

The Gardener appears to have received less attention from its creator. One reason may have been the haste with which Tagore compiled this and the subsequent volumes. 'One wishes,' writes Krishna Kripalāni 'that *Gitanjali* had not been followed by other translations, particularly of poetry, in such quick succession.'[12] These volumes seem to have been composed without enough thought to devising the mould that would best bring out their distinctive qualities. The same years also saw a spate of Bengali poems, plays, fiction, and nonfictional prose. Moreover, Tagore was now travelling incessantly to meet the ever-increasing demand for India's foremost representative in the West. All this could have left him little time to work on the translations.

The fact that the later volumes were not uniformly spiritual in content also made for a more tepid reception. Pound, who had the perspicacity to say in 1913 (after *The Gardener*) 'Let me deny that Mr Tagore is, in any exact sense, a mystic', could therefore retain his faith in Tagore's poetic genius:

> Why the good people of this island are unable to honour a fine artist as such; why they are incapable, or apparently incapable, of devising for his honour any better device than that of wrapping his life in cotton wool and parading about with the effigy of a sanctimonious moralist, remains and will remain for me an unsolvable mystery.[13]

In *The Gardener*, Tagore wished to prove himself to his Western readers as not only a mystical poet but a poet of love. He therefore chose poems that were romantic in bent and secular in mood, originally written over the two decades preceding the Bengali *Gitānjali*. There are extracts from verse plays, love lyrics, and narrative poems on romantic encounters. This makes the collection miscellaneous and eclectic, with no discernible plan of organization. Moreover, as Tagore indirectly admits in his brief preface, he now takes too much liberty with the original poems: 'The translations are not always literal – the originals being sometimes abridged and sometimes paraphrased.'[14] There are many infelicitous lines like 'O Farthest end, O the keen call of thy flute!'[15] and 'Come as you are, do not loiter over your toilet'.[16] Finally, there is a sameness in the diction and sound patterns, making the poems monotonous when read sequentially. One misses the clear thematic intent of the *Gitanjali* poems, where the style and diction validate a pervasive spirituality.

The lack of variety in sound and diction is equally apparent in *The Crescent Moon*. Here Tagore does achieve a unity of theme: these are mostly thoughtful poems about children and childlike states of mind. But the volume repeats a couple of mystical poems about children that had already appeared in the English *Gitanjali* (#60 and #61), thereby risking a reversion to the sameness of texture. Readers can be forgiven for a sense of *déjà vu*.

Not surprisingly, the volume had a mixed reception. *The Nation* (13 December 1913) thought William Blake provided the only fit English parallel, while the *TLS* reviewer (14 May 1914) dismissed the poems as more 'childish than childlike'. Shishirkumār (Sisir Kumar) Dās comments: 'The quality of the translation cannot be rated very high considering the fact that the original poems [unlike the English] show subtle variations in rhythm and rhyme, metrical structure and stylistic levels.'[17] Kripalani (225) notes that around this time, Tagore imagines himself in a Bengali poem as 'carrying his burden of wares and hawking them from place to place'.[18] We cannot but conclude that the damaging haste was owing to the rising demand for his poems in the West, which aided his purpose of raising money for his school in Santiniketan.

Fruit-Gathering, the next collection, brings together some of Tagore's best-known devotional song-lyrics; ballad-like poems about revered figures such as the Buddha or the saint Narottam; other narrative poems with spiritual themes; and some recently composed meditative poems. Again, the translations miss out on the distinctive qualities of the originals and the difference in their sources and subject matter. Nor does their sequence show the kind of integral structure that made *Gitanjali* so compelling. The translations themselves are of unequal quality. They might succeed in conveying their moral or spiritual theme, but they scarcely suggest the modernizing experiments with form and diction in the source volumes like the celebrated *Balākā* (1916). Inelegant phrasings mar the effect: 'Jewels are woven into the carpet where stands my king, but there are patient clods waiting to be touched by his feet'[19] and 'I had my face turned from you, therefore I read the letters awry and knew not their meaning'.[20]

Lover's Gift and Crossing, which followed, shows an even steeper fall in quality. As Das observes, this collection is even more miscellaneous than the preceding ones; moreover, '[t]he quality of translation is poor, many of the poems in English are [mere] paraphrases of the original Bengali and some ... have been so radically changed in the translation that it is quite difficult to locate the source'.[21] Far too many pieces border on plain prose and seem less and less like authentic prose poems. Four of them are not even sourced from Tagore.[22] Intended as a gesture of regard to fellow poets, they end up striking a dissonant note. Some of the translations seem eminently designed for unpopularity. *Lover's Gift* #15, which in Bengali is one of Tagore's best-loved songs, has lines like this: 'The pulse of the air boded storm. She rushed out of the hut, when she heard her dappled cow low in dismay.'[23] The opening of *Lover's Gift* #47 may have struck some English readers as quaint but could have disconcerted others: 'The road is my wedded companion. She speaks to me under my feet all day, she sings to my dreams all night.'[24]

The inclusion of poems by other hands in *Lover's Gift and Crossing*, and the earlier translations in *One Hundred Poems of Kabir* (1914),[25] showcasing the fourteenth-century mystic poet Kabir, point to another feature: through his English translations, Tagore wished to introduce poets and poems to which he felt temperamentally akin and which, he felt, might interest Westerners who had appreciated *Gitanjali*. This aim of promoting traditional poets, who would have otherwise gone unnoticed in the anglophone world, also appears in the next volume, *The Fugitive* (1921). It contains five songs (#1.22) by medieval Bengali poets on the spiritually infused love of Krishna and Rādhā; nine by the mystically inclined mendicant community of Bāuls (#2.34); and three by Jnānadās, another old Vaishnava poet (#3.38).

The opening poem of *The Fugitive* resumes the mystical and visionary vein – in fact, heightens it in comparison with its original, *Balākā* #8. In the English, it is not even readily apparent that the poem is addressed to a river. But *Fugitive* #1.9 takes us back in a more romantic vein to the world of the ancient poet Kalidāsa, and #1.11 addresses the mythical Urvashi as an archetype of female sexuality. Several pieces[26] translate verse dialogues between mythological and epic characters, chiefly taken from *Kāhini*. As before, however, such poems are interspersed with emotive lyrical pieces. Poems whose originals span some two decades are commingled without regard for their very different poetic trajectories. The result was another volume that received an indifferent reception.

In the remaining twenty years of his life, Tagore did not bring out any major volume of translations of his poems.[27] The decline of interest in the West must have disheartened him. Moreover, he seems to have felt unhappy about the quality of the translations and their lack of appeal for discerning readers in the age of literary Modernism. In fact, already after *The Gardener*, he had voiced such apprehensions to Rāmānanda Chattopādhyāy in a letter of November 1913: 'I had my fears about these translations. That the *Gitanjali* translations lacked metre was not so crucial, but I cannot surmise how mere prose versions of *Kshanikā* or *Sonār tari* will sound to the Western reader.'[28] The accolades achieved by *Gitanjali* attracted readers to the next few volumes, but the attraction soon began to fade. Buddhadeb Basu perhaps got it right when he noted that the English collections following *Gitanjali* were gleaned from 'wrong books, wrongly served'.[29] Tagore felt increasingly that he had done himself a disservice in his later volumes of English poetry. Radice cites a telling confession in a letter to Sturge Moore (24 May 1921): 'I myself in my translations have done grave injustice to my own work. My English is like a frail boat – and to save it from an utter disaster I had to jettison most part of its cargo. But the cargo being a living one it has been mutilated: which is a literary crime that carries its own punishment.'[30]

The posthumously published *Poems* (1942), however, display a somewhat different poet in its opening number, translated from 'Patra' (The Letter) in *Punascha*. The tone is refreshingly colloquial. The opening lines address the reader directly:

> Here I send you my poems
> densely packed in this writing book
> like a cage crowded with birds.

The poet laments wryly that he was 'hopelessly born in the age of the busy printing press, – a belated Kalidasa' addressing a beloved who is 'utterly modern', so that his muse must travel 'on trams and buses' to keep tryst with her.[31] In both subject matter and verbal register, such poems can be found all through Tagore's Bengali oeuvre; the novelty lies in its appearance in his English work. *Poems* gives us glimpses of the very different English-language poet that Tagore could have opted to be.

The new idiomatic tone is present in quite a few pieces. This simple but moving translation of another much-loved Bengali lyric is a good example:

Waves rise and fall,
the flowers blossom and fade
and my heart yearns for its place
at the feet of the Endless.[32]

The next poem presents the serenity and philosophic depth that readers admire in *Gitanjali*, but now in a new poetic key:

The night is upon me.
My desires that wandered all day have come back to my heart like
     the murmur of the sea in the still evening air.
One lonely lamp is burning in my house in the dark.
The silence is in my blood.
I shut my eyes and see in my heart the beauty that is beyond all
     forms.[33]

The following rendering of a poem from *Prāntik* is utterly unlike anything admitted to the earlier English collections. The poet had not struck this vein even in his earlier Bengali poetry.

When my mind was released
from the black cavern of oblivion
and woke up into an intolerable surprise
it found itself at the crater of a volcanic hell-fire
that spouted forth a stifling fume of insult to Man....[34]

Poems is a deliberately eclectic collection, intended as a representative, chronologically arranged selection of Tagore's poems in translation. Being a posthumous publication, the volume had the benefit of editorial input from Krishna Kripalani, assisted by Amiya Chakrabarti and others. In fact, 9 of the 122 poems are translated by Chakrabarti. The second edition added ten poems (three of them translated by Chakrabarti) and omitted one.

Tagore wrote a substantial English poem in 1930 entitled *The Child*, after watching a play about the Passion of Christ in the German village of Oberammergau. Immensely moved by it, he composed the first draft 'in the course of one night'. The poem makes no mention of Christ and has no localized setting. Rather, as Kripalani says, it is 'a product of Biblical inspiration and Hindu imagination, in which the memory of Jesus anticipates Gandhi's fate'.[35] *The Child* was performed on 1 December 1930 at the Carnegie Hall, New York, where the poet recited it to the accompaniment of music. It was published from London in 1931; in 1932, it was transformed into the Bengali 'Shishutirtha' in *Punascha*, reversing Tagore's usual practice. *The Child* embodies great imaginative power from the very start:

> A lurid glow waxes and wanes in the horizon –
> is it an ultimate threat from an alien star,
> or an elemental hunger licking the sky?
> Things are deliriously wild,
> they are a noise whose grammar is a groan
> and words smothered out of shape and sense.[36]

The following passage again demonstrates Tagore's English verse at its best in its visual sweep and sonorous movement:

> They come from the valley of Nile and the banks of the Ganges,
> from the snow-sunk uplands of Thibet,
> from high-walled cities of glittering towers,
> from the dense dark tangle of savage wilderness.[37]

What one notices above all are the cadences, of the quality of *Gitanjali* but adapted to a very different context.

Different again, indeed unique among the English poems, are the matching volumes *Stray Birds* (1916) and *Fireflies* (1928). *Stray Birds* was dedicated to Hara Tomitoro, Tagore's host in Yokohoma. Some of its short epigrammatic poems are sourced from *Kanikā* ('Particles', 1899) and a few from *Lekhan* (1927). As Das notes, they can be 'directly linked with the epigrammatic and didactic traditions of Sanskrit and also of Persian poetry prevalent in nineteenth-century Bengali literature'.[38] However, as Das also points out, the Japanese connection indicates a possible influence of the haiku. The imagist poems the poet came across in his visits to England and America might have influenced him too. Whatever the precise chemistry, the poems evince a terse, visually vivid expressiveness: 'What is this unseen flame of darkness whose sparks are the stars?'[39] or 'Our desire lends the colours of the rainbow to the mere mists and vapours of life'.[40] These are two of the 'stray birds' that have not been traced to any Bengali source.

In an article in the journal *Prabāsi* (Kārtik 1335/October–November 1928), Tagore describes how in Japan, he was often asked for autographed verses, usually in Bengali, on paper, silk, or fans. Such is the origin of many poems in *Lekhan*. But some of the poems are in English, like those he would later write in Italy. The Bengali source of *Fireflies* is almost exclusively

Lekhan, but many of its epigrams seem to be original English compositions. Its title poem is also the first poem in *Lekhan*:

> My fancies are fireflies, –
> Specks of living light
> twinkling in the dark.[41]

The poems in *Fireflies* vary within their brief compass. Some are succinct: 'The butterfly counts not months but moments and has time enough';[42] or, reflecting Tagore's eco-religious consciousness:

> Trees are the earth's endless effort to speak
> to the listening heaven.[43]

Others are longer, more relaxed in tone and wide-ranging in imagery:

> In the mountain, stillness surges up
> to explore its own height;
> in the lake, movement stands still
> to contemplate its own depth.[44]

Both volumes show Tagore writing pensively but fluently in English, using the language to convey incisive insights.

ENGLISH PROSE

Tagore's nonfictional prose covers a range of genres. It chiefly consists of the essays, lectures, and talks demanded of him once the success of the English *Gitanjali* won him worldwide fame. Some project him as the wise man of the East addressing unquiet but spiritually inclined Western audiences in need of healing words and spiritual anchoring. Others go further to articulate his deepest thoughts on religion, culture, and education. Some express his antipathy to the militant nationalism of the West and his fear that the contagion would soon engulf Asia as well. Yet others are autobiographical in intent or efforts to bond with the kind of spiritually inclined audience who had welcomed the *Gitanjali* poems so warmly.

    Sadhana: The Realization of Life (1913) is based on lectures in the United States to the Illinois Unitarians, subsequently converted into eight lectures at Harvard; the source lies in Tagore's Bengali discourses at Santiniketan. Sections of *Sadhana* were translated by members of Tagore's circle, the sixth essay entirely by Surendranāth Tagore.[45]

Tagore's purpose was to acquaint Westerners with the spiritual tradition he had inherited. The first essay, on 'The Relation of the Individual to the Universe', expounds the organic nature of his spiritual belief, based on the harmony between humans and the natural world. Quoting extensively from the Upanishads, but also citing the Buddha and Christ, Tagore underscores their common vision of a unity of being and the consequent release from materialism. The second essay, 'Soul Consciousness', defines the path whereby the self merges with the infinite by realizing God's presence. The third explores 'The Problem of Evil', seeing evil and death negated in the ultimate scheme of things and emphasizing a wholeness that transcends temporal barriers. Again, Tagore strives to link Hindu belief with Buddhist and Christian teachings. The fourth essay, on 'The Problem of Self', underlines the dangers of solipsism, or taking one's self to represent a distinct and ultimate value. The Buddha is cited yet again, invoking his goal of enlightenment through *nirvāna* and his concept of realizing one's *dharma*, which Tagore blends with Upanishadic teaching.

These lectures would have struck a chord in an American audience familiar with their own transcendentalist tradition in thinkers like Emerson. Snatches of the fourth essay recall Emerson's homiletic lyricism:

> This old, old day of our earth is born again and again every morning. It comes back to the original refrain of its music.... But every morning the day is reborn among the newly-blossomed flowers with the same message retold and the same assurance renewed....[46]

We can compare the strikingly similar passage from Emerson's 'The American Scholar':

> Every day, the sun; and, after sunset, Night and her stars. Ever the winds blow; ever the grass grows. Every day, men and women, conversing – beholding and beholden.[47]

The fifth essay, too, is lyrical in extolling the spiritual life of human beings, with a concomitant attack on mechanical civilization. It validates its theme, 'Realization in Love', by the basic premise that 'the world in its essence is a reconciliation of pairs of opposing forces'.[48] By reconciling this dialectic, the One can appear in the many.

The sixth essay, 'Realization in Action', expands the concept of the active soul, quoting verse 2 of the *Isha upanishad*, 'In the midst of activity alone wilt thou desire to live a hundred years',[49] and reinforcing the idea through a chiasmus: 'to work we must live, to live we must work'.[50] However, whereas activity in the West seeks worldly power, in Eastern thought it is geared to realizing the infinite in the finite world, and attainment of the unity of all beings. 'Let our newly awakened powers,' Tagore concludes, 'cry out for fulfillment in leaf and flower and fruit.'[51]

'The Realization of Beauty', the seventh essay, dwells on a sense of beauty springing from a sense of joy. Such beauty inheres in the totality of things, erasing local distinctions between beauty and ugliness: 'Beauty is omnipresent, therefore everything is capable of giving us joy.'[52] Even the most mundane object therefore appears precious. Validating Keats's famous line, Tagore asserts: '[W]e must ever know that "beauty is truth, truth beauty"; we must realize the whole world in love.'[53] As he later reaffirms in *Creative Unity*, again in a Keatsian context: 'Beauty is no phantasy, it has the everlasting meaning of reality.'[54] Illustrating the point that 'music is the purest form of art', Tagore's English prose turns musical at this point of *Sadhana*:

> When in the rainy night of July the darkness is thick upon the meadows and the pattering rain draws veil upon veil over the stillness of the slumbering earth, this monotony of the rain patter seems to be the darkness of sound itself.[55]

Tagore concludes *Sadhana* by urging the renunciation of a limited utilitarian outlook, and pursuit of the Infinite in order to attain wholeness in life as in art. The final chapter can therefore be titled 'The Realization of the Infinite'. Tagore makes the point with a favourite analogy:

> The bird, while taking its flight in the sky, experiences at every beat of its wings that the sky is boundless.... Therein lies its joy. In the cage the sky is limited; it may be quite enough for all the purposes of the bird's life, only it is not more than is necessary.[56]

Like the English *Gitanjali*, *Sadhana* was received enthusiastically in the West, being reprinted eight times within a year and adding to Tagore's growing international fame. This was no doubt owing to its spiritual tenor, but the quality of the writing must have played a part. As with the English *Gitanjali*, Tagore seems to have composed the lectures at his own pace, with enough attention to the form and language. Parts, as noted earlier, were by other hands. However, as Krishna Kripalani observes, both *Gitanjali* and *Sadhana* 'slanted' Tagore's reputation in the West: he was henceforth 'obscured in the cloak of a religious philosopher'.[57] The Western public would be less appreciative when he cast aside that cloak to address other issues.

Like the post-*Gitanjali* verse collections, *Personality* (1917), Tagore's next English publication in prose, did not attract as much attention as *Sadhana*. Like *Sadhana*, it originated in lectures delivered in North America. The volume covers a formidable range of subjects: besides spiritual musings on the extra-natural world and the importance of meditation, it contains Tagore's thoughts on art and on personality formation, his educational philosophy, and his views on women. But this assorted material does not quite gel, and Tagore appears to have given little thought to their ordering.

Nevertheless, for anyone trying to understand him as a thinker and creative artist, these lectures have much to offer. The first, 'What is Art?', views art as the expression of human feelings in excess of the purely utilitarian, seeking outlet in a 'flood-tide'.[58] Art is an expression of personality, but also a dialogue with the world and an endeavour to unite with the universal soul.[59] The second lecture, 'The World of Personality', validates the volume's title by seeing the artist's perception of the infinite as mediated by his unique personality. The 'absolute infinite' is an emptiness; it acquires meaning through union with the finite – a premise running through the course of his Bengali poetry. Tagore cites the *Isha upanishad*, verses 11, 14:

> He who knows that the knowledge of the finite and the infinite is combined in one, crosses death by the help of the knowledge of the finite and achieves immortality by the help of the knowledge of the finite.[60]

Again Tagore's American audience might have been reminded of Emerson's concept of the Oversoul. Perhaps also in an attempt to bond with his American audience, in this lecture Tagore alludes repeatedly and explicitly to Whitman. More importantly, he cites *Leaves of Grass* to bond with Whitman himself through a vision of art as projecting a mind that incorporates the universe:

> Beginning my studies the first step pleas'd me so much,
> The mere fact, consciousness, these forms, the power of motion,
> The least insect or animal, the senses, eyesight, love,
> The first step, I say, aw'd me and pleas'd me so much....[61]

He says of Whitman: '[I]n the centre of his world dwells his own personality. All the facts and shapes of this world are related to this central creative power, therefore they become interrelated spontaneously.'[62] This matches Tagore's rapture, at the climax of this essay, at his own sense of joyful oneness: 'Have I not known the sunshine to grow brighter and the moonlight deeper in its tenderness when my heart was filled with a sudden access of love assuring me that this world is one with my soul?'[63] The third lecture, too, celebrates the nexus between instinctual and material perception on the one hand and moral and creative expression on the other: human beings articulate their yearning for the infinite by apprehending their dual status in the natural order.

> In man, the life of the animal has taken a further bend. He has come
> to the beginning of a world, which has to be created by his own will
> and power.[64]

These three lectures have a kind of unity, developing the topic of the title in manifold ways; the fourth one breaks new ground. It discusses Tagore's disenchantment with conventional education, and the ideas that led to his school in Santiniketan. It takes off from the basic principle of the earlier lectures: the ideal school should inculcate in the young mind 'the idea that it has been born in a human world which is in harmony with the world around it'.[65] This harmony implies a rejection of the excesses of material civilization, in a vein recalling Thoreau's idea of 'voluntary poverty' in a way his audience would have appreciated: 'I had to provide for this great teacher, – this bareness of furniture and materials, – not because it is poverty, but because it leads to personal experience of the world.'[66]

The fifth lecture stresses the importance of meditation in accessing 'the Supreme Truth':[67] it almost takes the form of an extended prayer. The final lecture, 'Woman', associates the male of the species with 'a civilization of power' and urges a heightened role for women in redressing the balance, initiating a 'new task of building up a spiritual civilization'.[68] One wonders how women audiences in America, who had already encountered first-wave feminism, reacted to the idea.

Taken as a whole, *Personality*, like the volumes of poetry succeeding the English *Gitanjali*, must have struck a Western readership, especially in Europe, to be far removed from their daily engagement with the trauma of the First World War. This would not be the case with *Nationalism* (1917), a collection of lectures delivered in Japan and the United States. Indeed, the lectures appear relevant even now, a century later.

Nationalism registers Tagore's anguished response to the national mood he discerned in his two visits to Japan in 1916 and 1917 and his second trip to the United States in 1916. But the denunciatory tone of these lectures must have drawn their inspiration, at least in part, from his experience of British colonial nationalism in his own land. It may also reflect his disenchantment with nationalism in Bengal. After all, he had been an active anticolonial campaigner in his own country for a period, until put off by the excesses and bigotry he saw around him.

In fact, the first chapter, 'Nationalism in the West', begins with the Indian subcontinent's own age-old problems of race and caste. However, Tagore sees the burgeoning nationalism there as part of a tide sweeping the world. This tide emanated from the West, where 'the national machinery of commerce and politics turns out neatly compressed bales of humanity which have their use and high market value'.[69] In other words, it was the acquisitive spirit of industrial capitalism that fuelled nationalism and financed imperial ventures: a 'pack of predatory creatures let loose that must have its victims'.[70] Tagore seems even to have anticipated later critics of globalization in depicting a 'wealth-producing mechanism ... incessantly growing into vast stature, out of proportion to all other needs of society'.[71] At any rate, he leaves the reader in no doubt that this great evil has emanated from the West. He vehemently arraigns his Western audience: 'You, the people of the West, who have manufactured this abnormality, can you imagine the desolating despair of this haunted world of suffering man possessed by the ghastly abstraction of the organizing man?'[72]

In Japan, Tagore was dismayed to see the self-serving, self-perpetuating spirit of nationalism infect a nation he had ardently admired for its civilizational virtue. He is not against the modernization of the country, but does not believe it has to import nationalism from the West as part of a package deal: he urges his Japanese audience to choose from the West 'according to your genius and your need'.[73] His rhetoric is now still more strident: the monster of nationalism is 'carnivorous and cannibalistic in its tendencies, it feeds upon the resources of other peoples and tries to swallow their whole future'.[74] He is alarmed too by 'the mad orgies of militarism',[75] another infectious import from the West, that seem to be an inevitable concomitant of nationalism. He exhorts the Japanese to hold on to their traditions, cultivate even more the refinement of their artistic inheritance, and promote the ideal of *maitri* (Sanskrit 'friendship, affinity') that lay at the root of a once thriving pan-Asiatic culture.[76] However, he does not condemn modernity outright. Rather, he counsels his audience with epigrammatic emphasis: 'True modernism is freedom of mind, not slavery of taste. It is independence of thought and action, not tutelage under European schoolmasters.'[77] His peroration is both rousing and lyrical:

> I watched the sunset in your southern sea, and saw its peace and majesty among your pine-clad hills.... [T]he music of eternity welled up through the evening silence, and I felt that the sky and the earth and the lyrics of the dawn and the dayfall are with the poets and idealists, and not with the marketmen robustly contemptuous of all sentiments....[78]

The last chapter, 'Nationalism in India', begins like the first by acknowledging the caste problem that has bedevilled India, but rebukes the West for stigmatizing it while ignoring its own problem of race. He condemns all such divisive attitudes, grandly declaring: 'There is only one history – the history of man. All national histories are merely chapters in the larger one.'[79]

He emphasizes the need to rise above 'the fractional groups of nationality' to achieve 'the spiritual unity of all human beings'.[80] Again, he stresses the importance of idealism and humanism, and the need to curb nationalistic and imperialist appetites. Much less denunciatory in tone than in the previous lectures, he ends by proposing a model for Indian society:

> Let our life be simple in its outer aspect and rich in its inner gain. Let our civilization take its firm stand upon its basis of social coöperation and not upon that of economic exploitation and conflict.[81]

Despite such appeals in the name of humanity, many among the American and Japanese public were stung by these exhortations, and in India no less. To quote Das, 'Tagore's forthright denunciation of nationalism provoked violent attacks in the American press and severe criticism by the Japanese intellectuals. This work made him unpopular ... also in India where nationalism had already entered a new phase of growth.'[82] Kripalani considers the lectures 'ill-timed', 'though he was right, prophetically right, in what he said': Europeans were dying in thousands and could not stand being berated thus.[83] He also instances a distinguished Japanese admirer, Masakiyo Miyamoto of the University of Osaka, who was imprisoned for attempting a translation of the lectures.[84] Yet *Nationalism* has proved the most enduring of Tagore's prose works. It has been quoted with approval by many recent thinkers. Edward Said, for instance, calls these 'great lectures' a call for 'a creative solution to the divisiveness produced by racial consciousness'.[85]

Tagore's next work of English prose, *Creative Unity* (1922), is again based on tour lectures, this time from his third North American visit (1921–2). The topics are mostly familiar and non-controversial: his religious beliefs, his art, his views on women and East–West relationships. There is also an essay on 'The Nation'. The first piece, 'The Poet's Religion', cites Wordsworth, Shelley, Keats, and lesser-known English poets from Arthur Quiller-Couch's *Oxford Book of English Verse*, alongside Vedic hymns and mystical folk poets of Bengal, and his own poems in English renderings. This feat of inclusiveness is to illustrate, from as wide a range of examples as possible, the transcendent beauty of nature and the limitations of a materialistic outlook.

In 'The Religion of the Forest',[86] Tagore contrasts the unity of all things and human proximity to nature, as depicted in classical Indian literature, with the disjunction between human beings and nature in Shakespeare and Milton. He considers the Romantic Movement unique in this respect in European cultural history, attributing the change 'in the main to the influence of the newly discovered philosophy of India'.[87] 'An Indian Folk Religion' is a tribute to the Baul singers of Bengal and their journey from 'the finite nature of the individual self' to union with the infinite through love.[88] 'East and West' deplores the ravages of the First World War: Tagore had recently visited the site of the French battlefields. He acknowledges the West's gift of enlightenment and humanism to the world but regrets the 'passion for power and wealth'[89] that diverted this to a mission of mass destruction. He disagrees unequivocally with Kipling's assertion that the East and West shall never meet; rather, he urges a union of the two 'not merely in the fulness of physical strength, but in fulness of truth'.[90] The true incompatibility, he declares, is not between East and West but between man and machine. Following this line of thought, 'The Modern Age' begins by examining a range of evils, from the pollution of Kolkata's riverbanks by capitalist industry to the 'debauchery of destruction'[91] in the First World War. It ends by urging his audience to learn 'the truth of love'[92] from the Buddha and Christ.

Creative Unity updates the ideas in Tagore's earlier prose writings with images and examples from the post-war period. But 'An Eastern University', the last essay of the volume, is different. It articulates the formative ideas behind Visva-Bharati, the university he had recently founded. He explains how his originary impulse was to create an 'International University' whose goal would be 'promoting mutual understanding between the East and the West':[93] a purpose reflecting the title *Creative Unity*. An Indian university along these lines would afford Western students 'intellectual hospitality', offering 'their [Indians'] wealth of mind to others, and ... in return ... receiv[ing] gifts from the rest of the world'.⁹⁴ Turning to a favourite analogy, superbly developed in his parable 'Totākāhini' ('The Parrot's Training'), he declares the university 'must not be a dead cage in which living minds are fed with food artificially prepared', but 'an open house, in which students and teachers are at one'.⁹⁵ He also stresses the cultivation of indigenous knowledge and vernacular languages while recognizing the importance of a 'common language', like Sanskrit in ancient India and English in parts of the West in his own day.⁹⁶ He would like Indians

> not to resist the Western culture, but truly to accept and assimilate
> it; to use it for our sustenance, not as our burden; to get mastery over
> this culture, and not to live on its outskirts as the hewers of texts
> and drawers of book-learning.⁹⁷

Thus his ideal university would be 'a world in itself, self-sustaining, independent, rich with ever-renewing life, radiating life across space and time, attracting and maintaining round it a planetary system of dependent bodies'.⁹⁸

Tagore's next substantial collection of English prose, *Thoughts from Rabindranath Tagore*, is very different in nature. First published in 1921 as *Thought Relic*, it was enlarged considerably in 1929. As the title indicates, the contents are brief exercises in the *pensée* tradition, carrying on from *Stray Birds* (1916): in fact, the two titles were reprinted together in 1924. But unlike *Stray Birds*, most of the *Thoughts* were originally composed in English,⁹⁹ indicating Tagore's growing confidence in the language. They are various in nature – autobiographical, spiritual, philosophic. There are simple records of a moment's inspiration: 'I need have no anxiety about the world of Nature. The sun does not wait to be trimmed by me.'¹⁰⁰ But unlike in *Stray Birds* or *Fireflies*, these epigrammatic snatches are drawn out in a slightly more extended format.

Thoughts reflects his aversion to materialism and power-mongering, and his cherishing of beauty, the arts, and human bonding through love. Poetry can become a metaphor for love: 'We are like a stray line of a poem, which ever feels that it rhymes with another line and must find it, or miss its own fulfilment.'¹⁰¹ But the idiom of human union expands into that of religious consummation. The *Thoughts* recoil from blindness and worldliness, pointing to a union with the ultimate, marking humanity's place in the cosmic plan: 'The *I AM* in me realizes its own extension, its own infinity, whenever it truly realizes something else.' Art provides a constant trope for all kinds of experience, including universal synchrony:

> The rose appears to me to be still, but because of its metre of composition it has a lyric of movement within that stillness, which is the same as the dynamic quality of a picture that has a perfect harmony. It produces a music in our consciousness by giving it a swing of motion synchronous with its own.[102]

Thoughts celebrates rhythm and music, and reveals Tagore's aversion to an artificial, imitative world. They consistently project the author as a self-reflexive artist weaving his creations from the material around him but moving towards his own perfected thoughts, as in #102, which begins by seeing the world as 'a stream of sounds in music' but concludes by observing 'It is the unity of melody which ever survives the fleeting notes.'[103]

Despite its focused insights and succinct language, *Thoughts* disappeared from view after an expanded reprint; but *The Religion of Man* (1930), the Hibbert Lectures at Oxford, has found lasting favour. As with the English *Gitanjali*, this may have been because when these lectures appeared, they appealed to a readership wary of another war, seeking a salve for old wounds that seemed to be opening up again. The lectures could also be seen as a summation of Tagore's ideas on religion, a return to the wellspring of the spiritual beliefs in his Bengali oeuvre and earlier English writings. The Upanishads, the mystic folk traditions of Bengal, and the teachings of prophets from the East (Zarathustra makes an extended appearance,[104] indicating an interest Tagore would develop further on his 1932 trip to Iran) all appear in the book, as well as Christ.

Tagore states his basic thesis quite simply at the start: 'The idea of the humanity of our God, or the divinity of Man the Eternal, is the main subject of the book.'[105] The next chapter, on 'The Creative Spirit', is an extended meditation on the implications of the theory of evolution for life and creativity. Evolution is a differentiating, multiplying process that enhances the living world quantitatively. But 'an indefinite pursuit of quantity creates for Life, which is essentially qualitative, complexities that lead to a vicious circle'.[106] Release from this mere multiplication of species comes when Life encounters Mind, which is 'essentially qualitative'. So is Life: both have their 'meaning in freedom', but Mind 'missed [this freedom] in its earliest dealings with Life's children'. The freedom is realized only in humankind,[107] because human life extends beyond the physical to something greater, what

Tagore calls 'surplus',[108] thereby attaining a 'larger self'[109] that implies union with the divine – a merger of finite and infinite, each realized in the other.

The subsequent chapters pursue this belief in various ways, citing visionary moments in Tagore's own life and articulating his belief in a *jiban-debatā*, or 'god of life', a divine presence within him that impels him forward. 'My religion is a poet's religion,'[110] declares Tagore, but he also registers in passing his distaste for the grotesque and 'contagious' 'disillusionment' that he finds in modern literature,[111] whose practitioners have abandoned the quest for the infinite and are trapped in solipsism. The concluding chapter, by way of contrast, describes a transcendence whereby the self merges with the infinite by attaining to 'profound love, which is the intense feeling of union, for a Being who comprehends in himself all things that are human in knowledge, will and action'.[112]

Dutta and Robinson report that 'all three lectures had standing room only'.[113] The published book, too, was received warmly, being continuously reprinted to this day. It was Tagore's last major work of English prose. Occasional writings were published from time to time, individually (like *Man*, 1937, based on lectures delivered at Andhra University in 1933) or in collections (like the substantial earlier volume, *Talks in China*, 1925), but proved ephemeral in their impact. None met with the acclaim of *Sadhana* or *The Religion of Man* or even the opposition aroused by *Nationalism*.

VARIED FARE

In the first twelve years after *Gitanjali* made him famous in the West, Tagore translated and published a number of his plays.[114] *Chitra* (1913), like the English *Gitanjali*, was published by the India Society and then by Macmillan. However, this rendering of the Bengali *Chitrāngadā* was not acclaimed like *Gitanjali*, perhaps because Tagore failed to cast it in a theatrical mould. The Bengali originals of this and the other plays are full of music (in Bengali, *Chitrāngadā* was later transformed into a dance drama), but the English versions are confined to stilted dialogue in an archaic idiom. Even *Chitrāngadā*'s romantic plot seems diffused in the English version. This is even truer of *Sanyasi or the Ascetic* (1917), a drastically condensed version of the Bengali *Prakritir pratishodh*. Its archaic English seems designed to put off any audience, from the very opening soliloquy:

> I ran about, madly chasing my shadow. Thou drovest me with thy lightning lashes of pleasure into the void of satiety. And the hungers, who are thy decoys, ever led me into the endless famine....[115]

Sanyasi is one of four works in the collection *Sacrifice and Other Plays* (1917). These translations, like the poetical collections following the English *Gitanjali*, were rushed into print, mangling and truncating the original plays in the process. Animal sacrifice, at the heart of the title play, *Sacrifice* (*Bisarjan*), is a perennially topical issue; here it also recalls the human sacrifices of the First World War. However, the play is disfigured in translation. 'There is a loss of coherence here,' says Radice, 'a muddling of the clear thought' behind Tagore's condemnation of a controversial ritual.[116] The two other plays in the volume, *Malini* and *The King and the Queen* (*Rājā o rāni*), also suffer from drastic abridgement and indifferent translation.

It is neither parochial nor platitudinous to say that to one who knows the original Bengali plays, the English renderings seem sadly inadequate. The freshness of plot and theme in the Bengali versions, their abundant lyricism and moments of high drama, do not survive translation. This is a pity when we consider how prescient Tagore was in choosing his themes. *The Waterfall* (1922), based on the Bengali *Muktadhārā*, is today more topical than ever for its theme of environmental justice, as conveyed through the story of a dam that impedes the free flow of a river, threatening the people who live downstream. *Red Oleanders* (1925), based on *Raktakarabi*, deals with the exploitation of the earth's resources and the enslavement of common people by the powerful. This political concern usefully reinforces the play's central theme, which is philosophical and even mystical.

In 'Red Oleanders: An Interpretation', a talk delivered in Argentina in 1924, Tagore explains that he is dramatizing the exploitation of 'the resources of the underworld, of nature, of the mind, of science, and of human physique and intelligence, using all the weapons of organization and the elaborate machinery of a highly centralized bureaucracy' geared solely to augmenting the king's wealth.[117] Tagore's remarkable anticipation of today's movements for environmental justice makes the play as topical now as when it was printed. Yet as Das reports, its English reception 'was generally lukewarm, and some of the reviews were very harsh'.[118] The reason might lie yet again in the awkward translation, though the dialogue can be direct and effective on occasion:

It puzzles me to see a whole city thrusting its head underground, groping with both hands in the dark. You dig tunnels in the underworld and come out with dead wealth that the earth has kept buried for ages past.[119]

The symbolic mode and unfamiliar stage language, unlike anything experienced by the anglophone public of the day, might also have put them off.

Tagore chiefly left his fiction to be translated by his associates, himself rendering only four short stories. They offer no clue to his importance as a fiction writer, whose novels and short stories are distinguished by their realism and the complex depiction of man–woman relationships. 'Giribala' and 'The Patriot' translate two of the less-celebrated stories, 'Mānbhanjan' and 'Sangskār'. The other two pieces are allegorical or quasi-allegorical: 'The Parrot's Training' mentioned earlier, a satire on education, and 'The Victory' ('Jay-parājay'), about a battle of poets.

Of enduring interest, however, are the letters assembled in volumes 3 and 4 of the *English Writings*: *Letters to a Friend*, collected with a commentary by their recipient, C.F. Andrews, is especially valuable, depicting the poet in many moods and expressing some of his deepest concerns simply and directly. The language can be pithy ('Movement is the only cure when life becomes heavy with *débris*'[120]) or lyrical and symbolic:

Night, with its phantoms of false mystery of exaggeration, slinks away in shame when Morning appears in her simple robe of white.[121]

At times Tagore virtually echoes his Bengali poetry in celebrating his oneness with nature: 'It is becoming easier for me to feel that it is I who bloom in flowers, spread in the grass, flow in the water, scintillate in the stars, live in the lives of men of all ages.'[122] He can also reach deep within him, in almost confessional mode:

Believe me, I have a strong human sympathy, yet I can never enter into such relations with others as may impede the current of my life, which flows through the darkness of solitude beyond my ken.... I have a force acting in me, jealous of all attachments, a force that ever tries to win me for itself, for its own hidden purpose.[123]

The *English Writings* also abound in lectures, addresses, and messages that Tagore chiefly delivered as a public figure in India and abroad. Among the most eloquent is his open letter to Lord Chelmsford, Viceroy of India, on 30 May 1919, condemning the massacre of unarmed Indians at Jaliānwālā Bāgh and renouncing his knighthood in protest in these memorable lines:

The time has come when badges of honour make our shame glaring in the incongruous content of humiliation, and I for my part wish to stand, shorn of all special distinctions, by the side of those of my countrymen who, for their so-called insignificance, are liable to suffer degradation not fit for human beings.[124]

His Nobel Prize acceptance speech, delivered years after the award in May 1921, is no less impressive, though in very different vein:

And in the evening during the sun-set hour I often used to sit alone watching the trees of the shadowing avenue, and in the silence of the afternoon I could hear distinctly the voices of the children coming up in the air, and it seemed to me that these shouts and songs and glad voices were like those trees, which come out of the heart of the earth like fountains of life towards the bosom of the infinite sky. And it symbolized, it brought before my mind the whole cry of human life, all expressions of joy and aspirations of men rising from the heart of Humanity up to this sky.[125]

Notable too is the summing up of his public role at home and abroad: a chief purpose of all his mature writing, but more especially his English works. He feels he was invested with a God-given role to 'have been an instrument to bring together, to unite the hearts of the East and the West'.[126]

Though he lived another twenty years, this passage can be read as his last will and testament as poet and thinker. It is confirmed in a gravely different key by some lines composed four months before his death. The English text of 'Crisis in Civilization', translating the Bengali 'Sabhyatār sangkat', is not his own work. It was drafted by Kshitish Rāy and Krishna Kripalani but extensively revised by Tagore himself. It expresses his agony at the outbreak of another World War, but sets this, even now, against his undying faith in humanity. The peroration, in particular, has the authentic ring of his own voice and his own English prose:

As I look around I see the crumbling ruins of a proud civilization strewn like a vast heap of futility. And yet I shall not commit the grievous sin of losing faith in Man.[127]

CONCLUSION: AN ASSESSMENT

There were scattered attempts to observe the Tagore sesquicentenary in 2011 outside South Asia and revive interest in his multifaceted, still deeply relevant works. The English-speaking world saw a handful of anthologies and a flurry of scholarly papers, along with a few competent translations. However, Tagore's own English writings, despite their bulk and historical value, command very little attention today.

How enduring, then, will they be in the future? The English *Gitanjali* may continue to hold special place for those attracted to its meditative and musical elements. *Nationalism* will merit attention from students of culture with a postcolonial perspective or those critiquing the nexus between capitalism, industrialization, and politics in an endlessly globalizing world. The spectre of nationalism still haunts us: that gives the book its most direct relevance. People of philosophic or spiritual bent may be drawn to the line of titles from *Sadhana* to *The Religion of Man*.

Much of the remaining contents of the *English Writings* will probably lie neglected and, however deplorably, forgotten. Much of this material was compiled from scattered sources only through the assiduity of Shishirkumar Das and Nityapriya Ghosh and the laudable programme of the Sahitya Akademi. They are likely to be studied only by Tagore scholars or by cultural historians interested in the short-lived Tagore phenomenon in the West and Far East, the controversies he generated, and the adulation he received because of the 'spirit of the times'.

Tagore himself expressed lasting unease about the quality of his English writings on a number of occasions. His self-doubts emerge repeatedly in his letters in both English and Bengali. I have cited his remark to Thomas Sturge Moore that his English was 'like a frail boat'[128] and, again on 20 May 1924, that he did not trust his own judgement about anything he wrote in that language, whether verse or prose.[129] Even as the English *Gitanjali* was winning acclaim in England, he wrote to his niece Indira on 6 May 1913 about the work: 'I still don't know how I wrote it, or why people like it so much. It's so obvious that I can't write English that I don't even have the vanity to feel ashamed about it.'[130]

However, this disclaimer may seem somewhat disingenuous. Tagore must have had a basic confidence in his mastery of English. The way leading writers and intellectuals lavished praise on *Gitanjali*, *Sadhana*, or *The Religion of Man* must have reassured him further. He also knew there were people outside India who valued his labours to present his thoughts and beliefs to the world through the English language. That is no doubt why he had baulked at the idea of someone like Edward Thompson translating his work. As he wrote to this well-meaning admirer, 'There is a grave risk of my overlooking crudities of language – the evidence of which you will find in *The Gardener* – but still I must go on with my work [of translating

his poems] unaided till I have done what is in my power to do.'[131] He even
wrote to James Drummond Anderson, a lecturer in Bengali at Cambridge
whom he respected and corresponded with for a long time, that he found it
a 'delightful task ... to mould [his] Bengali poems into English prose form',
capturing 'the clearness, strength and the suggestive music of well-balanced
English sentences'.[132]

Undoubtedly, not a few of Tagore's English writings will endure. They
deal with matters of continuing and compelling interest in language that
can often be vivid, persuasive, and even moving. Whether commenting
on the common human concern about our place in the universe, the life
of the spirit, and the nature of humans as sentient beings, capable of love
and self-realization; or whether deploring the human capacity for self-
destruction, and the obsession of some nations to expand at the expense
of others, Tagore's poetry and prose in English treat of aspects of existence
still relevant in our times. Moreover, despite the infelicities that mar his
English writings on occasion, one finds in many of them abundant evidence
of the artistry and eloquence suffusing the intensely felt insights of works
like the English *Gitanjali* and *The Religion of Man*, or the indignation that
animates *Nationalism* and the letter renouncing his knighthood. And, of
course, the translated works give readers who cannot access the Bengali
text at least some sense of the range and depth of his original writings. Any
survey of his work must conclude, as this one does, that there is much to
be savoured and treasured in Tagore's English writings, for their riches of
expression as well as thought. Many of his English works resonate in our
lives even now, and are likely to do so in times to come.

NOTES

1. *Collected Poems and Plays of Rabindranath Tagore* (London: Macmillan, 1936).
2. My discussion of this work draws heavily on the essay 'The *Gitanjali* in Translation: A Miracle of Transformation', in my book *Rabindranath Tagore and National Identity Formation in Bangladesh* (Dhaka: Bangla Academy, 2012), 127–44.
3. Ten, including the then unpublished *Gitimālya* and *Utsarga*, though the sole poem (#102) from the latter had appeared in *Kābyagrantha*, ed. Mohitchandra Sen (Kolkata: Majumdar Library 1903).
4. Buddhadeva Bose, *An Acre of Green Grass and Other English Writings*, ed. Rosinka Chaudhuri (New Delhi: Oxford University Press, 2018), 5.
5. *CP* 5:20.
6. See the detailed stylistic analysis in 'The *Gitanjali* in Translation'.

7. *TLS*, November 1912: cited in *SL* 100, n. 2.

8. A somewhat different collection with that title had appeared from Santiniketan c.1919.

9. Kshitish Chandra Sen, *Fifteen Poems of Rabindranath Tagore* (Mumbai: privately printed, 1928); Nagendra Nath Gupta, *Sheaves* (Allāhābad: Indian Press, 1929); Bhabani Bhattacharya, *The Golden Boat* (London: George Allen & Unwin, 1932).

10. See Shyamal Kumar Sarkar, 'On the Autograph Manuscript of *Song Offerings*' (1977–8), in *Collected Papers on Rabindranath Tagore* (Kolkata: Dey's, 2013), 9–32; Rabindranath Tagore, *Gitanjali*, tr. William Radice (Gurgaon: Penguin, 2011), xlvi–xlvii, 215–32.

11. A reading of single poems like the oft-quoted #35 ('Where the mind is without fear', translating *Naibedya* #72) obscures the devotional narrative of the whole.

12. Krishna Kripalani, *Rabindranath Tagore: A Biography*, 2nd rev. ed. (New Delhi: Visva-Bharati and UBSPD, 2012), 213.

13. Ezra Pound, 'Rabindranath Tagore: His Second Book into English', *The New Freewoman*, 1 (1913), 187–8.

14. *EW* 1:81.

15. *Gardener* #5, *EW* 1:85 (*Utsarga* #8, *RRVB* 10:17).

16. Ibid. #11, *EW* 1:88 ('Chirāyamānā', *RRVB* 7:323).

17. For this and the two foregoing references, see *EW* 1:604.

18. *Gitimālya* #31.

19. *Fruit-Gathering* #3, *EW* 1:157 (song from *Rājā*, *RRVB* 10:222).

20. Ibid. #5, *EW* 1:158 (*Naibedya* #40, *RRVB* 8:36).

21. *EW* 1:609.

22. In *Lover's Gift*, the original of #21 is by Debendranāth Sen, of #31 and #53 by Satyendranāth Datta, and of #50 by Dwijendralāl Rāy.

23. *EW* 1:199 ('Krishnakali', *RRVB* 7:297).

24. *EW* 1:210, loosely rendering *Gitāli* #83, *RRVB* 11:275.

25. The translations are attributed solely to Tagore on the title page but build substantially on the earlier renderings of Ajitkumār Chakrabarti (see *EW* 1:623).

26. *Fugitive* #1.20, #2.29, #2.32, #3.25, #3.28.

27. *Fireflies*, epigrammatic pieces translated from *Sphulinga* and *Lekhan* with some original English additions, appeared in 1928. Ten previously unpublished poems were included in *Collected Poems and Plays* (1936).

28. *CP* 12:43.

29. Bose, *Acre of Green Grass*, 10.

30. *SL* 273.

31. *Poems* #1, *EW* 1:325–6 ('Patra', *RRVB* 16:18).

32. Ibid. #33, *EW* 1:339 (*GB*, 'Pujā' #248).

33. Ibid. #34, *EW* 1:339 (*GB*, 'Pujā' #256).

34. Ibid. #107, *EW* 1:381 (*Prāntik* #17, *RRVB* 22:18).
35. Kripalani, *Rabindranath*, 367.
36. *EW* 1:479.
37. *EW* 1:481.
38. *EW* 1:615.
39. *Stray Birds* #81, *EW* 1:406.
40. Ibid. #214, *EW* 1:422.
41. *Fireflies* #1, *EW* 1:439; *Lekhan*, *RRVB* 14:159.
42. Ibid. #8, *EW* 1:440; *Lekhan*, *RRVB* 14:159.
43. Ibid. #60, *EW* 1:447; no source identified.
44. Ibid. #19, *EW* 1:441; *Sphulinga* #249, *RRVB* 27:61.
45. Das, *EW* 2:770.
46. *EW* 2:314.
47. Ralph Waldo Emerson, 'The American Scholar', in *The Essential Writings of Ralph Waldo Emerson*, ed. Brooks Atkinson (New York: Random House, 2000), 44–5.
48. *EW* 2:316.
49. *EW* 2:327.
50. *EW* 2:328.
51. *EW* 2:333.
52. *EW* 2:334.
53. *EW* 2:336.
54. *EW* 2:500.
55. *EW* 2:336.
56. *EW* 2:340.
57. Kripalani, *Rabindranath*, 209.
58. *EW* 2:354.
59. *EW* 2:355–7.
60. *EW* 2:369.
61. Walt Whitman, 'Beginning My Studies', in *Leaves of Grass*, intr. Carl Sandburg (New York: Modern Library, 1921), 7.
62. *EW* 2:366.
63. *EW* 2:376.
64. *EW* 2:381.
65. Lecture 4, 'My School', *EW* 2:390.
66. Ibid.; *EW* 2:393.
67. Lecture 5, 'Meditation', *EW* 2:404.
68. *EW* 2:416.
69. Ch. 1, 'Nationalism in the West', *EW* 2:420.
70. Ibid., *EW* 2:426.
71. Ibid., *EW* 2:422.
72. Ibid., *EW* 2:428.
73. Ch. 2, 'Nationalism in Japan', *EW* 2:439.

74. Ibid., *EW* 2:440.

75. Ibid., *EW* 2:442.

76. Ibid., *EW* 2:445.

77. Ibid., *EW* 2:446.

78. Ibid., *EW* 2:452.

79. Ch. 3, 'Nationalism in India', *EW* 2:453.

80. Ibid., *EW* 2:455.

81. Ibid., *EW* 2:465.

82. *EW* 2:771.

83. Kripalani, *Rabindranath*, 245.

84. Ibid., 254, n. 19.

85. Edward Said, *Culture and Imperialism* (London: Vintage, 1994), 259.

86. Closely based on 'Tapoban', *Shāntiniketan*. The same theme is treated more expansively in English in 'The Message of the Forest', a 1919 lecture at Bengaluru.

87. *EW* 2:517.

88. *EW* 2:522.

89. *EW* 2:532.

90. *EW* 2:536.

91. *EW* 2:540.

92. *EW* 2:543.

93. *EW* 2:557.

94. *EW* 2:559.

95. *EW* 2:563.

96. *EW* 2:564.

97. *EW* 2:565.

98. *EW* 2:569.

99. See Das, *EW* 3:969.

100. *Thoughts* #5, *EW* 3:30.

101. *Thoughts* #16, *EW* 3:33.

102. *Thoughts* #161, *EW* 3:73.

103. *EW* 3:57.

104. Ch. 5, 'The Prophet', *EW* 3:113–19.

105. Ch. 1, 'Man's Universe', *EW* 3:88.

106. Ch. 2, 'The Creative Spirit', *EW* 3:95.

107. Ibid., *EW* 3:97.

108. Ch. 3, 'The Surplus in Man', *EW* 3:103–8.

109. Ch. 4, 'Spiritual Union', *EW* 3:112.

110. Ch. 6, 'The Vision', *EW* 3:121.

111. Ch. 8, 'The Music Maker', *EW* 3:136.

112. Conclusion, *EW* 3:172.

113. Krishna Dutta and Andrew Robinson, *Rabindranath Tagore: The Myriad-Minded Man* (London: Bloomsbury, 1995), 292.

114. *Dākghar* was translated as *The Post Office* (1914) by Debabrata Mukhopādhyāy (Devabrata Mukerjea) and *Rājā* as *The King of the Dark Chamber* (1914) by Kshitishchandra Sen, though the latter's title page says it was 'translated by the author'. Two other plays, unpublished in Tagore's lifetime, were intended for performance by the boys at Santiniketan: *The Crown* (1918), translated from *Mukut*, and *King and Rebel* (1912–13), an original English work.

115. *EW* 2:57.

116. William Radice, '*Visarjan* and Sacrifice', *VBQ*, 45 (1979), 13.

117. *EW* 4:336.

118. *EW* 2:768.

119. *EW* 2:212.

120. *EW* 3:248.

121. *EW* 3:236.

122. *EW* 3:250.

123. *EW* 3:239.

124. *EW* 3:751.

125. *EW* 3:962.

126. *EW* 3:965.

127. *EW* 3:726.

128. *SL* 273.

129. *SL* 311.

130. *CP* 5:19.

131. Uma Das Gupta, ed., *A Difficult Friendship: Letters of Edward Thompson and Rabindranath Tagore 1913–1940* (New Delhi: Oxford University Press, 2003), 52.

132. *SL* 196.

9 Tagore and Indian Literature
Influence and Presence
HARISH TRIVEDI

TAGORE: ACHIEVEMENT AND REPUTATION

Rabindranāth Tagore is the most widely renowned writer of modern India. In a career spanning more than six decades, he wrote poems, songs, plays, novels, short stories, essays, memoirs, and travelogues, besides a vast number of letters. He wrote primarily in Bengali, but his writings in English, including self-translations, fill four large volumes. Virtually no other major Indian writer has been so prolific. His Nobel Prize for Literature in 1913 – still the only award to an Indian – was cherished by his compatriots as being, among other things, a validation of India's cultural standing and even a sort of (post)colonial triumph. Tagore became a national icon, one of a trinity together with Mahātma Gāndhi and Jawāharlāl Nehru, despite the fact that not only did he not join Gandhi's movement for freedom, but engaged in public controversy with him in 1921. Already in 1917, his lectures titled *Nationalism* had denounced all forms of nationalism as both selfish and self-destructive.

Such apparent disengagement from worldly issues reinforced his image as a man of transcendent spiritual vision, an impression already generated by his first slim volume in English translation, *Gitanjali: Song Offerings* (1912), which sufficed to win him the Nobel Prize. In the West, even more than in India, he was seen as a sage and prophet of universal brotherhood, travelling far and wide to preach his message of love and harmony. He seemed to build on and outdo Vivekānanda's pioneering assertion of Indian spirituality at Chicago in 1893. For his admirers, Tagore was not merely a writer, not even only a *guru* or spiritual guide, but a *gurudev*, with the aura of a *deva* or (demi)god. The institution he founded in Santiniketan was at core an *āshrama*, a holy retreat. He inspired a reverence not remotely commanded by any other writer in modern times unless, like Sri Arabinda (Aurobindo), they acquired an overriding identity as a spiritual leader.

These matters have a bearing on the nature and extent of Tagore's *literary* influence, which this essay proposes to examine. Tagore wrote numerous works, especially fiction, political essays, and travelogues, which have little overt spiritual content. He also had a robust sense of comedy and humour. But he still has many admirers whose veneration is based solely on the English *Gitanjali*. For them, as for others who may not have read him at all, Tagore remains typecast as a devotional and mystical poet. In what follows, I attempt – necessarily in a highly selective manner – to trace his wider impact in some Indian languages other than Bengali.

This impact was substantially different at home and abroad, as what appeared novel to Western readers was often familiar to Indians, or vice versa. I will review the range of his influence across India and then consider in more detail his much-debated role in a prominent literary movement in Hindi, a language geographically and culturally close to Bengali. This movement was *Chhāyāvād*, 'penumbral' or symbolic poetry marked by romantic mysticism.

The case of Tagore raises some questions of terminology. Terms such as 'impact', 'influence', 'imitation', and 'emulation' all seem inadequate. What Tagore truly exercised was a persistent and pervasive *presence*, both dominating and inspirational. We need to unpack, complicate, and theorize this presence in indigenous ways rather than by invoking phenomenological cognition as expounded, for instance, by Maurice Merleau-Ponty, Hans-Georg Gadamer, and Andy Clark in their very different Western philosophical contexts. It may be more helpful to think of 'presence' in Sanskritic–Bengali terms like *astitva*, '(just) being', and *upasthiti*, 'being there', or in Arabic–Persian terms like *huzoor*, 'presence (of a person of high authority)',[1] who exercises power around him simply by being *haazir* or present. For not only was Tagore's appearance in Indian literary history uniquely compelling in his time, but its impact and influence are an abiding presence to this day.

THE NOBEL AND NEWNESS

It has been suggested that Tagore's pre-eminence in Indian literature is chiefly owing to the Nobel Prize. This is not entirely true. He was already a celebrated poet in Bengali even if purists derided his stylistic innovations, like the professor who reportedly asked examination candidates to 'correct the errors' in a passage by Tagore. A few of his works had been translated into other Indian languages even before the Nobel award. The play *Chitrāngadā*, for example, was translated into Hindi in the 1890s.[2] In Andhra, Mutnuri Krishnarāo, patriot and journalist, toured Bengal extensively with Bipinchandra Pāl from 1905 to 1911, during and after a mass movement against the proposed partition of Bengal. Returning to Andhra, he published some translations of Tagore and articles about him in his Telugu journal *Krishna patrikā*.[3]

Nevertheless, the award of the Nobel Prize was entirely unexpected. The nomination was made in a somewhat informal manner, but *Gitanjali* so overwhelmed the prize committee that norms were relaxed. Per Hallström, a member of the Swedish Academy, noted in his report that Tagore was 'an Indian saint', that in *Gitanjali* '[e]very poem is a prayer', and that the book possessed 'a primitive greatness'.[4] He was even apologetic about sullying the poet's other-worldly sanctity by the award: '[I]t goes against the grain to associate a monetary prize with this purely religious poetry. It is like paying for the psalms [of David] or the songs of Saint Francis.'[5]

Such fanciful appreciation was inspired by W.B. Yeats's introduction to the English *Gitanjali*, a flagrant attempt at exoticizing and orientalizing India. This was partly owing to wishful, compensatory myth-making on Yeats's part: he deplored that Western literature had not retained such spirituality and himself strove to resuscitate Celtic mythology. However, he finally grew disenchanted with Tagore, even to observing that the Nobel award was an act of 'wise imperialism from the English point of view'.[6]

Meanwhile, the myth-making had succeeded: Tagore's reputation as a poet-prophet and saint swept the West in the decade that followed. His reputation in India, too, instantly rose sky-high. But realization soon dawned on Indian readers that the religious-mystical vein that struck the West as a novelty was as old as the Vedas and the Upanishads and, unlike in the West, had never fallen into desuetude. Tagore's crown of renown in foreign lands turned out to be old hat at home. But this prophet continued to be honoured in his own country for the somewhat misplaced reason that in colonial India, especially among its anglophone elite, what was honoured in the West was doubly revered at home.

The history of Tagore's impact on Indian literature is thus filtered, mediated, and even determined by his impact in the West. (The nearest parallel is the acclaim accorded to Salman Rushdie in postcolonial India after the Booker prize of 1979.) The work by Tagore most often translated into other Indian languages remains *Gitanjali*, usually not from the substantially different Bengali volume but from the English collection of that name, drawn from ten Bengali collections. This was so inadequate and so oriented to Western readers that Tagore came to repent his Frankensteinian creation. He wrote to his biographer Edward Thompson in 1921:

> [W]hen I began this career of falsifying my own coins I did it in play.
> Now I am becoming frightened of its enormity and am willing to

make a confession of my misdeeds and withdraw into my original vocation as a mere Bengali poet.[7]

Needless to say, it was too late to shut the stable door on the horse of his renown, which had long bolted to gallop towards worldwide conquest as in the *ashvamedha yajna* of ancient India. Tagore's reputation at home and abroad is thus based substantially on ever-multiplying replications of his own professed mistranslations.

Despite his repeated pleas of *mea culpa* as a translator, and his 'complicity in the projection of the image of a "spiritual poet"',[8] Tagore never retreated from his exalted place on the world's stage into being a 'mere' Bengali poet again. Through repeated tours in India and abroad, he exploited his reputation not only for himself personally but also to raise funds for his financially precarious institution, Visva-Bharati. The 'false coin' of his translations and their retranslations remained in wide circulation, succeeding like success.

TRANSLATIONS AND MEDIATION

Tagore's serial textual misrepresentations, which go far beyond the 'loss' entailed in all translation, are mitigated by the fact that several Indian admirers actually travelled to Santiniketan to benefit from his reverend presence at that *āshram*. Some of them stayed long enough to learn Bengali and translate directly from the originals. V.K. Gokak names as many as twelve practising and future writers in Kannada, Telugu, Malayālam, and Gujarāti who went to study at Visva-Bharati at a time when it had no statutory status; several others in different parts of India learnt Bengali to access his work in the original, and often translate it as well.[9] Many other eminent Indian writers translated Tagore from the English, thus further celebrating and transmitting his work. This literary galaxy included half a dozen stars who went on to win the Jnanpith award after its institution in 1965: Masti, Kuvempu, and Bendre in Kannada and Sumitrānandan Pant, Mahādevi Varmā, and Agyey in Hindi.

Of the early translators, Subramania Bhārati (1882–1921) stands out. The reverence in which he is held by Tamil readers fully matches that accorded Tagore in Bengali. Unlike Tagore, Bharati was a proudly nationalist poet and journalist, self-exiled at one point to the French territory of Pondicherry (now known as Puducherry) to avert imminent arrest by the British. He twice translated into Tamil Bankimchandra Chattopādhyāy's nationalist hymn 'Vande Mātaram'. But he also translated parts of Tagore's *The Crescent Moon*, and then in 1918, two volumes of selections from Tagore, one comprising eight short stories and the other, in a rare choice, five essays, both with substantial annotation. In 1921, he hailed a European tour by Tagore in an essay titled 'Sri Ravindra Digvijayam' (Tagore's World-Conquest):

> If one attains fame it should be like that of the great Ravindrar.... His fame has spread across this earth.... What the world has seen are only translations. And yet this fame...! Ravindrar has established to the world that India is the world's teacher [*loka guru*]. May the flowers at his feet be praised![10]

There is a paradox at work here, which characterized the reception of Tagore throughout India. Even if one did not value his writings or disagreed with them, one took patriotic pride in his international acclaim. A.R. Venkatachalapathy remarks: 'For Bharati, Tagore's greatest achievement was fame.'[11]

The sheer quantity of Tagore translations is remarkable. No complete bibliography is available, but a team of scholars at the University of Delhi led by T.S. Satyanāth recorded 673 renderings of various works in ten selected Indian languages (including English) between 1900 and 1950. This may seem low, but the catalogues of some major collections like the Indian National Library in Kolkata, the British Library, and the University of Chicago Library show still lower numbers. Satyanath's database (in progress) has most items from the four major Dravidian languages: Telugu (161), Kannada (101), Tamil (93), and Malayalam (73). There follow Gujarati (70), English (64), and Hindi (53), trailed by Marāthi (27), Panjābi (20), and Sindhi (11).[12] These figures may be far from final, but they indicate the general trend and broadly suggest the degree of receptivity in each language to Tagore through translation.

The business of translating him into Indian languages may have passed its peak, but it continues in new hybridized ways. A significant example is a Hindi translation (2003) of *Gitanjali* by the poet Prayāg Shukla, who was born and brought up in Kolkata, has a degree from the University of Calcutta, and is fully competent in Hindi, Bengali, and English. This facing-page edition has the Bengali original, transcribed in the Devanāgari script, alongside the Hindi translation. We see how a large proportion of Tagore's Sanskritic register can be retained in Hindi without any change. (This is largely true of not only the Sanskrit-derived north Indian languages but also the Dravidian languages in their formal literary diction.) In the opening of the first poem, *ashesh* (endless) and *lilā* (divine sport) remain the same, while *jiban naba* (new life) becomes *nava-jeevan* to suit the Hindi rhyme and metre.[13]

But in the famous poem #35[14] ('Where the mind is without fear...'), the ending follows not the Bengali original but Tagore's truncated, self-censored English version, omitting the line that William Radice (who thoroughly deconstructs Tagore's English version) renders as 'with pitiless blows, Father, from your hand'.[15] Shukla explains that he has adhered to the English version here and throughout, not only because it has acquired historical value but also because it has 'the poet's own sanction [*kavi pramān*]'.[16] Shishirkumār (Sisir Kumar) Dās said that Tagore was initially regarded in India 'as an imposition by the Western world on [the] Indian literary scene'.[17] In the case above, the Western Tagore still interposes himself between the sister languages Bengali and Hindi.

RECEPTION AND RESISTANCE

Another aspect of such continuing Western imposition is that in the discourse on Tagore in the English language, whether generated in the West or in India, his reception in the West eclipses his reception in India. In the magnificent birth centenary volume published by the Sahitya Akademi in 1961, there are thirteen essays on 'Tagore in Other Lands' from Brazil to Vietnam but not a single essay on his reception in any Indian language. The journal of Tagore's own university, the *Visva-Bharati Quarterly*, contented itself in 1961 with reprinting some old essays from 1942–3, written after Tagore's death in 1941. Commemorative conferences and publications, 50 years after Tagore's death or 150 years after his birth, have focused predominantly on his place in the West, his message of universalism, or his relevance in the contemporary world.

In his wide-ranging survey marking Tagore's birth centenary, Gokak made some perceptive observations on the nature of Tagore's achievement and influence. Tagore, he said, was not only a poet of genius but the 'literary spokesman of the Indian renaissance par excellence';[18] his work reflected the 'Time-Spirit' and was thus 'also the birthright of his contemporaries and immediate successors';[19] and his chief legacy was not his themes or images but 'the freedom and confidence that he brought to the Indian aesthetic personality'.[20] He added that not only the left-leaning 'progressive' writers but many others later found his influence 'oppressive', that his mysticism and universalism had come to seem 'facile', and that there was now need for another synthesizer, a 'greater Tagore'.[21]

The scholars who assessed Tagore's influence on the literature of their respective languages shortly after his death adopted different approaches and attitudes. R.S. Joag spoke of a general antithesis between the 'emotional idealism' of Bengal and the 'rugged realism' of Mahārāshtra, and the foundational influence of the novelist Hari Nārāyan Apte (1864–1919) on Marathi literature, but he also noted that Apte had translated the English *Gitanjali* and that Tagore's epigrams in *Kanikā* had a vogue in Marathi, though the imitations were 'not noticed as serious poetry'.[22] By contrast, V.N. Bhushan, who had himself translated, staged, and written on Tagore in Telugu, recalled that Rāyaprolu Subbārāo (1892–1984), who stayed for a period in Santiniketan, had inaugurated a 'Romantic and Mystic school' in Telugu poetry, and that there had been 'circles of Tagore-intoxicated young Andhras' who would recite 'portions of the *Gitanjali* in the same spirit in which they do the Gāyatri', the seminal Vedic mantra.[23] Such 'reverential rapture' was owing to the fact that what was new in Tagore was nevertheless all too familiar, for he represented 'primarily the ageless poetic mood of India'; his 'essential Indianness ... stirs a responsive echo in the heart of every Indian'.[24] Rām Panjwāni similarly recalled that when Tagore arrived on the Sindhi scene, 'he became one with our Sufi poets – a part of our traditions': when he sings 'God stands outside the door', 'he is saying nothing new for us'.[25]

The Oriyā response to Tagore, suggested H.C. Barāl, was slow and limited because 'something like a renaissance era in Oriya literature had [already] been inaugurated' by its own writers.[26] In Kannada, on the other hand, R.V. Jāgirdār noted that a new stimulus came not from English but from the 'sister literature' of Bengali.[27] However, although the influential poet B.M. Srikāntaiāh did translate *Gitanjali*, he truly revolutionized literary taste in 1921 by rendering in Kannada a selection of the English Romantic poets under the title *English gitagulu*.[28] In Tamil literature, P.N. Appuswāmi noted that Tagore's influence had bred 'pseudo-mystics and pseudo-poets', while his influence on established Tamil writers was 'stimulative rather than directive'.[29]

Several common strands emerge from these responses. Tagore's dramatic appearance on the Indian literary scene in 1913 caused a sensation across India. The mystic-romantic element in his poetry had an immediate popular appeal that swept many admirers off their feet while encouraging facile imitators. The apparent devotion to an abstract god seemed deeply familiar to readers well versed in earlier Indian literature. But even those not much moved by these factors could not deny their effect in the West. Everyone seemed enthused by a contemporary Indian writer's attaining worldwide fame. Again we see how Tagore's Indian reputation fed directly on his acclaim elsewhere in the world.

THE CASE OF HINDI: *CHHĀYĀVĀD*, NIRĀLĀ, PANT, AND PREMCHAND

Perhaps the impact of Tagore was nowhere felt more strongly than in the vast Hindi region that starts at Bengal's doorstep. The pilgrimage cities of Vārānasi and Allāhābād (Prayāgrāj) had large Bengali populations. The prominent Bengali journal *Prabāsi* (1901–61), where many of Tagore's writings first appeared, was published from Allahabad. Tagore visited Allahabad for a month in 1914, during which time he wrote four celebrated poems to be found in his volume *Balākā*, including one on the Tāj Mahal (*Balākā* #7). In turn, Kolkata since the early nineteenth century had a large Hindi-speaking population including many writers and publishers; in fact, the first Hindi journal *Udant mārtand* appeared from Kolkata in 1826. It is in this long-shared literary context that Tagore's impact on Hindi literature needs to be seen.

Early in his poetic career, Tagore had attempted to emulate old Vaishnava poetry. These Chattertonian imitations, contained in *Bhānusingha thākurer padābali* (1884), are composed in a language he called 'imitation Maithili',[30] Maithili being a variety of Hindi spoken in parts of Bihar. (It gained the status of an independent language in 2003.) Shortly after the Nobel award, Tagore co-translated with Evelyn Underhill *One Hundred Poems by Kabir* (1914), a mystical-devotional medieval Hindi poet he had long admired.

Among Tagore's contemporaries, the Hindi poet who had the most complex literary relationship with him (although they never met) was Suryakānt Tripāthi 'Nirālā' (1899–1961). He was born and brought up in Bengal, in Mahishādal in Medinipur district where his father was a guard at the local rājā's palace. Throughout his life, he had an intense dialogic relationship with Tagore and can thus be regarded as a lightning rod of Tagore's influence. If a single writer from any Indian language can be designated as a principal beneficiary/victim and witness of Tagore's impact, it is him.

Nirala began his literary career in Kolkata as part of the core group of young contributors to the journal *Matvālā* (Intoxicated), established in 1923. Along with Sumitranandan Pant (1900–77), he was immediately identified as a leading poet of a new Romantic movement in Hindi poetry called – originally by its detractors – *Chhāyāvād* (Shadow-ism), that is, obscure mystical poetry written in the shadow of poets from England and from Bengal: the latter were widely recognized as the filter or clearing house for English cultural influence.

In his magisterial history of Hindi literature, Rāmchandra Shukla charged *Chhāyāvād* with being doubly derivative, in its mysticism and symbolism (*rahasyavād aur pratikvād*) and its exclusive concentration on the emotion of love, whether divine or secular (*laukik yā alaukik prem*).[31] Tagore acknowledges that he was in his youth especially attracted to the English Romantic poets: he was even called 'the Bengal Shelley',[32] while the influence of Keats has been persuasively demonstrated.[33] Ipshitā Chanda confirms this chain of influences in what is probably the most detailed study of Tagore's influence on Nirala. Even when under severe attack, Nirala proves himself a sophisticated arbiter of transactions between different literary systems. Not only he but even Omar Khayyam, Wordsworth, Shelley, Michael Madhusudan Datta (Dutt), and Rabindranath, he says, suffered the 'onslaught of poison-drenched arrows of criticism from the public' for not following convention in their poetic work.[34] Adding an equally vital indigenous influence to the mix, Nirala elsewhere highlights how much Tagore owed to Hindi poetry in the first place: 'Kavivar Rabindranath owes an immense debt to these [Hindi/Brajbhāshā Vaishnav poets] but he hasn't paid a single paisa as interest.'[35]

This did nothing to protect Nirala from the charge of purloining sentiments and ideas (*bhāv*) from Tagore. Nirala's biographer recounts how in 1924, on getting wind of a forthcoming article seeking to demonstrate his debt to Tagore, he decided to pre-empt the attack by publishing in *Matvālā* a letter acknowledging that in a few poems, he had indeed incorporated some lines and phrases from Tagore. When the article attacking him appeared shortly afterwards, all it said was that at several places, Nirala might have derived an idea from Tagore (*bhāvāpaharan*) but had treated it in his own way, so that finally, it was no more than a coincidence of ideas, *bhāvon ki bhidant*.[36] Of course, this may have been meant ironically, as another twist to the knife.

Nirala's reputation suffered from this controversy but not for long. In any case, what are commonly regarded as his greatest poems bear no resemblance to anything in Tagore. These are a self-reproachful elegy on his young daughter; a long poem on Rāma's worship of Shakti, seeking the goddess's blessings in his battle with Rāvana; and another long poem celebrating Tulsidās, the poet closest to Nirala's heart, author of the Hindi *Rāmcharitmānas* on the life of Rama. But Nirala continued cheerfully to recite large chunks of Tagore's poetry in Bengali, sing his songs, and offer him the highest praise, even allowing him to be greater than Shakespeare or Kālidāsa though not Tulsidas.

In 1929, Nirala published *Ravindra-kavitā-kānan* (The Garden of Tagore's Poetry), the first Hindi book on Tagore. He quoted copiously from Bengali in the Devanagari script, sometimes without translation and nearly always with unqualified appreciation. Occasionally, he introduced a comparative dimension as when, in the context of Tagore's poem on Urvashi, the heavenly courtesan, he cited sensuous descriptions of feminine beauty by older Sanskrit and Hindi poets and also queried a hyperbolic estimate of the poem by Ajitkumār Chakrabarti.[37] But the book was written in a hurry, as Nirala urgently needed money (as had Bharati when translating Tagore's short stories): he was being paid four annas a page. The worldly succour that Tagore afforded his translators and critics might be adjudged another of his contributions to Indian literature.

So far as the strain of mystic devotion was concerned, which constituted Tagore's primary appeal, Nirala soon drifted closer to the modern saint and devotee Rāmkrishna Paramhamsa, whose *Kathāmrita* (oral religious discourses) he translated into Hindi. Soon afterwards, he diverged yet again to write poems on subaltern characters like a woman breaking stones by the roadside on a hot day or a free-wheeling satirical poem like 'Kukurmuttā' (a mushroom, but literally 'dog's piss' in Hindi), and then in his final phase, devotional poems in the manner of Tulsidas. If anything rankled, it was Tagore's aristocratic and elitist advantages over a chronically indigent and feckless poet like himself. While staying at the Ramakrishna Math at Belur in the 1920s as editor of their journal *Samanway*, he reportedly used to say, 'If I were the [grand-]son of Prince Dwārakānāth Tagore and rich, people would have thought me great.'[38]

Tagore's influence on *Chhāyāvād* was not confined to Nirala. Sumitranandan Pant, who too lived in Allahabad and with whom Nirala had a fond relationship of comradely rivalry, vied with him in his admiration for Tagore: they exchanged banter on who had plagiarized more from Tagore. When Pant visited Santiniketan in the 1930s, Nirala jokingly challenged his entitlement to go where Nirala himself had never been. Eclectically open to influences, Pant was briefly a Marxist in the 1930s, during which time he wrote a condemnatory poem on the Taj Mahal very different from Tagore's. He then returned to Gandhi and finally sought inspiration from Sri Aurobindo. A younger *Chhāyāvādi* poet, Mahadevi Varma (1907–87), also wrote mystical poetry in a distinctive gendered voice while expressing reverence towards Tagore, whom she met in Allahabad as well as at Santiniketan. However, at thirty-five, at the peak of her powers, she abruptly stopped writing poetry, as if it were an indulgence, to devote herself to the

Gandhian nationalist cause. Her brief memoir of Tagore makes no reference to either his poetry or her own.

The Hindi writer personally closest to Tagore was Hajāri Prasād Dwivedi (1907–79). Tagore wanted a bright young Sanskrit pandit straight from Kāshi for Santiniketan, and Hajari Prasad fitted the bill. From 1930 to 1950, he taught Hindi at Visva-Bharati, served as the resident expert on all matters relating to the *shāstra*s, or Hindu scriptures, including *panchānga* (astrological almanacs), and grew specially close to Tagore's associate Kshitimohan Sen. His collection *Mrityunjay ravindra* (The Immortal Tagore) comprises twenty-eight notes and essays on various aspects of Tagore as a person and a writer, including one on Tagore's services to Hindi such as founding a Hindi Bhavana at Visva-Bharati. There is also a quizzical piece on Tagore's horoscope, expounding the planetary conjunction at vital moments like his marriage, the Nobel award, and his death.[39]

A 1942 essay by Hajari Prasad, whose title translates as 'Rabindranath as an Inspirer of Modern Hindi Literature', remains the *locus classicus* on the subject. Here he adjudges Munshi Ajmeri's Hindi translation of *Gitanjali* as surpassing all others.[40] *Gitanjali*, he declares, has spawned 'a plethora of mushroom poets' in Hindi, but *Chhāyāvād*, too, derived its 'inner radiance' from Tagore, even if the English Romantic poets had a more direct influence on Hindi poetry. Nirala had 'drunk deep at the springs of Bengali poetry old and new', and Sumitranandan Pant had 'studied' Tagore to comprehend his genius, whereas Mahadevi Varma was a true mystic whose 'genius ... was quite independent'.[41] Together with the fourth, elder *Chhāyāvādi* Jayshankar Prasād (1890–1937), who wrote a mythological epic and also plays, these three had worked 'a complete metamorphosis' in Hindi poetry: they were not mere imitators, of Tagore or anyone else.[42]

Hajari Prasad noted the allegation that Tagore had 'secured an easy fame by ingeniously polishing the 'rugged' ideas of Kabir with the borrowed lustre of Western mysticism,[43] and that his poems were a restatement of Vaishnavite devotion. He finally observed:

> The greatest service that Rabindranath has rendered to Hindi literature is to have emboldened it to the realization of its distinctive existence, contribution and mission, and taught it to stand on its own legs.... [U]nder his benign and invigorating influence, Hindi cast off the slough of diffidence.[44]

An older contemporary of these poets was the novelist Premchand (1880–1936), who towers above all other modern Hindi writers. Though he often referred with due respect to 'Dr Tagore', he also said more than once that there was too much of an emotional 'feminine' strain in Bengali writers like Tagore and Sharatchandra Chattopādhyāy. That should not be the path for Hindi literature: Premchand wanted it to be 'masculine'.[45] In 1918, Gandhi had already begun projecting Hindi as the national language, after consulting several eminent contemporaries, including Tagore who returned a qualified yes. Premchand's own novels, with titles such as *Rangabhumi* (Playground) and *Karmabhumi* (The Arena of Action), depicted various vigorous aspects of the national struggle for freedom.

CONCLUSION

Tagore's death on 7 August 1941 moved the Gujarati teenager Niranjan Bhagat (1926–2018), himself later an acclaimed poet, to write his first poem.[46] The Urdu poet Sanāullāh Sāni Dar 'Meerāji' (whose non-Urdu pen-name honoured a Bengali girl named Mira Sen whom he had loved fleetingly and unrequitedly) composed a *nauhā*, or traditional Muslim lament, in which he called Tagore an incarnation of Vishnu.[47] On the whole, however, Tagore's poetry, for long his major claim to fame, has receded from the Indian literary consciousness outside Bengal.

Unlike his poems, commonly on philosophic themes, the novels and short stories address contemporary social and even political issues, and also translate better. But Tagore's impact as a novelist has been eclipsed by that of two other Bengali writers, Bankimchandra Chattopadhyay (Chatterjee), often adjudged the father of the Indian novel, and Sharatchandra Chattopadhyay, whose moving depictions of wandering heroes and spirited 'fallen' women were phenomenally popular across India. But Mulk Rāj Ānand lauded Tagore the novelist for not merely narrating events but engaging with ideas, as Anand himself claimed to do. He therefore featured in Anand's canon of the Indian novel, consisting of 'the two Chatterjees, the two Banerjees, Tagore, Premchand, and myself'.[48]

As for the other spheres of Tagore's phenomenal creativity, the vast corpus of his songs with their distinctive style of rendering was apparently one of the inspirations behind *bhāva-geet*, a subgenre of emotive lyrics in Telugu and Kannada. As Tagore had rendered many of these songs in heightened English prose in the English *Gitanjali*, such prose poems too acquired a fortuitous vogue in some languages. Some of Tagore's essays on the literature, culture, and history of India also had a substantial effect in other languages. For example, his essay 'Kābyer upekshitā' (Women Characters Neglected in Poetry) led to Maithilisharan Gupta's Hindi epic *Sāket* (another name for Ayodhyā: 1932).This poem does not follow Rāma,

Lakshman, and Sitā into forest exile but focuses on Lakshman's grieving wife, Urmilā, left behind in Ayodhya, and gives her a voice. Another sort of influence led certain Indian writers, following Tagore's example, to translate their own works into English, without getting anywhere near the Nobel so far. The Marathi novelist Bhālchandra Nemāde has wondered about the effect on Indian literature if Premchand, Mohammad Iqbāl, or any other Indian writers had also won the Nobel Prize.[49]

In today's India, Tagore is most compellingly present in 'Jana-gana-mana-adhināyaka' (The leader of the hearts of the people), the song he wrote for the Kolkata session of the Indian National Congress in 1911. The first of its five stanzas was adopted as India's national anthem in 1950, heedless of Tagore's own opposition to any form of nationalism. Jawaharlal Nehru recalled that at his last meeting with the poet, shortly before his death, he had 'requested him to compose a National Anthem for the new India'. Nehru clearly did not then have 'Jana-gana-mana' in mind, but he was happy at the choice (made after Tagore's death and India's independence), partly 'because it is a constant reminder to all our people of Rabindranath Tagore'.[50] As happens with national anthems, many who hear and sing this toponymic and (in the Indian context) virtually language-neutral song do not know who the author was. Besides, as the postcolonial Hindi poet Raghuvir Sahāy (1929–90) satirically asks in his poem 'Adhināyak': 'Who is this in our anthem then / This *Bhārata-bhāgya-vidhāta*, / That every rag-clad urchin sings / So blithely his *guna-gāthā*?'[51] But such are the ironical ways of fame, remembrance, and persistent presence.

NOTES

1. R.S. McGregor, *Oxford Hindi–English Dictionary* (Oxford: Oxford University Press, 1993).

2. Hajari Prasad Dwivedi, 'Rabindranath as an Inspirer of Modern Hindi Literature', *VBQ* 7 (3) (1942); rpt. ibid., 26 (3–4) (1961), 246.

3. V.N. Bhushan, 'Tagore and Telugu Literature', *VBQ* 7 (3) (1942); rpt. ibid., 26 (3–4) (1961), 260–1.

4. Per Hallström, 'Tagore and the Nobel Prize', tr. Arvid Hallden (1913); rpt. *Indian Literature* 4 (1961), 12, 18.

5. Ibid., 11.

6. See Harish Trivedi, 'Nationalism, Internationalism, Imperialism: Tagore on England and the West', in *Colonial Transactions: English Literature and India* (Manchester: Manchester University Press, 1995), 63.

7. Letter of 2 February 1921: Uma Das Gupta, ed., *A Difficult Friendship: Letters of Edward Thompson and Rabindranath Tagore 1913–1940* (Delhi: Oxford University Press, 2003), 128.

8   Sabyasachi Bhattacharya, '"The Frail Boat": Tagore on Translation as a Link
    with the World', in *Tagore's Vision of the Contemporary World*, ed. Indra
    Nath Choudhuri (Delhi: Indian Council for Cultural Relations/Har-Anand
    Publications, 2016), 69.
9   V.K. Gokak, 'Tagore's Influence on Modern Indian Poetry', *Indian Literature*
    4 (1961), 101–4.
10 Cited in A.R. Venkatachalapathy, *Who Owns That Song? The Battle for
    Subramania Bharati's Copyright* (New Delhi: Juggernaut, 2018), 73–4.
11. Ibid., 74.
12. T.S. Satyanath, unpublished paper presented at a conference on 'Tagore in
    the Mirror of Our Times', Martin Luther University, Halle-Wittenberg, 2011,
    and personal communication.
13. Prayag Shukla, tr., *Gitānjali: nāgari mne mool tathā hindi padyānuvād*
    (*Gitānjali*, with the original in Nāgari script and translation in Hindi verse;
    Bikāner: Vāgdevi prakāshan, 2002), 16–17.
14. In the English *Gitanjali*. The Bengali original is *Naibedya* #72.
15. Shukla, *Gitānjali*, 92–3; William Radice, tr., *Gitanjali: Song Offerings [by]
    Rabindranath Tagore* (Delhi: Penguin, 2011), 94–5.
16. Shukla, *Gitānjali*, 8.
17. Sisir Kumar Das, *A History of Indian Literature, 1911–1956* (Delhi: Sahitya
    Akademi, 1995), 192.
18. Gokak, 'Tagore's Influence', 166.
19. Ibid., 169.
20. Ibid., 171.
21. Ibid., 177–8.
22. R.S. Joag, 'Tagore and Marathi Literature', *VBQ* 7 (3) (1942); rpt. ibid., 26
    (3–4) (1961), 255, 258.
23. Bhushan, 'Tagore and Telugu Literature', 261, 264–5.
24. Ibid., 265.
25. Ram Panjwani, 'Tagore and Sindhi Literature', *Indian Literature* 4 (1961),
    187, 189.
26. H.C. Baral, 'Tagore and Oriya Literature', *VBQ* 9 (1) (1943); rpt. ibid., 26 (3–4)
    (1961), 273.
27. R.V. Jagirdar, 'Tagore and Modern Kannada Literature', *VBQ* 9 (1) (1943); rpt.
    ibid., 26 (3–4) (1961), 269.
28. Vanamala Viswanatha and Sherry Simon, 'Shifting Grounds of Exchange: B.M.
    Srikantiah and Kannada Translation', in *Post-Colonial Translation: Theory
    and Practice*, ed. Susan Bassnett and Harish Trivedi (London: Routledge,
    1999), 170–2.
29. P.N. Appuswami, 'Tagore and Tamil Literature', *VBQ* 9 (1) (1943); rpt. ibid.,
    26 (3–4) (1961), 268.
30. Rabindranath Tagore, *My Reminiscences*, tr. Surendranath Tagore (New York:
    Macmillan, 1917), 138.

31. Ramchandra Shukla, *Hindi-sāhitya kā itihās* (A History of Hindi Literature), rev. ed. (Allahabad: The Indian Press, 1940), 805.
32. Tagore, *My Reminiscences*, 249.
33. Taraknath Sen, 'Western Influence on the Poetry of Tagore', in *Centenary*, 260.
34. Cited in Ipshita Chanda, *Reception of the Received: European Romanticism, Rabindranath and Suryakant Tripathi 'Nirala'* (Kolkata: Department of Comparative Literature, Jadavpur University, 2006), 30.
35. Cited in ibid., 146.
36. Rāmbilās Sharmā, *Nirālā ki sāhitya sādhnā* (Nirala's Literary Pursuit), 3rd ed. (New Delhi: Rājkamal, 1969; rpt. 1979), 1:89–93.
37. *Ravindra-kavitā-kānan* (1929): *Nirālā rachanābali* (Collected Works of Nirala), ed. Nandkishor Naval (New Delhi: Rajkamal, 1983), 5:104.
38. Cited in Sharma, *Nirālā*, 539.
39. Hajari Prasad Dwivedi, *Mrityunjay ravindra* (1963), rpt. in *Hajāri Prasād Dwivedi rachanāvali*, ed. Mukund Dwivedi (New Delhi: Rajkamal, 1998), 8.269–449.
40. Dwivedi, 'Rabindranath as an Inspirer of Modern Hindi Literature' (1961), 246.
41. Ibid., 249.
42. Ibid., 250.
43. Ibid., 251.
44. Ibid., 253.
45. Cited in Harish Trivedi, 'Tagore's Nationalism – and Premchand's: A Complementary Comparison', in *Tagore and Nationalism*, ed. K.L. Tuteja and Kaustav Chakraborty (Shimla: Indian Institute of Advanced Study, 2017), 211.
46. Rita Kothari, 'Bengali into Gujarati: Unequal Transactions', in *Translation and Culture: Indian Perspectives*, ed. G.J.V. Prasad (Delhi: Pencraft International, 2010), 47.
47. Sanaullah Sani Dar Meeraji, 'Tagore kā nauhā' (Urdu elegy on Tagore), in *Kulliyat-e meerāji*, ed. Jameel Jalibi (London: Urdu Markaz, 1988), 740–1.
48. Sourced from personal conversations.
49. Bhalachandra Nemade, 'Indian Literature and Universalism', in *Interdisciplinary Alternatives in Comparative Literature*, ed. E.V. Ramakrishnan, Harish Trivedi, and Chandra Mohan (New Delhi: Sage, 2013), 146.
50. Jawaharlal Nehru, 'Introduction', in *Centenary*, xvi.
51. Raghuvir Sahay, 'Adhināyak' (Leader, 1967), rpt. in *Pratinidhi kavitāyen* (Representative Poems: New Delhi: Rajkamal, 1994); my translation. The untranslated phrases mean 'arbiter of India's destiny' (a phrase from the song) and 'songs of praise'.

10 Rabindranath Tagore and Literary Communication across Borders

SUBHA CHAKRABORTY DASGUPTA

Literature, to Rabindranāth Tagore, is an expression of being-in-relation. According to him, affective bonds with truth lead to relations of reciprocity where one wants to give back to the world in equal measure what one has received, piling up the offerings with 'word and voice, brush and hone'.[1] What, we wonder today, could be the implications of his idealistic standpoint across borders, in the context of global reception? This essay will take up the question and situate it within the matrix of interliterary communication from several perspectives. It will focus on the various premises of communicative acts with relation to literature in multiple reading communities, and the consequent areas of interaction involving hermeneutic impulses in approaching the texts. It will then take up areas of mutuality and transformation, the function and value of Tagore's texts in different cultures, instances of non-communication, and, finally, shifts in the mechanism of transfer in the contemporary context. This study will help us to look at the dynamics of interliterary communication in the global context, framed by organizational structures on the one hand and, on the other, by literature's ability to create its own relations and extend in many directions, generating semantic and cultural tensions as well as resolutions.

There are layers of interculturality at the core of Tagore's literary work. Before looking at his communication with the wider world, we need to briefly consider the meaning and function of his *oeuvre* in its immediate cultural milieu. He produced an immense body of work in almost every conceivable verbal genre. But to his own people, he is primarily a poet, and his greatest gift to them, across socio-economic groups, is a major corpus of song poems. His community found in his works a new language for a meaningful, layered, and sophisticated expression of the many varied moments of its intimate experiences, and it is this that has ensured his lasting living presence among the people of Bengal. At the same time, he played an important role in the life of the nation and was drawn into larger civilizational questions in complex circumstances during and between the two Great Wars. His creative endeavours spilled over to the nurturing of an innovative system of education in harmony with natural surroundings and a university that would be the meeting place of teachers, artists, and community workers from all over the world. He also turned to painting in his last years. Given this range of activity, his reception in Bengal was not univocal at any point of time. He had many critics in his day: littérateurs, social reformers, and activists opposed him for his unconventional approach to form, content, and issues, while the modern poets of the early and mid-twentieth century criticized him for the same reasons as their European counterparts, except that the Bengali writers often also found themselves going back to him.

FIRST ENCOUNTERS AND HERMENEUTIC IMPULSES

The early rhythm of communication of Tagore's work in the English-speaking world is well documented. It moved from a surge of admiration among a few to large-scale public attention after the Nobel award in 1913, followed by a gradual petering out of enthusiasm with some outright rejections, and finally his reappearance in a different persona, particularly after the publication of his lectures on *Nationalism* (1917). There are other stories within this broad outline: of friendship and communication, and attempts by friends familiar with his land and language to present his works in a more acceptable form and idiom.

A circuit of communication was already in place between artists, poets, translators, and private individuals from both England and Bengal. Tagore was thus prepared for interliterary exchange with a cultural community that had ceased to be a complete 'other' in his imagination. The translations that went into the English *Gitanjali* were the work of a multilingual and multicultural imagination. To this was added an attempt to address the Western metropolis as a poet from the outside, a colonial voice that had to make itself heard. For this metropolis on the threshold of modernity that had grown used to regarding itself as the centre, the first glimpses of an outside world were bound to be marked by a tentativeness, a fragility. Hence the history of Tagore's reception in England is marked by great initial enthusiasm on the part of the literary elite, but then a moving away, an inability to explore further, to probe beyond the first hesitant dialogic attempts at translating a distant language and culture.

Several decades would pass before the English-speaking world resumed its attempts at meaningful communication with the 'other' within a new circuit of world literature, and tried to revisit the texts that had once briefly touched Western culture, learn their languages, go into their history, and retranslate them. Even then, the task remained difficult. Tagore, on his part, could not enter into dialogic communication with modern poetry as taking shape in the work of Yeats, Pound, or Eliot. The impending war led him in new directions: in his communication with the outer world, he found himself striving for agency to bring about a more just and violence-free world. A sustainable interliterary relation could only develop after many meetings and withdrawals. However, the first accommodative gestures from a few poets, artists, and scholars in England, broadly well-disposed to India and its cultural ethos, were historically of great magnitude. They marked the beginning of a cross-cultural dialogue that would enhance the cause of a global modernity.

William Butler Yeats's Introduction to the poems of *Gitanjali: Song Offerings* (1912) became the classic point of entry to the world of Tagore in most international contexts. Despite their differences, Yeats and Tagore had several features in common. Both belonged to colonized nations; both had noble visions of poetry and its function in the community; both subscribed to a certain notion of the 'essential', free of unnecessary embellishments; and in both, one encountered an aesthetic fusion of the sensuous and the spiritual. The first expression of Yeats's support to Tagore may be seen as the celebration of certain ideals that he cherished, but in the larger context, his introduction supplied a matrix of reception mediating between the strange and the familiar, between existing Western paradigms of the primeval East and the modern West. However, the tropes relating to the Orient were now invested with a different function: they helped in the figuration of a poetic ideal for reconstructing a Celtic sensibility.

Significantly, at the start of his introduction to the English *Gitanjali*, Yeats cites a Bengali doctor as saying, *inter alia*, 'He [Tagore] is as great in music as in poetry.'[2] Yeats himself foresees that 'travellers will hum [Tagore's songs] on the highway and men rowing upon rivers'.[3] He says this in the context of an 'unbroken', unified culture. Despite the homogenizing bent of the reference, it identifies an important feature of the general communicative process in later periods. Musicality also figured in Ezra Pound's reading of the poems. He thought that the poems should be read aloud, for as he observed, 'the apparently simple English translation has been made by a great musician, by a great artist who is familiar with a music subtler than our own'.[4] Pound sent six poems from the *Gitanjali* manuscript to Harriet Monroe for inclusion in the Chicago-based journal *Poetry*, along with a short article he had written.[5] But Pound's perspective on the poet was very different from Yeats's. In an essay in *The New Freewoman* in November 1913, he spoke against viewing Tagore as a mystic; instead, he preferred to set him in the context of imagism, with which Pound was engaged at this time. However, as with Yeats, Pound's appreciation of Tagore was quite short-lived. It is significant that Yeats included seven of Tagore's later poems in the *Oxford Book of Modern English Verse* (1936), suggesting that in his later years, Yeats rejected a certain kind of Tagorean poetry while recognizing the general worth of Tagore's poetic contribution.

Both in England and in the United States, *Gitanjali* began to be read in a context of mysticism – a word used by many on their first encounter with the work or even the personality of the poet. The impression crystallized through a review by Evelyn Underhill, the author of several books on mysticism. In the review, she alluded to a number of Christian contemplatives and mystics, along with the Persian poet Jalāluddin Rumi and the Hindu mystical tradition, emphasizing that Tagore deviated from the Hindu concept by moving away from a 'static and transcendent Absolute' to an 'energetic Spirit of life'.[6] Tagore's poems, it may be mentioned, drew freely from several local traditions, including *bhakti* and its energizing potentials, but invested them with new meanings centred on the human and the creative. Other reviewers, poets, and critics added to the allusions, spoke of the fusion of Eastern and Western elements, and in at least one statement, drew him into the Western fold, saying there was no 'radical difference between his lyrical art and that of Europe'.[7] The strangeness had to be dissolved and rendered familiar for a literary work from a different culture to be acceptable.

In the popular imagination, the mysticism associated with *Gitanjali* merged with other dimensions of spirituality treated in *Sadhana* (1913). Reviewers also drew parallels with the Psalms and other aspects of Christianity. However, the notion of mysticism itself was configured at different places and times with different nuances and in a fluid manner, including union with the absolute, spiritualism of a general order, infinite longing, and occasionally pantheism. Mysticism was also seen both as leading to a passive attitude and as an incentive for positive action. Tagore's poems could be seen as accommodating all these nuances selectively, and praised or critiqued accordingly. The Arabic literary community, in these early years of reception, often emphasized the hope and aspirations, the love and happiness in the poems along with love for the divine. There were debates related to his pantheism as well.[8] In the public imagination, the figure of Tagore as an Eastern mystic or sage also acquired a certain dimension of the performative, the considered construction of the poet's self 'from the outside'. His audience would often comment on the attraction of his personality, the iconic image of other-worldliness, even inviting comparisons with the figure of Christ. Later, in several cases, the sense of the iconic would be reversed.

Before we leave this topic, it would be pertinent to mention Tagore's links with the Unitarians in the context of their connection with the Brahmo Samaj to which Tagore belonged. The Unitarians played an important role early in the trajectory of his interaction with the United States. Recently, three songs of Tagore – English *Gitanjali* #67 and #70 and *Crossing* #71– were rediscovered in the hymnbooks of the First Unitarian Church of Pittsburgh, *Hymns for the Celebration of Life* (1964) and *Singing the Living Tradition* (1993).[9]

The award of the Nobel Prize to Tagore in 1913 took the fraternity of poets and critics in many parts of the world by surprise. To reporters, the name appeared strange and difficult to pronounce. We need not go into the details but only highlight the fact that the recognition bestowed on his works primarily rested on their capacity to be completely assimilated within the Western canon. This is evident in the Nobel citation, stating that the prize was given to Tagore 'because of his profoundly sensitive, fresh and beautiful verse, by which, with consummate skill, he has made his poetic thought, expressed in his own English words, a part of the literature of the West'.[10] A similar hermeneutic impulse is seen in the contention of several reviewers that the inspiration behind the poems in *The Gardener*, *The Crescent Moon* (both 1913), and *Stray Birds* (1916) was derived from Western, not Eastern traditions. With a few exceptions, there was ambiguity in the reception of two of his plays, *The King of the Dark Chamber* and *The Post Office* (both 1914),[11] because their symbolic structure was not in accord with the Western concept of drama, although Maeterlinck's name was evoked once or twice. A reviewer's comments on *The King of the Dark Chamber* asserted: 'Drama the play is not: poem it is not: true allegory it is not. It lives only by the lyric flame which destroys it.'[12] That this response represents an early stage of intercultural communication becomes evident if we juxtapose the remark with that of a reviewer in the *New York Times* in 1961 who called the play 'a striking amalgamation of mime, song, dance and poetry. Its appeal is to the mind as well as to the senses.'[13] This assessment illustrates the effect of several meetings of cultures and an opening up of the canon in the interim. Ludwig Wittgenstein had come across the same play in October 1921 and it became his cherished possession, where he probably discovered a shared area of thought and feeling.

After 1913, several volumes of Tagore's poems, short stories, plays, philosophical writings, and an autobiography were published by the Macmillan Company of London in quick succession. The haste with which they were published sometimes compromised the quality of the books. It seemed that the Nobel Prize brought in its wake a process over which the poet himself had no real control. The interliterary communication bore the marks of this phenomenon for many decades. In England, the channel of communication was also affected by a host of political incidents involving the colonizer and the colonized. Responses to Tagore's work became muted or negative, even as his own views underwent a substantial change. The situation continued for several decades till the 1980s, when new translations and studies began to appear, from both Bengal and the English-speaking world, owing to a renewed interest in global interliterary relations. The efforts of James Talarovic, William Radice, Joe Winter, Ketaki Kushāri Dyson, Krishnā Datta and Andrew Robinson, Kāiser Haque, Sukānta Chaudhuri and his panel of translators, Ānanda Lāl, Rādhā Chakrabarti, and Fakrul Ālam, among many others, created a rich body of translations that set Tagore within a larger and more detailed textual landscape. William Radice's efforts in his revised translation of *Gitānjali* (2011) to give back to the poems the element of song marked an important new turn. Interventions from the global Indian diaspora, and its role in enhancing the amalgamation of cultures, further helped to change aesthetic norms and values. There were also contributory factors, such as the films of Satyajit Rāy, which opened a multilevel channel of communication for the texts.

LITERATURE AND COMMUNICATION IN EUROPE IN THE INTERWAR PERIOD

It was in Germany, as Martin Kämpchen states, that Tagore was most successful in Europe 'as an author', with his books selling more than one million copies between 1914 and 1923.[14] As a pre-text to this interliterary relationship, one needs to remember the long history of intercultural communication between India and Germany, and the latter's engagement with ancient Indian literary texts such as Kālidāsa's play *Shakuntalā*, along with those on philosophy and religion. In the popular German psyche, Tagore was in many ways an ideal image of the Indian with spiritual and philosophical bearings. He was also regarded as a poet of peace, who brought solace to a people passing through difficult times.

Sales might have dwindled after 1923, but one could come across personalities like Helene Meyer-Franck (1873–1946), who learnt Bengali to read and to translate Tagore, and published fourteen translations; her husband, Heinrich Meyer-Benfey (1869–1945), who collaborated with her in compiling Tagore's collected works in German in eight volumes; and in recent times Martin Kämpchen (b. 1948), who has translated, researched, and brought several texts on Tagore before a large reading public. He has also co-edited with Imre Bangha the volume *Rabindranath Tagore: One Hundred Years of Global Reception* (2014), which can today form the basis of a different kind of research on Tagore, and to which this article is greatly indebted.

In 1921, Tagore was invited by Count Hermann Keyserling to Darmstadt, where Keyserling had founded his School of Wisdom in 1920 with aims similar to those of Visva-Bharati – to foster the individual's emotional and intellectual potential, and create a space where the East and the West could meet and strive for certain ideals. There was an overwhelming note of adulation in the reception accorded to Tagore at Darmstadt that did not go uncriticized, impacting negatively on a considerable section of intellectuals who felt it betokened a less than literary appeal. Stefan Zweig, an Austrian writer and an advocate of peace, while commenting on the German translation of *Sadhana*, wrote an imaginary dialogue on the issue between an older and a younger writer. The younger speaker, who had once appreciated the poems of Tagore, could not come to terms with this adulation: he declared that what pleased the masses must have some element of the false, and that facile expression of matters that called for depth could be suspect. The older poet tried to justify Tagore but agreed that one did not encounter in his work the deadly, agonizing struggle of mankind against disorder. His final comment was that not everything should be judged in terms of literary value. Tagore should be appreciated for giving them what no one else had done: the grace of his words and the pure breath of his humanity.[15]

Not all would agree with Zweig, particularly those who resented Tagore's pacifist outlook at their hour of defeat, and some Christian groups who were not too happy with his popularity as a prophet. The young Bertolt Brecht, reviewing *The Gardener*, talked enthusiastically about the flow of melody in the poems, replete with love and joy in the middle of the chaos and uproar of war. It seemed unnatural, even untrue, yet it touched the people, taking them to a sunlit peaceful world tinged with sadness. Tagore himself was touched by the spontaneous reaching out of the people towards him: it confirmed that he had something to contribute to the international scene, and probably made him feel less of a poet from the outside. On his last visit to Germany in 1930, he was deeply moved by the Passion Play in Oberammergau, which led him to compose his English poem *The Child*.

It was also during Tagore's Darmstadt visit that Paul Natorp, the German philosopher and educationist, met him and wrote on him. He drew attention to the specific communicative attributes of music in Tagore's poetry, the unique melody characteristic of the language and structure that he analysed in detail.

The fact that Tagore's works had a significant presence in Europe between the wars, as testified by their reception in Germany, adds another dimension to the communicative aspect of his work across borders. The anecdotes about the war poet Wilfred Owen's pocketbook with a verse from *Gitanjali*, returned to his mother after his death in action, or a rise in the sales of *Gitanjali* before soldiers left for the battlefield in Czechoslovakia, are instances calling for greater engagement with the notion of literature during war. Of these deeper communications, none perhaps has influenced the worldwide reception of a text more than the example of Janusz Korczak, who made the children of an orphanage in the Warsaw Ghetto perform *The Post Office* three weeks before they were taken to the extermination camp in Treblinka. Korczak accompanied the children to the camp. About his choice of play, he is reported to have said that he 'wanted to help the children accept death'.[16] This incident changed the reception of the play for future generations and the reception of its performances. It also occasioned other films and plays.

ACTUALIZING THE MODERN IN THE COMMUNICATIVE CHANNEL: GAPS AND FISSURES

According to Saint-John Perse, French readers in the early days detected in Tagore's poetry 'a new intonation of the universal soul'.[17] At the time of Tagore's birth centenary, Perse stated that the glory of Tagore inhered in the fact that he lived his poems in an integrated manner. Perse's interest in Tagore can be ascribed to his own search for the poetics of a new humanism and his faith in the 'divine spark' that lived forever in poetry. He was instrumental in getting *Gitanjali* translated by André Gide. Tagore was important to Gide, the author of *La Symphonie Pastorale*, not as an exponent of ancient Indian thought but because of what he had to offer to him. In the introduction to *Gitanjali*, Gide talks of discerning the quivering of an intimate music in certain verses, evoking a melody of Schumann or an aria from a Bach cantata. He focuses on the semi-pantheistic note of certain poems highlighting Tagore's relationship with the external, physical world. He talks about Tagore's reflection on the two antithetical faces of nature, externally active all along with complete silence and peace within, incorporating both submission and freedom, in passages of *Sadhana* and in lines such as 'You are the sky, you are also the nest'.[18] In this context, he makes a passing reference to Schopenhauer's 'le motif et le quietif'. Gide does not elaborate, but one finds in this allusive reading hints of the emergence of the afterlife of a text and an exercise in situating the text within a framework of the contemporary, while still allowing for differences. The poem 'Early in the day it was whispered'[19] reminds him of the last poem of Baudelaire's *Les fleurs du mal*, although again he is quick to admit the gulf between the two.

Significantly, Gide also underscores the engagement with death in the last poems of the English *Gitanjali*, commenting: 'I do not think I know, in any literature, a more solemn and more beautiful accent.'[20] In *The Post Office*, he finds all forms, all modes of waiting a trope replete with possibilities, here (we may add) in stark contrast with the absurd with which it comes to be associated after Beckett's *Waiting for Godot*. Yet the communication with Gide was short-lived. Gide writes in a diary entry of 1918: 'Read the Reminiscences by Tagore. But this Indian Orient ['Orient des Indes'] is not made to suit me.'[21] The East and the West remained far apart, and other efforts would have to be made to bridge them. Tagore never gained popularity in France. Yet Gide's translation of *Gitanjali* continued to circulate, and stimulated other acts of communication in other parts of the world. Tagore would also come back to France later with his drawings and paintings, revealing an almost Baudelairean preoccupation with the hidden depths of darkness in the individual psyche. His poems, too, would enter the public domain in adaptations for voice and piano, and musical pieces would be composed around them.

Tagore's communication with France also included his interactions with Romain Rolland. The pacifist Rolland, at a turbulent moment in his nation's history, drafted a document entitled 'Declaration for the Independence of the Spirit', asserting the bonds of common humanity even in such times of strife. In June 1919, after reading *Nationalism*, he wrote requesting Tagore to sign this declaration alongside many European intellectuals.[22] It was an important moment in world history, a moment of reciprocity and a response to Tagore's invitation to a dialogue, at a time when *Nationalism* was arousing strong reactions in several metropolitan centres.

We will only get a partial picture if we leave out the countries outside the metropolitan centres of Europe, but it is almost impossible to work out those lines of interliterary communication within the span of this essay. We can only consider a few powerful and relevant instances. There is, for example, the famous Dutch psychiatrist and poet Frederik van Eeden, who came to know of *Gitanjali* in early 1913 and was profoundly moved by the poems. He translated *Gitanjali* followed by several other texts, gave talks on Tagore, and for a short while experimented with a commune in

Bussum like Tagore at Santiniketan. This translation, in turn, was read by the Indonesian poet and writer Noto Soeroto, who wrote on Tagore and translated his 'The Parrot's Training' ('Totākāhini') into Dutch.[23] His poetry also drew inspiration from Tagore.

There was a different need for communication, arising from aesthetic-ethical visions of the future, on the part of a politically subjugated people in many European countries outside the metropolitan centres. One of the most relevant examples, studied in detail by Ana Jelnikar, is the universalist aspiration implicit in the young Slovenian poet Srečko Kosovel's engagement with Tagore.[24] Kosovel was trying to communicate with Tagore in order to find guidance on such issues as creativity and agency, transactions between the local and the international, and a different kind of truly cosmopolitan universalism at the threshold of a global modernity. The possibility of a different notion of universality was present in some of Tagore's writings in general and specifically in his essay 'Bishwasāhitya' mentioned earlier. There he talked about the edifice of world literature where the plan was not particularly stated, where it was both absent and present, universalist and contingent at the same time. And because it was always in the process of being constructed, it precluded exclusionary articulations of universality.

In Czechoslovakia as well, as Martin Hříbek tells us, Tagore's reception 'was located in the discourse of Czech national revival and the role that imagination of and knowledge about India had to play in it'.[25] For this study, where the intermedial nature of communication is often evident, it is important to note the reaction of the renowned Czech composer Leoš Janáček, who heard Tagore reciting his poems in Bengali in 1921 in Prague and was overwhelmed by the melody of the words. Janáček wrote an essay on his experience. He also got hold of a Czech translation of 'The Wandering Madman'[26] and set it to music. The motif would return in his opera *The Cunning Little Vixen*. A large number of Tagore's works were translated into Czech from Bengali by Vincent Lesný (1882–1953) and Dušan Zbavitel (1925–2012). Zbavitel translated many of Tagore's texts covering different genres, but his approach to Tagore was coloured by the Marxian narrative of social progress: in a monograph and other writings on Tagore, he presents him as starting out as a lyricist and gradually moving towards critical realism, probably influenced by his visit to Russia. Tagore's favourable reception in Czechoslovakia was marked by his expression of solidarity with the people on several occasions such as the Munich Treaty (1938) and the earlier call for peace in the winter of 1937.

Tagore's works were widely translated in Russia between 1913 and the late 1920s, but no new books appeared between 1929 and 1955. Thenceforth, because of friendly Indo-Soviet relations, several works were translated anew from Bengali: twelve volumes came out between 1961 and 1965. These were sometimes politically monitored, presenting Tagore as a progressive writer linked with the national independence struggle.[27] However, a deeper mediatory relation with Tagore appeared in a large body of musical compositions.

Hungary is important in this account, because as with Janáček in Czechoslovakia, a poetry reading by Tagore in Vienna inspired the translator Vilmos Zoltán (1869–1929) to render a volume of his poems in 'traditional Hungarian patterns close to the rhythm of folk songs'.[28] But it was the rewritings of Dezső Kosztolányi (1885–1936), who heard Tagore in Budapest and recreated his poems in more intense and melodious iambic strophes, that became popular and inspired composers, some of whom also went back to folk models.

MUTUALITY, TRANSFORMATION, AND CO-CONSTRUCTION

Tagore had a very dynamic reception in Spanish-speaking countries. Two poets stand out in this history: Juan Ramón Jiménez and Victoria Ocampo.[29] The poet and translator Zenobia Camprubí Aymar approached Jiménez, then an established poet, to help her translate *The Crescent Moon*, to which he readily agreed. She later became his wife, and the collaboration continued for almost two decades. After the success of *The Crescent Moon*, Jiménez decided that only Aymar's name would appear as the translator, while he would write a poem prefacing each book as a kind of paratext. The paratexts entered into a tangential relationship with the poetic universe of the text, but also consciously stood apart, creating a cultural space of difference and initiating a conversation. Jiménez can be seen as drawing Tagore into his poetic universe, or perhaps, conversely, his vision of that poetic universe may have been cast in sharper focus through contact with Tagore. His opening verses to *La luna nueva* (The New [that is, crescent] Moon), addressed to a child, may serve as an example:

You are here, yes; we feel you are amongst us, but where are you? Are you playing in your village among the sun-bathed lilies, and we hear you speaking to yourself, when the breeze unfolds the layers of sand on the beach, the breeze that guides your tiny paper boats; or are you already in the sky, boatman of the moon, pouring a blue ray into the vigil of your mother?

An infinite freshness and endless tenderness tell us you exist.
But I do not know how or why. But where, where are you? I think I
know you, but do you know us?[30]

Jiménez was dependent on Aymar's interpretations of the English
versions, but nonetheless, he captured the essence of the poems, the
realization of the child in the man. This perception would be central to
the reception of Tagore in the Spanish popular psyche for a long time to
come. Aymar and Jiménez, it is to be noted, did not start with *Gitanjali* but
with *The Crescent Moon* and then *The Post Office*. The translations were
an immediate success. They caught the attention of the philosopher José
Ortega y Gasset, who wrote three articles on them in the literary section of
the daily *El Sol*, with illuminating insights. For instance, he added another
layer of meaning to *The Post Office* by saying that like Amal, the child in
the play, each individual was constantly waiting for the King, the figure of
the Impossible, to interrupt one's mundane life: that expectation was the
last refuge of one's existence. The Amal within one waited for the King's
letter every day.

Jiménez was drawn to both Yeats and Tagore. There were many layers to
this modern poet who went through phases moving between sensuousness
and melancholy to attain to a textual space of ideal beauty. His poetic ideal
gradually moved towards the simplicity of a 'poesia desnuda', a poetry
without ornaments as in English *Gitanjali* #7 ('My song has put off her
adornments')[31] or Yeats's poem 'A Coat'. While translating Tagore's poems,
Jiménez was also writing his most popular work *Platero y yo* (1917), which
(like Tagore's English renderings) was an exploration of the boundaries of
prose and poetry.

Critics have sometimes argued against the impact of Tagore on Jiménez.
Tagore has encountered strong opposition from the upholders of Spanish
modernist poetry and the realist–naturalist trend in Spanish narrative
literature. But as far as Jiménez is concerned, the depth of the communicative
process can hardly be denied. It is evident in his poem 'Cenizas [ashes] de
Rabindranath Tagore', written after Tagore's death, where he speaks of his
hands that 'moulded the rhythm of his [Tagore's] soul's immensity' into a
Spanish frame.[32]

Tagore's relationship with the Argentinian writer, editor, and literary
personality Victoria Ocampo began in 1924. But his poems had already
travelled to Latin America through Spanish and French translations: Ocampo
speaks of their impact on her even in 1914. The first translation of Tagore
in Argentina, *Cien poemas de Kabir* (*One Hundred Poems of Kabir*) by

Joaquín V. González, appeared in 1915. It was through the medieval *bhakti* poet that Argentina first engaged with Tagore.

Tagore was warmly received on his arrival in Buenos Aires in 1924 but fell ill soon after. Ocampo, who deeply admired his poems, took charge of his convalescence, and a friendship grew between them. Each sustained the other: Ocampo shows traces of Tagore's deep impact on her thoughts, personality, and writing, even as Tagore wrote numerous poems dedicated to her. As Ketaki Kushari Dyson points out, Ocampo's allegorical play *La laguna de los nenufares* (The Water-lily Pond), written before her meeting with the poet, bears a spiritual resemblance to his plays, so that it can almost be taken 'as a last play of Tagore's'.[33]

Ocampo made a particularly notable contribution to the intertextual network of Tagore's reception outside Bengal, by reading him in the interstices of her deep engagement with Proust. In her book *Tagore en las barrancas de San Isidro* (1961),[34] she says that Tagore offered her a respite after long days with Proust, as though in a cool shady grove after a fascinating but polluted city. The lingering despair at the heart of rich and diverse nuances of love in Proust is set against the sorrow-tinged joy even in the experience of unrequited love in Tagore's *Chitra*.[35] But having laid out the difference, she links the two authors by the function of music in their art. She recalls a composer who had told her that when a subject receives form in music, in some great melody, the difference between joy and sorrow, happiness and despair is erased. In the language of music, all is joy – probably because the depth and expanse of melody takes us into an unfathomably deep world. Rabindranath, she says, believed this, as also of love. When love crosses all boundaries, it receives truth, as in the vision of Kabir. Proust too found an affinity with the infinite when speaking of music. Great musicians, says Ocampo, seek a deep darkness, out of which they pluck the hidden radiance of life. A poem by Tagore identifies that light, emerging from darkness, as a source of joy.[36] This, for Ocampo, is the greatest of discoveries and one mediated by Tagore. It seems that Tagore, for her, is not a poet 'from the outside' but almost a kindred spirit showing her the way, even if only for a short while.

Ocampo touches on another point as well: the question of identity, evoked by the poet's quest to discover what was essentially Argentinian. Latin American identity, as distinct from the European, was becoming an important issue. However, Ocampo also notes Tagore's observation that each country needed the other to survive. Eventually in 1931, Ocampo brought out the influential literary journal *Sur* (The South), publishing Spanish American works and foreign texts in translation. *Sur* was instrumental in disseminating the works of Tagore in Latin America. Ocampo also helped Tagore organize his exhibition of paintings in Paris, as earlier she had led Tagore to explore the pictorial potential of his manuscript doodles.

Tagore had an impact also on the Chilean poet, diplomat, educator, and humanist Gabriela Mistral, who declared in her autobiography of 1930 that her masters in art and life were the Bible, Dante, Tagore, and the Russians. She included several poems by the poet in a collection for schoolchildren and thought that his poems on love would give direction to the 'new woman' of the future.[37] Pablo Neruda, the renowned Chilean poet, paraphrased Tagore's poem 'You are the evening cloud floating in the sky of my dreams'[38] and gave it new meaning; that version, in turn, made its way back to the Bengali literary circuit with translations by Bishnu De and Shakti Chattopādhyāy.

Mention must also be made of José Vasconcelos, Mexican writer, philosopher, and politician who, as Secretary of Education from 1921 to 1924, tried to bring about changes in the field of education by a diffusion of cultures. He supplied copies of *The Crescent Moon* and *Nationalism* to libraries meant for teachers in Mexico.[39] Even if not widely popular, Tagore remained a presence in Latin America, particularly in the context of education and a humanist approach to life and literature.

Tagore's own engagement with education gradually received more and more attention in both the North and the South. His theory of education was linked with the notion of creativity, hence imbued with resonances of his poetic universe. This is notably exemplified by Martha Nussbaum, who in recent years has developed a new reading of Rabindranath's life and work. She celebrates his educational method for inculcating a 'more inclusive sympathy' by fostering the imaginative faculty through various activities related to the arts, the notion of interrelatedness of all things, and the ability to move beyond narrow boundaries and engage with problems as a 'citizen of the world'.[40] Nussbaum's reading suggests that Tagore's experiment at Santiniketan eventually did create a level playing field for the post-colonial agent, even if in retrospect after a century.

RENEWED CHANNELS OF COMMUNICATION: EAST AND SOUTH EAST ASIA

Rabindranath's communication with East and South East Asia had a somewhat different trajectory. Here Tagore was primarily a receiver, taking in the many different forms of art expressions, with cultural nuances that were similar though different. His pacifist and optimistic world view was not often favourably received in colonized countries, but again, the pattern of communication would change over the years. As a scholar suggested with reference to the art of Bagyi Aung Soyi, the pioneer of modern art in Myanmar, Tagore and the entire Santiniketan school introduced 'a competing point of reference in reinterpreting and reframing modern South East Asian art'.[41] Tagore's literary *oeuvre*, extending beyond the print medium to dance dramas and song plays, was part of this effort at a collective construction of modern South and South East Asian expressive forms, drawing on elements of both tradition and modernity.

In both Japan and China, Tagore was viewed through a double lens: his reception in Europe and what he might contribute to the emerging contours of the culture of those countries. His importance was acknowledged because of his recognition in Europe; but in both countries, his works were known before he won the Nobel Prize. There was a 'Tagore boom' in the sale of his books in Japan before his visit in 1916.

Yet it was Japan in particular where many people questioned his ideas of the unity of Asia, and the 'East' vis-à-vis the 'West'. They argued that India's experience of the West was different from that of Japan, hence their ideas of the East were conceptually not the same. Tagore's strong critique of Japan's militant nationalism alienated many intellectuals even more. But there were many young men and women who crowded the halls when he spoke, and his speech on 'The Message of India to Japan' (11 June 1916), where he referred to Japan's mission for Asia, received extensive coverage in the Japanese press.[42] There were a few minor scholars who wrote favourably about his lectures even while disagreeing with some of his points. The future Nobel laureate Yasunari Kawabata, then a youth of sixteen, was among the many who listened to his talk: years later, he recalled the impression left on him by the visit. He acknowledged his debt to Tagore for pointing out to him the evolved sense of beauty in Japanese culture, linking it with the perception of truth. This is borne out by Tagore's comments on the paintings he saw in Japan, which seemed to convey the very essence of art, and the same aesthetic sense reflected in the objects and practices of everyday life.[43] When he stayed at Sankei-en, the garden house of the wealthy cultural patron Hara Tomitoro, he had hosts of creative individuals visiting him. During his 1924 visit, he delivered a special lecture on women's issues that was attended by about two thousand women. There were dedicated Japanese translators of Tagore such as Mashino Saburo (1889–1916), Miura Kanzo (1883–1960), and Yamamuro Shizuka (1906–2000). During the poet's centenary, Watanabe Shoko (1907–77) did a complete translation of *Gitānjali* from the Bengali and placed it alongside the Japanese translation of the English version to demonstrate the importance of looking at Tagore's works in Bengali. Much later, there have been Azuma Kazuo (1931–2011) and his team, Morimoto Tatsuo (b. 1928) and others.[44]

Today, scholars in Japan and China are trying to create new perspectives on their intercultural communications with Tagore, beyond the story of the 'unwelcome guest'. The negative reception is being analysed to provide layered explanations of past events, and uncover certain undercurrents of interaction that connect recent attempts at building a structure of deep and meaningful communication. A new enthusiasm is evident today with new studies of Tagore, an interest in his plays among a section of people, and the appearance of Rabindrasangit exponents.

Tan Chung, the Chinese scholar long resident in India, has described Tagore's visit to China as 'a cultural movement' viewed through the 'prism of a geo-civilisational paradigm'. He had in mind the close friendship between Xu Zhimo (1897–1931) and Tagore, each representative of a particular aspect of their civilizations.[45] The friendship between the two had far-reaching consequences, allowing the conversation between the two civilizations to be taken up once more despite the spate of articles and student protests rejecting Tagore because of his opposition to material culture and technology. Xu Zhimo, Tagore's interpreter during his visit, was the driving spirit behind the 1923 avant-garde Xinyueshe or Crescent Moon Society, which, along with others, pioneered the new poetry movement in China. In an essay 'Taige'er Lai Hua' (Tagore Is Coming to China) written on 6 July 1923, he stated that among the 'new poems at least 8 or 9 out of 10 are directly or indirectly influenced by him' [Tagore].[46] During his visit, Tagore also came in touch with Guo Moruo (1892–1978), whose life and writings were deeply inspired by the poet before Moruo joined the Communist Party of China. Moruo was the initiator of another avant garde literary society. The third important poet to hold deep communication with Tagore was Bing Xin (1900–99). An eminent translator of Tagore, she published two collections of 'little poems', *Fan Xing* (Twinkling Stars, 1922) and *Chun Shui* (Spring River, 1923), which received great attention as poems for children, a distinct and independent form emerging in China during this period. Bing Xin acknowledges Tagore's influence in the 'Preface' to *Fan Xing*. Tagore's notion that life and death, finite and infinite are integrated in a rhythm is reflected in her essay 'Yaoji Yindu zheren Taige'er' (To the Indian Philosopher Tagore Afar) in which she 'seemed to be having a dialogue with Tagore on the boundary line of "infinite life"'.[47] The communication continues: in 2016 alone, thirty-three volumes of Tagore translations were published by eighteen Chinese translators fluent in Bengali.

SHIFTS IN THE MECHANISM OF TRANSFER

There are various kinds of communicative frames. Communication with people who are peripheral to certain cultural circuits may be functional in many other ways, and play an important role in later periods in determining the pathways of reception. There was, for instance, the Swiss farmer in a tiny village on the border between Switzerland and Italy who, as Rathindranāth and Pratimā Tagore discovered, had in his possession all the German translations of Tagore's books along with a whole range of classical Sanskrit works, and whose sister would often visit village homes in the evenings to read out passages from Tagore's plays and novels.[48] Today we can cite the instance of the Japanese sophomore Mika Sasaki, who found it remarkable that a genre of songs exists in Bengal that can be labelled neither 'popular' nor 'classical' and is always contemporary to members of the community. She came to India to research the phenomenon of Rabindrasangit to incorporate in a film entitled *Tagore Songs*; interviewed a large number of people, often from the fringes of society; and compiled a moving series of images that brought out the enabling potential of the songs in the lives of the Bengali people.

Interliterary communications take on a new form and dimension in the digital environment. Studies have shown that Tagore's works, both as texts and in different multimedial forms, are reaching a new set of recipients today. Translation into English may not always work with 'distant' languages, and sometimes a community may not wish to yield its most precious cultural resource to an indifferent reading in a metropolitan language. In such cases, multimedial modes can be a viable option. Also, an attempt at communication through an entry into Bengali will take one further towards building the edifice of world literature.

NOTES

1. Rabindranath Tagore, 'Bishwasāhitya' (World Literature), *RRVB* 8:379.
2. *EW* 1:38.
3. *EW* 1:40.
4. Ezra Pound, 'Rabindranath Tagore', *Fortnightly Review*, 11 April 2013, available at Fortnightlyreview.co.uk/2013/04/Rabindranathtagore/, accessed 1 September 2018.
5. Ezra Pound, 'Tagore's Poems', *Poetry* 1 (3) (1912), 92–4.
6. Evelyn Underhill, 'An Indian Mystic', *The Nation*, 16 November 1912, 320; quoted in Kalyan Kundu, Sakti Bhattacharya, and Kalyan Sircar, eds, *Rabindranath Tagore and the British Press (1912–1941)* (London: The Tagore Centre, 1990), 10.

7. Lascelles Abercrombie, 'The Indian Poet', *Manchester Guardian*, 14 January 1913, 6; quoted in Kundu et al., *Rabindranath and the British Press*, 12.

8. See Ahmad Rafiq Awad, 'Arab Countries', and Md. Badiur Rahman, 'Egypt', in *100 Years*, 117–42 and 143–61.

9. Nita Vidyarthi, 'Hymns by Tagore', *The Hindu*, 20 April 2018.

10. Available at https://www.nobelprize.org/prizes/literature/1913//tagore/facts, accessed 31 August 2018.

11. Translations of *Rājā* (1910) and *Dākghar* (1912). The translations were by Kshitishchandra Sen and Debabrata Mukhopādhyāy (Devabrata Mukerjea) respectively.

12. Review in *Manchester Guardian*, 16 October 1914; quoted in Kundu, Bhattacharya, and Sircar, *Rabindranath and the British Press*, 85.

13. Howard Taubman, review of 'The King of the Dark Chamber', *New York Times*, February 1961; cited in Anna Feuer, 'United States of America', in *100 Years*, 602.

14. Martin Kämpchen, *Rabindranath Tagore in Germany* (Shimla: Indian Institute of Advanced Study, 1999), 82.

15. Cited in Samir Sengupta, *Rabindrasutre bideshirā* (Kolkata: Sāhitya samsad, 2010), 391–4, from Martin Kämpchen, ed., *Rabindranath Tagore and Germany: A Documentation* (Kolkata: Max Mueller Bhavan, 1991).

16. Website of the Janusz Korczak Communication–Center, url: http://korczak. com>JanuszKorczak>Biography>DasPostamt and http://korczak.com/englisch. htm>JanuszKorczak>Biography>ThePostOffice, accessed 19 September 2018.

17. Saint-John Perse, 'Hommage à la Mémoire de Rabindranath Tagore', *Hommage de la France à Rabindranath Tagore pour le centenaire de sa naissance* (Paris: Institut de la Civilisation Indienne, 1961), 9.

18. *Naibedya* #81 (English *Gitanjali* #67).

19. *Gitānjali* #83 (English *Gitanjali* #42).

20. André Gide, 'Introduction', *L'Offrande Lyrique* (Paris: Éditions de la Nouvelle Revue Francaişe, 1917), xxxiii.

21. André Gide, *Journal*, 1:644 (1918); quoted in France Bhattacharya, 'France', in *100 Years*, 453.

22. See Bhattacharya, 'France', 462.

23. See also Barnita Bagchi, 'Rabindranath Tagore, Cosmopolitanism, and Utopia: Some Considerations', in *Tagore: The World as His Nest*, ed. Sangeeta Datta and Subhoranjan Dasgupta (Kolkata: Jadavpur University Press, 2016), 61–73.

24. See Ana Jelnikar, *Universalist Hopes in India and Europe: The Worlds of Rabindranath Tagore and Srečko Kosovel* (New Delhi: Oxford University Press, 2016).

25. Martin Hříbek, 'Czechoslovakia', in *100 Years*, 333. References to Tagore's reception in Czechoslovakia are from this article.

26. *The Gardener* #66, tr. of 'Parashpāthar' (The Philosopher's Stone), *Sonār tari*.
27. See Sergei Serebriany, 'Tagore's English Gitanjali in Russia: A Story of Censorship', in *Tagore and Russia*, ed. Reba Som and Sergei Serebriany (New Delhi: ICCR, 2016), 175–85.
28. Imre Bangha, 'Hungary', in *100 Years*, 323. References to Tagore's reception in Hungary are from this article.
29. See Shyama Prasad Ganguly, ed., *The Kindred Voice: Reflections of Tagore in Spain and Latin America* (New Delhi: CSPILAS, JNU, 2011); Shyama Prasad Ganguly, 'Spain and Latin America', in *100 Years*, 476–98.
30. English tr. by Shyama Prasad Ganguly and Sisirkumar Das; quoted in Sisirkumar Das, 'Jimenez and Tagore', in *Profile of Rabindranath Tagore in World Literature*, ed. Rita Sil (New Delhi: Khama Publishers, 2000), 72.
31. *Gitānjali* #125.
32. Quoted by Das in Sil, *Profile*, 69.
33. Ketaki Kushari Dyson, *In Your Blossoming Flower-Garden: Rabindranath Tagore and Victoria Ocampo* (New Delhi: Sahitya Akademi, 1988), 348.
34. Tr. by Shankha Ghosh as *Okāmpor rabindranāth* (Kolkata: Dāsgupta, 1973). My account is based on this Bengali version.
35. The English version of the play *Chitrāngadā*.
36. *Gitāli* #99 (*Fruit-Gathering* #58).
37. See Nilanjana Bhattacharya, 'Exploring a South–South Dialogue: Spanish American Reception of Rabindranath Tagore', *Revista de Lenguas Modernas*, 25 (2016), 81–9.
38. *GB*, 'Prem' #36 (*Gardener* #30).
39. See Xicoténcati Martínez Ruiz, 'Mexico', in *100 Years*, 587–92.
40. Martha Nussbaum, *Not for Profit: Why Democracy Needs the Humanities* (Princeton: Princeton University Press, 2010), 68.
41. Yin Ker, 'Śāntiniketan and Modern South-East Asian Art: From Rabindranath Tagore to Bagyi Aung Soe and Beyond', *Artl@s Bulletin*, 5 (2) (2016), 11, available at docs.lib.purdue.edu/atlas/vol5/iss2/2/, accessed 2 September 2018.
42. Rabindranath Tagore, *The Message of India to Japan: A Lecture* (New York: Macmillan, 1916). This lecture was incorporated in *Nationalism*, Lecture 1, 'Nationalism in Japan', #1.
43. See his *Jāpān-jātri* (1916–17), especially letters 13 and 14.
44. See Kyoko Niwa, 'Japan', in *100 Years*, 3–24; Kyoko Niwa, 'Jāpān bhramane rabindranath o jāpāner janya kabir bārtā', in *Rabindranāther jāpān, jāpāner rabindranāth*, ed. Manzurul Haque (Dhākā: Prathamā, 2011), 34–63.
45. Tan Chung, 'Telepathy between Rubidada and Sushima: A Geo-civilizational Perspective', in *Tagore and China*, ed. Tan Chung, Amiya Dev, Wang Bangwei, and Wei Liming (Peking and New Delhi: Central Compilation & Translation Press and Sage, 2011), 108.

46. Xu Zhimo, *Zhimoquanji* (Tianjin: Tianjin People's Press, 2005), 1:292; quoted in Chung, 'Telepathy', 101.

47. Zeng Qiong, 'Tagore's Influence on the Chinese writer Bing Xin', in *Tagore and China*, ed. Chung, Dev, Bangwei, and Liming, 263.

48. Rathindranath Tagore, *On the Edges of Time*, 2nd ed. (Kolkata: Visva-Bharati, 1981), 142.

11 Tagore and the Visual Arts

R. SIVA KUMAR

Rabindranāth Tagore's contribution to the visual arts in India is twofold: his own work as a painter and his role in bringing about a new turn in Indian art. These two achievements cannot be separated. His role as a critical interlocutor must be considered alongside his success in becoming an acknowledged painter after having failed initially. Given his multifaceted creative personality, his paintings must also be related to the rest of his works.

Tagore began to paint only in 1928, at the age of sixty-seven. He held his first exhibition in Paris two years later and left an oeuvre of more than 2,300 paintings.[1] However, his interest in painting has a longer history. In his reminiscences, he mentions drawing as an item in the all-round education he received at home as a boy.[2] As with literature and music, he was first drawn to painting by the activities of his elders. His brother Jyotirindranāth, who had a pervasive influence on him, and his cousin Gunendranāth, whose sons Abanindranāth and Gaganendranāth became pioneers of modern art in India, were amateur painters of talent. Rabindranath recollects how, even as he was first gaining recognition as a writer, he would spend afternoons with a drawing book, 'toying with the desire to make pictures'. He significantly continues: 'The most important part was that which remained in the mind, and not a line of which got drawn on paper.'[3] At thirty-nine, he writes to Jagadishchandra Basu (Bose) that his artistic impulse remained as ineffectual as before.[4] Soon after, he gave up the effort until, almost surprising himself, he resumed it successfully in late life.

Abandoning his initial efforts to become a painter did not end his interest in art. His continuing engagement as a critical viewer and interlocutor helped not only to develop a new trajectory of Indian art but also to discover new expressive possibilities in himself. His early response to art was, however, no different from that of other members of his class and time. His first recorded comment on modern Indian art is an appreciative response to Ravi Varmā,[5] who imported the British academic style into Indian art and applied it to Indian subjects, especially mythological. Tagore followed this up with appreciations of G.K. Mhātre in 'Mandirābhimukhe' (Towards the

Temple) in 1898 and J.P. Gangopādhyāy (Gangooly) in 'Kādambarichitra' in 1900. Both Mhatre and Gangooly were known for their application of Western methods of representation to Indian subject matter.

These responses, made between 1893 and 1900, are consonant with Tagore's own efforts at drawing at this period. Even as he commends these artists' skill in realistic rendering, bemoaning his own lack of such ability, he writes to Jagadishchandra in 1900 that he is sitting with a sketchbook, drawing. He confesses he uses the eraser more than the pencil: no Paris salon will covet his pictures nor need they trouble Raphael in his grave, but 'as a mother lavishes most affection on her ugliest son, so one feels drawn to the skill that does not come easily. That is why, having resolved on a period of absolute idleness, after much thought I settled on drawing pictures.'[6]

Despite its mock-serious tone, this passage explains why Tagore initially failed to become an artist, and also how he overcame this failure. First, it reveals that his early model was Raphael, the epitome of visual realism and elegance. He attempted to emulate these values but rightly realized he lacked the skills. The few drawings attributed to him from this period are pencil portraits, like those by his brother Jyotirindranath but less accomplished. Now if we turn to his professed weaknesses – the cultivation of ugliness rather than beauty, mental idleness rather than engagement, skill in erasure rather than delineation – it is not hard to see that his eventual success came by harnessing these 'negative' traits and turning them into strengths. But it happened only after some twenty years of engagement with the art of many cultures and periods.

Just when Ravi Varma had succeeded in universalizing the Indian taste for realism in art through mass-produced oleographic reproductions of his paintings, a new challenge was launched by Abanindranath. Although trained in realistic painting by European teachers, Abanindranath, influenced by early nationalist aspirations, had by 1896 begun to question the cultural fitness of painting Indian subjects using Western techniques. Drawing upon the language of Mughal miniature painting, he developed a new model of painting that was Indian in both subject matter and style. This development, and his own involvement in the Swadeshi movement at the turn of the century, led Rabindranath to reconsider his early artistic preferences. He supported Abanindranath's agenda, and the arguments of nationalist art writers such as E.B. Havell and Sister Niveditā in support of Indian artistic values, as a necessary corrective to colonial belittlement. However, his intuition as a writer questioned the revivalism and cultural insularity invoked by such an agenda.

In the 1890s, Tagore shifted base from Kolkata to the villages of eastern Bengal, thereby encountering rural life and nature as none of his predecessors or contemporaries had done. This experience had a profound impact on his career as a writer. It also changed his understanding of the writer's role in society: the new nationalist movement in art seemed urban, elitist, and limited in outlook, with little connection to the larger world. This position can already be discerned in the piece on Mhatre. He argues there that modern Bengali literature had ceased to be parochial. It afforded its readers a freedom of knowledge, broadening of emotions, and expansion of the imagination, but art, although intrinsically universal, was yet to achieve this advance in India.[7] Any culture, he believed, should direct us towards a greater humanity.

To encourage this, he invited Abanindranath and Gaganendranath to illustrate his writings revolving around local visual and social experiences. He also invited them to the family estates in rural Bengal, for the same transformative experience from which he had benefited as a writer. When they failed to respond, being homebound urban artists, he turned to younger Indian artists to share his rural experiences. This was more fruitful. Nandalāl Basu (Bose), in particular, enthusiastically embraced this expanded vision of art. Tagore had already set up his experimental school at Santiniketan, where nature and the arts were used to help the students negotiate the urban–rural divide. He invited Nandalal to help with its work. Further, especially after his visit to Japan in 1916, he felt the need for a new programme of art education to connect the arts to general education and social needs in a meaningful way.

In Japan, Tagore discovered a model for Indian art to follow. Although there had been contacts between Japanese and Indian art since 1903, his first-hand experience of the Japanese art scene was a revelation. He discovered that Japanese artists responded to nature with great sensitivity. They worked on a more ambitious scale than their Indian contemporaries. Their aesthetic refinement extended to every aspect of their lives: Japanese objects of everyday use were not merely functional but exquisite. He wrote enthusiastic letters to his nephews, encouraging them to visit Japan and explaining what could be learned. To Abanindranath he wrote:

> The winds of art have not blown in our country: art has no vital links with our social life, ... therefore you can never draw full sustenance from its soil.... The whole Japanese nation is nurtured by art; their whole life speaks through art. Had you come here, a thick veil would have been lifted from your eyes, and the goddess of art within you

would have received her true homage. After coming here, I have realized that your art has not found itself fully, sixteen annas to the rupee.[8]

In another letter to his son Rathindranāth, Tagore wrote:

Our new Bengal art should have a little more force, courage and expansiveness.... We have focused excessively on small things. Taikan's and Shimomura's paintings are very large in size and yet very precise. There are no useless peripheral objects. Only the idea most clearly revealed to the artist's mind is expressed forcefully on the canvas...; there is no hide-and-seek or haziness, no medley of colours: only a lot of empty space on the huge white canvas, and the picture standing out forcefully against this background. Had Nandalal come, he could have grasped this aspect [of their art] well. It's very necessary that one of them [Gaganendranath, Abanindranath, and Nandalal] should come here, otherwise there's a risk of our art getting cramped in a corner.[9]

Following his visit to Japan, Tagore was more determined than ever to bring about a radical change in modern Indian art. In 1919 he established a new art school at Santiniketan and invited Nandalal to head it. He wanted the school to be the hub of a new movement and not merely a teaching institution. Nandalal proved an able lieutenant, and over the next two decades made Santiniketan the locus of a new movement in which nature and local life, rather than history, became the basis of one's cultural identity. Art moved out of the studio into community spaces in the form of murals and open-air sculptures, while the boundaries between art and craft were erased with a whole spectrum of designing activities involving illustrated books, textiles, ceramics, furniture, stage sets, costumes, and pageants. Under Nandalal, Santiniketan came to realize Tagore's vision of a modernism universal in substance not form, preserving local history and realities yet open to other cultures.

Tagore's encounter with Japanese art helped in shaping this new development, but it was his wider engagement with world art that unlocked his own artistic genius. In his first two trips to Europe, he did not see much art, and his response to what he saw was tentative. The only work he marked out was a nude by Carolus Duran, not to praise its artistic merit but to berate Indians for their puritanical attitude to the human body. Art was more of a concern on his visit to England and America in 1912–13, undertaken with the specific aim of building cross-cultural relations with the West. He seems to have missed the opening of Roger Fry's second Post-Impressionist exhibition during his last days in London, but he visited the Armory Show at the Art Institute of Chicago.[10] Covering everything from Impressionism to the most avant-garde works of Picasso, Matisse, and Duchamp, the Armory Show was the world's first comprehensive exposition of Western modern art, and Tagore was the only Indian artist to have seen it at first hand. On his return to England from America, he made an effort to meet Rodin, who was then in London.[11] His changed taste in art also appears in a letter to Abanindranath, commenting on two sculpture portraits of him by Leonard Jennings and Jo Davidson: he praises Davidson's work as being in the manner of Rodin.

Tagore's familiarity with modern art grew in the years that followed. Four of his poems were printed in the February 1914 issue of *Der Sturm*, a magazine devoted to Expressionism and other avant-garde movements in art and literature. This number carried a work of Schmidt-Rottluff, one of the Die Bruke group of Expressionists, on its cover. The Expressionists would have not only taught him the role of primitive art in shaping the expressive rigour of modern painting but also encouraged him to take note of various traditions of 'primitive' art, through books and visits to ethnological collections.[12] He took time to internalize these lessons – not surprising when one considers that the impact of the Armory Show became widely visible in American art only in the early 1940s. However, this exposure certainly demolished his taste for representational realism. It prepared him for a sympathetic response to Japanese art in 1916, with its ability to slide smoothly from selective naturalism in painting to decorative abstraction in the decorative arts. Japanese art, in turn, should have prepared him for Art Nouveau, ubiquitous in various forms in Europe and America in the first two decades of the last century.

Simultaneously, Tagore also explored the conceptual differences underpinning the various art practices he encountered. Kandinsky's *Concerning the Spiritual in Art* (1911), of which he had a copy, was one source. Kandinsky begins by saying that 'each period of culture produces an art of its own which can never be repeated'; hence the past should not be imitated. This agreed with Tagore's view of new Indian art. However, Kandinsky also argues that similar moral and spiritual ideals between two periods could lead to a similarity of external forms, hence the modern artist's empathy with the primitives who sought 'in their work only internal truths, renouncing in consequence all consideration of external form'. For Kandinsky, modern art is essentially an effort at giving expression to the artist's personality and inner experiences, in the non-mimetic language of colour and form.[13]

The second source was Stella Kramrisch. Tagore invited the young Viennese art historian to teach at Santiniketan after hearing her lecture in London in 1920. Kramrisch arrived in Santiniketan in December 1921 and, at Tagore's request, delivered a series of forty-three lectures on Western art from the Gothic to the post-Cubist. Tagore not only attended the lectures but also served as her interpreter. He clearly wanted to share his discovery of modern Western art with other artists and students through these lectures, just as after his earlier discovery of Japanese art. Kramrisch, in turn, played a key role in bringing an exhibition of the Bauhaus artists to Kolkata in 1922 with the help of Johannes Itten, a founding member of the Bauhaus. Itten was interested in Tagore and attended his poetry reading at Weimar in 1921. Itten was also influenced by Franz Seizk, pioneer in the study of child art, and by Freud. Tagore met both, and their work contributed to his development as a painter.

To understand how these experiences were internalized, transforming his sensibility and helping him to become a painter, we must look at a type of corrections in his poetical manuscripts. Soon after giving up his early efforts at drawing, he began turning crossed-out words and lines in his manuscripts into doodles. At first they were small independent decorative motifs, floating on the page like little islands, but they gradually combined into more elaborate shapes. By the early 1920s, they had begun to exhibit two distinct trends: one towards lyrical Art Nouveauesque patterns, the other towards complex, composite zoomorphic forms like those of 'primitive' art. These doodles emerged spontaneously during editing of the texts: they projected what had been internalized over long years of looking at art.

In a manuscript of the play *Raktakarabi* from late 1923 or early 1924, a doodle covering a large part of the page assumes the form of a menacing animal (Figure 11.1). It marks a serious return to image-making. In the manuscript of *Purabi*, his next book of poems, the doodles proliferate, vying for space with the text. Sometimes they take over the whole page, submerging the texts in a web of pen-play. These doodles already display an element of conscious shaping. Their artistic merit was first recognized by Victoria Ocampo in 1924 while Tagore was her guest in San Isidro, Argentina. As she writes:

I was impressed by the copy-book where he was writing his *Puravi* poems in Bengali. He played with the erasures, following them from verse to verse with his pen, making lines that suddenly jumped into life out of this play: prehistoric monsters, birds, faces appeared. The cancelled mistakes in Tagore's poems gave birth to a world of forms that grinned, frowned or laughed at us in a mysterious fascinating way.... That copy-book, I think, was the beginning of Tagore the Painter.[14]

Encounter with Japanese decorative arts and Art Nouveau would have taught Tagore that all art is not based on realistic representation. Some were based on nuanced rhythmic articulation of lines: a skill he too possessed with his fine cursive handwriting. Similarly, 'primitive' art would have told him how varied, expressive, and widespread such practices have been, and how distortions of form can be deeply expressive. Modern artists like Gustav Klimt, Matisse, Kandinsky, and the Expressionists harvested these possibilities to add rigour and strength to their work. Tagore acknowledges this by tracing the origins of his art to his training in rhythm. Introducing his paintings in 1930, he writes:

The only training which I had from my young days was the training in rhythm in thought, the rhythm in sound. I had come to know that rhythm gives reality to that which is desultory, which is insignificant in itself. And therefore, when the scratches in my manuscript cried, like sinners, for salvation, and assailed my eyes with the ugliness of their irrelevance, I often took more time in rescuing them into merciful finality of rhythm.... I came to discover one fact, that in the universe of forms there is a perpetual activity of natural selection in lines, and only the fittest survives which has in itself the fitness of cadence....[15]

Like 'primitive' and modern artists, Tagore places expression above beauty, rhythm, or cadence above verisimilitude, compelling presence over certainty of meaning. The doodles embody this erasure of meaning and espousal of presence. To a writer who had marshalled words to create meaning all his life, this would have been an alien idea and a difficult process: it took him nearly two decades of doodling to arrive at painting.

However, this trajectory was not entirely novel. That doodling lowered the threshold of intentionality, opening the mind to suggestions and stimulating the imagination, was first recognized by Leonardo da Vinci. With the privileging of imagination over technical virtuosity in modern art, it was openly embraced at various levels by artists like Picasso, Paul Klee, André Masson, Joan Miró, and Jackson Pollock. Each in his own way

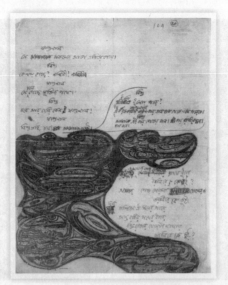

Figure 11.1   Doodle from the Manuscript of *Raktakarabi*

Ms 151(vii), page 104, ink on paper, 22.7 x 18 cm, 1923–24. Coll. Rabindra Bhavana Archive.

Figure 11.2   Landscape with Lake and Trees

Crayon, watercolour, coloured ink, and poster colour on paper, 35.2 x 52.1 cm, c. 1935. Coll. Rabindra Bhavana, Acc. No. 00-1865-16.

Figure 11.3 Fantastic Creature in Silhouette

Coloured ink on paper, 55.3 x 37.5 cm, c. 1929–30, sgd. Sri Rabindra. Coll. Rabindra Bhavana, Acc. No. 00-1893-16.

Figure 11.4 Portrait of a Woman

Coloured ink and opaque white on silk, 90.5 x 60.5 cm, sgd. Rabindra, 7-9-1934. Coll. Rabindra Bhavana, Acc. No. 00-1849-16.

Figure 11.5 Dramatic Scene with Five Figures

Coloured ink and poster colour on paper with transparent varnish, 56 x 54.7 cm, sgd. Rabindra, 12 November, 1934. Coll. Rabindra Bhavana, Acc. No. 00-1854-16

tried to privilege the play of motor actions and serendipity over thought-led image-making. However, once this becomes part of one's artistic process, intentionality cannot be entirely ruled out. An artist might begin without a plan, but a fortuitous discovery follows and conscious endeavour takes over. Tagore acknowledges this in a letter to Nirmalkumāri (Rāni) Mahalānabish:

> The subject-matter of a poem is generated in the mind, however hazily at first....
>
> The pictures I try to draw follow the reverse process. First, the hint of a line appears at the tip of the pen; then the more it takes form, the clearer it becomes to my conception. The mind is rapt with wonder at this creation of form.[16]

Tagore's first dated paintings are from 1928. It took him four years to move from advanced doodling to painting, from pen and ink to brush and coloured ink, from lines to dabs, and from dabs to strokes and touches. Gradually, gouache and crayon are added to the repertoire; rags and fingers are used occasionally; but coloured ink remains his favoured medium and paper the preferred surface, no doubt owing to his familiarity with their behaviour and his habit of executing several paintings at one sitting.

Most of the subjects persist too, but preferences shift and the nature of the images changes. Masks, landscapes, and composite or imaginary animals dominate his early paintings. The masks and animals carry resonances of 'primitive' art; the landscapes, fewer in number and without human presence, convey a sense of vastness and solitary communion with nature (Figure 11.2). The arabesque and the geometrical, the lyrical and the grotesque mark their formal and expressive latitudes. Animation rather than anatomical accuracy add liveliness and expressiveness to the forms (Figure 11.3). There is abundant trans-coding or cross-projection of the movement or expression of one thing or being onto another: he thereby creates expressive visual metaphors and bestows sentience on non-living objects. Thus imagination and inventiveness make good the lack of representational skills: as in all good art, expression exceeds the means at his disposal.

Tagore gradually grows more adept at handling materials and develops a personal technique: tentativeness gives way to greater assurance. This leads to a string of changes: the solitary landscapes bathed in twilight glow assume a more compelling presence, hovering between the ominous and the absorptive. Masks are supplanted by faces that are individualistic in typology and expression: animation and gesticulation give way to definitive gestures. Flat surfaces and planes, with segregated figures, make way for suggestions of immersive space. Figures become either iconic or interactive, mingling with their settings to evoke moods or interacting with each other to suggest dramatic moments.

All this does not make Tagore a narrative painter; rather, the ambivalence grows deeper and more enigmatic. The paintings still begin fortuitously, and the finding of forms is still largely serendipitous; but once recognized, he guides them into finality with greater resourcefulness. He becomes more adept at overlaying coloured inks to produce different shades and luminosities and to manipulate textures with greater subtlety. If something goes wrong, he salvages it – say, if over-layering makes the painting smudgy or tenebrous, he applies dabs of brighter gouache pigments or rubs crayons over the area. This resourcefulness, however, is in aid of serendipity: his paintings never proceed to plan. In other words, his method as a painter never becomes as assured as his method as a writer.

Tagore acknowledged the difference by refusing to name his pictures. The closest he came was in the short verses accompanying a small selection of paintings in *Chitralipi* (Visva-Bharati, 1940), the only volume of reproductions published in his lifetime. These are not descriptive elucidations but broad gestures towards the nature of his visual imagination. One, for instance, reads: 'I have searched out the cave of the primitive/ in my mind/with its etchings of animals.' Another says: 'The phantoms of faces/come unbidden into my vacant hours.' Naming the paintings, he believed, would erase the element of serendipity in their finding, impute to them a purposefulness and preconceived meaning where none existed. He wanted the serendipity that brought them into being to extend to the viewers' reception. They should project their memories and experiences into the paintings as he had done his.

The refusal to name his paintings can also be seen as Tagore's acceptance of the modernist idea of medium-based autonomy of the arts, keeping his paintings separate from the rest of his oeuvre. Of course the paintings benefited from his work in other mediums: it added to their thematic richness. The later portrait-like individualistic faces, where an inner world is captured within the confines of physiognomy, owe much to his exploration of the inner world of his fictional characters and the people he met (Figure 11.4). Similarly, his long experience as a theatre person fed his use of gesture and accoutrements in the paintings to suggest encounters between figures and to invoke charged dramatic moments without slipping into narrative (Figure 11.5). Above all, as I have described, his training in rhythm as a writer and musician, the calligraphic quality of his writing, and his experience as a composer and choreographer of dance dramas helped to infuse rhythmic articulation into his painted images.

Tagore's paintings are not narratives in themselves, nor do they illustrate his writings or his theatre: they are wholly and autonomously visual. Yet they are suffused with his experience of other arts. Nor are they all dark and melancholic, as often suggested. There is as much sensuality and tenderness, pleasure and beauty, playfulness and humour in them as there is suffering and anger, fear and conflict, the grotesque and the surreal. Like the rest of his oeuvre, his paintings open up a whole world of moods and emotions. To Tagore, all art was expression of the artist's personality, and he defined personality as the sum total of the world brought within the ambit of one's emotions. It was great or small according to the magnitude of this assimilation.[17]

The range of his emotions and concerns did not shrink even in the last decade of his life when the spectre of death stalked him. What mattered was the means at his disposal and the different possibilities made available by writing and painting. As a writer, his aim was the pursuit of meaning in a world where experiences were signs to be deciphered; as a painter, it was to acknowledge the concrete presence of things. The speaking subject of his writings becomes a mute observer in his paintings. While meaning has to be mined from the depths of language, presence is immediately and intuitively grasped by the senses. In a letter to the artist Jāmini Rāy written only months before his death, he writes:

[W]hen I turned to painting, I at once found my place in the grand cavalcade of the visual world: trees and plants, men and beasts, everything vividly real and in their own distinct forms.... There was no further need to elucidate their *raison d'être* once the artist discovered his role as a beholder pure and simple.[18]

He concludes by observing that the artist's role was 'to compel the unperceiving majority to share his joy in the visible, concrete world, directly perceived'. Painting gave him a new tool to express his personality. It amplified his aesthetic sensibility, kept it purely affective and universally accessible without slipping into the discursive and didactic. However, this also meant that as a painter, he worked within greater restrictions, while as a writer, he could address a wider range of issues with more confidence and subtlety.

Tagore was keenly aware that his paintings were different from those of his contemporaries. He first showed them to Nandalal and a few artists visiting Santiniketan such as Marguerite Milward, a student of Antoine Bourdelle; and though Nandalal proposed to organize an exhibition, Tagore was apprehensive of the reception in India and preferred to show them first in Europe. His earlier success with the English *Gitanjali*, and an awareness of the similarity of his paintings with those of modern Western artists, were probably the key factors in this decision. His first exhibition, organized with help from Ocampo, opened on 2 May 1930 in Paris, the acknowledged capital of modern art in Europe. This was followed by twelve other exhibitions across Britain, Germany, Denmark, Switzerland, Russia, and the United States over the next eight months. The first exhibition in India was held only in December 1931 at Kolkata.

Responses varied. In Paris, Henry Bidou's review dwelt at length on the doodles and imputed a surrealist slant to Tagore's work. In Germany, critics like Max Osborn compared him to the Expressionists. In England, Joseph Southall stressed his powerful imagination and the freshness of his vision, comparing his sense of rhythm and pattern to that of Persian and Indian textiles. And Ānand K. Coomaraswamy (Kumāraswāmi), writing in the catalogue of the American exhibition, drew attention to the childlike quality of the paintings, describing them as 'genuine examples of modern primitive art' that were 'not pictures about things but pictures about himself'.[19]

In India the initial response was less enthusiastic, as Tagore had anticipated. Apart from his close associates, the first Indian artist to admire his paintings was Amritā Sher-Gil, who saw them in Paris. The first critic to study them in the context of modern Indian art was W.G. Archer. He hailed Tagore's paintings as 'the first modern art to be produced in India'. However, to Archer, their strength came from their roots in the unconscious. Tagore's greatest paintings, by this view, were done between 1928 and 1930, and disaster followed as soon as he adopted a conscious approach to painting, following the success of his first exhibitions.[20]

Others have disagreed. Timothy Hyman, who includes Tagore in his book on twentieth-century figurative painting, reverses Archer's judgement: for him, 'after his first exhibition in 1930, Tagore's handling became more fluid. Tone and touch developed the image more unpredictably', his work became more atmospheric, and light assumed a 'new dimension in his imagery – building the surface by veils of transparent colour'. Borrowing a phrase from Joseph Herman, he describes Tagore as one of the 'last inheritors of a pre-verbal culture', who, 'so eloquent in verse and prose fiction, in song and in his essays, became in the 1930s the *elective mute* of twentieth century art'.[21]

Indian artists since the 1940s have seen him as a precursor. For them Tagore was an archetypal modernist who broke new ground by addressing the fundamental issues of art afresh, refusing to be culturally insular in the name of nationalism. He demonstrated that imagination and discernment were at least as important as training and skill, and above all encouraged his successors to pursue their personal visions with conviction. They admired the sense of freedom he demonstrated and the expressive distortions he achieved. Like Tagore, many of them were committed to communicating human experience without resorting to narrative; yet, to achieve this end, again like him, many marshalled the power of human postures and gestures to create dramatic moments pregnant with narrative possibilities. They saw Tagore as the first Indian artist to recognize the new possibilities which the modern period opened up to art.

NOTES

1. There are over 1,600 paintings and drawings in Santiniketan and nearly 200 in other public collections in India. We can estimate about 500 more in public and private collections across the world.
2. Rabindranath Tagore, *My Reminiscences*, tr. Surendranath Tagore (London: Macmillan, 1917), 38; *Jibansmriti*, RRVB 17:285.
3. Tagore, *My Reminiscences*, 264; RRVB 17:427.
4. *CP* 6:8.
5. *CPBLI* #94, 8 May 1893. Tagore later changed his mind about Ravi Varma: see the adverse comments in 'Mandirābhimukhe' (*RRVB* 29:396), and in the commemorative speech on Havell, 1939 ('I. bi. hyābhel', *RRVB* 31:156).
6. Letter of 1 Āshvin 1307 (17 September 1900), *CP* 6:8.
7. *RRVB* 29:398.
8. Letter to Abanindranath from Japan, 8 Bhādra 1323 (24 September 1916), in *Rabindranāther chintā-jagat: shilpachintā*, ed. Satyendranāth Rāy (Kolkata: Granthālay, 1996), 269.
9. Letter of 6 Bhādra 1323 (22 August 1916), *CP* 2:46–7.
10. Tagore gave a reading of *Chitrā* (a translation of his play *Chitrāngadā*) on 2 April 1913 at the Art Institute of Chicago, and returned to see the Armory Show the next day.
11. Count Herman Keyserling wrote to Tagore on (?)9 June 1912 inviting him to tea with Rodin, but there is no record of the meeting: see *RJPP* 6:807–8.
12. He owned copies of Friedrich Ratzel's *History of Mankind* (1896) and Walter Lehmann's *The Art of Old Peru* (1924). In 1924 in Argentina, he saw a collection of Peruvian artefacts and textiles. He would also have seen ancient Chinese bronzes earlier that year and Javanese art in 1927. All these have features in common with 'primitive' art. He may also have visited ethnographic museums in Europe, though there is no record.

13. Wassily Kandinsky, *Concerning the Spiritual in Art*, tr. Michael T.H. Sadler (Auckland: The Floating Press, 2008), 22–3.
14. Victoria Ocampo, 'Tagore on the Banks of the River Plate', in *Centenary*, 40.
15. 'My Pictures', *EW* 3:635.
16. Letter of 21 Kārtik 1335 (7 November 1928): Rabindranath Tagore, *Nijer kathā* (Kolkata: Mitra o ghosh, 2011; rpt. 2015), 164.
17. This is a concern of 'What Is Art?' *Personality* (1916): see *EW* 2:355–6.
18. Letter to Jamini Ray, 7 June 1941; reproduced in translation in *Rabindranath Tagore on Art and Aesthetics*, ed. Prithwish Neogy (Kolkata: Orient Longman, 1961), 107–9.
19. Early responses to his paintings are collated in *Paintings of Rabindranath Tagore: Foreign Comments* (Kolkata: Art Press, 1932).
20. W.G. Archer, 'Art and the Unconscious', in *India and Modern Art* (London: George Allen and Unwin, 1959), 72–4.
21. Timothy Hyman, *The World New Made: Figurative Painting in the Twentieth Century* (London: Thames and Hudson, 2016), 172–3; italics in original.

Part II
Studies

12 Women, Gender, and the Family in Tagore

HIMANI BANNERJI

Today I feel that a new age has begun. [N]ew ages have come ... by opening the door to eradicating differences.... Human beings cannot be alone. The truth of their condition is to grow by connecting with others; fulfilment comes by merging with everyone. That is the *dharma* of humanity.[1]

This essay examines Rabindranāth's views on women, gender, patriarchy, and the family, situating them in the ideas and practices of social reform in nineteenth-century Bengal. Rabindranath aimed to create new values and practices among colonized peoples and thus usher in a new age.[2] The condition of women in brahminical families in Bengal forms an important part of this decolonizing agenda and the social critique underlying it.

Social reform, a modernist project in nineteenth-century Bengal, was vigorously contested by revivalist and traditionalist Hindu orthodoxy. The reformers were concerned with both religious and everyday life, but they focused most intently on family mores centred on brahminical patriarchy and ordering of gender. This contestation, resulting from the encounter between British capitalist colonialism and pre-capitalist Bengali society, gave rise to new social formations, creating new professional and trading classes (the *bhadralok*) and new forms of consciousness.

The results were varied, embracing all aspects of life. Colonial capitalism engendered a new state apparatus. This created a third space, that of civil society,[3] comprising both the urban middle classes and a new land-owning rural gentry created by the Permanent Settlement (1793). This social space lay outside the immediate purview of the state and the economy, but was created through the interaction of the two. The central institution of civil society was the family, structured by brahminical patriarchy with its distinctive casteist character and gender values. Both reform and revivalism operated within this civil society, giving rise to serious controversies; yet the two trends could not be kept entirely apart. Reformers like Rabindranath, advocating a foundational social change, had to negotiate these complexities. Thus his critique of gender, patriarchy, family norms, and the condition of women could not follow a linear path.

Although the revivalists accused the reformers of being submissive colonial subjects, the latter did not passively follow in the wake of social legislation; their independent agenda progressed alongside the legislation and often actively advanced it. The most important legislations centred on women and the family. They comprised the banning of *satidāha* or widow-burning (1829), legalizing widow remarriage (1856), and determining the minimum age of marriage (1860) and the age of consent (1891). There followed legislation on polygamy, rape, and prostitution. These legislations, and the controversies erupting from them, provided the basis for the 'woman question' in Bengal and India. Eventually, the 'woman question' expanded to take in issues like women's individual status or personhood and their legal rights within and outside marriage. For both rulers and subjects, the cultural identity of the *bhadralok* had a strong gynocentric dimension. The education of women, both formal and informal, acquired priority in the reformists' agenda. All these issues affected the division of social space between the home and the world, the private and the public.

Rabindranath's social thought, like his artistic sensibility, evolved in complex interaction with this milieu. He developed a universal humanism that could sustain his critique of the condition of women, as of patriarchy and other unequal relations of power. His literary works explore the formative relations between immediate and particular experiences of social organization and a larger philosophical understanding. In the following account, I will focus on Tagore's fiction, referring to his poems, plays, and essays as necessary.

RABINDRANATH'S FICTION AND SOCIAL REFORM

Rabindranath grew up in the heart of the Brahmo Samaj, in an environment of social reform. What we call modernity in art and social outlook in Bengal was largely pioneered by his family. He concurred with the Brahmo Samaj's attempts to bring about transformation in the lives of women and generally in society. His fiction affords critical insights into everyday life.

Some stories are told by female narrators, others in the critical voices of reformed men. Gender relations are seen within the hierarchy of caste and kinship. The figure of the woman serves as a metaphor for Tagore's entire humanist–aesthetic philosophy, making her a locus of the oppressive aspects of social life as also of their critique. Going far beyond reportage, moral exhortation, and legislative demands, Tagore projects the need for a radical social transformation. His short stores bring out the oppression of women and girls within and outside the family, exposing multiple patriarchal oppressions in daily life. The family becomes the habitus and matrix of patriarchal normativity, the microcosm of an unbalanced and unjust social macrocosm.

The novels provide detailed studies of the psychology, the familial and social milieu, and the self-discoveries of men and women who live in this repressive world, but the short stories afford crucial snapshots of their condition. Rabindranath does not offer a single typology of women but a rich spectrum of which the girl child, before or after puberty, married or unmarried, is an important element. For example, in 'Khātā' (The Exercise-Book), little Umā's delight in writing is cruelly destroyed after her marriage into a family opposed to women's education. There are brides whose families cannot pay the dowry demanded or whose male guardians did not arrange their marriage in due time. 'Haimanti' presents such an older bride, whose unworldly father proves to be less rich than her in-laws expected; Haimanti therefore undergoes constant humiliation. Her love of reading also incriminates her, like an older Uma. Her modern-minded educated husband loves her but cannot protect her from his father's injunctions. Haimanti dies without any medical treatment in this rich, high-caste home.

This was also the fate of Nirupamā in the earlier story 'Denāpāonā' (Debts and Dues). Her father had been unable to pay off her dowry; when he finally came to do so, his daughter herself dissuaded him, and died in consequence after persecution and neglect. Rabindranath relentlessly analyses the institutions of the brahminical family, not excluding marriage itself. Its sanctity is torn apart:

> In our country, once a man is married, ... his feelings about his wife
> become like those of a tiger that has tasted human flesh.[4]

In such a dispensation, motherhood, especially of male children, is the most coveted status a woman can acquire. Yet premature motherhood posed a severe risk of lifelong illness or death in childbirth. In 'Madhyabartini' (She in the Middle), the chronic illness of Nibāran's first wife, Harasundari, makes her unable to conceive. Their conjugal life is therefore invaded by a girl-bride, Shailabālā, who dies in childbirth. Her presence after death continues to divide the surviving couple.

After much vehement debate, the age of marriage was fixed by law first at ten years and then at twelve. Thus a girl's childhood ended when she was barely aware of her own body, let alone her sexuality. As no age of marriage was prescribed for men, there could be glaring sexual and mental asymmetry between the couple. The stories present figures of little girl-brides or would-be brides looking like dolls, with silver ribbons in their braids, encouraged to play rather than be with their husbands, like Shailabala in 'Madhyabartini', Kāshishwari in 'Pātra o pātri' (Groom and Bride), or the imagined daughter-in-law once desired by Kshemankari in the novel *Naukādubi* (The Boat-Wreck).[5] Brahminical injunction placed the girl-bride at the discretion and mercy of her husband. In these circumstances, there was more than a possibility of marital rape. Actual or potential trauma, physical and mental, haunted the married lives of all too many women. Yet returning to the natal home was cause for disgrace; very few families would take in their daughters in such a situation. In 'Aparichitā' (The Unknown Woman), a rare father of progressive views refuses his daughter in marriage in protest against the humiliating exaction of dowry. The daughter, Kalyāni, grows up as a spirited, self-reliant person. Dipāli in 'Pātra o pātri' is another such woman, though she finally marries.

Some women in the stories are married to enlightened men, who understand and sympathize with their state and work towards a loving relationship. Such alternative conjugality allows love and companionship to develop even in this uncongenial atmosphere. Banawāri in 'Hāldārgoshthi' (The Hāldār Clan) is deeply moved by his wife's beauty and intelligence:

> His wife did not only please him, she overwhelmed him. He too wanted to overwhelm her. His wife did not have to put in any special effort for that – her youthful grace overflowed spontaneously, her meticulous care of him showed spontaneously as well.[6]

There are other such men with strong nurturing impulses towards their mothers, sisters, wives, daughters, and others. In particular, men's love for their children (of both sexes) can shine through the distance imposed by patriarchy. The father in 'Boshtami' (The Vaishnav Woman) takes care of his son as the negligent mother does not. Loving fathers unable to pay the agreed dowry are mortified by their daughters' resultant plight, as in 'Denāpāonā' and 'Haimanti': they never blame their daughters for their own humiliation. In the poem 'Shesh chithi' (The Last Letter, *Punascha*), the grieving father of the dead Amalā, packed off to boarding school after her mother's death, is another such affectionate and committed parent.

Motherhood, the generative source of family life and the pivot of its nurturing domesticity, was and is a polyvalent trope, as Jasodharā Bāgchi demonstrates.[7] Social discourses invest heavily in it, and the fragmented state of the Bengali middle classes offered many models of parenting for Rabindranath to portray. There are women effectively incarcerated by motherhood, like Kumu in *Jogājog* (*Relationships*). Tagore presents the mother in a double role: she is the hub of family life, yet lacking any form of economic and social independence, and usually without formal education. But most heroines in the novels have progressed well beyond literacy, often through schooling at home by male relatives or mentors. Hidden creativity emerges in Chārulatā in *Nashtanirh* (Broken Nest) and Nirjharini in 'Darpaharan' (Destruction of Pride): their writings achieve print, though Nirjharini burns hers because they excel her husband's. Nirjharini was schooled by her father-in-law, who praised her work and encouraged her to write. Her prize-winning story tells of her girl cousin's oppression by the latter's husband. This sombre strain provides an undercurrent to the story's ironic tone, producing (for once) a comic inconclusiveness of response.

Many mothers are shown as having imbibed an education of sentiment and general awareness, who can therefore confer on their children a critical perception of gender and caste. A powerful example is Ānandamayi in *Gorā*, who infuses her mothering with a non-possessive, universal, humanist love extending beyond the family, indeed beyond biological and ethnic boundaries: Gorā is an Irish orphan adopted by her during the Uprising of 1857.

Anandamayi has male counterparts: Jagamohan in *Chaturanga* (Quartet), who admirably 'fathers' his nephew Shachish, and Paresh Bābu in *Gorā*, who brings up Sucharitā, not his own daughter, with deep emotional and spiritual nurture. Rabindranath delinks parenthood from a gendered biological identity and extends it far beyond narrow possessiveness. But he also depicts fraught relationships between mothers and daughters, or fathers and sons. Both educated and uneducated, Westernized and 'traditional' mothers exhibit this tension, often within the same text. In *Gorā*, Baradāsundari, a Westernized Brahmo woman, and Harimohini, a widow committed to brahminical rituals, fail equally to form a nurturing relationship with their daughters and daughter figures; so does Elā's mother in *Chār adhyāy* (Four Chapters). The trope of motherhood embraces self-waste and danger along with self-sacrifice and love.

Nineteenth-century Bengali literature is full of widows, like the society it depicted, owing to the marked disparity in age between husbands and wives, and the proscription against widow remarriage. Many widows were young and often childless, exacerbating general fears about female sexuality. These problems are reflected in Bankimchandra Chattopādhyāy's influential novel *Krishnakānter uil* (Krishnākanta's Will). Hence widows became a two-headed symbol: of a disembodied, sexless purity transcending physical needs, but also of moral pollution, as dangerous unchaste figures at the margins of the family – themselves in danger of 'falling' and endangering the men portrayed as victims of their allure.[8] On the patriarchal moral scale, the young widow was the 'bad' woman providing a foil to the 'good' wife.

Male members of the reformist intelligentsia, however, approached the plight of widows sympathetically and constructively. The primary solution they advocated was widow remarriage,[9] together with the prevention of child marriage, thereby narrowing the age gap between husband and wife. Controversies raged around legislation on these issues, as orthodox Hindus considered marriage and the family structure as non-negotiable private institutions beyond legislation and civic reform. This explains why Ishwarchandra Vidyāsāgar's campaign for widow remarriage was so fiercely attacked. Ironically, through their vociferous disagreement, orthodox Hindus made sex and sexuality dominant public issues.

Rabindranath explored the theme of widowhood in his novels with sympathy, delicacy, and insight. In *Naukādubi*, when Ramesh discovers that the 'wife' he is living with is another man's widow (as he thinks), he is cast in a profound quandary as to whether he can continue living with her as man and wife. There is also Manjulikā in the poem 'Nishkriti' (Release, *Palātakā*), though she finally remarries happily. Widowhood is central to *Chokher bāli*, where Binodini plays out a complex dynamic of thwarted womanhood, a mixture of sexual desire, anger, and seduction, until she succeeds in capturing Mahendra, but then renounces that achievement. Her longing for sexual love and domesticity is briefly redirected towards social good and then more conclusively to withdrawal and renunciation.

In *Ghare-bāire* (At Home and in the World) and *Jogājog*, the attachment of young widows to their brothers-in-law reflects not only physical need but genuine love. Tagore does not favour a typology of widowhood. *Chaturanga*, for example, has two young widows of very different personalities. One commits suicide to avoid remarriage because she cannot forget her seducer, who refuses to marry her. The other aggressively pursues her desire for the hero, who spurns her. Thwarted in her love, she marries their common friend, finding thereby a life-affirming love instead of a self-consuming passion.

WOMEN, GENDER, AND THE FAMILY IN THE NOVELS

Rabindranath's narrative exploration of brahminical patriarchy is at its core an exploration of the relationship between the self and the other in the context of power. In his writings, gender and sexuality in various figurations become an expressive device for exploring certain aspects of this power relationship. In his major novels, plot complications and the details of domestic life are minimized to clear an ample space for depicting sexual and gender dynamics in different perspectives. In *Ghare-bāire*, sexuality is placed in both familial and political contexts; in *Chār adhyāy*, in the arena of violent nationalist struggle; in *Chaturanga*, in a religious setting; and in *Jogājog*, as imbricated in class relations and their impact on familial norms and forms.

Rabindranath reaches no clear resolution of these complications, nor does he force any. Though many of his novels are a species of *Bildungsroman*, the process of self-development and of relating the self to the other(s) is left to evolve further, as a projection beyond the text. These novels narrate the mental journeys of the protagonists, with varying degrees of recognition between the self and the other. The issue of self-recognition features most prominently among women characters. Tagore attributes an undeniable centrality to a woman's quest to find her self: it epitomizes such quests in general. Bimalā (*Ghare-bāire*), Dāmini (*Chaturanga*), and to some extent Elā (*Chār adhyāy*) grow up or find themselves in the course of their stories. They experience pain and sorrow, indeed devastation, in their selves and in the world around them. Particularly in *Gorā* and *Ghare-bāire*, they reflect on their own and others' experiences, and grasp the social and psychological forces active in themselves and in society. But by the time they arrive at this post-catastrophic understanding, it is too late for them to actualize their wisdom, at least within their textual lives. The lesson, however, continues to resonate with the readers.

The narrative of these novels moves on two planes. On one, the subject's will and desires are repressed by regulative social forces; on the other, s/he aspires to dominate them. Rabindranath seeks to free the subject from the imperatives of power, but again he does not impose a contrived resolution. Hence his characters rarely achieve harmony either within their selves or with others. Contrary to gender stereotypes, the women – Bimala, Damini, or Ela – are as impassioned as the men if not more so. In their pursuit of desire, they risk not only their social respectability but also their familial moorings and physical safety. Even at the end, we cannot tell clearly where the narrative is moving: the endings are catastrophic yet charged with new beginnings, where individuals can be transformed by confronting their own will and desire or that of others.

Masculinity and femininity gain substance through each other in Tagore. In *Ghare-bāire*, Bimala faces two male characters who are others to herself. Married to Nikhilesh, who exemplifies a new modernist masculinity,[10] she is a source of irresistible sexual attraction for his friend Sandip, a stereotypically masculinist figure advancing a violent communalist nationalism. His patriarchy appears in his aggressively acquisitive attitude towards both women and political territory. Bimala eroticizes Sandip's will to power and abets his base actions in the name of nationalism. Nikhilesh, the enlightened husband and constructive supporter of *swadeshi*, is no less patriarchal, using Bimala as a subject for his experiment in modernism. He deliberately breaks the prohibition on introducing male outsiders into the family space, although (or because) he is secretly convinced that Bimala would 'freely' prefer him to Sandip. When the opposite happens, despite his seeming unconcern he is affected to the point of growing careless of his own life. The novel ends with Nikhilesh's plunge into self-sacrifice, Sandip's callous departure, and Bimala's critical recognition of herself and the real nature of her two others. She would now indeed 'freely' choose Nikhilesh but cannot actualize that choice because of his impending death and her own expulsion from the social interior of the family. The ending is left open: the novel straddles the boundary between being and becoming, and admits no resolution.

The same themes of sexual and political passion merge in *Chār adhyāy*, but outside the sphere of domesticity. Ela, already a transgressive and wilful character, is alienated from herself and has moved away from ordinary life into the world of armed nationalists. She cannot tell the difference between her martyr's politics and her passion for Indranāth, a charismatic figure who has come to fetishize violence. Identifying with Indranath's cause, Ela becomes his recruiting decoy, unconscious of being a pawn in his game or of deriving her glamour from his reflected glory. Among her admirers is the gentle and imaginative Atin, but his sincere love is treated dismissively by Ela, who is attracted to dominating masculinity and sees gentleness in men as a sign of effeminacy. The turn of events, however, makes Atin the leader of the group. They are finally betrayed to the colonial authorities, when Atin visits Ela on a mission of liquidation. The danger excites Ela's sexuality: her impassioned self-offering to Atin is a violent act, identifying her sexual surrender with physical annihilation. In *Chār adhyāy*, unbalanced gender relations reflect a basically unbalanced and corrosive relationship between self and other. To the end, Ela remains a severely divided being, her love for the other compromised by her distorted understanding of her own and male sexuality. The novel lacks a redemptive moment: the emotional wasteland that Ela inhabits is the charred landscape of sexual and social war.

The earlier *Chaturanga*, too, had largely been located outside of family life, in an ashram dedicated to Krishna as a god of love, where four unconnected individuals come together in attachments of love and sexual desire. Their relations are complicated by a homosocial tinge to the friendship of the chief male characters, Shachish and Shribilās. Shachish is a figure of sovereign will, and Shribilas submits readily to all his wishes. The heroine, Damini, a young widow whose beauty is compared to lightning,[11] loves Shachish with unrestrained passion. The guru of the ashram, to whom Damini was entrusted by her late husband, is himself in unrequited love with her. In such an atmosphere, redolent with a discourse of love untempered by family mores, the characters act out their passions to their extremes. The narrative reaches a climax when Shachish, choosing spirituality over human love, journeys forth as a *sanyāsi*: his virility is sublimated into a religion of service to the masses.[12] Damini, too, undergoes a sentimental education: consumed by her own fiery passion and Shachish's rejection, she marries Shribilas, whom she had hitherto dismissed as an emasculated person with no will to power. She thereby gains insight into a nurturing love that can stably relate the self to the other. This love is in no way connected to the *bhakti* cult of the Krishna temple: it is a relationship between two ordinary people in a humble space in a large city.

Jogājog traces the workings of gender and sexuality in terms of family and class relations in a historical context.[13] The novel starts with the birthday of the son and heir of a businessman's family and flashes back to the story of his conception. But *Jogājog* is much more than a searing exposure of unwanted pregnancy within an arranged marriage. It humanizes and concretizes its themes by following the marriage of Kumudini (Kumu), daughter of the declining feudal rentier class, to Madhusudan, a member of the rising comprador business class. Class and sexuality are placed in a constitutive relation. Through the marriage, colonial comprador capitalism exacts vengeance on its erstwhile feudal oppressors.

But class relations also underscore an unrelenting confrontation of the self and the other. Kumu's brother, Bipradās, deep in debt, cannot provide an adequate dowry for her: Madhusudhan displays his class power by paying off Bipradas's debts and waiving the dowry, thereby reducing Kumu to a purchased woman. But unexpectedly, Madhusudan is not satisfied with possessing Kumu; he clumsily falls in love with her. Despite his wealth and marital patriarchal rights, his wife remains utterly beyond his reach. His ungainliness and rude masculinity provide a foil to Kumu's refined beauty. He makes matters worse by his stereotypical notions of what pleases a woman, buying her flashy jewellery: the disparity extends beyond wealth to culture. Kumu retains in her person her refined upbringing, innocence and artistic sensibility, and a delicate beauty cultivated through many generations of feudal marriages. The *nouveau riche* Madhusudan is utterly unprepared for such a wife: the distance between the self and the other is excruciating.

Kumu's position is further compromised by her having lived in isolation with her unworldly, reclusive, older artist-philosopher brother, Bipradas. The intimacy of their relationship almost hints at subliminal incest. Material disengagement and the triumph of art is his legacy to Kumu. She has no access to her sexual-emotional self except indirectly through the medium of music, in songs of lovers' separation and reunion.

It is not surprising, then, that she should find the sexual act repulsive and incomprehensible, although she is well into her womanhood. Her physical desires have been displaced into the mythical love of Rādhā and Krishna as expressed in the songs of the legendary queen Mirābāi, who became a mendicant devotee of Krishna. It is also in keeping with brahminical tradition, where the husband is viewed as the wife's personal god. Despite this religious legitimation, Kumu is unable to love and serve her husband: nothing can dispel the shocking discrepancy between Madhusudan and Krishna. The arbitrary consummation of an arranged marriage fills her with dread, converting the prospect of sexual pleasure into the actuality of marital rape. It is within her inert body that Madhusudan plants his seed, leading to the conception of the son whose birthday opens the novel.

GENDER AND FREEDOM

This account of Rabindranath's fiction indicates how he does not abide by consistent gender categories. He speaks in different registers at different times. It would be a mistake to try to systematize his views, because he is himself reluctant to do so. In romantic contexts, he draws on the conventional view of masculinity and femininity, emphasizing women's beauty, sweetness, and loving-kindness in accepting male fallibility, as also men's strength of body, handsomeness, protectiveness towards women, and intellectual capacities. On this plane, men are active subjects who wish to prove themselves through their achievements. In other contexts, for example in their love of reading, curiosity about the world, and interaction with others, both sexes can behave in similar ways. This varying projection prompts us to ask how Rabindranath's notion of gender balances biological and social factors. He certainly stresses the latter, but to what extent do these overrule biology? One point, however, is clear: whatever the slippages in Rabindranath's understanding of gender, there is no ambiguity in his rejection of power and domination in all human relations. He roundly rejects patriarchy, of the brahminical or any other variety.

Rabindranath's variations on the theme of gender are illustrated by the different types of women in his fiction. Some are 'traditional', like Kamalā in *Naukādubi*, who abides by time-honoured wifely norms to the point of self-effacement. Others are unconventional, like Lalitā in *Gorā*, who chooses her own husband in the face of social opprobrium. A self-driven desiring woman like Damini seeks sexuality outside of domestic life. Contravening the division between masculine and feminine, she is an egotist fascinated by power and eroticizing it. As the self is an essential element in her passionate love, she is thereby also in the process of discovering herself. Such characters are full of both tragic and creative potential. They stand on the edge of a yet unevolved self and society, to be brought to life by their own actions and interactions. In breaking the mandates of brahminical patriarchy, these women exceed their counterparts, the new men, who align with them but take less risk both in their personal lives and their projects of social reform. As Haimanti's ineffectual husband says: 'I didn't have to give up anything, neither relatives, nor habits, nothing at all, [while] she sat on a bed of thorns and I shared that bed with her.'[14]

Rabindranath's views regarding *stri swādhinatā* are relevant here. This phrase can be translated in two ways, overlapping yet different: 'women's liberation' and 'women's freedom'. 'Liberation' premises an initial stage of bondage, while 'freedom' points outward: it is an enabling concept. We need to complicate both notions to grasp how Rabindranath applies them to the condition of women. The instance of Ela in *Chār adhyāy* illustrates how Rabindranath decries a public political role for women, even in the cause of national freedom. Freedom for women does not, for him, translate into their suffrage, citizenship, or other political rights: such matters are connected with the state, and the state for Rabindranath is not a source of profound social transformation. For Rabindranath, freedom (*swādhinatā*), for both men and women, is not a political question. It is more a matter of self-emancipation, of a change of consciousness at the level of civil society, everyday life, and aesthetic creation, through engagement with the other on both a personal and a broader social plane.

It is in this context that the evolving self seeks liberation from social institutions that would destroy it, like brahminical patriarchy. The story 'Strir patra' (The Wife's Letter) offers an unqualified condemnation of traditional conjugality in an upper-class brahminical family. A woman's conventional roles are divided here among three characters: the narrator Mrināl, the privileged wife; Bindu, an unwanted dependent relative; and Mrinal's sister-in-law, who is also Bindu's sister. Despite their different positions in the familial hierarchy, these women are connected at the root: conjoined in unquestioning domestic servitude, socially and sexually obedient to patriarchy. The story outlines their terrible helplessness: they cannot protect Bindu from being married off to a mental patient, leading to her suicide in a no-exit situation. Her death is brushed away from the surface of family life. Mrinal, however, effects an exit by leaving her marital home, empowered by anger and disgust. She speaks for all the women in the story, and many more, in the letter she leaves for her husband: 'How negligible is my daily life, how trivial its fixed regulations, fixed habits, fixed cant, its habitual blows – but will this bondage to meanness be allowed to win? ... Why should I die little by little in this world behind a curtain of bricks and wood?'[15] The relation between self and other in this story has two aspects: one, with an othered self in the harsh grasp of patriarchy; the other, of a loving relationship between Mrinal and Bindu. Their common humanity bonds together a beautiful and a homely, a rich and a penniless woman. Mrinal leaves her dehumanizing environment without fear or regret, vowing never to return. The two meanings of *swādhinatā* come together in her liberation from self-alienation into self-affirmation and self-expression. Her letter is a work of art: it gives aesthetic shape to her own experience, speaking to the experiences of others. The story 'Paylā nambar' (House Number One) presents another example of a woman who goes away, abandoning both her husband and her supposed lover, in search of an independent life. But she leaves behind no letter or explanation – the implicit explanation comes from the unedifying account of her husband, the narrator.

Rabindranath's understanding of gender is anchored in his universalist philosophy of nature. Nature, for him, has two aspects: one biological, physical, and instinctual, the other reflective and imaginative, as well as social and ethical. The human rational and aesthetic faculties are natural endowments, their social and creative capacities a peculiarity of their species being.[16] They can interpret, critique, and shape nature according to their needs and imagination. However, the dialectic between the human and the social other does not necessarily result in a positive or liberating outcome. In the play *Raktakarabi* (Red Oleanders), greed and instrumental rationality, instinct and intellect conjoin and impact on the earth in industrial mining for gold, producing an anti-human society. This inhumanity does not come from outside nature, but from a particular deployment of natural capacities and resources within the species being of the human. Similarly, gender binaries, which restrain and rigidify human nature, obstruct the path to a full and free humanity. The human within the gendered self is distorted and reified by hostility between the self and the other.

Equally, human love, including sexual love, can be joyous if it is mutual. In their sensuous union, both masculinity and femininity are marked by empathy and liminality. These are essential features of the same human capacities that create home, art, knowledge, and spirituality. Deprived of these features, gender becomes rigid, the self narcissistic, sexuality egotistical, and desire an instrument of property and power. Rabindranath seems to envision a reverse transformation towards an imaginative, empathic encounter with the other. His narratives explore the possible routes towards this goal.

For Rabindranath, the basic problem seems to lie not in the qualities coded in gender terms, but in their attachment to certain physical bodies, that is, an equation of sex with gender. He challenges this affixation by giving so-called maternal qualities to fathers or supposedly masculine will to power or strength of mind and reason to women. Reason and imagination, rationality and emotion, tenderness and strength, nurturing and disciplining become potentially meaningful attributes of all individuals in all societies; they are immutably attributed to one or other sex through specific types of social organization and social consciousness. A society marked by constitutive relations of power, such as patriarchy, caste, class, and property, will not only define social functions and institutions in terms of gender but express that gendering in hierarchic relationships within and outside the family. But if gender is unmoored from specific body types, every kind of mental and practical potentiality becomes fluid and generally available. In such a world, the young boy Āshu in 'Ginni' (The Housewife) would not be taunted at school for playing with dolls to amuse his little sister. Nurturing would not be invariably expressed through motherhood, or disciplining through fatherhood; nor would initiating a sexual relationship be the prerogative of men and a sign of depravity in women. Hence too, sexual love would not be defined in heteronormative terms.

The problem is presented early on in an unusual reverse perspective in the musical drama *Chitrāngadā*. The princess Chitrāngadā, brought up according to a model of heroic masculinity, is disconcerted by her sudden desire for the hero Arjuna, who spurns her for her lack of femininity. She is endowed with feminine beauty and seductiveness by the god of love at the cost of the other part of herself. Refusing to accept this contradiction between her external and internal self, Chitrangada reassumes her authentic identity as her partner's equal.

> I am the princess Chitrangada: not a goddess, nor any ordinary woman. You cannot raise me aloft by worshipping me, nor keep me[17] neglectfully yet make me follow you.[18]

Arjuna accepts her need to be her own authentic self; the play ends in a harmony or balance of gender roles. *Chitrāngadā* offers us the possibility of combining the characteristics of both sexes in the same person, irrespective of biology. Masculinity and femininity are brought into reflexive relations with each other, problematizing the notions of inner and outer beauty, nurturance and acts of valour.

Rabindranath suggests that social transformation is possible through changes in consciousness and in social relations and practices. His fiction traces the decline of the old feudal household and the new familial structures of the middle class, the rise of women's education, and new mores of conjugal relations. He thus projects complex possibilities of change, challenging Hindu cultural-nationalist claims of the fixed ontology of patriarchy and the family. His universal humanism is not an ungrounded ideological position, but based upon human capacities for the creation of society, culture, and history. Women's urge for freedom and selfhood, reason and creativity, become homologous with this greater project. In the essay 'Nārī' (Woman) in *Kālāntar* (Change of Era), Rabindranath describes how the conventional roles of women are undergoing a paradigm shift, with women adopting new roles and functions hitherto the prerogative of men. In this way, he concludes, a new age has dawned on the world.[19]

However, Rabindranath does not go beyond a premonition of this new age. He brings us to the point where, blinders and barriers removed, women and men may see themselves in the clear light of day. What may happen thenceforth remains a challenge for Rabindranath's readers to meet. At no point does he trade off a fantasy for history. As we see in his later writings, disappointment and failure are not alien to him. But he still proclaims that the 'human' is our only principle of hope.

NOTES

1. 'Nabajug' (The New Age), 1933, *RRVB* 24:456–7.
2. See Himani Bannerji, 'A Transformational Pedagogy: Reflections on Rabindranath's Project of Decolonisation', in *Tagore: The World as His Nest*, ed. Sangeeta Datta and Subhoranjan Dasgupta (Kolkata: Jadavpur University Press, 2016), 24–60.
3. I follow Antonio Gramsci's application of the term 'civil society' to the social and cultural sphere.
4. 'Haimanti', *RRVB* 23:220.
5. See also the poem 'Naba banga-dampatir premālāp' ('The Love-Talk of a Newly Married Bengali Couple'), *Mānasi*.

6. *RRVB* 23:202.

7. Jasodhara Bagchi, *Interrogating Motherhood* (New Delhi: Sage, 2017).

8. See Tanika Sarkar, 'Wicked Widows', in *Rebels, Wives, Saints* (New Delhi: Permanent Black, 2009), 121–52.

9. Rabindranath himself arranged his son Rathindranāth's marriage with a young widow, Pratimā Debi.

10. See Sumit Sarkar, 'Nationalism and Stri-Swadhinata', *Beyond the Nationalist Frame* (Delhi: Permanent Black, 2002), 112–53.

11. *RRVB* 7:454. *Dāmini* means lightning.

12. See Indira Chaudhuri, *The Frail Hero and Virile History* (Delhi: Oxford University Press, 1998).

13. See Supriya Chaudhuri's introduction to her translation of the novel, *Relationships* (Oxford: Oxford University Press, 2006).

14. 'Haimanti', *RRVB* 23:230–1.

15. *RRVB* 23:260.

16. See Himani Bannerji, 'Beyond the Binaries', in *Marxism: With and Beyond Marx*, ed. Amiya Kumar Bagchi and Amita Chatterjee (London: Routledge, 2014), 25–56.

17. The Bengali word, *pushiyā*, is used of pet animals.

18. *RRVB* 3:200.

19. *RRVB* 24:382.

13 On the Seashore of Endless Worlds

Rabindranath and the Child

SIBAJI BANDYOPADHYAY

A MESSAGE FROM THE KING

A darkness, impenetrably dense, was about to descend.

13 June 1940. The next day, the Nazi army would occupy Paris. As though to send out a call to the threatened population, a call full of trepidation but also with the hope of deliverance, the French translation of a Bengali play was broadcast on French radio.[1]

That is not all. In March 1942, the Nazis established their first extermination camp, surpassing in cruelty the concentration camps in operation since 1933. Leaving no exit route, the extermination camp was, by definition, a 'non-place'. But among those about to enter these waiting rooms of death, the same Bengali play, on a wait for death of a very different kind, found an audience. It was staged in Polish on 18 July 1942 in a Jewish orphanage in the Warsaw Ghetto just before its children went to the gas chamber. Translated five times into Polish till date, the play still retains a place in 'collective Polish remembering'.[2]

A peculiar chemistry of emotions must have been at work. Else how could a drama full of indomitable optimism become so compelling at a time when destruction proceeded so rapidly as to make a mockery of the very idea of death? The clue to the paradox lies in the figure of a child: a child simultaneously restive and immobilized.

~

The play was Rabindranāth Tagore's *Dākghar* (1912), translated by Debabrata Mukhopādhyāy (Devabrata Mukerjea) as *The Post Office*. Its child protagonist (whose very name, Amal, means 'pure') is terminally ill and confined indoors, yet deeply drawn to the world outside: 'I would rather go about and see everything that there is.'[3] Sitting by his window, Amal watches a new building come up across the road. He learns it is a *dākghar*, a post office set up by the king. He is attracted by the word *dāk*, which in Bengali means both 'call' and 'letter': he longs to receive a letter with a call from the king. Rabindranath spoke of the genesis of *Dākghar* in a 1915 talk at Santiniketan. He observed that the play had no story as such: it was a prose lyric. He was driven to write it by the premonition of a catastrophe, perhaps his own death. Writing the play came as a great relief.[4]

~

The English version was staged in 1913 in Dublin and London, four years before the original was staged in Kolkata. Since the English *Gitanjali* (1912) and the Nobel Prize (1913), Rabindranath was venerated in Europe as a messiah from the East, epitomizing whatever was *not* characteristic of the 'sick' West. This imputed mystic allure – though it might have led to the swift subsequent decline of Tagore's standing in the West – was perhaps what prompted the Dublin and London productions. W.B. Yeats said in his preface to the English version (1914) that some friends of his 'discovered much detailed allegory' in the play, but he himself considered it 'less intellectual, more emotional, ... convey[ing] to the right audience an emotion of gentleness and peace'.[5]

André Gide, whose translation of *Dākghar* was aired on French radio on 13 June 1940, found it a 'strange play', although 'entirely modern in its appearance'.[6] He felt its strangeness would be highlighted by a line from poem 44 of the English *Gitanjali*: 'This is my delight, thus to wait and watch at the wayside.'[7]

The general consensus, in the second decade of the twentieth century, was that the distinguishing feature of *Dākghar* was its untroubled serenity. Yet the text so hailed on the eve of the First World War seemed charged with a sense of entrapment, with no possible escape, at the time of the Second World War. The theme of waiting unfolded in the play spanned everything from elation to despair.

Decidedly, this was uncanny.

COLONIAL SUBJECTS: GOPAL AND RAKHAL

Sigmund Freud suggests in his 1919 essay 'The Uncanny' that a symbol that 'takes over the full functions of the thing it symbolizes' counts as 'uncanny'.[8] If so, one such revealed symbol in the colonial period was that of the child.

The British colonizers embraced the mission of civilizing and educating their childlike subjects. Their contrarious means of setting about the task was to instil an incurable syndrome of dependency and imitation. It was with this aim that Macaulay, in his portentous Minute on Education, proposed to establish English education in India in the hope of creating a 'class [of] interpreters' between the English and the Indians: 'Indian in blood and colour, but English in taste, in opinions, in morals, and in intellect'.[9]

Despite his pragmatism, Macaulay failed to foresee that the art of mimicry was a double-edged sword.

~

1855: The two-part Bengali primer *Barnaparichay* saw the light of day. Authored by Ishwarchandra Vidyāsāgar, the crusader for justice for women and the spearhead of many reform movements, the primer's conceptual impact is evident in Bengali society even today.

Two leading figures in *Barnaparichay* are the boys Gopāl and Rākhāl.[10] Gopal plies his books and conforms to the patriarchal order governed by his father and his teacher: he is 'good', while Rakhal, who defies this order, is 'bad'. The Gopal–Rakhal pair constitutes a perfect binary. The moral seems to be that the lads have absolute freedom to carve their own destinies, but their only choice is between these polar opposites. Any middle path is excluded.

There are three remarkable blank spaces in *Barnaparichay*. First, not once does a girl peep in to sully the boys' social space. Second, up to the eighth edition, Gopal and Rakhal bear caste appellations that later disappear. And third, *Barnaparichay* is thoroughly secular in temper: God, afterlife, and prayers to divinities are completely absent. For the emerging middle class, *Barnaparichay* held out the promise of a new mode of social mobility, however narrow in scope, actualized by English education. Colonial 'interpreters'-in-the-making could seize the opportunity to become Gopal-like on their own impetus: studious, cultivated *bhadralok*, the petty bourgeoisie.[11]

Yet 'goodness' being defined so narrowly, the horizon of 'badness' becomes infinitely stretchable. Whatever may have been the author's intention, the scales are tipped in favour of the 'bad'. It is not the admirable Gopal but the derided and rejected Rakhal who looms large in *Barnaparichay*. It is Rakhal, again, who keeps alive the possibility of the explosive return of the repressed.

~

1895: In a lecture paying homage to Vidyasagar, Rabindranath launches a blistering attack on Gopal: 'There is no dearth of goodie-goodie boys like Gopal in inoffensive Bengal.... No doubt they pass their exams, find well-paid jobs and get lots of dowry in marriage.' But he identifies Rakhal, Vidyasagar's scorned antihero, with his creator himself: 'In this feeble-spirited land, only the rise of unruly boys like Rakhal and his biographer Ishwarchandra can rid the Bengali race of the stigma of pusillanimity.'[12]

THE PARROT'S TRAINING

Within two and a half months of staging the Bengali *Dākghar* under his own direction in October 1917, Rabindranath published the parable 'Totākāhini' and translated it the same year as 'The Parrot's Training'. 'Totākāhini' begins like a *rupkathā* or fairy tale: 'Once upon a time there was a bird.'[13] It dances and prances about, lacks propriety, and never recites the scriptures. As is the wont in fairy tales, there now appears a villain, the king himself. Incensed at the bird's useless and uncouth antics, he decides to educate it.

His fearsome command 'Shikshā dāo' means both 'Educate' and 'Teach a lesson'. The ambiguity evokes the pedagogic ideal of Macaulayan liberals in the cause of Utilitarian market economics. A host of panjandrums cluster around the bird, now imprisoned in a great golden cage. Copying from books and copying those copies, scribes pile the cage with manuscripts 'to an unreachable height'. The world gathers to exclaim in rapture, 'Culture, captured, and caged!'[14]

Yet '[w]hatever may be its other deficiencies, the world is never in want of fault-finders'.[15] They start gossiping: sure, there's hectic activity around the cage, but what about the bird? The perturbed Raja goes to check on the creature. It is an impressive sight: the cage is empty of grain and water, while reams of paper are shoved down the bird's throat. It cannot scream, let alone sing: it is coming to resemble the half-dead *bhadralok*. Finally, nobody knows just when, it exhales its last sigh.

The fairy-tale opening might have led us to expect that the bird would live happily ever after. Instead, Rabindranath crafts a mock-*rupkathā*, a bitter farce on the way children are tutored in modern times. Only the closing sentence marks an abrupt change of register. It is poetic in flavour, its irony implicit: 'Outside the window, the murmur of the spring breeze amongst the newly budded *asoka* leaves made the April morning wistful.'[16]

Building on the idea that the uncanny was something 'meant to remain secret and hidden but ... now come out into the open', Freud broadened its scope to include effacement of 'the distinction between imagination and reality'.[17] The uncanny side to *Dākghar* needed the extraordinary historical circumstance of Nazi rule in order to be revealed. 'Totākāhini' exposes the 'secret and hidden' element in what society has accepted as normal.

JOYFUL LEARNING

Bengali *shishusāhitya* or children's literature is not overdetermined by the word *shishu*, 'child'. Themes that seem suitable only for adults are also found there – sometimes openly, sometimes beneath the surface. The person who did most to free children's reading from the stranglehold of dry textbooks and didactic preaching was Rabindranath. It was his 'inspiration and patronage' that inaugurated the 'golden age' of Bengali children's literature.[18]

In Rabindranath, the child is the victim of cruel and insensitive forces, but also an active agent, resilient enough to outgrow victimhood. Across his writings in all genres, he mounts an incisive critique of the external world with which the child must engage. Yet he invariably tinges his depictions of little ones living at the mercy of the big ones with sharp wit or gentle humour. Adopting the persona of a young-at-heart grandfather, the twenty-four-year-old Rabindranath has this to say about genteel Bengali society:

> Ours is a phlegmatic temperament, we lack in fads. We are very sedate and respectable [bhadra], very intelligent, not crazy about anything. We pass exams, earn money, and smoke the hookah. We will not lead but follow, not work but advise. We are not into murderous riots, but very much into lawsuits and backstabbing.... Clearly, [as an antidote,] our principal need is to cultivate eccentricity.'[19]

It is thus no wonder that the primers Tagore wrote are free from top-down diktats. Instead of boring the students with didactics and moralizing, they cultivate a line of whimsy.

Rabindranath's search for the aesthetic proper to joyful learning is best realized in his Bengali primer *Sahaj path* (Simple Reading, 1930). In contrast to the arid terrain of Vidyasagar's *Barnaparichay*, the landscape of *Sahaj path* is lush green. The details directly pertaining to nature are not merely descriptive but poetically evoked. The prose is rhythmic; the poetry, besides being limpid and full of pictures, is replete with exciting prosodic variations, starting with an ingenious series of couplets introducing the Bengali vowels and consonants. All this was only achieved through arduous experiment, as evident from a notebook of 1895–6 with many rejected alternatives.[20] It took years of poetic practice before Rabindranath could produce a primer to effectively displace Vidyasagar's.

Tellingly, the noun 'reading' and associated words occur eighty-six times in the two-part *Barnaparichay* but only once in the two-part *Sahaj path*. We have seen how in his 1895 lecture 'Bidyāsāgarcharit', Rabindranath had roundly expressed his disdain for the bookworm Gopal. This contempt is implicit in two other primers he wrote, for English and Sanskrit. *Sangskrita-*

shikshā (1896) has an exasperated-sounding Sanskrit example that translates as 'Only Gopal has come, no-one else'.[21] In *Ingreji-sahajshikshā* Part 2, which appeared in 1930 just a month before *Sahaj pāth*, the English verb 'read' has the common noun 'boy' as its subject ('The boy reads', 'The boy is reading'), but 'sell' has a proper noun, none other than 'Gopal': 'Gopal sells', 'Gopal is selling'.[22] It is pertinent to recall that in the Bengali original of 'The Parrot's Training', the king is concerned because the untamed parrot eats wild fruit, causing losses in the king's fruit market.

Abjuring punishing drills and preset routines to instil conformity, Rabindranath's primers are imbued with the spirit of *chhuti* or holiday.

RELEASE: THE OPEN ROAD

In Rabindranath's lexicon, *chhuti* (holiday) connotes release from a confined space. It can be a forced, final exit or a voluntary withdrawal. The first implies witting or unwitting homicide; the second, an anarchic impulse to upset the status quo.

The short story 'Chhuti' (1892) narrates the short life of a wayward village boy who neglects his studies. Hoping to reform the lad, his uncle brings him to Kolkata, but no matter how hard his custodians try, nurture can never stick on him. His benefactors' attempts to turn him into a bookish Gopal fail miserably, while the boy, no less miserable in the alien metropolis, slips away quietly, gaining the *chhuti* that only death can grant.

If 'Chhuti' is 'Totākāhini' shorn of its allegory, the short story 'Atithi' (The Guest, 1895) is broadly akin to *Dākghar*. Chancing upon a handsome roving adolescent boy, a wealthy couple are charmed by him. They bring the teenager home, arrange for his education, and plan to marry him to their only daughter. But Tārāpada is no fairy-tale prince, to settle down comfortably on gaining the princess and half the kingdom. Foiling the conspiracy to bind him in a net of affective ties and reduce him to a tame family man, Tarapada spurns his prospects and seeks *chhuti* by taking to the road again.

Rabindranath's oeuvre is replete with the call of the open road, most manifestly in his songs. A Eurocentric view would attribute this feature exclusively to Western Romanticism. But for Rabindranath, that influence combines with the model of the *shramana* drawn from early Buddhism and Jainism. In revolt against the ritual-bound structure of an indolent homekeeping brahminism, the *shramana*s adopted a nomadic life, rejecting caste divisions and celebrating nonviolence. Such abjuration was possible even to the scholar who had not completed his student life.

Extending to the full this latent trait within the child figure, Rabindranath creates characters who, though young and unpractised, are stricture-defying rebels with an irrepressible wanderlust, physical as in Tarapada or imaginative as in Amal. However, Tagore detested the ideal of the unattached recluse. Combining these factors, the operational category crucial to his writings for children is *khelā* – 'play' or, more specifically, 'engaged play'.

PATRIARCHY: DREAM AND REALITY

The bulk of poems in the collections *Shishu* (1903) and *Shishu bholānāth* (1922) present a boy-child giving free rein to his imagination. The audience for his unchecked fancy is his bemused mother; with her quiet encouragement, he speaks his mind without fear. This secret understanding is enabled by the physical *absence* of the third party, the father. Borrowing a fairy-tale device, the child speaker in the poem 'Rāja o rāni' (King and Queen) describes the situation: 'Once there was a Raja. The other day, he punished me.... When the trial was over, she came, voice broken, eyes red. Who was that Rani? I know, I know, I know.'[23]

In the poet's philosophic imagination,

On the seashore of endless worlds children meet....

Tempest roams in the pathless sky, ... death is abroad and children play.[24]

But in the real world, the scope for play is limited, above all by the patriarchal family. The amazing achievement of *Shishu* and *Shishu bholānāth* is that by foregrounding 'conversations' between mothers and sons, both mandated to keep decorous silence before male elders, these poems penetrate the mystique of patriarchy to the heart of the humanity it overlays. Crafting a novel dialectic between silence and deafness, they reveal that in actuality, the dependents are loquacious but the guardians are hard of hearing.

There is an interesting reversal of these dynamics in 'Duorāni' (The Neglected Queen, *Shishu bholānāth*). In *rupkathā*, the *duorāni* is the meek queen discarded by the Raja, over whom the conniving *suorāni* or favoured queen, often a demoness in disguise, has cast a spell. Exiled from the palace, the *duorāni* suffers uncomplainingly till one day the *suorāni*'s spell is broken, the Raja drives her out, and recalls the long-suffering *duorāni*. In Tagore's poem, however, the boy wishes that his mother might be ill-treated like the *duorāni*, so that they can both escape the irksome rule of the father-king. They will live in the woods, and the son will step into his father's shoes and protect his mother from all dangers. The Freudianism is most piquant at the end: the little boy enjoins that when he falls asleep, his head on her lap, she must not slip back to the father!

There are other ways too in which a boy might wish to supplant the father, moulding himself in his image. In the hilarious 'Chhotobarho' (Big and Small),²⁵ a little boy contemplates life once he grows up to be his father's age, 'much older than my big brother'. He conjures up many gleeful fantasies: when the teacher tells him to ply his books, he will retort, 'I'm no longer a child, I'm as big as father is', but if his elder brother shirks his studies, he will scold him. On 'the day I first grow up', he will have learnt to open the safe and dole out money, with every assurance of earning more.

~

Besides translating *Gitanjali* and *Dākghar* into Spanish, Juan Ramón Jiménez composed sixteen odes in tribute to Rabindranath. One of them was addressed to the child in *Shishu*. 'I know you are here,' Jiménez tells the child, 'I feel it. But where are you? You're speaking to yourself, aren't you, O my boatman of paper-rafts?'²⁶ Jiménez's emphasis on the 'infinitely green, illimitably delicate' in *Shishu* was not misplaced. But that alone does not encompass all the subtleties of *Shishu* or *Shishu bholānāth*, or *Sahaj pāth* for that matter.

Take, for example, the poem in lesson 11 of *Sahaj pāth* Part 2. In a dream, a Kolkata boy witnesses an incredible scene:

> Roof-beams knocking, pushing, shoving,
> Kolkata has started moving!
> The houses, brick-built rhinos, rushing:
> Doors and windows come down crashing.
> The roads wriggle like python snakes,
> Tramcars tossing on their backs.

But this merry vision of sheer motion does not last long: the boy wakes to find 'Kolkata back in Kolkata'.²⁷

Just as there are roads that can swing to the imagination, so also are there roadblocks.

RULE AND REBELLION

The year was 1913. Rabindranath was in England. From there he sent the manuscript of a short play to Santiniketan, for the entertainment and edification of early learners of English there. Despite its straightforward pedagogic purpose, Tagore's sole English play, *King and Rebel*, is a subtle work of art.

The play is constructed as a game of make-believe by a band of boys. Its two chief characters are Rājen and Hem. The play begins with Rajen proclaiming to the people, 'I am your King.' Hem immediately registers his protest, but cowed down by Rajen's humbug, the people accept him as their ruler. There follows a period of utter confusion. Protected by loyal soldiers and assisted by corrupt underlings, Rajen does whatever he pleases. The compliant commoners sing in unison, 'Long live His Majesty King Rajen. May his shadow never grow less, and may his sneezes ever be attended with loyal snapping of fingers!'[28]

Tired of peace, Rajen longs for war. He chastises his general: 'You are a fine general if you have to wait for a cause to fight. Can't you create enemies?'[29] Although no one follows his reasoning, Rajen brands Hem a 'rebel', even though by now he is an obedient subject. But the declaration of war against Hem stirs up the people. Sensing that everything is rotten with their state, they start to demand 'justice'. They ask Rajen whether what he is set on doing is right. 'Right!' retorts Rajen. 'The King is never wrong.'[30]

Most people join Hem, switching camps: they defeat Rajen's army. The vanquished king hands over the crown to the jubilant rebel. But once Hem assumes the throne, the masses are visited by a replay of Rajen's reign. One of Hem's acolytes reports to him how an offender has had the audacity to sneeze twice while his Majesty was passing by. In fact, sneezes are the constant stuff of crimes under both kings, so that Hem's displeasure is ironic: 'Indeed, this case has no parallel in the history of our realm.'[31]

Written on the eve of the First World War, *King and Rebel* is a play about power-play, a farce about challenging authority under cover of upholding it. There is something Kafkaesque about the playlet. Written ostensibly to help young Bengalis hone their skills in English, it would have taught them many profounder lessons in the ways of the world.

~

All this attests to the complexities of framing a child's aesthetic of resistance. The framing is mostly from a boy's standpoint. The girl child found no mention in Vidyasagar's *Barnaparichay*, and as though following this precedent, she has remained heavily underrepresented in Bengali juvenile literature. Rabindranath does raise the issue in *Se* (He, 1937), even if he dodges it with a weak apologia.

Se is a peerless book of nonsense and fantasy. It chronicles the tall tales of a chatty grandfather to the little girl Pupe, a clear reflection of Rabindranath himself and his granddaughter Nandini. She enters into the fiction and even adds to it, but also offers her own critique. Grandpa says:

> 'Don't you remember the tiger that was so scared of your stick that he slunk away and hid under Aunt Nutu's bed?'
>
> Our heroine was gratified to hear this. She reminded me about the bear who, trying to run away in fright, fell into the bathtub.[32]

The protagonist of the tales is a man indicated only by the third person singular, *se*. Blessed with 'a matchless gift for telling fibs', he not only joins Grandfather and Pupe in weaving crazy tales but makes himself the protagonist.

> I only have to signal for him to say with a straight face that at the pilgrim's fair at Kanchrāpārhā, a crocodile seized him by the top-knot when he went to bathe.... Press him a little more, and he'll tell you how a sahib diver from a man-o'-war searched in the mud for months and rescued the top-knot, all but five or six strands of hair. He was tipped three and a quarter rupees.[33]

Bengali pronouns being genderless, a stand-alone *se* can refer to a person of either sex. The 'Se' of the book is a man, but the narrator exploits the opacity surrounding the pronoun when he says: 'In all the world, there's only one me and only one you; all others are *se*. The *se* in our story stands surety for every *se*.'[34] And yet....

There is also a boy in *Se*. Named Sukumār, he is near cousin to Amal in *Dākghar* and Tārāpada in 'Atithi'. We learn at the end that by way of preparing to land on the moon, Sukumar has left home and is training himself by flying round the earth. Noting that Grandfather is more taken up with Sukumar than with her, Pupe remarks resentfully: 'I know, I know, Sukumar-da had much more in common with you than I did.' The embarrassed grandfather protests it was bound to be so as they shared the same male 'mould' (*chhānch*), different and therefore distant from Pupe's. Forgiving the old man's gender bias, Pupe says simply: 'Never mind all that now.'³⁵ She could instead have said: if the gender divide is so very restrictive, how come male writers launch full-blast sallies into the minds of adult females? Why are they so reticent only when it comes to the girl child?³⁶

DESTRUCTION

In the last two years of Rabindranath's life – with the Second World War raging, Hitler and Mussolini making huge advances – he published several titles whose target audience could well be non-adults: *Chhelebelā* (Childhood: 1940), *Galpasalpa* (Tales: 1941), and *Chharhā* (Rhymes: 1941), the last of which appeared after his death. *Chhelebelā* is an account of Rabindranath's own childhood in scintillating prose, neither sentimental nor nostalgic.

Like *Se*, the stories in *Galpasalpa* are told to a little girl by her grandfather. A poem follows each of the anecdotal pieces. At points in both *Se* and *Galpasalpa*, as though to contest the language of warfare and exploitation, Tagore deliberately breaks with standard Bengali syntax and vocabulary. His indignation never cramps the wit to create meaningful nonsense: one after another, the angry old man coins fantastic words that defy all lexical binds. In *Galpasalpa*, he thoughtfully affords us an English instance, a translation from the Bugbulbuli language by the Sanskrit pundit Vāchaspati: 'The habbarfluous infatuation of Ākbar dorbendically lazertized the gorbandism of Humāyun.'³⁷

On 17 March 1935, Rabindranath drew a grotesque pen-and-ink figure. While he generally avoided naming his artworks, he made an exception in this case: the cartoonish creature is identified as 'Mussolini'.³⁸ Poem 6 in *Chharhā* has a curious combination of elements. Each stanza recounts a series of bizarre happenings, but ends with just two lines of running commentary on Hitler's ongoing massacres, followed by two more lines on caged birds. Nothing is omitted: the toothbrush moustache, the cacophany of German radio, bombs, machine guns, slit throats, sinking ships. And then comes the summing up: 'Everything turns topsy-turvy across the seas: they are crushing bones to build up a whole new universe from them. The truth there is tremendously true, the false fearsomely false.'³⁹

BY WAY OF AN ENDING

Rabindranath wrote *Shishu bholānāth* to find relief from his exposure to acquisitive capitalism in the United States.⁴⁰ For this uncompromising critic of nationalism and mindless mechanization, the return to childhood was an act of catharsis.

Flouting the codes that would shelter children from the dark side of life, the grandfather in *Galpasalpa* presents the reality of war in the story 'Dhwangsa' (Destruction):

> Everyone was amazed on calculating the force of civilization. A long-distance cannonball landed from twenty-five miles away. This showed the progress of the times![41]

The accompanying poem says that civilization (the poet uses the English word) is endowed with nothing except the might of machines. Its greatest task is to oppress humanity.

Today, we may be about to cross the last of many Rubicons. The consequences of Macaulay's agenda for postcolonial societies are all too apparent. Neo-liberal market economics dominates the globe. Neo-nationalism is entrenched in almost every country. Man-made machines are devastating the earth's climate. Nervously awaiting a macabre dance of death, *Homo sapiens* is intent on annihilating the planet.

In this 'crisis in civilization', to reapply Tagore's own title for his last diatribe on the world he had lived to see, a few lines from a 1930 poem seem relevant. It is Tagore's only major poem originally written in English:

> 'What of the night?' they ask.
> No answer comes.
> For the blind Time gropes in a maze and knows not its path or
>   purpose.
>
> ...
>
> A ray of morning sun strikes aslant at the door.
> The assembled crowd feel in their blood the primaeval chant of
>   creation:
> 'Mother, open the gate!' ...
> The poet strikes his lute and sings out:
> 'Victory to Man, the new-born, the ever-living.'[42]

The title of the poem is 'The Child'.

NOTES

1. France Bhattacharya, 'France', in *100 Years*, 457. A memorial report going back to the same source says the play was actually performed: see Maitreyi Debi, *Mangpute Rabindranāth* (1943; rpt. Kolkata: Rupa, 1967), 187–8.
2. Elżbieta Walter, 'Polish Reception of Rabindranath Tagore', 2000, available at https://weblearn.ox.ac.uk/access/content/group/123d20aa-ac83-481d-80bf-3168eaa53a58/Polish.doc, accessed 2 September 2018.
3. *The Post Office*, tr. Devabrata Mukerjea (London: Macmillan, 1914), 13.
4. *RRGWB* 16:688–9.
5. *The Post Office*, v–vi.
6. *L'offrande Lyrique* (*Gitanjali*), tr. André Gide, 2nd ed., 1914, Introduction; tr. Chinmoy Guha, available at sesquicentinnial.blogspot.com/2011/08/andre-gides-intrduction-to-his-french.html, accessed 2 September 2018.
7. *EW* 1:56 (*Gitimālya* #7, *RRVB* 11:134).
8. Sigmund Freud, 'The Uncanny' (1919), tr. Alix Strachey, in *Sigmund Freud: Art and Literature*, ed. Albert Dickson (Harmondsworth: Penguin, 1985), 367.
9. Thomas Babington Macaulay, *Prose and Poetry*, ed. G.M. Young (London: Rupert Hart-Davis, 1952), 729.
10. All *Barnaparichay* references to the 1858 edition as in *Banglā prāimār sangraha*, ed. Āshish Khāstagir (Kolkata: Paschimbanga bānglā ākādemi, 2006).
11. See Sibaji Bandyopadhyay, *The Gopal–Rakhal Dialectic: Colonialism and Children's Literature in Bengal*, tr. Rani Ray and Nivedita Sen (New Delhi: Tulika Books, 2015), 127–33.
12. 'Bidyāsāgarcharit' (Life of Vidyasagar), *RRVB* 4:488.
13. *EW* 2:272 (*Lipikā*, *RRVB* 26:132).
14. Ibid.
15. Ibid. (*RRVB* 26:133).
16. Ibid., *EW* 2:274 (*RRVB* 26:135).
17. Freud, 'The Uncanny', 367.
18. Mānabendra Bandyopādhyāy, *Rabindranāth: shishusāhitya* (Kolkata: Papyrus, 1970 rpt. 2000), 12.
19. *Chithipatra* (Letters), *RRVB* 2:523. This *Chithipatra*, an imaginary exchange of letters between a grandfather and grandson, is different from the collection of Tagore's letters under that title.
20. *RRGWB* 16:1259–60.
21. *RRVB* A2:244.
22. *RRVB* A2:455–6.
23. *Shishu bholānāth*, *RRVB* 13:91–2.
24. English *Gitanjali* #60, *EW* 1:63, also as 'On the Seashore' in *The Crescent Moon*, *EW* 1:129 (Introductory poem, *Shishu*, *RRVB* 9:5–6).

25. *Shishu, RRVB* 9: 32–4; tr. as 'The Little Big Man', *Crescent Moon, EW* 1:146.
26. Translated by the author from the Bengali translation in *Juān rāmon himenether kabitā: shikarher dānā*, tr. Debiprasād Bandyopādhyāy (Kolkata: Chitrak, 1972), 91.
27. *RRVB* A2:637–8.
28. *EW* 2:754.
29. *EW* 2:751.
30. *EW* 2:755.
31. *EW* 2:758.
32. *RRVB* 26:187.
33. *RRVB* 26:189.
34. *RRVB* 26:190.
35. *RRVB* 26:292.
36. Sibāji Bandyopādhyāy, *Bāngla shishusāhityer chhoto meyerā* (Kolkata: Gāngchil, 2017), 126.
37. *RRVB* 26:344.
38. *Rabindra Chitravali: Paintings of Rabindranath Tagore*, ed. R. Siva Kumar (Kolkata: Pratikshan, 2011), vol.3, plate 265.
39. *RRVB* 26:20–3.
40. See *Pashchim-jātrir dāyāri, RRVB* 19:404–5.
41. *RRVB* 26:354.
42. *EW* 1:479, 485–6.

14 Tagore's View of History

SABYASACHI BHATTACHARYA

Rabindranāth Tagore's writings on history cover three chief areas of interest. One is his philosophy of history, particularly in the context of free will and determinism. Here he basically asks the question: Is a human being and a citizen a free agent, or is he an instrument of the historical forces of his times? A second area covers issues arising out of historical narrative: events, personalities, and the long-term course of history. Here his chief focus of interest is the history of Indian civilization, but some of the most valuable discussions relate to global history, European civilization in particular. The third area extends beyond history to historiography: Tagore is critical of the colonial school of writing and offers his own interpretive approach. These three strands are interwoven and cannot be studied in isolation from each other. They are necessarily combined in the account that follows.

We must also bear in mind that Tagore was essentially a poet, and his perception of history finds expression not only in his discursive prose but also in his poetry, fiction, and literary criticism. There was a time in India when works of history were written in verse. In Tagore's poems based on historical annals and legends, most memorably collected in *Kathā o kāhini* (1908), one can discern traces of that centuries-old tradition. He sourced many verse-tales from Buddhist legends in texts such as the *Avadānashataka, Bodhisattva-avadāna, Mahāvastu*, and *Divyāvadānamālā*. On another plane, he imbibed and extended the nascent nationalism that found soil in the history of the Sikhs and the Marāthās, and the historical legends and folk traditions of Rājasthān. Perhaps more importantly, he found a major source of inspiration for his poems and songs, with actual formal models, in the medieval saintly traditions associated with Kabir, Tulsidās, and others, and the Vaishnavite poetry and culture of Mithilā and Bengal.

In an essay on the historical novel ('Aitihāsik upanyās'), Tagore observes that a disconnect between actual history and fiction based on history is natural and inevitable. He quotes the English historian E. Augustus Freeman's comment that if anyone wishes to learn about European history at the time of the Crusades, he must studiously avoid reading Scott's *Ivanhoe*.[1] Tagore recognized the educational value of historical tales and dramas.[2] But he did not try to replicate historical narrative in his poems; he only derived material and drew inspiration for the latter from the accounts of history. In his poetic creations, history is reincarnated in a form all his own. 'The form and *rasa* of *Kathā o kāhini* stirred waves of joy only in Rabindranath's particular mind. This was not owing to history, but to Rabindranath's core being (*antarātmā*).'[3]

However, this also implies that his intellectual and political engagement with history is apparent not so much in his poems as in his philosophical vision of the present and the past. In the rest of this essay, I will focus on the interpretation of history in his discursive writings in English and Bengali, which have received less attention than they merit from professional historians.

We can start with Tagore's critique of the school of colonial historians. Tagore never wrote history in narrative form: his interventions in historiography were chiefly in the form of critique. He conceded that English scholars of Indian history had added to our store of knowledge about historical events, but he felt that racial bias often caused misjudgements or misrepresentation of the native players on the stage of history. The colonial historians constructed a chronicle of the triumphal advent of European powers in the Indian subcontinent. As might be expected, their story glorified the role of the conquering race, the might of British military power, and the moral and material progress achieved by India under British rule. Tagore wrote a few articles in his youth – at least one while in his teens[4] – contesting the colonial historians' view of prominent Indian personalities, but his criticism acquired substance only when Indian historians began to produce regional history, often in regional languages.

At the turn of the century, Mahādev Govind Ranade in Mahārāshtra and Akshaykumār Maitreya in Bengal began to write history from the Indian point of view. In January 1899, just over thirteen years from the foundation of the Indian National Congress, Akshaykumar launched the quarterly *Aitihāsik chitra* (Images from History), the first historical journal in the Bengali language. Tagore supported him morally and materially in this effort: a critical approach to colonial historiography was an item of their common agenda. We can no longer be content, writes Tagore, to see our country through others' eyes. Indian history as written by Indians might be biased, but it was still better than the opposite bias imbued with hatred and lack of empathy.[5]

Tagore wrote a series of essays in 1898–9 celebrating this new trend.[6] He perceived in it 'a hunger for history' (*itihāsbubhukshā*): a new interest in the history of the country, a new stage in the growth of historical consciousness. Most importantly, he saw it as indicating the growth of productive nationalist sentiment: 'The [Indian National] Congress has not merely been sending fruitless appeals to the royal palace year after year without any result. It has also ... planted the seed of a new consciousness in our minds.'[7]

The central point he often made was that colonial historians offered a textbook account of the external events of Indian history. Indian students crammed those books to pass examinations, but that did not enlarge their deeper knowledge of their own country through history. 'In a country favoured by fortune, people perceive in their histories their own country as shaped by its past.... In our country, the opposite has happened. Writings on history hide our country from our vision.'[8] History-writing in colonial times is chiefly concerned with conquerors and their battles. It presents the outsiders' view of India's past, excluding things central to the civilization of the country:

> We are not weeds and parasites on India's soil: we have sent a myriad roots down to its core over many centuries. But by ill fortune, we have to study a version of history whereby this is precisely what our children forget. We feel we are people of no importance in India: the conquerors are all.[9]

Second, Tagore argued that colonial historians focused attention only on the state and the political order; in that state-centred narrative, the history of Indian society, culture, and way of life were marginalized if not totally absent. Yet it was the continuity and stability of society (*samāj*) that had always sustained Indian civilization, sometimes without the aid of the state. The defining characteristic of India's civilization was that it was held together by the *samāj* at its core. Colonial historians failed to appreciate that fact; and having failed to find in India the familiar history of state-building and political power, they concluded that India has no history at all.[10] As Tagore quips in 'Bhāratbarsher itihās', it was as though they were searching for aubergines in a paddy-field, and failing to find what they wanted, dismissing paddy as a useless crop.[11]

While Tagore was critical of nineteenth-century British historians for these reasons, he also charged Indians with exoticizing their own history to weave 'a huge web of illusion' out of a narrative of heroes, rulers, and warriors, of stirring and romantic events – a kind of *Arabian Nights*.[12] Tagore deplored the absence of a truly critical reading of Indian history geared to its distinctive character, social rather than political or military: there were too many gaps and uncertainties, which could only be made good from the researches of foreign historians. Hence he asks: 'Will we always be reliant on others for learning about the history of our own country?'[13]

About the substantive content of the version of Indian history accepted in his times, Tagore had little to say. He wrote isolated pieces on the rise of Shivaji in Maratha country, or Sikh history, or Lakshmibāi, the warrior-queen of Jhānsi during the uprising of 1857,[14] but they do not add up to any systematic contribution. What is outstanding in this area of Tagore's thought is his thesis of a historical trend that characterizes India's civilization. This trend, he submitted, was the search for unity among a plurality of cultures. Indian society and the Indian ethos took into their midst a succession of ethnic groups that came and settled in the land: Tagore idealizes this unifying tendency as epitomizing India's spirit of syncretism. It is an overarching theme in his writings from 1898 ('Aitihāsik chitra') through 1902 ('Bhāratbarsher itihās', where the view is perhaps most clearly expressed) to 1912 ('Bhāratbarshe itihāser dhārā', The Course of Indian History). It reappears in markedly different guise in the 1930s in the essays collected in *Kālāntar* (Change of Era, 1937), the title essay in particular. Tagore saw Indian civilization as a ceaseless interplay between the individuality of each of its myriad cultures and ethnicities and the tendency towards their unification. He insisted no less that in India, differences were not ironed out by a flattening process of assimilation; they were preserved within the whole.

> Bhāratvarsha [India] has attempted the bonding of dissimilars. Where there is a genuine difference, it is possible to accommodate it in its appropriate place and thereby bring it within the unity. You cannot legislate unity into existence.[15]

Tagore extended the idea to argue that India's quest for unity is diametrically different from that in many other parts of the world. The Western colonial powers sought first of all to destroy the peoples whose lands they had overrun:

> What happened in America and Australia? When Europeans set foot there, they were Christians, versed in the doctrine of loving their enemies. But they did not rest till they had totally extirpated the original inhabitants of America and Australia, slaughtering them like animals. These original inhabitants could not be assimilated into the nations set up in America and Australia.[16]

Where the Other could not be totally eradicated, it was unified with the dominant group by a species of 'assimilationism', whereby newcomers gained entry at the price of abandoning their original culture, as in the United States.[17] As Tagore phrased it elsewhere, Europe and America have raised high walls on the foundation of their nationalism.[18] India, by contrast, was hospitable to differences: here various peoples could live together with their separate identities within the all-inclusive compass of a syncretic civilization:

> India has always sought one thing only: to establish unity in diversity,
> to direct many paths towards the same goal, to perceive the one
> among the many indubitably and profoundly – to secure the intrinsic
> affinity without destroying external differences.[19]

The notion of plurality and syncretism as the basis of Indian unity became a cornerstone in the construction of nationhood in the hands of Jawāharlāl Nehru and other nationalist thinkers. This concept is Tagore's outstanding and lasting contribution to the interpretation of Indian history, as incorporated in the fabric of the living nation. At the same time, we must recognize that in late life, roughly from 1925 onwards, Tagore radically revised his notion of the fundamental civilizational unity of India. The revision was forced upon Tagore by the rising tide of casteism and religious conflict. These faults in the social fabric had largely been ignored in the vision of India's syncretic unity found in his earlier writings. In the later essays collected in *Kālāntar* (1937) but often written much earlier, such as 'Shudradharma' (The Dharma of the Shudras, 1925), 'Swāmi Shraddhānanda' (1926), and 'Hindumusalmān' (Hindus and Muslims, 1931), Tagore conceded the need to rethink the idealistic postulation of India's fundamental unity in his early writings.

The ideal unity of Indian civilization is now presented more as an unattained goal than a realized and evolving model:

> The fact of the matter is that we are not as one, there is no end to the
> divisions between us. I said at the outset that division is sorrow, it is
> sin, whether between ourselves and foreigners or among ourselves.[20]

Tagore sees the Hindu and the Muslim as coexisting for centuries in India, side by side, without a true mingling of hearts.[21] For this he blames brahminical Hinduism, bound by rejections and prohibitions, as much as the doctrinal restrictions of Islam.[22] He recognizes equally the continuing insult heaped upon the lower castes in the name of religion, even by the educated.[23] He feels that Indians have thereby demeaned themselves and impeded their quest for true independence, as opposed to mere freedom from foreign rule:

> In the land where humanity has enslaved itself in its sense of *dharma* as well as in a practical sense, it does not possess within itself the true strength to demand the right to governance. It has to rely on the goodness of others to grant it such a right.[24]

'When we want independence for the nation,' he writes, 'we do not want a negative independence.'[25]

In the essays in *Kālāntar*, this concern with India meshes with Tagore's view of the wider world. Another of his major tasks was to locate colonial India in the global context of East–West civilizational relationships. The broad historical perspective underlying that endeavour is based on deep and extensive readings in modern history, along with personal observations and experiences during his travels overseas. He did not fail to connect the history of imperialism with the growth of industrial power and commercial prosperity among a few countries in Europe, as analysed in *Kālāntar*. However, his focus is not so much on the political economy of imperialism as the concomitant moral degradation of the West, as shown in the contrast between Europe in the nineteenth and early twentieth centuries and Europe prior to that. He recalls that modern Europe was the origin of ideas upholding liberty and democracy, the abolition of slavery, and much more, setting the world on a new path of progress. He also recalls in the essay 'Kālāntar' the human values that India imbibed from the West, inspiring its own reawakening in the nineteenth century.[26] He contrasts this with instances like the experience of China during the Opium Wars or Congo under Belgian rule or the hegemony acquired in Persia by the European powers.[27]

The ideological cause of Europe's moral decline was, by Tagore's diagnosis, nationalism. Nationalism is a theme that figures prominently in Tagore's writings on the modern world. No account of his view of history can afford to leave it out, though only a brief outline can be offered here. His basic position on this subject is summed up in his lectures in Japan and the United States in 1916–17, which he put together in the book *Nationalism* (1917). The first chapter is about the general Western concept of nationalism, the second about the spread of nationalism in Japan and its consequences, while the third addresses the issues faced by Indian nationalism.

'Society as such,' says Tagore, 'has no ulterior purpose.... It is a spontaneous self-expression of man as a social being. It is a natural regulation of human relationships, so that men can develop ideals of life in cooperation with one another.' When that society comes to constitute a 'political and economic union ... for a mechanical purpose', it becomes a nation.[28] A nation represents 'the organized self-interest of a whole people, when it is the least human and the least spiritual'.[29] Society then becomes a mechanical order whose sole aim is to excel in competition. Tagore describes the consequences as witnessed in recent history:

> This history has come to a stage when the moral man, the complete man, is more and more giving way, almost without knowing it, to make room for the political and the commercial man, the man of the limited purpose. This, aided by the wonderful progress in science, is assuming gigantic proportion and power, causing the upset of man's moral balance, obscuring his human side under the shadow of soul-less organization.[30]

As he has already observed, this marks 'an evil day for humanity'.[31]

Tagore turns next from Europe to Japan. He lauds her modernization and resistance to foreign domination but condemns her voluntary surrender to the doctrine of nationalism. As regards nationalism in India, he boldly says that India 'has never had a real sense of nationalism'.[32] Nationalism was an outcome of European history: the spread of nationalist sentiment in India leads him to protest that 'we cannot borrow other people's history'.[33] Tagore's position on nationalism was developed further through his interaction with Gāndhi from 1919 onwards. While they disagreed on certain basic issues like the effectiveness of non-cooperation with the British and the utility of the *charkhā*, or spinning wheel, they agreed that the constraints of nationalist ideology might misguide India into abandoning humanist values.

Another recurrent theme in Tagore's writings on history is the intellectual contribution of some late medieval religious preceptors. They upheld a kind of universalist humanism upon which Tagore elaborates in his own philosophical writings like the Hibbert Lectures at Oxford published as *The Religion of Man* (1930) and the Kamalā Lectures at Calcutta University published as *Mānusher dharma* (1933). For their resistance to blind obscurantism, casteist exclusion, and priestly tyranny, Tagore particularly celebrates spiritual leaders like the Sikh Guru Nānak and the Vaishnavite Chaitanya, pietists and poets like Kabir, Tukārām, Rabidās, Dādu and the latter's Muslim disciple Rajjab, and the Bāul community of

Bengal.[34] He himself translated *One Hundred Poems of Kabir* into English. But in the last analysis, although these personalities often appear in Tagore's writings, he does not integrate them to their historical context as his total historiography allowed him ample scope to do. His interest was focused on their spiritual message.

As E.P. Thompson points out in his introduction to the 1992 edition of the book, *Nationalism* was largely provoked by the First World War. The War, said Tagore, exposed the true nature of European civilization:

> The political civilization which has sprung up from the soil of Europe and is over-running the whole world ... is carnivorous and cannibalistic in its tendencies, it feeds upon the resources of other peoples and tries to swallow their whole future.[35]

Tagore returned to the theme in his last public statement shortly before his death, 'Sabhyatār sangkat', translated as 'Crisis in Civilization' (1941). Here Tagore recalls how Indians of his generation had looked up to Europe, the home of the progressive ideas that inspired the reawakening of the Indian mind in the nineteenth century. He deplores the contrasting impact of the rise of imperialist aggression in and from Europe, and the record of imperial rule in India:

> From one end of the world to the other the poisonous fumes of hatred darken the atmosphere. The spirit of violence which perhaps lay dormant in the psychology of the West, has at last roused itself and desecrates the spirit of Man.
>
> The wheels of Fate will some day compel the English to give up their Indian empire. But what kind of India will they leave behind, what stark misery? ... I had at one time believed that the springs of civilization would issue out of the heart of Europe. But today when I am about to quit the world that faith has gone bankrupt altogether.[36]

Beyond this message for his times, and the increasingly sombre vision of history impelling it, Tagore shows originality in dealing with some broader philosophical issues in history. One of these is the classic problem weighing the freedom of the individual in history against historical necessity. Tagore tends to emphasize his freedom as an individual mind with an autonomous trajectory of its own: 'In the core of my being I am a poet and nothing else. There I am a creator: I am singular and free, not wrapt in the web of external events.'[37] The creative mind selects and uses certain elements from history and from the social environment around him, but that mind retains its freedom in the act of creation. As he puts it in the same essay, 'The light glinting on the leaves of the coconut trees in [Tagore's] garden was not an official import of the British government. It emerged from some mysterious history of my deepest spirit.'[38] In his creative writing, he continues – the short stories, for instance, mainly concerned with common people's existence – he did not try to narrate political history, though that history was undoubtedly buffeting those lives. Distinct and separate from the history of Mughal or British rule, there was a stream of life experiences that he aimed to capture in his fiction. The significant history was that whose course through immensity was charioted by creative humanity – a history beyond history, at the core of the human spirit. The Upanishads knew this; the poet received the message of the Upanishads by his own volition, by exercising his own mastery over it.[39]

Tagore wrote this in May 1941, shortly before his death. He refrained from pushing the argument further. Despite his assertion of individual autonomy, he accepts that the human mind is conditioned by historical circumstance: 'My writings have taken many shapes, many twists and turns owing to the changing situation and environment around me, and the variety of new experiences.'[40] Tagore clearly aimed at striking a balance between necessity and freedom: historical determination on the one hand and the mind's freedom on the other.

Beyond such philosophical issues, Tagore's view of history has an epistemological dimension as well. He does not seem to consider the impact of Leopold von Ranke on historical methodology of great import, although his contemporaries like the historian Jadunāth Sarkār were deeply influenced by Ranke's stress on sources and documents. Tagore's interest in the history of culture and ideas led him to place more value on writers like Ernest Renan, Auguste-Réal Angers, and Herbert Spencer.[41] Broadly speaking, his focus was on the history of India as a civilization, which he tried to place in the context of global history. Crucial concomitant themes in this exploration are the relationship between the civilizations of the East and the West, and the distortions introduced into their exchanges and affinities by militant nationalism and imperialism.

In 1923, Tagore wrote a memorable English poem addressed to the historical past, appended to his essay 'A Vision of India's History':

Tumultuous years bring their voice to your bosom,
    Unfathomed Past!
In what dark silence do you keep it gathered, covering it

> Under your brooding wings? ...
> You come to write stories of our fathers in unseen script
>   On the pages of our destiny....
> Is not the restless Present itself your own visions
>   Flung up like planets that arise from the bottom of dumb night?[42]

This draws loosely on a Bengali poem of 1903[43] but introduces ideas of its own, especially the arresting notion in the last lines. They admirably reflect Tagore's view of the present as set in the past and deriving from it, making real the latent potential of earlier times. But already in the first line, the poet has validated the most crucial arena of the historical process: the interior of the human sensibility, impacted by history, yet never shaped by it to the extent of surrendering freedom and individuality.

NOTES

1. *RRVB* 8:447.
2. See 'Itihāskathā' (Historical Tales), *RRVB* 12:520.
3. 'Sāhitye aitihāsikatā' (Historicity in Literature), *RRVB* 27:283. Tagore is referring to himself in the third person.
4. 'Jhānsir rāni' (1877), *RRVB* 30:317.
5. 'Aitihāsik chitra', *RRVB* 9:511–12.
6. They include 'Aitihāsik chitra', 'Aitihāsik chitra: suchanā' (foreword to the first number of the journal *Aitihāsik chitra*), 'Bhāratbarsher itihās' (The History of India), and two reviews of Akshaykumar's historical novel *Sirājaddaulā*.
7. 'Aitihāsik chitra', *RRVB* 9:509.
8. 'Bhāratbarsher itihās', *RRVB* 4:379.
9. Ibid., *RRVB* 4:378.
10. 'Bhārat-itihās-charchā' (The Study of Indian History), *RRVB* 32:238.
11. *RRVB* 4:380.
12. Ibid., *RRVB* 4:379.
13. 'Bhārat-itihās-charchā', *RRVB* 32:238.
14. See the poem 'Shibāji-utsab' (Celebration of Shivaji) and the essays 'Bir guru' (The Heroic Guru), 'Shikh-swādhinatā' (Sikh Independence), and 'Jhānsir rāni' (The Queen of Jhansi).
15. 'Bhāratbarsher itihās', *RRVB* 4:382.
16. 'Bhāratbarshiya samāj' (Indian Society), *RRVB* 3:521; see also 'Bhāratbarsher itihās', *RRVB* 4:383.
17. 'Bhārat-itihās-charchā', *RRVB* 32:237.
18. *Bishwabhārati* 10, *RRVB* 27:383.
19. 'Bhāratbarsher itihās', *RRVB* 4:381.

20. 'Samasyā' (1923), *RRVB* 24:345.
21. 'Kālāntar' (1933), *RRVB* 24:243-4.
22. 'Hindumusalmān', *RRVB* 24:375-6.
23. 'Kālāntar', *RRVB* 24:247.
24. 'Bātāyaniker patra' (Letters of a Watcher at the Window), *RRVB* 24:316.
25. 'Samasyā', *RRVB* 24:342.
26. *RRVB* 24:244-8.
27. 'Swādhikārpramattah' (Reckless of One's Rights), *RRVB* 24:395.
28. 'Nationalism', Lecture 1, *EW* 2:421.
29. Ibid., *EW* 2:423.
30. Ibid., *EW* 2:424.
31. Ibid., *EW* 2:422.
32. Ibid., Lecture 3, *EW* 2:456.
33. Ibid., *EW* 2:456-7.
34. For references to the personalities named, see 'Bhāratbarsher itihās', *RRVB* 4:378; 'Path o pātheya' (The Way and the Means), *RRVB* 10:452; 'Mahātmā gāndhi', *RRVB* 27:295; 'Brāhmasamājer sārthakatā' (The Fulfilment of the Brahmo Samaj), *Shāntiniketan*, *RRVB* 16:377. He has many writings on the Bauls, for example, 'Bāul gān' (Baul Songs), 'Bāuler gān' (The Song of the Baul), and *The Religion of Man*, ch. 7, 'The Man of My Heart'.
35. 'Nationalism', Lecture 2, *EW* 2:440.
36. *EW* 3:726.
37. 'Sāhitye aitihāsikatā', *RRVB* 27:281.
38. Ibid., *RRVB* 27:283.
39. Ibid., *RRVB* 27:284.
40. Introduction (1939) to vol. 1 of his Collected Works, *RRVB* 1:ix.
41. For Renan, see 'Neshan ki' (What Is a Nation), *RRVB* 3:515; for Angers, 'Birodhmulak ādarsha' (An Ideal Based on Conflict), *RRVB* 10:592; for Spencer, 'Rājā o prajā' (King and Subject), *RRVB* 10:545, and 'Ghushāghushi' (Coming to Blows), *RRVB* 19:610. His use of these thinkers is far from uncritical, as the reference to Spencer in 'Rājā o prajā' testifies.
42. *VBQ* 1 (1923), 32. A revised version is found in *Poems* (1942), #37.
43. Introductory poem, *Kathā*, *RRVB* 7:9.

15 Tagore's View of Politics and the Contemporary World

SOBHANLAL DATTA GUPTA

I

Rabindranāth's encounter with a larger world, beyond his own country, began at a very early age and continued all through his life. Hence the interrelation between his political thought and his view of the world is an exciting but challenging issue, for at least two reasons. First, Tagore was not a political activist, nor did he attach primary importance to politics in his thought. Hence apart from his lectures collected as *Nationalism*, delivered as the First World War was approaching its end, there is hardly any other text where he reflects exclusively on politics. The importance of this text notwithstanding, it is perhaps time to consider his political standpoint from other angles, by looking at many other sources that are not primarily political. Among these are his essays, mostly in Bengali, and his lectures and addresses delivered abroad in the period between the two World Wars. During this time he travelled extensively to both the East and the West, following the award of the Nobel Prize in 1913 and his desperate search for funds for his dream project of Visva-Bharati in Santiniketan.

Second, there is a methodological dimension to this exercise, which in turn is twofold. At one level, Tagore was a product of Indian and specifically Upanishadic tradition together with Western modernity, a mix that characterized the Tagore family. At another level, he was writing as a colonized subject in British India, experiencing colonial rule at first hand and the responses it evoked at various levels in his own country. He therefore had two rather easy options open before him. The first was to accept British rule in a spirit of servility like any 'brown sahib' of his day; the second, to completely reject the West, turning instead to nationalism or uncritical nativism. Tagore took neither of these two paths. His position on colonialism, more specifically on colonial modernity, was mediated through a total worldview evolving since his youth.

Tagore's contemporaries viewed India on an existential level through their lived experience of colonialism, and hence often resorted to nationalism by rejecting the West; but for Tagore the global citizen, the East–West binary was methodologically irrelevant. He attempted to blend critical readings of both Indian and Western tradition, culture, and values, viewing India in the world's mirror and thereby analysing her maladies, and also *vice versa*. He could thus be critical of what the West lacked and advocate what it could learn from the East, India in particular. At the same time, while he loved his own country and detested colonialism, he never limited his attack on the latter to the narrow confines of nationalism or nativism. His questioning of the East–West binary was guided by a larger vision of a new world of the future, free from the crude arrogance, power, and materialism of the West as well as the conservatism and stagnation that plagued the East, synthesizing instead the best that was cultivated by both West and East. Tagore thus belongs to the model of humanity represented by Romain Rolland or Albert Schweitzer. His view of politics was utopian and futuristic, to the exasperation of his own countrymen no less than the Western world.

2

Viewed in this light, Tagore's engagement with both the West and the East was a dialectical process, endorsing some points and rejecting others, weighing the positive against the negative. In his 1916 lecture on nationalism in Japan he said: 'Europe is supremely good in her beneficence where her face is turned to all humanity; and Europe is supremely evil in her malefic aspect where her face is turned only upon her own interest, using all her power of greatness for ends which are against the infinite and eternal in Man.'[1] These 'supremely good' and 'supremely evil' elements were analysed in some early Bengali essays like 'Akāl kushmānda' (Ripe Too Early, 1884) and 'Hāte kalame' (Hands On, 1884), then in the many pieces collected between 1905 and 1908 in *Ātmashakti* (Inner Strength), *Bhāratbarsha* (India), *Rājā prājā* (Rulers and Subjects), *Samuha* (Collection), *Swadesh* (Homeland), and *Samāj* (Society). Here he identified a set of ideas and institutions that were Western in nature and origin, distinct from anything in the East. Chief among them were notions of the individual and the collective entity; of politics, the state and the nation; and the public.

Tagore brought out the distinctiveness of the Western attitude towards labour and consumption, as contrasted with India:

Europe is individual in consumption, collective in labour. India's case is opposite. India shares its consumption, but labours individually. Europe's wealth, comfort and happiness are individual, but her philanthropy, her schools and colleges, religious practice, trade and commerce are collective exercises. Our wealth and happiness are not individual, but our philanthropy, scholarship and discharge of duty are.[2]

Another essay in *Bhāratbarsha* made an even more crucial distinction:

> Just as 'politics' and 'nation' are European expressions, *dharma* is an Indian expression. Just as 'politics' and 'nation' cannot be translated into our language, it is impossible to find a synonym for *dharma* in any European language. So we mistakenly imagine *dharma* to be the English 'religion'.[3]

Many of the essays argued that while the West focused on the state, power, and the individual, in India the accent was on *samāj*, *dharma*, and social accountability. He followed up the idea in *Nationalism*, characterizing Western civilization as 'political' or state-centric, unlike the Eastern model 'whose basis is society and the spiritual ideal of man'.[4] The word 'society' indicates that he had in mind the Indian concept of *samāj*, which, for him, is a non-political, non-statist category. To be more precise, *samāj* meant the totality of the structure of Indian society that constituted and defined its people. Unlike the 'state', which is external to the individual, *samāj* and the people are inseparable, organically connected. For Tagore, the West's understanding of nationhood involved a notion of exclusiveness and universalization. This led to disrespect for others, and a justification of domination and arrogance that, he felt, was inapplicable to the East. The traditions of the East did not support this outlook.

This understanding led him to highlight two points. First, he cautioned Indians against uncritically emulating the West. He held up Japan as an example in this regard. In *Jāpān-jātri* (Traveller to Japan, 1919), he admired how Japan had emulated the most potent expressions of Europe's prowess, everything that could benefit and empower her: its weapons and military discipline, industries and offices, even the cultivation of science.[5] Yet far from blindly imitating the West, Japan had preserved the essence of her own culture and ethos – what two years earlier, in *Nationalism*, Tagore had called her 'vital nature'.[6] In other words, Tagore distinguished between what was and was not necessary or appropriate for the East to value and absorb. He could therefore observe that India had more to learn from Japan than from Europe.[7]

In 'Akāl kushmānda', he ridiculed the Indian tendency to draw mechanical analogies between eminent Indians and their Western counterparts: 'Bengal's

Byron , 'Bengal's Demosthenes', and so on.[8] He felt this practice implied that Indians were soliciting the blessing and patronage of the British in a spirit of servility, even though the latter were averse to admitting Indians to their cultural sphere.[9] Tagore brilliantly anticipated today's postcolonial perception that the West has dominated the East by universalizing itself through a cultural strategy whereby the East is persuaded to look upon the West as its model and mentor.

Second, Tagore sought the cause of the West's closed mind vis-à-vis the East in its premising the centrality of the state, with its concomitant display of power, arrogance, and hegemony, as against the all-embracing humane institution of the *samāj*. The consummation of the Western ethos was militant nationalism and intolerance. In an appendix to the essay 'Swadeshi samāj' (Indigenous Society, 1904), he wrote:

> The repository of Europe's strength is the *state*,[10] that is, the government. It is the state that has taken up the responsibility of all welfare activities in the land: the state gives out doles, the state provides education, the state even protects religion. So for European civilization to survive, it is imperative to make the rule of the state powerful, efficient and alert in every way, to protect it from internal failures as well as external aggression.
>
> In our country, the power to do good lies with the *samāj*. It pervades our entire society in the form of *dharma*. Hence all these ages, India has considered the protection of *dharma* and the *samāj* to be the means of her survival. It has focused not on statehood but on the *samāj*.[11]

But here too, Tagore's stand is suitably critical. In 'Hāte kalame', he deplores the absence of the force that in Europe would be called the 'public':[12] it is in some ways similar to *samāj*, but a more active and assertive force that can take initiatives, protest, or campaign for a cause in a way he does not find in Indian society.[13] The European concept, he explains, envisaged people consciously coming together in an express show of solidarity for attaining a certain objective. In India there was no such sense of bonding. So although the word 'public' was frequently used in India, it was only as a figment of the imagination. A spirit of conscious, collective engagement at the heart of citizenship flourished in the West but was lacking in India.

For all these reasons, Europe could not provide the model for writing India's history: the two traditions were completely different, as Tagore argued at length in 'Bhāratbarsher itihās' (The History of India). Even more crucial than the interpretation of the past were the implications for the future. In *Kālāntar* (Change of Era, 1937), he wrote in a spirit of anguish that for the non-European world, those who were not kin (*anātmiya*) to the European, 'it became gradually evident that ... the torch of European civilization aimed not to show the light but to set on fire'.[14]

For Tagore, the uniqueness of the East lay in its alternative understanding of freedom. Unlike the West's focus on activism, materialism, individualism, and utilitarianism, the East viewed freedom as the spiritual liberation of the self, which in turn was integrally associated with the idea of social and moral responsibility as enshrined in the collective.[15] Tagore lamented that his countrymen were not aware of this ideal of their own, and thus suffered from self-denigration. He observed in the essay 'Shikshār herpher' (The Vicissitudes of Education) that there were Indians versed in Western education, inclined towards Western materialism but blind to the true wealth of Western culture and civilization. Yet alongside this, they clung to outdated Indian customs and practices instead of developing their own true inheritance. They thus steered themselves into a situation of ludicrous self-contradiction. What Tagore espoused instead was not any dichotomy of East and West but a negotiation between them. He thereby distanced himself from mere nativism, while granting due honour to nativist tradition, culture, and values.

Tagore's political standpoint could easily have been infected with the virus of nationalism. A sample of the provocations he sustained is found in the account in the early *Yurop-jātrir dāyāri* (Diary of a Traveller to Europe, 1891) of his indignation on hearing a stout Englishman tell his female companion how Indian punkah-wallahs (fan-pullers) habitually fell asleep at work and had to be punished by a stick or a kick.[16] His sustained revulsion against the entire colonialist programme, most strikingly manifested in his unsparing condemnation of the Jaliānwālā Bāgh massacre of 1919, could have led him to justify a kind of Eastern nationalism in the name of patriotism. But as Amartya Sen points out,[17] Tagore never carried his patriotic fervour to excess, since that would have obstructed his critical engagement with the West on the cultural plane. That, in turn, would have blurred his view of India in the world's mirror.

3

In Tagore's understanding of politics, shaped by his total vision of the world, there was no scope for ambiguity. But a pertinent question arises at this point: While Tagore's condemnation of Western arrogance and violence stemmed both from his experiences in India and his travels abroad, what were the means by which the West developed its impression of Tagore? How did it react to his idea of a dialogic encounter of the East and the West?

After the Nobel award of 1913, Tagore could no longer be ignored; yet he was chiefly known in the West through a very selective body of work, most notably the English *Gitanjali*. The other means of direct access was his lectures and addresses on his trips abroad. In these, he iterated the themes he had already developed in the aforementioned Bengali essays from the pre-Nobel period. The image of Tagore formed in the West from these twin sources was not consensual. The overwhelming impression was of an oriental mystic who, with his sermonizing on East–West relations and his attack on the West's power, arrogance, and materialism, invoked the wrath of the Western press. For them this was an anti-modernist position, an unacceptable exercise in oriental obscurantism. There was a minority opinion shared by Romain Rolland, Gilbert Murray, Hermann Keyserling, and others, who deeply admired his position from a standpoint of humanism and the syncretism of East and West.

Recent research throws interesting light on this issue.[18] It was in the interwar years that the West encountered Tagore's politics of peace, harmony, and humanism, with its concomitant condemnation of the West. In the immediate aftermath of the First World War, when an exhausted Europe was gasping for peace, Tagore's apparently 'mystical' ideas initially found favourable response. To many Europeans he appeared almost like a messiah, his innate grace and exotic attire lending credence to the image. But as Europe recovered from the War, Tagore's political philosophy began to lose its appeal. The West was faced with new misgivings: political unrest, the decadence of the capitalist order, the challenge of Bolshevism, the menace posed by fascism to the values of liberal democracy, forebodings of another World War – all these demanded a kind of politics that had to be specifically political or ideological rather than high-soundingly moral or spiritual.

This was most strongly evident in the responses evoked by Tagore in Britain, the United States, Germany, and Italy, as also in China and Japan. The British press grew severely critical of his views after his 1930 address 'Civilization and Progress' at Birmingham,[19] his critique of power and the machine in his Hibbert Lectures at Oxford the same year (published as *The Religion of Man*), and his general condemnation of colonial oppression, expressed in action in his renouncing his knighthood after the Jalianwala Bagh massacre. In the United States too, his two lecture-series *Sadhana* and *Nationalism* were seen as glorifying the East and vilifying the West.

By the end of his many visits to both countries, these responses totally frustrated Tagore.

In Germany, again, as Martin Kämpchen recounts, his three visits in 1921, 1926, and 1930 created the image of an oriental mystic, a contemplative, and a venerator of nature. Tagore, in other words, was the 'Other' of the German spirit, and thereby a curious object in the public eye. His spiritual aura aroused resentment on the following grounds:

(1) Tagore, a Hindu, wanted to influence Christians in their faith and ultimately convert them to Hinduism. (2) German writers deserved a slice of the Indian writer's enormous fame, as they were no less talented and relevant in their writing. (3) Tagore's seeming 'oriental lethargy', 'bloodlessness', 'Indian mildness' was inimical to European 'dynamism', to its 'action-oriented' mindset. This European mindset was desperately needed to support the reconstruction of the German nation after the First World War.[20]

Interestingly, the response in China and Japan was no different. In China the Left intelligentsia, many of them associated with the newly formed Chinese Communist Party (CPC), did not look favourably upon Tagore's critique of the West. Even Chen Duxiu, a founder of the CPC and among the earliest Chinese admirers of Tagore's poetry, found his political position unacceptable. His advocacy of *dharma* was construed as a defence of traditionalism, hence inimical to China's quest for Western modernity (of which Marxism too was a product).[21] Japan had already taken a positive stand towards Western culture and science. Tagore's critique of Western imperialism did not agree with that perception, despite the poet Noguchi's apparent appreciation.[22]

In fact, the appreciation of Tagore in Japan was rather limited, being confined to select literary figures; on the other hand, the reaction to his lectures and his views was overwhelmingly hostile, chiefly for two reasons. First, Tagore's critique of Western civilization as aggressive and violent, and his projection of the East as an alternative to the West, was unacceptable to the Japanese: Japan, unlike India, was not a colony of the West, and found the roadmap of its future in Westernization. Second, Tagore's denunciation of nationalism hurt Japan's own patriotic pride and imperialist ambitions, especially when the country was at war with China. So, for Tagore, the visit to Japan was no less frustrating, if not more, than that to China. Even Noguchi tilted more towards nationalism through the 1920s and 1930s and hence became increasingly critical of Tagore.

His interaction with Italy was especially noteworthy. While critiquing statism, Tagore had proposed a leader or head of society (samājpati) who would lead the samāj in the right direction. He might be good or bad but could do no lasting harm if the samāj was alert.[23] Giuseppe Flora has shown how this romantic view of a 'leader' provides an interesting clue to Tagore's visits to fascist Italy in 1925 and 1926 and his initial weakness for Mussolini. He had very little earlier knowledge of the fascist state in Italy. Moreover, as Flora observes, 'The emphasis on personality along with a certain encrustation of romanticized history, in the wake of Carlyle's hero worship, might have misguided Tagore's judgment on Mussolini in 1925 and soon after.'[24] In an interview given to Giacinta Salvadori, wife of Guglielmo Salvadori, at Zürich on 5 July 1926, he said of Mussolini:

> His personality was striking. As an artist, the human element – even in politics – touches me more deeply than abstract theories.... Therefore personality is always interesting to me.... Moral judgment and the interest invoked by a dramatic personality are two entirely different things. Now Mussolini struck me as a masterful personality. I felt that he must have great strength to obtain such a perfect control over a whole people. But this does not necessarily justify his activities from an ethical point of view.[25]

By this time Tagore was disillusioned with Mussolini, primarily because of Romain Rolland's intervention; on 5 August 1926 he issued a disclaimer in the Manchester Guardian. The initial warmth shown to him by Mussolini's Italy immediately vanished: he was now branded a 'sly hermit' whom stupid people 'had made into a great man' and who, after recrossing the border, came under 'the bastard pressure of his superiors ... and obeyed their orders by speaking with great venom against Italy'.[26]

The East European response was rather different. With some exceptions, it did not seize on his mystical image and romantic veneration of nature. One explanation might be that the industrialized western Europe viewed eastern Europe itself as its 'other'; another, that in the authoritarian regimes of the east, Tagore's message of freedom inspired the common people. Thus in Bulgaria, Vicho Ivanov recollects,

> after the defeat of the People's September Uprising of 1923, ... every interpretation and presentation of the humanistic ideas, the ideas of a world-wide regeneration held up by this Indian author, found a ready response among our progressive audiences. Tagore's optimism,

his love of the Indian people and all liberty-loving mankind, his
devotion to the progressive traditions of the philosophical thought
and culture of ancient India, acquired the significance of a call for
sorrowing Bulgaria.[27]

In the introduction to Ivanov's book, Lyudmil Stoyanov, a Bulgarian poet,
writer, and critic, observed that the aim of Tagore's teaching was not the
passive contemplation generally associated with Eastern thought. Rather,
it was a call for active participation in life, which brought his philosophy
close to the best traditions of the West, since 'he rates freedom higher
than goodness and preaches not a denial of the world and Nirvana, but the
affirmation of the world in joy'.[28]

In this interpretation of Tagore, some East European scholars have found
echoes of European romanticism, different from the passive, contemplative,
nostalgic romanticism of the Orient. The Latvian scholar Viktor Ivbulis has
argued that Tagore's concept of *jiban-debatā*, the 'god of life', reflected the
European spirit of romanticism, which put responsibility for development
not on society but on the human personality: the poet's creative, subjective
impulse gave birth to art and literature, which were expressions of the
Universal Man.[29] This is further corroborated by the Slovenian scholar
Anna Jelnikar:

> [F]rom its beginning, Tagore's popularity amongst the Slovenes was
> connected less with the romantic side of Orientalism ... [than] with
> a sense of identification ... derived from a perceived common goal of
> striving for political and cultural independence.[30]

She further points out, citing a 1914 article by Janko Lokar, that Tagore's
winning the Nobel Prize was valued by the Slovenes as the defeat of the rival
nominee, the Austrian poet Peter Rosegger, who, for them, was not so much
a literary figure as an advocate of Austria's Germanization policy. Tagore,
accordingly, became for the Slovenes an icon of protest and liberation: Lokar
called him 'a spiritual giant of enormous horizons' in contrast to Rosegger,
who 'fans the flames of nationalist hatred'. Tagore 'bleeds from the love of
his fettered country', yet 'firmly acknowledges the rights of the opponents,
even stresses them'. His songs were not 'boisterous fighting hymns' but
perfect expressions of 'his universalism'.[31]

Jelnikar also recounts in detail how the Slovenian writer Srečko Kosovel
found in Tagore 'a voice that shared some of the age's deepest cultural and
intellectual concerns, ... that helped him [Kosovel] articulate both a critique

of Europe and ... a solution to it'.[32] She cites a tradition harking back to the Enlightenment, whereby eastern Europe or 'the Balkan East' was considered 'the Western half's lesser other'.[33] 'Germans and Italians were regarded as cultural equals ... while Slavs were backward peasants, lacking national consciousness, and Eastern.'[34] Thus Tagore's critique of the aggressive, violent aspects of Western modernity, which evoked an unkind if not hostile reaction in Western Europe, had just the opposite effect in Slovenia.

The significance of such an understanding is twofold. First, this alternative action-oriented reading of Tagore's romanticism added a new dimension to his critique of the West. Stripped of the orientalist, pacifist, mystic image in vogue in western Europe, he was now projected as a symbol of struggle and emancipation. Second, his critical stand on nationalism opened up the route to internationalism, and celebration of the universal cause of humanity and human liberation, which the oppressed could invoke against the oppressor nation. But this revolutionary romanticism was also Western in spirit and was applied in European contexts. The image of a demystified, activist Tagore facilitated a new synthesis of East and West, in place of one couched in terms of 'East versus West'.

The East European deconstruction of the 'oriental' Tagore was not, however, uniform. In Romania, for instance, while Tagore's critique of nationalism was endorsed, a section of the intelligentsia could not accept his equation of nationalism with chauvinism. Besides, his early sympathy for Italian fascism and his Russian visit in 1930 irked many Romanian intellectuals who believed in the West and were scared of Russia's 'red imperialism'. For them, Romanian nationalism was guided by the instinct for self-preservation and hence quite different from Western or Russian nationalism.[35] In Hungary, Georg Lukács in his review of the novel *Gharebāire* (At Home and in the World) castigated Tagore as an intellectual agent of British imperialism, and considered Indian culture as antithetical to the spirit of communism. In other words, in Hungarian literary circles from the late 1920s, Tagore continued to be regarded as the typical Indian mystic steeped in exotic romanticism, notwithstanding the fact that even this 'orientalism' implied a censure of Western civilization.[36]

In Czechoslovakia, however, Tagore was not regarded as an oriental mystic or seer, but a critic of the crises that plagued modern Europe, Pan-Germanic imperialism being the most aggressive. But even there, the Czechoslovak Left criticized him as a spokesman for the religious-minded East, different from the revolutionary East represented by Russia.[37] In Russia itself, his 1930 visit was treated with caution by the Soviet authorities. In the novel *The Little Golden Calf* (1931) by Ilya Ilf and Yevgeni Petrov, Tagore is portrayed as 'a funny pseudophilosopher who was completely irrelevant to the real life in Russia'.[38] *Rāshiār chithi* (Letters from Russia) contained some critical remarks on the Soviet system. Letter 13, in particular, observed that the Soviet rulers had failed to distinguish the individual from the collective, and by endowing the collective with absolute value, they, like the fascists, had ruthlessly repressed individual freedom. Moreover, he added, Russia was witnessing dictatorship as wielded by a powerful man. These passages were excluded from the Russian version of the work, and the highly critical interview that Tagore gave to *Izvestiya* on 25 September 1930 was published only in 1988 in the Gorbachev era.

4

Tagore's view of politics was certainly futuristic if not utopian. Consequently, he was misunderstood by his own countrymen as well as the Western intelligentsia. His vision comprised two distinct elements. One was his focus on engagement, dialogue, and negotiation between East and West rather than treating the two as incompatible binaries. The other element was the critical spirit that permeated this understanding. At one level, he deplored the uncritical acceptance of what the East, and specifically India, stood for. This led to his alienation in his own country, since his lifelong engagement with the West, anchored as it was in science and reason, did not conform to the nativism dominating the Indian mind. At another level, he was a ruthless critic of how Western imperialism treated colonized peoples as its inferior 'others', implying a binarity that he rejected. As its corrective, he proposed the positive elements of the East's cultural and spiritual legacy. This, in turn, irked the uncritical Western champions of modernity.

In fact, the irony of Tagore's position is that he has been misinterpreted by both the Western modernists and the postcolonialists. While the modernists accuse him of not being sufficiently modern, steeped as he is in Eastern nativism, the postcolonialists question his derivative modernity since, for them, Tagore was not ready to shed the trappings of the Enlightenment. What is missing in both these positions is the failure to understand that Tagore refused to take an undifferentiated view of modernity. He always distinguished between the dark and the bright side of modernity, between reason and unreason, between hope and despair – all of them outcomes of Western modernity itself.

Particularly relevant in this context is Gāndhi's position on modernity, and the Gandhi–Tagore relationship in this regard. Especially in postcolonial literature, Gandhi is generally seen as the exponent of an alternative modernity, since his critique of the West was deeply anchored in a rejection of the modern industrial society generated there. His position had two chief thrusts: an almost total rejection of Western modernity as an idea or philosophy and, arising from that, a nativism expressed, for instance, by espousing *swadeshi* (indigenous manufactures) and urging the boycott of foreign goods. Such premises were unacceptable to Tagore. For him, while it was important to recognize the nativist tradition, upholding it to the exclusion of the West implied a reactionary conservatism.

While Tagore and Gandhi held each other in great esteem, and Gandhi admired Tagore's project at Visva-Bharati, they were poles apart in their understanding of modernity. Gandhi's strategy, with its focus on the *charkhā* or spinning wheel and on village and community life, made him a political icon in the eyes of the ordinary Indian, the peasant in particular: they could readily connect the Gandhian ideas to their existential identity. For the freedom struggle too, Gandhi's anti-West stance, his espousal of *swadeshi* and the boycott of foreign goods, enabled him to reap rich political dividends, emerging as the father figure of Indian nationalism. Tagore, who was not a political leader, did not subscribe to this populist stance of the Mahātma. Instead, he was guided by a broader and deeper philosophical vision at whose heart lay the idea of conflation rather than confrontation of East and West. But he always viewed this engagement in a critical and non-partisan spirit: he deplored the evils of the machine in the play *Muktadhārā* (The Free Stream), while not sparing *swadeshi* and the boycott movement in *Ghare-bāire*.

The contrast is most starkly manifest in the ways Gandhi and Tagore viewed the Sabarmati *ashram* and Visva-Bharati respectively. To summarize Shailesh Pārekh's succinct analysis, in the Gandhian ambience of Sabarmati the stress was on

> *achar*, conduct – simple, transparent and righteous. On the other hand, at the core of the credo of Visva-Bharati is the concept of one world and synthesis between various paths leading to truth.... For Tagore and Gandhiji, both, Truth was of utmost importance as they were both travellers in quest of Truth. Gandhiji asserts that Truth is God and goes on to specify how to practise Truth in life. Tagore merely asserts that Truth can be approached from many paths, that knowledge from East as well as West can lead to Truth, and describes the gains of realizing Truth.[39]

Ultimately Tagore emerges as a visionary, advocating a kind of politics that had little to do with *realpolitik*; yet he nurtured a political vision whose growing relevance we may come to value in an age increasingly marked by violence and intolerance, repression and domination. Despite his personal celebrity, his contemporary world was inimical to him and all that he stood for. Again and again he sought refuge in a world vision, a synthesis of cultures, a plurality of ideas and values that celebrate the cause of humanity and civilization. The clues that he provided to an alternative politics – anti-statism, community feeling, solidarity, and moral activism, whose roots he traced to the East as against the materialistic, utilitarian mindset of the West – were unacceptable to the Western mind for obvious reasons.

But what needs to be stressed is that European modernity was not merely synonymous with statism, individualism, and utilitarianism. There was an alternative modernity that questioned this outlook, its focal point being collectivity, a deep moral concern for society and a sense of solidarity. This tradition descended from Aristotle through Rousseau, and acquired a distinct shape in Marx. This alternative current of modernity has usually remained marginalized. Tagore's own vision derived primarily from the East but was compatible with this alternative current of Western modernity. Yet it failed to consider that current, reflecting a different tradition altogether. To be more exact, Tagore's critique was aimed against the liberal current of modernity. What it failed to consider was the alternative current, and the different tradition it represented.

The tragedy of Tagore was that his notion of politics, as it impacted his contemporary world, made him a *persona non grata* both at home and abroad. But he neither relented nor abandoned his unique perspective of politics as viewed in the mirror of the world. By the mid-1930s, when his health put a stop to his foreign travels, he became increasingly wedded to the cause of anti-fascism on a global scale. The brutalities of the Spanish Civil War, followed by the advent of the Second World War in 1939, two years before his death, led him to denounce these outbreaks of European militarism in absolute terms. Yet he did not abandon the cause of modernity and humanism, as evidenced in 'Sabhyatār sangkat' ('Crisis in Civilization'), composed months before his death. Even while the War was raging, he condemned the instrumentalist use of modernity in the cause of humanity. He reposed his faith in humanity till the end, reiterating his conviction that 'Man will retrace his path of conquest, despite all barriers, to win back his lost human heritage.'[40]

NOTES

1. *Nationalism*, ch. 2, 'Nationalism in Japan', *EW* 2:442–3.
2. 'Nababarsha' (The New Year), *RRVB* 4:371.

3. 'Dhammapadang', *RRVB* 4:462.
4. *Nationalism*, ch. 2, *EW* 2:440.
5. *RRVB* 19:337, 352–3, 357.
6. *Nationalism*, ch. 2, *EW* 2:437–8.
7. *Jāpān-jātri*, *RRVB* 19:350.
8. *RRVB* 30:172.
9. 'Ingrāj o bhāratbāsi' (The English and the Indians), *RRVB* 10:401.
10. Tagore uses the English word.
11. *RRVB* 3:552–3.
12. Here too he uses the English word.
13. *RRVB* 30:189.
14. *RRVB* 24:250.
15. See the following essays in *Bhāratbarsha*: 'Nababarsha' (The New Year), 'Prāchya o pāschātya sabhyatā' (Eastern and Western Civilization), and 'Bāroāri-mangal' (The Common Good).
16. *RRVB* 1:611–15.
17. 'Tagore's criticism of the British administration of India was consistently strong and grew more intense over the years. [But] he made a special effort to dissociate his criticism of the Raj from any denigration of British – or Western – people and culture. Even in his [last] powerful indictment of British rule in India in 1941, ... *Crisis in Civilization*, he strains hard to maintain the distinction between opposing Western imperialism and rejecting Western civilization.' Amartya Sen, 'Tagore and His India', *New York Review of Books*, 26 June 1997.
18. For a global account of Tagore's travelogues, lectures, and addresses, with the response in the countries he visited, see *100 Years*; Rita Banerjee, *Rabindranath Tagore's Lectures Abroad: A Critical Encounter* (Kolkata: Seribaan, 2018).
19. *The Friend*, 23 May 1930: see Kalyan Kundu, Sakti Bhattacharya, and Kalyan Sircar, ed., *Imagining Tagore: Rabindranath and the British Press (1912–1941)* (London: Tagore Research Centre and Kolkata: Sahitya samsad, 2000), 469.
20. Martin Kämpchen, 'Tagore's Reception in Germany', in *Rabindranath Tagore: Reclaiming a Cultural Icon*, ed. Kathleen M. O'Connell and Joseph T. O'Connell (Kolkata: Visva-Bharati, 2009), 270. See also Martin Kämpchen, 'Germany, Austria and Switzerland', in *100 Years*, 389–410; Banerjee, *Tagore's Lectures*, 276–332.
21. See Tan Chung and Wei Liming, 'China', in *100 Years*, 38–56. See also Banerjee, *Tagore's Lectures*, 539–77.
22. See Kyoko Niwa, 'Japan', in *100 Years*, 3–24; Banerjee, *Tagore's Lectures*, 483–538.
23. 'Swadeshi samāj', *Ātmashakti*, *RRVB* 3:540–1.
24. Giuseppe Flora, 'Rabindranath Tagore and Italy', in *Rabindranath Tagore*, ed. O'Connell and O'Connell, 305.

25. Cited in ibid., 299.

26. Mario Prayer, 'Italy', in *100 Years*, 430. See also Banerjee, *Tagore's Lectures*, 216–58.

27. Vicho Ivanov, *Rabindranath Tagore's Wisdom* (Sofia, 1926), cited in Anna Nikolaev and Nikolay Nikolaev, *Rabindranath Tagore and the Bulgarian Connection: Facts and Documents* (Kolkata: Visva-Bharati, 2009), 69–70. See also Nikolay Nikolaev, 'Bulgaria', in *100 Years*, 263–74.

28. Alexander Shurbanov, 'Tagore in Bulgaria', in *Rabindranath Tagore in Perspective* (Kolkata: Visva-Bharati, 1989), 211.

29. Viktors Ivbulis, 'Tagore's Western Burdens', in *Rabindranath Tagore: A Timeless Mind*, ed. Amalendu Biswas, Christine Marsh, and Kalyan Kundu (London: Tagore Centre, UK, with Indian Council for Cultural Relations, 2011), 157.

30. Anna Jelnikar, *Universalist Hopes in India and Europe: The World of Rabindranath Tagore and Srečko Kosovel* (Delhi: Oxford University Press, 2016), 179–80.

31. Ibid., 179.

32. Ibid., 277.

33. Ibid., 203.

34. Glenda Sluga, *Difference, Identity, and Sovereignty in Twentieth-Century Europe* (New York: SUNY Press, 2001), 2, cited in Jelnikar, *Universalist Hopes*, 203.

35. See Liviu Bordas, 'Romania', in *100 Years*, 236–62.

36. See Imre Bangha, 'Hungary', in *100 Years.*, 320–32.

37. See Martin Hříbek, 'Czechoslovakia and its Successors', in *100 Years*, 333–56.

38. Sergei Serebriany, 'Russia', in *100 Years*, 215.

39. Shailesh Parekh, 'Tagore and Gandhi: An Engaging Enigma', in *Rabindranath Tagore and His Circle*, ed. Tapati Mukhopadhyay and Amrit Sen (Santiniketan: Rabindra-Bhavana, 2015), 150–1.

40. 'Crisis in Civilization', *EW* 3:726.

16 Tagore's Santiniketan
Learning Associated with Life
KATHLEEN M. O'CONNELL

I started with this one simple idea that education should never be dissociated from life. I had no experience of teaching, no special gift for organisation, and therefore no plan which I could put before the public.... The institution grew with the growth of my own mind and life.[1]

Describing his educational experiment in Santiniketan, Rabindranāth Tagore has indicated that he started with the intention of creating an educational system that was connected to life's totality, and that the institution had grown with his own 'mind and life'. Accordingly, this overview of Tagore's educational theory and practice will follow the unfolding of his educational experiment in Santiniketan in conjunction with the personal growth of his rich and multifaceted life and personality. It will explore the ways in which his educational theory and method evolved and were affected by an ever-widening sense of inclusivity that developed as a result of his poetic sensitivity to nature and the arts, as well as his experiences with colonial education, aggressive nationalism, international travels, and Gāndhi's Non-cooperation Movement, among other factors.

Tagore would appear to hold a distinctive position among educators as being the only internationally renowned poet and artist to create an educational system. His profound sensitivity to nature and special connection to the creative arts, as well as his strategies for developing global networks of cooperation, give him a special position in educational theory. His role in the history of international education will be considered, as well as his methods for developing creativity and awareness in the Santiniketan students through outdoor classes in a beautiful natural setting, along with music, seasonal festivals, dance dramas, student publications, and global interconnection.

Rabindranath's first major address on education,'Shikshār herpher' (The Vicissitudes of Education), delivered in 1892, was one of the first comprehensive critiques of English-medium education in India. It lays out a number of the educational ideals that would later play a part in his Santiniketan experiment. The address provides a strong critique of English-medium education and the disassociation that results from learning in a foreign curriculum, where the language and images are disconnected from a Bengali environment. A child's linguistic medium, argues Rabindranath, should be associated with his/her social and cultural environment. 'Shikshar herpher' argues against the mechanical and narrow purpose of colonial education, proposing instead an educational framework that allows for mental space and freedom for students to achieve physical development, psychic well-being, and nurturing of their creative and critical powers. Human beings develop, he observes in 'Shikshār herpher', through constant stimulation from 'many colours, many forms, many fragrances; through a variety of movements and songs; and through affection and happiness'.[2]

THE FOUNDING OF THE BRAHMA VIDYALAYA, DECEMBER, 1901

In 1890, before he had written 'Shikshār herpher', Tagore was put in charge of the family estates in east Bengal, where he set up a home school for his children, and also began to consider a boarding school for other children. The initial model that Rabindranath had in mind during this period contains various levels of influence, including what he termed 'the living university': that is, the rich cultural environment that he had experienced in the joint family at Jorasanko. Concurrently, one of the strongest influences at this time stemmed from the currents of nineteenth-century Hindu nationalism and the need to develop national leaders. In a letter to his scientist friend Jagadishchandra Basu (Bose), dated August 1901, Tagore described his plans for a school modelled on ancient lines to train *brahmachārins*, celibate spiritual-minded scholars, and develop *karma yogis*, heroic social crusaders like Bāl Gangādhar Tilak and Shivrām Mahādev Parānjape of Mahārāshtra. The whole system will be just like that of the ancient resident guru-schools, he wrote: 'If *brahmacharya*[3] is not undertaken from childhood, we will never become real Hindus.'[4]

The initial enrolment of the *brahmavidyālaya* or *brahmacharyāshram*, as it was called at the time of its inauguration in 1901, consisted of five boys. Though set in the beautiful natural environment of Santiniketan, the tone of the institution, as reflected in Rabindranath's first detailed statement of the school in the form of a constitutional letter written in 1902, was decidedly different from the one presented in 'Shikshār herpher'. The emphasis here is less on joyous learning and more on discipline and devotion to one's country, with clear nationalistic aims:

The students of the Brahma Vidyālaya must be made especially faithful and devoted to their own country.... It is precisely by giving our own nature its fullness in terms of that special nobility of our country that once existed that we may rightly rise up within humanity as a whole.... Therefore, it is better to be excessively devoted to the ways of one's country than to think oneself glorified through a spellbound imitation of the foreigner.[5]

In 1905, the British government sought to stem nationalistic endeavours through a proposal to divide Bengal along communal lines, fomenting a resistance that constituted an early phase of the nationalist Swadeshi Movement and led to India's full-fledged struggle for independence. Tagore initially took an active role, composing songs, initiating new ceremonies such as rākhi-bandhan (tying fraternal wrist bands), supporting boycotts, encouraging active student involvement, and even leading demonstrations. One of the Santiniketan teachers, Ajitkumār Chakrabarti, has described the anti-partition spirit and activities within Santiniketan with Rabindranath as 'its high priest', noting that '[t]he country-consciousness surged high in the asram'.[6] However, as the initial resistance degenerated into factionalism, terrorism, and Hindu–Muslim conflict, Tagore turned his attention more and more to inclusive education, rural outreach, and literary pursuits. As he wrote to a friend: 'Having seen all this at first hand, I no longer feel any desire to "idealise" the Hindu samāj through delusions pleasant to the ear but ultimately suicidal.'[7]

Rabindranath resigned from the National Council of Education,[8] which he felt placed too much emphasis on Western-style higher education at the expense of primary education. He also withdrew from political and Brahmo Samaj activities, and he sent his son Rathindranāth to study agriculture at the University of Illinois. He poured his thoughts concerning the negative aspects of Hindu fundamentalism and aggressive nationalism into fictional writing such as the novels Gorā and Ghare-bāire (At Home and in the World), an anti-fundamentalist drama Achalāyatan, and related essays. He also focussed on new curricular initiatives.

A PARADIGM SHIFT: FROM BRAHMA VIDYALAYA TO A POET'S SCHOOL, 1907–1912

After 1907, a definite shift in Tagore's educational priorities was manifested in various ways. Outreach efforts at village reconstruction were started by the teachers and students of Santiniketan, which would lead to later developments at Sriniketan. There was a new spirit of community building and cosmopolitanism. Special days were set up to honour significant religious figures such as Christ, the Buddha, and Chaitanya,[9] and there was a new emphasis on critical thought and *ātmashakti* (confident self-autonomy).

Perhaps the most significant shift was to a curriculum more in line with Tagore's prodigious artistic personality and his conviction that learning must be intimately connected with nature. As he had argued in 'Shikshār herpher', rather than confining a child within an unsuitable system, immersion in nature at a time when the child's senses were fresh would produce happier, healthier, and more intelligent children. In other essays, he further developed the themes of simplicity, empathy, and the development of the aesthetic imagination, arguing that education should not merely provide information but should bring our lives into harmony with existence:

> From our very childhood habits are formed and knowledge is imparted in such a manner that our life is weaned away from nature and our mind and the world are set in opposition from the beginning of our days. Thus the greatest of educations for which we came prepared is neglected, and we are made to lose our world to find a bagful of information instead. We rob the child of his earth to teach him geography, of language to teach him grammar.[10]

To encourage an intimacy with nature, the daily schedule provided for fifteen minutes of morning and evening meditation, where the children were encouraged to exert self-control and remain quiet for that period, 'even though instead of contemplating on God, they may be watching the squirrels running up the trees'.[11] Children were introduced to an Upanishadic mantra to facilitate a direct perception and appreciation of nature:

> The self-expressive Spirit that is in fire and in water, that permeates the entire world, that is in the plants and trees: reverence, reverence to that Spirit.[12]

Tagore felt that one of the seminal lessons children learn from holding classes under the trees is improvisation without the 'constant imposition of the ready-made':[13] it allows them to explore their abilities and to observe creative patterns in life. Nature walks and excursions were built into a flexible class schedule, and students were encouraged to study and document the life cycles of birds, insects, and plants. There were also outdoor evening events, such as literary nights on the day of the full moon, and other evening events to study astronomy.

The students were indeed privileged to have a future Nobel laureate as their mentor. Tagore composed and directed plays on site, which the students staged and performed, thus providing an in-depth educational experience. He instinctively realized the way in which participation in the arts provides multidimensional learning in so many areas, mental, physical, and artistic, besides facilitating cooperation. The students were the first to hear readings of his work, to learn his musical compositions, and to participate in newly created festivals that celebrated the nuances of nature. There was the spring festival, Basanta-utsab, and rain festival, Barshāmangal. A special tree-planting ceremony, Briksharopan, was introduced, where each child was encouraged to nurture a tree. As part of the rural outreach, Tagore later created the Halakarshan festival to mark the spring ploughing and planting, and a Nabānna ceremony to celebrate the new rice crop.

During this period, *brahmacharya* was mentioned less frequently, though the ideals of self-discipline and self-restraint were upheld. The notion of a *brahmacharyāshram* was further diminished in 1909 when six girls were admitted to the school, and Rabindranath began a drama programme involving female characters. In general, it was a time for curricular experiments. Students were allowed to participate in particular classes according to their ability rather than age, making it possible for a student good at maths or some other particular subject to study with a more advanced class. There were also pioneering efforts in student self-government, as well as experimental forays into arts-based education.

TRAVELS ABROAD, WORLD FAME, THE FIRST WORLD WAR, AND GANDHI'S NON-COOPERATION MOVEMENT

Following his trip to England and the United States in 1912, and the award of the Nobel Prize in 1913, Tagore's life changed dramatically in the face of world recognition. One of the objectives of his travels abroad had been to explore alternative educational models, and he sent back various educational materials to the Santiniketan teachers. He became aware of the work of Maria Montessori, and a detailed article on Montessori's methodology appeared in the *Tattwabodhini patrikā* in 1913, while he was the editor. The article, written by Tagore's student and future biographer Prabhātkumar Mukhopādhyāy, describes Montessori's work in Rome and the use of 'sense training' to develop practical independence and literacy. Montessori, the first female M.D. in Italy, became widely known for her work with illiterate children in Rome. She developed a method involving special educational toys that encouraged the use of all the senses in the learning process. Though

Rabindranath did not employ special educational toys, he devised various strategies within a natural setting to develop the students' powers of touch, sight, and smell, enabling them to make subtle distinctions and trained estimates of size and number. It is likely that he became familiar with the educational work of John Dewey during his visit to Chicago in 1912, when he wrote back about a school that emphasized role-playing and hands-on learning.

Tagore was deeply affected by the outbreak of the First World War in August 1914. His experiences with the Swadeshi movement of 1905–6 had convinced him of the dangers involved in mass political demonstrations and aggressive nationalism, and his determination to develop strategies for global cooperation and mutual understanding in the Santiniketan curriculum became a priority.

In 1915, boys from Gāndhi's Phoenix School were relocated to Santiniketan from South Africa. This came about through the efforts of C.F. Andrews,[14] who worked closely with both Rabindranath and Gandhi, and an initial meeting between the two took place on 6 March. Although deeply respectful of one another (Tagore had been one of the first to call Gandhi 'Mahātmā'), their personalities and cultural backgrounds were vastly different. Gandhi did not hesitate to point out some shortcomings in Santiniketan, which acted as a catalyst for some changes, while Tagore, who had moved beyond the *brahmacharyāshram* days, questioned Gandhi's authoritarian approach with his students. He felt that strict discipline imposed from outside stunted the boys' imaginations and was unsuccessful in the long term, and that discipline was most effective when it came from within and developed organically. As he wrote to Andrews concerning the Phoenix students: 'They are trained to obey, which is bad for a human being; for obedience is good, not because it is good in itself, but because it is a sacrifice. These boys are in danger of forgetting to wish for anything and wishing is the best part of attainment.'[15]

The differences between Gandhi and Tagore became more evident as Gandhi was developing his Non-cooperation Movement within India, just as Tagore was expanding his notion of global intercommunication and cooperation during a tour of Europe and America. After witnessing Europe's devastation after the war, and coming into contact with like-minded individuals through his travels, Rabindranath began to conceive of a multicultural network centred in Santiniketan to bring together individuals from different races and cultures, with a goal of mutual understanding and the creation of non-violent networks in aid of global peace and cooperation. One of his first statements concerning the establishment of an international centre to counter aggressive nationalism came in a 1916 letter written from Los Angeles to his son Rathindranath:

I wish to make the school at Santiniketan a link between India and the world. A centre must be set up there to study humanity across all races and nations [*sarbajātik*]. The age of narrow-minded nationalism is approaching its end. The first preparation for the great future ceremony of universal union will take place in the fields of Bolpur. I plan to locate that spot beyond all societal and geographical limits, and plant there the first victory-flag of universal humanity. It will be the task of my last years to break the python-coils of nationalistic pride crushing the world.[16]

In 1919, Rabindranath delivered a seminal address in Adyar, near Chennai, entitled 'The Centre of Indian Culture', which provided a blueprint for an educational centre modelled on sustainability and cultural collaboration. Though phrased in theoretical terms, the address laid the groundwork for the future of his own institution, Visva-Bharati, which had been inaugurated in 1918 on an informal basis, when a group of Gujarati boys was admitted to the school. 'A Centre of Indian Culture,' he argued, should be in touch with complete life:

> Education can only become natural and wholesome when it is the direct fruit of a living and growing knowledge.... [O]ur education should be in full touch with our complete life, economical, intellectual, aesthetic, social and spiritual; and our educational institutions should be in the very heart of our society, connected with it by the living bonds of varied co-operations. For true education is to realize at every step how our training and knowledge have an organic connection with our surroundings.[17]

Such a centre of Indian culture would aim to give a prominent place to aesthetic education, but its basis should be rooted in economic cooperation with a 'social objective of improving housing, sanitation, and the moral and intellectual life of the villages'. Making a distinction between nationalism and culture, Tagore argued that nationalism as a construct produces the most aggressive and selfish elements in individuals, whereas 'culture' remains dynamic and open-ended, allowing for creative sharing and the building of international alliances. 'We forget,' he wrote, 'that the mission of all education is to lead us beyond the present date.'[18] And again: 'culture, which is the life of mind, can only be imparted through man to man.... Culture grows and moves and multiplies itself in life.'[19] Rather than having to go abroad for Indological studies, the centre would provide a place within India where such study could be carried out in depth. The overall goal would be intellectual cooperation, which would require cooperation within India and a synthesis of diverse elements:

> So, in our centre of Indian learning, we must provide for the co-ordinated study of all these different cultures – the Vedic, the Puranic, the Buddhist, the Jain, the Islamic, the Sikh, and the Zoroastrian. And side by side with them the European – for only then shall we be able to assimilate the last.... Along with study of our living languages, we must include our folk literature, in order truly to know the psychology of our people and the direction towards which our underground current of life is moving.[20]

As Tagore continued his travels abroad, his letters began to focus increasingly on Gandhi's Non-cooperation Movement. He wrote to Andrews about the negative character of the movement and its similarity to the Swadeshi movement, lamenting the irony that he 'should be preaching co-operation of cultures between East and West on this side of the sea just at the moment when the doctrine of non-co-operation is preached on the other side'.[21] Upon his return from Europe in July 1921, he faced strong criticism for his stance on non-cooperation. Although his trip had brought him into contact with like-minded people who would later play a role in Visva-Bharati, it had not been successful financially, since his warnings about nationalism had not been well received. His dialogue with Gandhi continued. There were many affinities between the educational models used by Gandhi and Tagore: both rejected English models as inadequate for India's needs, placing new emphasis instead on vernacular expression and social uplift. However, their approaches differed on major issues such as civil disobedience and non-cooperation, the use of authority, plying the *charkha*, or spinning-wheel, the burning of foreign cloth, Hindu–Muslim relations, Basic Education,[22] and science and technology.

1921: INAUGURATING VISVA-BHARATI

The institution at Santiniketan was officially re-inaugurated as Visva-Bharati on 22 December 1921, signalling a vastly broader paradigm for global education. The terms *Visva* and *Bharati* can be variously translated to represent different levels of exchange: the culture and learning of the world, or of all India, or all cultures.[23] The motto of the university expressed the global scope of its mission: *yatra vishvam bhavatyekanidam*, 'where the world comes together in a single nest'. Its constitution designated the following goals:

(a) To study the mind of Man in its realisation of different aspects of truth from diverse points of view.
(b) To bring into more intimate relation with one another, through patient study and research, the different cultures of the East on the basis of their underlying unity.
(c) To approach the West from the standpoint of such a unity of the life and thought of Asia.
(d) To seek to realise in a common fellowship of study the meeting of East and West, and thus ultimately to strengthen the fundamental conditions of world peace through the free communication of ideas between the two hemispheres.
(e) And with such Ideals in view to provide at Santiniketan a centre of culture where research into the study of the religion, literature, history, science and art of Hindu, Buddhist, Jain, Zoroastrian, Islamic, Sikh, Christian and other civilizations may be pursued along with the culture of the West, with that simplicity of externals which is necessary for true spiritual realisation, in amity, good-fellowship and co-operation between the thinkers and scholars of both Eastern and Western countries, free from all antagonisms of race, nationality, creed or caste and in the name of the One Supreme Being who is *Shantam, Shivam, Advaitam* [supremely peaceful, good and indivisible].[24]

Visva-Bharati was structured to operate on three levels. The basic level was to provide an Indian university. In aid of this, he slowly built up a network of Indian scholars to teach Indian religions, languages, and folk culture, as well as a collection of Indian texts. Kala Bhavana became the centre for art and music, with dance introduced in the early 1920s. The music and dance sections separated from Kala Bhavana in 1934 and became known as Sangit Bhavana.

At another level, Visva-Bharati was to operate as an Eastern university. The study of Eastern cultures was begun and a library of Eastern texts was initiated with foreign professors invited to give courses. An important link between India and China was set up through the Chinese Buddhist scholar Tan Yun-Shan, who came to Santiniketan from China in 1928, later becoming the first Director of Cheena Bhavana. Others on the staff included a growing number of visiting scholars and artists from various Eastern countries. The extensive library of Eastern writings also incorporated material on arts and crafts from Japan, China, Malaya, Thailand, Java, and Sumatra.

The most inclusive level was the global one, the result of a shared vision of Tagore and C.F. Andrews, who held many positions at Visva-Bharati, both academic and administrative, until his death. By 1924, the academic curriculum included modern and classical languages, logic, philosophy, political economy, sociology, and science. The faculty and students came from different parts of India and the world. The effectiveness of the Santiniketan environment and curriculum have been attested to by various distinguished alumni such as Indirā Gāndhi, Satyajit Rāy, and Amartya Sen, who later went on to impact global affairs and the arts.

A further extension of the ever-widening circles of inclusion included the rural areas surrounding Santiniketan, which had been a concern of Tagore's for many years. Formal recognition of this came with the inauguration of a Centre for Rural Reconstruction in Sriniketan in February 1922. Tagore's concern with rural uplift gained momentum when he met Leonard Elmhirst, a British agronomist studying at Cornell University, and invited him to oversee the rural programme. Elmhirst accepted, and the Rural Reconstruction Centre was inaugurated in February 1922.[25] The stated objectives were to make the villages 'self-reliant and self-respectful, acquainted with the cultural traditions of their country and competent to make use of modern resources for improvement of their physical, intellectual, and economic conditions'.[26] There was also an unstated goal to engage the students in constructive nation-building rather than political agitation.

Tagore had earlier urged informal vernacular education through *melā*s (country fairs), folk plays, songs, and lantern-slide exhibitions. He had also set up an agricultural bank with the Nobel Prize money, establishing a model for micro-credit. A pioneering educational project, Shikshā-satra ('where education is given freely'), was started in July 1924, with a learning framework that reflected a more practical adaptation to village life. An early form of distance education was initiated and women's educational projects, such as nutrition, maternity and child care, literacy, and so forth, were handled by the Mahilā Samitis (women's committees).

TAGORE AS INTERNATIONAL EDUCATOR AND PIONEER

The roots of international education go back to the nineteenth-century humanist-progressive movement, which challenged authoritarian methods and advocated a more democratic child-centred form of education. It is indebted to such figures as Jean Jacques Rousseau, Johann Pestalozzi, Friedrich Froebel, and others. But from the nineteenth century, nationalism gained momentum in educational thinking: there was pressure to develop pedagogical methods and theories that would further the interests of a given nation. A group of educational pioneers, however, began to counter such trends by developing alternative paradigms that privileged humanity over the nation state. D.G. Scanlon, a contemporary historian of international education, has described this group as being out of step with the nineteenth century:

> In an era of provincial loyalties, they argued for loyalty to mankind. In an era of nationalism, they spoke of internationalism. And in an era of mass education for patriotism, they contended that the school was the only agency capable of advancing education across national boundaries. Little wonder that their proposals were viewed as radical, visionary, and utopian.[27]

These educators, who sought to create a curriculum that prioritized internationalism, social inclusiveness, human freedom, and creativity, included such figures as John Dewey, Leonard and Dorothy Elmhirst, Paul Geheeb, Nikolaj Grundtvig, Aldous and Dora Huxley, Maria Montessori, Rudolf Steiner, and, of course, Rabindranath Tagore, who was connected to these educators in various ways.[28] His global travels gave him insight into the urgency for developing cooperative modes of cultural communication that do not predispose people towards aggressive nationalistic postures. As he wrote:

> When races come together, as in the present age, it should not be merely the gathering of a crowd; there must be a bond of relation, or they will collide with each other.... Education must enable every child to understand and fulfil this purpose of the age, not defeat it by acquiring the habit of creating divisions and cherishing national prejudices.[29]

Beyond the influence of progressive Western educational theory, Tagore used his own experiences within the Jorasanko joint family, the model of the *tapovana* or forest hermitage, as well as the ancient Buddhist monastic universities of Nālandā, Takshashilā, and Vikramshilā as prototypes of Indian hospitality, cosmopolitanism, scholarship, and a harmonious relationship with the local community.

Given his extensive cosmopolitan experiences and quest for balance, Tagore's educational paradigm demonstrated a unique sensitivity towards environment, race, language, cultural differences, economic disparity, as well as political and gender imbalance. It presented one of the earliest comprehensive paradigms for international education and global collaboration. The relational qualities such as empathy, cooperation, creativity, and cosmopolitanism, along with humanities-based education, which Tagore had prioritized so many years ago, cannot be underestimated. It is noteworthy that recent psychological and neuroscientific studies of cognition are validating the educational priorities he had articulated so many years ago. Scientific studies like those done by the Harvard professors Howard Gardner, Professor of Cognition and Education, and psychologist Daniel Goleman have documented the way in which a child's intellect simultaneously functions at very different levels, as well as the importance of harmonizing thought and emotions in the learning process. Tagore would have agreed with Gardner's cosmopolitan statement that educators should 'pay close heed to the biological and psychological proclivities of human beings and to the particular historical and cultural context of the locales where they live'.[30] Goleman, much in keeping with Tagore's ideas regarding joyous learning at critical stages in a child's development, advocates a 'flow' model of education predicated on a child's interests.

Neuroscience has also made it possible to measure the ways in which the brain is altered through arts education and the benefits that accrue from art and music education for overall brain development. Studies such as the 2008 *Neuroeducation: Learning, Arts and the Brain* by the Johns Hopkins School of Education have been able to document how arts training such as music and dance improves attention and increases generalized overall intelligence, and how the executive functioning demanded by the arts relates to other areas such as mathematics and language. The significant findings from this group support insights regarding education and human consciousness that Tagore had articulated and put into practice many years earlier.

Tagore stated that he wanted to create an educational system connected to life's totality and his own 'mind and life'. From the early *brahmavidyālaya* days, which were strongly influenced by Hindu nationalism, to the inauguration of Visva-Bharati, this overview has traced how Tagore's own broadening outlook has been reflected in curricular shifts towards environmental sensitivity, non-sectarian orientation to religion and culture, rural outreach, coeducation, and a democratic structure. His evolution towards greater pluralism and inclusion has reflected in the educational idiom of his institution. The inauguration of Visva-Bharati, reflecting his own associations with global culture, deepened its emphasis upon the arts and its linguistic and cultural links with other parts of Asia to become an Eastern university, while identifying with all humanity in its activities as a global learning centre. Tagore's desire to overcome social and material poverty, and to break down the barriers between the urban elites and the uneducated rural population, was expressed through the rural reconstruction ventures at Sriniketan.

Though Tagore's life and mind undoubtedly outdistanced their practical working out in his educational institution, he was (and remains) one of a handful who put their theories into constructive practice, not only at the primary and secondary levels but also in one of the earliest initiatives of international tertiary education. As well as providing a model for humanities and arts-based education, Santiniketan promoted educational reform. It provided a model for vernacular instruction and the development of Bengali textbooks, and it offered one of the earliest coeducational programmes in South Asia. The establishment of Visva-Bharati and Sriniketan led to pioneering efforts in many directions, including distinctively Indian models for higher education and mass education, as well as pan-Asian and global cultural exchange.

Tagore's attempts to associate education with the totality of life continue to inspire us today. The fundamental questions he asked regarding a child's well-being, what constitutes a meaningful life and how we can create peaceful channels of cooperation, are at least as relevant today as when he asked them so many years ago. Perhaps Tagore's most enduring contribution to education and the learning process comes from his role as a great artist, and his being one of the most balanced thinkers of our times, something that enabled him to explore still-relevant issues with such depth, breadth, and perception.

NOTES

1. Letter to Patrick Geddes, 9 May 1922, *SL* 291–2.
2. *RRVB* 12:280.
3. *Brahmacharya* refers to a stage in life, usually coinciding with student life, characterized by rigorous and celibate spiritual discipline.
4. Anāthnāth Dās, ed., *Shāntiniketan bidyālayer shikshādarsha* (Kolkata: Visva-Bharati, 1989), 3.
5. For a translation of the full document, see Kathleen M. O'Connell, *Rabindranath Tagore: The Poet as Educator* (Kolkata: Visva-Bharati, 2002), 127–42.
6. Ajitkumar Chakravarty, review of W.W. Pearson's *Shantiniketan*, *Modern Review* 22 (July 1917), 46–8.
7. Letter to Manoranjan Bandyopādhyāy, 30 Asharhh 1315/mid-July 1908: quoted in Sumit Sarkar, *The Swadeshi Movement in Bengal* (New Delhi: People's Publishing House, 1973), 348.

8. The National Council of Education had been initiated in 1906 by the Dawn Society, an important forum in Bengal for the ideas of nationalist education and Swadeshi activities; Rabindranath had helped to draft the first constitution. It published many of the general criticisms of the English-medium educational system. Such criticisms against the English system described it as overliterary and under-technical in content and contrary to an integrated national development. However, the Council placed heavy emphasis on Western-style higher education, whereas Tagore felt the emphasis should be on indigenous forms of mass education and breaking down the gulf between the educated elite and the rural population.

9. See Ajitkumar Chakrabarti, *Brahmabidyālay* (Kolkata: Visva-Bharati, 1951), 49.

10. 'My School', *Personality*, EW 2:391.

11. Ibid., EW 2:402.

12. *Shvetāshvatara upanishad* 2:17: cited in Tagore's letter to Kunjalāl Ghosh, a teacher at the *brahmacharyāshram*, 13 November 1902 (CP 13:168). This letter was later proposed by Tagore to Kshitimohan Sen as the basis of a 'constitution' for the school (RJPP 6:17).

13. *Religion of Man*, ch. 12, 'The Teacher', EW 3:159.

14. C.F. Andrews had gone to India in 1904 as an Anglican missionary and begun teaching at St. Stephen's College, Delhi. After meeting Tagore in London in 1912 at the famous poetry reading at William Rothenstein's house, he decided to join Rabindranath's educational experiment and make Santiniketan his base in India.

15. Letter to Andrews, 15 November 1914: Rabindra Bhavana Archives, Andrews Papers, file 3 image 33.

16. Letter to Rathindranath Tagore, 11 October 1916, CP 2:70.

17. *The Centre of Indian Culture*, 1, EW 2:469.

18. Ibid., 4, EW 2:475.

19. Ibid.

20. Ibid., 15, EW 2:487.

21. Letter to C.F. Andrews from Chicago, 5 March 1921: *Letters to a Friend*, EW 3:287.

22. Gandhi's 'scheme of Basic Education' advocated seven years of compulsory education and emphasized the economic self-sufficiency of both students and their teachers. It placed considerable emphasis upon disciplined technical training and craft apprenticeship, whereas Tagore's educational priorities focussed more on the full development of a child's creative potential.

23. *Visva* has the connotations of 'world', 'universe', 'all', 'every', 'entire', or 'whole'. *Bhārati* can have the meanings of 'India', 'culture and learning' (as represented by the goddess Saraswati), 'eloquence', and 'narrative'.

24. From the first Visva-Bharati prospectus, 1922.

25. The name 'Sriniketan' was given later by Tagore.

26. 'Aims and Objects', *Visva-Bharati Bulletin* 11 (December 1928), 1.

27. D.G. Scanlon, *International Education: A Documentary History* (New York: Columbia University Bureau of Publications, Teachers College, 1960), 3–4.

28. See Kathleen O'Connell, 'Tagore as International Educationist: The "Bond of Relation"', in *Rabindranath Tagore – Envoy of India*, ed. Radha Chakravarty (New Delhi: Indian Council of World Affairs, 2015).

29. 'My School' (lecture in Tokyo, June 1924), *EW* 4:522.

30. Howard Gardner, *Frames of Mind: The Theory of Multiple Intelligences* (New York: Basic Books), 393.

17 Tagore and Village Economy

A Vision of Wholeness

SOURIN BHATTACHARYA

Rabindranāth Tagore was born and brought up in a city: Calcutta, now Kolkata, the erstwhile second city of the British empire. He belonged to the third generation of a propertied family. His grandfather 'Prince' Dwārakānāth Tagore built up the family fortune in the modern sense of the term. Dwarakanath's eldest son, Debendranāth, was Rabindranath's father. It is well known that Rabindranath never felt close to his grandfather in spirit. He felt greater affinity with his philosophic father: the two had a warm relationship over some forty years.

Young Rabi was brought up on disciplinarian but markedly unorthodox lines. The child's unusual nature made him resist institutional education. He was almost entirely taught at home in many fields – general education, science, music, painting – but in an unconventional way, neither ordered nor complete, nor even always rigorous. This recipe for disaster turned out wonderfully well in his case. It conditioned him to break conventions, as evident in all his creative work: poetry, music, painting, theatre, and even dance.

This chapter concerns his ideas on rural welfare and development in India. It may appear a strange concern for a literary personality of Rabindranath's stature; even more that he should pursue it with the zest of an activist. In fact, his engagement with such action-oriented projects was part of a grander design for a complete and harmonious life in society as a whole. This made village work as creative for Rabindranath as writing poetry and composing music. They all contributed to his project of wholeness.

THE ESSENCE OF *SHRI*

I have mentioned the related concepts of wholeness and harmony. Rabindranath's life's project took shape as a comprehensive endeavour towards those goals, absorbing almost anything that came his way – many strands of thought and practice, derived from both East and West. The spirituality of Upanishadic tradition, acquired from family sources, fed an aesthetic consciousness that was, at the same time, deeply rooted in socio-political reality. But his abiding concern all through was the notion of *shri*, which can be defined as grace, harmony, and well-being informed by a sense of inner truth. This commitment to truth made him look critically at the ritualistic aspects of not only religious practices but all spheres of social and political life. Instead of heeding the mystic call of an inner voice, he directed a rational, critical gaze at the reality around him.

Rabindranath was well aware of the evils of the brahminical hierarchy with its oppressions and injustices. A society mired in ritualistic practice was transmitting the lifeless baggage of custom from generation to generation. The vast majority of people were bereft of any meaningful education, drained of self-confidence, and virtually reduced to despair. Where society is utterly without vibrancy and well-being, any search for grace and harmony must be futile. The fairly early poem 'Ebār phirāo more' (Now Turn Me Back) projects this bleak reality:

> See the dumb hordes with bowed heads, their dimmed faces inscribed with the pain of a hundred centuries. The more burdens are heaped on their shoulders, they trudge along bearing them as long as they have life; then bequeath them to their children, generation after generation. They do not blame fate nor upbraid the gods or humankind, only eke out their painful lives, picking at a few grains of rice.[1]

Our attitude to the poor, as also towards village-dwellers, often smacks of the paternalistic. Our models of development make it important to provide people with more and more goods. We do not care whether they feel it benefits them or whether they have the confidence to take their own decisions instead of relying on external authorities. The driving force of their destiny seems to lie outside themselves. That imbalance cannot be corrected by external agency.

An impassioned formulation of the idea of *shri* is found in a short message sent by Rabindranath in 1921 to the workers of the central cooperative at Visva-Bharati. It was republished posthumously in 1954 to introduce the collection *Samabāyniti* (Principles of the Cooperative).[2] Rabindranath was already haunted by the image of the *yakshapuri*, later the setting of his play *Raktakarabi* (Red Oleanders): a mining city named after *yaksha*s, mythic underground creatures obsessively protective of wealth. In his 1921 message, Rabindranath deplores the tussle between Kubera, god of material wealth, and Shri, an appellation of Lakshmi, goddess of true prosperity and well-being:

Kubera, the lord of wealth, has captured our countrymen's minds with the *yakshapuri* of the city. We have long forgotten how to invoke the worship of Shri in the rice-fields.[3]

Conventional economics does not look beyond material success, driven by competition, efficiency, and skill; it is unmoved by the poverty that stems from a lack of *shri*. Rabindranath's economics, on the contrary, commences with the quest for *shri*. He writes in a 1923 essay on the cooperative movement:

> Wherever people have thought 'I will outvie others in wealth or power', humanity has wounded itself, for no person is self-sufficient.... If wealth or strength were sought collectively by everyone in society, each individual would enjoy the abundant fruits of that collective effort in the natural way.[4]

The discipline of economics began with the idea of a household (Greek *oikos*), a unit of settled life in a community. This harmonious community life is central to the notion of *shri*.

STATE AND *SAMĀJ*

Rabindranath was critical of both religion and state. They are institutions working through external process, the rituals of religion, and the laws of state. Both are designed to ensure the harmonious functioning of society, but in both, more often than not, mere adherence to externals replaces the essence of the practice. They are sites of endless divisions and vying interests; hence neither provides a suitable basis for social unity. Instead, Rabindranath wishes to found human unity on the 'religion of economics' – the universal search for livelihood, valid beyond all compulsions and divisions. He grounds it in the village community, close to basic nature, free of the falsity of ritual:

> [T]he religion of economics is where we should above all try to bring about this union of ours ... for here high and low, learned and ignorant, all have their scope. If ... there we can prove, that not competition, but co-operation is the real truth, then indeed we can reclaim from the hands of the Evil One an immense territory for the reign of peace and goodwill.... [T]his is the ground whereon our village communities had actually practised unity in the past. What if the thread of the old union has snapped? It may again be joined together; for such former practice has left in our character the potentiality of its renewal.[5]

In the essay 'Bhāratbarsher itihās' (The History of India), he observes that foreign invasions only affected India at the level of politics and warfare, leaving unimpaired 'the life that flowed through the real India, the waves of effort, the changes in society'.[6] Politics only touched the surface of social life; it could not permeate its deeper layers. Rabindranath identified this as the site of a constructive *swadeshi* (indigenous) movement.

To reach out to one's *swadesh* (homeland), one must know it and bond with it. That calls for a shared social or community life that Rabindranath calls *samāj*. This was more likely, he felt, to be realized in the simplicity of village life: 'When life is simple, wealth does not become too exclusive, and individual property finds no great difficulty in acknowledging its communal responsibility, rather, it becomes its vehicle.'[7] Such a life is also more likely to be free of greed and bring us closer to our true selves. Rabindranath's Upanishadic nurturing made the concept of selfhood central to his ideas of village reform.

His ideas in this respect may be compared to those of Marx, Tolstoy, and Gāndhi. Marx is centrally concerned with re-establishing need as a corrective to the alienation brought about by capitalist property relations.[8] The idea of committing surplus wealth to communal needs is also germane to Gandhi's idea of trusteeship. Tolstoy too, in later life, renounced the identity of a count and devoted himself to the education of peasant children. However they diverged among themselves, these great men were remarkably alike in locating the village community as the site for their creative revolutionary work. Even Marx, in his late correspondence with Vera Zasulich, admitted the possibility of a direct transition to socialism from the Russian village community without going through the pangs of capitalist development.[9]

EDUCATION AND *ĀTMASHAKTI*

The shift from state to *samāj* began to germinate in Rabindranath's mind around 1890 when he came to manage his family estates in eastern Bengal, affording him first-hand knowledge of life in rural Bengal. In the poem 'Ebār phirāo more', he lists, almost as in a manifesto, the things lacking in that life: food, life, light, fresh air, health, strength, joyous longevity, and a courageous heart. Throughout his writings, he seems to have considered two things essential to ensure these: education and self-reliance. Education, for him, did not involve the intellect alone but the total being: it was a fulfilment of mind and body, in joyful harmony with nature and humankind. Such creative nurture would equip the young with full confidence in themselves, taking responsibility for their own decisions.

This involves the notion of *ātmashakti*, 'one's own strength' or inner strength: not merely self-reliance for one's material needs, but an awakening of the mind. This is as true for a community as for an individual: *ātmashakti* must operate at the level of the village collective. The collective must be confident and self-reliant in functions like providing pure drinking water, malaria control, and meaningful education for the young. Such ideas occupied Rabindranath at least since his 1904 lecture 'Swadeshi samāj':

> In our country, warfare, defence of the realm and the dispensation of justice were carried out by the king; but everything else from education to water supply was provided by the *samāj*, so naturally that even the flood-tide of regimes engulfing us ... could not destroy our *samāj* and reduce us to vagrant wretches. Kings have fought endlessly; but amidst our murmuring bamboo groves and shade-giving mango and jackfruit trees, temples have been built, guest houses established, ponds dug; schoolteachers have taught arithmetic, tols [Sanskrit schools] have studied the scriptures, the *Rāmāyana* has been read in community halls.... The *samāj* did not look for external aid, nor did it lapse from *shri* through external menace.[10]

Tagore encountered a problem of terminology in regenerating the *swadeshi samāj*: the relevant idioms, both linguistic and social, needed to be indigenized. A *melā* or fair, he suggests, rather than a conference, would open up the village community to an equitable exchange with the world, both material and cultural: in selling farm produce and other wares, spreading the message of public health, and rewarding bards, singers, and folk actors. 'A *melā* is the time to fill the heart of the village with the ideas of the world, as the ponds are filled in the time of the rains.'[11]

Rabindranath is cautious about proposing a fit leadership for the *samāj*. The leader should be an honourable person who commands authority. Such a person may not be readily available: the people themselves may require to shape their leader. The golden pitcher on the temple spire is only as high as the temple itself.[12] The leader is as great as the community and vice versa: the spirit of the community is realized in him.

COOPERATION

The idea of *swadeshi samāj* took shape in an ambience charged with patriotic feeling. There are two risks latent in such a milieu. One is the valorization of 'ours' over 'theirs'. This is understandable in a time of exploitative foreign rule, but it can degenerate into nationalistic chauvinism. The other danger is of authoritarianism, viewing the leader as a superhero moulding the people's destiny. That would mean the end of *ātmashakti*: the people would lose their innate power, whereas in a true *swadeshi samāj* the leader's decision should carry the stamp of collective authority. Excessive stress on the indigenous or nationalistic, along with excessive authority of the leader, is a fearful combination for any polity, let alone the *swadeshi samāj*.

Rabindranath found an escape route from these dangers in the principle of cooperation:

> The symptoms of our miseries cannot be removed from the outside; their causes must be extirpated from within. If we wish to do this, we must undertake two tasks: first, to educate everyone in the land, so as to unite them mentally with all the world.... Secondly, to unite them among themselves in the sphere of their livelihood, so as to bring about their union with the world through their work.[13]

This is taken from a 1918 essay on the cooperative movement where he describes international practices of mechanized farming, with the sharing of machinery and pooling of land holdings to make it possible.

Such unity is the basis of cooperation. Cooperative societies formalize the communal collective. In his essay 'Charkā', Rabindranath recalls how, while mulling the idea of the cooperative, he chanced upon AE (George Russell)'s book *The National Being*. It struck a sympathetic chord, for he had already reached the point where he could say: 'Cooperation is an ideal, not a mere system, and therefore it can give rise to innumerable methods of its application. It leads us into no blind alley; for at every step it communes with our spirit.'[14]

For Rabindranath, cooperation allowed the individual to relate organically with the community. Further, it rendered this relationship in material terms. AE was a poet and activist involved in the Irish Agricultural Organization Society, a successful dairy cooperative. Its slogan was 'Better Farming, Better Business, Better Living'. AE's book inspired Tagore, who was already thinking on similar lines:

> There I could see a great concrete realization of the co-operative living of my dreams. It became vividly clear to me what varied results could flow therefrom, how full the life of man could be made thereby. I could understand how great the concrete truth was in any plane of life, the truth that in separation is bondage, in union is liberation.[15]

The cooperative ideal thus held out a visionary promise for the poet: 'If any true devotee of our motherland should be able to eradicate the poverty of only one of her villages, he will have given permanent wealth to the thirty-three crores of his countrymen.'[16]

EXPERIMENTS ON THE TAGORE ESTATE

Rural life and the village economy engaged Rabindranath's thought from the time he began supervising the family estates in 1890. His ideas had a long gestation: the 1904 essay 'Swadeshi samāj' was based on fourteen years of rural experience. It was a time of burgeoning national sentiment, striving to revive native institutions at the risk of lapsing into xenophobia. Rabindranath's focus was on collective regeneration, not mere resistance to foreign rule; hence his agenda had to be sited outside formal politics. This potentially anarchist tendency, turning from the state to the *samāj*, brought him into frequent confrontation with almost every shade of politics of the day, including many views held by Mahātmā Gandhi. Rabindranath could not accept Gandhi's advocacy of the *charkhā*, or spinning wheel, to revive indigenous industry, nor could he support the Non-cooperation Movement and boycott of foreign goods. He aimed to rebuild society from within through meaningful education and constructive reform. The quest for material prosperity must rest on the spiritual foundation of *ātmashakti*.

However, the practical agenda for implementing his scheme on the family estates was worked out in detail: there was even a formal constitution.[17] Membership rules, subscriptions, a levy to meet common expenses, and punishment for offences were all clearly laid down. Living as he did on his Shilāidaha estate, for part of the time with his family, he was no absentee landlord but an active participant. He started projects for silkworm breeding and improving the quality of potatoes, though admittedly without much success.

These efforts did, however, give his ideas a chance to mature. In 1908, he planned a total reorganization of two *parganā*s (territories) within his estates, Birahimpur and Kāligrām. He writes to Manoranjan Bandyopādhyāy, a teacher at Santiniketan, on 14 July 1908 that he proposed to divide the *pargana* into five circles, each under a *pradhān* or head. The *pradhān* would organize the village community or *pallisamāj* (formalized at Kaligram as a *hitaishi sabhā* or welfare committee) for public tasks like building and repairing roads, ensuring water supply, adjudicating disputes, establishing schools, clearing overgrowth, and setting up public kitchens in time of famine. The experiment foundered at Birahimpur but was successful at

Kaligram, where within a few years, several schools and dispensaries were set up, roads built, wells dug, ponds cleared, and a dispute redressal system put in place.[18]

The collective initiative of the community was the keyword in this experiment. Leadership is commonly conceived hierarchically. The leader–follower combination is usually unidirectional, the follower a mere instrument without initiative or autonomy. This undermines the operation of the entire system. The Kaligram welfare committee, instead, was designed to function at the beneficiaries' impetus. Its long-term success was limited, but it set up a working model of an integrated rural community.

This relates to the ideal of holistic human development guiding the educational experiment already started in Santiniketan. 'In our school,' Tagore writes in the letter to Manoranjan Bandyopadhyay, 'the *bhadralok* children [that is, of the educated middle class] have become non-*bhadra* to some extent, and the non-*bhadralok* partly *bhadra*. I am trying to bring the two classes together in this way.'[19] This is an important insight. Under the colonial dispensation, the *bhadralok* were trained in limited professional skills: manpower was manufactured for a specific purpose like any other commodity. Rabindranath's goal, by contrast, was to let the child grow naturally into the fullness of humanity.

THE EXPERIMENT AT SRINIKETAN

'It has been my earnest desire for long that we in this country should deal with the problems of agriculture in a big way.'[20] Rabindranath said this in 1922 while introducing Leonard Elmhirst to the Santiniketan community on the latter's arrival to take up village regeneration work. Ten years earlier, Rabindranath had purchased a plot of land with a farmhouse at Surul village, close to Santiniketan. He meant to use this land for experiments in agricultural development. He had sent his son Rathindranāth and Santoshchandra Majumdār, the son of a close friend, to train in agricultural science at the University of Illinois.

In New York in 1921, he made the crucial acquaintance of Elmhirst. Elmhirst's varied early career included time in India in 1915, when he saw the plight of the Indian farmer and thought of devoting himself to the cause of Indian agriculture. In Allāhābād, he met Samuel Higginbottom, a missionary and agricultural scientist. Higginbottom advised Elmhirst, a Yorkshireman who had read history at Cambridge, to acquire training in agricultural science and return to India. Elmhirst went to Cornell University for this purpose. At their very first meeting, Rabindranath invited him to India to endow her villagers with 'the tools, and perhaps the ideas, whereby they could re-establish their economy, their social balance and their creative arts'.[21]

The poet exhorted Elmhirst to travel out 'tomorrow', but the latter naturally took time to decide. On 3 April 1921, he wrote to Rabindranath with his own notion of the man needed for the task: 'a man of intense devotion and of great selflessness, ... a school teacher, extension worker and agriculturist [with] enough real sympathy with suffering and poverty'.[22] It was with this commitment that he finally arrived in Santiniketan in November. Rathindranath and Santoshchandra had also returned. Together with Kālimohan Ghosh, Gaurgopāl Ghosh, and Santosh Mitra, this was the founding team of the Institute of Rural Reconstruction, otherwise Sriniketan (home of *shri*), inaugurated on 6 February 1922 with Elmhirst as Director. Shortly before, Visva-Bharati, the parent institute at Santiniketan, had itself been reconstituted as a public body under a Parishad (council) established on 23 December 1921.

As we have seen, Rabindranath's engagement with rural uplift had a long history; he brought to the Sriniketan experiment a broad vision and mature approach. He was now thinking on a worldwide scale, whereas earlier he had only sought relief for the people of his estate. Now he realizes that a different order of life is both possible and imperative for humankind as a whole. Contemporary civilization, marked by the crudest greed for wealth and power and the sharpest concomitant inequality, was set on a suicidal course. Sriniketan was conceived as an alternative way of life. In his speech prefacing a lecture by Elmhirst, Rabindranath refers to King Janaka of the *Rāmāyana*, who 'combined his quest for the highest truth (*Brahma*) with his knowledge of agriculture'.[23] Janaka cultivated the soil equally with the soul: a combination embodied in the synchronized binaries of Visva-Bharati and Sriniketan.[24]

A landmark in the development of this idea was a lecture by Elmhirst at Kolkata on 28 July 1922, entitled 'The Robbery of the Soil'. Rabindranath wrote an introduction for the printed text. Lecture and introduction both point to a truth engaging many people today, especially since the equivocal experience of India's Green Revolution. It was rightly diagnosed by Rabindranath and Elmhirst that many ills of modern civilization are due to unacceptable levels of social and economic inequality, reflected in the inharmonious growth of cities at the expense of villages. Elmhirst emphasized the importance of nature for human life to continue. The soil needs to be husbanded; if we rob it instead, it will take its revenge, sooner rather than later. As Rabindranath writes in his introduction:

A living relationship, in a physical or in a social body, depends upon
sympathetic collaboration ... between the various individual organs or
members.... Whenever some sectarian ambition for power establishes
a dominating position in life's republic, the sense of unity, which can
only be generated and maintained by a perfect rhythm of reciprocity
between the parts, is bound to be disturbed.[25]

The problem has grown vastly more intense between Elmhirst's time and
ours. Tagore relates this devouring process to the destruction of democracy.
He apprehends the manipulation of public institutions almost prophetically
when he writes: 'Man has been digging holes into the very foundations not
only of his livelihood but of his life. He is now feeding upon his own body.'
He places his own work in this perspective: 'We have started in India, in
connection with Visva-Bharati, a kind of village work the mission of which
is to retard this process of race suicide.'[26]

Even in the down-to-earth context of rural reconstruction, so direly
envisaged, Rabindranath lays stress on a total creativity of being:

Our object is to try to flood the choked bed of village life with streams
of happiness. For this the scholars, the poets, the musicians, the
artists as well as the scientists have to collaborate.[27]

In creativity is happiness. It is a displacement of priorities to relate happiness
merely to material goods. Rabindranath adopts the counter-stance that
material goods acquire value only when they release human capabilities.[28]

Visva-Bharati and Sriniketan were thus conceived as a composite project
across conceptual boundaries: one was not complete without the other.
Colonial education and culture had opened a yawning gap between tertiary
education and research on the one hand and vocational or manual training
on the other: a gap marked by class segregation, and an epistemological
hierarchy valuing the intellectual over the manual. The twin projects aimed
to bridge this gap.

At Sriniketan itself, rural development embraced agricultural education,
health, and social awareness. The farm at Surul started cultivating *jowār*
(a millet) and jute. Experiments were made in switching from chemical
fertilizers to organic manure. Malaria eradication was pursued seriously.
A dispensary was established in 1923 and health cooperatives set up from
1932. These activities and innovations were not confined to Sriniketan but
extended to the neighbouring villages through volunteer cadres: nineteen

such bands were in existence in the 1930s. The power of *ātmashakti* was harnessed thereby: it was for the people to conquer their own problems.

Besides the core programme of agricultural activities, Sriniketan came to embrace four centres of instruction in its early years. At the most basic level was the Shikshā-satra or 'open public centre for education', founded near Santiniketan in 1924 for the village children and shifted to Sriniketan in 1927 after Santoshchandra Majumdar's untimely death in 1926. The Lokshikshā Sangsad (People's Education Council), established in 1936, was an extra-mural centre where one could pursue courses without being regular students. Shikshācharchā Bhavan (Teachers' Training Institute) was established in 1937 to train elementary school teachers; a diploma course in rural organization commenced in 1922. But perhaps the most important branch was the Shilpa Bhavana (Institute of Arts and Crafts), founded in 1922, for training in rural industries: leathercraft, handloom operation, bookbinding, needlecraft, woodcraft, pottery, lac craft, and block printing. The Shikshā-satra and Shilpa Bhavana continue to the present. Needless to say, more centres of activity have been added subsequently.

Sriniketan also conducted an apprenticeship programme and educational training camps catering to the surrounding villages. In 1924, Kalimohan Ghosh organized three such camps for thirty-four apprentices from twenty-two villages. At Shilpa Bhavana, a leading figure was Lakshmishwar Sinha. Inspired by Gandhi's Non-cooperation Movement, he left the state educational system and eventually joined Sriniketan, devoting himself to village welfare and learning woodcraft in his spare time under the Japanese master Kasahara. Lakshmishwar championed woodcraft with almost missionary zeal: he started classes and wrote a pioneering book on the subject, *Kāther kāj* (Woodcraft, 1925). In his foreword to the book, Rabindranath hoped such pursuits would go a long way to bridge mental and manual exercises.

Rabindranath urged Lakshmishwar to study the Sloyd educational system, based on the ideas of the Finnish educationist Uno Cygnaeus (1810–88) and similarly combining the mental and the manual. On the poet's advice, Lakshmishwar left for Sweden in March 1928 and rejoined Visva-Bharati on his return in early 1937. His chief centre of activity was now the Shilpa Bhavana, but he soon left Santiniketan to join Gandhi's centre for basic education at Wārdhā.

The Shikshā-satra found a special place in Rabindranath's educational scheme. It aimed at 'the wholeness of human individuality', which could not be properly attained in the middle-class milieu of the Santiniketan school. 'I had to start a parallel school,' wrote Rabindranath, 'where the

villagers who do not have ambitions for finding Government employment
or employment in merchants' offices, come and join. There I am trying to
introduce all my methods which I consider to be absolutely necessary for
a perfect education.'[29]

In a 1924 essay on the Siksha-satra, Elmhirst outlined the philosophy
infusing not only that centre but the entire Tagorean quest for 'a perfect
education':

> The aim, then, of the Sikshá-Satra is, through experience in dealing
> with this overflowing abundance of child life, its charm and its
> simplicity, to provide the utmost liberty within surroundings that
> are filled with creative possibilities...; to give the child that freedom
> of growth which the young tree demands for its tender shoot, that
> field for self-expansion in which all young life finds both training
> and happiness.[30]

It is remarkable that Elmhirst's essay resonates with a message of freedom
among trees, the same natural growth and freedom sought in Rabindranath's
educational experiments. Shortly afterwards, this idea finds poetic
expression in *Banabāni* (The Message of the Forest), a book filled entirely
with poems on trees, written between 1926 and 1928. The same sensibility
seems to flow naturally into the ceremonies of Briksharopan (tree planting)
and Halakarshan (ploughing) commenced at Sriniketan respectively on 14
and 15 July 1928. The superbly perceptive preface to *Banabāni* (adapted
from a letter to the tree lover Tejeshchandra Sen) invokes ancient sayings
like *Yadidam kincha sarvam prāna ejati nihsritam* (All that there is comes
out of life and vibrates in it) [31] and *Keno prānah prathamah praitiyuktah*
(From where does the first life force come into this world?).[32] Upanishadic
insight is linked to the poet's project of educating the young in a remote
corner of Bengal.

The work at Sriniketan, though begun in right earnest, suffered many
tensions and conflicts from the start. There was tension between Santiniketan
and Sriniketan: the former, bound by middle-class aspirations, saw the latter
as a vocational centre for the less privileged. The complementarity of the
two, so basic to their founder's thought, was not easily granted by many
others in that ambience. There was also the destabilizing impact of Gandhi's
Non-cooperation Movement, which took the country by storm: Santiniketan
could hardly remain isolated. Yet, despite its limited and unreplicated
success, Rabindranath's experiment and its theoretical foundation cannot
lose their value for human aspiration and even human survival.

The author is indebted to Professor Kumkum Bhattacharya for helpful discussion on the Sriniketan story.

NOTES

1. *RRVB* 4:33.
2. *Samabāyniti* was also the title of a 1929 pamphlet, reprinted in the 1954 volume.
3. *RRVB* 27:449.
4. *RRVB* 27:458.
5. 'The Cult of the Charka', *EW* 3:543-4.
6. *RRVB* 4:378.
7. 'City and Village', *EW* 3:511.
8. Karl Marx, *The Economic and Philosophic Manuscripts of 1844*, first published 1932, English translation 1959.
9. Marx-Zasulich Correspondence in *Late Marx and the Russian Road*, ed. Teodor Shanin (New York: Monthly Review Press, 1983).
10. 'Swadeshi samāj', *RRVB* 3:526-7.
11. Ibid., *RRVB* 3:532.
12. Ibid., *RRVB* 3:544.
13. 'Samabāy' (The Cooperative) 1, *RRVB* 27:456.
14. 'The Cult of the Charka', *EW* 3:544; 'Charkā', *RRVB* 24:409.
15. Ibid., *EW* 3:545; *RRVB* 24:409.
16. Ibid., *EW* 3:546; *RRVB* 24:411.
17. See *RRWBG* 16:1187-9.
18. See *RJPP* 6:15, 20-1.
19. *CP* 13:71.
20. L[eonard] K[night] Elmhirst, 'Siksha-Satra, A Home School for Orphans', *VBQ* 2 (1924), 136.
21. *RJPP* 8:65.
22. *RJPP* 8:145. The Elmhirsts, Leonard and Dorothy, founded Dartington Hall in Devon, England, in 1935 on the model of Sriniketan.
23. *EW* 3:759.
24. See Umā Dāsgupta, *Shāntiniketan o shriniketan* (Kolkata: Visva-Bharati, 1984).
25. 'The Robbery of the Soil', *EW* 3:868.
26. Ibid., *EW* 3:871.
27. Ibid.
28. A major thinker in this tradition is Amartya Sen, who commenced his life and education at Santiniketan. See his *Commodities and Capabilities* (Oxford: Oxford University Press), 1999.
29. Prasanta C. Mahalanobis, ed., 'Rabindranath Tagore in Russia', *Visva-Bharati Bulletin*, 15 (1930), 33; cited in *RRPM* 4.125.

30. 'Siksha Satra, Home for Orphans', *VBQ*, 2 July 1924; cited in Rebantakumār Chattopādhyāy and Chandankumār Dās, eds, *Sikshā-satra shashthibarshapurti smārak grantha* (Santiniketan: Visva-Bharati, 1984), 50.
31. *Katha upanishad* 2.3.2 as translated by Rabindranath in *The Religion of Man*, ch. 4, *EW* 3:110.
32. *Kena upanishad* 1.1 as interpreted by Rabindranath in the preface to *Banabāni* (*RRVB* 15:114).

18 An Ecology of the Spirit

Rabindranath's Experience of Nature

ASEEM SHRIVASTAVA

It is the tears of the earth that keep her smiles in bloom.[1]

The fallen petals that Rabindranāth gathers in the flower basket of *Stray Birds* are imbued with poignant insights into the nature of existence. Some of these aphorisms were composed during the First World War – 'the war to end all wars' – when a self-destructively ambitious, globally avaricious Europe was savaging itself over the division of the spoils of colonial conquest. The spectacle of violent nationalistic greed – a forerunner of today's warring world – prompted Tagore to write: 'I thank thee that I am none of the wheels of power but I am one with the living creatures that are crushed by it.'[2] This expression of gratitude, which is equally a declaration of loyalties, is preceded by another valiantly humble line: 'The stars are not afraid to appear like fireflies.'[3]

Rabindranath is not an environmentalist as sometimes claimed. Some of his work – prominently the plays *Muktadhāra* and *Raktakarabi* – takes up, almost prophetically, environmental issues of great relevance in our own time, like giant dams and mining. But his fundamental commitment is to nothing less than the elusive simplicity of everyday sentience, *ecological living and dying* – something rendered remote, or even impossible, by the technocratic colonization of the planet in the twenty-first century. His poetry delivers what only poetry can: a mode of apprehension beyond scientific cognition, expressing what we *are* as against what we merely think about. It takes a poet to remind us of our myriad ecological responsibilities as speaking beings.

ECOLOGY AND COSMOLOGY, LIFE AND DEATH

Rabindranath's ecological vision is impossible to grasp unless one recognizes the cosmology in which it lives. He experiences life in wholes larger than his mortal self, feeling and thinking holistically in the most generous and expansive sense of even that inclusive term. This enables him to understand human life and death, as well as our place in nature and the broader scheme of things, in an ecological key. In varied genres of creativity, he demonstrates what it means not just to think but to *live and die* ecologically, never forgetting the power of nature within and around us.

In his attitude to nature, Rabindranath is anything but a sentimentalist or a blind romantic. He does not allow his tenderness and empathy for all things natural to prevent himself from clearly acknowledging the harsh realities that the elements impose on all creatures. The signature poem *Patraput* #3 (otherwise 'Prithibi', Earth) is one of the most detailed expressions of this outlook:

> You make human life toss in unbearable conflict.
> You fill the cup of nectar with your right hand,
> then smash it with your left....
> You have hidden in your plants the struggle inhering in every
>   moment,
> attaining garlands of victory in fruit and crops.
> Both land and sea are your unsparing battlefields,
> where triumphant life proclaims its victory in the face of death.[4]

The blinding ferocity of the elements is balanced by the love songs of the spring breeze and the celestial nectar bubbling over from the moon's goblet. The moral ambiguities of creation do not prevent the poet from offering it the unconditional tribute of his 'scarred life's homage'. His liberation lies in complete submission and surrender to nature, freeing himself of self-centred illusions, 'little cages of fragmented time':[5]

> I will not demand immortality at your door ...
> only that you should place a holy mark with your clay upon my
>   forehead.
> That mark will be effaced
> on the night when all signs merge in the all-fulfilling unknown.[6]

In 1993, at the age of ninety, the ecological philosopher Hans Jonas gave an award acceptance speech titled 'The Outcry of Mute Things'. He ended with the following words of caution, his last public utterance before his death a few days later:

> It was once religion which told us that we are all sinners.... It is now the ecology of our planet which pronounces us all to be sinners

because of the excessive exploits of human inventiveness.... The latest revelation ... is the outcry of mute things themselves that we must heed by curbing our powers over creation, lest we perish together on a wasteland of what was creation.[7]

That humanity belongs to nature (and not the other way around) is an ancient truth found in all traditional cultures. That humanity also belongs to a cosmos beyond the earthly world of organic life is a yet greater truth admitted down the ages. For Rabindranath this cosmos transcends the earth both materially and spiritually. This belief makes him not so much a pantheist as a *panentheist*, someone to whom the divine is not merely present in all creation, but exceeds all that exists.

It was the ancient forest sanctuary of India that taught us panentheism: 'the wisdom, which grew up in the quiet of the forest shade, came out of the realization of this Greater-than-all in the heart of the all.'[8] For Rabindranath there can be no lasting peace in the human realm unless and until we draw upon the reserves of eternity hidden in the heart of a nature that also includes ourselves. He draws extensive lessons from the *tapovana*, the ancient Indian idea of the forest hermitage:

[T]he ideal hermitage of ancient India ... establish[ed] a harmony between all our energies and the eternal reality. That is why the relations of Indian humanity with beast and bird and tree had attained an intimacy which may seem strange to people of other lands.... [T]he emotional quality peculiar to the forest-retreat is Peace ... where man was not separate from, and had no quarrel with, the rest of his surroundings.'[9]

Our freedom (*mukti*) lies in this peaceful transcendence, which offers the master key to Tagore's spiritual ecology. It is possible to appreciate his ecology without knowledge of his cosmology, but the former's full significance can only be divined, and its vital relevance to a mortally imperilled modernity grasped, when contextualised within a cosmic frame of reference. This is readily illustrated from a celebrated song:

Amidst the sky full of suns and stars, the world full of life,
I have found a place:
That is why my song wakes in wonder.
The swaying rhythm of endless time, that rocks all creation in its
  ebb and flow,

Tugs at my pulse:
That is why my song wakes in wonder.
I have laid my feet on the grass as I walked down forest paths,
My heart has thrilled at the sudden scent of flowers.
Gifts of delight are scattered everywhere:
That is why my song wakes in wonder.[10]

Wonder at the unfathomable mystery of existence is woven into the most mundane, everyday experience of nature: it awakens a liberating melody in the poet's heart.

Inspired by the grandeur of the river Padmā, Rabindranath writes in a similar vein in an 1895 letter to his niece Indirā Debi. These letters, collected in *Chhinnapatrābali* ('Scattered Leaves' as well as 'Scattered Letters'), were written by the poet to Indira between 1889 and 1895 from his family estate at Shilāidaha in eastern Bengal. They are full of insights into his understanding of nature; hence I quote them extensively. This was the time when, in the words of Satyajit Rāy, 'from this intimate contact with the fundamental aspects of life and nature ... a whole new world of sights and sounds and feelings opened up before him'.[11]

> We can draw a deep and secret joy from nature only because we feel a profound kinship with it. [T]hese green, fresh, ever-renewing trees, creepers, grasses and lichens, these flowing streams, these winds, the ceaseless play of light and shade, the cycle of the seasons, the stream of heavenly bodies filling the limitless sky, the countless orders of life – we are related to all this through the blood-beat in our pulse – *we are bound by the same rhythm as the entire universe.*[12]

Such a truth cannot be attained by mere reason. Tagore suggests it can be divined joyfully by the poet's heart at one with the immensity of existence around him. This joy results from his discovery that the Infinite is present in every particle of finite life – an idea that recurs through his works and, above all, in what he regarded as his life's axial work, the *tapovana* of Santiniketan itself.

CHHINNAPATRĀBALI: APPROACHING NATURE

How does Rabindranath arrive at this realization? The unity of humanity, nature, and the universe seems to elude virtually everyone, especially in the highly processed, man-made environment of today's metropolitan world.

The world we cognize seems misaligned with the way a poet of the Eternal perceives nature. Where he is greeted by an overarching unity, we encounter difference if not outright alienation.

Perhaps what is required is a sentient outlook where affection and empathy supersede intellection. A basic prerequisite is a feeling of inner reverence towards our natural surroundings. 'There is in nature an accessible and an inaccessible. Be careful to discriminate between the two; be circumspect and proceed with reverence.... [N]ature has ever in reserve something problematical which man's faculties are insufficient to fathom.' This was Goethe's advice to Eckermann in 1827.[13] Rabindranath could not agree more with such a view.

In an evocative letter in *Chhinnapatrābali*, Rabindranath expresses his feeling for nature, religious in a very special sense:

I have a very deep, intimate, truly living relationship with all nature, and I know and feel that affection, that bond to be my truest and best dharma.... It is a constant, everyday dharma: its observance is my constant act of worship. Yesterday, a mother goat was sitting on the grass by the road – serene, tender, entirely at ease – with her infant snuggling against her in total comfort, total security. The profound love and wonder, replete with *rasa*, that the sight aroused in me is what I would call my religious observance.[14]

The poet then warns against superfluous intellection. His love and wonder at the sight of the mother goat with her young is enough to evoke his own distinctive religious feelings. He needs no support from '*dogma*s [using the English word] that I neither know nor understand': the clarity of his emotively charged experience is quite enough.[15] In fact, the 'perceptible truth' at the heart of that experience is jeopardized by any overlay of the analytical mind.

Gifted with the universe itself, Rabindranath is acutely sensitive to the grandeur of creation and bemoans the fact that we are usually so utterly blind to the enormous beauty that surrounds us.

All these colours, this light and shade, this silent grandeur filling the skies, this peace and beauty infusing both heaven and earth – how much groundwork does it all need! ... This vast and wonderful process is happening every day outside us, but we scarcely respond to it fittingly from within, so far removed are we from the universe! The light of a star reaches this earth after travelling through the infinite darkness for hundreds of thousands of years, but it cannot enter our hearts, as though that were another hundred thousand leagues away! ... The people inhabiting this world to which I have been consigned are very strange creatures. Day and night, they are busy constructing rules and walls, assiduously putting up curtains so that their eyes might not catch sight of anything.... It's remarkable that they have not screened off flowering plants, or set up a tent to shut out the moon.[16]

The beauty of nature is an intoxicant for Rabindranath. Soaking it in, he reflects on the way in which the human mind, busy raising its cognitive partitions, represses its feelings towards the natural world.

Central to this repression is the fact that the modern imagination is metropolitan, the city being its cognitive axis: Rabindranath himself was a city-bred creature from colonial Kolkata. Every visit to Shilaidaha gives him pause to reflect on his own urban background:

The quacking of ducks in this village afternoon, the call of birds, the sound of clothes being washed, the water lapping as boats go by, the far-off commotion of cows fording the stream, the lazy wistful hum of songs inside my head – I couldn't imagine any of this amid Kolkata's daily grind, monotonous, colourless, cluttered with tables and chairs. Kolkata is very civilized and very ponderous, like a government office. Every day there seems to be of the same size and mould, like gleaming coins emerging from the mint: silent, lifeless days....[17]

During his long stays in rural east Bengal, the poet has to unlearn his urban conditioning in order to rediscover our 'deep age-old relationship' with the natural world. Not only that: 'the thousand intricate, unexampled, immeasurable processes of the human mind' only manifest themselves to Rabindranath when he finds himself alone in nature. The direct solitary experience of nature is essential for discovering our relationship with it, for attaining to both self-knowledge and knowledge of the natural world:

We have a deep age-old relationship with this earth, this sea: how can we possibly express it unless we feel it deep inside us, face to face with solitary nature? When there was no soil on the surface of the earth, when the ocean was all alone, my heart, so restless today, would be rocked inarticulately on the waves of that uninhabited mass of waters.... Today, the sea within me is being rocked in the same

way as I sit here alone. Something seems to be in creation there....
We cannot really perceive this immense hidden mystery within us
unless we sit in solitude on the shore of the vast ocean or under the
open sky.[18]

To the receptive mind, nature provides an inner spiritual perspective
bafflingly different, distant, and sometimes contrary to the familiar. As the
poet observes self-mockingly,

It seems highly inappropriate to bring clothes for the body and food
for the stomach into a discourse on spiritual matters, yet the soul
and the hungry stomach have always coexisted. My estates extend
just where the moonlight falls; but the moonlight says 'Your landed
property is a lie', and the property says the moonlight is nothing
but a fraud.[19]

In another letter, the poet imagines himself as a tree that grew out of the
ancient, sea-drenched earth, an intimate witness to the drama of the latter's
childhood, the very earth that is later viewed as a mother:

I drank in the first sunlight that touched the earth with my entire
body under the blue sky, stirred by a blind joy in living, like a newborn
child. I clutched this mother of mine, this clay, with all my roots and
sucked at her breast.... Ever since, I have been born on this earth's
soil with every new era. I seem to recall that old relationship, little
by little, when I sit face to face with her in solitude.[20]

The poet finds meaningful delight in a lively, historicized anthropomorphism,
helping the reader imagine the primordial history of the earth's flora. While
the evolutionary sciences look for remote evidence, the poet's imagination
evokes pictures out of the unvisualized facts of earth's distant pre-human
past. Empathy 'shows' what geological history hides. As matter and mind
converge in a moment of experiential singularity, we snatch a glimpse of
the poet's 'somatic unconscious'.[21]

The intimate sensuousness of Rabindranath's experience of nature is
hard for the twenty-first-century metropolitan mind to appreciate: evening,
beside the Padma, stands close to him, like a human presence,

with such intensity that the whole vast scene, from the starry realm
of the sky to the distant shaded shoreline of the Padma, encloses me
like a secret, secluded, restful little room. The two beings within me,

I and my soul dwelling in me, have this entire room to ourselves:
everything comprised in the scene, all birds and beasts and other
creatures, become part of our being.[22]

Does nature aid self-knowledge? Here is one response:

I was thinking yesterday that the human mind too is mysterious,
just like the vast world of nature. There's an unending play of
illusion everywhere.... The blood flows in a roaring tide, the nerves
quiver, the heartbeat rises and falls, the seasons change within the
mysterious being of man. We don't know what gale may suddenly
rise, or from where.[23]

The poet shows striking poise in the face of this great mystery of being
human. Far from making him anxious, it propels him energetically towards
many an imaginative adventure. 'Know thyself? If I knew myself, I'd run
away,' Goethe is reported to have said. When he was thirteen, Rabindranath
rebelled from acquiring such 'knowledge' in a Macaulayite school but later
willingly embraced the prospect in the lap of nature.

THE REPRESSION OF FEELINGS TOWARDS NATURE

Can we even be human if nature is absent from our immediate surroundings?
What will the young learn if they grow up in such barren places? Rabindranath
repeatedly asks this fundamental question – a concern that leads him to
locate his educational experiment in the rural setting of Santiniketan and
not in urban Kolkata. To him, open skies, planted fields, and swaying
palms are more essential to untrammelled learning and the formation of
the mind than the hectic cultural exchanges a modern metropolis affords
(and a village denies).

The poet sees the ecologically alienating influence of cosmopolitan
'civilization' as robbing humanity of its spiritual wealth:

Give back the wilderness, take away the city....
Cruel all-consuming one,
Restore all sylvan, secluded, shaded and sacred spots
And traditions of innocence....
We'd rather get back the strength that we had,
Burst through all barriers that hem us in and feel
This boundless universe's pulsating heartbeat![24]

This poem is one among countless songs, poems, plays, and stories where Rabindranath illustrates how metropolitan humanity is enfeebled by its growing estrangement from the earth, draining it of the vitality it can regain only if ecological integrity is restored to our relationship with nature.

Rabindranath believes that the ecological alienation of metropolitan life profoundly cripples our sensibility, leaving humanity in a self-destructive state of spiritual destitution. Engagement with the natural world from a formative age is the only way to restore humanity to spiritual and ecological health. This is the core of his spirituality as well as his pedagogy. In *Creative Unity*, he writes about the university he set up in Santiniketan:

> This religion of spiritual harmony is not a theological doctrine to be taught, as a subject in the class, for half an hour each day. Such a religious ideal can only be made possible by making provision for students to live in intimate touch with nature, daily to grow in an atmosphere of service offered to all creatures, tending trees, feeding birds and animals, learning to feel the immense mystery of the soil and water and air.[25]

In his insistence that the participative presence of the natural world is essential for a fully realized human life, Rabindranath is perhaps unique among modern philosophers. More than his vast literary corpus and his music, it was Santiniketan that Rabindranath regarded as his life's main work. In unpropitious modern conditions, it was his unique experiment with the ancient Indian idea of the *tapovana* or forest hermitage. Santiniketan was not synthetically abstracted from the natural world in the manner of modern educational institutions: its programme included daily outdoor instruction in the midst of nature. Its twin village Sriniketan was dedicated to agriculture and the revival of rural life and crafts.

The only sensible way to educate the young, Rabindranath felt, was to not sequester them in dull, four-walled Macaulayite classrooms, but to sit with them under a banyan or peepul tree and take them for walks in the woods and fields. In Santiniketan, the transition from one season to another (natural events that go unnoticed in most schools around the world) was marked by festivals, many of which Rabindranath had himself initiated. For instance, the Briksharopan, or tree-planting ceremony, was held as part of the Barshāmangal (auspicious rain) celebrations at the start of the monsoons. The practice is responsible in no small measure for turning the dry red laterite soil of Birbhum to the partial verdure that survives a century on. At neighbouring Sriniketan, the coming of the rains was marked by the Halakarshan, or ploughing ceremony.

In 'Aranyadebatā' (The God of the Forest), a prescient speech at the Halakarshan and Briksharopan ceremony in Sriniketan in 1938, Rabindranath extols the life lived in everyday kinship with the natural world. He points out that in the past, humankind lived in physical proximity to forests. Children were born there. This inspired a creaturely affection and empathy (*mamatwabodh*) with the forest, besides dependence upon it for countless material needs. Such a life recognized the need to nurture its habitat. Since the onset of modern urbanization, this symbiosis declined and grew remote: with greater ecological distance, *mamatwabodh* mutated into *nirmamatā* (mercilessness). Remarkably anticipating the insights of modern ecological science, Rabindranath cites instance after instance of the damage caused by deforestation: the desertification of tracts of North America, the increasingly hotter summers of northern India, and the 'exposed skeleton' of the soil in the region around Santiniketan itself. He concludes this Briksharopan speech by invoking a feeling of remorse among his listeners and calling on people to replant the region, to help heal the pain and scars (*kshatabedanā*) of Mother Earth.

Globalized metropolitan life and the growing urbanization of the mind (which today impacts on villagers too) cause a physical and psychological estrangement from the very natural world that supports human life among all other things. Such alienation nurtures ecological ignorance at a cognitively formative age. In the prophetic 1922 lecture 'The Robbery of the Soil',[26] an introduction to his associate Leonard Knight Elmhirst's paper of the same name, Rabindranath points out that villages are 'nearer to nature than the towns'; 'the cradle of the race' thus lies 'in their keep'. He draws particular attention to the cultural gulf that modern cities consciously cultivate with respect to the rural hinterlands that support them: the 'epidemic of voracity that has infected the total area of civilization', wherein 'the very shriek of advertisement' prompts wasteful 'unlimited production' for 'a whole population of gluttons'. The price is paid in Asia and Africa, 'where human flesh is cheap' and the 'happiness of entire peoples is sold for the sake of providing some fastidious fashion with an endless supply of respectable rubbish'. An 'illusion of wealth' is thereby created, 'as certain portions grow large on their robbery of the whole'.

> The city, in its intense egoism and pride, remains blissfully unconscious of the devastation it is continuously spreading within the village, the source and origin of its own life, health and joy.[27]

Rabindranath continues:

> True happiness is not at all expensive. It depends upon that natural
> spring of beauty and of life, harmony of relationship. Ambition
> pursues its own path of self-seeking by breaking this bond of
> harmony.... Being wasteful it remains disruptive of social life and
> the greatest enemy of civilization.[28]

These ideas resound through the lectures and speeches that Rabindranath
gave over decades of sustained work in Santiniketan and Sriniketan.[29]
His writings in various genres are closely intertwined with his intimate
experience of the natural world.

Another such instance is the short story 'Balāi' about a motherless boy
brought up by his aunt. He is so much in love with nature, so attuned to
her inner movements, that he has to hide his true emotions from his friends
when they slash roadside shrubs with a cane, or break the branch of a *bakul*
tree, just to tease him. He grows especially attached to a silk-cotton tree
in their garden: he will not allow his uncle to cut it down. But once Balāi
leaves home to study at Shimlā, the uncle proceeds to do so, to the utter
devastation of his wife, Balai's aunt, for whom the tree had become a symbol
of her nephew away from home. In remorse, she does not eat for two days.[30]

In stories like 'Balāi', poems ranging from the philosophic 'Brikshabandanā'
(Hymn to the Tree) – and the collection *Banabāni* (The Voice of the Forest)
generally – to the children's poem 'Tālgāchh' (The Palm Tree), or the
letters gathered in *Chhinnapatrābali*, Rabindranath brings out the ancient
existential bond between nature and humankind. For him, humankind is
properly naturalized only when the natural world is reciprocally personified,
when humanity awakens to its liberating destiny as a witness to the sentient
order of creation. For Rabindranath, in keeping with the Vedas and the
Upanishads, the same consciousness that we experience as human beings
permeates the entire natural world and the cosmos. This great truth is
obscured from us by certain endemic illusions: we need to see past those
illusions to realize ourselves by accepting the unity of all creation. Hence
it is impossible to be properly human without the constant daily touch of
the natural world into which we are born, and without which we cannot
live for a day, though we may be seduced into believing otherwise. Modern
society routinely represses its feelings for nature to the point where it is
no longer conscious of them. Humanity thereby suffers an inner spiritual
impoverishment, which allows it to connive blindly and passively with the
organized forces of ecological destruction.

Ever the prophet of renewal, Rabindranath's poetic vision is a challenge to the calculative utilitarian environmentalism in vogue at the present day. His is an invitation to a spiritual ecology, urgently needed to rescue imperilled humankind from its predicament in the anthropocene.

SUMMING UP

This essay is not a comprehensive account of Rabindranath's ecological vision,[31] but a few concluding remarks may be in order.

To Rabindranath, nature was never merely an object for fragmented study in laboratories and conference rooms. Respectful of science and the valid knowledge with which it has gifted humanity, he was less reverential of the countless ways in which its technological applications in a man-made world have made life easier for a growing minority, while rendering humanity as a whole increasingly inert, diminished, and redundant. Visiting Europe in the early days of the fascist era, an alarmed Tagore said to Giacinta Salvadori in a 1926 interview that Europe – and with it, the entire modern zeitgeist – needed to be rescued 'from the dominion of the machine'.[32] He had made the point in a lecture in China in 1924: the Western world had been acquainted in the past with a more enlightened culture, but in the two previous centuries, 'the West found access to Nature's storehouse of power, and ever since all its attention has irresistibly been drawn in that direction'.[33]

For Rabindranath, science and its applications have their place. But he had already made his definitive pronouncement on the matter in *Sadhana*:

> The man, whose acquaintance with the world does not lead him deeper than science leads him, will never understand what it is that the man with the spiritual vision finds in these natural phenomena. The water does not merely cleanse his limbs, but it purifies his heart; for it touches his soul. The earth does not merely hold his body, but it gladdens his mind; for its contact is more than a physical contact – it is a living presence.[34]

In passages like this (and there are many), Rabindranath imparts a poetic and philosophic dimension to ideas waiting to be articulated, in more earthbound vein, by ecologists half a century later. He pre-endorses their scientific findings even as he soars beyond them in his philosophic imagination.

NOTES

1. *Stray Birds* #4, *EW* 1:397.
2. Ibid., 48, *EW* 1:402.
3. Ibid., 49, Ibid.
4. *RRVB* 20:12.
5. This phrase as translated by William Radice in Rabindranath Tagore, *Selected Poems* (London: Penguin, 1985), 101.
6. *RRVB* 20:15.
7. Cited in Rabbi Lawrence Troster, 'Hans Jonas: The Most Inspiring Teacher I Never Met', *Jewish Standard*, 6 April, 2006, available at http://jewishstandard. timesofisrael.com/hans-jonas-the-most-inspiring-teacher-i-never-met/, accessed 31 January 2018.
8. 'The Message of the Forest', *EW* 3:399.
9. Ibid., *EW* 3:394.
10. *GB*, 'Prakriti' #8.
11. Quoted in Krishna Dutta and Andrew Robinson, *Rabindranath Tagore: The Myriad-Minded Man* (London: Bloomsbury, 1995), 109.
12. *CPBLI* #227. Italics mine.
13. Johann Wolfgang Von Goethe, *Conversations of Goethe with Johann Peter Eckermann*, tr. John Oxenford (New York: Da Capo Press, 1998), 188–9.
14. *CPBLI* #187.
15. Ibid.
16. *CPBLI* #55.
17. *CPBLI* #114.
18. *CPBLI* #91.
19. *CPBLI* #182.
20. *CPBLI* #74.
21. 'Somatic unconscious' is used here to mean something like the 'subtle body' (*sukshma sharir*, as opposed to the *sthula sharir* or gross body) in yoga. Carl Jung uses the expression while discussing Nietzsche: 'The part of the unconscious which is designated as the subtle body becomes more and more identical with the functioning of the body, and therefore it grows darker and darker and ends in the utter darkness of matter.... Somewhere our unconscious becomes material, because the body is the living unit, and our conscious and our unconscious are embedded in it: they contact the body. Somewhere there is a place where the two ends meet and become interlocked. And that is the [subtle body] where one cannot say whether it is matter, or what one calls "psyche". ' Carl Jung, *Nietzsche's Zarathustra* (Princeton: Princeton University Press, 1988), 1:441.
22. *CPBLI* #145.
23. *CPBLI* #119.

24. 'Sabhyatār prati' (To Civilization), *RRVB* 5:17–18; tr. Fakrul Alam in *The Essential Tagore*, ed. Fakrul Alam and Radha Chakravarty (Cambridge, MA: Harvard University Press, 2011), 240.

25. 'An Eastern University', *Creative Unity*, EW 2:568.

26. *EW* 3:866–72.

27. *EW* 3:869.

28. Ibid.

29. Many of these talks (like 'Aranyadebatā') have been collected as *Palliprakriti*. The title is difficult to render in English. Literally, it can mean 'the nature of villages' but, more basically, 'nature in the villages' or 'rural nature', implying that villages are closer to the natural world than cities. ('Shahar-prakriti' or 'urban nature' would make little sense.)

30. The story was written by Tagore in 1928 to be narrated at the *Barshā-utsab* in Santiniketan, a festival to celebrate the arrival of the monsoon.

31. That is the goal of a forthcoming book by this author.

32. *EW* 3:903.

33. 'Civilization and Progress', *Talks in China*, EW 2:626.

34. 'The Relation of the Individual to the Universe', *EW* 2:283.

19 Rabindranath and Science

PARTHA GHOSE

SCIENCE IN THE POET'S CHILDHOOD

In 1925, Rabindranāth Tagore wrote to Praphullachandra Rāy, the distinguished chemist: 'I was sitting reading *Scientific American* when I noticed an envelope from the University College of Science [where Praphullachandra taught].'[1] How many poets read *Scientific American* as a pastime, one wonders. But for Rabindranath, it followed naturally from his childhood training and bent.

In the introductory epistle to his only book on science, *Bishwaparichay* (1937), Rabindranath describes how science had fascinated him since childhood. His science tutor would thrill him with simple demonstrations like making the convection currents in a heated glass of water visible by using fine sawdust. The differences thereby made visible between the layers of an apparently undifferentiated mass of water filled him with a sense of wonder. This was when he first realized that things we take as evident are, in fact, often not so. The discovery set him wondering forever.

The next wonder came when at the age of twelve he stayed with his father, Debendranāth, at Dalhousie in the Himalayas. At night, Debendranath would point out to him the constellations and the planets, telling him about their distances from the sun, their periods of revolution, and other such things. The fascinated boy began writing down what he learnt. He is thought to have penned his first long essay, on the possibility of extraterrestrial life, at the age of twelve and a half.[2] It started to be published in serial form in *Tattwabodhini patrikā*, a journal established by Debendranath, but did not progress beyond the first instalment.

As he grew older, the young Rabindranath started reading every book on astronomy that he could lay his hands on, his favourite being Sir Robert Ball's work. He persisted even when the mathematics proved difficult. Then he discovered Thomas Huxley's essays on biology. Astronomy and biology became, and remained, the scientific subjects that fascinated him and found reflection in his mature writings, especially his poetry. These studies did not afford a rigorous grounding in science, but they helped him acquire a scientific mindset that served him well through his life without impairing his poetic genius. It led him to develop a distinctively new philosophy in which the tenets of modern science were seamlessly integrated with the ancient wisdom of the Upanishads.

SCIENTISTS AND THE POET

The originality of Rabindranath's philosophy attracted the leading European scientists of his time, grappling with the profound philosophical problems unleashed by their scientific discoveries. Einstein wrote in 1926 expressing a desire to meet, and Arnold Sommerfeld actually did so in Kolkata in 1928. So did Werner Heisenberg in 1929, shortly after his discovery of the 'Uncertainty Principle', at the root of the breakdown of determinism at the level of individual events in quantum mechanics. His 'long conversations' with Rabindranath brought him great comfort.

> He began to see that the recognition of relativity, incommensurability, interconnectedness, and impermanence as fundamental aspects of physical reality, which had been so difficult for himself and his fellow physicists, was the very basis of the Indian spiritual traditions. 'After these conversations with Tagore,' he said, 'some of the ideas that had seemed so crazy suddenly made much more sense. That was a great help for me.'[3]

Rabindranath's celebrated dialogues with Einstein are recounted below. But needless to say, his most sustained interaction was with the preeminent Indian scientists of the day, Jagadishchandra Basu (Bose) and Prashāntachandra Mahalānabish (Prasanta Chandra Mahalanobis) above all.

Jagadishchandra, arguably India's first modern scientist, conducted major research in electromagnetic radiation and the electrophysiology of plants. The poet had been daunted at the prospect of meeting him, but

> to my relief, I found in him a dreamer, and it seemed to me, what surely was a half-truth, that it was more his magical instinct than the probing of his reason which startled out secrets of nature before sudden flashes of his imagination.[4]

The two became close friends. Rabindranath's friendship, writes Jagadishchandra, was an unfailing support in his 'ceaseless efforts during which I gained step by step a wider and more sympathetic view of continuity of life and its diverse manifestations'.[5] He dedicated his work

The Nervous Mechanism of Plants (1926) to Rabindranath, who responded enthusiastically: 'I realized this is where our truth lies, this light, this life – this is India's essence.'[6] He dedicated two books to Jagadishchandra and addressed six poems to him – the greatest number to any person. Most important is the poem entitled 'Jagadishchandra' in *Banabāni* (The Message of the Forest):

> You have brought the eager tidings of life to sight
> across darkness, from its mute inner chamber.
> It speaks to the radiant genius of your mind
> about the kinship of the plants' murmur
> and the core of humanity:
> evidence of their oldest, most primordial relations.[7]

Banabāni is entirely about plants: Jagadishchandra's inspiration clearly underlies the entire volume. When the scientist established his own research institute, the frescos and other artwork in the main auditorium were executed by Nandalāl Basu (Bose) and Surendranāth Kar, the famous artists from Santiniketan. Rabindranath composed the opening song: 'Make the holy precinct of the mother's temple shine supremely bright today'.[8] It is a patriotic song, but in its context, the patriotic effort is channelled through scientific enquiry. The 'mother' is both the motherland and mother nature.

Rabindranath knew the other pre-eminent Bengali scientist of the time, the chemist Praphullachandra Ray, and made him a patron of the Department of Agriculture at Visva-Bharati, but there is no evidence of their close interaction. The unmarried Praphullachandra may have been the model for the absent-minded, benevolent elderly bachelor Chandranāth in Rabindranath's play about a league of bachelors, *Chirakumār sabhā* (The Bachelors' Club). But Ray's protegé Rājshekhar Basu won the poet's admiration. Rajshekhar held successful charge of the Bengal Chemical Works founded by Praphullachandra, and played a key role in the history of printing in Bengal. But he was also a writer, a humorist *par excellence*, a lexicographer, and a Sanskrit scholar. Tagore warmly praised his works, particularly his first book of comic stories, *Gaddalikā*, and his Bengali dictionary, *Chalantikā*. This prompted an amusing exchange of letters between Rabindranath and Praphullachandra, each playfully charging the other with poaching young talent from his field.

One of Rabindranath's regrets was that he could not introduce full-fledged science teaching at Santiniketan for lack of funds. Rajshekhar donated five thousand rupees' worth of new equipment for physics, chemistry, and botany, besides some old instruments. The laboratory built to house them was named 'Rājshekhar Vigyān Sadan'.[9] It was later shifted elsewhere without acknowledging the benefaction; the original laboratory has disappeared without trace.

A major scientist who developed a lifelong relationship with Rabindranath was Prashantachandra Mahalanabish, physicist and statistician. Their families had long known each other, and Rabindranath was drawn to the young Prashanta by his combination of a love of literature with a flair for logical analysis. Prashantachandra, in return, worked to rehabilitate Rabindranath in the Brahmo Samaj, from which he had been ostracized for his liberal views. Together with the poet's son Rathindranāth, Prashantachandra served as joint secretary of Visva-Bharati for ten years from 1921, and accompanied Rabindranath on several visits abroad. When Prashantachandra founded the Indian Statistical Institute in December 1931, it was Rabindranath who coined the Bengali word for statistics, *rāshibijnān* or *rāshibidyā*, and wrote a foreword for the inaugural issue of the institute's journal, *Sankhyā*.

In the early days of Visva-Bharati, Rabindranath also gained from his close friendship with the Scottish polymath Patrick Geddes, biologist, sociologist, and town planner. Geddes impressed on him the need for planning in order to regenerate the rural communities in Bengal, including training opportunities to integrate sustainable agriculture with village industries. This became the founding principle of Sriniketan. But a single encounter between Rabindranath and the physicist Meghnād Sāhā held more significance for the development of modern India. The two met in Munich in 1921 on Sommerfeld's introduction, but only in 1938 did Meghnad go to Santiniketan to solicit Tagore's support for a Planning Commission for India, to ensure planned industrial growth on scientific lines. This agenda was favoured by Subhāshchandra Basu (Subhas Chandra Bose), the then president of the Indian National Congress, in sharp counter to Mahātma Gāndhi's call to make the spinning wheel and village industries the foundation of India's economy. Rabindranath was openly critical of this aspect of Gandhi's vision, especially after visiting the Soviet Union in 1930 (accompanied by Prashantachandra) and admiring its industrial progress. The plan was to use Rabindranath's influence with Gandhi to win his continuing support for Subhash. The poet wrote to both Gandhi and Jawāharlāl Nehru. The political ploy failed, but it is now history how later, as prime minister of independent India, Nehru championed the cause of planning and industrial growth. India's Second Five-Year Plan was largely the work of Prashantachandra.

Rabindranath also requested Meghnad Saha to lecture during his Santikinetan visit. Reiterating the views of his teacher Praphullachandra, Meghnad vehemently attacked the brahminical tradition in his talk, holding it responsible for India's backwardness. This led to a controversy from which Tagore kept himself aloof.

Rabindranath seems to have had little or no interaction with the physicist and Nobel laureate C.V. Raman, though he taught at Calcutta University. But the poet did interact with Satyendranāth Basu (Bose) after the latter shot to fame for his epochal work on quantum statistics. He invited him to Santiniketan on several occasions, and dedicated *Bishwaparichay* to him. This was no doubt owing to Satyendranath's interest, even then, in propagating science through the mother tongue.

CONVERSATIONS WITH EINSTEIN

Of all Rabindranath's encounters with scientists, intellectually the richest by far was with Albert Einstein. The two iconic figures of the twentieth century met at least five times in Europe and America, and held many ideas in common. Both publicly voiced concern at the spread of militant nationalism, and defended human rights and creative freedom in the cause of world peace. In 1919, at Romain Rolland's invitation, they signed a document against aggressive nationalism, 'La Déclaration de l'indépendance de l'Esprit'.

More crucially, they shared a communion of spirit. 'He seemed to me a man who valued human relationship and he showed toward me a real interest and understanding,' wrote Rabindranath about their first meeting in Germany. On that occasion they discussed, and agreed on, the need for 'modern industrial improvements to help us in our modern life'.[10] But their celebrated dialogue on the nature of reality took place at a later meeting in 1930 in Einstein's house at Caputh near Berlin. Einstein's stepson-in-law Dmitri Marianoff and Rabindranath's companion Amiya Chakrabarti both took notes, which were later approved by both poet and scientist. There are slightly different accounts in various sources, but the lines of discussion are clear.

Rabindranath began by contrasting Einstein's pursuit of 'the two ancient entities, Time and Space' with his own concern with 'the eternal world of Man, the universe of Reality'. The Divine is part of this universe:

The infinite personality of Man comprehends the Universe. There cannot be anything that cannot be subsumed by the human personality, and this proves that the truth of the Universe is human truth.[11]

He illustrated this with 'a scientific fact':

> Matter is composed of protons and electrons, with gaps between them; but matter may seem to be solid. Similarly humanity is composed of individuals, yet they have their inter-connection of human relationship.... The entire universe is linked up with us in a similar manner, it is a human universe.[12]

But, said Einstein,

> There are two different conceptions about the nature of the universe: (1) The world as a unity dependent on humanity. (2) The world as a reality independent of the human factor.[13]

Hence, 'if there is a *reality* independent of man there is also a truth relative to this reality'.[14] Tagore's response, essentially, is that such truth is not humanly apprehensible, so 'for us it is absolutely non-existing'.[15] The individual human strives to attain to truth by 'the standard of the Eternal Man whose experiences are through our experiences'.[16]

An impression has gained ground that the conversation was a failure, perhaps because of Marianoff's comment, 'It seemed to an observer as though two planets were engaged in a chat.'[17] A serious discussion with fundamental differences is of far greater value than polite agreement, as evident from the famous debate between Einstein and Niels Bohr. Unlike a brief afternoon chat between a man of science and a poet, the Bohr–Einstein debate extended from 1927 to 1955 between two founding fathers of quantum theory. But the theme of both dialogues was essentially the same: the role of an observer in the description of nature. Bohr kept pressing his point about the essential role of observations in describing nature, while Einstein stuck to his conviction of an observer-independent reality. The debate is still very much alive among physicists and philosophers, which may be why they are still attracted to the Tagore–Einstein conversation. Einstein was disturbed by the fact that the vast majority of physicists shared Bohr's point of view. Perhaps it was this anxiety that made him raise the question with Rabindranath. The latter's stand has been upheld by several later scientists including two Nobel laureates, Brian Josephson and Ilya Prigogine.[18]

It is important to grasp that in the dialogue with Einstein, Rabindranath's position is not merely emotive or spiritual. He credits Einstein with 'what might be called a transcendental materialism, which reaches the frontiers of metaphysics, where there can be utter detachment from the entanglement

of the world of self'.[19] Tagore, on the contrary, advocates knowledge through
an enlargement of the Self in the Universal Man, who alone is the repository
of truth. This, too, is a grounded and rational quest with the same objective
as science:

> The Unknown has led Science, no one can deny that.... Man's
> movement is always progressively toward an objective reality. His
> steadying pivot is his belief that Truth is there which beckons him
> even when he does not see it. This is the call to the Individual from
> the Universal Man – and it is this call that carries us toward the
> Universal.[20]

Like Einstein, Rabindranath can conceive of new paradigms of reality:

> an existence where Space is not the factor, but where Time reigns
> as it does in music. It is not impossible that a mind can live in time
> and have no notion of space. For such a mind, existence might be
> the kind comprehended in music.[21]

The only difference is that such a truth would be validated by man, as music
is, being an aspect of the objective truth validated by Universal Man.

Einstein sent the following note for *The Golden Book of Tagore*, the
commemoration volume for Rabindranath's seventieth birthday:

> Man defends himself from being regarded as an impotent object in
> the course of the Universe. But should the lawfulness of happenings,
> such as unveils itself more or less clearly in inorganic nature, cease
> to function in front of the activities in our brain? ... [D]eterminism
> does not stop before the majesty of our human will.
>
> May be, that we and the human society require the illusion of
> the freedom of human activities!

He continues: 'The conviction about the law of necessity in human activities
introduces into our conception of man and life a mildness, a reverence, and
an excellence, such as would be unobtainable without this conviction.' He
makes this premise of his own conviction the basis of a moving tribute to
the poet who disagreed with it:

> Thou sawest the fierce strife of creatures, a strife that wells forth from
> need and dark desire. Thou sawest the escape in calm meditation

and in creations of beauty ... spreading everywhere a gentle and free thought in a manner such as the Seers of thy people have proclaimed as the ideal.[22]

SCIENCE, TECHNOLOGY, AND TWO TAGORE PLAYS

Tagore wrote two powerful symbolic plays which reflect his rejecting science as a machine (not merely the machines created by science) and affirming his faith in the human spirit. *Muktadhārā* (The Free Stream) was written in 1922 and *Raktakarabi* (Red Oleanders) in 1923. They are his finest protests against totalitarianism and the use of machines to subjugate human beings.

In *Muktadhārā* the 'machine' is a dam across a mountain stream with which the greedy king tries to subjugate the people downstream. His plans are foiled by Dhananjay, an apostle of non-violence who inspires the people to fight for their lawful rights, and the anointed prince Abhijit after he learns of his castaway status. Abhijit eventually breaks the dam but gets swept away by the flood. In *Raktakarabi* the greedy king, lurking behind a screen, reduces mine workers to cogs in a wheel of exploitation symbolized by a gold mine. A revolt is engendered by a young woman called Nandini, the embodiment of love and beauty, who steals into the mine like a breath of fresh air and arouses everybody to revolt. Eventually even the king surrenders to her charm, but her own love, Ranjan, is killed.

The lesson of these plays must not be interpreted in a simplistic spirit. To reject science as a machine is not to reject science. The British classical scholar Gilbert Murray asked Rabindranath in 1934 whether he hated machines as such. Tagore replied:

> My occasional misgivings about the modern pursuit of Science is not against Science, for Science itself can be neither good nor evil, but its wrong use.... It is this spirit of man which has refused to recognize the boundaries of nature as final.[23]

This refusal, says Rabindranath in *Personality*, means that science has broken down 'the prison of matter' only to operate 'in the rubbish heap of the ruins'.

> At the invasion of a new country plunder becomes the rule of the day. But when the country is conquered, things become different, and those who robbed act as policemen to restore peace and security. Science is at the beginning of the invasion of the material world and

there goes on a furious scramble for plunder.... But the day will come when some of the great powers of nature will be at the beck and call of every individual, and at least the prime necessaries of life will be supplied to all with very little care and cost. To live will be as easy to man as to breathe, and his spirit will be free to create his own world.[24]

When that time comes, Abhijit and Nandini need have no quarrel with the technology they oppose at such cost to themselves, for the science guiding that technology will have become a humanely enlightening force aiding the liberation and well-being of humankind.

THE UNIVERSE IN THE SCHOOL

In *Personality*, Tagore puts that quintessentially poetic object, a rose petal, to strictly scientific application.[25] As one zooms in on the petal through a microscope, it is seen in an ever-expanding space, and at the limit of infinite space it is neither a rose petal nor anything else. It acquires the character of a rose petal where infinity meets finitude at a particular point; when we move away from that point towards the smaller or the larger, the petal begins to lose its reality. To Tagore this fading away of the reality and beauty of a rose petal into scientific abstractions appeared as a serious limitation of the scientific viewpoint. It is like Keats's objection to Newton unweaving the rainbow by reducing it to 'cold philosophy',[26] but there is an important difference. To Tagore it is not only the beauty of a rose that vanishes under scientific analysis, but its very reality.

In *Personality*, Tagore writes:

> [T]he world is not atoms and molecules or radio-activity or other forces, the diamond is not carbon, and light is not vibrations of ether. You can never come to the reality of creation by contemplating it from the point of view of destruction.[27]

It is from this perspective that Tagore attempted to teach science in his school at Santiniketan.

> The boys of my school have acquired instinctive knowledge of the physiognomy of the tree. By the least touch they know where they can find a foothold upon an apparently inhospitable trunk; they know how far they can take liberty with the branches.... [They] make the

best possible use of the tree in the matter of gathering fruits, taking rest and hiding from undesirable pursuers.... I consider it as a part of education for my boys to let them fully realize that they are in a scheme of existence where trees are a substantial fact, not merely as generating chlorophyll and taking carbon from the air, but as living trees.[28]

He composed songs, wrote plays, and organized seasonal festivals in Santiniketan so that the students could be acquainted with nature by direct experience and emotional involvement rather than from the cold resources of printed books alone. Some of these festivals have become public attractions, like the spring festival (Basantotsab) and the winter festival (Paush melā). Even more significant, however, are the festivals of the rainy season including the tree planting ceremony (Briksharopan) and ploughing the fields (Halakarshan).

BISHWAPARICHAY

Such was the form taken by the very first attempt at environmental education in India. As Tagore writes in the dedicatory epistle to *Bishwaparichay* (Introducing the Universe, 1937):

> It is extremely important for those who have just started their learning process to enter, right from the beginning, not perhaps into the storehouse of science, but into its courtyard.[29]

The book was written to impart the rudiments of physics and astronomy to young learners, at Santiniketan school and elsewhere, and also to develop a model for scientific prose in Bengali, which would infuse a literary flair into science. The latter aim has remained largely unfulfilled except in the writings of Satyendranath Basu, to whom Rabindranath dedicated the book.

The five chapters take us through the entire realm of science: from the intricacies of atomic structure to the mysteries of distant galaxies, then narrowing focus from the solar system and the other planets to the earth. In the epilogue he sums up the key points by quickly surveying the emergence of life, wondering how the primitive living cells appeared from the dumb and the inert with miraculous powers of assimilation, adaptation, and growth, branching out into endless forms most beautiful and wonderful. He then brings in the inevitable heat death of the universe (the second law of thermodynamics, which Eddington famously called 'the arrow of time') and wonders if that means the eventual disappearance of life from the universe forever. Regarding the emergence of the mind and consciousness, he says the human mind refuses to believe in the appearance of something totally unrelated to everything else that exists. He offers his conjecture that mind and consciousness must have been immanent in very subtle forms in the primitive light energy that pervaded the early universe when there was nothing else. In today's terms, this is the cosmic microwave background radiation, the fossil of the hot Big Bang, which was conjectured by Gamow in 1946 but discovered only in 1957.

Where did Tagore get this idea from? Already in 1910 he had composed a song about the primitive radiative energy that pervaded the skies.[30] He also mentions the various attempts to calculate the age and lifespan of the universe and the solar system, and comments on their utter futility. To him the ultimate beginning and ultimate end of a limitless universe made no sense. He favours the ancient Indian view of endless cycles of creation, sustenance, and dissolution, which make such calculations seem pointless. Finally, he writes about the difficulties in putting together a satisfactory theory of solar system formation by collisions of stars, as first proposed by James Jeans and later extended by Lyttleton. He mentions Henry Norris Russell, director of the Princeton University Observatory, who had shown in a paper written as recently as 1936 how the temperature generated by stellar collisions would make the atoms and molecules fly apart violently and make it impossible for them to congeal into planets. He concludes that Russell's criticisms have struck at the very roots of the Jeans-Lyttleton theory, which, like so many other theories, may have to be relegated to oblivion.

Tagore thus works an entire philosophy of science into a book ostensibly designed for schoolchildren. It is little wonder that it celebrates the intellectual curiosity that impelled a world-renowned poet and artist, at the age of seventy-six, to inspire his young readers with the same enthusiasm. He writes in the Introduction:

The human being is the only creature that has suspected its own simple perception, opposed it and been delighted to defeat it. To transcend the limits of simple perception, humanity has brought near what was distant, made the invisible visible, and given expression to what is hard to understand: forever probing the depths of the unmanifest world behind the manifest, and thereby uncovering the fundamental mystery of the universe.[31]

SCIENTIFIC *MĀYĀVĀDA*

What follows a few pages later is truly challenging: 'Today, at the end of my life, my mind is overwhelmed with the new theory of nature, with scientific *māyāvāda*.'[32] The use of the adjective 'scientific' to qualify *māyāvāda* is extremely significant, taking us beyond Rabindranath's use of the word *māyā* in his conversation with Einstein. Rabindranath rejected the ancient *māyāvāda* of Shankarāchārya, which dismisses the world as an illusion. Here lies the originality of his synthesis of the Upanishads with modern science in a new paradigm where the two illuminate each other. Modern science revealed to him a deeper level of reality than our senses can detect – the invisible differences between layers of a continuous mass of heated water; the stars, galaxies, and their movements that lie beyond our gaze; the microscopic world of atoms and molecules that are too small for us to see.

These phenomena are invisible to us, but they are not illusions. They are material phenomena which, through the revelations of science, we can perceive with the mind and the mind alone. They may be said to have always existed within the Universal Mind, and are now come within reach of ours. Modern science seems to be effecting a resolution of Rabindranath's controversy with Einstein: it is pointing to a synthesis of the truth implicit in both epistemologies.

SCIENCE INTO POETRY

In 'The Realization of Beauty' in *Sadhana* (1913), Rabindranath writes:

> When I went to sleep I closed my eyes with this last thought in my mind, that even when I remain unconscious in slumber the dance of life will still go on in the hushed arena of my sleeping body, keeping step with the stars. The heart will throb, the blood will leap in the veins, and the millions of living atoms of my body will vibrate in tune with the note of the harp-string that thrills at the touch of the master.[33]

He had put the same idea in a poem published twelve years earlier:

> The waves of life that course night and day through my veins are also rushing to conquer the world, dancing through the universe in exquisite beat, pace and rhythm. It joyfully infuses a myriad blades of grass in every pore of the earth's clay; ... it sways to the ebb and flow of the ocean tide of life and death across the universe. That mighty throb of the aeons is now dancing in my pulse-beat.[34]

The imagery recurs in even more striking form in a classic song of 1927 on Shiva as the cosmic dancer Natarāj:

Rebellious atoms turn beautiful, enthralled by your dance.
The sun and the moon ring out like bells in your luminous anklets.
The inert world awakens into consciousness at the living touch of
    your dance.
Through ages and time, in music and rhyme,
Your eternal bliss breaks into waves of joy and sorrow.[35]

The language of *Bishwaparichay* is lively, imaginative in its use of metaphor, but never merely 'poetic': on the contrary, it is focused on scientific facts and concepts. But almost inevitably, the same ideas transformed in the imaginative writings above occur from time to time in more literal form in *Bishwaparichay*, as in this account of cosmic rays:

There is no object or creature that they do not touch: they even strike
upon the atoms of metals and excite them. Perhaps they enhance
the life of created beings, perhaps they destroy them: we don't know
what they do, only that they impinge on them. The mystery of their
origin remains unknown; but we have come to know of their gigantic
energy – how they spread all across the skies, enter into all substances
in water, earth and air.[36]

There is no gap, let alone conflict, between Rabindranath's poetic imagination and scientific perception: the latter is woven seamlessly into the greater fabric of the former.

One can cite only a few outstanding examples where his poetic vision of the universe, or of nature around him, is not only compatible with scientific insight (such instances are too numerous to list) but, it seems, directly inspired by it and incorporates it.[37] Some of these poems seem to mesh with the physical sciences, astronomy and cosmology in particular; others with the life sciences, celebrating the order and energy in the living world of nature. One long excerpt must serve for them all. *Shesh saptak* #28 is addressed to the evening star that is also the morning star, but it becomes an emblem of both the universal creative force and its manifestation in the world of homely nature and humanity:

Wise men call you the planet Venus. They say you are immense, swift
and venerable in your vast orbit. You are the earth's fellow-traveller as

350 Partha Ghose

you circle the sun in prayer: the jewelled garland of daylight, woven of sunbeams, dangles from your neck.

In the arena of great time where you carry out your cosmic commerce, you are distant and aloof, hidden in the manless mystery of thousands and millions of years. But when, today, at the border of approaching night, you inspire the poet's heart with the silent message of peace – at that moment, unknown to us, the cycle of the changing seasons is generating the variety of creation in your water, land and air....

We know you are the planet of scholars, an astronomical truth proved by mathematics. But this is also true, even more true, that you are our morning star and evening star. There you are small and beautiful, to be compared to late autumn's dewdrop and early autumn's *shiuli* flower.[38]

This poem serves as well as any to illustrate how Rabindranath is different from a scientist. The insights of science are a noteworthy part of his greater mental universe. As he puts it in *Personality*: 'The prosody of the stars can be explained in the classroom by diagrams, but the poetry of the stars is in the silent meeting of soul with soul.'[39]

NOTES

1. Subrata Ghosh, *Rabindranāth o prajukti* (Kolkata: Signet Press, 2017), 99.
2. 'Grahagan jiber abāsbhumi' (The Planets Are the Home of Life), *Tattwabodhini patrikā*, 8:4 (Paush 1281/December 1873–January 1874), 161–3. Rabindranath's authorship has been questioned: see *RJPP* 1:202–3.
3. Heisenberg's interview to Fritjof Capra, in Fritjof Capra, *Uncommon Wisdom: Conversations with Remarkable People* (1988; rpt. New York: Bantam, 1989), 43.
4. 'Jagadish Chandra Bose', *EW* 3:826.
5. J.C. Bose, 'A Homage to Rabindranath Tagore', in *The Golden Book of Tagore*, ed. Ramananda Chatterjee (Kolkata: Golden Book Committee, 1931), 16.
6. *CP* 6:72.
7. *RRVB* 15:119.
8. *GB*, 'Swadesh' #17.
9. See Dipankar Chattopādhyāy, *Rabindranāth o bijnān* (Kolkata: Ānanda Publishers, 2000), 322.
10. Rabindranath Tagore, 'My Memories of Einstein' in 'Portfolio: Einstein and Tagore, "Endless Dawns" of Imagination', intr. Wendy Singer, *Kenyon Review* n.s. 23 (2001), 16. Tagore says here that he met Einstein 'during my first visit

to Germany after the War' – that is, in 1921. However, the general consensus is that they first met during Tagore's second visit in 1926.

11. *EW* 3:911. The fullest transcript of the Tagore–Einstein dialogues, with other material on their interaction, is to be found in Singer, 'Portfolio'.
12. *EW* 3:911.
13. Ibid.
14. *EW* 3:912.
15. *EW* 3.913.
16. *EW* 3.911.
17. Dmitri Marianoff, 'Einstein and Tagore Plumb the Truth', *New York Times*, 10 August 1930, 3.
18. Brian Josephson, '"We Think That We Think Clearly, But That's Only Because We Don't Think Clearly": Mathematics, Mind, and the Human World', available at https://arXiv:1307.6707, accessed 30 September 2018; Ilya Prigogine and Isabelle Stengers, *Order Out of Chaos: Man's New Dialogue With Nature* (London: Fontana, 1985), 293.
19. Tagore, 'My Memories', 17.
20. Ibid., 18.
21. Ibid., 19.
22. *Golden Book of Tagore*, 12.
23. *East and West, EW* 3.347–8.
24. 'The Second Birth', *Personality, EW* 2:382.
25. 'The World of Personality', *Personality, EW* 2:364.
26. John Keats, *Lamia*, 2:230.
27. 'The World of Personality', *Personality, EW* 2:366.
28. 'My School', *Personality, EW* 2:391–2.
29. *RRVB* 25:347.
30. *GB*, 'Pujā' #470.
31. *RRVB* 25:348.
32. *RRVB* 25:350.
33. *EW* 2:337.
34. *Naibedya* #26, *RRVB* 8:27–8.
35. *GB*, 'Bichitra' #2.
36. *RRVB* 25:373.
37. For a few prominent examples, see *Patraput* #3, #7; for cosmology and astronomy, *Patraput* #11, 'Prashna' ('Question', *Nabajātak*) and *Janmadine* #5; for nature and animal life, 'Pākhir bhoj' ('The Birds' Banquet', *Ākāshpradip*). Of the numerous poems on the plant world, the biggest group is found in *Banabāni*.
38. *RRVB* 18:57–8.
39. 'The World of Personality', *Personality, EW* 2:370.

20 Rabindranath Tagore as Literary Critic

SWAPAN CHAKRAVORTY

Rabindranāth Tagore believed that literature, if not all art, was free play (*lilā*) and led to joy (*ānanda*). Derived from the Upanishads and introduced to him by his deeply religious father, Debendranāth, these notions would later be fused with his own reading of Indian and Western texts. A phrase in the *Mundaka upanishad* (2:2:7), one that Tagore recalled on countless occasions,[1] describes the infinite as the immortal manifested in joyous form: *ānandarupamamritam yadvibhāti.*

Play connects freedom with the joy we experience in what is functionally a surplus. Humans need the face for physical functions, but it is also the theatre of emotions. 'Muscles are essential, and they have plenty of work. But we are enchanted only when the play of their movements expresses the body's music.'[2] Tagore said this in the 1924 address 'Srishti' (Creation) delivered at Calcutta University. Freedom, play, and joy are invoked in the same address: 'This release from the fetters of fact into the world of abiding joy is no small freedom. Human beings composed songs and painted pictures to remind themselves of this freedom.'[3] He defended the idea of poetry as play with unperturbed humour in 1915, in reply to the social scientist Rādhākamal Mukhopādhyāy's attack on his literary thought and practice as indifferent to social reality and uncaring of human suffering. Radhakamal seemed annoyed that Tagore used words such as play (*khelā*), holiday (*chhuti*), and joy (*ānanda*) far too often in his writings. 'If that is so', answered Tagore in 'Kabir kaiphiyat' (The Poet's Defence), 'one is to understand that I am possessed by some truth.'[4]

Tagore also employed the word *rasa* in talking of art, though not always in the sense one finds in classical Sanskrit aesthetics. *Rasa* for him was not simply the eight affective 'essences', such as compassion or fury, mentioned in Bharata's manual *Natyashāstra*, and the ninth added to it by Abhinavagupta. For Tagore, any mixture of these or even a new *rasa* may lead to *ānanda*. *Rasa* in poetry is at its most intense when it pleases the ears and satisfies our intellect and emotions through its *bhāva*, that is, its feeling and idea.[5] Tagore wrote something similar (without mentioning *bhāva*) to the younger poet Sudhindranāth Datta in July 1928.[6] He even insisted that 'pure thought' (*shuddha chaitanya*), understood in the ancient Indian use of the word *chaitanya*, may be emotionally experienced. Delinking *rasa* from questions of ethics and profit, he says that 'value' is of three kinds. Material demands fix the market value of something, ethical factors determine social value, and *rasa* its especial value for the individual. An intellectual element constitutes part of this last value, but the major element is the form (*rupa*), which, however, excites interest only when fused with *rasa*. Tagore was then sixty-seven, and literature still remained for him relatively autotelic, a production that exceeded its ostensible function, a surplus that refused to be consumed by mere usefulness. He sought to discover the formless in aesthetic form. He observes in 'Srishti' that just as science has discovered non-matter behind material nature and claimed it as the 'truth', so does art point to a *rasa* beyond form as its truth: 'truth frees us from form when it appears in form'.[7]

Tagore's aesthetics, though not always uniform, poses two major obstacles for the literary critic. How does a critic communicate a sense of *lilā* and *ānanda*, or their absence, in the work of other writers without creating a new and possibly irrelevant work of art in the name of criticism? Second, even if one uses Tagore's norms to judge a literary work, it is difficult to maintain a critical distance from it if the text necessarily demands joyous immersion or, if the work is indifferent, cold dismissal.

Tagore wrote a great deal and often seemed to contradict himself. In a letter of 1891, when he was only thirty, he confided to the author Pramatha Chaudhuri that he felt torn between renunciation and attachment, Indian placidity and European zest, philosophy and poetry.[8] On occasions, self-doubt haunted him. He felt the need to distance himself from his everyday identity to escape his conscious social self. In October 1929, in his sixty-eighth year, he wrote to Nirmalkumāri Mahalānabish that his innermost self was like an open chamber with no marked entrance or exit. Unbidden guests swarmed in so that he might observe all and depict all.[9] Plenitude requires distance, and entails the occasional contradiction. However, a few ideas endured. On 24 May 1941, two and a half months before his death, Tagore wrote to the younger poet, novelist, and critic Buddhadeb Basu (Buddhadeva Bose) that what human beings gathered for their livelihood defined them outwardly, but their true identity belonged with 'useless' things, easy to dismiss, which constitute their *lilākshetra*, field of play.[10]

Tagore had a way out of the difficulty created for criticism by the criteria of joy and free play. Literature is a means of union with fellow humans; the Bengali word *sāhitya* is derived from *sahit*, 'with (someone or something)'. In 'Bānglā jātiya sāhitya' (Bengali National Literature) he writes, '*Sahitatwa* or union is the main ingredient of *sāhitya*'.[11] This idea is supplemented by the Sanskrit word *sahridaya*: literally, a companion of the writer's heart. Abhinavagupta, in his commentary on Ānandavardhana's *Dhvanyāloka*, defined the word as the reader or listener who felt one with the subject matter or, if the poet were the subject, with the poet.[12] Literature unites human beings in their common humanness, which includes their bond with the universe. Vedāntic precepts made Tagore think of creation as the one manifested in the various: 'The one that is within me also wishes to find its own self in the many.'[13] The consummation of that union causes that especial *frisson* – *ānanda* reached through creativity freed of immediate needs. 'Knowledge is this union of reason with the universe, and it is in this union that our rationality finds joy,' writes Tagore in the essay 'Bishwasāhitya' (World Literature). 'Likewise, it is the nature of the human soul to seek a union of its particular humanness with all humanity: in this lies its true joy.'[14]

This might sound a touch too exalted for the practising critic, but Tagore places writers in their milieu by employing the same principle of union. In *Panchabhut* (The Five Elements, serialized 1892–5), a poem by one of the five interlocutors stimulates variant readings in the other four. The fictional poet concludes, 'Poetry has this virtue, that the poet's creativity stimulates the reader's own.'[15] A poem, like a flame, ignites a range of fireworks in readers, and all readings are legitimate if true to the pleasure the text generates. This passage is close to another in 'Sāhityasrishti' (Literary Creation, 1907), an essay published more than a decade later.

> Thus throughout human society, the thoughts of one mind strive to find fulfilment in another, thereby so shaping our ideas that they are no longer exclusive to the original thinker.... In fact, what we say is shaped by the conjunction of speaker and listener.[16]

This is followed by a paragraph in which a popular writer of *pnāchāli* or mythological ballads, Dāsharathi Rāy, is linked to the society of his time. Dasharathi's *pnāchāli* 'is not Dasharathi's sole possession; it is written in collaboration with the society that listens to it.... [T]he love, hate, piety, belief, and taste of a given circle at a given time find spontaneous expression within it.'[17] One may be reminded of Eliot's dry remark on critics of his times who demanded that poetry be 'representative of its age' rather than 'well written'.[18] Tagore makes no such demands. He simply uses the principle of commonalty and union to explain the *sahitatwa* of *sāhitya* – the paradox of free bonds that literature forges with its mileu, an idea alien to Tagore's critic

Radhakamal Mukhopadhyay, and to the categories of Western sociology he specialized in, such as class and ethnicity.

Tagore sought in art, or at least in literature, freedom in an unfree country. A tacit compact between the literatures of unequal peoples may upset the best-laid plans of rulers and induce resistance, not by inflaming short-lived literary excitement or breeding militant groups, but by freeing literature from the narrow confines of race and 'national' identities into a liberating kinship with the world. Tagore extended such bonds beyond literature, although in his philosophy, literature might have a special claim. The bonds of union, unlike those of 'patriotism', were for him those of liberty. Faith in such kinship inspired much of Tagore's work: his attempt to join love with knowledge of nature in his school in Santiniketan; his university Visva-Bharati where he hoped the world might find a home; and rural reconstruction in the extensive tracts in eastern Bengal that the Tagores held under the *zamindāri* settlement. He wished to unite tenants and landlords in a concern for the collective good, a bond he termed *kalyānsambandha*. Applying Lenin's comment on Tolstoy, one might say that Tagore's equal concern for the welfare of unlettered peasants and plundering landlords mirrored the contradictions of a semi-feudal colony,[19] were it not the case that Tagore pioneered cooperative farming, rural banks, skill-training, small-scale enterprise, and, curiously enough, techniques of mass education that he witnessed on his visit to Stalin's Russia in 1930.

Resistant to summary assessments, the prophet of free play and joy turns social scientist in the essay 'Kabi-sangit' (The Songs of Kabiyāls).[20] *Kabigān* was a lapsed variant of rural lyric and song adapted to bourgeois life. It entertained traders, moneylenders, and merchants' agents, an unrefined species of consumers spawned by colonial commerce in the new capital, Kolkata. Tagore appears suspicious of popular culture, admittedly debased, in a city of new money. Tārāshankar Bandyopādhyāy, a younger writer whose short stories Tagore admired,[21] tried to show in his novel *Kabi* that the genre belonged to a fallen rural culture too, and that even a depressed countryside could produce poets from the most disadvantaged sections of people. Tagore was clear-eyed about the rude demands of commercial art. Nevertheless, he remained committed to a 'non-useful' literature that, as Pierre Bourdieu thinks, classifies, and in so doing classifies the classifier as the product of social privilege.[22] All the same, Tagore believed that the class and breeding of consumers should not define aesthetic judgement. Such judgement, even of popular forms, depended on the capacity of the arts to produce *ānanda*, joy. This is evident in the other essays in the volume *Lokasāhitya* (Popular Literature), which contains 'Kabi-sangit'. Tagore's aesthetics and the entertainment market remained unreconciled in many ways. His plays failed on the commercial stage in his lifetime, unlike his brother Jyotirindranāth's. His music found only a minority audience until the 1960s. The current popularity of his music, a lucrative genre and yet a source of deep joy and solace, has lessons for sceptics who dismiss his aesthetic ideas as mystifying.

Tagore made his debut as literary critic with a review of three books of verse by three different poets.[23] The review appeared in 1876, when Tagore was fifteen. It is a defence of the lyric, which he believed was the genre that the Sanskrit playwright and poet Kālidāsa and medieval Vaishnav poets such as Barhu Chandidās of Bengal and Vidyāpati of Mithilā had gifted Bengali poetry. The progress of the lyric, destined to 'improve' in step with civilization, was being regrettably impeded by Bengalis biased towards the Western variety of the epic. Tagore quoted Shakespeare, Robert Herrick, and Thomas Moore, and cited Moore's *Lalla Rookh* and Milton, not to speak of Jayadeva and other Indian poets. He declared that drama and epic represented others; the lyric, the self. Shakespeare was an indifferent lyric poet; Byron, an inferior dramatist.

The review by a fifteen-year-old school dropout shows which way the apprentice poet was heading. Tagore took literary criticism seriously, just as the great novelist Bankimchandra Chattopādhyāy had done before him. Bankimchandra had written an essay on the lyric, entitled 'Abakāshranjini', three years back in his journal *Bangadarshan*. This essay, later published as 'Gitikābya' (The Lyric), argued that an epic like Vālmiki's *Rāmāyana* could express both action and hidden emotions, unlike Bhavabhuti's lyrical *Uttararāmacharitam*, the Sanskrit play derived from the *Rāmāyana*: drama, such as Shakespeare's *Othello*, avoided burdening the action with excessive verbal effusions or commentary. Hence, Milton's *Comus* and Byron's *Manfred* were not drama proper. The lyric takes personal emotions as its province. Bengali literature needed the lyric, but Bankimchandra placed the genre in a hierarchy topped by the epic.[24] Tagore was questioning that hierarchy.

In 1881, Tagore published a praise of Tennyson's 'De Profundis' (revised in 1907). The idea of the human individual emerging from a mass of vapours, from an immanent first cause, overwhelmed him. Milton's epic similes may compare a giant to a mountain and his staff to a tree, but *Paradise Lost* is inferior in sublimity.[25] The next year saw, among other pieces, a comparative estimate of the two major Vaishnav poets Chandidas and Vidyapati.[26] Here again, he challenges Bankimchandra's conclusion in the latter's essay 'Bidyāpati o jayadeva' (1873)[27] that Jayadeva was extrovert and sensuous and Vidyapati the poet of hidden desire and suffering. Tagore insisted that all genuine poets were inward-looking. Chandidas, sad and wistful even in the presence of his love, was the superior poet.

Little wonder then that the reviewer's next target should be the other big name in Bengali literature of the time – Michael Madhusudan Datta (Dutt) and, particularly, his epic *Meghnādbadh kābya* (*The Slaying of Meghnad*, 1861). However tempered Tagore's later view of Michael might be, in his early years he attacked him twice: in an essay in six instalments in the magazine *Bhārati* in 1877, when he was sixteen, and in another assessment in *Bhārati* in 1882. Tagore accused Michael of domesticating the grandeur of the *Rāmāyana* with trite comparisons. The critic had an imperfect grasp of the simultaneity of strangeness and familiarity, epic extension and dramatic contraction demanded by the epic simile. Further, he accuses Michael of inconsistent portrayal of Rāvana and other characters, shallow thought, and lack of spontaneity. In the second essay, Tagore says that no epic is purely or consistently poetical.[28]

The details of the immature critic's charges are of minor consequence, although in 1934 the seventy-three-year old poet seems still unreconciled to Michael's sonorous style.[29] The odd thing is that he should care more for the songs of Bāuls, followers of an esoteric cult with their own music on which he wrote a review essay in 1883, or even for rural balladeers, than for the work of the first great modern in Bengali poetry, simply because Michael was renowned more for his Western-style epic than his accomplished sonnets, lyrics, and plays. Kierkegaard believed that tragedy made the universal ethical burden manifest through the individual who is at other times immediate and concealed as physical being.[30] For the young Tagore, ontological manifestation called for the lyric idiom. It was *prakāsh*, revelation of the individual as unique yet joined to fellow humans, the Creator, and the universe. Tagore's insistence on the supreme consciousness would weaken with time. The faith in the lyric mode as the primary means of manifesting the union of the individual with other humans and with the universe would last longer. As adolescent critic, Tagore did not pick on the weak, and his daring takes one's breath away.

The more substantial of Tagore's early critical essays were collected in *Samālochanā* (1888), a book Tagore later discarded. The second formal phase starts in 1891 with the essay on Kalidasa's *Meghadutam* and ends in 1906. The output was collected in three volumes published in 1907 – *Prāchin sāhitya* (Ancient Literature), *Lokasāhitya* (Folk Literature), and *Ādhunik sāhitya* (Modern Literature). In addition, several of his earlier essays of criticism and review appear in *Sāhitya* (Literature, 1907). Literary criticism appears in less formal sources – letters, memoirs, travelogues – both during the second phase and later. Tagore's comments on literature and literary aesthetics were spread across his works in other genres, and he never stopped writing on literary philosophy. An instance is the book *Sāhityer pathe* (On the Road to Literature, 1936), which includes many of his more theoretical essays and addresses on literature. However, one misses the sixteen-year-old critic who had the nerve to say that Bengalis led unexciting, constricted lives, and to ask: 'How many poems do we have in the Bengali language? And how many of them could we count as first-rate?'[31]

Tagore withdrew from literary polemics but not from criticism. He retained his admiration for Bankimchandra for creating a discerning reading public and rescuing Bengali criticism from the pundits who judged modern literature by the principles of Sanskrit poetics. Yet at times, even the young Tagore seemed allergic to the idea of criticism. On 7 May 1886, he wrote to his friend Shrishchandra Majumdār that one's spontaneous response to literature is killed by criticism which murders texts in order to dissect them. Then there are the 'Yes, but....' qualifications and corrections, not from others as postulated by F.R. Leavis,[32] but from doubts in the critic's own mind, which empty the text of all blood. Even when readers take delight in a text, the critic in them feels constrained to deny that enjoyment in the interest of analysis.[33]

What, then, is the function of criticism? The Bengali words for 'criticism' that Tagore uses are *samālochanā*, the act of organizing one's observations and expressing them, and *bichār*, the act of judging. In 1929, Tagore would write in the essay 'Sāhityabichār' (Judging Literature) that *bichār* aimed at a faithful account of the work: the critic's task was more interpretation than analysis, which, like the psychoanalysis of fictional characters, loses sight of wholeness.[34] But when in 'Rāmāyan' (1903) he makes an exception for the *Rāmāyana* and the *Mahābhārata*, texts which the critic must interpret in reverent obeisance,[35] the *bichār* strikes one as less than critical. Tagore was praising the *Rāmāyana* while introducing Dineshchandra Sen's *Rāmāyani kathā* (On the *Rāmāyana* Stories); perhaps he was expressing the sentiments of his so-called revivalist phase, which ended around 1905–6. But the context matters little when he declares that the critic's task is not comparative assessment, in which he had himself led the way in 'Chandidās o bidyāpati'. A charitable, though hardly comforting, conclusion would be that since Tagore expected his ideal literary critic to adopt the criteria of *rasa* and *ānanda*, only a pious commentator could address the *rasa* of devotion, although devotion was not the only thing the *Rāmāyana* and the *Mahābhārata* were about.

This is seemingly at odds with a statement in the 1903 essay 'Sāhityer bichārak' (The Judge of Literature). Education and talent enable the critic to discover the timeless elements in a work and ignore the ephemeral.[36] The creative and the critical are seen as distinct activities. In the major essays in *Prāchin sāhitya*, the ancient works studied are like flames to ignite creative digressions. Does the critic always need to be true to the text? While introducing his essay (in the journal *Sādhanā* in 1894) on Bankimchandra's novel *Rājsingha*, Tagore had complained that he was afraid to undertake the task, as he would be expected to unearth some secret from the novel about which both author and readers were in the dark.[37] Shortly before his death, in a second essay entitled 'Sāhityabichār' (Judging Literature),[38] he flatly admitted that although critics ought to be disinterested, they were likely to be prejudiced by class, taste, and training. It was wiser to forsake the pretence of objectivity and make criticism itself into an occasion for producing good literature. Till the end, Tagore remains hard to pin down. In stressing disinterestedness, he departs from the goal of communicating pleasure, yet returns to it through a detour viewing criticism as contemplative creativity.

Good instances of 'creative criticism' in *Prāchin sāhitya* are 'Meghdut' (The *Meghadutam*) and 'Kābyer upekshitā' (The Ignored Woman in Poetry). 'Meghdut' praises Kalidasa, but hardly assesses the poem critically. Instead, Tagore creates a myth of love out of Vaishnav themes and what reads like neo-Platonic motifs, which he may have derived from his close reading of Shelley. The *yaksha* parted from his beloved yearns for her because of the incompleteness of human lives and the desire they are therefore destined to suffer: '[W]e feel that we all belonged once to the same realm of the mind, and are now banished from it.'[39] 'Kābyer upekshitā' is a meditation on ignored women in Sanskrit poetry, such as Urmilā, Lakshman's wife in Valmiki's *Rāmāyana*, and Shakuntalā's friends Anasuyā and Priyamvadā in Kalidasa's *Abhijnānashakuntalam*. The meditation is profound, yet it remains fanciful, since the secret lives of these characters are not a textual fact.

On the other hand, in 'Rāmāyan' and 'Kumārsambhab o Shakuntalā', Tagore is more concerned to justify the ways of ancient poetry against the modern. In the latter essay, the 'union' in Kalidasa's two plays is achieved through happy and virtuous domesticity. In 'Shakuntalā', Tagore shifts the union to a different plane. Bankimchandra had written a memorable essay in 1875 comparing Shakuntala to Shakespeare's Miranda and Desdemona. Tagore agrees with Goethe that Shakuntala is different from Miranda in uniting youth and maturity in her nature. Tagore had translated Shakespeare in his earlier years and had alluded to him many times. His admiration for Shakespeare notwithstanding, he felt Kalidasa passed the test of *sahitatwa* (union) better. 'In *The Tempest*, man has not extended himself into the universe in a beneficent bond of love, and thus grown great; he has tried to become lord of the universe by curbing and oppressing it.'[40]

Tagore's discrepant statements stemmed partly from his restless versatility, pursuing disparate texts and approaches at almost the same time. Take the essay 'Grāmyasāhitya' (Rural Literature), written just five years before 'Rāmāyan'. Tagore was perhaps the first critic in Bengal to see that rural literature was not 'rural' because of its subject matter, but for being the collective production of a community, even when a text can be attributed to an individual author. Its naïve nature, like that of the children's rhymes discussed in 'Chhelebhulāno chharhā' (Children's Rhymes), was related to its expression of love and pleasure unconfined by codified religion. Instances are the traditional Bengali rural verses about Krishna and Rādhā or Shiva and Pārvati. Manu's writ does not run there: Tagore was never conservative enough to abandon his creed of aesthetic freedom.

Ādhunik sāhitya contains Tagore's assessments of his precursors and near-contemporaries. 'Bihārilal', his tribute to Bihārilal Chakrabarti as the first modern lyric poet in Bengali, surprisingly ignores the devotional lyrics of Rāmprasād Sen (*c.*1720–81), the songs of Rāmnidhi Gupta (1741–1839), and the more recent lyrical *oeuvre* of Michael Madhusudan Datta.[41] What appealed to Tagore was that Biharilal's inward-looking verse worked more through suggestion than statement, leaving the reader's imagination free. Tagore was quick to see that Biharilal, like Michael, showed in his long stanzaic poem *Sāradāmangal* (1870–9) that Bengali, lacking long vowels, relied on conjunct consonants for metrical variation.[42]

Ādhunik sāhitya includes reviews and essays on writers as different as the historian-turned-novelist Shibnāth Shāstri and the dramatist Dwijendralāl Rāy, and on scholars like Akshaykumār Maitreya and Abdul Karim.[43] There is also an essay on Joseph Joubert. Tagore liked the French thinker's idea that there is a sublime uncertainty in the style of genuinely great writers. But the dominating figure in the collection is Bankimchandra. The essay 'Bankimchandra' is a classic tribute to Bankimchandra as novelist and as the creator of an educated reading public through his journal *Bangadarshan*. 'Rājsingha' is a brilliant analysis of the novel's narrative structure, although Tagore downplays the historical element. He emphasizes the historically minor characters, especially Zebunnisā.

What is it, then, that characterizes the historical novel? Tagore addresses the question in an 1898 essay, 'Aitihāsik upanyās' (The Historical Novel). He believes that the particular and contingent truth of history is less crucial than the constant or eternal truth of literature.[44] The novelist may be free with facts as long as he infuses the novel with the *rasa* of history, which is different from mere knowledge of facts. Both Scott and Bankimchandra are held to fall short of the ideal combination of the particular and the perennial that Tagore demands of the historical novel but does not clearly define.

Perhaps the finest essay in the collection is the one on Bankimchandra's *Krishnacharitra* (The Nature of Krishna). Bankimchandra wrote the book over the years 1884 to 1892; Tagore's critique appeared in 1895. Tagore deplored the educated Bengali's indiscriminate glorification of the Hindu past, attempting to compensate for the Hindu's political powerlessness by a false sense of superiority in social and religious matters. Bankimchandra's corrective, said Tagore, had been to demonstrate Krishna's historicity by subjecting the *Mahābhārata* to the protocols of textual criticism. Bankim's lucidity is sometimes marred by tirades against Indian superstition and intemperate digs at Europeans; but despite blemishes, Tagore sees *Krishnacharitra* as establishing the sovereignty of the intellect – a virtue in the critic that Tagore had occasionally underrated in the past.

Tagore was a world figure after the Nobel award of 1913. Hostility at home followed international renown. In 1918, he advised Pramatha Chaudhuri to ignore reviews in periodicals. Nearly all their authors, he deplored, were lacking in intellect: quote undigested bits from Dostoevsky, Ibsen, Maeterlinck, and Bernard Shaw, and Bengal hails you as a critic.[45] Tagore continued to comment on literature in letters and essays, but wrote formal criticism sparingly. One major essay that he wrote in 1932 for the magazine *Parichay* was 'Ādhunik kābya' (Modern Poetry), where he discusses modernist Western verse. Tagore had always read and translated European poetry, besides translating from Sanskrit, Hindusthani, Maithili, and, using mediate sources, Punjabi and Marathi. He had translated more than two dozen poets writing in English from Caedmon to Hārindranāth Chattopādhyāy, from Shakespeare to T.S. Eliot (including the latter's 'The Journey of the Magi').[46] He loved his Shakespeare, Wordsworth, Keats, and Shelley[47] and studied contemporary poets. He wrote an essay on Yeats ('Kabi yets', 1912), who wrote an introduction for the English *Gitanjali*. Tagore valued Yeats, who was yet to write his best verse, as a poet resorting to the well-spring of poetry rather than the modish world of letters. Tagore found more of Wordsworth than of Swinburne in Yeats.

On 12 January 1935, the seventy-four-year-old Tagore was writing to the modernist poet Sudhindranath Datta of his admiration for Wordsworth's poems and Lamb's essays.[48] Earlier, he had written on a staggering range of European writers including Dante, Petrarch, and Goethe.[49] He translated several passages from Dante and Petrarch and poems by Heine and Hugo.[50]

We learn from the essay 'Bihārilal' that as a child he had loved Krishnakamal Bhattāchārya's Bengali translation (1868–9) of Bernardin de Saint-Pierre's novel *Paul et Virginie*. Tagore's brothers Satyendranāth and Jyotirindranath knew French; Jyotirindranath translated Molière; his niece Indirā and her husband Pramatha Chaudhuri helped him with his own translations. Tagore had read Pascal, Gautier, Maupassant, Anatole France, Renan, and Amiel. He was translated by Gide and counted Rolland among his friends. He seems to have disapproved of Zola's novels[51] and Baudelaire's poetry.[52] Nor did he enjoy *Anna Karenina*.[53] However, he was admired and translated by Pasternak.

At the time of writing 'Ādhunik kābya', Tagore seemed anxious to defend himself from the charge of obsolescence brought against him by the fictional hero in his own novel *Shesher kabitā* (The Last Poem). On 6 January 1935, he complained to the younger poet Amiya Chakrabarti of a lack of universal appeal in contemporary Western verse. On 23 February 1939, he wrote to Amiya that the samples of recent verse the latter had sent him had reassured him that he was not that outmoded after all. However, he warned Amiya, Bengali poets must not lose the organic touch in trying to imitate Eliot, Pound, and Auden.[54]

In 'Ādhunik kābya', Tagore describes the 'modern' as a bend in time's river.[55] Romanticism was a turn towards self-expression. Modernism pretends to scorn sentimentality, what Eliot would call 'a turning loose of emotion'.[56] Tagore was unwilling to forsake the norms of *rasa* and *ānanda* in the name of 'science'. The scientific mind finds pleasure in inquiry, not in kinship of spirit. After a virtuoso display of translations, occasionally relying on memory, from Orrick Johns, E.A. Robinson, Amy Lowell, and Eliot's 'Preludes' and 'Aunt Helen', and a brief comment on Pound, the essay clears a space for Tagore's own poetic faith. He says that Eliot, unlike Bridges, has accepted the modern creed of ridding poetry of embellishments but has thereby let in a tawdry world for which Tagore cannot hide his disgust. Tagore seems unwilling to concede that the aridity of Eliot's urban landscape was the point from the start and presumably the source of his own admiration for Eliot. A turn away from genteel diction is welcome, says Tagore, but extreme hostility to the world rings false. He quotes from the ancient Chinese poet Li Po to argue that being dispassionate is the best recourse, though the virtue is not exclusive to European modernism, or best exemplified there. Europe may have achieved a dispassionate mind in science, but not as yet in poetry.

'Ādhunik kābya' is distant from the reviews and essays of Tagore's first phase and the collections published in 1907. His late views are dispersed in his correspondence with the Bengali poets and novelists he encouraged and argued with: Pramatha Chaudhuri, Sudhindranath Datta, Amiya Chakrabarti, Buddhadeb Basu, and Dhurjatiprasād Mukhopādhyāy. He was most relaxed when writing or talking to young members of his extended family or with Santiniketan inmates. On 8 April 1925, in a conversation with the poet and composer Dilipkumār Rāy, he remarked that songs were too culture-specific to be universal; hence European music was alien to Indians since they had not studied it like, say, Keats's odes.[57] He also suspected that the appeal of lyric poetry of a certain period would fade as conventions and idioms wore out. It was only when a text brought fully rounded characters alive that the possibility of renewed interpretations was ensured: Kālidāsa's *Shakuntalā* and characters from the *Mahābhārata* would outlast the lyricist's bag of tricks, he observed on 24 April 1941 to Rāni Chanda, the painter and writer trained in Santiniketan.[58]

Tagore passed away three and a half months later, on 7 August, having written four poems between 13 and 30 July. They were all lyrics, four of his best.

NOTES

1. As in 'The Problem of Self', *Sadhana*, *EW* 2:311; 'Saundarjya' (Beauty), *RRVB* 13:522; 'Bairāgya' (Renunciation), *RRVB* 14:352; 'Sāhitya' (Literature), *RRVB* 23:378.
2. *RRVB* 23:397, trans. by the present author in Rabindranath Tagore, *Selected Writings on Literature and Language*, ed. Sisir Kumar Das and Sukanta Chaudhuri (New Delhi: Oxford University Press, 2001), 270 (henceforth *SWLL*).
3. *SWLL* 267; *RRVB* 23:394.
4. *SWLL* 275; *RRVB* 23:370.
5. 'Bikār-shankā' (The Peril of Perversion), *RRVB* 13:478–9.
6. See *CP* 16:20–1.
7. *SWLL* 269; *RRVB* 23:396.
8. *CP* 5:149–51.
9. Rabindranath Tagore, *Nijer kathā*, ed. Amitrasudan Bhattāchārya (Kolkata: Mitra o ghosh, 2011), 234–5.
10. *CP* 16:161.
11. *SWLL* 181; *RRVB* 8:417.
12. J.L. Masson and M.V. Patwardhan, *Aesthetic Rapture: The Rasadhyaya of the* Natyashastra (Pune: Deccan College, 1970), 6.
13. 'Sāhityatattwa' (The Philosophy of Literature): *SWLL* 294; *RRVB* 23:435.
14. *SWLL* 141; *RRVB* 8:376.

15. 'Kābyer tātparjya' (The Significance of a Poem), *Panchabhut*, *RRVB* 2:610.

16. *SWLL* 152; *RRVB* 8:401.

17. *SWLL*, 153; *RRVB* 8:401.

18. T.S. Eliot, *The Use of Poetry and the Use of Criticism*, 2nd ed. (1933; London: Faber and Faber, 1964), 25.

19. Vladimir Ilyich Lenin, *Leo Tolstoy as the Mirror of the Russian Revolution (1908): Collected Works*, vol. 15 (Moscow: Progress Publishers, 1973), 202–9.

20. *RRVB* 6:632–8.

21. See Rāni Chanda, *Ālāpchāri rabindranāth*, 2nd ed. (1942; Kolkata: Visva-Bharati, 1971; rpt. 2010), 127.

22. Pierre Bourdieu, *Distinction: A Social Critique of the Judgement of Taste*, tr. Richard Nice (Cambridge, MA: Harvard University Press, 1984), 5–6.

23. 'Bhubanmohinipratibhā, abasarsarojini o duhkhasangini', *RRVB* 29:79–82.

24. Bankimchandra Chattopādhyāy, *Bankim-rachanābali*, ed. Jogeshchandra Bāgal, vol. 2 (Kolkata: Sāhitya samsad, 1954; rpt. 1998), 163–5.

25. *RRVB* A2:97–105, see especially 104–5.

26. 'Chandidās o bidyāpati', *RRVB* A2:110–21.

27. *Bankim-rachanābali*, 2:167–9.

28. See *RRVB* 29:82 and *RRVB* A2:73 respectively.

29. 'Bānglā chhander prakriti' (The Nature of Bengali Metre), *Chhanda*, *RRVB* 21:358–9.

30. Søren Kierkegaard, *Fear and Trembling*, tr. Walter Lowrie (Princeton: Princeton University Press, 1941), 79, 124–5, 131–3.

31. 'Bāngāli kabi nay' (Bengalis are not Poets), *RRVB* 29:206.

32. F.R. Leavis, 'Valuation in Criticism' (1966), in *Valuation in Criticism and Other Essays*, ed. G. Singh (Cambridge: Cambridge University Press, 1986), 277.

33. Rabindranath Tagore, *Chhinnapatra* (Scattered Leaves: Kolkata: Visva-Bharati, 1968), 13.

34. *RRVB* 23:418–20.

35. *RRVB* 5:503.

36. *RRVB* 8:354.

37. *RRVB* 9:559.

38. *RRVB* 27:272.

39. *RRVB* 5:510.

40. *RRVB* 5:528–9.

41. See the critique of Tagore's history of the Bengali lyric in Satyendranāth Rāy, *Sāhityasamālochanāy bankimchandra o rabindranāth* (Kolkata: Sāraswat Library, 1974), 284–5.

42. *RRVB* 9:418–20.

43. 'Jugāntar' (Shibnath); 'Ārjyagāthā' and 'Mandra' (Dwijendralal); 'Sirājaddaulā' (Akshaykumar), 'Musalmān rājatwer itihās' (Abdul Karim).

44. *RRVB* 8:447.

45. *CP* 5:240.
46. See *RRVB* 28:106–292, 30:53–91, 32:41–76, 16:95.
47. See Taraknath Sen, 'Western Influence on the Poetry of Tagore', in *Centenary*, 251–75.
48. *CP* 16:61–2.
49. 'Biyātriche, dānte o tnāhār kābya', 'Pitrārcā o larā', 'Gete o tnāhār pranayinigan': respectively, *RRVB* 29:138–52, 152–61, 161–70.
50. For Dante and Petrarch, see note 49; for Heine, *RRVB* 30:87–91; for Hugo, *RRVB* 28:275–7, 285–6, 30:86–7.
51. 'Patrālāp: Lokendranāth pālitke likhita' (Letters Exchanged with Lokendranāth Pālit) 4, *RRVB* 8:484–5
52. See Victoria Ocampo, 'Tagore on the Banks of the River Plate', in *Centenary*, 44.
53. *CPBLI* #3.
54. *CP* 11:135, 238–9.
55. *SWLL* 280; *RRVB* 23:420.
56. T.S. Eliot, 'Tradition and the Individual Talent', in *The Sacred Wood* (New York: Alfred A. Knopf, 1921), 52.
57. *RRVB* 28:785–6. Cf. a slightly different approach to the subject in Chanda, *Ālāpchāri rabindranāth*, 95–8.
58. Ibid., 95–7, 99–100.

21 Tagore's Aesthetics

JAYANTI CHATTOPADHYAY

I

Rabindranāth started writing critical and analytic pieces on literature and art from the very outset of his career. His first published prose composition, in 1876, was a review of three contemporary poetical works.[1] From that time till his death in 1941, his critical writings appeared in a steady stream alongside his creative works. In June 1941, some two months before his demise, he wrote his last critical essay 'Satya o bāstab' (Truth and Reality), first published in the journal *Prabāsi* as 'Sāhitya, shilpa' (Literature, Art). His critical essays comprise some hundred items. There are also countless remarks and discussions of literature and art in his poems, novels, short stories, and plays, even his letters and diaries.

Despite this abundance of material, there are some problems in understanding Tagore's views on the subject. The first and most fundamental might well be his distinctive style of writing. In 1881, he wrote in the essay 'Sangit o kabitā' (Music and Poetry): 'Reason at its height finds expression in prose, emotion at its height in poetry.'[2] However, he did not always follow this precept in his own work. Buddhadeb Basu (Buddhadeva Bose) once remarked that 'Rabindranath could not fully reconcile the roles of poet and prose writer: ... the clash between the two has done harm to his novels.'[3] The harm to his critical writings might have been greater, as they often do not embody the clear reasoned discourse we might expect.

For example, in 1926, at the convention of Bengali writers living outside Bengal, Amal Hom attacked the upcoming young writers, especially Modernists associated with the journal *Kallol*, as 'vacuous and lacking in taste'. Needless to say, those writers were vocal in their defence. As the protests mounted, Rabindranath (some say at the behest of Amal Hom and his supporters) wrote two essays admonishing the Modernists, 'Sāhityadharma' (The Inherent Nature of Literature) and 'Sāhitye nabatwa' (Novelty in Literature). The first wraps its critical message in an allegorical tale. A king's son, a general's son, and a merchant's son set out in search of a princess, or rather 'a truth called a princess'.[4] The general's son has the mind of a detective. He applies anatomy and physiology to his study of the princess's beauty and psychology to her mental qualities. But this analysis shows all women in the world to be the same: it is the path of inquiry, not of artistic appreciation. The merchant's son, in his turn, values everything in terms of gain, an approach that 'has neither inquiry nor emotion'. For him, the princess is judged by her utility, her skill in cooking and housekeeping. There remains the king's son. He has made the perilous journey for neither gain nor knowledge, but for the princess herself.

In other words, for Rabindranath literature has no external or material value: it can only be felt and valued in and for itself. But in the polemical context of the allegory, the young writers derided this indirect, trope-laden manner of expression. Nareshchandra Sengupta published a rejoinder titled 'Sāhityadharmer simānā' (The Boundaries of the Inherent Nature of Literature) in the journal *Bichitrā*, reworking Tagore's own title, where he attacks not so much Tagore's argument as the alleged lack of argument:

> Rabindranath's writings have never shown much by way of a clear conclusion in lucid language. His plain purpose is carefully concealed in a forest of charming, skilfully ordered rhetoric and poetic sentiment, conveyed through hints and gestures. It is thus impossible to make out his precise intention, unambiguously stated.[5]

Tagore's critical prose raises other problems besides this poetic and metaphoric style of discourse. Most of his writings are redactions of speeches and articles composed at different times in specific situations, often polemical. They are accordingly self-contained, without thought of what the writer might have said elsewhere; hence they show a great deal of overlap and repetition. Sometimes this results in the extension and enrichment of an idea after a long gap. For instance, in discussing the comic villain Bhnāru Datta in Mukundarām Chakrabarti's medieval mythological narrative, the *Kabikankan-chandi*, he writes in 1907 that the man is 'astute, selfish, and unflagging in his role of village busybody' – in a word, a thoroughly dislikeable character. Yet, says Tagore, he comes to life because 'he appears to us in a single integrated image, freed of all unnecessary trappings'.[6] The restrictively drawn figure acquires a paradoxical totality. In the introduction to the volume *Sāhityer pathe* (On the Road to Literature, 1936), he again refers to Bhnaru Datta. The external world, he says, combines the beautiful and the ugly, the noble and the trivial, but our insensitive minds pass it all by equally. Only its focused, concentrated treatment in literature arouses the sensitivity that enables us to define the world clearly in our understanding.[7] The same idea is elaborated over a span of twenty-nine years.[8]

At other times, there are inconsistencies or even contradictions in the use of specific terms and concepts over a period of time. Tagore's views on literary realism are a case in point. In the 1914 essay 'Bāstab' (The Real), he considers the reality of things to be a valuable resource of literature: 'The absence of the real is a kind of fraud.'⁹ Again, he writes in 'Sāhityatattwa' (The Theory of Literature, 1933): 'From infancy, humanity has derived pleasure from the direct perception of reality.'¹⁰ But in 'Sāhityer tātparjya' (The Significance of Literature, 1934), he rejects this value of the real: 'The eternal human is not realistic in outlook; the eternal human is a creature of thought', and literature deals with this eternal human.¹¹ To take another instance, his collection of essays *Ādhunik sāhitya* (Modern Literature, 1907) includes a piece on the medieval poet Vidyāpati's treatment of Rādhā. He does not explain how this relates to 'modern' literature. The term is taken in yet another sense in the 1932 essay 'Ādhunik kābya' (Modern Poetry). Scholars have noted Tagore's varying use of the term *ādhunik* (modern), with many shifts and inconsistencies. Yet they have found it possible to extract a consistent set of thoughts and principles on literature and art from this profusion. This chapter proposes to do the same, drawing as relevant on earlier studies.

2

Many scholars of Rabindranath's literary ideas see 1907 as a watershed. From 1876 to 1906, many of his writings in this field were assessments of particular works, the last being his review of Sharatkumāri Chaudhurāni's novel *Shubhabibāha* in the journal *Bangadarshan* in 1906.¹² The next year saw his collection of critical writings, *Sāhitya* (Literature).¹³ The first edition contained eleven essays; more were added in later editions, bringing the final tally to twenty-six. The essays in *Sāhitya* treated of general issues, often of a theoretical bent. Henceforth, Rabindranath's substantive literary criticism, in particular the development of his literary ideas, focused on such broader matters, though he continued writing reviews and review articles on particular works all his life.

Of the essays initially included in *Sāhitya*, only two, 'Saundarjya o sāhitya' ('Beauty and Literature') and 'Sāhityasrishti' ('Literary Creation'), date from 1907. The rest had been written and published earlier; most of those added in later editions are of still earlier date. Other early pieces, published in *Bhārati* and *Bangadarshan*, remained unanthologized, but even these foreshadow certain ideas that later assumed importance. For instance, the 1880 essay in *Bhārati*, 'Bāngāli kabi nay' (The Bengali Is Not a Poet),[14] denies that there can be any such entity as a 'silent poet':

> No-one can be called a poet without publishing poetry.... Ideas that have not been expressed in language cannot constitute poetry, and a person who has not expressed ideas in language is not a poet.[15]

In Bengali, both 'expression' and 'publication' are commonly indicated, as here, by the same word, *prakāsh*. Later on, this word, in the former and primary sense, became an important component of Tagore's critical thought. Again, he says in the same essay that imagination (*kalpanā*) is a chief ingredient of poetry, but 'powerful imagination by itself does not make a poet': it must be suitably trained and refined.[16] Two years later, in 'Chandidās o bidyāpati' in the same journal, he writes:

> The power to enter into one's own life, the life of others, and the life in nature is called the poetic faculty.... The imagination required to enter into the heart of something is called the poetic imagination.[17]

Nonetheless, it is in the essays in *Sāhitya* that Rabindranath focuses exclusively for the first time on critical and aesthetic issues, as the very titles of most of the items indicate. Two later collections address the same range of concerns, *Sāhityer pathe* (On the Road to Literature, 1936) and the posthumously published *Sāhityer swarup* (The True Being of Literature, 1943). These three collections are the chief source texts for his thoughts on the subject, though there is a great body of other writings not collected in his lifetime. The problem is that they do not offer a consistent, worked-out theory of literature. Nor did Tagore write any full-length work laying out his critical position *in extenso*. This was perhaps inevitable, for his impatience with systematic theory or critical principles is well known. He has himself acknowledged it more than once. As said above, most of the essays were written at different times in different situations, sometimes polemical; they do not look beyond their immediate context. At the same time, they are heavily tinged with his thoughts on other subjects: his aesthetics is inseparable from his views on spiritual and philosophical issues, in fact his total engagement with life, nature, and the universe. Despite this, or perhaps because of this, his writings on literature yield a rich set of interrelated ideas, most visibly conveyed by certain recurrent terms and concerns, treated sometimes briefly, sometimes at relative length. These terms thereby acquire a contextual or conceptual meaning beyond the everyday lexical sense. They offer the best means of entry into Rabindranath's concept of literature.

The first such term is *sahitatwa*, an abstract noun derived from *sahit*, 'with'. It means 'with-ness', 'togetherness', 'accord' – that is to say, in the terms used by Rabindranath in 'Sāhityer tātparjya', 'closeness' (*naikatya*) or 'coming together' (*sammilan*). Tagore uses this root meaning to explore the implications of the Bengali word for literature, *sāhitya*.[18] 'Bānglā jātiya sāhitya' (Bengali National Literature), his address at the 1895 annual meeting of the Bangiya Sāhitya Parishat (Bengali Academy of Literature), opens thus: '*Sāhitya* is derived from *sahit*. The etymological sense imparts a notion of unity to the word *sāhitya*.'[19] Certain classical Sanskrit rhetoricians had defined the *sahitatwa* of literature in terms of the accord of word and meaning. Tagore, however, takes it in a much deeper sense:

> It is not only the accord of idea with idea, word with word, work with work. *Sāhitya* alone can work the profound, intimate accord between one human being and another, between the past and the present, the near and the far.[20]

In the essay 'Bishwasāhitya' (World Literature), he extends the idea still further to the accord between writer and reader, the union of the 'human truth' (*mānabsatya*) inhering in their individual beings.

> Our innate faculties are given us only so that we can set up links with everyone. It is through this coming together that we become true and attain truth. Otherwise, whether I exist or not is a matter of no consequence.[21]

Going even further, literature can thus connect one reader with another, and thus form a bond between readers from different times and places – finally, all readers from all times and places. The most crucial benefit deriving from this union emerges in the 1934 essay 'Sāhityer tātparjya': it is a coming together for no external purpose, only to share the sense of a common humanity. 'Humans have to meet for many purposes; but they also need to meet purely for the sake of meeting, for *sāhitya*.'[22]

The second term, which we have already encountered, is *prakāsh*. Its basic meaning is the bringing out of what was absent or concealed, hence a divulging or expressing. For Tagore, the word means something more: what is expressed or divulged is the truth. The essay 'Sāhitya' in *Sāhityer pathe* opens by alluding to the trifold Upanishadic division of the nature of Brahma – truth, knowledge, and infinity – reflected in a trifold division of human functions that he phrases in English as 'I am, I know, I express'.[23] Human creative expression mirrors the expression of the divine in creation:

> If you can entirely surrender your mind to the universal flow and play (*lilā*) of expression (*prakāsh*), the surge of expression will be quickened within you: one light ignites another.... The artist's dedicated endeavour (*sādhanā*) is to receive this universal expression within his mind.[24]

This is linked to the notion of a shared human identity conveyed by *sāhitya*:

> The ennoblement resulting from a sense of union with others is the soul's treasure. Inspired by that union, humanity keeps expressing itself. Where a human is alone, there is no expression.[25]

Much earlier, he had clarified in an essay fashioned as a letter to his friend Lokendranāth Pālit that 'the end of literature is not to express the writer's individuality, but to express humanity.... The writer is only the pretext, the real concern is the human.'[26] He had therefore originally entitled this essay *mānab-prakāsh*, 'the expression of the human'. Or as he argues in another letter in the collection, the life of literature lies in the attempt to express the whole of humanity.[27] But this expression is to be sought for human fulfilment in and for itself, not to meet any material need:

> There is no impediment to human self-expression in literature.... Alongside the economy (*sangsār*) dictated by need, humanity constructs an economy of literature free of need.[28]

The much later 'Tathya o satya' (Fact and Truth) adds another new element to this idea:

> I give the name *rasasāhitya* ['affective literature', literature appealing to the sensibility] to the literary output resulting from an effort at expression that aims to give form not to my need but to my joy (*ānanda*).[29]

Ānanda (variously joy, delight, or bliss) is the third fundamental term in Tagore's aesthetics. According to him, our relation to the world is threefold: of intellect, of need, and of joy. The first generates power, the second applies this power to the reality of our condition, while the third enables us to know others and let them know of us. It is, therefore, through *ānanda* that we expand our beings. Hence too, *ānanda* must embrace the totality of our experience; we cannot restrict it to only a part:

> There is a difference between happiness and *ānanda*. Sorrow is the opposite of happiness but not of *ānanda*. *Ānanda* can readily absorb sorrow, as Shiva drank poison. In fact, it is through sorrow that *ānanda* fulfils itself and achieves perfection.[30]

Ānanda is both the origin and the end of literary creation, which achieves the goal of togetherness (*sahitatwa, sāhitya*) by means of expression (*prakāsh*) – though of course, togetherness is also a means and expression a goal of the creative exercise. The joy thereby attained is its own end:

> The culmination of expression (*prakāsh*) is joy (*ānanda*). It is thus pointless to ask whether *art* [using the English word] is of benefit to us.[31]

The fourth pivotal term in Tagore's aesthetics is *lilā* (play, sport). This too is linked to the absence of need. God has not created the world from any sense of need or lack but from the free play of his will and pleasure, solely to delight in realizing the infinite potential of his being. All creation is, therefore, the free joyful expression of his wealth of being. The human being feels an analogous impulse of joyful creative play. All other human activities are driven by need; only art and literature are born out of 'desire for the unnecessary', the desire for joy.[32] The artist who writes poems, composes songs, paints pictures or sculpts in stone is reflecting the *lilā* infusing divine creation.

> Our scriptures call the creator sportive, *lilāmay*.... The human being too is *lilāmay*. The history of that *lilā* is inscribed in human literature and *art* [using the English word].[33]

Another essay in the same collection links *lilā* to the togetherness of *sahitatwa* and *sāhitya*:

> It is through the imagination that we achieve a sense of oneness with all that is separate from us.... This play [of the imagination] is the human *lilā*: in this *lilā* is human joy (*ānanda*).[34]

Again there is the sense of the greatest fulfilment arising by cultivating that for which there is least need, for that very reason:

> The human task that can be called *lilā*, that is to say, that for which there is no need, gradually takes principal place, exceeding the pursuit of one's material life. That becomes the mark of human excellence.[35]

Besides these four pivotal terms, there are many other important concepts scattered through Tagore's critical writings. One constant premise is the opposition between the individual and all humankind. For Rabindranath, it is almost always the individual that creates; but beyond that circumscribed entity of the self is the vastness of all that remains, all that is 'not-I'. The individual cannot but be a slave to necessity, yet is endowed with a native impulse towards creation or expression. Art allows the individual to exceed the confines of the self, thereby comprehending oneself as well as connecting with other humans, other recipients of that art – not only in one's immediate milieu but across time and space, thus striving towards a timeless truth.

Ultimately, Rabindranath's philosophy of literature derives from his philosophy of life, in particular his faith in humanity. He holds the human mind to be inherently creative. This creativity is the field and means of human self-realization, of autonomy and liberation of being. That is why the concept of *prakāsh* or expression is so basic to his thought. He considers human potential to be infinite, hence human art and literature of infinite promise, with no predetermined bounds or rules. Through art, the 'I' and 'not-I' can merge in a totality of being, a perfect *sahitatwa*.

3

So far, I have presented Rabindranath's views on literature, only cursorily touching on their bearing on the other arts. Can they be applied more fundamentally to the two other arts he practised extensively, music and painting? What other factors enter into his concept of those arts? Do practitioners of various arts simultaneously bring the same mind to bear on them all? Are their basic assumptions similar, different, or even opposed? Bimalkumār Mukhopādhyāy, who investigated these issues in relation to Tagore, drew attention to the poet's observation, late in his life, that every art form is singular; the very singularity of each allows for exchange between them, giving to and receiving from one another.[36] Given Tagore's assumption of such interaction of the arts, Bimalkumar concludes that his views on music and painting can be deduced from his extensively stated views on literature, though he seldom discusses 'art' generally.[37] (When he does, he sometimes uses the English word.)

Without question, certain observations in Tagore bear out this interpretation. In an earlier 1903 essay also titled 'Sāhityer tātparjya', he finds music and visual form to be constituent parts of literature or poetry:

> To express in language what is beyond language, literature commonly mingles two elements with language, image (*chitra*) and music.[38] Pictures[39] can bring out what words cannot. There is no end to drawing pictures in this way in literature.... And needless to say, literature must have recourse to music in order to arrange words in metrical form.... Hence image and music are major ingredients of literature.... Image is its body, music is its life.[40]

On 25 April 1941, two and a half months before his death, we find him repeating the same idea in 'Sāhityer mulya' (The Value of Literature):

> In my youth, I named one of my books *Chhabi o gān* (Pictures and Songs). If one thinks about it, it will appear that the extent of all literature can be demarcated by these two words.[41]

Shankha (Sankha) Ghosh found the realm of poetry and the realm of visual form to come very close to each other in the late book of poems *Sānāi*.[42]

At the same time, Tagore has continually distinguished between literature, music, and the visual arts, compared and evaluated them against one another, and judged their relative merits and potential. As early as 1894, he observes in a letter that painting and music are pure arts, literature is not: 'Language is much more articulate than the brush or the voice; hence we mix many other things with literature. On the pretext of expressing beauty, we purvey information, offer advice, talk about all kinds of things.'[43] Twenty years later, he writes in *Jāpān-jātri* (Traveller to Japan):

> Painting belongs where the infinite is contained in the finite, song where the infinite is without bounds. Painting is the art of the realm of forms, song of the realm beyond form. Poetry is amphibious: it walks with painting and flies with song.[44]

Again, on 7 October 1924, he writes in *Paschim-jātrir dāyāri*:

> What we call song is the pure play of creative energy (*srishtililā*).... When the mind looks for the enlivening spirit (*rasa*) of this causeless,

purposeless play, it sits down to compose a song, like an emperor with no other employment.⁴⁵

He is talking about *gān* (literally 'song'), but he appears to have all music in mind, in fact 'pure' music without the addition of words. Later still, in the passage from 'Sāhityer mulya' cited earlier, he grants music and visual form still greater prominence, virtually defining literature in their terms. He almost seems to have lost faith in the independent power of words.

In many of these passages, Tagore is talking in the same breath of image and music, painting and song. But there seems to be a fundamental difference between his verbal and musical universe on the one hand and that of his paintings on the other. Barring a few youthful efforts, his engagement with the visual arts is confined to the last fifteen years of his life, when over 2,000 paintings of a highly unconventional nature flowed from his brush. Poetry and song, however, commonly in association, had been his mother element since childhood. In an early essay in the journal *Bhārati*, he writes that poetry and song are twin brothers.⁴⁶ The titles of some of his early volumes of poetry contain musical terms: *Shaishab sangit* (Childhood Songs), *Sandhyāsangit* (Evening Songs), *Prabhātsangit* (Morning Songs), *Karhi o komal* (Sharps and Flats); so do late titles like *Purabi* (the name of a raga) and *Shesh saptak* (The Last Octave). But though he continually composed poetry and song side by side, they do not always bear the same formal relation. There can be a perceptible difference in the tone and structure of poems and songs composed on the same day. Again, the same basic composition can assume different forms as 'read' poetry and as song, as though the first is facing outward to the world and the latter towards the inward self. But then again, the two streams commingle in a new synthesis in the *Gitānjali* period, in the volumes *Gitānjali*, *Gitimālya*, and *Gitāli*.⁴⁷

Can we postulate the same affinity, in either theory or practice, between Tagore's conception of the visual arts and that of either poetry or song? Dhurjatiprasād Mukhopādhyāy argued for an affinity, citing certain poems from *Prāntik* in support, chiefly for the way they reflect the unconscious.⁴⁸ Shankha Ghosh finds other poems, from *Rogshajyāy* and *Janmadine* (but not *Prāntik*), evincing the same primordial imagination as projected in the paintings, but nonetheless sees an essential conflict between the aspects of Tagore's genius that find expression in his poetry and his paintings: 'a conflict of himself with himself, and of himself with his times'.⁴⁹ This is closer to the position of art critics who have seen the paintings as Tagore's effort to break away from the accustomed course of his literary and musical creation, set by this time on a particular plane despite endless innovations.

But in his paintings, says Shibnārāyan Rāy,[50] he is entirely 'un-Indian, un-Bengali, un-Hindu', drawing on the contemporary European art of his day rather than on any Indian tradition. It is a fact that Tagore's paintings had an impact on European connoisseurs that his poetry, after a brief vogue, did not.

This does not mean that Tagore's paintings are unrelated to the thought and sensibility infusing every other aspect of his creative life, but it does mean we must define that relationship in a new way, perhaps without much reference to other contemporary Indian thinking on the visual arts. Tagore began to paint regularly from 1927 or 1928, after a build-up when he was working the deletions in his poetic manuscripts into doodles and moving on to stand-alone sketches. The Santiniketan artist Binodbihāri Mukhopādhyāy finds in these doodles a resemblance to the designs in African or Australian aboriginal tattoo art.[51] Their stark contrast of black and white (though a few manuscript sketches use coloured inks), and the imposition of one medium upon another, sets the stage for a bold and untrammelled innovation in the paintings that followed, a protest against conventional aesthetics that often finds vent in the grotesque and fantastic. Only a handful of pieces are conventionally composed and executed. For the most part they present bizarre birds and animals, anatomically distorted human figures, and landscapes with unfamiliar contours and lights.

The spirit of such constructs can range from pleasurable whimsy and fancifulness to irony, terror, and perturbation at the artist's own condition and that of the world. They suggest the 'artless' designs of child art and the surfacings of the subconscious. In his 1928 short story 'Chitrakar' (The Artist), Rabindranath describes the pictures drawn by Satyabati in secret exercises with her young son Chunilāl: 'animals not yet created by man, where the shapes of a cat and a dog might merge, or a fish be hard to tell from a bird'. The mother's own native artistic bent had been fed by the love of things 'without need and without cause'.[52]

But this unclouded, untrammelled freedom of imagination was overcast by the disapproval of Chunilal's mercenary uncle, who may be seen as a symbolic or at least a representative figure in this context. From 1935 onwards, sinister human faces begin to proliferate in the paintings, expressive of greed, hate, and suspicion, suffused with the artist's own irony and antipathy. Behind them we can sense the troubles of the age, the debasement of the human spirit and the 'crisis in civilization' that troubled Rabindranath more and more in his late years.

In a late song, the poet speaks of 'the ocean of peace' lying ahead.[53] Does this peace appear at all in the paintings? The manuscript of the song has a doodled sketch of a creature like a four-legged duck, even suggesting a dodo. It testifies to an alternative yet simultaneous creative energy – ironic, subversive, innovative. There are subterraneous links between the two aesthetic universes.[54] The late poetry too is marked by profound innovation, in ways often impinging on the vision distinguishing the paintings. Ultimately, the paintings do not simply disrupt that other world but extend, enrich, and problematize it. The ways in which this happens largely remain to be explored.

NOTES

1. 'Bhubanmohinipratibhā, abasarsarojini o duhkhasangini', *RRVB* 29:79.
2. *RRVB* A2:89.
3. Buddhadeb Basu, *Rabindranāth: kathāsāhitya* (Kolkata: New Age, 1955), 13.
4. *RRVB* 23:401.
5. Nareshchandra Sengupta, *Jugaparikramā*, part 1 (Kolkata: Firma KL Mukhopadhyay, 1961), 151.
6. 'Saundarjya o sāhitya' ('Beauty and Literature'), *RRVB* 8:397.
7. *RRVB* 23:356–7.
8. The example is cited by Shankha Ghosh, *Nirmān ār srishti* (Santiniketan: Rabindra Bhavana, 1982), 221.
9. *RRVB* 23:361.
10. *RRVB* 23:445.
11. *RRVB* 23:463.
12. Most of these pieces were collected in volumes 2, 3 and 5 of his 1907 Collected Prose Works (*Gadyagranthābali*) under the titles *Prāchin sāhitya* (Ancient Literature), *Lokasāhitya* (Folk Literature), and *Ādhunik sāhitya* (Modern Literature).
13. This appeared as volume 4 of the *Gadyagranthābali*.
14. In the collection of Tagore's youthful writings later 'withdrawn from circulation' (*achalita sangraha*), this essay is entitled 'Nirab kabi o ashikshita kabi' (The Silent Poet and the Untrained Poet).
15. *RRVB* 29:201.
16. Ibid.
17. *RRVB* A2:110.
18. *RRVB* 23:451.
19. *RRVB* 8:415.
20. Ibid.
21. *RRVB* 8:372.
22. *RRVB* 23.451.
23. *RRVB* 23:375.
24. *Paschim-jātrir dāyāri* (Diary of a Traveller to the West), *RRVB* 19:451.
25. 'Sāhitya' (Literature), *RRVB* 23:375–6.

26. 'Patrālāp' (Exchange of Letters), RRVB 8:487.
27. Ibid., RRVB 8.479.
28. 'Bishwasāhitya', RRVB 8:382.
29. RRVB 23:382.
30. 'Dui ichchhā' (Two Desires), RRVB 26:499.
31. 'Sāhitya', RRVB 23:381.
32. 'Dui ichchhā', RRVB 26:499.
33. Sāhityer pathe, dedicatory epistle, RRVB 23:358.
34. 'Sāhityer tātparjya', RRVB 23:456.
35. Mānusher dharma (The Religion of Man), RRVB 20:377. These Kamalā Lectures, delivered at Calcutta University in 1933, are different from the 1930 English work with a synonymous title.
36. 'Rupshilpa' (Visual Art), Prabāsi, Asharhh 1346 (*June 1939); quoted in Bimalkumar Mukhopadhyay, Rabindranandantattwa (1972; rpt. Kolkata: Dey's, 1991), 318–19.
37. Ibid., 325.
38. Here and later, sangit is translated as 'music' and gān as 'song'.
39. Here and later, chhabi is translated in its primary sense of a picture or painting, though Tagore's ideas can usually apply to all visual arts.
40. RRVB 8:341.
41. RRVB 27:277.
42. Shankha Ghosh, 'Ekti raktim marichikā', in E āmir ābaran, 3rd ed. (Kolkata: Papyrus, 1991), 83–4.
43. CPBLI #131, 18 July 1894.
44. RRVB 19:348.
45. RRVB 19:402–3.
46. 'Sangit o kabita', RRVB A2:91.
47. See Shankha Ghosh, 'Nibhrita prāner debatā', E āmir ābaran, 28–33.
48. Dhurjati Prasad Mukerji, Tagore – A Study (Mumbai: Padma Publications, 1943), 140.
49. Ghosh, Nirmān ār srishti, 98.
50. Shibnarayan Ray, Anihshesh rabindranāth (Kolkata: Renaissance, 2003), 157–68.
51. Binodbihari Mukhopadhyay, 'Rabindrachitrer bhitti', in Chitrakathā (Kolkata: Arunā, 1984), 291.
52. RRVB 24:227, 225.
53. Shesh lekhā #1, RRVB 26:39; GB, p. 866.
54. See Sukanta Chaudhuri, The Metaphysics of Text (Cambridge: Cambridge University Press, 2010), 194–6.

22 Rabindranath, *Bhakti*, and the *Bhakti* Poets

FRANCE BHATTACHARYA

The word *bhakti*, as a common noun, means the intense love that one feels for one's god, the supreme attachment to a divinity. This god may be the formless Absolute, infinite, and eternal – *nirguna*, without attributes or qualities. The devotee may also address devotion towards a god made manifest in human form, with a name and a mythology. The god is then *saguna*, with attributes and qualities.

In Bengal, Vishnu's incarnation Krishna has always been the object of the deepest religious fervour. At the end of the twelfth century, the poet Jayadeva composed the *Gita govinda* in Sanskrit in honour of Krishna-Govinda. Jayadeva was the initiator of a devotion to Krishna that coloured the whole of eastern Indian Vaishnavism with its emotional quality and lyrical beauty. Later, Vaishnavite poetry of a very high order was also composed in Bengali and in Brajabuli, an artificial language mixing Maithili and Bengali. The poets mostly wrote about Krishna's love affair with Rādhā, his beloved, and his play with the other *gopis*, or cowherd women, on the banks of the Yamunā. The eroticism was imbued with spiritual and mystical meaning.

These love poems composed during the medieval period, mostly during and after the life of the great mystic Shrikrishna Chaitanya (1486–1534), did not fail to move the young Rabindranāth. As a young man, he was moved to joy on reading a collection of ancient lyric poems composed by the poets of the Vaishnav sect. He writes:

> I was sure that these poets were speaking about the supreme Lover, whose touch we experience in all our relations of love – the love of nature's beauty, of the animal, the child, the comrade, the beloved, the love that illuminates our consciousness of reality.[1]

At the age of sixteen, he composed a number of poems, in the same vein and language as the medieval Vaishnav lyrics, which were collected (along with a few later pieces) as *Bhanusingha thākurer padābali* (1884). He published eight of the poems anonymously in the family magazine *Bhārati* in 1877–8 (and a few later), giving the impression that they had been composed by an ancient poet named Bhānusingha. The mature Tagore was not very proud of this work, but he did not disown it. He allowed it to be included in the main sequence of his Bengali works (*Rachānabali*) published in his lifetime, rather than among the early works later withdrawn from circulation (*Achalita sangraha*).

All his life, Rabindranath continued to be moved by the beauty of the Krishna story, not as a devotee but as a *rasik*, an aesthete. But he could not fail to value the philosophical content of the myth. In his Santiniketan talk 'Sāmanjasya' (Harmony), he lauds the 'amazing courage and candour' with which Vaishnav spirituality proposes the idea that 'God has bound himself to the living being (*jiva*)': that is the 'supreme glory' upon which the latter's existence rests.[2] In the 1904 short story 'Boshtami' (The Vaishnav Woman), he recounts his encounter with a married Vaishnav woman who had to leave her village home because her husband's guru was lusting after her. She brought fresh flowers to the poet but did not allow him to discard the old ones in which she saw her beloved god. In *Creative Unity*, Rabindranath says of the real woman underlying this fictional character: 'I felt that this woman, in her direct vision of the infinite personality in the heart of all things, truly represented the spirit of India.'[3] He continues:

> The Vaishnav religion ... carries the same message: God's love finding its finality in man's love. According to it, the lover, man, is the complement of the Lover, God, in the internal love drama of existence.[4]

However, Rabindranath did not care for the purely emotional *bhakti* of some of Chaitanya's later disciples. In another Santiniketan talk, he condemns the sentimental intoxication of such devotees. He writes to Hemantabālā Debi, an aristocratic lady of Vaishnav faith, decrying her selfish devotion and urging her to bring relief to Kolkata's poor rather than play with an idol in her closed room, priding herself in 'the indulgence of emotive *rasa* on the pretext of religion'. This kind of devotion has weakened India, he continues. 'I say: Enough of devotion, enough of rites. Let us obtain true divine favour by serving humanity.'[5]

Despite his great debt to Vaishnav poetry and tradition, especially in his earlier period, Rabindranath's *bhakti* is more akin to the *sādhanā* or spiritual quest of *nirguna* devotees. The Bhakti Movement of the fifteenth to seventeenth centuries produced a number of holy men and women (*sants*), who were also poets of a high order. The one who most engaged Tagore was Kabir, a fifteenth-century Muslim weaver and family man who lived most of his life at Vārānasi. Among the other male poets were Nāmdev, Dādu,

Dadu's disciple Rajjab, Ravidās, and Nānak, the first Sikh guru; among the women, Mirābāi, Janābāi, Lālleshwari (Lāl Ded) and, of considerably earlier date, Andāl. Rabindranath asked his friend Kshitimohan Sen, professor at Santiniketan and founder of its Hindi Bhavana, to collect Kabir's songs. In 1910–11, Kshitimohan toured the whole of north India and collected many such verses, mostly from oral transmission. Rabindranath himself translated *One Hundred Poems of Kabir*,[6] published in 1915 by Macmillan with an introduction by Evelyn Underhill, an English writer on spiritual topics. Later, he wrote an essay on the north Indian mystic poets as the introduction to Kshitimohan's compilation of Dadu's works (1935).[7]

Since receiving the Nobel Prize in 1913 for the English *Gitanjali*, Rabindranath became known in the West as a religious poet. Whether in *Gitānjali* (Bengali and English) or other poetical collections before and after, such as *Naibedya, Kheyā, Gitimālya,* and *Gitāli;* in his talks at Santiniketan; in his lectures in the United States published as *Sadhana: The Realisation of Life* (1913); in *The Religion of Man,* his 1930 Hibbert Lectures at Oxford; the synonymously titled *Mānusher dharma,* his 1933 Kamalā Lectures at Calcutta University; or in his translations of Kabir, Rabindranath voices his deep spiritual engagement, where the *bhakti* poets were a considerable presence. Kshitimohan Sen's article 'Dadu and the Mystery of Form', from the *Visva-Bharati Quarterly,* was reprinted as the third appendix to *The Religion of Man.* But it was Kabir whom Rabindranath appreciated the most among all the north Indian *sant*s. The spirituality of the poems of the *Gitānjali* period has much in common with the utterances of Kabir.

The French scholar Charlotte Vaudeville doubts the authenticity of many songs collected by Kshitimohan and feels that Rabindranath has added much of his own in his translations of Kabir. The American scholar J.S. Hawley concludes that the several thousand songs now attributed to Kabir are a construction of collective memory.[8] Leaving aside the question of authenticity, our essential concern is the deep agreement between the medieval *sant* and the modern Bengali poet. For both, all religions have only one aim: union with the divine. Kabir denies all value to theologies, rituals, priests, pilgrimages, and places of worship. For him, these are only outward forms, whereas true religious revelation is an individual experience. His religion is a pure monotheism: he is accounted a follower of the *nirguna* school. The Rāma to whom he, the originally Muslim poet, ceaselessly prays is not the hero of the *Rāmāyana* but the invisible and eternal Absolute, both immanent and transcendent. According to an ancient tradition, Kabir became the disciple of Rāmānanda, a south Indian brahmin who advocated the philosophical path of the *vishishtadvaita* or qualified non-dualism.

Rabindranath, though born into the Brahmo Samaj, refused, like Kabir, to be bound to a sect with its texts, rituals, and set beliefs:

> Leave this chanting and singing and telling of beads! ... Open thine eyes and see thy God is not before thee!
>
> He is there where the tiller is tilling the hard ground and where the path-maker is breaking stones.[9]

According to him, all human beings, whatever be their country, caste, or social origin, can experience within themselves the divine presence by pursuing their *sādhanā* or spiritual quest:

> the ultimate truth in man is ... in his illumination of mind, in his extension of sympathy across all barriers of caste and colour; in his recognition of the world ... as a habitation of man's spirit, with its eternal music of beauty and its inner light of the divine presence.[10]

He explains his position in *The Religion of Man*:

> The vision of the Supreme Man is realized by our imagination, but not created by our mind. More real than individual men, he surpasses each of us in his permeating personality which is transcendental.[11]

The divine essence 'is definite and finite at the same time, the Eternal Person manifested in all persons'.[12] Rabindranath calls this Person 'the infinite ideal of Man towards whom men move in their collective growth, with whom they seek their union of love as individuals, in whom they find their ideal of father, friend and beloved'.[13] He often calls his god *satya*, both Truth and Reality, the *nirguna* seeker's name for the Absolute; at other times, the god is a friend, as eager for a meeting as the poet. The divine friend is a solitary wayfarer in a rainy, deserted landscape: 'Oh, my only friend, my best beloved, the gates are opened in my house – do not pass like a dream.'[14]

Tagore was not a pietist, lost in meditation. After describing the *sādhanā* of the pure non-dualists, he observes: 'But such an ideal of the utter extinction of the individual separateness has not a universal sanction in India. There are many of us whose prayer is for dualism so that for them the bond of devotion with God may continue forever.'[15] Often, he advocates the life of a *karmayogi*, one who seeks spiritual fulfilment through work in the world, and writes: 'I am sure that it was this idea of the divine Humanity unconsciously working in my mind, which compelled me to come out of the seclusion of my literary career and take my part in the world of practical activities.'[16] He did not agree to call religion 'the endeavour ... to merge completely [one's] individual personal self in an impersonal entity which is without any quality or definition'.[17] But as his letter to Hemantabala Debi indicates, he did not approve either of a purely emotional *bhakti* that takes its devotees away from the affairs of the world, blinds their intelligence and makes them forget themselves by indulging in devotional *rasa,* the flow of emotions. He derives his definition of a religious life from his favourite Upanishad: 'As the Ishopanishat declares, a man must live his full term of life and work without greed, and thus realize himself in the Being who is in all beings. This means that he must reveal in his own personality the Supreme Person by his disinterested activities.'[18]

Kabir was of the same opinion. Like Tagore, he does not think that one should leave one's home to find the Lord:

> In the home is the true union, in the home is enjoyment of life: why should I forsake my home and wander in the forest? ...
>
> The home is the abiding place.... So stay where you are, and all things shall come to you in time.[19]

He draws a caustic portrait of a yogi who 'dyes his garments, instead of dyeing his mind in the colours of love'.[20] So does Rabindranath write in that magnificent poem, *Naibedya* 30:

> Deliverance is not for me in renunciation....
>
> No, I will never shut the doors of my senses. The delights of sight and hearing and touch will bear thy delight.[21]

The vein continues even more strongly in *Gitimālya*:

> Who is it that scatters love with both hands from the skies? Its light spreads from world to world.[22]

The beauty of nature played an important part in awakening Rabindranath's spirituality. His first decisive religious experience was at the age of twenty-one, when he felt 'the sudden expansion of my consciousness in the super-personal world of man'.[23] The poem 'Nirjharer swapnabhanga' (The Awakening of the Waterfall) expresses his feelings after this momentous happening. He describes another such epiphanic experience in *The Religion of Man*:

I felt sure that some Being who comprehended me and my world was seeking his best expression in all my experiences, uniting them into an ever-widening individuality which is a spiritual work of art.[24]

Rabindranath's spiritual life was fostered by natural beauty, but the sustaining force was ethical: a fight against the five enemies of anger, pride, lust, ignorance, and greed, from which Kabir also seeks release.[25] Rabindranath is convinced that a proud ego will never reach the Lord:

He whom I enclose with my name is weeping in this dungeon. I am ever busy building this wall all around; and as this wall goes up into the sky day by day I lose sight of my true being in its dark shadow.[26]

Humbly, he prays: 'Let only that little be left of me whereby I may name thee my all.'[27] For Kabir, too, the greatest enemy is the same: the ego, the individual self that must be defeated and made to vanish before the union with the real Self can take place:

There one loses one's self at His feet....
The lover is never slow in offering his head for his Lord's service.[28]

Tagore is equally aware that this ego always follows the 'I' and 'adds his loud voice to every word that I utter'.[29] The soul, different from the ego, is the great principle of unity in every man: 'When we are conscious of our soul, we perceive the inner being that transcends our ego and has its deeper affinity with the All.'[30] This transcending of the ego is possible through love, *prem*: love for nature, for humanity as a whole, and for the infinite Brahman. This love which is not that of our individual self is the source of *ānanda*, joy.

At times, both Tagore and Kabir speak a monistic language, stressing the fundamental identity of the Absolute and of man: 'The creature is in Brahma, and Brahma is in the creature: they are ever distinct, yet ever united.'[31] At other times, both poets address the Infinite Being in the manner of dualist (*dvaitavādi*) devotees, who see the divine entity as distinct from the human soul; hence the poet addresses God as father, friend, or beloved. They can speak as a woman in love mourning the absence of her beloved. Says Kabir:

A sore pain troubles me day and night, and I cannot sleep;

I long for the meeting with my Beloved, and my father's house gives me pleasure no more.[32]

and Rabindranath:

> Clouds heap upon clouds and it darkens. Ah, love, why dost thou let
> me wait outside at the door all alone? ...
> I keep gazing on the far-away gloom of the sky, and my heart wanders
> wailing with the restless wind.[33]

But there can also be a tumultuous union of the soul with the divine, a
tryst where the impact of the Vaishnav poets comes out in passionate self-
surrender:

> The storm tosses away my veil from my face: I cannot draw it back.
> My modesty is lost, my garments swept away.... Let all that I have
> be scattered in the night sky; let the utterance of my heart sound
> amidst this tumult, defying all bonds.[34]

In poems like this, it is the yearning soul that seeks the divine. But Tagore's
work abounds in poems (often songs) where the lover, implicitly the deity,
comes to the beloved, seeking union:

> You have come to me hidden in the darkness of night, My Friend!
> You draw me to your bosom with your firm strong hands, My Joy![35]

Biraha, the longing consequent on absence or separation, and *milan,*
union, are essential moments in this spiritual love-quest. In Rabindranath,
biraha is voiced as often as *milan,* because he feels his pride or conceit
prevents him from attaining the vision. But he is sustained by the thought
that God too loves man and needs him. Love is as essential to the Creator as
to the creature: 'Thus it is that thy joy in me is so full. Thus it is that thou
has come down to me. O thou lord of all heavens, where would be thy love if
I were not?'[36] Hence *biraha* or separation, too, can be a fulfilling experience:

> My body thrills, my eyes grow languorous.... With what deception,
> today, does joy wish to shed tears; separation grows sweet and fills
> my heart.[37]

If such love exists, the Absolute divinity cannot be a mere concept.
Rabindranath did not value love for a divine Person who, though seen as
beyond an individual, yet is given a biography with precise happenings and
circumstances. For him, such myths diminish the divine. Rather, he sees

the soul as the great principle of unity within every man. Alluding to the ancient sages, he writes:

> These ancient seers felt in the serene depth of their mind that the same energy, which vibrates and passes into the endless forms of the world, manifests itself in our inner being as consciousness; and there is no break in unity.[38]

Unity is a key word in Rabindranath's vocabulary: unity among humankind transcending caste and nation, unity between the individual human being and nature, and, above all, unity between the individual self and the Absolute.

Like Kabir who often hears the 'unstruck music'[39] that the true guru makes him hear, Rabindranath hears sounds played on various instruments and does not forget that he himself is a singer. He humbly admits that he has no other part to play in this world: 'I am here to sing thee songs.... In thy world I have no work to do.'[40] Sometimes it is the Master who sings while the disciple wonders: 'I know not how thou singest, my master! I ever listen in silent amazement.'[41] But when he should be the singer, he does not always succeed: 'The song that I came to sing remains unsung to this day. I have spent my days in stringing and in unstringing my instrument.'[42] He can only hope that when his last hour comes, he will not be found wanting: 'Let all the strains of joy mingle in my last song ... the joy that sets the twin brothers, life and death, dancing over the wide world ... and the joy that throws everything it has upon the dust, and knows not a word.'[43]

Besides the saint-poets of the Bhakti Movement, the Bāuls of Bengal were another set of devotees that attracted Rabindranath. They sang their love for the Man of the Heart, *maner mānush*, on the village paths. Their freedom from social and religious rules, their simple way of life in nature, and the beauty of their songs moved the poet. He did not probe their secret practices but took from them, as from the other proponents of *bhakti*, what he could appreciate and set aside the rest. An essay on the Bauls by Kshitimohan Sen, reprinted from the *Visva-Bharati Quarterly*, was appended to *The Religion of Man*. In chapter 7 of the main work, entitled 'The Man of My Heart', Tagore writes of his personal encounter with a Baul:

> [W]hat struck me in [his] simple song was a religious expression that was neither grossly concrete, full of crude details, nor metaphysical in its rarified transcendentalism. At the same time it was alive with an emotional sincerity. It spoke of an intense yearning of the heart

for the divine which is in Man and not in the temple, or scriptures, in images and symbols.[44]

Baul songs provide Tagore with a staple ingredient of his own songs, in form and structure even more than in content. But the content, too, constitutes a prominent vein of his spiritual songs, with a homely simplicity conveying a rare spontaneous mysticism. The *maner mānush* also comes like a lover, and union with him is tinged with *biraha*:

> He is the man of the heart, why do you keep him waiting at the door of your eyes? Call him to your breast, let your eyes flow with tears. When night has come and the lamps have burnt out, lay out a couch for him in your heart....[45]

The opening of the novel *Gorā* describes a Baul singing that his heart is like a cage where an unknown bird comes and goes; he wishes to bind it with bands forged in his mind. Binay wishes to call the Baul and learn the song from him but desists out of lethargy – a missed opportunity he later regrets. Maybe Rabindranath felt the same regret at not meeting Lālan, the greatest of the Bauls, who lived on the Tagore estates in east Bengal. But thanks to the poet and his friend Kshitimohan Sen, educated Bengali society discovered the Baul singers, as also the great *bhakta* Kabir and the other *sants*.

In a foreword to Kshitimohan Sen's *Medieval Mysticism of India*, Rabindranath analyses what is for him the nature of India's spiritual endeavour (*sādhanā*):

> But India has a *sādhanā* of her own and it belongs to her innermost heart.... [I]t does not glide along any embankment of scriptural sanctions, and the influence of scholasticism on it, if any, is very small..... [Nor is it] controlled by social laws of any kind. Its spring is within the innermost heart of the people whence it has gushed forth in its spontaneity and broken through the barriers of rules, prescriptive as well as proscriptive.
>
> Most of the persons from whose heart this spring has come forth belong to the masses and whatever they have realised and expressed was "not by means of intellect or much learning of the sacred lore" (*na medhayā na bahunā śrutena*).[46]

In the last chapter of *Sadhana*, entitled 'The Realization of the Infinite', Tagore defines what the worship of God means for him:

So our daily worship is not really the process of gradual acquisition of Him, but the daily process of surrendering ourselves, removing all obstacles to union and extending our consciousness of Him in devotion and service, in goodness and in love.[47]

In *Naibedya* #99, the poet offers a humble prayer that he might complete this process, accomplishing all that he needs to do before meeting his Lord:

Give me the strength lightly to bear my joys and sorrows.
Give me the strength to make my love fruitful in service.
Give me the strength never to disown the poor or bend my knees
    before insolent might.
Give me the strength to raise my mind high above daily trifles.
And give me the strength to surrender my strength to thy will with
    love.[48]

Here the poet's spirituality attains to the universal. Any believer of any faith could recite this prayer to his god without changing a word.

My account indicates what Tagore thought and felt in his mature years about the divine, and the world created by and infused with that divinity. The poet seems to be generally at peaceful harmony with himself and his Absolute – at times, overcome by an immense joy. But his life did not end in 1910–12 when he composed *Gitānjali*, nor in the 1930s when he wrote *The Religion of Man* and *Mānusher dharma*. Rabindranath died only in 1941 at the age of eighty. He lived through the First World War and the beginning of the Second. He was a witness to the struggle for India's independence, and the growing religious conflicts in the land. In his last years, the poet feared what the future held in store for his country and for the world. These fears overcloud his last Santiniketan address, *Sabhyatār sankat* ('Crisis in Civilization').

In one of his last poems, he writes:

On the bank of the Rupnārāyan, I awoke; I understood that the world was not a dream. I saw my own form in letters of blood. I knew myself through repeated blows, repeated sufferings. Truth [*satya*] is hard: I loved that hardness, it never cheats you. This life is a painful ascetic quest till death, to earn the terrible price of Truth, to pay, in death, all debts.[49]

The poet stands firm in the values and beliefs that impregnated his life, but one misses the joy that pervaded his earlier encounter with *bhakti*.

The last poem of his life moderates this bleakness. It is addressed to a deceitful goddess who also partakes of the cosmic and the divine, who has filled the path of her creation with traps and wiles. However,

> by this deceit, you have marked out the noble of spirit.... Your star lights for him the path within his heart: a path ever-clear, made radiant by simple faith.... He finds truth within his innermost heart, laved in its own light.[50]

The last words of Rabindranath thus come to blend with the words of Kabir: 'The Formless is in the midst of all forms. I sing the glory of forms.'[51]

NOTES

1. *The Religion of Man*, ch. 6, 'The Vision', *EW* 3:127.
2. *Shāntiniketan*, *RRVB* 13:471.
3. 'An Indian Folk Religion', *EW* 2:523.
4. Ibid., *EW* 2:526.
5. *CP* 9:159.
6. The translations owe much to the earlier work of Ajitkumār Chakrabarti (see *EW* 1:623).
7. 'Dādu', *RRVB* 32:244.
8. See Charlotte Vaudeville, ed., *Kabir Granthāvali (Doha)* (Puducheri: Institut français d'Indologie, 1957); Charlotte Vaudeville, *A Weaver Named Kabir* (Delhi: Oxford University Press, 1993); John Stratton Hawley, *A Storm of Songs: India and the Idea of the Bhakti Movement* (Cambridge, MA: Harvard University Press, 2015).
9. English, *Gitanjali* #11, *EW* 1:46 (*Gitānjali* #119, *RRVB* 11:94).
10. 'The Poet's Religion', *Creative Unity*, *EW* 2:505.
11. *Religion of Man*, ch. 10, 'Man's Nature', *EW* 3:144.
12. Ibid., ch. 12, 'The Teacher', *EW* 3:154. 'Definite' is probably an error for the manuscript reading 'infinite'.
13. Ibid.
14. English #*Gitanjali* #22, *EW* 1:49 (*Gitānjali* #18, *RRVB* 11:18).
15. *The Religion of Man* (New York: Macmillan, 1931), ch. 14, 'The Four Stages of Life', 200–1. This passage is missing in *EW*.
16. *The Religion of Man*, ch. 12, 'The Teacher', *EW* 3:154.
17. Ibid., ch. 7, 'The Man of My Heart', *EW* 3:133.
18. Ibid.
19. *One Hundred Poems of Kabir* #40, *EW* 1:517.
20. *Kabir* #66, *EW* 1:526.
21. English *Gitanjali* #73, *EW* 1:68 (*RRVB* 8:30).

22. *Gitimālya* #108, *RRVB* 11:210.
23. *The Religion of Man*, ch. 6, *EW* 3:121.
24. Ibid., *EW* 3:122.
25. See *Kabir* #5, #17.
26. English *Gitanjali* #29, *EW* 1.51 (*Gitānjali* #143, *RRVB* 11:112).
27. English *Gitanjali* #34, *EW* 1:53 (*Gitānjali* #138, *RRVB* 11:108).
28. *Kabir* #55, *EW* 1.522.
29. English *Gitanjali* #30, *EW* 1:51 (*Gitānjali* #103, *RRVB* 11:79).
30. 'Soul Consciousness', *Sadhana*, *EW* 2:291.
31. *Kabir* #7, *EW* 1:501.
32. *Kabir* #31, *EW* 1:513.
33. English *Gitanjali* #18, *EW* 1:48 (*Gitānjali* #16, *RRVB* 11:16).
34. *Gitimālya* #19, *RRVB* 11:149–50.
35. *EW* 3:957 (*Gitimālya* #47, *RRVB* 11:170).
36. English *Gitanjali* #56, *EW* 1:62 (*Gitānjali* #121, *RRVB* 11:96).
37. *Gitānjali* #42, *RRVB* 11:35.
38. 'The Relation of the Individual to the Universe', *Sadhana*, *EW* 2:289.
39. *Kabir* #54, *EW* 1:522.
40. English *Gitanjali* #15, *EW* 1:47 (*Gitānjali* #31, *RRVB* 11:27).
41. English *Gitanjali* #3, *EW* 1:43 (*Gitānjali* #22, *RRVB* 11:21).
42. English *Gitanjali* #13, *EW* 1:46 (*Gitānjali* #39, *RRVB* 11:33).
43. English *Gitanjali* #58, *EW* 1:62 (*Gitānjali* #134, *RRVB* 11:105).
44. *EW* 3:129.
45. *GB*, 'Pujā' 548.
46. Rabindranath Tagore, foreword to Kshitimohan Sen, *Medieval Mysticism of India* (1930; rpt. New Delhi: Oriental Books, 1974), i–ii.
47. *EW* 2:338–9.
48. English *Gitanjali* #36, *EW* 1:53 (*RRVB* 8:73–4).
49. *Shesh lekhā* #11, *RRVB* 26:48.
50. *Shesh lekhā* #15, *RRVB* 26:50.
51. *Kabir* #47.

23 Tagore and the Idea of Emancipation

NIRMALYA NARAYAN CHAKRABORTY

This essay is an attempt to understand Tagore's idea of emancipation, locating it against the trajectory of Indian philosophy. In both classical India and ancient Greece, philosophy had a distinctly practical motive. Although many issues come up for scrutiny in the Socratic dialogues, for example, one particular question has an overriding presence: the nature of the good life, and the superiority of a good life over other types of life. The classical Indian philosopher, in his turn, is preoccupied with the search for an ideal life that is not fraught with the vagaries of mundane existence. The ideal life is to be reached by breaking all shackles of material bondage and freeing oneself from suffering of all kinds (twenty-one kinds, for instance, in the Nyāya school of philosophy). Indian philosophy is thus moulded from the beginning by the search for an ideal life.

This practical motive has left a distinct mark on Indian philosophical speculation. Classical Indian philosophical theories never lost their touch with this ultimate goal of human life. This perhaps explains why Indian philosophy never had any concern with formal logic in the way Western philosophy has. The age-old debate in Western philosophical tradition between experience and reason as sources of knowledge is conspicuous by its absence in Indian philosophy. This can be explained by the Indian philosopher's attempt to treat epistemology as a branch of the psychology of knowledge. In India, we therefore have the kind of metaphysical speculation that is 'almost a matter-of-fact study of reality',[1] where it is argued that reals are either perceived or inferred from perceptual data or known through some other accredited sources of knowledge. There are held to be reliable sources of apprehension even in matters of faith. And where normal inferential methods are not applicable, we can try to grasp the truths intuitively through some esoteric exercises.

This also explains why poetry and philosophy are never at war with each other, unlike in the West: a point forcefully made by Tagore in his presidential address to the first Indian Philosophical Congress in December 1925.[2] From this perspective, Tagore can be placed very much in the tradition of Indian philosophical inquiry. In his philosophical essays, Tagore explores some of the fundamental metaphysical issues of Indian philosophy.

In the commentorial tradition of Indian philosophy, commentators on early texts – even if they be the founding texts of a tradition – reinterpret their basic insights in the light of new questions and challenges. At times, the commentator breaks radically from other interpreters to found a new school. He brings in fresh insights to extant ideas, thereby offering a creative interpretation of the earlier text. I wish to show how Tagore accomplishes this admirably in presenting his idea of emancipation (*mukti*), an idea that has been debated by classical Indian philosophers for over a thousand years. He blends his poetic sensitivity with Upanishadic monism and, along with this, the Vaishnav yearning for a personal God. He combines spiritualism and humanism in his idea of a 'surplus' in human life, resulting in a syncretic idea of emancipation where man, the world and the beyond are woven into a single fabric.

Since Tagore is not a philosopher in the technical sense, he does not offer arguments for rejecting alternative views. He is an artist who looks at man and his surrounding world from his distinctive perspective. His ideas are steeped in his private feelings and intense realizations: he articulates in his writings whatever has been revealed to him through his personal experience. He accepts that many will not agree with his way of looking at things, but he pleads that he is not a logician making fine distinctions: he views the universe as a whole. 'I am a poet, I don't know logic. I see this world in its true and total identity.'[3] This holistic perspective is of profound importance in his thought. 'Harmony' (*sāmanjasya*) is a key word in Tagore's philosophy. Each and every element in this world is related to every other. Inanimate things, plants, animals, and everything else in nature are bound together in a grand unity. This sense of unison or accord is central to Tagore's philosophy of emancipation.

When we seek emancipation, what do we want to be free from? It is only in the state of liberation[4] that one realizes that there is a state called bondage. Our wrong knowledge and consequent craving for wrong or inappropriate things are the causes of bondage. Classical Indian philosophers generally hold that we want freedom from suffering. Almost all the ancient Indian philosophers talk about a wrong knowledge of 'I' being the source of suffering.

While accepting this general position, Tagore finds a positive element in pain and suffering that can actually aid emancipation. A person who has not suffered any pain has missed out on something important. The more one tries to avoid pain, the more one falls prey to it. Tagore exhorts us to embrace pain with a positive attitude. Truth can be realized only by welcoming pain.

I can bear still more pain, still more.... Let all my laments take flame, let the winds roar: rouse the whole sky and spread your fullness through it.[5]

In his *Gitānjali* phase, we find the idea that when suffering engulfs our existence, it disturbs our peace and slumber. Only then do we become conscious of the love that lies beyond and reach out to it. Thus freedom from pain is achieved not by evading pain but by living through it.

My incense does not give scent until it is burnt; my lamp does not give light till it is lit.[6]

That we do not grasp this is owing to our ignorance and restricted vision. Our small 'I' impedes our vision and stops us from assimilating ourselves to the total 'I' implicit in creation. This total picture of the universe would enable us to see our pain in perspective. Thus a perception of unity facilitates emancipation.

This comprehensive vision is advocated by another path. Like the silkworm, humans are entangled in the net they themselves create:

Like the silkworm, I weave a subtle net around me. I stay immersed in my own sweet darkness and do not see the gigantic life of the universe.[7]

The instrument of our bondage emanates from within us, and the path to salvation also lies within. The root cause of this bondage is, again, our ignorance of the unity of creation. When we blend with this unity that binds nature, man, and all creation, we attain emancipation. Such blending is achieved through love and results in bliss.

God, humanity, and nature form a triangle in Tagore's philosophy. The Upanishadic message of unity had a profound influence on him. Since his early days, he had an intense sense of affinity between his own being and external nature, a sense inspiring overwhelming bliss. He describes the visionary experience of his youth that led to the composition of 'Nirjharer swapnabhanga' (The Awakening of the Waterfall): looking out on a morning scene,

suddenly in a moment, it was as if a veil was removed from my eyes. I saw that the entire creation is covered with a splendid glory, waves of joy and beauty suffusing everything.... That very day, the poem 'Nirjharer swapnabhanga' began to flow like an actual spring.[8]

After that experience, says Tagore, nothing seemed to him to be undesirable or unloveable. The mundane world showed itself in a new light: from seeing only with his eyes, he came to perceive things with his entire consciousness, with an inwardness of vision. Our gross outward perception cannot grant us the vision of truth in its totality.

But Tagore emphasizes the relation that holds not only between humanity and nature but also within humanity, between one individual or group and another. As he says in another poem from this time, 'How my heart has opened up today: the whole world comes to embrace there.'[9] He relates himself to people of all kinds: being with people, working with people, feeling an accord with them. When he fails to achieve it, he feels a sense of loss or failure. The human being wants a response to his yearning, which is available only from fellow humans. So meditating in seclusion does not bring about emancipation.

Since truth is to be realized in and through its infinitely various manifestations in creation, truth defies any particular form. In this sense, it is formless. At the personal level, Tagore realizes this truth when he feels himself in closest communion with the divinity within him, which he calls the god of his life or *jiban-debatā*; at the cosmic level, the same divinity permeates the minute recesses of all creation. Thus the opposition of externally and inwardly directed perception falls through. Whatever is outside is also inside: the inner and the outer mingle in one.

Tagore warns us not to rationalize these ideas. He is neither proposing any theory nor engaging in a debate between monism and dualism. He only rejoices in this affective perception, an all-embracing love and bliss:

> I have no command of metaphysics. I will keep silent during any argument about dualism and monism. I am saying only, on the basis of my experience, that my inner god finds bliss in being manifest in myself. This bliss, this love have overwhelmed my whole body, my mind, and my intelligence, my world that I perceive, my past without beginning and my future without end.[10]

Many Indian philosophers, including the Buddhists, argue that emancipation consists in freeing oneself from the circle of birth and death. Tagore takes a different stand. For him, *becoming* is the essence of emancipation. If emancipation inheres in apprehending the truth, that truth is not a static idea. It is a dynamic entity in a constant state of becoming.

> Liberation comes to many people in many guises, not in the same way. The nectar of fulfilment flows through the worlds in many flavours, many streams.[11]

Truth permeates all the various manifestations of becoming in every sphere of life. Truth is not a theoretical construct; it is the realization of the unifying force in creation, the universal self to which we attain by passing beyond the narrow, egoistic 'I'. As we have already seen in this brief account, Tagore returns to this idea of the expansion of the self through many paths, in many contexts.

If the divine manifests itself in this creation, the world of shape and form is not false. Motion – that is to say, displacement and transience – signifies the abundance of life. Tagore senses the presence of motion throughout creation and human life – indeed, even in death, for the stream of life flows from birth through death to eternity. In other words, this motion itself brings an end to the tenure of the small 'I' and facilitates its merger with nature and humanity in general. Hence motion is crucial for attaining emancipation, which is not a static condition. There is no finality in emancipation. It is always in a state of becoming.

All through his life, Tagore declares his love of life and the world around him: from the early expression in *Karhi o komal*, 'In this beautiful world, I do not wish to die but to live amidst humanity',[12] to the echo of the Rig-Veda in the late *Ārogya*: 'This sky is full of sweetness, full of sweetness the earth's dust.... The joyful manifestation of truth has taken form in this dust.'[13] Does this love not create bondage, narrowing one's vision to the mundane, immediate, and contingent? For Tagore, it does not: love, for him, is an expansive, unifying force that binds life and the world together. It takes us out of our narrow beings and enlarges our vision, transporting us from microcosm to macrocosm, from the finite to the infinite, from the immediate to the entire. His life and the surrounding environment intermingle in the intensity of love, linking him with the sun, moon, and stars.

> [When we see God] in his blissful manifestation (*ānandarup*) in the universe, ... we achieve an emancipation (*mukti*) that is not disaffection (*bairāgya*) but love, not renunciation but attachment (*jog*), not the surrender but the manifestation of identity.[14]

Losing this kind of love makes life meaningless. Without this love, everything is mere abstraction: 'If you have not given love to my life, why have you filled the morning sky with songs?'[15] This all-encompassing love inspires the realization of unity in which lies emancipation.

Tagore hears the music of liberation in the sighing of leaves and the movements of the stars. All creation is dancing in the waves of this sea:

> When the mind dances to its own music in many movements on the universal tide – in that rhythm is my bondage, in that my liberation.[16]

Thus Tagore discovers unfathomable bliss (*ānanda*) in liberation through union with the living universe.

> Emancipation lies on the shore of that great ocean of life, whose surface sways with the colourful waves of sportive beauty, and whose depths harbour *shāntam shivam advaitam*: the peaceful, the beneficent, the one. In that play of beauty there is no rapacity, no addiction, no inertness, only the sway of that great power's inexhaustible bliss.[17]

Discursive knowledge delinks humanity from the universe by inducing a sense of his separate and unique existence and of the elements of nature as equally separate and disjunct entities. But when truth dawns again in its totality, it reunites man with everything else. When man confines himself to his own narrow demands, he aspires after his own happiness. And then the conflict between good and evil, pleasure and pain appears. In this clash, man looks for his own good or well-being. But, according to Tagore, achieving this restricted good cannot be the ultimate goal: the *summum bonum* is to attain to a state of harmony. Life and death, pleasure and pain are equally the accompaniments of this state: they all have their roles to play. In this totality lies emancipation. Hence emancipation does not and cannot imply any loss or impoverishment; rather, it fosters a sense of totality and concord.

Unrestrained pursuit of one's own will does not lead to happiness. We are happy only when our will is in tune with that of others – in other words, when it fulfils itself in love. This sacrifice of will is an act of the will. Distinguishing 'sacrifice' from 'resignation' (he uses the English words), he writes:

> The Upanishads teach us not to accept sacrifice as a sorrow to which we pledge ourselves, but as something to partake of or enjoy. The sacrifice enjoined by the Upanishads is a fuller form of acceptance: there is in it a deeper joy.[18]

Hence Tagore distinguishes emancipation from freedom. Freedom (*swādhinatā*), for Tagore, is a political concept; it is located in a social and political space. Emancipation or liberation (*mukti*), on the contrary, marks the fulfilment of the individual: its sphere is the social in one aspect and the mental and ethical in another. Even where Tagore applies the word *swādhinatā* to the latter state, it is only to contrast it with political freedom:

> For India, true freedom is social freedom (*samājer swādhinatā*): the freedom to do good, the freedom to preserve our *dharma*.[19]

Mere political freedom, like that which Indians sought from British rule in Tagore's day, would not ensure this freedom of the spirit.

Hence, emancipation for Tagore is not anarchy. Defying all rules does not bring freedom. We seek freedom from the law only when we consider it an external imposition and feel enslaved by it. In the state of emancipation, laws are internalized and become part of our being – felt in the pulse, so to speak. They stop feeling like chains: the emancipated soul follows them of its own accord, as part of its existence, without having to be forced.[20] The free exercise of willpower whereby we subject ourselves to this discipline testifies to our emancipation: we realize the all-encompassing nature of the law and try to integrate with it. This can be called the unqualified aspect of emancipation. Placing oneself within this rule, the human being can then turn to creation through love and action. The greater 'I' now shines forth in him. This is called the qualified aspect of emancipation.[21]

That greater 'I', the One, has made himself subservient to rule by creating the world:

> Our master himself has joyfully taken upon him the bonds of creation;
> he is bound with us all for ever.[22]

To emulate divine creativity, we must make ourselves similarly subject to rule. Emancipation is creative, a condition of the artist reflecting that of the world artist. In *Shesh saptak* #8, the poet speaks of how ancient cave artists immerse themselves in their art, abjuring their personal identities, like the creator himself at work on the universal picture (*bishwa-chhabi*): by this immersion in their art to the exclusion of self, they afford the poet a taste of emancipation (*mukti*) from the illusory bond (*māyābandhan*) of personal names.

It is only when the strings of a sitar are placed and plucked in accord with a set of rules that melody results, yielding the truth in the sitar.

When the strings of a sitar are truly strung, when there is not the least lapse of principle in stringing them, those strings play music, and through that music the sitar transcends itself: it acquires emancipation (*mukti*). It is because it is firmly confined to order on the one hand that, on the other, it can be expansively liberated in music.[23]

If the mundane world cannot be ignored, nor can the actions performed in that world. Borrowing ideas from the Upanishads, Tagore holds that Brahman, the ultimate reality, is the cause of all beings; all the beings disappear in this reality; all the beings want to know this reality. This reality is the base of all actions. But then is not Brahman bound by the imperatives of his actions? Tagore would reply that there are two kinds of action: action arising out of lack and action arising out of plenty. Action merely to supply a lack or want consigns us to bondage; action performed out of a sense of plenty brings emancipation. The Brahman, while creating the world, keeps himself engaged in the world. The world-creating Brahman does not lack anything; his acts of creation are not undertaken from a sense of want, but a sense of bliss. Creation is his *lilā*, action not performed for any end but only for the sake of bliss, the pleasure arising out of a creative act. He has everything, and he wants to share that plenitude with all. He unfolds himself in the multiplicities of creation. When humans perform actions, it is to satisfy some lack, implying a state of bondage or victimhood. But when man relates himself to his action through bliss and love – for instance, by sacrificing himself for others' well-being – his action does not arise out of any lack. Such actions signify liberation, allying one to the all-pervading divine: human action merges with world action, leading to liberation and bliss.

This unison is also present in time, in the flow of life from one age to another. Even though individual lives are subject to constant change, there is an overriding continuity that unifies the entire evolutionary process. An individual human life gains value only as part of the great stream of humanity encompassing past, present, and future. Moreover, this flow of humanity is related to the cosmic flow, the movement of the heavens.

Since, for Tagore, a dynamic process of *becoming* is what constitutes emancipation, the prospect of freedom from the cycle of birth and death does not attract him. If we regard our very being in the world as a cause of pain, the creation of the poem that is this world by the world's great Poet would become meaningless. Instead of maligning this 'world poetry', Tagore asks us to grant that its music can lead us to emancipation.[24] The mundane world, instead of being the cause of bondage, then becomes the pathway to emancipation: the poison becomes the nectar. The idea finds classic expression in a celebrated song:

> My liberation is in the light of this sky. My liberation is in the dust, in the grass.... My liberation is in the minds of all, in hard acts that make light of sorrow and danger.[25]

Tagore recalls Buddha's exhortation to love and to practise compassion towards fellow creatures, thereby casting off the slough of the petty 'I' so that the great 'I' may shine through:

> Draw aside this veil of illusion, draw it aside. Let me see your beautiful face to my eyes' content. Look into my heart, O look.[26]

Once the veil is removed, truth shines in all creation and also within oneself. By breaking the illusory barriers of the 'petty I', we come to see the divine beauty that lies beyond it as immanent *within* us.

Since Tagore's emancipation is located in the world and not beyond it, he does not advocate asceticism: 'Liberation through denial – that is not for me.'[27] Denial or renunciation of the world carries no appeal for him. Since the world is the creation of Brahman, denying the world means denying Brahman. Rather, it is by comprehending the world in its totality that the individual transcends the addictions and limitations of the petty 'I' for the expansive knowledge of the greater 'I'. We return to the same recurrent premise: this becoming, this transformation of the petty 'I' to the universal 'I' is emancipation.

Tagore admits two paths to emancipation, the path of love and the path of beauty. Love is truth in the sense that love inspires us to constantly sacrifice ourselves. The creator is constantly sacrificing himself in his creation by manifesting himself in various forms, compromising his remote abstract perfection. The poet's *jiban-debatā* reaches out from his lonely throne to the music of the seasons and the life of the speaker.[28] Much later, in the poem 'Āmi' (I), the poet imagines how, after the annihilation of the cosmos, the creator, in a universe devoid of poetry, will recreate nature – an object to whom he can say, 'You are beautiful' and 'I love you'.[29] In other words, the divine act of creation is an act of love. Hence one can unite with this all-loving creator only through the path of love. Love makes one give up many things, and in this forgoing one finds bliss. This giving up is actually getting back something important: by this surrender, one realizes the greater 'I' within one.

Through evolution over time, life has manifested itself in an awe-inspiring variety of beauty, which, within humankind, has transformed itself into boundless love. Humanity has tried to unite with cosmic life through the pursuit of beauty, and to unite with the Universal Man through love. For Tagore, humankind has two aspects, the animal and the human. The animal existence appears in a concern with narrow selfish knowledge and action.

> That which distinguishes man from the animal is the fact that he expresses himself not in his claims, in his needs, but in his sacrifice, which has the creative energy that builds his home, his society, his civilization. It proves that his instinct acknowledges the inexhaustible wealth of a positive truth which gives highest value to existence.... For rampant individualism is against what is truly human – that is to say spiritual – it belongs to the primitive poverty of the animal life, it is the confinement of a cramped spirit, of restricted consciousness.[30]

To transcend animality is to achieve liberation, to escape 'the confinement of a cramped spirit, of restricted consciousness' – in other words, to achieve emancipation, passing beyond absorption in our immediate needs and interests. We can plunge into the pursuit of a higher ideal and face adversities in order to realize this ideal. This ideal humanity is projected by Tagore in the figures he calls the 'Great Man' (*mahāmānab*) and the 'Universal Man' (*bishwamānab*). These are Tagore's most powerful tropes for the divinity he finds in man: 'The idea of the humanity of our God, or the divinity of Man the Eternal, is the main subject of this book.'[31] This is the ideal moral hero projected in Tagore's last poem: 'He finds truth within him, bathed in its own light.'[32]

It is clear from this account that for Tagore, emancipation is not the final state that one could arrive at. There is a constant play of opposites in human existence, swinging to and fro between liberation and bondage. Only a poet could have realized such a notion. In the poem 'Muktitattwa' (The Doctrine of Emancipation) opening the musical spectacle *Natarāj riturangashālā* (Natarāj and the Theatre of the Seasons), the poet calls himself a disciple of Natarāj, the dancing Shiva.[33] That dance embodies a constant play of opposites, the bonds of all creation being girded and ungirded through time. In this dance, creation proceeds by accepting bondage. There remains nothing permanent to hold on to: with one dance step, the external world is evoked in all its variety; in the next, the inner world in its array of thought and beauty: laughter and tears, good and evil, birth and death alternate with each other. By participating in the dance of Nataraj, one realizes one's unity with the life-flow that runs through the universe. We come back to the same idea: this unison with the whole is emancipation. All the apparent binaries like birth and death, laughter and tears, good and bad, bondage and liberation meld in one indivisible flood of creation, ever manifesting itself, where the new is born and reborn eternally.

To summarize: for Tagore, emancipation results from the perception of unity with all creation. Expanding oneself into the great or the total (*bhumā*) results in emancipation. But this emancipation is not a final state; rather, it is an ever-unfolding disclosure. The liberated soul is constantly at move, proceeding on an unending journey.

An underlying assumption of all Tagore's writings on the subject is that the human individual is essentially liberated. Liberation is not an accidental quality of the human soul. But because of the veil put up by the small 'I', the individual fails to realize one's own essence in the greater or universal 'I'. That veil is removed only with the expansion of the indvidual's own small 'I'. Then and then alone can one see everything in its true nature, assessing one's acts in their true perspective: one could be one's own true essence.

The term 'emancipation' has a positive connotation. It does not merely imply the relinquishing of attachments, nor does it call for asceticism. Instead, it engages with the entire world in a different way. An emancipated soul links itself with its environment through bonds of love and beauty. Love of nature manifests itself in the appreciation of beauty; love of the creator manifests itself in action. Such action arises out of bliss (*ānanda*), the expanding of oneself in others. This is not due to any lack. Thus Tagore can be seen as engaged in explicating the idea of emancipation, an idea that has shaped classical Indian philosophical thought. But he brings in fresh ideas, ideas that are formulated according to his own poetic sensitivity and aesthetic perspective.

NOTES

1. Kalidas Bhattacharyya, 'An Outline of Indian Philosophy', *Bulletin of the Ramakrishna Mission Institute of Culture* 16 (1965), 93.
2. 'The Philosophy of Our People', *EW* 3:559–69.
3. *Rogshajyāy* #21, *RRVB* 25:24.
4. I am using the terms 'liberation' and 'emancipation' interchangeably.
5. *Gitānjali* #90, *RRVB* 11:71.
6. *Gitānjali* #91, *RRVB* 11:72.
7. 'Swapnaruddha' (Bound in a Dream), *Karhi o komal*, *RRVB* 2:99.

8. *Jibansmriti* (Reminiscences), *RRVB* 17:396.

9. 'Prabhāt-utsab' (The Morning Festival), *RRVB* 1:62.

10. *Ātmaparichay* (An Account of Myself) #1, *RRVB* 27:194–5.

11. 'Mukti'(Emancipation), *RRVB* 14:75.

12. 'Prān' (Life), *RRVB* 2:31.

13. *Ārogya* #1, *RRVB* 25:41.

14. 'Mukti', *RRVB* 14:446.

15. *GB*, 'Puja' #521. See also Kshitimohan Sen, *Balākā kābya parikramā*, 7th ed. (Kolkata: A. Mukherji, 1996), 149.

16. 'Pāntha' (The Wayfarer), *RRVB* 15:168.

17. Preface to *Banabāni* (The Forest's Message), *RRVB* 15:113.

18. 'Tapoban' (The Forest Retreat), *RRVB* 14:466–7.

19. *Ātmashakti* (Inner Strength), *RRVB* 3:553.

20. 'Niyam o mukti' (Rules and Release), *RRVB* 14:429–30.

21. 'Jagate mukti' (Emancipation in the World), *RRVB* 14:297–8.

22. English *Gitanjali* #11, *EW* 1:46 (*Gitānjali* #119, *RRVB* 11:95).

23. 'Karmajog' (The Mission of Work), *RRVB* 16:350.

24. 'Muktir path' (The Road to Emancipation), *RRVB* 14:446–7.

25. *GB*, 'Pujā' #339.

26. *GB*, 'Pujā' #423.

27. *Naibedya* #30, *RRVB* 8:30.

28. 'Jiban-debatā', *RRVB* 4:106.

29. *RRVB* 20:67.

30. *Religion of Man*, Appendix VII/IV (sermon at Manchester College, Oxford, 25 May 1930), *EW* 3:186–7.

31. *Religion of Man*, ch. 1, 'Man's Universe', *EW* 3:88.

32. *Shesh lekhā* #15, *RRVB* 26:51.

33. *RRVB* 18:195.

24 Tagore's Thoughts on Religion

SHEFALI MOITRA

I

When writing in English on Rabindranath Tagore's thoughts on religion, most scholars prefer to focus on his 1930 Hibbert lectures at Oxford, published as *The Religion of Man*. His second major work on religion, *Mānusher dharma*, the Kamalā Lectures at Calcutta University (1933), is an expansion rather than merely a translation of the former as its synonymous title might be taken to imply. The poet's ideas on the religion of humanity did not come to a standstill at this point: he continued to develop his ideas through the rest of his life. Some scholars even believe that he ultimately became an atheist, having arrived at a human-centric 'religion of Man' towards the end of his life.[1] Others think his position can be interpreted either for or against atheism.[2] There were shifts in his position both before and after the Hibbert lectures. He was constantly engaging with new ideas and insights across an expanding horizon of lived experience. All of this was factored into his religious sensibility without any break in continuity.

When the Brahmo Samaj, known as a neo-Vedantic institution, split into the Ādi Brahmo Samaj and the Bhāratvarshiya Brahmo Samaj in 1866, Rabindranath was five years old. His father Debendranāth Tagore led the Adi Brahmo Samaj. This group claimed that they were Hindus and that their reading of the Vedas was the authentic one, unlike the convoluted interpretation of orthodox practising Hindus of that period. Debendranath contributed to the development of a monotheistic religion based on the philosophy of the Upanishads. Rabindranath was initiated to the Upanishadic teachings by his father at an early age: he actively participated in all the religious activities conducted by his father at the Samāj. In 1884, at the age of twenty-three, he was appointed secretary of the Adi Brahmo Samaj. This started the first phase of his public engagement with religion. During this period his thoughts were traditional, with hardly any trace of individuality.

As secretary of the Adi Brahmo Samaj, Rabindranath was drawn into various debates of the time. A major debate took place with Bankimchandra

Chattopādhyāy (Chatterjee), the leading novelist, thinker, and public intellectual of the day. Bankimchandra argued that truth is related to the welfare of the people. What is not conducive to the welfare of the people is false, even though it may outwardly appear to be true. Rabindranath, on the contrary, claimed that Truth is not contextual but immutable. The exchange was about to take a bitter turn when Rabindranath silently disengaged himself from the controversy.[3] His faith in immutable Truth never faltered; yet at the same time, his position was unconventional, almost paradoxical, in that Truth, for him, was also dynamic.

After establishing his school at Santiniketan in 1901, his focus of responsibility shifted from the Adi Brahmo Samaj to his newly founded institution. At the turn of the century, with the increased intensity of the Nationalist Movement, leading thinkers veered towards Hindu conventionalism. Rabindranath was no exception. In the initial years of his school, he did not allow practices that were contrary to traditional Hindu rituals. Whether this diktat was motivated by conviction or by extraneous pragmatism is hard to judge. But from approximately 1907, Rabindranath began to move away from Hindu conservatism. This was when he started on the novel Gorā. In the final chapter of the novel, Gorā says, 'Today I am truly an Indian. There is no conflict in me between Hindu, Mussulman, and Christian. Today all castes in India are my caste, everyone's food is my food.'[4] There is scathing criticism of decadent Hindu religious practices in his play Achalāyatan (The Immovable Institution, 1912). In his response to a review article on this play, Rabindranath remarks that rituals are meant to help the growth and vitality of a religion; when a religion outgrows this need, rituals weaken and restrict its further growth.[5]

Always a champion of personal freedom, he describes in the Hibbert Lectures how he refused to accept his family orthodoxy and says he refused to accept an idea 'merely because people in my surroundings believed it to be true', and insisted on 'freedom from the dominance of any creed [sanctioned by] the definite authority of some scripture, or in the teaching of some organized body of worshippers'.[6] Hence his life 'has always realized its religion through a process of growth and not by the help of inheritance or importation'.[7] In Rabindranath we find a creative reception and commingling of elements from three sources: religious texts, intellection, and personal religious experience. The end result is in no way eclectic. It is an accomplished synthesis, every bit an expression of his first-hand lived experience, what he called 'the living face of truth'.[8]

First through the efforts of Rāmmohan Rāy, then of Debendranath and the Brahmo Samaj, and later of Rabindranath, the Upanishads gained a central place in the religious culture of Bengal. On 8 November 1931, Rabindranath writes in a letter to Hemantabālā Debi, 'I consider the Upanishads to be the foundation of all religions.'[9] He was especially drawn by the *Isha Upanishad*, of which he had his own unique interpretation, as explained in *Personality*[10] and in a letter to Mahādev Desāi, Gāndhi's personal secretary.

Rabindranath believed the *Isha Upanishad* provided the means of bringing the East and the West together. According to him, 'Ishopanishat has, from human point of view, divided truth into two aspects: – one dealing with life and another with immortality.'[11] These aspects have to be perfected and harmonized. By its emphasis on science, the West can achieve the fulfilment of our rational and moral life; similarly, the East can achieve its fulfilment through emphasis on the spiritual realization of the infinite. Rabindranath says, 'The salvation of humanity lies in the meeting of the East and West in a perfect harmony of truth.'[12] This implies the harmonious mingling of the scientific world view with the spiritual: the worlds are identical although the views are different. Both views are necessary in an individual's life.

2

Between 1901, when Rabindranath shifted to Santiniketan, and 1907, when he began writing *Gorā*, he wrote a number of poems on religious themes that were included in *Naibedya* (1901) and *Kheyā* (1906). During these years, he also wrote a number of important essays on religious and devotional themes that were collected in *Dharma* (1909). These writings provide a prelude to *Gitānjali*. The Bengali volume of that name appeared in 1910. In 1912, the poet gathered many of its poems, with some from *Naibedya* and eight other volumes including the yet unpublished *Gitimālya*, into an English collection also called *Gitanjali*, for which he received the Nobel Prize in 1913. *Naibedya* was Rabindranath's first volume in any genre chiefly devoted to religious themes. The poems in this collection tend to the abstract, with relatively less room for personal emotions and lived experience. Here the poet's religious experience is repeatedly expressed in terms of the father–son relationship. The underlying tenor is of submission and devotion, in return for fatherly love and guidance from above.

The *Gitānjali* poems, along with *Gitimālya* and *Gitāli* (both 1914), mark a shift from filial devotion to a paternalistic god, to a more equal and intimate friendship between the human artist and the divine creator. The deity is now addressed as *bandhu* (friend) or *parānsakhā* (companion of my life).[13] The friendship grows. The poet writes, 'Drunk with the joy of singing I forget myself and call thee friend who art my lord.'[14] There is mutual affection and respect, an appreciation of each other's creative expressions: the one complements the other's actions. This mutual affection often extends to something like romantic love, speaking of the experience of togetherness (*milan*) and separation (*biraha*). It is a genuine mutuality: God does not enjoy a superior position. Nor is there any compulsion: humans are free to accept or to reject God's love. Rabindranath says, 'It is the man's self from which God has withdrawn his commands, for there he comes to court our love.'[15]

A relationship of love can only be sustained through constant creativity leading to greater and greater unity – unity with the external world and within ourselves. These two spheres of unity are distinct yet related. Creative self-expression lends vitality to love. The human spirit seeks to achieve unity and harmony without surrendering freedom: to integrate freedom and unity becomes a lifelong endeavour. This is only possible in love. The long-drawn process is painful as well as rewarding.

The pain involved in creativity is no mundane pain. For Rabindranath, the pain associated with poverty, weakness, or disease is caused by discord between our individual self and our universal self, so that 'it kills and consumes till nothing remains but ashes'.[16] By contrast, the pain involved in creative self-expression and in love are sublimating emotions. Suffering is the language of imperfection, and imperfection always points to the contrasting condition of perfection. The journey from imperfection to perfection, from dark to light is the journey from the finite to the infinite. The human soul is not a beggar who begs the love of the friend, the *parānsakhā*: love is acquired through pain. Pain 'is the hard coin which must be paid for everything valuable in this life.... [I]n pain is symbolised the infinite possibility of perfection.'[17] Hence perfection is the painstaking achievement of the individual; pain is neither designed nor imposed by the friend. The poet writes:

Thou didst well to turn me back when I came begging.
In thy parting glance I saw a smile; and since then
I have learnt my lesson. I break my old alms bowl,
I wait for my chance to give what is mine.[18]

One who is not willing to accept this pain, which is also a pleasure and an honour, is doomed to spiritual frustration. In his later years, Rabindranath writes: 'Today I gain you truly/for with my sorrow I have paid the price of your love.'[19]

3

Rabindranath did not express his thoughts on religion in an academic format. He never intended to offer a philosophy of religion; he refers to his position as a 'poet's religion'.[20] His religious ideas are better expressed in poems and songs than in his essays and addresses. Between 1909 and 1916, he delivered weekly talks or sermons to the students of Santiniketan. These were later published in seventeen small volumes with the title *Shāntiniketan*. Two English works, *Sadhana* (1913) and *Personality* (1917), may be grouped with them. But more than these talks and discursive writings, his religious thought and sensibility in those years are best reflected in the three poetical volumes of the *Gitānjali* phase – *Gitanjali*, *Gitimalya*, and *Gitali* – continuing, with important formal changes, into the next collection, *Balākā* (1916), and even beyond.

Rabindranath's devotional poems are often restrained in expression. He objected to all forms of mesmeric devotion. He tells his god, '[Y]our heaven is in my secret heart; it slowly opens its buds in shy love.'[21] And again:

Not for me is the love that knows no restraint....

Send me the love that would soak down into the centre of being, and from there would spread like the unseen sap through the branching tree of life....[22]

Communication with the deity takes place in the innermost solitude of consciousness, where there is no language except the music of silence. But he also departs from this vein, in relatively early poems like 'Jiban-debatā' (The God of Life) in *Chitrā* (1896), intermittently in poems of the *Gitānjali* triad, and continuing in poems like *Balākā* 29, where the love is more ardent and passionate. The distance between the individual and the beloved is obliterated. There is no need to sit waiting for the beloved or woo him with the creations of art. He is no longer 'out there'; he resides in the very being of the individual. The Creator, who was being addressed as the king, as the all powerful, is now within; he is the King of all kings, the 'Maharaja' who has 'come to the palace of my heart' (*GB*, 'Pujā' #522). Rabindranath also calls the *jiban-debatā* 'the Man of my Heart',[23] whom we must not confuse with a personal God. The Man of the Heart (*maner mānush*) is a mystic concept of the Bāul community of devotees. Rabindranath renders the idea as 'the divine which is in Man and not in the temple, or scriptures, in images and symbols'.[24]

Yet humanity generates forms, images, and meanings. Without human presence, the universe is a nebulous whole without vibrancy, form, or colour. The poet writes:

When I first met you it was in the solitude of a pathless dark. My wish was to light my one lamp to you, even though you had no need.[25]

In order to experience variety and plurality, to realize this potential within his own self, the Creator had to create a human world. In order to enjoy his own wealth, the infinite Personality chooses to be seated in the heart of the finite, route his creation through the human poet's: 'My songs are the same as are the spring flowers, they come from you. Yet I bring these to you as my own.'[26]

The poet writes, 'You did not know yourself when you dwelt alone, ... I came and you woke, and the skies blossomed with lights.'[27] The infinite is incomplete without the love of the individual: without love, it misses its full splendour. 'O thou lord of all heavens, where would be thy love if I were not?' Hence the infinite greatly treasures the love of the individual. Just as the individual craves for a union with the infinite, the infinite too is in search of the individual. There is a two-way journey. The finite individual is striving to realize infinitude, and the infinite is striving to captivate the heart of the individual: 'thou who art the King of kings hast decked thy self in beauty to captivate my heart.' The two-way journey ends in a relationship of mutual love: 'thy love loses itself in the love of thy lover.'[28]

Since the infinite has no desires, it lacks emotions. Emotions only arise in course of relationships with individuals. Rabindranath says, 'The consciousness of personality, which is the consciousness of unity in ourselves, becomes prominently distinct when coloured by joy or sorrow, or some other emotion.'[29] And again: 'What I mean by personality is a self-conscious principle of transcendental unity within man.'[30] Personality keeps extending itself beyond itself through knowledge, love, and action. The finite personality seeks the infinite Personality, just as the infinite Personality seeks the finite.

The manifestation of the divine within the human in the notion of *jiban-debatā* explains the genesis of 'the idea of the humanity of our God' as expounded by Rabindranath in *The Religion of Man*.[31] The corollary of the humanization of God is the divinity of the human. The divine being might be manifested in other worlds too, but we humans can never imagine or know those manifestations. For us, it is the 'direct communication of the person with the Person' that opens up 'a new world ... of light and love'.[32]

The poet writes: 'When my heart did not kiss thee in love, O world, thy light missed its full splendour.'[33]

One may ask, is this not an extremely individual-centric position? Should not an individual, in that case, worship herself or himself alone? But for Rabindranath, the individual is never the goal: the soul reaches out beyond itself to a greater whole, the infinite. Hence the individual anxiously asks the lord of his heart whether the deity's wish has been fulfilled in him.[34] Doubtless this reflects an individual relationship with the Creator. But although the Creator is intimately related to each individual, he is not exclusively related to any single one. He is in the heart of all persons, even though each has a world related to his or her own personality.

The god–individual relationship, self-contained yet limited and inadequate owing to its exclusiveness, thus inspires a journey or quest seeking unity with the whole. In *Gitāli* #95, Rabindranath refers to such a seeker as the *pānthajan* or traveller, and to the Creator as *pānthajaner sakhā*, the traveller's friend; elsewhere the Creator is *pather sāthi*, 'companion of the road'.[35] It is an introspective journey towards self-realization, guided by an inner light. Rabindranath speaks of the faculty of 'luminous imagination'.[36] In religious matters each individual must proceed independently. Religion is a journey of the solitary individual. This has been eloquently expressed by Rabindranath in a poem in *Sphulinga*: 'Burn thy self like a lamp. You will have to provide the light for your own journey.'[37] The affinity between this notion and the Buddhist notion of *Ātmadipa bhaba*, 'Be a lamp unto thyself', is unmistakable.

4

At the age of seventy-five, Rabindranath gives a succinct account of his religion in *Patraput* #15. He speaks of two mysteries. One is the initial mystery of creation, the manifestation of light; the second is the final mystery of creation, the flowing of the nectar of love and the realization of truth through love.

The metaphysical underpinning of Rabindranath's position is found in his distinctive theory of cosmology and evolution, as expounded at the opening of *The Religion of Man*.[38] He finds a 'divine principle of unity' manifested in the interrelationship of all creatures and objects. The first phase of this unity evolved on the inanimate physical plane; then came the infusion of life in the physical universe. Man interacts with the physical universe, but transcends it to attain to a universe of the spirit, what he elsewhere calls the 'sky of the mind', *chidākāsh*.[39] The human being is both a biological animal guided by natural laws and a spirit with a surplus far in excess of his or her biological needs. The spirit of mind with its surplus makes us intensely conscious of our intrinsic freedom and turns the course of evolution into a different path, the path of creativity.

It is sheer pleasure to witness the replay of God's creativity in human creations. By utilizing the surplus of its being, humanity creates new relationships in tandem with the principle of unity manifested in divine creation. The power of creation thus vests in the created human being as much as in the Creator. Rabindranath writes:

> To all things else you give; from me you ask.

> The harvest of my life ripens in the sun and the shower till I reap more than you sowed, gladdening your heart, O master of the golden granary.[40]

The matter can be expressed in another way. The finite and the infinite are two sides of the same reality. Rabindranath admits that this is a paradox – the paradox of reality. Freedom, reason, and creative imagination are the defining features of humankind. Freedom is experienced differently in its finite mode and in its infinite mode. In the finite mode, the individual employs freedom for emancipation from the oppression of physical nature. Such freedom enables the individual to choose the manner in which to engage with the external world. In its finite aspect, the self attempts to achieve greater distinction than others.

This finite freedom moves on to freedom in its infinite aspect. The goal of freedom shifts from separateness to harmony. Harmony cannot be achieved through compulsion, but only through independence. 'We must have the possibility of the negative form of freedom, which is licence, before we can attain the positive freedom, which is love.'[41] We pass from the freedom of separation to the positive freedom of creative imagination, with which is associated the 'freedom of view'.[42] God creates the natural world; we receive it and make it our own. Negative or finite freedom functions in the domain of the natural world. But 'in the creation of the spiritual domain, we are God's partners'. This partnership has to be acquired through the individual's effort: the individual's will has to be 'made free of all contrary forces of passions and desires', the consciousness cleared of all delusions. This can be a long and painful process. Nevertheless, God 'has to wait for our will to harmonize with his own'. Through the positive freedom gained thereby, the individual 'meet[s] God where he creates.... He gives us from His own fullness and we also give him from our abundance'.[43]

'Love is the perfection of consciousness', according to Rabindranath.[44] He often speaks of detachment as the necessary condition of pure love. He was greatly attracted by the Upanishadic teaching 'Tena tyāktena bhunjitah. Mā gridah' (*Isha Upanishad* 1), which he interpreted as 'You shall gain by giving away; you shall not covet.'[45] The love relation between the individual and the infinite is essentially reciprocal. The individual approaches God as the beloved and God relates to the individual as the beloved: the being of each is extended by surrendering to the other. This is because the unity of the universe requires the unity of the finite and the infinite. Neither the finite nor the infinite is complete when not related to the other. The relationship needs to be one of genuine togetherness.

In the initial stages of human evolution, freedom is expressed through the severance of relationships with nature for the purpose of controlling nature; in the higher stages, a new freedom forges new participatory relationships with humankind's surroundings. This is a yet higher freedom, a freedom of unity. As we pass from the freedom of separation to the freedom of unity, our perception of the world is transformed: from perceiving the finite, we pass to the perception of the infinite. This is a qualitative change, from an atomistic way of looking at things to a holistic way. There is no need to transcend the world to gain this holistic perception. Rabindranath realized that the modern world was no longer attracted by the prospect of a holistic perception. Nevertheless, he felt we must aim at a perfect order of interdependence, mutual understanding and cooperation, of harmony and unity. 'In the human world,' he says, 'only a perfect arrangement of interdependence gives rise to freedom.'[46] We must aspire to this higher freedom of unity: there is no other remedy for the state of the times.

There is no pre-set road map to this end. *Sadhana* proposes three ways to reach the goal: through love, through action, and through beauty. These paths need not be followed sequentially; they are simultaneously present in different phases of Rabindranath's writings. Sometimes Rabindranath sees the universe through music, sometimes he celebrates Shiva in his aspect of Natarāj, the cosmic dancer; at times he looks at the universe through the relation of a lover and his beloved, and occasionally he takes the path of the devotee. There is no conflict between these paths.

Rabindranath consistently speaks of a future state where all disharmony will be resolved in unity. Unity does not entail uniformity, nor does it imply a pre-established harmony waiting to be discovered. Human consciousness and human freedom generate the capacity to create new relationships through love, to forge new and various unities. Rabindranath did not dream of the kind of seamless globe we witness today, dominated by market forces.

Some unities are based on utilitarian demands, but Rabindranath feels the human entity is imperfectly revealed through utilitarian relationships. Similarly, science and commerce can create a certain power-giving unity, but this too is not a desired end. The only means to harmony is the realization of spiritual unity. The opposition between power and love, death and life, self-interest and well-being (*kalyān*) can only be meaningfully reconciled by a religious sensibility, culminating in absolute peace, blessedness (*mangal*), and unity.

This joyful human unity is gained by realizing ourselves in others. For the poet, 'this is the definition of love'.[47] He dreamt of a world without barriers, '[W]here the world has not been broken up into fragments by narrow domestic walls'.[48] He even thought of taking up a project of unifying the scattered religions of Asia; but as his friend C.F. Andrews comments, 'his comprehensive vision could not stop at any horizon that was less wide than humanity'.[49]

The realization of unity is an unending process. Death is not the culmination of the journey; it simply marks the passage from life to a new beginning. In his poem 'Jiban-debatā', Rabindranath writes:

> But have my days come to their end at last …?
> Then break up the meeting of this languid day.
> Renew the old in me in fresh forms of delight;
> and let the wedding come once again
> in a new ceremony of life.[50]

Our present is part of an endlessly unfolding future.

Rabindranath raises the question, '[W]hat is the ultimate end of the freedom which has come into man's life?' The simple answer is that the end of freedom is to know that 'I am'.[51] But what am I? What is the nature of humankind, its *dharma* or essential quality? Rabindranath says, 'Humanity is the *dharma* of human beings.'[52] It is to know my nature, the nature of humanity – to know that I am both finite and infinite, and that I am free. How does this knowledge impact my action? He says, 'This freedom is not perfect in its mere extension, but its true perfection is in its intensity, which is love.'[53] Freedom gains perfection through love for nature, love for fellow human beings, and love for the Person, the infinite. In the absence of relationships there can be no love. The day humankind departs from the universe, all colour will be wiped away and the world will be bereft of poetry. Expressions like 'You are beautiful' or 'I love' will no longer be heard.[54]

The year 1922 marked a watershed in Rabindranath's search for unity. It was the year he founded the Institute of Rural Reconstruction at Sriniketan. He was now looking beyond the unity between the individual and the Creator. Instead, he sought to bond with common humanity, the toiling masses. The search was not new, only its intensity had increased. He had written as early as 1910: 'He [God] is there where the tiller is tilling the hard ground.... Meet him and stand by him in toil and in sweat of thy brow.'[55] The search for unity had to embrace a search for equality. Besides his experience at Sriniketan, several other factors – India's freedom struggle, the devastation of the First World War, the rise of aggressive nationalism across the world, and, somewhat later, his trip to Russia in 1930 – all fed this sustained urge to connect with the masses. In *Stray Birds* #317 he writes, 'Man's history is waiting in patience for the triumph of the insulted man.'[56] As long as there is suffering, deprivation, and lack of dignity in this world, a single individual cannot gain deliverance in isolation.[57]

History has never been a linear progression towards the goal of unity. There have been many blunders and obstructions; even so, we attempt to trace a progression towards a world of new relationships based on love. After a lifelong assertion of this uplifting view of humanity, did Rabindranath find conclusive evidence to sustain it? At the age of eighty, just before his death, he says in his last major utterance on the state of the world: 'As I look around I see the crumbling ruins of a proud civilization strewn like a vast heap of futility.' Some commentators focus on this utterance to establish Rabindranath's loss of faith in his final years. However, as we must not fail to notice, he hastens to add: 'I shall not commit the grievous sin of losing faith in Man.'[58]

NOTES

1. Ābu Sayeed Āyyub, 'Pānthajaner sakhā', in *Pānthajaner sakhā* (Kolkata: Dey's, 1973), 119–76; Sukumāri Bhattachārya, 'Rabindrakābye mānush o naitikatā', in *Prabandhasangraha*, vol. 3 (Kolkata: Gāngchil, 2014), 339–50.

2. Shashibhushan Dāsgupta, *Upanishader patabhumikāy rabindra mānas* (Kolkata: Supreme Publishers, 1992); Satyendranāth Rāy, ed., *Rabindranāther chintājagat, dharmachintā: rabindrarachanā-sankalan* (Kolkata: Granthālay, 2007).

3. For a detailed account of this exchange see Ray, *Rabindranāther chintājagat: dharmachintā*, 21–2.

4. *RRVB* 6:570.

5. Letter to Lalitkumār Bandyopādhyāy, *RRVB* 11:504–5.

6. *The Religion of Man*, ch. 6, 'The Vision', *EW* 3:120.

7. Ibid.
8. *The Religion of Man*, ch. 7, 'The Man of My Heart', *EW* 3.129.
9. *CP* 9:116.
10. 'The World of Personality', *EW* 2:363–74.
11. Letter to Mahadev Desai, *EW* 3:810.
12. Ibid., *EW* 3.811.
13. As in *Gitānjali* #20, *RRVB* 11:19 (English *Gitanjali* #23, *EW* 1:49).
14. English *Gitānjali* #2, *EW* 1:43 (*Gitānjali* #78, *RRVB* 11:63). Unless otherwise specified, all translations of Tagore's poems are his own renderings.
15. 'Soul Consciousness', *Sadhana* (London: Macmillan, 1913), 41. The quoted portion is part of two pages of the 1913 text missing at the expected point in *EW* (2:296).
16. 'The Creative Ideal', *Creative Unity*, *EW* 2:509.
17. 'The Problem of Evil', *Sadhana*, *EW* 2:305.
18. *Poems* #36, *EW* 1:340: lines added in the English to the Bengali original, *Utsarga* #20.
19. *Poems* #99, *EW* 1:374 (*Shesh Saptak* #1, *RRVB* 18:3).
20. See the chapter of that name in *Creative Unity*.
21. *Fruit-Gathering*, #81, *EW* 1:188 (*Balākā* #33, *RRVB* 12:55).
22. *Fruit-Gathering* #63, *EW* 1:182 (*Naibedya* #45, *RRVB* 8:40).
23. Title of ch. 7 of *The Religion of Man*: *EW* 3:129.
24. Ibid.
25. *The Fugitive* (Bolpur edition, ?1919), #79, *EW* 1:574 (*GB*, 'Pujā' #59).
26. *Crossing* #65, *EW* 1:236 (*Gitānjali* #97, *RRVB* 11:75).
27. *Fruit-Gathering* #80, *EW* 1:188 (*Balākā* #29, *RRVB* 12:50–1).
28. English *Gitānjali* #56, *EW* 1:62 (*Gitānjali* #121, *RRVB* 11:96).
29. 'The Creative Ideal', *Creative Unity*, *EW* 2:506.
30. *Religion of Man*, ch. 8, 'The Music Maker', *EW* 3:134.
31. Ibid., ch. 1, 'Man's Universe', *EW* 3:88.
32. 'The World of Personality', *Personality*, *EW* 2:374.
33. *Crossing* #72, *EW* 1:238 (*Balākā* #17, *RRVB* 12:37).
34. See the opening of 'Jiban-debatā' (*Chitrā*, *RRVB* 4:107–8), tr. in *The Religion of Man*, ch. 6, 'The Vision', *EW* 3:123.
35. *Crossing* #78 (*Gitāli* #98).
36. *Religion of Man*, ch. 1, 'Man's Unverse', *EW* 3:88.
37. *Sphulinga* #26, *RRVB* 27:7 (translation mine).
38. *EW* 3:87–8.
39. 'Tintalā' (The Third Storey), *Shāntiniketan*, *RRVB* 14:339.
40. *Fruit-Gathering* #78, *EW* 1:187 (*Balākā* #28, *RRVB* 12:50). The harvest image is found only in the English version.
41. 'The Problem of Self', *Sadhana*, *EW* 2:312.
42. 'The World of Personality', *EW* 2:374; *Religion of Man*, ch. 3, 'The Surplus in Man', *EW* 3:104.

43. 'The Second Birth', *Personality*, EW 2:386.
44. 'Realization in Love', *Sadhana*, EW 2:321.
45. The passage is usually interpreted in another way.
46. *Religion of Man*, ch. 13, 'Spiritual Freedom', EW 3:164.
47. Ibid., ch. 2, 'The Creative Spirit', EW 3:102.
48. English *Gitanjali* #35, EW 1:53 (*Naibedya* #72, RRVB 8:56).
49. C.F. Andrews, Introductory Notes, *Letters to a Friend*, ch. 5, EW 3:257.
50. 'Jiban-debatā', tr. in *The Religion of Man*, EW 3:123.
51. 'The Second Birth', *Personality*, EW 2:384.
52. *Religion of Man*, ch. 10, 'Man's Nature', EW 3:148.
53. 'The Second Birth', EW 2:384.
54. See the poem 'Āmi' (I), *Shyāmali*, RRVB 20:65.
55. English *Gitanjali* #11, EW 1:46 (*Gitānjali* #119, RRVB 11:94–5).
56. EW 1:434.
57. See *Mānusher dharma*, RRVB 20:415.
58. 'Crisis in Civilization', EW 3:726.

25 Rabindranath Tagore and Humanism

SARANINDRANATH TAGORE

> An act of hospitality can only be poetic.
>
> – Jacques Derrida

I

The idea of the human, which played a central role in the thought-world of Rabindranāth Tagore, was invoked by him in 'Sabhyatār sangkat' ('Crisis in Civilization', 1941), his last address in Santiniketan, to envisage a possible future on the other side of a global civilizational crisis:

> As I look around I see the crumbling ruins of a proud civilization strewn like a vast heap of futility. And yet I shall not commit the grievous sin of losing faith in Man. I would rather look forward to the opening of a new chapter in his history after the cataclysm is over and the atmosphere rendered clean with the spirit of service and sacrifice.... A day will come when unvanquished Man will retrace his path of conquest, despite all barriers, to win back his lost human heritage.[1]

Tagore did not live to see the full genocidal impact of the Nazi regime, but had he done, he might still not have endorsed the anti-humanist sweep of Adorno's famous observation on the silencing of poetry, the most refined expression of human language: '[T]o write a poem after Auschwitz is barbaric, and that corrodes also the knowledge which expresses why it has become impossible to write poetry today.'[2] To revivify civilization cannot be anything but a human project; crisis, however deep, can only be contested in Rabindranath's thinking by the figure of the human. Yet the idea of the human, at least in its essentialist formulation, has been under severe pressure in recent times. The attack took its sustenance from Nietzsche, one of the first architects of the anti-humanist gesture.

In European modernity, the human, in its essentialist formulation, travels from Renaissance painters and thinkers to the Cartesian discovery of the centred *cogito* to the ethics of human dignity propounded by Kant. Each of these conceptions argues for a common presence of the human across histories and cultures, subverting the idea of difference. Nietzsche famously questioned this idea of 'man as an *aeterna veritas* [eternal truth], as something constant in the midst of all flux, as a sure measure of things'[3] by noting the lack of historical sense in philosophers and concluding that there are no eternal facts, just as there are no absolute truths. Thus Nietzsche sets the stage for more recent anti-humanism, perhaps enunciated most powerfully by Michel Foucault:

> One thing in any case is certain: man is neither the oldest nor the most constant problem that has been posed for human knowledge.... As the archaeology of our thought easily shows, man is an invention of recent date. And one perhaps nearing its end.[4]

If Nietzsche cites historical variations to attack the essentialist concept of the human, Foucault mounts a similar assault using movement, marked by ruptures, of discursively formed epistemes. Jean-François Lyotard, the quintessential postmodern philosopher, advances and critiques the 'modern' idea of a meta-narrative with the transcendental function of legitimizing one perspective, theoretical or otherwise, over another. Such legitimization constructs unities through the removal of difference.[5] The essentialism inherent in humanism faces the danger of excluding difference in the very act of unifying the human. In the face of these and allied philosophical pressures, I will interrogate the nature of Rabindranath's faith in the 'human heritage', and ask how it can be preserved.

2

Rabindranath's poem 'Ami' (I), written in 1936 and included in the collection *Shyāmali*, opens thus:

> My consciousness turns the emerald green,
> Ruby deep red.
> I turn my gaze to the sky – it lights up
> from east to west.
> 'Lovely', I say looking at the rose –
> and it grows lovely.
> You'd complain it's mere theory, not a poetic utterance.
> I'd say it's the truth, hence this is poetry:

such is my conceit [*ahankār*],
which I feel on behalf of mankind.[6]

These few lines present three fundamental philosophical ideas, remarkably condensed, that are important for grounding Tagore's conception of the human. First, the 'I' consciousness (the *cogito* in the Cartesian-Husserlian vocabulary) enables the formation of meaningful experience: my consciousness provides the condition for the possibility of the emerald's green, the ruby's red, the sky's light, the rose's beauty. Second, in suggesting these might be philosophical truths and not the utterances of poetry, the poet settles on the idea, remarkably reminiscent of the late Heidegger's invocation of Hölderlin, that these words form a truth that only poetry can show forth. Third, the 'I' is not merely Rabindranath Tagore, the individual subject uttering the words; here 'I' names the human.

It is worth pausing over the last two lines quoted above. The word *ahankār* can mean pride or conceit; by this reading, the poet says that the creative aspects of consciousness make him proud of the productive values of humans in general. But the reading that interests me more, which can be broadly called a phenomenological reading, suggests that *ahankār*, trading on the Upanishadic *aham* (self), is human consciousness, a sense of selfhood, doubling as the organizing principle of all possible experience. In this way, particularity is linked to universality. The 'I', then, is the subjective 'I', but its constitution is strictly commensurable with all other 'I's, which together make up the figure of the human. Thus the lines do not invoke solipsist isolation, rather the truth that all possible meanings must rise from the crucible of the human.

Rabindranath made the same point in his famous remark to Albert Einstein that 'if there be some truth which has no sensuous or rational relation to the human mind it will ever remain as nothing so long as we remain human beings'.[7] The phenomenological reading of the human also serves well in interpreting the humanist concept of *jiban-debatā*, wherein Tagore aligns his metaphysical assertions in opposition to the notion of ineffability found in Advaita philosophy:

> According to some interpretations of the Vedanta doctrine Brahman is the absolute Truth, the impersonal It, ... having no other quality except its ineffable blissfulness.... But, as our religion can only

have its significance in the phenomenal world comprehended by our human self, this absolute conception of Brahman is outside the subject of my discussion.... [W]hatever name may have been given to the divine Reality it has found its highest place in the history of our religion owing to its human character.[8]

Advaita philosophy endorses a strict metaphysical monism. Applying metaphysics to the philosophy of religion, an Advaita interpretation of the Upanishads would regard ultimate reality (Brahman) as escaping all qualifications (*nirguna*): an ineffable conception of ultimate Being located outside the meaning-making flow of human consciousness, thereby rendering it 'as nothing so long as we remain human beings'.[9] For Rabindranath, on the contrary, any assertion concerning Being must be relatable and commensurable with the possibilities of the human. In this phenomenological sense, no truth can be 'extra-human':

[H]ow shall we call extra-human the world whose fundamental truths are found by man in conformity with the innate principles of his thought? That is why a modern scientist describes the universe as the creation of [a] mathematical mind. But even this mathematical mind is not beyond the bounds of the human mind. If it were, then we could not have at all known the scientific theory of the world.[10]

By favouring the 'human', which is open to endless qualifications, in contradistinction to the 'impersonal it', Rabindranath adopts a counter-Advaita position.

For Rabindranath, the human, understood as the unfolding of consciousness, is primarily an autonomous agent of creativity, free of historical and political pressures. This humanism that rests upon autonomy is most clearly described by Rabindranath in another very late essay, 'Sāhitye aitihāsikatā' (Historicity in Literature, 1941). In a refined example of phenomenological description, Rabindranath describes the miraculous in the everyday in an experience of his childhood:

I had come back from school at four-thirty. The first thing I saw was a dark blue cloudbank suspended above the third storey of our house. What a marvellous sight that was! I still remember the day, although no second person in its history saw those clouds with the same eyes or felt the same rapture. Rabindranath alone broke upon the scene.[11]

The human, in this reckoning, is not the product of discursive formations informed by the agencies of history and politics, but is constituted by a singular response to the world. Rabindranath proceeds to talk about another such event, stressing its singularity:

> The history of that day did not divulge to anyone else the deep significance of the sight. In his own field of creativity, Rabindranath was alone, not tied by history to any public. Where history was public, there was a *British subject*, but not Rabindranath.... The light glinting among the coconut fronds was not a statist import of the *British Government*. It emanated from some mysterious history of my innermost soul.[12]

Cutting across the political and its allied historiography, literature emerges as a supreme humanist project, which describes the agency of everyday consciousness:

> It was not some feudal or statist order that *Galpaguchchha* [his collection of short stories] mirrored; it was created out of the history of human joys and sorrows that has always transcended all other history and come to appear in farmlands and village festivals, forever expressing its utterly simple humanity – sometimes in the time of Mughal rule, sometimes of British.[13]

Rabindranath's conception of the human opens up a space prior to the political by emphasizing a history of an 'inner soul', which runs a different course from political history. This characterization of humanity can be properly called ontological because it traces the humanist context to its original sense of an embodied, meaning-forming, worldly entity that lies prior to and makes possible any other description of the human, which need not be reduced to the singular.

For Rabindranath, literature emerges as textured by humanist sensibilities precisely because in its profoundest sense, language in its poetic deployment can alone recover the voice of history that signifies the daily 'weal and woe [*prātyahik sukhduhkha*] of human life' untouched by political history. Such an ontological retrieval of the human resists the flattening effect of essentializing gestures: no one else saw those clouds in the same way or was similarly thrilled. Humanism, ontologically construed, inscribes difference in the figure of the human. It names a range, however vast, of possible experiences; thus by its very nature the human must contain multiplicities, irreducible to any one epistemic formation.

3

Although literature is infinitely attentive to the 'weal and woe of human life', the human in its meaning-forming particularity, Rabindranath was also concerned with the unity of the human consolidated by the universal, what he calls the universal human (*mahāmānab*).[14] He gave a helpful formulation of this concept in a 1933 lecture at Andhra University:

> In the world of Man individuals are conscious of a comprehensive truth which is spiritual and whose members they are themselves. The best expression of Man therefore is that which does not exclusively represent an isolated mind, but can be accepted by the minds of men of all times.[15]

The idea here is that individual expressions can possibly relate to all minds at all times: in other words, universal humanity does not erase everyday particularity. Rather, the universal marks out possible commensurability between individual particularities. Rabindranath's humanism elicits the lesson that the universal and the particular can embrace each other, recalling the Upanishadic conception of the Atman wherein everyday consciousness of intentional particularity is undergirded by the witnessing function (*sākshin*) of universal consciousness:[16]

> The *Upanishad* says that when we know united in completeness *asambhuti*, the unmanifested infinite, and *sambhuti*, the manifested finite, we know truth, in a reconciliation of the duality. He who is infinite in man must be expressed in the finitude of human life, of human society.[17]

Hence the tropes of universalizing unity need not erase particularizing difference. Rabindranath insists that there are two kinds of unities; their difference animates many strands of his thought, which maintains at all levels this harmony of the universal and the particular. The first conception can be called the imperialist conception of unity, which is to be rejected:

> Uniformity is not unity. Those who destroy the independence of other races, destroy the unity of all races of humanity. Modern Imperialism

is that idea of Unity, which the python has in swallowing other live creatures.... [W]hen we respect the true individuality of men, then we can discover their true unity.[18]

Humanism militates against imperialism – or imperialism follows an anti-humanist trajectory – because its conception of humanity follows a reductive agenda, textured by essentialist constructions. Rabindranath proposes an alternative humanism that can shield against imperialist violence. This calls for a different articulation of unity:

> When the science of meteorology knows the earth's atmosphere as continuously one, affecting the different parts of the world differently, but in a harmony of adjustments, it knows and attains truth. And so, too, we must know that the great mind of man is one, working through the many differences which are needed to ensure the full result of its fundamental unity.... [P]erfection of unity is not in uniformity, but in harmony.[19]

This unity through adjustment universalizes without doing violence to the difference inscribed in particularities: here the universal is not hegemonic and the particular is not divisive. What is the value of a humanism so construed, that can accommodate the universal in the particular?

4

Humanism, at least in Rabindranath's variant, is virtuous because it makes intercultural conversation possible. More pointedly, it opens up the possibility of an expanded and expanding account of identity wherein the individual (the quotidian human of the *prātyahik*) can aspire towards the universal (*mahāmānab*). Indeed, Amartya Sen has argued, very much following in the footsteps of Rabindranath, that realization of identity in the multiple can reduce real violence in the world.[20] Rabindranath captures the possible movement of the individual aspiration towards the universal in a letter to C.F. Andrews:

> Whatever we understand and enjoy in human products instantly becomes ours, wherever they might have their origin. I am proud of my humanity, when I can acknowledge the poets and artists of other countries as my own.[21]

One need not be an essentialist to admit this all-embracing view of the human. Yet it carries the possibility of a contestation of attitudes that signals the debate between the Enlightenment, hence modern, valuing of reductive unity and the postmodern defence of pluralism. In Lyotard's manifesto of postmodernism, modernity legitimizes certain narrative threads and marginalizes others, creating a specious and reductive unity that activates the history of violence. Against these grand narratives of legitimation, Lyotard proposes to build global culture on little narratives where each cultural formation follows localized rules.

The constituting trope of humanism, the figure of the human, is deeply – perhaps centrally – implicated in this contest. While the postmodern insistence that reductively articulated conceptions of the human need to be resisted give pause for thought, it is not at all clear how removing all nodes of commensurability across human expressions can remove the danger of violence, political or otherwise. In this dialectic, particularity is erased in the movement of the universal on the one hand, and saved through the erasure of the universal on the other. Rabindranath's humanism cuts a path between these two formations. Rabindranath never underestimated the relationship between the human and the violent, even while insisting that humanism need not therefore be set aside:

> I had sighed with the great poet Wordsworth, who became sad when he saw what man had done to man.... Men are ever the greatest enemy of Man.... [A]ll the same, there was a hope, deep in my heart, that I should find some place, some temple, where the immortal spirit of man dwelt hidden like the sun behind clouds.[22]

Far from being discounted, humanism should be emphasized and nurtured in this context of violence.

The human is a figure intensely particular; but the nature of particularity is such that it can move without obstruction beyond its own cultural habitation. I have argued elsewhere that the humanist position so understood makes for a cosmopolitan sensibility which refuses to reify human otherness (alterity).[23] Rabindranath brings this humanism to the service of literature: 'I am proud of my humanity, when I can acknowledge the poets and artists of other cultures as my own.' Accordingly, there is an aesthetic dimension to Rabindranath's account of humanism, related to the contest between particularity and universality just indicated. Literature connects the *prātyahikatā* of particularity with the *bishwa* of the universal. Rabindranath famously said, 'My religion is a poet's religion.' He described that religious state in this moving way:

> In the night we stumble over things and become acutely conscious of their individual separateness, but the day reveals the great unity which embraces them. And the man, whose inner vision is bathed in an illumination of his consciousness, at once realizes the spiritual unity reigning supreme over all differences of race and his mind no longer awkwardly stumbles over individual facts of separateness in the human world, accepting them as final.[24]

Rabindranath's intervention powerfully suggests that the unity of the human, as motivating a religion of art, cannot be determined by deploying a syllogism; rather, poetry or literature (*sāhitya*) discloses a space where the unity of the human manifests itself. 'If we grasp that universal humanity finds expression in literature, we shall be able to discern in literature what we rightfully should.'[25] Here we are reminded of a conception of art's ontology which runs parallel to the later Heidegger's reconfiguration of thought as poetic, summarized by Calvin Schrag with exemplary economy as a form of thinking that 'commemorates but does not represent; it is a matter of showing rather than referring; it is a setting forth instead of an explaining; it is evocative rather than demonstrative'.[26] In Rabindranath's vocabulary, the illumination of consciousness, like the revelatory possibility of daylight, is a modality of disclosure activated by poetry or literature. His description of this event of disclosure is centrally humanist in implication, showing forth the human as a field of commensurable difference. Art acquires meaning by invoking this dynamics of difference, not in terms of separateness but of an intrinsic unity. By this view, art can be truth-tracking, not in the sense of propositional logic, but of an ontological disclosure where the particular and the universal together constitute the fabric of the human, not through essentializing gestures but through the making of art, where quotidian particularity, the *prātyahik*, indeed has universal significance.

Rabindranath writes in the 'The Meaning of Art' (1926): 'The *I am* in me realizes its own extension, its own infinity whenever it truly realizes something else.'[27] Art gives expression to these 'extensions', not forever fractured but unified in harmony, thereby producing the shape of the human. Ranajit Guha notes this deep connection that literature discloses between particularity and universalist solidarity, as illustrated in Rabindranath's short stories:

When village women meet for a short afternoon break between domestic chores, it is *sukhduhkha* that they talk about. So do people among themselves in the intimate circles of their friends and families, neighbours, and colleagues. Thus the discourse of weal and woe, *sukhduhkher kathā*, has come to signify the concern that characterizes the solidarities of a shared world.[28]

Guha is arguing that the late essay 'Sāhitye aitihāsikatā' premises a position where literature can invest the everyday with 'historicality', so that one can argue for a historiography emulating literature, removing the need for 'statist blinkers'. However, it needs to be added that such a conception of the everyday is made possible by a humanism that resists the destruction of the particular by an essentializing universality. Rabindranath uncompromisingly states: 'Individuality is precious, because only through it we can realize the universal.'[29]

In Rabindranath's reckoning, the human, as the trope of this transcendence, motivates the idea of universal literature (*bishwasāhitya*):

> It is time we resolved to make it our goal to view universal humanity
> in universal literature by freeing ourselves from a rustic limitation
> of outlook – to recognize each author's writings as an integral whole,
> and perceive in that unity the interrelations binding all human efforts
> at expression.[30]

This vision is possible because 'it is the natural bent (*dharma*) of the human soul to find its own particular humanity fully united with all humankind'.[31]

5

Rabindranath's humanism, disclosing the human in the enactments of literature, informs the entirety of his myriad-minded thought. Most importantly, his articulation of universal humanism nurtured an ethics of cosmopolitanism. Cosmopolitanism derives from a concept of universality that disregards the rootedness of tradition. This binary between the universal and the particular mirrors the contest between essentialist constructions of the human and postmodern rejections of a reductionist unity. A cosmopolitanism sustained by universalist premises of the Enlightenment, such as the transcendental inscriptions of reason, runs the risk noted by postmodern critics of erasing the formations of tradition that contribute to the making of the human.[32] Humanism of Rabindranath's kind teaches that ethical sensibilities can be nurtured in a space wherein the particularity of tradition need not negate the prospect of cosmopolitan solidarity. Isaiah Berlin perceptively describes this interstitial posture: 'Tagore stood on the narrow causeway, and did not betray his vision of the difficult truth.'[33] Standing on this causeway, Rabindranath refused to define the human through essentialist gestures of legitimation; rather, he insisted that the universal emerges from the everydayness of the particular, *prātyahik sukhduhkha*, as disclosed in the acts of literature. The argument for cosmopolitan solidarity binding the human proves, at base, a poetic conviction of unity-as-harmony.

Within the concrete and contemporary, Rabindranath states the problem in the language of diagnosis. First comes the observation:

> The most difficult problem for India is, that both Hindus and Mahomedans, when they reach the full consciousness of their individuality, become, in the natural course of things as they exist today, mutually exclusive and antagonistic.

Then, with great assurance, arrives the humanist remedy:

> There must be something radically wrong in our mental and social life when such can be the case. It must be the result of some narrowness of vision, some distrust of human nature in its universal aspect, which distracts our sympathy from the great course of its development that is to comprehend all humanity.[34]

For Rabindranath, cosmopolitan solidarity, however illuminated through poetic disclosure, can never be a given; it is always an achievement in process through a 'great course of development'.

At this juncture of the argument, the great humanist arc of Rabindranath's thinking attains closure in his philosophical and practical interventions in education. He connects the possibility of cosmopolitan achievement with the contours of pedagogy. In the essay 'Shikshār milan' (Union in Education), Rabindranath conceives of the educational institution (*bidyāniketan*) as primarily a space of hospitality: 'Countries cannot rest content with their own dinner hall; they need guesthouses to welcome the world.'[35] In the same essay on the philosophy of education, hospitality in the context of education is defined with great consistency in humanist terms, summoning at once the binaries of particularity and universality, unity and difference:

There can be genuine harmony only where each is distinct in its own space. Similarly, we can achieve true unity between humans where they are one, only by accepting their individuality where they are individual.[36]

The ethics and practice of hospitality, a natural extension of Rabindranath's universal humanist project, shaped his thinking on education as expressed in a Tokyo address on 'The Ideals of Education': there are 'golden crops' of the spirit

that have developed in different forms and in different soils but whose food value for man's spirit has the same composition. These are not for the local markets but for universal hospitality.... [H]uman civilization is a spiritual feast the invitation to which is open to all, it is never for the ravenous orgies of carnage where the food and the feeders are being torn to pieces.[37]

Beyond curricular issues, education for Rabindranath must foster a culture of hospitality in order to achieve cosmopolitan solidarity. Rabindranath calls this attitude formation *bhābshikshā* and invokes it in his other great essay on education, 'Shikshār herpher' (The Vicissitudes of Education):

If along with language instruction, one is educated from childhood in attitude formation (*bhābshikshā*), and if one's entire life is governed by this attitude, only then can a true balance be established in life; we can then live naturally and apprehend the true measure of all things.[38]

Rabindranath's philosophy of education conceived of humanism not only as a philosophical figure whose truth is to be captured by the artist or writer, but also as a moving force to conceive of a world where the proposition that 'men are ever the greatest enemy of Man' can be cast aside. In other words, humanism as an ethical achievement is impossible without pedagogy.

One of the last honours bestowed on Rabindranath was an honorary doctorate from the University of Oxford. The encomium at the degree ceremony, held in Santiniketan, profiled the polymathic nature of Rabindranath's genius:

Here before you is the myriad-minded poet and writer, the musician famous in his art, the philosopher proven both in word and deed, the fervent upholder of learning and sound doctrine, the ardent defender of public liberties, one who by the sanctity of his life and character has won for himself the praise of all mankind.[39]

I would suggest that the connecting thread relating all these different Rabindranaths is his understanding of humanism, which navigates between the signatures of essentialism and fragmentation. Universalist identification need not elide the richness of individuality: the truth of humanism can simultaneously comprehend the distinctive autonomy (*swatantratā*) of the particular and the oneness (*aikatā*) of the universal. Rabindranath sums it up in a notable play on Bengali words, 'Ekākār haoā ek haoā nay': to be thrown together is not to be united.[40]

NOTES

1. *EW* 3:726.
2. Theodor Adorno, *Prisms*, tr. Samuel Weber and Shierry Weber (Cambridge, MA: MIT Press, 1967; rpt. 1983), 34.
3. Friedrich Nietzsche, *Human, All Too Human*, tr. R.J. Hollingdale (Cambridge: Cambridge University Press, 1986 rpt. 1996), 12–13.
4. Michel Foucault, *The Order of Things*, English tr. (London: Tavistock Publications, 1970 rpt. 1985), 386–7.
5. This oft-quoted passage captures the idea: 'I will use the term *modern* to designate any science that legitimates itself with reference to a meta discourse … making an explicit appeal to some grand narrative, such as the dialectics of Spirit, the hermeneutics of meaning, the emancipation of the rational or the working subject, or the creation of wealth.' Jean-François Lyotard, *The Postmodern Condition* (Minneapolis: University of Minnesota Press, 1984), xxiii.
6. Tr. Kaiser Haq, in *The Essential Tagore*, ed. Fakrul Alam and Radha Chakravarty (Cambridge, MA: Harvard University Press, 2011), 297. Bimal Krishna Matilal has philosophically analysed this poem in 'A Man-Centric View: Poet and Scientist', tr. Amiya Dev, in *Tagore, Einstein and the Nature of Reality*, ed. Partha Ghose (Abingdon: Routledge, 2019).
7. *EW* 3:913. For a more extensive discussion of this conversation in the light of Rabindranath's conception of the human, see Saranindranath Tagore, 'Why the Moth Cannot Be a Poet', in *Tagore, Einstein and the Nature of Reality*.
8. *The Religion of Man*, ch. 15, 'Conclusion', *EW* 3:172.
9. Tagore–Einstein dialogue, 14 July 1930: *EW* 3:913.
10. *Man*, Lecture 2, 'Supreme Man', *EW* 3:204.
11. *RRVB* 27:282.
12. *RRVB* 27:283; italicized words in English in the original.

13. *RRVB* 27:284.
14. The word '*mahāmānab*' ('great man' or 'supreme man') appears in a late poem (*Shesh lekhā* #6, *RRVB* 26:43) celebrating the advent of the universal human, appended to 'Sabhyatār sangkat', the Bengali version of 'Crisis in Civilization', when it was first published in *Prabāsi*. The poem does not appear in the English version.
15. *Man*, Lecture 1, 'Man', *EW* 3:193.
16. Shankara writes in *Upadeshasāhasri*: 'Being the witness of all cognitions, it is changeless and all-pervading. If it were to change, it would have become of limited knowledge like the intellect': tr. Bina Gupta, *The Disinterested Witness: A Fragment of Advaita Vedanta Phenomenology* (Evanston: Northwestern University Press, 1998), 37.
17. *Man*, Lecture 3, 'I am He', *EW* 3:215.
18. 'The Union of Cultures' (1921), *EW* 3:435.
19. 'An Eastern University', *Creative Unity*, *EW* 2:557.
20. Amartya Sen, *Identity and Violence* (New York: W.W. Norton, 2007).
21. Letter of 13 March 1921, *Letters to a Friend*, *EW* 3:289.
22. 'The Voice of Humanity' (1925), *EW* 3:521.
23. Saranindranath Tagore, 'Tagore's Conception of Cosmopolitanism: A Reconstruction', *University of Toronto Quarterly*, 77 (2008), 1070–84.
24. 'The Religion of an Artist', ch. 1, *EW* 3:689.
25. Tagore, 'Bishwasāhitya' (World Literature), *RRVB* 8:384.
26. Calvin Schrag, *Philosophical Papers: Betwixt and Between* (Albany: State University of New York Press, 1994), 172.
27. *EW* 3:582.
28. Ranajit Guha, 'The Poverty of Historiography', in *History at the Limit of World History* (New York: Columbia University Press), 93.
29. 'The Way to Unity' (1923), *EW* 3:461.
30. 'Bishwasāhitya', *RRVB* 8:387.
31. Ibid., *RRVB* 8:376.
32. For a discussion of Rabindranath's conception of cosmopolitanism see Saranindranath Tagore, 'Tagore's Conception'.
33. Isaiah Berlin, 'Rabindranath Tagore and the Consciousness of Nationality', in *The Sense of Reality* (New York: Farrar, Strauss and Giroux, 1996), 265.
34. 'The Way to Unity', *EW* 3.461.
35. 'Shikshār milan', *RRVB* 28:426.
36. Ibid., *RRVB* 28:423.
37. 'The Ideals of Education', *EW* 3:613.
38. *RRVB* 12:284. *Bhāb* can also be translated as 'sensibility', but 'attitude' captures better the overall philosophical sense of the passage.
39. See Krishna Dutta and Andrew Robinson, *Rabindranath Tagore: The Myriad-minded Man* (London: Bloomsbury, 1995), 353.
40. 'Shikshār milan', *RRVB* 28:422.

List of Tagore's Works Cited, with Index

SOURCES OF INFORMATION

Dates of composition (especially of poems) often accompany the text in *RRVB*. Other major sources of information have been:

- the bibliographical notes ('Granthaparichay') comprising *RRWBG* vol. 16
- the bibliographical notes ('Granthaparichay') in each volume of *RRVB*
- the bibliographical compilations of Pulinbihāri Sen, collected in his centenary volume *Pulinbihāri: janmashatabārshiki shraddhārgha*, ed. Anāthnāth Dās and Subimal Lāhiri (Kolkata: Visva-Bharati, 2009)
- Swapan Majumdār, *Rabindragranthasuchi* (Kolkata: National Library, 1988)
- information in *RJPM* and, more particularly, *RJPP*
- for drama, the appendices to *Rabindranath Tagore: Three Plays*, tr. and ed. Ananda Lal (Kolkata: M P Birla Foundation, 1987)
- *Bichitra*, the Tagore Online Variorum hosted by Jadavpur University

This is not an exhaustive list of sources.

PRACTICES AND CONVENTIONS

All conventions noted at the start of the book apply also to the list of works. The following additional points should be noted.

1. Each section of the list is structured as appropriate to its contents – for example, whether individual works or collections. Some types of material require additional items – for example, for plays, the date of first performance; for translations, the original work.

The sequence of elements in each section, with the relevant symbols, is indicated at the start of the section.

2. All single works have been listed together, whether short pieces or volume-length: for example, novels and individual short stories under Individual Works of Fiction, but collections of short stories under Prose Collections.

3. Exact dates of composition are available in a surprising number of cases; but in many others, we can only specify a (usually Bengali) month or span of months. Dates can rarely be ascertained for the English poems. For essays originating in talks or lectures, the date of delivery has often been taken by default as the date of composition. Only the month and year have been cited in volume publications; exact dates may appear to be available, but are often unreliable (for example, in Bengal Library Catalogue entries).

4. Tagore continually revised his work. This list does not take note of revisions. The text of the earliest published version can be different, often very different, from that in *RRVB*, perhaps with other versions in between.

5. Items quoted or cited in the text but named only in the corresponding note have been indexed under the note. Conversely, where the item is named in the text, the corresponding note has not been indexed.

BENGALI COLLECTIONS: POETRY AND SONGS

Sequence: Bengali Title (Translation of title). First publication. Location in Collected Works if applicable. Index references

Ākāshpradip (The Lamp in the Sky). Kolkata: Visva-Bharati, May 1939. *RRVB* 23. **72**

Ārogya (Recovery). Kolkata: Visva-Bharati, February 1941. *RRVB* 25. **76**

Balākā (A Flight of Geese). Allahabad: Indian Press, *May 1916. *RRVB* 12. **3, 20, 61–3, 73–4, 194, 407**

Banabāni (The Voice of the Forest). Kolkata: Visva-Bharati, *September 1931. *RRVB* 15. **65, 66, 70, 162, 320, 322n32, 333, 339, 351n37, 402n17**

Bhānusingha thākurer padābali (Bhānusingha Thākur's Verses). Kolkata: Adi Brahmosamaj Press, July 1884. *RRVB* 2. **50, 52, 131, 194, 379–80**

Bichitritā (The Pictured). Kolkata: Visva-Bharati, *July 1933. *RRVB* 17. **67–9, 70**

Bithikā (The Avenue). Kolkata: Visva-Bharati, September 1935. *RRVB* 19. **66, 69**

Chaitāli (Poems of Late Spring). In *Kābyagranthābali*, 1896. *RRVB* 5. **65, 75**

Chayanikā (Selections). Kolkata: Indian Publishing House, September 1909; various later editions. **41**

Chhabi o gān (Pictures and Songs). Kolkata: Adi Brahmosamaj Press, February 1884. *RRVB* 1. **374**

Chharhā (Rhymes). Kolkata: Visva-Bharati, *August 1941. *RRVB* 26. **264**

Chharhār chhabi (Pictures for Rhymes). Kolkata: Visva-Bharati, October 1937. *RRVB* 21. **75**

Chitrā (The Many-Pictured One). Kolkata: Adi Brahmosamaj Press, March 1896. *RRVB* 4. **52–4, 57, 63, 81n6**

Gāner bahi (Book of Songs). Published with *Bālmiki-pratibhā*. Kolkata: Adi Brahmosamaj Press, April 1893.

Gitabitān (Expanse of Songs). First ed. vols 1–2 *September 1931, vol. 3 *July 1932. Many later editions. Current standard 1-vol. ed. Kolkata: Visva-Bharati, *December 1973. **95–6, 99n63**

Gitāli (Collection of Songs). Allahabad: Indian Press, October 1914. *RRVB* 11. **59–61, 78, 96, 375, 381, 405, 407**

Gitalipi (Song-Scripts). 6 vols. Kolkata: various publishers, 1910–18.

Gitānjali (Song-Offering). Kolkata: Indian Publishing House, September 1910. *RRVB* 11. **5, 8, 37, 59–61, 73, 82n42, 96, 191, 197, 207, 216, 261, 375, 381, 388, 405, 407**

Gitimālya (Song-Garland). Kolkata: Indian Publishing House, July 1914. *RRVB* 11. **37, 59–61, 82n42, 96, 182, 375, 381, 405, 407**

Janmadine (On My Birthday). Kolkata: Visva-Bharati, 8 May 1941. *RRVB* 25. **20, 72, 76, 77, 375**

Kābyagrantha (Book of Poems), ed. Mohitchandra Sen. Kolkata: Majumdar Library, 1903. **182**

Kābyagranthābali (Collection of Poems), ed. Satyaprasād Gangopādhyāy. Kolkata: Adi Brahmosamaj Press, September 1896.

Kāhini: see *Kathā o Kāhini*. There is an entirely separate collection of short dramatic pieces also called *Kāhini* (1900).

Kalpanā (Imaginings). Kolkata: Adi Brahmosamaj Press, May 1900. *RRVB* 7. **52–3**

Kanikā (*Particles*). Kolkata: Adi Brahmosamaj Press, November 1899. *RRVB* 6. **166, 193**

Karhi o komal (Sharps and Flats). Kolkata: Adi Brahmosamaj Press, November 1886. *RRVB* 2. **35, 50, 375**

Kathā (*Kathā o kāhini*, Legends and Tales): as *Katha*, Kolkata: Adi Brahmosamaj Press, January 1900; with additional poems in two parts, *Kāhini* and *Kathā*, in *Kābyagrantha*, vol. 5 (1903); combined as *Katha o kahini*, Allahabad: Indian Press, 1908. *RRVB* 7. **74, 75, 268–9**

Kheyā (The Ferry). Bolpur: Brahmacharyashram, August 1906. *RRVB* 10. **5, 6, 7, 52–3, 59, 381, 405**

Kshanikā (Moments). Kolkata, July 1900. *RRVB* 7. **20, 164**

Lekhan (Writings). Budapest/Berlin, January 1927. *RRVB* 14. **166–7, 184n41, 184n42**

Mahuyā [a plant with intoxicating nectar]. Kolkata: Visva-Bharati, *September 1929. *RRVB* 15. **39, 63, 68, 70**

Swarabitān (Expanse of Notations). 66 + additional vols; ongoing. Kolkata: Visva-Bharati, 1935–. **95**

Utsarga (Offering). Kolkata: Indian Publishing House, May 1914. *RRVB* 10. **82n42, 182**

BENGALI COLLECTIONS: DRAMA

Sequence: Bengali Title (Translation of title). First publication.
Location in Collected Works. Index references

Byanga-kautuk (Satiric Charades). Kolkata: Majumdar Library, December 1907 (*Gadyagranthābali* vol. 7). *RRVB* 7. **104**

Hāsya-kautuk (Comic Charades). Kolkata: Majumdar Library, December 1907 (*Gadyagranthābali* vol. 6). *RRVB* 6. **104**

Kāhini (Tales). Kolkata: Adi Brahmosamaj Press, March 1900. *RRVB* 5. **128n14, 163**

BENGALI COLLECTIONS: FICTION

Sequence: Bengali Title (Translation of title). First publication.
Location in Collected Works. Index references
Volumes marked ¶ also contain poems or prose poems.

Galpaguchchha (Collection of Stories). Kolkata: Majumdar Agency, September 1900 and later editions; current standard edition from Kolkata: Visva-Bharati, 4 vols. *RRVB* 14–24, 27. **155n21, 420**

¶ *Galpasalpa* (Tales). Kolkata: Visva-Bharati, May 1941. *RRVB* 26. **264**

¶ *Lipikā* (Writings). Allahabad: Indian Press, August 1922. *RRVB* 26. **70**

¶ *Sahaj pāth* (Simple Reading). Kolkata: Visva-Bharati, May 1930. *RRVB* A2. **258, 261**

Tin sangi (Three Companions). Kolkata: Visva-Bharati, January 1941. *RRVB* 25. **39**

BENGALI COLLECTIONS: NON-FICTION

Format: Bengali Title (Translation of title). First publication.
Location in Collected Works if applicable. Index references

Ādhunik sāhitya (Modern Literature). Kolkata: Majumdar Library, October 1907 (*Gadyagranthābali* vol. 5). *RRVB* 9. **154n5, 357, 360, 368, 377n12**

Ātmaparichay (An Account of Myself). Kolkata: Visva-Bharati, April 1943. *RRVB* 27. **402n10**

Ātmashakti (Inner Strength). Kolkata: Majumdar Library, September 1905. *RRVB* 3. **280, 402n19**

Bhāratbarsha (India). Kolkata: Majumdar Library, ?February 1906. *RRVB* 4. **280**

Bichitra prabandha (Various Essays). Kolkata: Majumdar Library, April 1907 (*Gadyagranthābali* vol. 1). *RRVB* 5.

BENGALI POEMS AND SONGS: SINGLE ITEMS

Sequence: Bengali Title (Translation of title). ^Date of composition. †First publication. Volume where currently found. Reference in Collected Works. Index references
If the place of first publication is not separately indicated, it is the same as the volume where the item is currently found. For numbered poems in a collection ('Ārogya #1' etc.), that collection is the volume where the item is currently found. Songs are indexed under first lines when so cited in the text. All other songs cited by Gitabitān *(GB) section and number.*

Utsarga #24. †*Bangadarshan*, Shrāvan 1310. *RRVB* 10:41. **81n23**
Utsarga #45. ^?1902. †*Bangadarshan*, Bhādra 1309. *RRVB* 10:71. **65**

BENGALI DRAMA: SINGLE ITEMS

Sequence: Bengali Title (Translation of title). ^Date of composition. (Period of serialization is sometimes taken by default as period of composition.) †First publication. §First performance. Volume where currently found (if relevant). Reference in Collected Works. Index references
If the place of first publication is not separately indicated, it is the same as the volume where the item is currently found.

Achalāyatan (The Immovable Institution). ^June 1911. †*Prabāsi*, Āshvin 1318; Kolkata: Adi Brahmosamaj Press, August 1912. §Reading, Kolkata, 2 July 1911; staged Santiniketan, 26 April 1914. *RRVB* 11. **106, 296, 404**

Arup ratan (Formless Jewel). ^January 1920. †Kolkata: Chintāmani Ghosh [Indian Publishing House], *February 1920. §Reading with music and miming, Alfred Theatre, Kolkata, 15 September 1924; staged Santiniketan, 8 December 1935; New Empire Theatre, Kolkata, 12 December 1935. *RRVB* 13. **107, 116**

Baikunther khātā (Baikuntha's Notebook). ^? February 1897. †Kolkata: Adi Brahmosamaj Press, April 1897. §Reading, Kolkata, ?March 1897; staged Kolkata, ?May–June 1897. *RRVB* 4. **104**

Bālmiki-pratibhā (Vālmiki's Genius). ^?January 1881 (later expanded). †Kolkata: Adi Brahmosamaj Press, February 1881. §Jorasanko, 26 February 1881. *RRVB* 1. **87, 102, 111–12, 126**

Basanta (Spring). ^February 1923. †Santiniketan Press, February 1923. §Madan Theatre, Kolkata, 25 February 1923. *RRVB* 15. **106**

Bisarjan (Sacrifice). ^January–February 1890 (radically revised several times subsequently). Kolkata: Adi Brahmosamaj Press, May 1890. §Tagore family, October 1890. *RRVB* 7. **103, 113, 114, 119, 121, 122, 178**

Bnāshari. ^April–June 1933. ^Serialized *Bhāratbarsha*, Kārtik–Paush 1340. †Kolkata: Visva-Bharati, December 1933. §Reading, Santiniketan, 23 April 1933. *RRVB* 24. **108**

Chandālikā (The Chandāl's Daughter). ^August 1933. †Kolkata: Visva-Bharati, *August 1933. §Reading, Santiniketan, 17 August 1933; reading (by Tagore) accompanied by songs, Madan Theatre, Kolkata, 12 September 1933; full performance, Santiniketan, 16 March 1935. *RRVB* 23:131. Recast as a dance drama (*Nrityanātya Chandālikā*), ^January–February 1938. †Kolkata: Visva-Bharati, *February 1938. §Santiniketan, c. 2 March 1938. *RRVB* 25. **95, 99n62, 102, 103, 109, 128n17**

Chirakumār sabhā (The Bachelors' Club). ^Late 1924–early 1925. †Kolkata: Visva-Bharati, April 1926. §Star Theatre, Kolkata, 18 July 1925. *RRVB* 16. Adapted from an earlier work of prose fiction with the same title. **108, 124, 339**

Tapati. ^July–August 1929. †Kolkata: Visva-Bharati, *August 1929. §Reading, Santiniketan, 19 August 1929; acted Jorasanko, 26 September 1929. *RRVB* 21. **107–8, 113, 120, 128n15**

Tāser desh (The Land of Cards). ^August 1933. †Kolkata: Visva-Bharati, *August 1933. §Madan Theatre, Kolkata, 12 September 1933. *RRVB* 23. **108, 124**

BENGALI FICTION: SINGLE ITEMS

Format: Bengali Title (English translation). ^Date of composition.
(Period of serialization is sometimes taken by default as period of
composition.) †First publication. Volume where currently found.
Reference in Collected Works. Index references
If the place of first publication is not separately indicated, it is the same
as the volume where the item is currently found. Where a work has first
appeared in serial form, that span of dates is indicated by the symbol ^
and the date of first volume publication by †.

'Anadhikār prabesh' (Trespass). ^July 1894. †*Sādhanā*, Shrāvan 1301. *Galpaguchhha.*
RRVB 19:205. **136**

'Aparichitā' (Woman Unknown). ^c. 29 September 1914. †*Sabuj patra*, Kārtik 1321.
Galpaguchhha. RRVB 23:293. **145, 242**

'Atithi' (The Visitor). ^?c. 28 June 1895. †*Sādhanā*, Bhādra–Kārtik 1302.
Galpaguchhha. RRVB 20:243. **135, 259, 260, 263**

'Badnām' (Ill Repute). ^May–June 1941. †*Prabāsi*, Āshārhh 1348. *Galpaguchhha.*
RRVB 27:69. **39**

'Balāi'. ^14 July 1928. †*Prabāsi*, Agrahāyan 1335. *Galpaguchhha. RRVB* 24:220.
137, 333

Bauthākurānir hāt (The Young Queen's Market). ^Serialized *October
1881–*September 1882 (*Bhārati*, Kārtik 1288–Āshvin 1289). †Kolkata: Adi
Brahmosamaj Press, January 1883. *RRVB* 1:370. **34, 131, 132**

'Bhikhārini' (The Beggar Woman). ^?June–August 1877. †*Bhārati*, Shrāvan–Bhādra
1284. *RRVB* 27:103. **131**

'Boshtami' (The Vaishnava Woman). ^?June 1914. †*Sabuj patra*, Āshārhh 1321.
Galpaguchhha. RRVB 23:234. **242, 380**

Chār adhyāy (Four Chapters). ^May–June 1934. †Kolkata: Visva-Bharati, December
1934. *RRVB* 13:265. **43, 152–3, 156n60, 243, 245, 246, 249**

Chaturanga (Quartet). ^Serialized *November 1914–*February 1915 with separate
titles for each part (*Sabuj patra*, Agrahāyan–Phālgun 1321). †Allahabad: Indian
Press, 1916. *RRVB* 7:427. **20, 43, 44, 140, 145–6, 243, 244, 245, 246–7, 249**

'Chhuti' (Holiday). ^?June 1892. †*Sādhanā*, Paush 1299. *Galpaguchhha. RRVB*
17:229. **136, 259**

'Chitrakar' (The Artist). ^?October 1929. †*Prabāsi*, Kārtik 1336. *Galpaguchhha.*
RRVB 24:225. **376**

Chokher bāli (Grit in the Eye). ^Started by July 1899. ^Serialized April 1901–October 1902 (*Bangadarshan*, Vaishākh 1308–Kārtik 1309). †Kolkata: Majumdar Library, April 1903. *RRVB* 3:283. **14, 44, 138–40, 146, 155n23, 155n25, 244**

'Darpaharan' (Destruction of Pride). ^?December 1902–January 1903. †*Bangadarshan*, Phālgun 1309. *Galpaguchhha. RRVB* 22:263. **243**

'Denāpāonā' (Owed and Owing). ^May–July 1891. †*Hitabādi*, 1298. *Galpaguchhha. RRVB* 15:405. **136, 241, 242**

'Dhwangsa' (Destruction). ^6 March 1941. †*Galpasalpa. RRVB* 26:353. **265**

Dui bon (Two Sisters). ^October–November 1932. †*Bichitrā*, Agrahāyan–Phālgun 1339. †Kolkata: Visva-Bhārati, March 1933. *RRVB* 11:409. **14, 153**

Ghare-bāire (At Home and in the World). ^Serialized April 1915–*February 1916 (*Sabuj patra*, Vaishākh–Phālgun 1322). †Allahabad: Indian Press, ?April, 1916. *RRVB* 8:137. **20, 28, 39, 42–3, 44, 138, 140, 146–9, 244, 245–6, 288, 290, 296**

'Ghāter kathā' (The Ghat's Story). ^?September–October 1884. †*Bhārati*, Kārtik 1291. *Galpaguchhha. RRVB* 14:245. **133**

'Ginni' (The Housewife). ^May–July 1891. †*Hitabādi*, 1298. *Galpaguchhha. RRVB* 15:415. **251**

Gorā. ^Serialized *August 1907–*February 1910 (*Prabāsi*, Bhādra 1314–Phālgun 1316). †Incomplete ed., Kolkata: Kuntalin Press, April 1909; complete in 2 vols, Kolkata: Indian Publishing House, February 1910. *RRVB* 6:109. **6–7, 9, 11n36, 14, 16, 20, 41–2, 43, 140, 142–4, 146, 243, 245, 249, 296, 387, 404, 405**

'Haimanti'. ^May 1914. †*Sabuj patra*, Jyaistha 1321. *Galpaguchhha. RRVB* 23:220. **241, 242, 249**

'Hāldārgoshthi' (The Haldar Clan). ^April 1914. †*Sabuj patra*, Vaishākh 1321. *Galpaguchhha*. **145, 242**

'Jay-parājay' (Victory and Defeat). ^?*May 1892. †*Sādhanā*, Kārtik 1299. *Galpaguchhha. RRVB* 17:210. **179**

'Jibita o mrita' (The Living and the Dead). ^?*August 1892. †*Sādhanā*, Bhādra 1299. *Galpaguchhha. RRVB* 17:181. **136, 137**

Jogājog (*Relationships*). ^Completed by July 1928. †Serialized September 1927–March 1929 (*Bichitrā*, Āshvin 1334–Chaitra 1335). Kolkata: Visva-Bharati, *June 1929. *RRVB* 9:181. **20, 44, 138, 140, 149–52, 157n50, 157n51, 157n52, 243, 244, 245, 247–8**

Karunā. ^August 1877–August 1878. †Serialized September 1877–August 1878 (*Bhārati*, Āshvin 1284–Bhādra 1285). *Galpaguchhha. RRVB* 27:117. **131, 154n2**

'Khātā' (The Exercise-Book). ^May–July 1891. †*Hitabādi*, ?1298. *Galpaguchhha. RRVB* 18:317. **136, 241**

'Kshudhita pāshān' (Hungry Stone). ^?First half of 1895. †*Sādhanā*, Shrāvan 1302. *Galpaguchhha. RRVB* 20:231. **137**

'Lyābaretari' (The Laboratory). ^*c.*1 September 1940. †*Ānandabājār patrikā*, 15 Āshvin 1347; *Tin sangi. RRVB* 25:269. **137**

'Madhyabartini' (She in the Middle) ^?April–May 1893. †*Sādhanā*, Jyaistha 1300. *Galpaguchhha. RRVB* 18:257. **241, 242**

'Totākāhini' (The Parrot's Tale). ^?January 1918. †*Sabuj patra*, Māgh 1324. *Lipika*. *RRVB* 26:132. **179, 257, 259**

BENGALI NON-FICTION: SINGLE ITEMS

Format: Bengali Title (English translation). ^Date of composition.
(Period of serialization is sometimes taken by default as period of
composition.) †First publication. Volume where currently found.
Reference in Collected Works. Index references
If the place of first publication is not separately indicated, it is the same
as the volume where the item is currently found. Where a work has first
appeared in serial form, that span of dates is indicated by the symbol ^
and the date of first volume publication by †.

'Ādhunik kābya' (Modern Poetry). ^?April 1932. †*Parichay*, Vaishākh 1339. *Sāhityer pathe*. *RRVB* 23:420. **361–2, 368**
'Aitihāsik chitra' (Images from History [title of a journal]). ^?September 1898. †*Bhārati*, Bhādra 1305. *Ādhunik sāhitya*. *RRVB* 9:506. **271, 277n5, 277n6, 277n7**
'Aitihāsik chitra, suchanā' [foreword to the first number of the journal *Aitihāsik chitra*]. ^?December 1898. †*Aitihāsik chitra*, January 1899. *RRVB* 30:342. **277n6**
'Aitihāsik upanyās' (The Historical Novel). ^August–September 1898. †*Bhārati*, Āshvin 1305. *Sāhitya*. *RRVB* 8:446. **268, 360**
'Akāl kushmānda' (Ripe Too Early). ^23 March 1884. †*Bhārati*, Chaitra 1290. *RRVB* 30:166. **280, 281**
'Antar bāhir' (Within and Without). ^7 June 1912. †*Bhārati*, Shrāvan 1319. *Pather sanchay*. *RRVB* 26:502. **129n40**
'Aranyadebatā' (The God of the Forest). ^3 September 1938. †*Prabāsi*, Kārtik 1345. *Palliprakriti*. *RRVB* 27:545. **332**
'Ārjya gāthā' [Aryan Lays: review of a book of that title]. ^?November 1894. †*Sādhanā*, Agrahāyan 1301. *Ādhunik sāhitya*. *RRVB* 9:480. **99n7, 364n43**
'Āshirbād: harāmani' [Lost Jewels: Review of *Hārāmani*, a collection of Bāul songs]. ^^*March 1928. *Prabāsi*, Chaitra 1334. *RRVB* 32:258. **99n22**
'Ātmaparichay' I (An Account of Myself). ^?July 1904. †*Bangabhāshār lekhak*, Part I, ed. Harimohan Mukhopādhyāy (August 1904). *Ātmaparichay*. *RRVB* 27:187.
'Bairāgya' (Renunciation). ^27 February 1909. †*Shāntiniketan* 6, April 1909. *RRVB* 14:350. **363n1**
'Bāngāli kabi nay' (The Bengali Is Not a Poet). ^August 1880. †*Bhārati*, Bhādra 1287. *Samālochanā*. *RRVB* 29:199. **364n31, 369**
'Bānglā chhander prakriti' (The Nature of Bengali Metre). ^?15 September 1933. †(In part) *Udayan*, Vaishākh 1341. *RRVB* 21:351. **364n29**
'Bānglā jātiya sāhitya' (Bengali National Literature). ^7 April 1895. †*Sādhanā*, Vaishākh 1302. *Sāhitya*. *RRVB* 8:415. **353–4, 370**

'Jugāntar' (A Change of Era). ^?January–February 1995. †*Sādhanā*, Chaitra 1301. *Ādhunik sāhitya. RRVB* 9:476. **364n43**

'Kabi yets' (The Poet Yeats). ^4 September 1912. †*Prabāsi*, Kārtik 1319. *Pather sanchay. RRVB* 26:521. **361**

'Kabir kaiphiyat' (The Poet's Defence). ^?May 1322. †*Sabuj patra*, Jyaistha 1322. *Sāhityer pathe. RRVB* 23:368. **352**

'Kabi-sangit' (The Songs of Kabiyāls). ^?May 1895. †*Sādhanā*, Jyaistha 1302. *Lokasāhitya. RRVB* 6:632. **355**

'Kābyer tātparjya' (The Significance of a Poem). ^?November 1894. †*Sādhanā*, Agrahāyan 1301. *Panchabhut. RRVB* 2:603. **364n15**

'Kābyer upekshitā' (The Ignored Woman in Poetry). ^?May 1900. †*Bhārati*, Jyaistha 1307. *Prāchin sāhitya. RRVB* 5:548. **198, 359**

'Kādambarichitra' (An Image of *Kādambari*). ^?January 1900. †*Pradip*, Māgh 1306. *Prāchin sāhitya, RRVB* 5:537. **223**

'Kālāntar' (Change of Era). ^?July 1933. †*Parichay*, Shrāvan 1340. *Kālāntar. RRVB* 24:243. **272, 278n21, 278n23**

'Karmajog' (The Pursuit of Work). ?February 1911. †*Bhārati*, Phālgun 1317. *Shāntiniketan*, vol.13. *RRVB* 16:343. **402n23**

'Krishnacharitra' (The Nature of Krishna). ^?January–February 1895. †*Sādhanā*, Māgh–Phālgun 1301. *Ādhunik sāhitya. RRVB* 9:446. **361**

'Kumārsambhab o Shakuntalā'. ^November 1901. †*Bangadarshan*, Paush 1308. *Prāchin sāhitya. RRVB* 5:510. **359**

'Landane' (In London). ^c. 20–27 June 1912. †*Prabāsi*, Bhādra 1319. *Pather sanchay. RRVB* 26:513. **48n14**

'Lekhā kumāri o chhāpā sundari' (Miss Script and Madame Print). ^?May 1883. †*Bhārati*, Jyaistha 1290. *RRVB* 30:418. **33**

'Mahātmā gāndhi'. ^2 October 1936. †*Prabāsi*, Agrahāyan 1344. *Mahatmā gāndhi. RRVB* 27:289. **278n34**

'Mandirābhimukhe' (Towards the Temple). ^?December 1898. †*Pradip*, Paush 1305. *RRVB* 29:395. **222, 235n5**

'Mandra' [Review of Dwijendralāl Rāy's book of poems, *Mandra*]. ^?October 1902. †*Bangadarshan*, Kārtik 1309. *Ādhunik sāhitya. RRVB* 9:489. **364n43**

'Meghdut' (*The Meghadutam*). ^?November 1891. †*Sāhitya*, Agrahāyan 1298. *Prāchin sāhitya. RRVB* 5:508. **357, 359**

'Meghnādbadh kābya'. ^1877. † Serialized in *Bhārati*, 6 parts, Shrāvan–Phālgun 1284. *RRVB* 29:82. **357**

'Meghnādbadh kābya'. ^?July 1882. †*Bhārati*, Bhādra 1289. *Samālochanā. RRVB* A2:73. **357**

'Mukti' (Emancipation). ^20 April 1909. †*Shāntiniketan* 8, June 1909. *RRVB* 14:444. **402n14**

'Muktir path' (The Road to Emancipation). ^20 April 1909. †*Shāntiniketan* 8, June 1909. *RRVB* 14:446. **402n24**

'Musalmān rājatwer itihās' (The History of Muslim Rule). ^?July–August 1898.
†Bhārati, Shrāvan 1305. Ādhunik sāhitya. RRVB 9:494. **364n43**
'Nababarsha' (The New Year). ^14 April 1902. †Bangadarshan, Vaishākh 1309.
Bhāratbarsha. RRVB 4:367. **291n2, 292n15**
'Nabajug' (A New Age). ^23 December 1932. †Prabāsi, Māgh 1339. Kalāntar
(additions). RRVB 24:456. **252n1**
'Nāmāntar' (Change of Name). ^4 October 1927. †Bichitrā, Agrahāyan 1334. RRVB
9:544.
'Nāri' (Woman). ^2–10 October 1936. †Prabāsi, Agrahāyan 1343. Kalāntar. RRVB
24:377. **13, 252**
'Neshan ki' (What Is a Nation?). ^?July 1901. †Bangadarshan, Shrāvan 1308.
Ātmashakti. RRVB 3:515. **143, 148, 278n41**
'Niyam o mukti' (Rules and Release). ^12 April 1909. †Shāntiniketan 8, June 1909.
RRVB 14:429. **402n20**
Paschim-jātrir dāyāri (Diary of a Traveller to the West). ^24 September 1924–15
February 1925; serialized in Prabāsi, Agrahāyan 1331–Jyaistha 1332, Phālgun
1333. †Included in Jātri, Kolkata: Visva-Bhārati, *May 1929. RRVB 19:363.
267n40, 374–5, 377n24
'Path o pātheya' (The Way and the Means). ^25 May 1908. †Bangadarshan, Jyaistha
1315. Rājā prajā. RRVB 10:445. **6, 156n41, 278n34**
'Patrālāp: Lokendranāth pālitke likhita' (Letters Exchanged with Lokendranath
Palit). 1892. Sādhanā, Phālgun 1298–Āshvin 1299. Sāhitya (additions). RRVB
8:463. **128n19, 155n24, 365n51, 371**
'Pitrārcā o larā' (Petrarca and Laura). ^?July 1878. †Bhārati, Āshvin 1285. RRVB
29:152. **365n49**
'Prāchin bhārater ekah' ('The One' of Ancient India). ^22 December 1901.
†Bangadarshan and Tattwabodhini patrikā, both Phālgun 1308. Dharma.
RRVB 13:364. **5**
'Prāchya o pāschātya sabhyatā' (Eastern and Western Civilization). ^?May 1901.
†Bangadarshan, Jyaistha 1308. Bhāratbarsha. RRVB 4:416. **292n15**
'Rājā o prajā' (The King and the Subjects). ^?July 1894. †Sādhanā, Shrāvan 1301.
Samuha (additions). RRVB 10:542. **278n41**
'Rājbhakti' (Loyalty to the King). ^23 January 1906. †Bhāndār, Māgh 1312. Rājā
prajā. RRVB 10:435. **5, 11n32**
'Rājsingha' [title of Bankimchandra's novel]. ^?March 1894. †Sādhanā, Chaitra 1300.
Ādhunik sāhitya. RRVB 9:463. **359, 360**
'Ramābāier baktritā upalakshe' (On the Occasion of Ramābāi's Lecture). ^June 1889.
†Bhārati o bālak, Āshārhh 1296. Samāj. RRVB 12:450. **23n4**
'Rāmāyan'. ^20 December 1903. †Introduction to Dineshchandra Sen's Rāmāyani
kathā (1904). Prāchin sāhitya. RRVB 5:501. **358, 359, 360**
'Rangamancha' (The Stage). ^? December 1902. †Bangadarshan, Paush 1309.
Bichitra prabandha. RRVB 5:449. **40, 104–5, 112**

'Swādhikārpramattah' (Reckless of One's Rights). ^*December 1917. †*Prabāsi*, Māgh 1324. *Kālāntar* (additions). *RRVB* 24:392. **278n27**

'Swāmi Shraddhānanda'. ^?December 1926. †*Prabāsi*, Māgh 1333. *Kālāntar* (additions). *RRVB* 24:431. **272**

'Tapoban' (The Forest Retreat). ^1 December 1909. †*Shāntiniketan* 9, January 1910. *RRVB* 14:457. **185n86, 402n18**

'Tathya o satya' (Fact and Truth). ^2 March 1924. †*Bangabāni*, Bhādra 1331. *Sāhityer pathe*. *RRVB* 23:382. **371**

'Tintalā' (The Third Storey). ^22 February 1909. †*Shāntiniketan* 6, April 1909. *RRVB* 14:338. **414n39**

'Utsab' (Celebration). ^22 December 1905. †*Bangadarshan*, Māgh 1312. *Dharma*. *RRVB* 13:335. **5, 11n31**

Yurop-jātrir dāyāri (Diary of a Traveller to Europe). ^22 August–4 November 1890; serialized in *Sādhanā*, Agrahāyan 1298–Kārtik 1299. †Kolkata: Adi Brahmosamaj Press, September 1893. *RRVB* 1:584a(*ka*). **2, 283**

Yurop-prabāsir patra (Letters of a Sojourner in Europe). ^September 1878–March 1880. †Serialized in *Bhārati*, Vaishākh 1286–Shrāvan 1287. Kolkata: Sāradāprasād Gangopādhyāy, October 1881. *RRVB* 1:531. **20n3**

ENGLISH COLLECTIONS: POETRY AND DRAMA

Sequence: English Title. First publication. Reference in Collected Works. Index references

Collected Poems and Plays. London: Macmillan, 1936. *EW* 1, 2. **18, 19, 158**

Crescent Moon, The. London: Macmillan, November 1913. *EW* 1:129. **18, 160, 162, 190, 206, 212–13, 215**

Fireflies. New York: Macmillan, 1928. *EW* 1:439. **166–7, 175, 183n27**

Fruit-Gathering. London: Macmillan, 1916. *EW* 1:157. **160, 162–3**

Fugitive, The. New York: Macmillan, October 1921. A shorter collection 'for private circulation only' from the Santiniketan Press in 1918. *EW* 1:245, 545. **160, 163**

Gardener, The. London: Macmillan, October 1913. *EW* 1:80. **18, 160, 161–2, 164, 206, 208**

Gitanjali (Song-Offerings). London: India Society, (?1 November) 1912. *EW* 1:38. **18, 19, 36, 37–8, 44, 59, 60, 82n42, 158, 159–61, 162, 164, 167, 169, 171, 176, 177, 178, 181, 182, 187, 188, 189, 193, 198, 203, 204–5, 207, 209, 210, 213, 216, 234, 284, 361, 381, 405**

Lover's Gift and *Crossing*. London: Macmillan, April 1918. *EW* 1:195. **160, 163**

One Hundred Poems of Kabir. London: India Society, 1914. *EW* 1:487. **160, 163, 194, 197, 213–14, 275, 381, 383, 384, 386, 389n19, 389n20, 390n25, 390n28, 390n31, 390n32, 390n39, 390n51**

Poems. Kolkata: Visva-Bharati, 1942. *EW* 1:325. **160, 164–5**

Poems from Tagore. London: Macmillan, 1921. **160**

Sacrifice and Other Plays. New York: Macmillan, October 1917. *EW* 2:53. **178**
Stray Birds. New York: Macmillan, November 1916. *EW* 1: 397. **166, 175, 206, 323**

ENGLISH VOLUMES AND COLLECTIONS: NON-FICTION

*Sequence: English title. ^Period of composition if known. First
publication. Reference in Collected Works. Index references*

Creative Unity. New York: Macmillan, 1922. *EW* 2:493. **169, 174–5**
   Sectional headings:
   The Poet's Religion. *EW* 2:495. **174, 382, 414n20**
   The Creative Ideal. *EW* 2:506. **414n16, 414n29**
   The Religion of the Forest. *EW* 2:511. **128n23, 174**
   An Indian Folk Religion. *EW* 2:520. **127n4, 174, 380**
   East and West. *EW* 2:530. **174**
   The Modern Age. *EW* 2:538. **174**
   The Nation. *EW* 2:548. **174**
   An Eastern University. *EW* 2:556. **174–5, 331, 429n19**
East and West. ^August–September 1934. Paris: Institut internationale de
   coopération intellectuelle, 1935. **351n23**
Letters to a Friend. Letters written 1913–22. Chennai: S. Ganesan, 1922; enlarged,
   London: George Allen and Unwin, 1928. *EW* 3:219. **128n21, 129n57, 179,
   307n21, 415n49, 429n21**
Man. ^Lectures at Andhra University, 1933. Waltair: Andhra University, 1937.
   EW 3:191. **177**
   Sectional headings:
   'Man' (Lecture 1). *Visva-Bharati News,* May 1934. *EW* 3:193. **429n15**
   'Supreme Man' (Lecture 2). *EW* 3:203. **428n10**
   'I am He' (Lecture 3). **429n17**
Nationalism. ^June–December 1916. New York: Macmillan, September 1917. *EW*
   2:417. **171–3, 177, 181, 182, 187, 203, 210, 215, 273–4, 275, 279, 281, 284**
   Sectional headings:
   Nationalism in the West (ch. 1). *EW* 2:419. **148, 156n34, 172,**
   Nationalism in Japan (ch. 2). *EW* 2:436. **172–3, 220n42, 280**
   Nationalism in India (ch. 3). *EW* 2:453. **148, 173**
Personality. ^June–?December 1916. London: Macmillan, May 1917. *EW* 2:347.
   170–1, 344–5, 407
   Sectional headings:
   What Is Art? *EW* 2:349. **170, 236n17**
   The World of Personality. *EW* 2:363. **128n18, 170–1, 350, 351n25, 351n27,
      351n39, 414n10, 414n32, 414n42**
   The Second Birth. *EW* 2:377. **170-1, 415n43, 415n51, 415n53**
   My School. *EW* 2:389. **171, 307n10, 307n11, 351n28**

ENGLISH POEMS: SINGLE ITEMS

Sequence: English Title (Bengali original if any). ^Date of composition.
†First publication.   Volume where found. Reference in Collected
Works. Index references
If the place of first publication is not separately indicated, it is the same
as the volume where the item is currently found. For numbered poems
in a collection ('Crossing #65', etc.), that collection is the volume where
the item is currently found. Exact or even approximate dates for specific
poems are seldom available.

'Ama and Vinayaka': see *Fugitive* #2.29.

Child, The. ^July 1930. †London: George Allen and Unwin, 1931. *EW* 1:477. **79, 160, 165–6, 208, 265**

Crossing #65 (*Gitānjali* #97). *EW* 1:236. **414n26**

Crossing #71. *EW* 1:238. **71**

Crossing #72 (*Balākā* #17). *EW* 1:238. **414n33**

Crossing #78 (*Gitāli* #98). *EW* 1:240. **414n35**

Fireflies #1 ('Swapna āmār jonāki', *Lekhan*). *EW* 1:439. **184n41**

Fireflies #8 ('Prajāpati se to', *Lekhan*). *EW* 1:440. **184n41**

Fireflies #19 (*Sphulinga* #249). *EW* 1:441. **184n44**

Fireflies #60. *EW* 1:447. **184n43**

Fruit-Gathering #1 (*Balākā* #8). *EW* 1:245.

Fruit-Gathering #3 (song: 'Basante ki sudhui kebal', *Rājā*). *EW* 1:157. **183n19**

Fruit-Gathering #5 (*Naibedya* #40). *EW* 1:158. **183n20**

Fruit-Gathering #47 (*Smaran* #14). *EW* 1:176.

Fruit-Gathering #58 (*Gitāli* #99). *EW* 1:180. **220n36**

Fruit-Gathering #63 (*Naibedya* #45). *EW* 1:182. **414n22**

Fruit-Gathering #78 (*Balākā* #28). *EW* 1:187. **414n40**

Fruit-Gathering #80 (*Balākā* #29). *EW* 1:188. **414n27**

Fruit-Gathering #81 (*Balākā* #33). *EW* 1:188. **414n21**

Fugitive #1.9 ('Sekāl', *Kshanikā*). *EW* 1:248. **163**

Fugitive #1.11 ('Urbashi', *Chitrā*). *EW* 1:249. **163**

Fugitive #1.17 ('Sonār tari', *Sonār tari*). *EW* 1:252. **81n34**

Fugitive #1.20, 'Kacha and Devayani' ('Bidāy abhishāp'). *EW* 1:253. **183n26**

Fugitive #1.22 (translations of medieval Bengali Vaishnav songs). *EW* 1:260. **163**

Fugitive #2.29, 'Ama and Vinayaka' ('Sati', *Kāhini*). *EW* 1:271. **183n26**

Fugitive #2.32, 'The Mother's Prayer' ('Gāndhārir ābedan', *Kāhini*). †*Modern Review*, June 1919. *EW* 1:277. **183n26**

Fugitive #2.34 (translations of Baul songs). *EW* 1:283. **163**

Fugitive #3.25, 'Somaka and Ritvik' ('Narak bās', *Kāhini*). *EW* 1:297. **183n26**

Fugitive #3.28, 'Karna and Kunti' (Karna kunti sangbād', *Kāhini*). †*Modern Review*, April 1920. *EW* 1:303. **183n26**

Fugitive #3.38 (translations of Hindi songs by Jnānadās). *EW* 1:312. **163**

ENGLISH DRAMA: SINGLE ITEMS

Sequence: English Title (Bengali original). ^Date of composition.
†First publication. §First performance. Volume where currently found.
Reference in Collected Works. Index references

ENGLISH FICTION: SINGLE ITEMS

Sequence: English Title (Bengali original). ^Date of composition if known. †First publication. Volume where currently found. Reference in Collected Works. Index references

ENGLISH NON-FICTION: SHORT SINGLE ITEMS

Sequence: English Title (Bengali original if any). ^Date of composition if known. †First publication. Volume where currently found. Reference in Collected Works. Index references

Further Reading

These lists are necessarily selective. They only comprise material available in English. The works cited sometimes confine their own scope to English material, largely or entirely. Inevitably, most of them focus on relatively language-neutral aspects of Rabindranath's life and thought, rather than the core creative substance of his poems, drama and fiction. One feels compelled to add a statutory warning that even estimable studies and translations can be marred by error. One or two popular titles have been omitted for this reason.

Titles included in the List of Tagore's Works Cited have not been repeated below, except for special reasons.

WEBSITE

The online variorum *Bichitra* (bichitra.jdvu.ac.in), created by the School of Cultural Texts and Records, Jadavpur University, covers virtually all Rabindranath's Bengali and English writings. It provides scans of the manuscripts and early printed volumes, reading texts, a hyperlinked bibliography, a search engine, and a collation engine to compare variant readings. The site can be navigated in English as well as Bengali and Hindi.

See also Sukanta Chaudhuri, ed., *Bichitra: The Making of an Online Tagore Variorum* (New York: Springer, 2015).

MULTI-GENRE ANTHOLOGIES

Alam, Fakrul, and Radha Chakravarty, eds. *The Essential Tagore*. Cambridge, MA: Belknap Press, Harvard, 2011: the fullest collection.
Boundless Sky. Kolkata: Visva-Bharati, 1964.
Chakravarty, Amiya, ed. *A Tagore Reader*. London: Macmillan, 1961.
Chakravarty, Radha, ed. *Shades of Difference: Selected Works of Rabindranath Tagore*, with an audiovisual DVD. Delhi: Social Science Press, 2015.
Sinha, Arunava, tr. and ed. *Tagore for the 21st Century Reader*. Delhi: Aleph Books, 2014.
It is important to note that *The Collected Poems and Plays of Rabindranath Tagore* (London: Macmillan, 1936) has a grossly misleading title. It contains only translations by the poet himself published till that date, with a few additional items.

POETRY: RABINDRANATH'S OWN TRANSLATIONS

The English Writings of Rabindranath Tagore. Vols 1–3 ed. Sisir Kumar Das, vol. 4 ed. Nityapriya Ghosh. Delhi: Sahitya Akademi, 1994–2007.
The separate titles originally published by Macmillan (see List of Tagore's Works Cited), but now also reprinted by other publishers, are still readily available.

POETRY: OTHER TRANSLATIONS

Chaudhuri, Sukanta, ed. *Rabindranath Tagore: Selected Poems*, tr. by various hands. Oxford Tagore Translations. Delhi: Oxford University Press, 2004.
Dyson, Ketaki Kushari, tr. and ed. *I Won't Let You Go*. Newcastle upon Tyne: Bloodaxe Books, 1991.
Gitanjali (English), facsimile of the manuscript, ed. Abhik Kumar Dey. Kolkata: Shishu sāhitya samsad, 2009.
Kabir, Humayun, ed. *One Hundred and One Poems by Rabindranath Tagore*. Mumbai: Asia Publishing House, 1966.
Radice, William, tr. and ed. *Rabindranath Tagore: Gitanjali*. Gurgaon: Penguin Random House, 2011: contains Radice's own translations of the poems in the English *Gitanjali*, together with the manuscript versions of Rabindranath's translations and other material.
———, tr. and ed. *Rabindranath Tagore: Selected Poems*. Harmondsworth: Penguin, 1985.

PLAYS: TRANSLATIONS

The English Writings of Rabindranath Tagore (see earlier), vols 2 and 4, for plays translated by Rabindranath himself, or by associates but published under his name (see List of Tagore's Works Cited).
The separate titles originally published by Macmillan (see List of Tagore's Works Cited), but now also reprinted by other publishers, are still readily available.
Lal, Ananda, tr. and ed. *Rabindranath Tagore: Three Plays*. Kolkata: M P Birla Foundation, 1987; rev. but without musical scores and illustrations, Delhi: Oxford University Press, 2001: contains *Raktakarabi* (as *Red Oleander*), *Tapati*, and *Arup ratan* (as *Formless Jewel*).
Sykes, Marjorie, tr. and ed. *Rabindranath Tagore: Three Plays*. Mumbai: Oxford University Press, 1950: contains *Muktadhāra*, *Chandālikā*, and *Natir pujā*.
Tagore, Rabindranath. *Chandālikā*, tr. Ananda Lal, in *Shades of Difference* (see earlier, 'Multi-genre anthologies').
———. *Chandālikā*, tr. Arunava Sinha, in *Tagore for the 21st Century Reader* (see earlier, 'Multi-genre anthologies').
———. *Dākghar* (as *The Post Office*), tr. William Radice. Kolkata: Visva-Bharati, 2008.

————. *Grihaprabesh* (as *The Housewarming*). In *The Housewarming and Other Selected Writings*, tr. Mary Lago, Tarun Gupta, and Amiya Chakravarty. New York: New American Library, 1965.

————. *Tāser desh* (as *Card Country*), tr. William Radice. Kolkata: Visva-Bharati, 2008.

NOVELS: TRANSLATIONS

Tagore, Rabindranath. *Chār adhyāy* (as *Four Chapters*), tr. Surendranath Tagore. Kolkata: Visva-Bharati, 1950.

————. *Chaturanga*, translator unknown: serialized as *A Story in Four Chapters* in *Modern Review* 31 (February–May 1922); published as *Broken Ties* in *Broken Ties and Other Stories* (London: Macmillan, 1925).

————. *Chaturanga* (as *Quartet*), tr. Kaiser Haq. Oxford: Heinemann, 1993.

————. *Chokher bāli* (as *Eyesore*), tr. Surendranath Tagore: serialized in *Modern Review* 15–16 (January–December 1914).

————. *Chokher bāli* (as *Binodini*), tr. Krishna Kripalani. Delhi: Sahitya Akademi, 1959.

————. *Ghare-bāire*, tr. Surendranath Tagore, 'revised by the author': serialized as *At Home and Outside* in *Modern Review* 23–24 (January–December 1918); published as *The Home and the World* (London: Macmillan, 1919).

————. *Ghare-bāire* (as *Home and the World*), tr. Sreejata Guha. Delhi: Penguin, 2005.

————. *Ghare-bāire* (as *The Home and the World*), tr. Arunava Sinha in *Tagore for the 21st Century Reader* (see earlier, 'Multi-genre anthologies').

————. *Gorā*, tr. W.W. Pearson, rev. Surendranath Tagore. London: Macmillan, 1924.

————. *Gorā*, tr. Sujit Mukherjee. Delhi: Sahitya Akademi, 1998.

————. *Jogājog* (as *Relationships*), tr. Supriya Chaudhuri. Oxford Tagore Translations. Delhi: Oxford University Press, 2006.

————. *Naukādubi* (as *The Wreck*), tr. 'An Englishman' [J.G. Drummond]. London: Macmillan, 1921.

————. *Naukādubi* (as *The Wreck*), tr. Arunava Sinha. Noida: HarperPerennial, 2017.

————. *Shesher kabitā* (as *The Last Poem*), tr. Dilip Basu. Noida: HarperPerennial, 2011.

————. *Shesher kabitā* (as *Farewell Song*), tr. Radha Chakravarty. Delhi: Penguin, 2011.

SHORT STORIES: TRANSLATIONS

Bhattacharya, Sipra, tr. *The Return of Khokababu*. Noida: HarperPerennial, 2009.

Broken Ties and Other Stories, tr. by various hands (see earlier, 'Novels').

Chaudhuri, Sukanta, ed. *Rabindranath Tagore: Selected Short Stories*, tr. by various hands. Oxford Tagore Translations. Delhi: Oxford University Press, 2000.

Dutta, Krishna, and Mary Lago, trs. *Rabindranath Tagore: Selected Short Stories*. London: Macmillan, 1991.

Housewarming and Other Selected Writings, The, tr. by various hands (see earlier, 'Plays').

Hungry Stones and Other Stories, tr. by various hands. London: Macmillan, 1916.

Mashi and Other Stories, tr. by various hands. London: Macmillan, 1918.

Moitra, Somnath, ed. *The Runaway and Other Stories*, tr. by various hands. Kolkata: Visva-Bharati, 1959.

Quayum, Mohammad A., tr. and ed. *The Ruined Nest and Other Stories*. Kuala Lumpur: Silverfish, 2014.

Radice, William, tr. and ed. *Rabindranath Tagore: Selected Short Stories*. Harmondsworth: Penguin, 1991: use the 2nd or later editions.

Sen, Rajani Ranjan, tr. *Glimpses of Bengal Life*. Chittagong: Minto Press / Chennai: G.A. Natesan, 1913.

WRITINGS FOR CHILDREN: TRANSLATIONS

Chaudhuri, Sukanta, ed. *Rabindranath Tagore: Selected Writings for Children*, tr. by various hands. Oxford Tagore Translations. Delhi: Oxford University Press, 2002.

Tagore, Rabindranath. *Se* (as *He (Shey)*), tr. Aparna Chaudhuri; introduction by Sankha Ghosh. Delhi: Penguin, 2007.

AUTOBIOGRAPHY: TRANSLATIONS

Das Gupta, Uma, ed. *My Life in My Words*. Delhi: Penguin/Viking, 2006: a compilation of Tagore's autobiographical writings.

Tagore, Rabindranath. *Chhelebelā* (as *My Boyhood Days*), tr. Marjorie Sykes. Kolkata: Visva-Bharati, 1940.

———. *Chhelebelā* (as *Boyhood Days*), tr. Radha Chakravarty. Delhi: Puffin, 2007.

———. *Jibansmriti* (as *My Reminiscences*), tr. Surendranath Tagore. London: Macmillan, 1917.

NON-FICTION: TRANSLATIONS

Chaudhuri, Sukanta, and Sisir Kumar Das, eds. *Rabindranath Tagore: Selected Writings on Literature and Language*, tr. by various hands. Oxford Tagore Translations. Delhi: Oxford University Press, 2001.

Tagore, Rabindranath. *Jābhā jātrir patra* (as *Letters from Java*), with other material, tr. Indira Debi Chaudhurani and Supriya Roy. Kolkata: Visva-Bharati, 2010.

———. *Yurop-prabāsir patra* (as *Letters from a Sojourner in Europe*), tr. Manjari Chakravarti. Kolkata: Visva-Bharati, 2008.

———. *Pārasye* (as *Journey to Persia and Iraq*), tr. Surendranath Tagore and Sukhendu Ray. Kolkata: Visva-Bharati, 2003.

———. *Pather sanchay* (as *Gleanings of the Road*), tr. Somdatta Mandal. Delhi: Niyogi Books, 2018.

———. *Rāshiār chithi* (as *Letters from Russia*), tr. Sasadhar Sinha. Kolkata: Visva-Bharati, 1960.

Towards Universal Man, tr. by various hands. Mumbai: Asia Publishing House, 1961.

LETTERS AND INTERACTIONS

Chakravarty, Bikash, ed. *Poets to a Poet: 1912–1940*. Kolkata: Visva-Bharati, 1998: letters to Rabindranath from various Anglophone poets.

Das Gupta, Uma, ed. *A Difficult Friendship: Letters of Edward Thompson and Rabindranath Tagore 1913–1940*. Delhi: Oxford University Press, 2003.

Dutta, Krishna, and Andrew Robinson, eds. *Selected Letters of Rabindranath Tagore*. Cambridge: Cambridge University Press, 1997.

Dyson, Ketaki Kushari. *In Your Blossoming Flower-Garden: Rabindranath Tagore and Victoria Ocampo*. Delhi: Sahitya Akademi, 1988.

Guha, Chinmoy, ed. and part tr. *Bridging East and West: Rabindranath Tagore and Romain Rolland Correspondence (1919–1940)*. Delhi: Oxford University Press, 2019.

Lago, Mary, ed. *Imperfect Encounter: Letters of William Rothenstein and Rabindranath Tagore, 1911–41*. Cambridge, MA: Harvard University Press, 1972.

Majumdar, Sirshendu. *Yeats and Tagore: A Comparative Study*. Bethesda: Academica Press, 2013.

Tagore, Rabindranath. *Chhinnapatra*, selections (as *Glimpses of Bengal*), tr. Surendranath Tagore. London: Macmillan, 1921.

———. *Chhinnapatrābali* (as *Letters from a Young Poet 1887–1895*), tr. Rosinka Chaudhuri. Delhi: Penguin, 2014.

———. *Letters to A Friend*, ed. C.F. Andrews (1928), in *English Writings*, vol. 3: Rabindranath's Letters to C.F. Andrews, 1913 to 1923.

Thompson, E.P. *Alien Homage: Edward Thompson and Rabindranath Tagore*. Delhi: Oxford University Press, 1993.

RECEPTION

For Rabindranath's reception in India, see

Chakravorty, Swapan, ed. *Nameless Recognition: Rabindranath Tagore and Other Indian Literatures*. Kolkata: National Library, 2011.

Visva-Bharati Quarterly 7:3 (1942; rpt. in *VBQ* 26:3–4, 1961).

For his reception outside India, see

Aronson, Alex. *Rabindranath through Western Eyes*. Allahabad: Kitabistan, 1943.

Bharucha, Rustom. *Another Asia: Rabindranath Tagore and Okakura Tenshin*. Delhi: Oxford University Press, 2006: on Rabindranath's interaction with East Asia, Japan in particular.

Kämpchen, Martin. *Rabindranath Tagore and Germany: A Documentation*. Kolkata: Max Müller Bhavan, 1991.

Kämpchen, Martin, and Imre Bangha, eds. *Rabindranath Tagore: One Hundred Years of Global Reception*. Hyderabad: Orient Blackswan, 2014: a detailed account, country by country.

Kundu, Kalyan, Sakti Bhattacharya, and Kalyan Sircar, eds. *Imagining Tagore: Rabindranath Tagore and the British Press (1912–1941)*. Kolkata: Shishu sāhitya samsad, 2000: expanded from the earlier *Rabindranath Tagore and the British Press* (1990).

Mukherjee, Sujit. *Passage to America: The Reception of Rabindranath Tagore in the United States, 1912–1941*. Kolkata: Bookland, 1964.

COMMEMORATIVE VOLUMES (IN ORDER OF DATE)

Ramananda Chatterjee, ed. *The Golden Book of Tagore*. Kolkata: Golden Book Committee, 1931: to mark Rabindranath's 70th birthday.

Amal Hom, ed. *Calcutta Municipal Gazette*, special number after Rabindranath's death. Kolkata: Calcutta Corporation, 1941.

Visva-Bharati Quarterly 7:3 (1942): to mark Rabindranath's death in 1941.

Rabindranath Tagore: A Centenary Volume. Delhi: Sahitya Akademi, 1961.

Sangeet Natak Akademi Bulletin, Centenary Number: Rabindranath Tagore 1861–1961. New Delhi, 1961.

Indian Literature 4:1–2 (1960–1): Tagore Centenary number.

Visva-Bharati Quarterly, 2:1–4 (1991–2): 50th death anniversary number.

Udaya Narayana Singh and Sandeep Suri, eds. *Rabindranath Tagore: A Commemorative Volume*. Delhi: Ministry of External Affairs, 2011: to mark Rabindranath's 150th birth anniversary.

Amalendu Biswas, Christine Marsh, and Kalyan Kundu, eds. *Rabindranath Tagore: A Timeless Mind*. London: The Tagore Centre UK/Indian Council for Cultural Relations, 2011: to mark Rabindranath's 150th birth anniversary.

COLLECTIONS OF ESSAYS

Chaudhuri, Bhudeb, and K.G. Subramanyan, eds. *Rabindranath Tagore and the Challenges of Today*. Shimla: Indian Institute of Advanced Study, 1988.

Dasgupta, Sanjukta, Ramkumar Mukhopadhyay, and Swati Ganguly, eds. *Towards Tagore*. Kolkata: Visva-Bharati, 2014.

Datta, Sangeeta, and Subhoranjan Dasgupta, eds. *Tagore: The World as His Nest.* Kolkata: Jadavpur University Press, 2016.

Hogan, Patrick Colm, and Lalita Pandit, eds. *Rabindranath Tagore: Universality and Tradition.* Madison: Fairleigh Dickinson University Press, 2003.

Lago, Mary, and Ronald Warwick, eds. *Rabindranath Tagore: Perspectives in Time.* Basingstoke: Macmillan, 1989.

Quayum, Mohammad A., ed. *The Poet and His World: Critical Essays on Rabindranath Tagore.* Hyderabad: Orient Blackswan, 2011.

GENERAL STUDIES AND BIOGRAPHIES

Bhattacharya, Sabyasachi. *Rabindranath Tagore: An Interpretation.* Delhi: Penguin/ Viking, 2011.

Chakrabarti, Shirshendu. *Towards an Ethics and Aesthetics of the Future: Rabindranath Tagore 1930–41.* Shimla: Indian Institute of Advanced Study, 2015.

Kripalani, Krishna, *Rabindranath Tagore: A Biography* (1961; rev. 1980; rev.). Delhi: UBSPD with Visva-Bharati, 2012.

Lago, Mary. *Rabindranath Tagore.* Boston: Twayne Publishers, 1976.

Lesný, V. *Rabindranath Tagore: His Personality and Work*, trans. from the Czech by Guy McKeever Phillips. London: George Allen and Unwin, 1939.

Mukerji, Dhurjati Prasad. *Tagore: A Study.* Mumbai: Padma Publications, 1943.

Sen Gupta, S.C. *The Great Sentinel: A Study of Rabindranath Tagore.* Kolkata: A. Mukherjee, [1948].

Sykes, Marjorie. *Rabindranath Tagore.* Kolkata: Longmans, 1943.

CRITICISM AND INTERPRETATION OF THE LITERARY WORKS

Ayyub, Abu Sayeed. *Modernism and Tagore*, tr. Amitava Ray. Delhi: Sahitya Akademi, 1995.

———. *Tagore's Quest.* Kolkata: Papyrus, 1980.

Bhattacharya, Nandini, ed. *Rabindranath Tagore's* Gora: *A Critical Companion.* Delhi: Primus Books, 2015.

Bose, Buddhadeva. Essays in *An Acre of Green Grass and Other Writings*, ed. Rosinka Chaudhuri. Delhi: Oxford University Press, 2018: augmented edition of *An Acre of Green Grass* (1948).

Chaudhuri, Sukanta. Introduction to *Selected Writings for Children.* Oxford Tagore Translations (see earlier, 'Writings for Children').

Chaudhuri, Supriya. Introduction to *Jogājog.* Oxford Tagore Translations (see earlier, 'Novels').

Das, Sisir Kumar. Introduction to *Selected Writings on Literature and Language.* Oxford Tagore Translations (see earlier, 'Non-fiction').

Datta, P.K., ed. *Rabindranath Tagore's* The Home and the World: *A Critical Companion.* Delhi: Permanent Black, 2003.

Datta, Sudhindranath. Essays in *The World of Twilight*. Mumbai: Oxford University Press, 1970.

Dev, Amiya. *Rereading Tagore*. Delhi: Niyogi Books, 2018.

Ghosh, Sankha. Introduction to *He (Shey)* (see earlier, 'Writings for Children').

———. Introduction to *Selected Poems*. Oxford Tagore Translations (see earlier, 'Poems: other translations').

Ghosh, Tapobrata. Introduction to *Selected Short Stories*. Oxford Tagore Translations (see earlier, 'Short Stories').

Lal, Ananda. Introduction to *Three Plays* (see earlier, 'Plays').

Radice, William. *Gitanjali Reborn*, ed. Martin Kämpchen. Delhi: Social Science Press, 2017.

Sarkar, Shyamal Kumar. *Collected Papers on Rabindranath Tagore*. Kolkata: Dey's, 2013.

Thompson, Edward, *Rabindranath Tagore: Poet and Dramatist* (1926, rev. 1948; with introduction by Harish Trivedi). Delhi: Oxford University Press, 1992. This supersedes Thompson's controversial *Rabindranath Tagore: His Life and Work* (1921; rev. London: Oxford University Press, 1928).

EDUCATION

Elmhirst, Leonard K., ed. *Rabindranath Tagore: Pioneer in Education*. London: John Murray, 1961.

Nussbaum, Martha. 'Tagore, Dewey, and the Imminent Demise of Liberal Education', in *The Oxford Handbook of Philosophy of Education*, ed. Harvey Siegel, 52–63. Oxford: Oxford University Press, 2009.

O'Connell, Kathleen, *Rabindranath Tagore: The Poet as Educator*. Kolkata: Visva-Bharati, 2002.

HISTORY, POLITICS, SOCIETY

Banerjee, Arunendu. *Rabindranath Tagore and Patrick Geddes*. Kolkata: Asiatic Society, 2005.

Bhattacharya, Sabyasachi, *The Mahatma and the Poet: Letters and Debates between Gandhi and Tagore 1915–1941*. Delhi: National Book Trust, 1997.

Chakravarty, Chandrava, and Sneha Kar Chaudhuri, eds. *Tagore's Idea of the New Woman*. Delhi: Sage, 2017.

Chatterjee, Partha. 'Tagore's Non-Nation', in *Lineages of Political Society*, 94–126. Delhi: Permanent Black, 2011.

Collins, Michael. *Empire, Nationalism and the Postcolonial World: Rabindranath Tagore's Writings on History, Politics and Society*. Abingdon: Routledge, 2012.

Sen, Amartya. 'Tagore and His India', in *The Argumentative Indian*, 89–120. London: Allen Lane/Penguin, 2005.

Sen, Sochin. *Political Philosophy of Rabindranath*. Kolkata: Asher, 1929.

Tuteja, K.L., and Kaustav Chakraborty, eds. *Tagore and Nationalism*. Delhi: Springer, 2017.

PHILOSOPHY

Ghose, Partha, ed. *Tagore, Einstein and the Nature of Reality: Literary and Philosophical Reflections*. Abingdon: Routledge, 2019. There are also some perspectives on Tagore in the scientifically oriented *Einstein, Tagore and the Nature of Reality*, ed. Partha Ghose (Abingdon: Routledge, 2016).

Radhakrishnan, S. *The Philosophy of Rabindranath Tagore*. London: Macmillan, 1919.

ART

Archer, W.G. 'Art and the Unconscious: Rabindranath Tagore', in *India and Modern Art*. London: George Allen & Unwin, 1959.

Art of Tagore, The. Kolkata: Rupa, 2004: 72 reproductions.

Banerjee, Nilanjan, ed. *Wings of Mistakes: Doodles of Rabindranath Tagore*. Kolkata: Punascha with Visva-Bharati, 2011.

Parimoo, Ratan, ed. *Rabindranath Tagore (Collection of Essays)*. Delhi: Lalit Kala Akademi, 1989.

Siva Kumar, R., ed. *My Pictures: A Collection of Paintings by Rabindranath Tagore*. New Delhi: Viva Books with Visva-Bharati, 2005: 30 reproductions with notes.

———, ed. *Rabindra Chitravali: Paintings of Rabindranath Tagore*, 4 vols. Kolkata: Pratikshan Books, 2011: a near-complete set of reproductions with a comprehensive range of related textual material.

———, ed. *The Last Harvest: Paintings of Rabindranath Tagore*. Ahmedabad: Mapin Publishing, 2011.

Subramanyan, K.G. 'Tagore – the Poet Painter', in *Rabindranath Tagore: A Celebration of his Life and Work*, ed. Ray Monk and Andrew Robinson. London: Rabindranath Tagore Festival Committee/Oxford: Museum of Modern Art, 1986.

SONGS

Recordings of Rabindranath's songs, almost always in Bengali, abound on YouTube and other internet sites. The most comprehensive collection, with much information in English, is perhaps www.geetabitan.com (note the exact spelling).

CODA: THE CONTEXT OF TAGORE STUDIES

The lists above only cover material in English. They need to be seen in the total context of Tagore studies, chiefly and necessarily carried out in Bengali.

All serious engagement with Rabindranath must take account, directly or indirectly, of the complex chronology of his writings and other activities, attested by a great mass of records. The two authoritative biographies are *Rabindra-jibani* (4 vols, Kolkata: Visva-Bharati, final edition, 1970–94) by Prabhātkumār Mukhopādhyāy, one of the stalwarts of the early period of Santiniketan; and in stupendous detail, *Rabi-jibani* (9 vols, Kolkata: vol. 1, Bhurjapatra, vols 2–9, Ānanda Publishers, 1982–2001) by Prashāntakumār Pāl – sadly stopping short at 1926, Rabindranath's 65th year, owing to Prashantakumar's untimely death.

It is no less important to grasp not only the range and volume of Rabindranath's writings but their intricate intertextuality, and untiring revision often amounting to reinvention. The bibliographical researches of Pulinbihāri Sen, Sajanikānta Dās, Kānāi Sāmanta, Pashupati Sāsmal, Swapan Majumdār, Amitrasudan Bhattāchārya, and others have been brought together in the monumental volume 16 of the West Bengal Government edition of Rabindranath's works (*Rabindra-rachanābali*, Kolkata: Government of West Bengal, 2001).

In general criticism and interpretation, the pioneers, from the poet's lifetime, include Ajitkumār Chakrabarti, Kshitimohan Sen, Nihārranjan Rāy, and Pramathanāth Bishi. Of the Bengali modernist writers who have explored the work of their daunting predecessor, the most substantial contribution is by Buddhadeb Basu (Buddhadeva Bose). Of later scholars and critics, I will name only Ābu Sayeed Āyyub, Shankha Ghosh, and Ānisuzzāmān, seminal figures in a continuing line of scholarship. The wider purpose of a book like this is to help extend the line beyond the linguistic and geographical boundaries of Bengal, and make it more central to international literary scholarship.

General Index

Where a keyword has been indexed from the body of the text, its recurrence in an endnote (for instance, in a bibliographical reference) has not been indexed unless it adds substantive information. Editors and translators have not been indexed.

There is no entirely satisfactory way of indexing the names of women born or married into the Tagore family. They have been indexed under 'Tagore' (rather than 'Debi'), with the married names of the daughters in parentheses. Indira Debi Chaudhurani has been indexed under 'Chaudhurani' as being well known by that surname. Other women commonly known as 'Debi' have been so indexed.

Fictional characters have not been indexed. Journals are listed only when mentioned for themselves, not as part of a bibliographical reference.